Contents

The Blackwell Reader in Social Psychology

	Term-time opening hours:
...RY ... GE	Term-time opening hours:

The Blackwell Reader in Social Psychology

Edited by

Miles Hewstone
Antony S.R. Manstead
Wolfgang Stroebe

BLACKWELL
Publishers

Copyright © Blackwell Publishers Ltd, 1997

Editorial apparatus copyright © Miles Hewstone, Antony S.R. Manstead and Wolfgang Stroebe, 1997

First published 1997
2 4 6 8 10 9 7 5 3 1

Blackwell Publishers Ltd
108 Cowley Road
Oxford OX4 1JF
UK

Blackwell Publishers Inc.
350 Main Street
Malden, MA 02148
USA

Library of Congress Cataloging-in-Publication Data
Blackwell reader in social psychology / edited by Miles Hewstone,
    Antony S.R. Manstead, Wolfgang Stroebe.
        p. cm.
    Includes bibliographical references and index.
    ISBN 0-631-19997-7 (hard: alk. paper). – ISBN 0-631-19998-5 (pbk: alk. paper)
    1. Social psychology. I. Hewstone, Miles. II. Manstead, A.S.
R. III. Stroebe, Wolfgang.
HM251. B4764 1997
302-dc20   96-31873
                                                                              CIP

British Library Cataloguing in Publication Data

A CIP catalogue record for this book is available from the
British Library.

Commissioning Editor: Alison Mudditt
Desk Editor: Jack Messenger
Production Controller: Lisa Eaton

Typeset in 10 on 12 pt Garamond 3
by Best-set Typesetter Ltd, Hong Kong
Printed in Great Britain by T.J. Press Ltd, Padstow, Cornwall

This book is printed on acid-free paper

Preface

This volume is the third in a series of books we have published with Blackwell which are intended to contribute to the teaching of social psychology. The first (*Introduction to Social Psychology*, eds Miles Hewstone, Wolfgang Stroebe, Jean-Paul Codol and Geoffrey M. Stephenson, 1st edn 1988, 2nd edn 1996) has become a popular textbook throughout Europe. The second (*The Blackwell Encyclopedia of Social Psychology*, eds Antony Manstead and Miles Hewstone, published in hardback in 1995 and in paperback in 1996) is a comprehensive source book providing an in-depth account of the field. The present volume is designed to meet a different objective, namely to provide students of social psychology with the opportunity to read original articles – not only to find out first-hand how the research was done, but also in doing so to learn how to read original scientific articles.

Why a *Reader in Social Psychology*? First, students' desires to read original work are often frustrated because the library does not have the relevant volume of a particular journal, or because someone else has borrowed that volume (and there is a waiting list!). The provision of this relatively inexpensive volume will provide the student with immediate access to thirty-two original articles, spanning the whole field of social psychology. Second, the succinct style of journal articles, while necessary in a world of strict page limitations, can be off-putting to newcomers to the field. We have therefore been more ambitious than the editors of other readers we have seen in the way that we introduce each article. Instead of simply reprinting a set of key papers, we have provided introductions to each reading that guide the reader through the paper concerned. Most of the introductions are subdivided into the following sections: theoretical background, hypotheses, design, method, results, discussion, further reading, and references. In writing the introductions we have tried to make clear what was sometimes only implicit in the original, sought – where appropriate – to explain any complex forms of data analysis that were used, and spelled out what the study was about, how it was carried out, and what it actually found. We have often contacted the original authors to clarify certain matters of experimental design and analysis, and we have placed each article in the context of both previous and subsequent research.

Any choice of a set of articles to represent a field such as social psychology is bound to be somewhat contentious. We made our selection in the following way. First, we used the aforementioned *Introduction to Social Psychology* (referred to in our introductions as the 'textbook') as a framework, since that book covers what we regard as the core of the discipline as studied by students. We then allocated one article to each of the four introductory chapters in that book, and two articles to each of the subsequent chapters. This choice by no means limits the potential audience for this *Reader* to those who use the textbook, but taken together the two volumes should complement each other very well. Second, we wanted to include both 'classic' and 'contemporary' contributions. The former are of historical interest, often showing how a particular article opened up a new field or changed the direction of research; the latter are often technically more complex but of course do a better job of reflecting current knowledge. Third, we selected papers that we thought would be relatively easy to follow and understand. Thus the thirty-two articles included in this *Reader* are not necessarily our choice of the 'very best' of social psychology, and we are well aware that we have failed to include articles by some researchers who have had a massive impact on the field. But we have selected a series of articles that in our opinion are broadly representative of research in each area of social psychology, and that illustrate the varieties of social psychological research and its methods: laboratory and field studies, experimental and correlational research, basic and applied, and so on.

We are grateful to all those authors of the original articles who responded to what might have seemed to be slightly irritating tests of their long-term memory, and who encouraged us in this endeavour. We would also like to express our thanks to Alison Mudditt at Blackwell, who has been heavily involved in all three of the volumes mentioned above. She has perfected the art of when to send an inquisitive email, when to call to check we are still alive, and when to reward us with a good dinner!

Miles Hewstone, University of Wales, Cardiff
Antony S.R. Manstead, University of Amsterdam
Wolfgang Stroebe, Utrecht University

Acknowledgements

The editors and publishers gratefully acknowledge the following for permission to reproduce copyright material:

Ajzen, I. and Madden, T.J. (1986). Prediction of goal-directed behaviour: Attitudes, intentions, and perceived behavioural control. *Journal of Experimental Social Psychology* 22, 453–74. Copyright © 1986 by Academic Press, Inc.

Baron, R.S., Cutrona, C.E., Hicklin, D., Russell, D.W. and Lubaroff, D.M. (1980). Social support and immune function among spouses of cancer patients. *Journal of Personality and Social Psychology* 59, 344–52. Copyright © 1980 by the American Psychological Association. Reprinted with permission.

Berkowitz, L. and LePage, A. (1967). Weapons as aggression-eliciting stimuli. *Journal of Personality and Social Psychology* 7, 202–07. Copyright © 1967 by the American Psychological Association. Reprinted with permission.

Bradbury, T.N. and Fincham, F.D. (1992). Attributions and behaviour in marital interaction. *Journal of Personality and Social Psychology* 63, 613–28. Copyright © 1992 by the American Psychological Association. Reprinted with permission.

Breckler, S.J. (1984). Empirical validation of affect, behaviour, and cognition as distinct components of attitude. *Journal of Personality and Social Psychology* 47, 1191–1205. Copyright © 1984 by the American Psychological Association. Reprinted with permission.

Buss, D.M., et al. (1992). Sex differences in jealousy: Evolution, physiology and psychology. *Psychological Science* 3, 251–5. Reprinted by permission of Cambridge University Press.

Caporeal, L.R., Lukaszewski, M.P. and Culbertson, G.H. (1983). Secondary baby talk: Judgements by institutionalized elderly and their caregivers. *Journal of Personality and Social Psychology* 44, 746–54. Copyright © 1983 by the American Psychological Association. Reprinted with permission.

Cartwright, D. (1979). Contemporary social psychology in historical perspective. *Social Psychology Quarterly* 42, 82–93. Copyright © 1979 by the American Sociological Association.

Darley, J.M. and Batson, C.D. (1974). From Jerusalem to Jericho: A study of situational and dispositional variables in helping behaviour. *Journal of Personality and Social Psychology* 27, 100–108. Copyright © 1974 by the American Psychological Association. Reprinted with permission.

Darley, J.M. and Gross, P.H. (1983). A hypothesis-confirming bias in labelling effects. *Journal of Personality and Social Psychology* 44, 20–33. Copyright © 1983 by the American Psychological Association. Reprinted with permission.

Diehl, M. and Stroebe, W. (1987). Productivity loss in brainstorming groups: toward the solution of a riddle. *Journal of Personality and Social Psychology* 53, 497–509. Copyright © 1987 by the American Psychological Association. Reprinted with permission.

Ekman, Paul (1971). Constants across cultures in the face and emotion. *Journal of Personality and Social Psychology* 17, 124–9. Copyright © 1971 by the American Psychological Association. Reprinted with permission.

Gergen, K.J. (1978). Experimentation in social psychology: A reappraisal. *European Journal of Social Psychology* 8, 507–27. Copyright © 1978 by John Wiley & Sons, Ltd. Reprinted with permission.

Hamilton, D.L. et al.(1980). Cognitive representation of personality impressions: Organizational processes in first impression formation. *Journal of Personality and Social Psychology* 39, 1050–63. Copyright © 1980 by the American Psychological Association. Reprinted with permission.

Hazan, C. and Shaver, P. (1987). Romantic love conceptualized as attachment process. *Journal of Personality and Social Psychology* 52, 511–24. Copyright © 1987 by the American Psychological Association. Reprinted with permission.

Latané, B. and Rodin, J. (1969). A lady in distress: Inhibiting effects of friends and strangers on bystander intervention. *Journal of Experimental Social Psychology* 5, 189–202. Copyright © 1969 by Academic Press, Inc.

Latané, B., Williams, K. and Harkins, S. (1979). Many hands make light work: The causes and consequences of social loafing. *Journal of Personality and Social Psychology* 37, 822–32. Copyright © 1979 by the American Psychological Association. Reprinted with permission.

Lemyre, L. and Smith, P.M. (1985). Intergroup discrimination and self esteem in the minimal group paradigm. *Journal of Personality and Social Psychology* 49, 660–70. Copyright © 1985 by the American Psychological Association. Reprinted with permission.

Linder, Darwyn E. (1967). Decision freedom as a determinant of the role of incentive magnitude in attitude change. *Journal of Personality and Social Psychology* 6, 245–54. Copyright © 1967 by the American Psychological Association. Reprinted with permission.

Milgram, S. (1963). Behavioural study of obedience. *Journal of Abnormal and Social Psychology* 67, 371–8. Reprinted by permission of Alexandra Milgram.

Noller, P. (1982). Channel consistency and inconsistency in the communication of married couples. *Journal of Personality and Social Psychology* 43, 732–41. Copyright © 1982 by the American Psychological Association. Reprinted with permission.

Petty, Richard E. (1981). Personal involvement as a determinant of argument-based persuasion. *Journal of Personality and Social Psychology* 41, 847–55. Copyright © 1981 by the American Psychological Association. Reprinted with permission.

Rusbult, C.E. (1980). Commitment and satisfaction in romantic association: A test of the investment model. *Journal of Experimental Social Psychology* 16, 172–86. Copyright © 1980 by Academic Press, Inc.

Snyder, M. and Uranowitz, S.W. (1978). Reconstructing the past: Some cognitive consequences of person perception. *Journal of Personality and Social Psychology* 36, 941–50. Copyright © 1978 by the American Psychological Association. Reprinted with permission.

Storms, M.D. (1973). Videotape and the attribution process: Reversing actors' and observers' points of view. *Journal of Personality and Social Psychology* 27, 165–75. Copyright © 1973 by the American Psychological Association. Reprinted with permission.

Tajfel, H. (1970). The development of children's preference for their own country: A cross-national study. *International Journal of Psychology* 6, 245–53. Copyright © 1970 by the International Union of Psychological Science. Reprinted with permission.

Wilder, D.A. (1984). Intergroup contact: The typical member and the exception to the rule. *Journal of Experimental Social Psychology* 13, 131–40. Copyright © 1984 by Academic Press, Inc.

Zillman, D., Johnson, R.C., and Day, K.D. (1974). Attribution of apparent arousal and proficiency of recovery from sympathetic activation affecting excitation transfer to aggressive behaviour. *Journal of Experimental Social Psychology* 10, 503–15. Copyright © 1974 by Academic Press, Inc.

The publishers apologize for any errors or omissions in the above list and would be grateful to be notified of any corrections that should be incorporated in the next edition or reprint of this book.

Part I
Introduction

1 Introduction to a History of Social Psychology

Contemporary social psychology in historical perspective

D. Cartwright

Editors'
Introduction

Introduction

This personal, historical review of the field of social psychology offers a direct challenge to any student asking 'why should I read or know about history?' (for a more detailed treatment, see Farr's 1996 volume). Cartwright was an active player in the game for over forty years, and provides a historical perspective that is much more closely tied to the present than are most other historical pieces (see also Berscheid, 1992). His article also provides provocative answers to many of the questions that students might ask: how old is the empirical research area of social psychology? (now nearly a hundred years); what was the single most important influence on the development of social psychology?; and which person had the greatest impact on the field? But Cartwright also analyses less dramatic influences on the nature of the discipline (funding policies, journal practices and university promotion systems, for example), and he does so by analysing the issues as a social scientist (viewing social psychology as a 'social system', and treating his own subjective observations as the 'data' of a 'participant observer'). To understand the crucial contributions of key individuals, he argues, we have to understand the social system in which they worked and something about how scientific 'revolutions' occur (see Kuhn, 1962). Given the continuing emphasis on social psychology as an empirical, and largely experimental, discipline, it is worth noting Cartwright's view that we owe our relatively new discipline to 'a generational revolt against the arm-chair methods of social philosophy'.

Historical and Social Context

Cartwright identifies World War II as the most important single influence on the development of social psychology, and Adolf Hitler as the person who had the greatest impact. Why?

Social Psychology Quarterly (1979), 42:82–93.

Because the problems created by war forced the US government to include the developing field of social psychology in its search for solutions. New techniques such as the sample survey were pushed forwards, and the applications of social psychology became obvious, even if theory did not advance much in the process.

But above all the war forced the migration of Europe's leading scholars to the United States and it was there, in a more auspicious funding climate, that the discipline was able to advance, while in Europe it was left behind until later. This development had the disadvantage, Cartwright argues, of narrowing the essential breadth of perspective of social psychology. The discipline also became heavily influenced by American political ideology. This was seen in the opposition to instinct theories of aggression and is still seen in the controversy over whether social behaviour has a significant genetic basis (see the article by Buss, Larsen, Westen and Semmelroth in chapter 2). Moreover, the problems studied in social psychology became the social problems facing US society and, as Cartwright persuasively argues, different historical periods have thrown up their own research foci (for example, Senator McCarthy's 'witchhunts' in the 1950s spawned research on conformity; urban riots in the 1970s provoked research on frustration–aggression and violence). It is important to see how our past and present have been determined by social and historical factors.

Current State of the Field

Cartwright's evaluation of social psychology is one we, as editors, would endorse: positive, but critical. Much has been done, but much remains to be done, and 'all is not for the best in this best of all possible (social psychological) worlds'. We should acknowledge the positive progress made, and the continuing limitations, along key dimensions.

Research techniques

Advances in methodology, statistics and computational hardware and software have dramatically altered what we can study, and how we can study it. Yet Cartwright is surely correct to assert that the availability of these new tools should not determine the content of research. And we should try to make use of the variety of techniques (such as laboratory experiments and sample surveys), rather than specialize in one approach, in order to increase confidence in the generalizability of our findings (see Campbell and Fiske, 1959; and the reading by Gergen in chapter 4).

Substantive content

While acknowledging the 'vast storehouse' of well-established empirical findings in our discipline, Cartwright also highlights limitations – notably our general ignorance about how social processes unfold over time, and our lopsided focus on intrapersonal cognitions, even if this 'concern with the subjective world of individuals has constituted social psychology's unique contribution to the social sciences'.

Theoretical integration

Despite the growth in sophisticated theory, Cartwright regrets the lack of theoretical integration. While the goal of explaining all social behaviour in terms of one theory does seem hopelessly naive, as a discipline we do seem to spend much more time generating short- to middle-range theories, rather than worrying about how they fit together (see Pettigrew, 1991, for an exception). Matters get even worse when we think of the schism between two 'schools' of social psychology – 'psychological social psychology' and 'sociological social psychology' – which tend to ignore each other (but see Stephan et al., 1991), and are pursued by scholars working in separate disciplines (psychology and sociology).

Concluding Observations

Although having detailed criticisms of the field, Cartwright ends by emphasizing his positive outlook, based in part on the youthfulness of social psychology as a discipline (compared with physics, for example). While some of the criticisms are still as pertinent today – the susceptibility to fads and fashions (see Jones, 1985), and the reliance on a narrow data base (see Carlson, 1984; Sears, 1986) – others, such as the narrow demographic composition of researchers, have faded, as the 'truly international community of scholars' envisaged by Cartwright has come to pass. One should also emphasize that the field of social psychology has changed dramatically since Cartwright wrote this piece. For example, we do more field and longitudinal studies; evolutionary social psychology has arrived on the scene; and, due to meta-analysis, we realize that our research is much more cumulative (see Berscheid, 1992).

FURTHER READING

Berscheid, E. (1992). A glance back at a quarter century of social psychology. *Journal of Personality and Social Psychology, 63*, 525–33. Another personal retrospective, which highlights some different themes and complements Cartwright's article.
Stephan, C.W., Stephan, W. and Pettigrew, T.F. (eds) (1991). *The Future of Social Psychology* (pp. 13–27). New York: Springer-Verlag. This short book explores the relationship between 'psychological' and 'sociological' social psychology, and asks whether they can be (re)unified.

REFERENCES

Carnpbell, D.T. and Fiske, D.W. (1959). Convergent and discriminant validation by the multitrait–multimatrix method. *Psychological Bulletin*, 56, 81–105.
Carlson, R. (1984). What's social about social psychology? Where's the person in personality research? *Journal of Personality and Social Psychology*, 47, 1304–9.
Farr, R.M. (1996). *The Roots of Modern Social Psychology*. Oxford: Blackwell.
Jones, E.E. (1985). Major developments in social psychology during the past four decades. In G. Lindzey and E. Aronson (eds), *The Handbook of Social Psychology* (vol. 1 pp. 47–107). New York: Random House.

Pettigrew, T.F. (1991). Toward unity and bold theory: Popperian suggestions for two persistent problems of social psychology. In C.W. Stephan, W. Stephan and T.F. Pettigrew (eds), *The Future of Social Psychology* (pp. 13–27). New York: Springer-Verlag.

Kuhn, T.S. (1962). *The Structure of Scientific Revolutions*. Chicago: University of Chicago Press.

Sears, D.O. (1986). College sophomores in the laboratory: Influences of a narrow data base on social psychology's view of human nature. *Journal of Personality and Social Psychology*, 51, 515–30.

- - - - -
Primary
Reading
- - - - - - - -

The entire history of social psychology as a field of empirical research extends over a period of only approximately eighty years. And since most of its growth has occurred within the past four decades, it is largely the product of scholars who are still active in the field. In this paper, I would like to draw upon my own experience as a social psychologist over the past forty years to make some observations about the current state of the field and the problems it faces today. The data I shall be using are those of a participant observer and have the strengths and weaknesses of this method of research. Although they have the advantage of being derived from first-hand experience, they also reflect my personal biases, values, and aspirations for the field. A more detatched observer would undoubtedly view this period of history from a different perspective and might very well reach different conclusions concerning its significance.

In order to understand the nature of the developments of the past forty years, it is necessary to consider not only the findings, methods, and theories produced during this period but also the institutional changes occurring within the field itself. Social psychology, like any branch of science, is a social system whose primary objective is the production of a particular kind of empirical knowledge, and its history is more than a history of ideas and intellectual accomplishments. As I have observed the intellectual and professional activities of social psychologists over the years, I have been impressed by how much they have been influenced by such things as the policies of funding agencies, the editorial practices of journals and publishing houses, the monetary and symbolic reward system of university departments, the nature of the doctoral programs, and the demographic composition of the profession. I am not suggesting that all of these influences have been detrimental, but I do feel that it would be a mistake to underestimate the magnitude of their effects upon the problems that have been chosen for investigation, how they have been approached, the methods employed, the way research facilities have been organized, and the amount of time social psychologists have devoted to that old-fashioned activity known as scholarship.

It is true, of course, that the substantive content of the knowledge attained in any field of science is ultimately determined by the intrinsic nature of the phenomena under investigation, since empirical research is essentially a process of discovery with an internal logic of its own. But it is equally true that the knowledge attained is the product of a social system and, as such, is basically influenced by the properties of that system and by its cultural, social, and political environment. These influences are especially apparent when one attempts to understand the developments occurring within a limited period of time.

There are, I believe, certain pragmatic advantages to be gained from conceiving of a discipline as a social system. For one thing, it helps to establish realistic standards for evaluating a field's rate of progress. The production of scientific knowledge is a collective enterprise in which each contributor builds upon the work of others, and the amount of time required to produce empirical findings, to communicate them, and to permit others to assess their significance sets severe limits upon the rate of progress that can be realistically expected. Just how much time is consumed in this process has been documented by research conducted by the American Psychological Association under the supervision of Garvey and Griffith (1971). These investigators found that the average duration of a research project in psychology – from the time when someone gets a bright idea about how previous work on some topic can be extended up to the publication of an article – is approximately five years. This finding is important for any realistic evaluation of the progress made in social psychology during the past forty years, since it is obvious that the number of five-year intervals over this period is quite small.

Additional insight into the temporal constraints on scientific progress is provided by Kuhn's (1962) discussion of the history of scientific revolutions, in which he argues that truly fundamental advances in science occur as a result of rebellions staged by younger generations of scientists against older ones. Such rebellions grow out of a deep sense of dissatisfaction with the field's ability to deal with its basic intellectual problems and result in the establishment of a fundamentally new theoretical and methodological approach, or in Kuhn's words, a new paradigm. The emergence of social psychology as a distinctive field of empirical research around the turn of the century can be viewed, I believe, as a generational revolt against the arm-chair methods of social philosophy. It is possible that the so-called crisis in contemporary social psychology is the beginning of another generational rebellion, although I am more inclined to agree with Elms (1975) that the present crisis is actually one of a lack of professional self-confidence brought about by unrealistic expectations. But in any event, it is clear that social psychology is simply not old enough to have benefited from many revolutionary advances of the sort described by Kuhn.

A second advantage of this point of view is that it suggests where efforts might best be directed to bring about improvements in the intellectual performance of the field. It has been my experience that efforts to upgrade the quality of research by attempting to persuade scholars to mend their ways have never been very successful. And if I am correct in my assessment of the importance of the social system in shaping the thinking of individual social psychologists, it follows that fundamental improvements in the intellectual performance of the discipline as a whole will require changes in the system itself and the way it operates.

The third advantage of this approach is that, if it were generally accepted, it would help to counteract an unfortunate tendency on the part of some to divide the activities of social psychologists into two separate spheres – the sacred and the profane; or, in other words, those activities concerned with the substantive content of research, and those having to do with the construction and maintenance of the social system that makes research possible. Although these two kinds of activities undoubtedly call for different sorts of skills, it is important to recognize that each depends for its success upon the other, and that both are essential for scientific progress.

In adopting a system approach to the history of social psychology, I do not intend to minimize the contributions made by individual scholars, for social psychology has had its share of great names, and the field would now be in a sorry state indeed if it had not been for the work of these creative individuals. But if we are to understand how these people came to make their particular contributions and why they were so influential, we must examine the nature of the social system in which they worked, its stage of development, and its larger social setting.

Historical and Social Context

There can be little doubt that the most important single influence on the development of social psychology up to the present came from outside the system itself. I am referring, of course, to the Second World War and the political upheaval in Europe that preceded it. If I were required to name the one person who has had the greatest impact upon the field, it would have to be Adolph Hitler. There are several reasons why these events in the world at large were so important for social psychology: They came at a critical stage in its development; they were largely responsible for the spectacular increase in its rate of growth; they basically influenced the subsequent demographic composition of the field; and they have exerted a fundamental influence upon its entire intellectual complexion right up to the present.

During the first three or four decades of its existence, social psychology had been mainly concerned with the problem of establishing itself as a legitimate field of empirical research. Social psychologists had directed their attention primarily to the task of developing basic concepts and devising appropriate methods of research. By the mid-1930s, the field was prepared to undertake research on significant substantive problems. Within a period of less than ten years, Newcomb did his important research, that became known as the Bennington study; F.H. Allport and Sherif published their basic studies on social norms and conformity; Hyman conducted his work on reference groups; Murray reported the results of an impressive program of research on human motivation; the Yale group published their seminal work on frustration and aggression, and on social learning and imitation; Whyte did his participant observation research on street-corner society; and Lewin, Lippitt, and White undertook their classic experiment on styles of leadership. It was also during this time that Dollard published his book, *Caste and Class in a Southern Town*, Myrdal conducted his influential analysis of race relations in the United States, and the Clarks did their work on racial identification in black children. It was in 1936 that Gallup so dramatically demonstrated the possibility of using interviews with samples of the population to predict election results, and in 1939 that Likert began doing public opinion research for the federal government. The field was in a state of intellectual ferment, and social psychologists were well-prepared to respond to the events that followed.

It is difficult for anyone who did not experience it to appreciate the magnitude of the impact of the war upon American social psychology. The smoke had hardly cleared from Pearl Harbor before the government began recruiting social psychologists to assist in the solution of problems faced by a nation at war. As a result of this migration from the campuses, together with the military draft, academic research and the training of graduate students came to a virtual halt. The variety of topics investigated for the government almost defies description, but in a review of this work (Cartwright, 1948) undertaken immediately after the war, I was able to identify the following: Building civilian morale and combatting demoralization; domestic attitudes, needs, and information; enemy morale and psychological warfare; military administration; international relations; and psychological problems of a wartime economy.

Work on problems like these called for the sharpening of research tools only recently designed and the invention of new ones. It demonstrated the power of the sample survey as a technique of social science research. It resulted in the accumulation of a tremendous mass of new information, but I must add, not much in the way of theory. It opened up new fields of investigation such as organizational psychology, economic behavior, and political behavior. It provided concrete examples of the practical usefulness of social psychology. Most importantly, it fundamentally altered social psychologists' view of the field and its place in society, and established social psychology, once and for all, as a legitimate field of specialization worthy of public support.

When the war was over, the field was incomparably different from what it had been just three or four years before. Prospects were bright, morale was high, and social psychologists set about the task of converting into reality their new vision of what social psychology might become. They established new research facilities, such as the Survey Research Center, the Research Center for Group Dynamics, and the Laboratory for Social Relations. They began submitting research proposals to governmental agencies, foundations, and business firms, and received, for the most part, a warm reception. They organized doctoral programs in most of the leading universities, and within a few years had trained more social psychologists than there had been in the entire history of the field. And they began to publish large quantities of research.

It is clear that these developments would not have taken place if it had not been for the war, and they have important implications for social psychology today. As a result of the population explosion within the field over the past thirty years, something like 90% of all social psychologists who have ever lived are alive at the present time. The entire conceptual framework of social psychology, including all of the unexamined assumptions about its proper subject-matter and acceptable methods of research and most of its empirical findings, are therefore largely the product of a single generation of people who were trained by a relatively small group of teachers with a common background and a rather homogeneous point of view. And due to the social conditions of the time in which they entered the field, they are predominantly white, male, middle-class Americans, and thus reflect the interests and biases of this segment of the population. Their accomplishments are most impressive, but it is important to recognize that the field as it exists today is not God-given, nor even the best that could be devised by man.

No review of the historical forces that have shaped contemporary social psychology would be complete without consideration of another consequence of the war and the social upheaval that preceded it. The rise of Nazism in Germany, with its accompanying anti-intellectualism and vicious anti-Semitism, resulted as we all know in the migration to America of many of Europe's leading scholars, scientists, and artists. Although this massive displacement of intellectual talent had important effects upon all branches of science and culture, it was especially critical for social psychology. One can hardly imagine what the field would be like today if such people as Lewin, Heider, Köhler, Wertheimer, Katona, Lazarsfeld, and the Brunswiks had not come to the United States when they did. They not only brought to American social psychology a fresh and stimulating point of view at a time when it was about to embark upon a period of unprecedented growth, but they also exerted a direct personal influence upon many of the individuals who were to come to play a leading role in the subsequent development of the field, and through them, an indirect influence upon the training of the present generation of social psychologists. I cannot provide a complete list of those who had close personal association with these stimulating scholars, but it includes such names as Asch, Krech, Crutchfield, Merton, Campbell, Likert, Barker, Lippitt, French, Zander, Cook, Festinger, Kelley, Thibaut, Schachter, and Deutsch.

As a result of the war and the political events that preceded it, social psychology had become almost nonexistent on the continent of Europe, or, for that matter, anywhere outside of North

America, at the very time it underwent its most important developments. It had become primarily an American product, and when it was finally reestablished abroad it had a completely American flavor. This turn of events had profound implications for the field as we know it today. Social psychology, more than any other branch of science, with the possible exception of anthropology, requires a breadth of perspective that can only be achieved by a truly international community of scholars. Social psychologists are not merely students of society, they are also participants in it, and despite their best efforts to attain a detached objectivity in their research, their thinking is affected by the particular culture in which they live.

The fact that social psychology was so largely an American enterprise in its formative years means that its intellectual content has been greatly influenced by the political ideology of American society and by the social problems confronting the United States over the past forty years. The effects of these influences upon contemporary social psychology are pervasive. American political ideology is, of course, basically democratic. It emphasizes the importance of the individual; rejects the doctrine of the immutability of human nature; places great confidence in the belief that human progress can be achieved through rational problem solving, scientific research, and technology; and holds to the optimistic view that needed social changes can be brought about by public education.

These assumptions are reflected in the heavy concentration of social psychological research on topics of public opinion, attitudes, social learning, and attitude change. They account, in part at least, for the great interest in cognitive and motivational processes within the individual, although one should not underestimate the influence here of Gestalt psychology and Freudian theory that came with the migration of psychologists from Europe, nor should one overlook the importance of the invention of the computer. These ideological premises also help to explain the dominance of environmentalism in social psychological thinking. McDougall's theory of instincts never really had a chance, not so much because it was wrong, which it may very well have been, but because it was antithetical to American culture. One cannot but be impressed by the intense emotional fervor with which social psychologists react to the proposition that intelligence has a substantial genetic component, or to the claim by Lorenz and others that aggression is instinctive.

In calling attention to these ideological influences, it is not my intention to criticize democracy, for I am convinced that social psychology by its very nature cannot perform its essential task in an authoritarian society nor under a dictatorial form of government. Lewin was undoubtedly correct in his assertion that: "To believe in reason, is to believe in democracy, because it grants to the reasoning partners a status of equality" (1948:83). If as social psychologists we do believe in reason, it follows that we must do the best we can to distinguish between ideological assumptions and scientific evidence.

Since most social psychological research has been the product of American investigators, its substantive content has been influenced by the social problems confronting American society. These problems have not only affected the topics chosen for investigation, but have also created a willingness on the part of governmental officials and other financial gatekeepers to provide the support needed to do such research. We are all familiar with the strategic value of including in our research proposals a section on "social relevance" regardless of how irrelevant they might otherwise seem to be.

The effects of these social problems upon the content of research would be readily apparent if one were to do an archeological dig down through the accumulated literature of social psychology. One would find near the surface a concentration of material dealing with sex roles and the status of women; then a layer concerned with urban unrest, violence, and riots that was deposited during the sixties; a thick stratum of research on conformity from the heyday of McCarthyism in the fifties; and then, of course, the residues of all the work on the problems brought about by the Second World War. Running vertically through all of these artifacts, there would also be the products of research on such continuing problems as intergroup relations, prejudice, stereotypes, discrimination, and social conflicts of various kinds; the inefficiencies and pathologies of social institutions; the detrimental effects of modern society on mental health; and the persistent problems of delinquency and antisocial behavior. I am not suggesting that social psychologists have done research on all of the problems actually faced by American society during this period, for some of them were not generally recognized and others were simply too hot to handle. Nor am I proposing that our research has been concerned only with social problems. But there can be little doubt that the body of knowledge that we have today would be substantially different if it had been created in a different era or in a different social setting.

Current State of the Field

With this general historical orientation, I would like now to present some observations of a more evaluative nature concerning the state of contemporary social psychology. Let me begin by saying that my overall evaluation is definitely positive. I do not share the gloom of those who think that the field has reached a state of crisis. Social psychology is incomparably better-equipped to achieve its basic objectives than it was some forty years ago. We have better facilities, better methods for collecting and analyzing data, a vast storehouse of well-established empirical findings, more rigorous conceptual models, and much more sophisticated theory.

It is true that the general level of excitement that characterized social psychology immediately after the war has all but disappeared. But since this decline in enthusiasm actually began in the mid-1950s, as I noted in a review of the field at that time (Cartwright, 1961), it should not be taken as evidence of deficiencies in the work of recent years but, instead, as a by-product of moving from a programmatic stage of development to one described by Kuhn as "normal science" in which the field is engaged in the less glamorous task of collecting detailed data and testing rather limited theoretical hypotheses. In view of the inherent complexity of our subject-matter and the youthfulness of our discipline, I find it remarkable that so much progress has been made. I do not, of course, believe that all is well or that we can be content with what has been accomplished. For social psychology, as we know it today, does have deficiencies and does face some very difficult problems.

Research techniques

The early social psychologists have clearly been vindicated in their claim that important social phenomena can be subjected to empirical investigation. We no longer have to rely on intuition, anecdotes, and arm-chair speculation. The invention and refinement of techniques for conducting survey research have made it possible to obtain remarkably accurate estimates of the beliefs, attitudes, intentions, behavior, and even the quality of life of large populations on the basis of interviews with a relatively small number of people. Advances in experimental methodology now permit us to control and systematically vary many of the more important determinants of human behavior and thus to investigate causal relationships among variables. Our research has been substantially improved by work in the field of statistics on small-sample theory, experimental design, and multivariate analysis. As a result of these methodological developments, we now have a quite respectable body of firmly based empirical findings.

But these impressive gains in technical competence and sophistication have been, I fear, something of a mixed blessing, for the fascination with technique seems all too often to have replaced a concern for substantive significance. The literature is full of studies that do little more than demonstrate the technical virtuosity of the investigator, and one might think that our journals would have to go out of business if use of the analysis of variance were to be prohibited. We tend to forget that methods are, after all, only tools and, as such, should not determine the content of research or be used simply because they are there. The motivation of research should be different from that of mountain-climbing. One would hope that the obsession with technique is a temporary phenomenon, analogous to the conspicuous consumption of the *nouveau riche*, but I suspect that change will not come quickly, since it is much easier for research review committees, editors, and departmental executive committees to evaluate methods than the quality or significance of substantive content.

The preoccupation with method has not only had a detrimental effect on the work of individual investigators, it has also had consequences for the organization of the field as a whole. The discipline has become divided along methodological lines rather than by substantive problems. Social psychologists tend to specialize, usually in survey research or in laboratory experimentation, and to associate with others having similar skills. Although it is understandable why the field should be divided in this way, it is nonetheless regrettable. For, as Hovland (1959) showed in his comparison of the results of survey research and laboratory experiments on the topic of attitude change, research based on a single technique is especially vulnerable to methodological artifacts and theoretical preconceptions.

Over the years, social psychologists have developed a variety of other methods, such as the unobtrusive or obtrusive observation of behavior in naturalistic settings, field experiments, computer simulation, and the analysis of personal documents, case histories, and the products of the mass media. Some of these techniques have been employed rather extensively within certain subareas of social psychology. But this research has also suffered from the single-method approach. I am aware, of course, that it may not be possible, or even desirable, for every social psychologist to become proficient in all of these techniques, but I cannot believe that the discipline as a whole cannot find some better way to make use of the methods we now possess.

Substantive content

If one examines the total body of knowledge thus far acquired in social psychology, as presented in our textbooks and other systematic reviews of the literature, it is evident that it too has certain limitations. It is, for one thing, largely based on cross-sectional as opposed to longitudinal data. We have attained a good understanding of the nature of normative behavior, but we know virtually nothing about the conditions affecting the formation and decay of social norms or the determinants of their content. We recognize the importance of social roles in social interaction, but we know little about their development or why particular roles are found in particular circumstances. And we now have quite sophisticated theories about the processes involved in choosing among a set of alternatives with given utilities, but hardly any theory at all about the determinants of these utilities.

We have acquired considerable skill in predicting behavior in settings of our own fabrication, and a breath-taking ability to explain behavior after the fact. But we have not yet learned how to deal effectively with processes that take place over an extended period of time, and we are, I fear, no better than the intelligent layman in forecasting the course of future social developments. Although I would like to think that social psychologists should be at least as good as economists in the art of prognostication, the attainment of even this modest level of competence will require a substantial shift in our conceptual orientation and in our methods of research.

Some important progress has been made in this direction in research on voting behavior, consumer expectations, and organizational development through use of repeated measures, panel studies, and statistical procedures that employ time as a variable. And the work of Zajonc (1976) and his colleagues on the development of intellectual abilities suggests another promising approach, for even if their predictions of future trends in test scores should turn out to be incorrect, their conceptual model, unlike so many in social psychology, not only deals with time but also has the virtue that it can be proven wrong. The more extensive use and refinement of methods such as these would greatly improve the quality of our research.

The body of knowledge we now have is not only limited in its temporal depth, but is also disproportionately concerned with certain aspects of social behavior. A tabulation of how the field's intellectual and financial resources have been distributed according to substantive content would undoubtedly show that by far the largest proportion, especially in recent years, has been devoted to work on cognitive processes occurring within individuals, or on the product of these processes. We now have a large body of information about the beliefs, opinions, and attitudes of people in all walks of life and a reasonably good understanding of the ways in which individuals in various segments of society experience the social environment. The major theoretical advances in recent years have also been primarily concerned with cognitive processes within individuals. And although it would not be correct to say that other determinants of behavior have been completely ignored or that there has not been important work on social interaction, the fact remains that the central focus of attention has been on cognition.

The emphasis on subjective experience has a long tradition and cannot be attributed, as is sometimes claimed, to the popular appeal of dissonance theory and attribution theory. It can be found throughout the history of the field, as for example, in W.I. Thomas' stress on the importance of "the definition of the situation," G.H. Mead's theory of symbolic interaction, Lewin's concept of the psychological life space, and Heider's theory of naive psychology. It can be seen in such statements as that made by Newcomb when he said: "It seems to me to be a truism that no interpersonal behavior can be understood without a knowledge of how the relationship is perceived by the persons involved" (1947:74). It is also reflected in Asch's assertion that: "It is not possible, as a rule, to conduct investigation in social psychology without including a reference to the experiences of persons" (1959:374). There have, of course, been radical behaviorists who reject such statements as utter scientific nonsense, but their protests have not significantly affected the mainstream of social psychological research and theory.

If one looks more broadly at the intellectual context of the field, it is apparent that this concern with the subjective world of individuals has constituted social psychology's unique contribution to the social sciences. It is what is usually meant when one refers to the "social psychological point of view" in anthropology, economics, history, sociology, or political science, and we can be proud of the impact that social psychology has had upon these disciplines.

But having said all of this, I must admit to certain misgivings. For surely the view that human beings are merely information processors is too narrow, even when it is broadened to include the influences of motivation. We are correct, I believe, in our claim that in order to explain a person's behavior, one must relate it to the subjective environment of that particular individual. The cognitive representations of the external world together with motivational forces arising from needs and internalized values unquestionably exert profound influences on behavior. But behavior itself is a transaction between an individual and the *objective* environment, not its cognitive representation, and the effectiveness of *social* behavior depends upon much more than beliefs and intentions. It requires social skills, social support, the utilization of resources, the exercise of power, and collaborative effort. It brings about changes in the social environment that have consequences for the individual's physical and mental well-being, his relations with others, his position in society, and the resources he can employ in future transactions.

When these consequences combine to have adverse effects upon the environment shared by others, they constitute social problems, such as pollution, energy shortages, urban decay, crime, overpopulation, the restriction of freedom, and social discrimination of various kinds. If they are to be remedied, they require changes in the behavior of large numbers of individuals. The remedies most often proposed by social psychologists tend to reflect their concern with cognition and thus to rely heavily upon programs for changing beliefs and attitudes. But if it is true that cognition is only one of the proximal determinants of behavior, it follows that such remedies, by themselves, are not likely to be very successful, and the experience of recent years would seem to support this conclusion.

Theoretical integration

A third imperfection of our present body of knowledge is its lack of theoretical integration. For despite all of the good theoretical work that has been done, we simply do not have a comprehensive theoretical framework for the field as a whole. The early attempt to explain everything of interest to social psychology by means of what Gordon Allport called a "simple and sovereign" theory has long since been abandoned. Such explanatory systems, which view all social phenomena as manifestations of something like imitation, the drive for power, enlightened self-interest, the herd instinct, or learning, now seem hopelessly naive, except perhaps to a few undaunted Skinnerians.

Big theories that merely sketch out a global orientation to the field have given way to numerous smaller but more rigorous ones, such as balance theory, congruity theory, dissonance theory, attribution theory, social comparison theory, information integration theory, decision theory, reactance theory, equity theory, exchange theory, and the like. These miniature conceptual systems have served us well, for they are concerned with important problems and have generated a large amount of quite good research. But since they deal with only limited parts of the field's subject-matter and have little or no explicit relationship to one another, they do not provide theoretical integration for all of social psychology. Until we achieve a more comprehensive theoretical framework, we shall not have a firm basis for deciding which problems are most worthy of investigation.

In the absence of integrative theory, social psychologists have come to organize their intellectual activities around some specific substantive topic that happens to interest them at the time, or around some particular method of research. What is more important, they tend to identify with their own area of specialization rather than with the discipline as a whole. It is true, of course, that we all share a common tradition and that we are deeply interested in the welfare of the entire field. But even though we still use the label "social psychology" to refer to our own professional occupation, we are no longer exactly sure what this term means or where the boundaries of the field should be drawn. Research topics that were once seen as part of the central core of social psychology are now generally viewed as belonging to such specialties as organizational psychology, developmental psychology, cognitive psychology, or group dynamics, and some have been relegated to other disciplines such as anthropology, economics, or political science. Some forty years ago, Murphy, Murphy, and Newcomb (1937) described social psychology as consisting of a number of lonely and isolated peninsulas jutting out into the sea of knowledge, and although we have broadened these peninsulas and have constructed new ones, this metaphor seems even more appropriate today.

The present theoretical disorientation of social psychology has been exacerbated by the deep cleavage within the field between what, for the want of better terminology, may be called "psychological social psychology" and "sociological social psychology." Stryker (1977) and House (1977) have argued that this cleavage lies at the heart of the field's present state of malaise. And I tend to agree with this diagnosis, for even though the hostilities between proponents of these two basically different orientations have diminished, they have not been integrated to provide a comprehensive theoretical framework for the discipline as a whole.

Both of these approaches have a long history, going back to the very beginning of social psychology. But it was the intention of the founders of the discipline that they should be combined to provide an understanding not simply of the individual or society but of the relationship, or interaction, between the two. Comte, who is generally recognized as the intellectual father of social psychology, viewed man as both the creature and the creator of the social world in which he lives, and identified the central problem of social psychology as that of finding an answer to the question: How can the individual be both the cause and the consequence of society? And McDougall (1926), in one of the first textbooks, formulated social psychology's central mission as that of showing "how, given the native propensities and capacities of the individual mind, all the complex mental life of societies is shaped by them and in turn reacts upon the course of their development and operation in the individual" (1926:18).

This conception of the central mission of social psychology has been undermined, however, by theorists who maintain that all social psychological phenomena must be explained exclusively in terms of their antecedents either within society or within the individual. Thus, for example, Durkheim formulated what was to become the sociological approach when he asserted that "the determining cause of a social fact should be sought among the social facts preceding it and not among the states of the individual consciousness" (1895/1950:110). And Floyd Allport stated the essence of the psychological approach when he said, "I believe that only within the individual can we find the behavior mechanisms and consciousness which are fundamental in the interaction between individuals . . . There is no psychology of groups which is not essentially and entirely a psychology of individuals" (1924:vi).

Although these attempts to make social psychology a branch of one of its parent disciplines have not succeeded, they have influenced thinking up to the present time. Gordon Allport, in discussing the history of the field, observed that "with few exceptions social psychologists regard their discipline as an attempt to understand and explain how the thoughts, feelings, and behavior of individuals are influenced by the actual, imagined, or implied presence of others" (1968:3). This statement has often been taken as the definition of social psychology, but since it is not acceptable to those who adopt the sociological approach, we are left with two social psychologies rather than one.

Immediately after the Second World War several efforts were made to bring these two subdisciplines together by establishing doctoral programs intended to encompass all of social psychology. Although these programs produced some outstanding social psychologists and generated some important theoretical and empirical research, they did not accomplish the desired reorganization of the field. In looking back over this experience, I am now inclined to believe that it was unrealistic to hope to solve what is essentially a theoretical problem simply by having psychologists and sociologists collaborate in the training of graduate students. But whatever the reason for the failure of these programs, we should not be deluded into thinking that the problem went away with their termination.

It would be paradoxical if social psychology were ever to abandon the very task that constituted its original *raison d'etre* and were to accept either of these approaches as the sole basis for defining its proper subject-matter. But if this unfortunate eventuality is to be avoided, we must have a clear conception of the discipline's basic mission, or master problem, which will provide an organizing principle for all of social psychology. We need, in other words, a definition of the field that places the study of psychological processes within a proper social context and, at the same time, recognizes the critical role of these processes in interpersonal relations, social interaction, and social structure.

As a first approximation to such a definition, I would suggest something like the following: Social psychology is that branch of the social sciences which attempts to explain how society influences the cognition, motivation, development, and behavior of individuals and, in turn, is influenced by them. This definition, by focusing on the reciprocal relations between individuals and society, could, I believe, provide an organizing principle for all of social psychology, including its two main subdivisions and its several areas of specialization. But if it is to do so, we shall have to clarify two of our basic constructs that serve to relate the individual to society. These are the concepts: *social environment* and *social behavior*.

The term *social environment* is an extension by analogy of the concept *physical environment*, and refers to all those features of the external world that influence the social behavior and development of individuals. It consists of such things as social networks, groups, organizations, social structure, roles, norms, social pressures, social support, duties, and obligations. And although it has a long history in social psychology, its conceptual properties have not yet been well defined. A good beginning has been made, however, by Barker (1968) in his work on ecological psychology, by French and his colleagues (1974) in their research on person–environment fit, by Katz and Kahn (1978) and other theorists, such as Emery and Trist (1965), who view the individual and the social environment as an interdependent system, and by Berger and Luckmann (1966) in their theoretical treatment of the social construction of reality. Research such as this has made it evident that the social environment cannot be usefully described solely in terms of its physical properties since its significance for social behavior lies in its semantic content or social meaning. It differs from the physical environment in that it is largely a social product and must therefore be conceived as both the cause and consequence of social behavior.

The term *social behavior* refers to such things as asking questions, providing information, seeking or giving help, expressing hostility or affection, joining a group, enacting a role, performing acts of leadership, exercising power, voting, or participating in a social movement. Actions ⟨...⟩ ort are the means by which individuals adjust their relationships with the e⟨...⟩ ⟨...⟩ cannot properly be conceived merely as responses to stimuli. The essential ⟨...⟩ ere, as I see it, is to find an effective conceptualization of the processes by ⟨...⟩ individuals is converted, or transformed, into "social acts" which have ⟨...⟩ ture that they can have consequences for other people, groups, and ⟨...⟩ words, for the social environment. A proper understanding of these ⟨...⟩ e to any adequate theory of social power, leadership, group problem ⟨...⟩ ing, social effectiveness, and collective action. Without such a theory, ⟨...⟩ hological research are bound to have limited practical value.

Concluding Observations

In introducing this discussion of the current state of the field, I indicated that my overall evaluation is definitely positive. But since I have dwelt for the most part on deficiencies and unsolved problems, one may well ask what is the basis for all the optimism. Part of it results from the historical perspective described earlier. Social psychology is in an early stage of development and has not had time to solve all of its problems. Such defects as the susceptibility to fads and fashions, the obsession with technique, the reliance on a single method of research, and the disproportionate emphasis on cognition and other temporally proximal determinants of behavior are, I believe, symptoms of immaturity and can be expected to be remedied with the passage of time.

Most social psychologists today have come from a restricted segment of American society, and this has limited our theoretical perspective, contributed to an unfortunate degree of ethnocentrism, and greatly influenced the content of empirical research. But these, too, will be overcome as the demographic composition of the field is broadened to include more women, members of various minority groups, scholars from different cultures, and citizens of both the so-called developed and underdeveloped countries. Within the next few years, social psychology should become a truly international community of scholars, and every effort should be made to facilitate this accomplishment.

Perhaps the most important reason for optimism, however, derives from the demonstrated capacity of social psychologists to respond positively to challenge. From its very beginning, the field has confronted what must have appeared to be almost insurmountable theoretical, methodological, and institutional obstacles. But these have always served to stimulate innovation and creativity, and although the problems we face today are exceedingly difficult, I can see no reason to believe that social psychologists will not continue to respond to these challenges in the foreseeable future.

NOTE

This paper was presented as the 1978 Katz–Newcomb Lecture at the University of Michigan, where it was my great privilege to have been associated with Professors Katz and Newcomb for thirty years.

REFERENCES

Allport, F.H. (1924) *Social Psychology*. New York: Houghton Mifflin.

Allport, G.W. (1968) "The historical background of modern social psychology." Pp. 1–80 in G. Lindzey and E. Aronson (eds), *The Handbook of Social Psychology* (vol. 1, 2nd edn). Reading, Mass.: Addison-Wesley.

Asch, S.E. (1959) "A perspective on social psychology." Pp. 363–83 in S. Koch (ed.), *Psychology: A Study of a Science* (vol. 3). New York: McGraw-Hill.

Barker, R.G. (1968) *Ecological Psychology*. Stanford: Stanford University Press.

Berger, P.L., and T. Luckmann (1966) *The Construction of Reality*. New York: Doubleday.

Cartwright, D. (1948) "Social psychology in the United States during the Second World War." *Human Relations* 1:333–52.

——(1961) "A decade of social psychology." Pp. 9–30 in R.A. Patton (ed.), *Current Trends in Psychological Theory*. Pittsburgh: Pittsburgh University Press.

Durkheim, E. (1895) [1950] *The Rules of Sociological Method*. Tr. (1950) by S.S. Solvay and J.H. Mueller. New York: Free Press.

Elms, A.C. (1975) "The crisis of confidence in social psychology." *American Psychologist* 30:967–76.

Emery, F.E., and E.L. Trist (1965) "The causal texture of organizational environments." *Human Relations* 18:21–32.

French, J.R.P. Jr, W.L. Rogers, and S. Cobb (1974) "Adjustment as person–environment fit." In G. Coelho, D. Hamburg, and J. Adams (eds), *Coping and Adaptation*. New York: Basic Books.

Garvey, W.D., and B.C. Griffith (1971) "Scientific communication: Its role in the conduct of research and creation of knowledge." *American Psychologist* 26:349–62.

House, J.S. (1977) "The three faces of social psychology." *Sociometry* 40:161–77.

Hovland, C.I. (1959) "Reconciling conflicting results derived from experimental and survey studies of attitude change." *American Psychologist* 14:8–17.

Katz, D., and R.L. Kahn (1978) *The Social Psychology of Organizations* (2nd edn). New York: Wiley.

Kuhn, T. (1962) *The Structure of Scientific Revolutions*. Chicago: University of Chicago Press.

Lewin, K. (1948) *Resolving Social Conflicts*. New York: Harper.

McDougall, W. (1926) *An Introduction to Social Psychology* (rev. edn). Boston: Luce.

Murphy, G., L. Murphy, and T.M. Newcomb (1937) *Experimental Social Psychology*. New York: Harper.

Newcomb, T.M. (1947) "Autistic hostility and social reality." *Human Relations* 1:69–86.

Stryker, S. (1977) "Developments in 'two social psychologies': Toward an appreciation of mutual relevance." *Sociometry* 40:145–60.

Zajonc, R.B. (1976) "Family configuration and intelligence." *Science* 192:227–36.

2   Evolutionary Social Psychology

Sex differences in jealousy: Evolution, physiology, and psychology

D.M. Buss, R.J. Larsen, D. Westen and J. Semmelroth

Editors'
Introduction

Theoretical Background

While everybody knows about the cognitive revolution in social psychology, another revolution that has happened in our field has hardly been noticed. Social psychologists who until recently abhorred the idea that social behaviour might be to some extent influenced by genetic factors are suddenly embracing such ideas enthusiastically. Evolutionary social psychology is fast becoming an established area of psychology, enriching our understanding of many aspects of social behaviour (see Archer, 1996; Caporael and Brewer, 1991). There has certainly been a profound change in the intellectual climate of our discipline, facilitating the emergence of an evolutionary approach to social psychology. However, of equal importance has been the fact that evolutionary psychologists have begun to test their ideas experimentally.

The article by Buss and associates is an excellent example of the new breed of evolutionary social psychology. Basic to the evolutionary argument is the assumption that the genes underlying any traits which help individuals to survive and to produce numerous offspring (that is, increase 'fitness') will be more strongly represented in the next generation. In contrast, genes underlying traits which reduce the ability of the organism to survive and reproduce will be less strongly represented. For example, any gene which would make men jealously guard their women against being impregnated by other men should have a greater chance of being represented in the next generation than a gene which would lower their guard against being cuckolded. Jealousy would protect men against investing valuable resources in assumed offspring who might not even be genetically related to them, given that men cannot usually be certain that they are the biological father of a child. As a consequence, there should be 'strong selection pressure on males to defend against cuckoldry'.

Women, on the other hand, face entirely different problems. Although they can be certain that their offspring are genetically related to them, they run the risk of losing their own time and resources, and also of losing the commitment of the male, who may walk out.

Psychological Science (1992), 3:251–5.

Hypotheses

On the basis of such reasoning, the authors argued that men and women should differ in the type of infidelity which triggers most jealousy and subjective distress. Men should be more distressed by sexual infidelity, women by emotional infidelity signalling the development of a strong emotional attachment of their partner to another woman.

STUDY 1

Design

The study is a repeated-measures judgement task in which subjects are presented with certain stimuli (in this case imaginary stimuli) and asked to evaluate their reactions.

Method

Subjects were male and female undergraduate students who were asked to think of a serious, committed romantic relationship they had had in the past, currently had or would have liked to have had, and to imagine that their partner had become involved with someone else in one of two ways, namely (1) by forming a deep emotional attachment to that person or (2) by enjoying passionate sexual intercourse with that person. After subjects had indicated what would upset them more, they had to repeat this procedure with a second set of situations, namely (1) imagining their partner trying different sexual positions with that other person, (2) imagining their partner falling in love with that person.

Results

Data were analysed using chi-square tests. In line with predictions, 60 per cent of the men reported more distress about sexual rather than emotional infidelity, whereas more than 80 per cent of the women gave the reverse judgement, a difference which was highly significant. A similar pattern of significant differences emerged for the second set of situations.

STUDY 2

Study 2 is essentially a replication of study 1, except for a difference in dependent measures. Instead of using self-ratings, psychophysiological measures were used to assess emotional upset. Three types of physiological activity were measured: (1) electrodermal activity, better known as skin conductance – people produce more perspiration when emotionally aroused, which increases their skin conductance; (2) pulse rate, which quickens when people are emotionally aroused; (3) electromyographic activity – measuring movements of (facial) muscles, in this case the furrowing of the brow often seen in facial displays of negative emotions. Subjects were first asked to imagine an emotionally neutral situation to establish a baseline for the physiological measurement. They were then asked to imagine two infidelity images, one sexual and one emotional, with the order of presentation counterbalanced across subjects. The dependent measures were expressed in terms of the difference in physiological reactions to the neutral image as compared to each of the infidelity images. Data were analysed with *t*-tests. Findings replicated the patterns observed in study 1 (see table 2.1).

STUDY 3

This study tested the hypothesis that the sex differences observed for types of jealousy in studies 1 and 2 would emerge even more strongly for subjects who had been in a committed sexual relationship as compared to subjects who had not. As in study 1, data were analysed by chi-square tests. Overall the findings closely replicated those of the previous studies. When groups were divided into those who reported having been in a committed sexual relationship and those who had not, this factor made a big difference for men but not for women.

Discussion

The results of the three empirical studies provide consistent support for the hypothesized sex difference in the type of infidelity likely to produce the highest level of distress. However, one weakness of the present set of studies is that the evolutionary hypotheses were not tested against hypotheses derived from other types of theory. For example, one could argue that with a traditional distribution of marital roles, where women are the homemakers and men are the salary earners, women could have much more to lose financially than men. Thus, they may have every reason to worry more about a break-up of their marriages than their partners do. This alternative hypothesis could be tested by comparing jealousy in dual-earning versus traditional families.

FURTHER READING

Buss, D.M. (1995). *The Evolution of Desire*. New York: Basic Books. Presents Buss's view on the importance of evolutionary theory for understanding human nature.
Singh, D. (1993). Adaptive significance of female physical attractiveness: Role of waist-to-hip ratio. *Journal of Personality and Social Psychology*, 65, 293–307. Presents evidence that factors which determine female physical attractiveness (such as body fat distribution) are correlated with youthfulness, reproductive endocrinologic status and long-term health risk in women.

REFERENCES

Archer, J. (1996). Evolutionary social psychology. In M. Hewstone, W. Stroebe and G.M. Stephenson (eds), *Introduction to Social Psychology: A European Perspective* (2nd edn, pp. 24–45). Oxford: Blackwell.
Caporael, L.R. and Brewer, M.B. (eds) (1991). Issues in evolutionary psychology. *Journal of Social Issues*, 47 (3).

In species with internal female fertilization and gestation, features of reproductive biology characteristic of all 4,000 species of mammals, including humans, males face an adaptive problem not confronted by females – uncertainty in their paternity of offspring. Maternity probability in mammals rarely or never deviates from 100%. Compromises in paternity probability come at substantial reproductive cost to the male – the loss of mating effort expended, including time, energy, risk, nuptial gifts, and mating opportunity costs. A cuckolded male also loses the female's parental effort, which becomes channeled to a competitor's gametes. The adaptive problem of paternity uncertainty is exacerbated in species in which males engage in some postzygotic parental investment (Trivers, 1972). Males risk investing resources in putative offspring that are genetically unrelated.

These multiple and severe reproductive costs should have imposed strong selection pressure on males to defend against cuckoldry. Indeed, the literature is replete with examples of evolved anticuckoldry mechanisms in lions (Bertram, 1975), bluebirds (Power, 1975), doves (Erickson and Zenone, 1976), numerous insect species (Thornhill and Alcock, 1983), and nonhuman primates (Hrdy, 1979). Since humans arguably show more paternal investment than any other of the 200 species of primates (Alexander and Noonan, 1979), this selection pressure should have operated especially intensely on human males. Symons (1979); Daly, Wilson, and Weghorst (1982); and Wilson and Daly (in press) have hypothesized that male sexual jealousy evolved as a solution to this adaptive problem (but see Hupka, 1991, for an alternative view). Men who were indifferent to sexual contact between their mates and other men presumably experienced lower paternity certainty, greater investment in competitors' gametes, and lower reproductive success than did men who were motivated to attend to cues of infidelity and to act on those cues to increase paternity probability.

Although females do not risk maternity uncertainty, in species with biparental care they do risk the potential loss of time, resources, and commitment from a male if he deserts or channels investment to alternative mates (Buss, 1988; Thornhill and Alcock, 1983; Trivers, 1972). The redirection of a mate's investment to another female and her offspring is reproductively costly for a female, especially in environments where offspring suffer in survival and reproductive currencies without investment from both parents.

In human evolutionary history, there were likely to have been at least two situations in which a woman risked losing a man's investment. First, in a monogamous marriage, a woman risked having her mate invest in an alternative woman with whom he was having an affair (partial loss of investment) or risked his departure for an alternative woman (large or total loss of investment). Second, in polygynous marriages, a woman was at risk of having her mate invest to a larger degree in other wives and their offspring at the expense of his investment in her and her offspring. Following Buss (1988) and Mellon (1981), we hypothesize that cues to the development of a deep emotional attachment have been reliable leading indicators to women of potential reduction or loss of their mate's investment.

Jealousy is defined as an emotional "state that is aroused by a perceived threat to a valued relationship or position and motivates behavior aimed at countering the threat. Jealousy is 'sexual' if the valued relationship is sexual" (Daly et al., 1982, p. 11; see also Salovey, 1991; White and Mullen, 1989). It is reasonable to hypothesize that jealousy involves physiological reactions (autonomic arousal) to perceived threat and motivated action to reduce the threat, although this hypothesis has not been examined. Following Symons (1979) and Daly et al. (1982), our central hypothesis is that the events that activate jealousy physiologically and psychologically differ for men and women because of the different adaptive problems they have faced over human evolutionary history in mating contexts. Both sexes are hypothesized to be distressed over both sexual and emotional infidelity, and previous findings bear this out (Buss, 1989). However, these two kinds of infidelity should be weighted differently by men and women. Despite the importance of these hypothesized sex differences, no systematic scientific work has been directed toward verifying or falsifying their existence (but for suggestive data, see Francis, 1977; Teismann and Mosher, 1978; White and Mullen, 1989).

Study 1: Subjective Distress over a Partner's External Involvement

This study was designed to test the hypothesis that men and women differ in which form of infidelity – sexual versus emotional – triggers more upset and subjective distress, following the adaptive logic just described.

Method

After reporting age and sex, subjects ($N = 202$ undergraduate students) were presented with the following dilemma:

> Please think of a serious committed romantic relationship that you have had in the past, that you currently have, or that you would like to have. Imagine that you discover that the person with whom you've been seriously involved became interested in someone else. What would distress or upset you more (*please circle only one*):
> (A) Imagining your partner forming a deep emotional attachment to that person.
> (B) Imagining your partner enjoying passionate sexual intercourse with that other person.

Subjects completed additional questions, and then encountered the next dilemma, with the same instructional set, but followed by a different, but parallel, choice:

> (A) Imagining your partner trying different sexual positions with that other person.
> (B) Imagining your partner falling in love with that other person.

Results

Shown in figure 2.1 (upper panel) are the percentages of men and women reporting more distress in response to sexual infidelity than emotional infidelity. The first empirical probe, contrasting distress over a partner's sexual involvement with distress over a partner's deep emotional attachment, yielded a large and highly significant sex difference ($\chi^2 = 47.56$, $df = 3$, $p < .001$). Fully 60% of the male sample reported greater distress over their partner's potential sexual infidelity: in contrast, only 17% of the female sample chose that option, with 83% reporting that they would experience greater distress over a partner's emotional attachment to a rival.

This pattern was replicated with the contrast between sex and love. The magnitude of the sex difference was large, with 32% more men than women reporting greater distress over a partner's sexual involvement with someone else, and the majority of women reporting greater distress over a partner's falling in love with a rival ($\chi^2 = 59.20$, $df = 3$, $p < .001$).

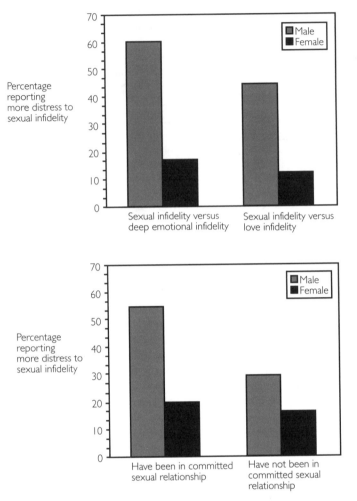

Figure 2.1 Reported comparisons of distress in response to imagining a partner's sexual or emotional infidelity. The upper panel shows results of Study 1 – the percentage of subjects reporting more distress to the sexual infidelity scenario than to the emotional infidelity (left) and the love infidelity (right) scenarios. The lower panel shows the results of Study 3 – the percentage of subjects reporting more distress to the sexual infidelity scenario than to the emotional infidelity scenario, presented separately for those who have experienced a committed sexual relationship (left) and those who have not experienced a committed sexual relationship (right)

Study 2: Physiological Responses to a Partner's External Involvement

Given the strong confirmation of jealousy sex linkage from Study 1, we sought next to test the hypotheses using physiological measures. Our central measures of autonomic arousal were electrodermal activity (EDA), assessed via skin conductance, and pulse rate (PR). Electrodermal activity and pulse rate are indicators of autonomic nervous system activation (Levenson, 1988). Because distress is an unpleasant subjective state, we also included a measure of muscle activity in the brow region of the face – electromyographic (EMG) activity of the *corrugator supercilii* muscle. This muscle is responsible for the furrowing of the brow often seen in facial displays of unpleasant emotion or affect (Fridlund, Ekman, and Oster, 1987). Subjects were asked to image two scenarios in which a partner became involved with someone else – one sexual intercourse scenario and one emotional attachment scenario. Physiological responses were recorded during the imagery trials.

Subjects

Subjects were 55 undergraduate students, 32 males and 23 females, each completing a 2-hr laboratory session.

Physiological measures

Physiological activity was monitored on the running strip chart of a Grass Model 7D polygraph and digitized on a laboratory computer at a 10-Hz rate, following principles recommended in Cacioppo and Tassinary (1990).

Electrodermal activity
Standard Beckman Ag/AgCl surface electrodes, filled with a .05 molar NaCl solution in a Unibase paste, were placed over the middle segments of the first and third fingers of the right hand. A Wheatstone bridge applied a 0.5-V voltage to one electrode.

Pulse rate
A photoplethysmograph was attached to the subject's right thumb to monitor the pulse wave. The signal from this pulse transducer was fed into a Grass Model 7P4 cardiotachometer to detect the rising slope of each pulse wave, with the internal circuitry of the Schmitt trigger individually adjusted for each subject to output PR in beats per minute.

Electromyographic activity
Bipolar EMG recordings were obtained over the *corrugator supercilii* muscle. The EMG signal was relayed to a wide-band AC-preamplifier (Grass Model 7P3), where it was band-pass filtered, full-wave rectified, and integrated with a time constant of 0.2 s.

Procedure

After electrode attachment, the subject was made comfortable in a reclining chair and asked to relax. After a 5-min waiting period, the experiment began. The subject was alone in the room during the imagery session, with an intercom on for verbal communication. The instructions for the imagery task were written on a form which the subject was requested to read and follow.

Each subject was instructed to engage in three separate images. The first image was designed to be emotionally neutral: "Imagine a time when you were walking to class, feeling neither good nor bad, just neutral." The subject was instructed to press a button when he or she had the image clearly in mind, and to sustain the image until the experimenter said to stop. The button triggered the computer to begin collecting physiological data for 20s, after which the experimenter instructed the subject to "stop and relax."

The next two images were infidelity images, one sexual and one emotional. The order of presentation of these two images was counterbalanced. The instructions for sexual jealousy imagery were as follows: "Please think of a serious romantic relationship that you have had in the past, that you currently have, or that you would like to have. Now imagine that the person with whom you're seriously involved becomes interested in someone else. *Imagine you find out that your partner is having sexual intercourse with this other person.* Try to feel the feelings you would have if this happened to you."

The instructions for emotional infidelity imagery were identical to the above, except the italicized sentence was replaced with "*Imagine that your partner is falling in love and forming an emotional attachment to that person.*" Physiological data were collected for 20s following the subject's button press indicating that he or she had achieved the image. Subjects were told to "stop and relax" for 30s between imagery trials.

Results

Physiological scores
The following scores were obtained: (a) the amplitude of the largest EDA response occurring during each 20-s trial; (b) PR in beats per minute averaged over each 20-s trial; and (c) amplitude of EMG activity over the *corrugator supercilii* averaged over each 20-s trial. Difference scores were computed between the neutral imagery trial and the jealousy induction trials.

Table 2.1   Means and standard deviations on physiological measures during two imagery conditions

Measure	Imagery type	Mean	SD
	Males		
EDA	Sexual	1.30	3.64
	Emotional	−0.11	0.76
Pulse rate	Sexual	4.76	7.80
	Emotional	3.00	5.24
Brow EMG	Sexual	6.75	32.96
	Emotional	1.16	6.60
	Females		
EDA	Sexual	−0.07	0.49
	Emotional	0.21	0.78
Pulse rate	Sexual	2.25	4.68
	Emotional	2.57	4.37
Brow EMG	Sexual	3.03	8.38
	Emotional	8.12	25.60

Measures are expressed as changes from the neutral image condition. EDA is in microsiemen units, pulse rate is in beats per minute, and EMG is in microvolt units.

Within-sex *t* tests revealed no effects for order of presentation of the sexual jealousy image, so data were collapsed over this factor.

Jealousy induction effects

Table 2.1 shows the mean scores for the physiological measures for men and women in each of the two imagery conditions. Differences in physiological responses to the two jealousy images were examined using paired-comparison *t* tests for each sex separately for EDA, PR, and EMG. The men showed significant increases in EDA during the sexual imagery compared with the emotional imagery ($t = 2.00$, $df = 29$, $p < .05$). Women showed significantly greater EDA to the emotional infidelity image than to the sexual infidelity image ($t = 2.42$, $df = 19$, $p < .05$). A similar pattern was observed with PR. Men showed a substantial increase in PR to both images, but significantly more so in response to the sexual infidelity image ($t = 2.29$, $df = 31$, $p < .05$). Women showed elevated PR to both images, but not differentially so. The results of the *corrugator* EMG were similar, although less strong. Men showed greater brow contraction to the sexual infidelity image, and women showed the opposite pattern, although results with this nonautonomic measure did not reach significance ($t = 1.12$, $df = 30$, $p < .14$, for males; $t = -1.24$, $df = 22$, $p < .12$, for females). The elevated EMG contractions for both jealousy induction trials in both sexes support the hypothesis that the affect experienced is negative.

Study 3: Contexts that Activate the Jealousy Mechanism

The goal of Study 3 was to replicate and extend the results of Studies 1 and 2 using a larger sample. Specifically, we sought to examine the effects of having been in a committed sexual relationship versus not having been in such a relationship on the activation of jealousy. We hypothesized that men who had actually experienced a committed sexual relationship would report greater subjective distress in response to the sexual infidelity imagery than would men who had not experienced a high-investing sexual relationship, and that women who had experienced a committed sexual relationship would report greater distress to the emotional infidelity image than women who had not been in a committed sexual relationship. The rationale was that direct experience of the relevant context during development may be necessary for the activation of the sex-linked weighting of jealousy activation.

Subjects

Subjects for Study 3 were 309 undergraduate students, 133 men and 176 women.

Procedure

Subjects read the following instructions:

> Please think of a serious or committed romantic relationship that you have had in the past, that you currently have, or that you would like to have. Imagine that you discover that the person with whom you've been seriously involved became interested in someone else. What would distress or upset you more (*please circle only one*):

    (A) **Imagining your partner falling in love and forming a deep emotional attachment to that person.**
    (B) **Imagining your partner having sexual intercourse with that other person.**

Alternatives were presented in standard forced-choice format, with the order counterbalanced across subjects. Following their responses, subjects were asked: "Have you ever been in a serious or committed romantic relationship? (yes or no)" and "If yes, was this a sexual relationship? (yes or no)."

Results

The results for the total sample replicate closely the results of Study 1. A much larger proportion of men (49%) than women (19%) reported that they would be more distressed by their partner's sexual involvement with someone else than by their partner's emotional attachment to, or love for, someone else ($\chi^2 = 38.48$, $df = 3$, $p < .001$).

The two pairs of columns in the bottom panel of figure 2.1 show the results separately for those subjects who had experienced a committed sexual relationship in the past and those who had not. For women, the difference is small and not significant: Women reported that they would experience more distress about a partner's emotional infidelity than a partner's sexual infidelity, regardless of whether or not they had experienced a committed sexual relationship ($\chi^2 = .80$, $df = 1$, ns).

For men, the difference between those who had been in a sexual relationship and those who had not is large and highly significant. Whereas 55% of the men who had experienced committed sexual relationships reported that they would be more distressed by a partner's sexual than emotional infidelity, this figure drops to 29% for men who had never experienced a committed sexual relationship ($\chi^2 = 12.29$, $df = 1$, $p < .001$). Sexual jealousy in men apparently becomes increasingly activated upon experience of the relevant relationship.

Discussion

The results of the three empirical studies support the hypothesized sex linkages in the activators of jealousy. Study 1 found large sex differences in reports of the subjective distress individuals would experience upon exposure to a partner's sexual infidelity versus emotional infidelity. Study 2 found a sex linkage in autonomic arousal to imagined sexual infidelity versus emotional infidelity; the results were particularly strong for the EDA and PR. Study 3 replicated the large sex differences in reported distress to sexual versus emotional infidelity, and found a strong effect for men of actually having experienced a committed sexual relationship.

These studies are limited in ways that call for additional research. First, they pertain to a single age group and culture. Future studies could explore the degree to which these sex differences transcend different cultures and age groups. Two clear evolutionary psychological predictions are (a) that male sexual jealousy and female commitment jealousy will be greater in cultures where males invest heavily in children, and (b) that male sexual jealousy will diminish as the age of the male's mate increases because her reproductive value decreases. Second, future studies could test the alternative hypotheses that the current findings reflect (a) domain-specific psychological adaptations to cuckoldry versus potential investment loss or (b) a more domain-general mechanism such that any thoughts of sex are more interesting, arousing, and perhaps disturbing to men whereas any thoughts of love are more interesting, arousing, and perhaps disturbing to women, and hence that such responses are not specific to jealousy or infidelity. Third, emotional and sexual infidelity are clearly correlated, albeit imperfectly, and a sizable percentage of men in Studies 1 and 3 reported greater distress to a partner's emotional infidelity. Emotional infidelity may signal sexual infidelity and vice versa, and hence both sexes should become distressed at both forms (see Buss, 1989). Future research could profitably explore in greater detail the correlation of these forms of infidelity as well as the sources of within-sex variation. Finally, the intriguing finding that men who have experienced a committed sexual relationship differ dramatically from those who have not, whereas for women such experiences appear to be irrelevant to their selection of emotional infidelity as the more distressing event, should be examined. Why do such ontogenetic experiences matter for men, and why do they appear to be irrelevant for women?

Within the constraints of the current studies, we can conclude that the sex differences found here generalize across both psychological and physiological methods – demonstrating an empirical robustness in the observed effect. The degree to which these sex-linked elicitors correspond to the hypothesized sex-linked adaptive problems lends support to the evolutionary psychological framework from which they were derived. Alternative theoretical frameworks, including those that invoke culture, social construction, deconstruction, arbitrary parental socialization, and structural powerlessness, undoubtedly could be molded post hoc to fit the findings – something perhaps true of any set of findings. None but the Symons (1979) and Daly et al. (1982) evolutionary psychological frameworks, however, generated the sex-differentiated predictions in advance and on the basis of sound evolutionary reasoning. The recent finding that male sexual jealousy is the leading cause of spouse battering and homicide across cultures worldwide (Daly and Wilson, 1988a, 1988b) offers suggestive evidence that these sex differences have large social import and may be species-wide.

ACKNOWLEDGMENTS

This research was supported in part by National Institute of Mental Health (NIMH) Grant MH-44206-02 to David M. Buss; Research Scientist Development Award KO1-MH00704 and NIMH Grant MH-42057 to Randy Larsen; and Biomedical Research Support Grant SO7 RR07050-25 from the National Institutes of Health to Randy Larsen and David M. Buss through the University of Michigan Office of the Vice President for Research. The authors thank Michael Chen, Martin Daly, Todd DeKay, Bruce Ellis, Arlette Greer, Kurt Hoop, Tim Ketelaar, Neil Malamuth, David Schmitt, and Don Symons for helpful suggestions on earlier versions of this article.

REFERENCES

Alexander, R.D., and Noonan, K.M. (1979). Concealment of ovulation, parental care, and human social evolution. In N. Chagnon and W. Irons (eds) *Evolutionary biology and human social behavior* (pp. 436–53). North Scituate, MA: Duxbury.
Bertram, B.C.R. (1975). Social factors influencing reproduction in wild lions. *Journal of Zoology*, 177, 463–82

Buss, D.M. (1988). From vigilance to violence: Tactics of mate retention. *Ethology and Sociobiology*, 9, 291–317.

Buss, D.M. (1989). Conflict between the sexes: Strategic interference and the evocation of anger and upset. *Journal of Personality and Social Psychology*, 56, 735–47.

Cacioppo, J.T., and Tassinary, L.G. (eds) (1990). *Principles of psychophysiology: Physical, social, and inferential elements*. Cambridge, England: Cambridge University Press.

Daly, M., and Wilson, M. (1988a). Evolutionary social psychology and family violence. *Science*, 242, 519–24

Daly, M., and Wilson, M. (1988b), *Homicide*. Hawthorne, NY: Aldine.

Daly, M., Wilson, M., and Weghorst, S.J. (1982). Male sexual jealousy. *Ethology and Sociobiology*, 3, 11–27.

Erickson, C.J., and Zenone, P.G. (1976). Courtship differences in male ring doves: Avoidance of cuckoldry? *Science*, 192, 1353–4.

Francis, J.L. (1977). Toward the management of heterosexual jealousy. *Journal of Marriage and Family Counseling*, 10, 61–9.

Fridlund, A., Ekman, P., and Oster, J. (1987) Facial expressions of emotion. In A. Siegman and S. Feldstein (Eds), *Nonverbal behavior and communication* (pp. 143–224). Hillsdale, NJ: Erlbaum.

Hrdy, S.B.G. (1979). Infanticide among animals: A review, classification, and examination of the implications for the reproductive strategies of females. *Ethology and Sociobiology*, 1, 14–40.

Hupka, R.B. (1991). The motive for the arousal of romantic jealousy: Its cultural origin. In P. Salovey (ed.). *The psychology of jealousy and envy* (pp. 252–70). New York: Guilford Press.

Levenson, R.W. (1988). Emotion and the autonomic nervous system: A prospectus for research on autonomic specificity. In H. Wagner (ed.), *Social psychophysiology: Theory and clinical applications* (pp. 17–42). London: Wiley.

Mellon, L.W. (1981). *The evolution of love*. San Francisco: W.H. Freeman.

Power, H.W. (1975). Mountain bluebirds: Experimental evidence against altruism. *Science*, 189, 142–43.

Salovey, P. (ed.) (1991). *The psychology of jealousy and envy*. New York: Guilford Press.

Symons, D. (1979). *The evolution of human sexuality*. New York: Oxford University Press.

Teismann, M.W., and Mosher, D.L. (1978). Jealous conflict in dating couples. *Psychological Reports*, 42, 1211–16.

Thornhill, R., and Alcock, J. (1983). *The evolution of insect mating systems*. Cambridge, MA: Harvard University Press.

Trivers, R. (1972). Parental investment and sexual selection. In B. Campbell (ed.), *Sexual selection and the descent of man, 1871–1971* (pp. 136–79). Chicago: Aldine.

White, G.L., and Mullen, P.E. (1989). *Jealousy: Theory, research, and clinical strategies*. New York: Guilford Press.

Wilson, M., and Daly, M. (in press). The man who mistook his wife for a chattel. In J. Barkow, L. Cosmides, and J. Tooby (eds), *The adapted mind: Evolutionary psychology and the generation of culture*. New York: Oxford University Press.

3 Developmental Social Psychology

The development of children's preference for their own country: A cross-national study

H. Tajfel, C. Nemeth, G. Jahoda, J.D. Campbell and N.B. Johnson

- - - - -
Editors'
Introduction
- - - - - - - -

Theoretical Background

To what extent is ethnocentrism (preference for one's own social group over others) something that emerges relatively early, independently of direct contact with other social groups? Children of 6 or 7 have relatively rudimentary concepts of nationhood, yet they already seem to exhibit clear preferences for their own nation over others. This raises interesting issues relating to prejudice, stereotyping and intergroup relations. If preference for one's own nationality emerges early, and relatively independently of a concept of nationhood, this suggests that children learn to prefer their own nationality not as a result of knowing what it means to be French, German, Dutch or whatever, but because they are exposed in the course of socialization to attitudes that are more favourable to their own nationality than to other nationalities. Tajfel and his colleagues wanted to study this phenomenon in 6–8-year-olds, and also in 9–12-year-olds, in order to see how preference for own nationality changes with age. One of the most interesting aspects of this study is the fact that it was conducted in six different countries. Showing that children in a variety of countries exhibit a preference for their own nationality over other nationalities rules out the possibility that such a preference is due to special factors that apply in one country.

Hypothesis

The authors expected children to exhibit a preference for their own nationality. They made no prediction concerning how the two age-groups might differ.

International Journal of Psychology (1970), 5:245–53.

Method

How does one examine children's preferences for their own nation in a way that does not fall foul of all the problems of demand characteristics (see Manstead and Semin, 1996, for a discussion of these problems)? Previous research used symbols of nationhood such as flags but there are strong normative pressures to respect and value such blatant national symbols. The researchers' solution was to ask children to perform two separate tasks, using the same set of stimuli – twenty-three photographs of young men. In one task (evaluative), the children had to sort these photographs into four categories, ranging from ones they liked very much to ones they disliked very much. In the other task (nationality assignment), children were asked to decide whether the man shown in each photograph was someone of their own nationality or of another nationality. The two tasks were separated by two to three weeks, in an attempt to minimize the chances that performance on one task would be influenced by performance on the preceding one. Furthermore, the order in which the two tasks were performed was 'counterbalanced', meaning that half the children first performed the evaluative task and then the nationality assignment task, whereas the other half did the tasks in the reverse order.

Two further points need to be noted. First, one of the countries involved in the study was Belgium. Because Belgium is a nation comprising two distinct linguistic and cultural communities (the French-speaking Walloons, and the Dutch-speaking Flemish), the concept of 'nationhood' is a complex one (one can be Flemish, as opposed to Walloon; but one can also be Belgian as opposed to, for example, English). To control for this issue, half the Flemish children were asked to make 'Flemish–not Flemish' choices in the nationality assignment task, while the other half were asked to make 'Belgian–not Belgian' choices.

The second point is that the Italian (Naples) group of children were added after data from the other five countries had been collected. This was to check whether certain regularities in the findings could be explained by the existence of regularities in the physical features of compatriots (such as blond hair) that are learned by older children. Because what the authors call the 'physiognomic ecology' (that is, the typical facial appearance of a local person) presumably differs between Italy and northern Europe, the addition of an Italian group allowed the authors to test their hunch.

Results

The main findings are the ones reported under the subheading 'Preference for own nationals'. In the first numbered paragraph the authors report differences between how much 'own nationality' and 'other nationality' photographs were liked, averaged across children. If children had not preferred their own nationality, the scores would be roughly zero. The fact that all means, except that for the Scottish (Glasgow) group, differ significantly from zero (assessed by means of a one-sample *t*-test) supports the authors' hypothesis. Another way of examining the same issue is to compute the correlation between liking and nationality scores. (Note that the unit of analysis here was each photograph, not each child.) These correlations are reported in Table 3.1 and are also broadly supportive of the hypothesis, although this time the results for the Dutch (Leiden), as well as the Scottish (Glasgow), children are not statistically significant. Table 3.2 shows the same correlations, this time separately for the two age-groups. Note that the liking–own nationality relationship is generally weaker in the older group. Table 3.3 shows that there is a high level of agreement within countries between the younger and older children in their liking ratings and their nationality judgements, with the exception of the Italian (Naples) group, where there was little consensus in nationality judgements. Table 3.4 shows that there is quite a high level of agreement between countries in the judgements that children made, although differences in size of correlation between younger and older children were quite variable for the liking judgements (sometimes the older children from two countries agreed more, sometimes the younger children). By contrast there is a clear trend for nationality judgements to be more highly correlated between countries among older children than among younger ones. The fact this was not true for the Italian children is consistent with the authors' conjecture that older children develop a 'physical stereotype' of their compatriots: for Italians this stereotype presumably differs from those held by northern European children.

Discussion

In general the findings support the authors' hypothesis. The main discussion points concern the findings for those national groups that diverge from the general trend. These were the Scottish children, the Flemish children, and the Italian children. The Scottish and younger Flemish children were less inclined than the other groups to show preference for their own nationality. The authors suggest that this may be due to the more complex nature of the nationality of these two groups (Scottish children are Scottish rather than English, but also British rather than French). The older Italian children were less likely than were older children in other countries to agree with their younger counterparts about who was or was not a compatriot. The authors suggest that this reflects the learning by older children of a physical stereotype of compatriots, a stereotype that was not well represented among the stimulus photographs.

Although the results of Tajfel et al.'s study do not pinpoint which processes or factors are responsible for this generally robust tendency for children to prefer their own nationality over other nationalities, it seems likely that children are socialized to adopt such own-nationality-preferring attitudes. A comparison can be made with work on gender socialization. Ruble (1987) argues that once children discover the significance of their own gender label, they start attending selectively to the behaviours of same-sex others, who provide them with information about what is expected from members of this social category. Likewise, it can be argued that once children have a sense of the fact that they are, say, British, they may actively attend to information relevant to this category. In this way they acquire the representations of nationhood that are shared in their society (cf. Emler et al., 1990) – representations that are likely to be more favourable with respect to one's own nationality than to other nationalities.

FURTHER READING

Aboud, F. (1988). *Children and Prejudice.* Oxford: Blackwell. An overview of theory and research on this topic.
Tajfel, H., Jahoda, G., Nemeth, C., Rim, Y. and Johnson, N.B. (1972). Devaluation by children of their

own national or ethnic group: Two case studies. *British Journal of Social and Clinical Psychology*, 11, 235–43. This paper reports research following up the present study, focusing on the exceptional cases where children devalue their own nationality.

REFERENCES

Emler, N.P., Ohana, J. and Dickinson, J. (1990). Children's representations of social relations. In G. Duveen and B.B. Lloyd (eds), *Social Representations and the Development of Knowledge* (pp. 161–83). Cambridge: Cambridge University Press.
Manstead, A.S.R. and Semin, G.R. (1996). Methodology in social psychology: Putting ideas to the test. In M. Hewstone, W. Stroebe and G.M. Stephenson (eds), *Introduction to Social Psychology* (2nd edn, pp. 74–106). Oxford: Blackwell.
Ruble, D. (1987). The acquisition of self-knowledge: A self-socialization perspective. In N. Eisenberg (ed.), *Contemporary Topics in Developmental Psychology* (pp. 281–312). New York: Wiley.

- - - - -
Primary
Reading
- - - - - - - -

There is general consensus in the literature that children come to "prefer" their own country to others well before they are able to form, understand and use appropriately the relevant concepts of countries or nations (for reviews of evidence, cf. Jahoda, 1963a, 1963b; Davies, 1968). This discrepancy between the development of concepts and of evaluations exists not only with regard to countries and nations but also in the case of attitudes pertaining to other large-scale human groups, racial, ethnic, religious and social (Proshansky, 1966). Several studies have shown that evaluations precede understanding whether the relevant groups are or are not in direct contact (e.g., racial, ethnic or religious groups living side by side as contrasted with nations), and whether clear-cut physical or behavioural cues do or do not exist to facilitate discrimination (e.g., racial groups in contact as contrasted with, for example, religious groups in contact). It seems that Horowitz's (1947) early dictum that "attitudes toward Negroes are now chiefly determined not by contact with Negroes, but by contact with the prevalent attitude toward Negroes" (p. 517) has a much more general application.

Studies such as those by Piaget and Weil (1951) and by Jahoda (1962) have shown that at the ages of 6–7 the concept of nation is still rudimentary and highly confused for most children. Our purpose was to show that, at the same age, there is already a highly crystallised and consensual preference in children for their own country, and to trace the course of development of this preference until about the age of twelve. Piaget once wrote that "what first interests a child in a country is the name" (1928, p. 128). It is this "nominal realism" underlying preferences that most probably accounts for their early existence and for their relative independence, already mentioned, of direct contact or of supporting cues. In the present study we wished to use no more than the "word" or the national label in order to elicit children's preferences, to do this in a manner which would not involve young children in complex verbalizations which are often equally complex to interpret, and to avoid as far as possible the weight on the children's responses of heavy normative pressures – such as exist when, for example, preferences for national flags are requested (Lawson, 1963). We also attempted to establish as much free choice of responses as possible by using stimuli which were highly ambiguous and by introducing a considerable time lag between the presentation of the national label and the relevant evaluations. At the same time we attempted to develop a method which would have the advantage of unambiguous comparability both cross-nationally and across age groups.

Method

Subjects

Subjects for the study were drawn from primary schools in Oxford (England), Leiden (Holland), Vienna (Austria), Glasgow (Scotland), Louvain (Belgium), and Naples (Italy). In each sample, half of the children were male and half female; they ranged from 6 to 12 years of age. The numbers of subjects in the various samples were as follows: 336 in Oxford, 136 in Glasgow, 120 in Leiden, 418 in Vienna, 110 in Louvain (Flemish subjects) and 118 in Naples.

Procedure

In each country the same experimental method was used. Twenty-three fairly standardised photographs of young men were prepared in Oxford for the purposes of the study and used in all the countries. Each child was tested individually in two successive sessions, the sessions being separated by two to three weeks. In one session, the child was presented with twenty photographs and asked to put each photograph in one of four boxes respectively labelled "I like him very much", "I like him a little", "I dislike him a little" and "I dislike him very much." In the other session, the child was told that some of the photographs were of people of his own nationality (e.g., English in England) and that some were not. He was then asked to decide whether or not each photograph was of his own nationality and then to place it in one of two boxes appropriately labelled (e.g., English and Not English). In the Louvain study, half the subjects sorted the photographs on the basis of Belgian–not Belgian, while the other half sorted them on the basis of Flemish–not Flemish. At the start of each session, the child was given three pilot photographs to ascertain his understanding of the instructions. Thus, for example, in the nationality assignment session for an English child, the experimenter first made sure that the child could read the labels on the boxes (i.e., English–not English). After the child was informed that some of the individuals in the photographs were English and some were not English, he was shown the first pilot photograph and was asked whether he thought the individual was English or not English. After the child responded, the experimenter asked him to put it in the appropriate box. The procedure was repeated for the three pilot photographs; if the child had difficulties, the prompting continued. Similar prompting occurred in the "like–dislike" session for the three pilot photographs. Here, the child was first asked to decide whether he liked or disliked the individual. If the child responded, for example, that he "liked him" he was instructed to hold the photograph near the two boxes for the "liked" people, and was then asked if he liked the person "very much" or "a little". After the child responded, he was shown the appropriate box for the photograph. This procedure was repeated for at least three pilot photographs; if the child had further difficulties the prompting continued. Half of the children in each of the national samples had the nationality assignment session first and the "like–dislike" session later; this order was reversed for the other half of the subjects. The photographs were presented in four different random orders.

Results

In all the samples the proportions of photographs assigned by the children to the categories of "own" nationals and of foreigners were each close to 50%.

Preference for own nationals

The analysis of data was done in two ways:

(1)   An index termed d-score was calculated for each child. The d-score consisted of the mean difference in liking between the photographs the child assigned to his own national category and those he assigned to "not own", (e.g., English as compared with not English, etc.). A score of 1 to 4 was assigned to the degrees of liking (from "I dislike him very much" to "I like him very much") in the like–dislike sessions; the d-score consisted of the mean difference in liking scores between the photographs assigned to own and not own nationality. Thus, a positive d-score reflected a preference in the like–dislike session for photographs assigned to own nationality in the nationality assignment session.

The overall mean d-scores for each of the samples are: Oxford +.30; Glasgow +.09; Leiden +.32; Louvain: Belgian +.24, Flemish +.19; Naples +.17; Vienna +.32. With the exception of Scotland, they are all highly significant ($p < .01$, on the basis of a two-tailed one-sample *t*-test). Thus children clearly prefer those photographs they classify as own nation to those classified as not own nation.

(2)   In order to facilitate comparisons across countries and age groups, a second index of preference was calculated by means of a correlation coefficient based not on individual data from the subjects but on the photographs. For each photograph the percentage of subjects that assigned it to own nation was correlated with the overall mean liking score for that photograph in each sample. Table 3.1 sets out these correlations. They are positive and again significantly different from 0 with the exception of the Scottish data; the Dutch data nearly reach significance. Thus the more a group of children classify a photograph as own, the more it is preferred.

Age trends

As can be seen in table 3.2, a fairly clear pattern emerges when the nationality–liking correlations for younger children are compared with those for the older age groups. With the exception of the Louvain samples, all correlations show a substantial *decrease* with age.

Table 3.1 Correlations (*r*) between liking and nationality (total samples)

Oxford	.82*		Belgian–not Belgian	.66*
Glasgow	.07	Louvain		
Leiden	.31		Flemish–not Flemish	.54*
Vienna	.76*	Naples		.51*

*$p < .05$.
N = 20 photographs.

Table 3.2   Correlations between liking and assignment to own nation

		Younger Ss (age 6–8)	Older Ss (age 9–12)
	Oxford	.923*	.726*
	Glasgow	.342*	.032
	Leiden	.465*	.174
	Belgian	.407	.739*
Louvain {			
	Flemish	.230	.530*
	Naples	.653*	.099
	Vienna	.779*	.657*

*p < .05.

Cross-national comparisons

The studies were first conducted in Oxford and in Glasgow, and later in Leiden, Louvain and Vienna. Of those six samples (i.e., including the Belgian–not Belgian and Flemish–not Flemish versions in Louvain) all excepting Glasgow showed a significant tendency to prefer photographs which were assigned to own national groups. Six kinds of correlation were run subsequently in order to assess and compare the extent of cross-age and cross-national preferences and of nationality assignments. They were as follows: (1) within each national group, a correlation between the younger and the older children of their liking of the twenty photographs; (2) within each national group, a correlation between the younger and the older children of the proportions of Ss who assigned each photograph to their own nationality; (3) correlations showing the extent of agreement in liking of the twenty photographs between the younger children for all pairings of national groups; (4) as (3), for the older children; (5) correlations showing the extent of agreement in assignment of the twenty photographs to own nationality between the younger children for all pairings of national groups; (6) as (5), for the older children.

Table 3.3 shows the correlations obtained for (1) and (2) above. Leaving the Naples data aside for the moment, it can be seen that all intranational correlations are positive and that, with the exception of the Flemish data, they are all statistically significant; i.e., there is fair agreement between the younger and the older children within each national group as to who they like and as to who is their compatriot. The sets of correlations (3), (4), (5) and (6) showed unexpected regularities which led to the decision of replicating the study in Naples. These correlations are reproduced in table 3.4. Ignoring once again for the moment the Naples data, the following can be seen from the tables: (1) the five samples (i.e., except Glasgow) which showed positive relationships between preference and national assignment display no clear-cut pattern of trend from the younger to the older age groups in their agreement as to who they "like". It can be seen in table 3.4(a) that out of the ten pairs of correlations between samples from Oxford, Leiden, the two Louvain samples and Vienna, there is an increase in the liking correlations from the younger to the older children for six pairs of countries, and a decrease for four; (2) the overall pattern is very different for the same ten pairs in the case of correlations of nationality assignments. It can be seen from table 3.4(b) that in *all* ten cases older children in

Table 3.3   Correlations between younger and older children (a) on liking, (b) on nationality assignment

	Oxford	Glasgow	Leiden	Louvain Belgian	Flemish	Naples	Vienna
(a)	.949*	.649*	.844*	.530*	.335	.846*	.881*
(b)	.804*	.581*	.680*	.666*	.383	.183	.802*

*p < .05.

Table 3.4   Correlations between various countries in younger (Y) and older (O) children (a) on liking, (b) on nationality assignment

	Dutch		Belgian		Flemish		Austrian		Italian		Scottish	
	Y	O	Y	O	Y	O	Y	O	Y	O	Y	O
(a)												
English	.574	.448	.507	.657	.506	.670	.733	.809	.667	.714	.813	.865
Dutch			.595	.332	.100	.104	.839	.616	.579	.579	.482	.505
Belgian					.282	.599	.652	.357	.790	.391	.369	.544
Flemish							.428	.501	.376	.645	.498	.577
Austrian									.803	.779	.682	.786
Italian											.579	.754
(b)												
English	.711	.782	.233	.493	.527	.574	.690	.715	.662	.551	.520	.450
Dutch			.332	.601	.212	.679	.431	.504	.487	.405	.255	.482
Belgian					.299	.653	.329	.508	.013	.365	.039	.044
Flemish							.526	.765	.343	.230	.368	.025
Austrian									.685	.491	.056	−.013
Italian											.306	.463

any two countries agree more than younger children do as to who are their compatriots. This was an intriguing finding, particularly in view of the absence of a similar pattern in the case of liking and of the general finding that the correlations between liking and nationality assignment decreased with age (see table 3.3).

One possible explanation of this regularity was that, with increasing age, children tend to learn some kind of a physical stereotype of their national group and that this stereotype may be similar in the four countries concerned – England, Belgium, Holland and Austria. In order to test this possibility, the study had to be replicated in another location in which two criteria would be satisfied: (1) the same photographs could still be used as presenting a credible choice in the assignment to compatriot and foreigner; and (2) the location should offer the possibility of finding a "physiognomic ecology" different from the first four countries. Thus, if it were true that children do acquire with age some form of a consensual physical stereotype of their national group which depends to some extent upon the cues which they learn in their environment, the agreement in national assignments between the new location and the other countries should *decrease* with age. The replication was conducted in Naples. Comparison of the data obtained there with the other data provides suggestive evidence that a certain crystallisation of physical stereotype may be taking place with increasing age and that this stereotype is not unrelated to what we called the "physiognomic ecology".

The younger and the older children in Naples strongly agree, as do the children in the other locations, as to who they like; they do not, however, agree – and in this they are the only exception – as to who are their compatriots (see table 3.3). In view of the general tendency for the assignments of younger children to be more closely related to affectivity than those of the older ones (see table 3.2), this finding lends support to the possibility that there is a crystallisation of a physical stereotype in the older age group. As stated above, in all ten pairs of correlations from Oxford, Leiden, Louvain and Vienna there is an increase with age of agreement about national assignments. Out of the five correlations with Naples, four show a decrease with age in this agreement (see table 3.4(b)). Once again, there is no sign of a clear-cut pattern for the corresponding set of correlations for liking (see table 3.4(a)).

Conclusions and Discussion

The main findings of the study are as follows:

1   In all the locations except Glasgow, there is a significant tendency to assign better liked photographs to own national category.
2   The strength of this tendency decreases with age with the exception of Louvain, where, in the case both of the Belgian and of the Flemish assignments, there is a marked increase of the correlations with age. For children tested in England, Belgium and Austria, the tendency is still strong and significant in the older age-range tested.
3   There is a marked agreement between all the locations in the selection of photographs that are liked.
4   There is also a marked agreement between all the locations, with the exception of Naples, in the assignments to own national category.
5   In all cases of positive relationships between liking and nationality assignment except Naples, the cross-national agreement in nationality assignment increases with age. No such general age tendency appears in the case of cross-national agreement on liking. The Naples data provide a marked exception to the assignment pattern: the comparisons of other locations with Naples show a tendency for a decrease with age of agreement in nationality assignments.
6   In all locations, there is a high agreement on liking between the younger and the older children. This also applies to nationality assignments with the exception of the data from Naples.

Discussion of these findings is bound to remain speculative without further data bearing on the various hypotheses that can be generated. This discussion must be mainly concerned with the various exceptions to general trends that were found in the data.

The general findings are as follows: through an association of national verbal labels with preference sorting of photographs one can elicit from young children a clear index of preference for their own national group. This relationship weakens with age. It would be naive to assume that this decrease is due to a decrease in "nationalism". It seems more likely that for the younger children both sets of judgements tend to be based more directly on the same affective criterion and that this is the way in which they solve the problem presented to them by the highly ambiguous task of nationality assignments. There is no doubt that this task is also an ambiguous one for the older children – as it would be for adults. But it is possible that in the older age group separate cues begin to function for liking and for nationality assignments, that an effort is made by the children to approach the two kinds of judgements with different criteria. There are indications in the data that a physical national stereotype develops in children with age. It is possible that the subtle cues for this stereotype do not fully overlap with the cues for liking of individual photographs, and that there is an area of random variation in the relationship between the two.

In addition, we know from previous studies, such as those of Piaget and Weil (1951) and of Jahoda (1963a, 1963b), that a "great intellectual distance [is] traversed within the span of a few years" (Jahoda, 1963b) with regard to the concept of nationality. A relatively mature concept of nation could be strongly related to positive attitudes towards one's own country without having to express itself through rudimentary preferences for photographs which appear – rather dubiously – to be of one's compatriots. It is likely that in younger children a more primitive kind of national preference which still remains at a preconceptual stage makes use of any simple affective symbols that it can find. This close relationship between rudimentary affectivity and national preference is by no means a phenomenon to be found only amongst children.

The agreement in national assignments between the first four locations in which positive results were obtained led to the Naples study. Cross-national comparisons of the Naples data with the others strengthened the case for the existence of a physical stereotype of own nation which develops with age. If this interpretation were to be supported by further research, it would lead to some interesting questions. Is this an "ideal" stereotype based on mass communication media such as comics, cinema, television, advertisements, etc., in which certain physical "types" are used, or is it based more directly on a distillation of cues from the "real" social environment? The second alternative does not appear very plausible unless one assumes a considerable uniformity in what we referred to above as "physiognomic ecology". Physiognomic problems of this nature have always presented extraordinary difficulties for research (e.g., Brunswik, 1956; Tagiuri, 1969). On the other hand, there also exists the possibility that a negative stereotype develops because of frequent presentation of "undesirable aliens" as having certain physical characteristics in comics, cartoons, films, etc. (e.g., Johnson, 1966). The difference in the physical stereotypes between Naples and the other locations could be explained on this basis only if it could be shown that the heroes and villains to whom the Neapolitan children are exposed in various forms of visual fiction look different from their equivalents in Oxford, Louvain, Leiden or Vienna. Alternatively, it is of course possible that the general physiognomic ecology of Naples is sufficiently different from that of the other European locations in which we worked to have produced the differences that were found.

The two main findings – of a significant relationship between preference and nationality assignments in the younger children and of its decrease with age – have two exceptions: in Glasgow, where this relationship hardly exists; and in Louvain, where it shows a considerable *increase* with age both for the Flemish and for the Belgian assignments. The common feature of Glasgow and Louvain is that, as distinct from the other four locations, nationality assignments present there a task which is altogether more complex. But the effects of this complexity are very different in Glasgow and in Louvain. The early confusion in Louvain (shown also by a weak correlation in the data from younger children between assignments as Flemish and as Belgian, and relatively weak correlations in liking between the younger and the older children in both the Belgian and the Flemish versions of the task) gives way in the older age groups to firm preferences for their own national group – whether expressed as Belgian or as Flemish. One can speculate that the lack of a simple and unique national label for the Flemish children combined with the high salience in the country of the binational issue and of the Flemish self-awareness (which, however, is not on the whole *un*Belgian) interferes, in the case of the younger children, with the simple affective reaction to the "word" or "label". "Flemish" may mean "not Walloon" but it is also a subcategory of "Belgian" of which Walloon is another subcategory; "not Flemish" may mean "Walloon" and/or "Belgian"; "Belgian" and "not Belgian" may present similar complexities. It is therefore a fair assumption that these difficulties of ethnic and national labels and relationship are sorted out only at later ages when both kinds of national concepts, assignments and preferences have become more firmly established.

The Glasgow children seem to react to a different kind of complexity by not showing a preference for their own national group. One possible reason for this lack of national preference may well be that the well-known phenomenon of the devaluation of ingroup which has been shown in many studies on children of minority or underprivileged groups (for recent examples, cf. Vaughan, 1964; Morland, 1966; Jahoda and Thomson, 1970) exists here in a rather unexpected context. As the Scots are by no means a minority in Scotland, nor are the intergroup tensions between the English and the Scots comparable to those which form the background of other studies on ingroup devaluation, the data we obtained may well constitute an important example of children's high sensitivity even to those aspects of social influence which remain fairly subtle as distinct from being an all-pervading consequence of a tense intergroup situation (Tajfel, 1969). It is because of this possibility that further studies specifically addressed to this problem were subsequently conducted in Scotland and in England as well as in Israel, where data were obtained from children of European and of Oriental origin (Tajfel, Jahoda, Nemeth and Rim, in preparation).

NOTES

We are greatly indebted to our colleagues who organised and conducted the studies in the various locations: Jos Jaspars and John van de Geer in Leiden; Jozef Nuttin, Jr. and Annie Janssen-Beckers in Louvain; Gustavo Iacono and Maria Barbiero in Naples; and Maria Simon in Vienna. Separate detailed reports exist of the various national studies: from Leiden, cf. J.M.F. Jaspars et al. (1965); from Naples, cf. M. Barbiero; and from Vienna, cf. M. Simon et al. (1967).

C. Nemeth and J.D. Campbell were in Oxford during part of the period when the present studies were conducted.

REFERENCES

Barbiero, M. National prejudice in the formative years. Unpublished manuscript, University of Naples.
Brunswik, E. *Perception and the representative design of psychological experiments*. Berkeley and Los Angeles: University of California Press, 1956.

Davies, A.F. The child's discovery of nationality. *Australian and New Zealand Journal of Sociology*, 1968, 4, 107–25.

Horowitz, E.L. Development of attitude toward Negroes. In T.M. Newcomb and E.L. Hartley (eds), *Readings in social psychology*, New York: Henry Holt, 1947. Pp. 507–17.

Jahoda, G. Development of Scottish children's ideas and attitudes about other countries. *Journal of Social Psychology*, 1962, 58, 91–108.

Jahoda, G. The development of children's ideas about country and nationality. I. The conceptual framework. *British Journal of Educational Psychology*, 1963a, 33, 47–60; II. National symbols and themes. *British Journal of Educational Psychology*, 1963b, 33, 143–53.

Jahoda, G. and Thomson, S.S. Ethnic identity and preference among Pakistani immigrant children in Glasgow. *European Journal of Social Psychology*, 1970, in press.

Jaspars, J.M.F., van de Geer, J.P., Tajfel, H. and Johnson, N.B. On the development of interpersonal attitudes. Report ESP n°001-65, University of Leiden, Institute of Psychology, 1965.

Johnson, N.B. What do children learn from war comics? *New Society*, July 1966, 7–12.

Lawson, E.D. The development of patriotism in children. A second look. *Journal of Psychology*, 1963, 55, 279–86.

Morland, J.K. A comparison of race awareness in Northern and Southern children. *American Journal of Orthopsychiatry*, 1966, 36, 22–31.

Piaget, J. *Judgement and reasoning in the child.* New York: Harcourt, Brace, 1928.

Piaget, J. and Weil, A.M. The development in children of the idea of homeland, and of relations with other countries. *International Social Science Bulletin*, 1951, 3, 561–78.

Proshansky, H.M. The development of intergroup attitudes. In I.W. Hoffman and M.L. Hoffman (eds), *Review of child development*, vol. 2. New York: Russell Sage Foundation, 1966. Pp. 311–71.

Simon, M., Tajfel, H. and Johnson, N.B. Wie erkennt man einen Osterreicher? *Kölner Zeitschrift für Soziologie und Sozial-psychologie*, 1967, 3, 511–37.

Tagiuri, R. Person perception. In G. Lindzey and E. Aronson (eds), *The handbook of social psychology*, 2nd edn, vol. 3. Reading, Mass.: Addison-Wesley, 1969. Pp. 395–449.

Tajfel, H. Cognitive aspects of prejudice. *Journal of Biosocial Sciences*, 1 Supplement monographs, No. 1, *Biosocial aspects of race*, 1969, 173–91, and *Journal of Social Issues*, 1969, 4, 79–97.

Vaughan, G.M. The development of ethnic attitudes in New Zealand school children. *Genetic Psychology Monographs*, 1964, 70, 135–75.

4 Methodology in Social Psychology: Putting Ideas to the Test

Experimentation in social psychology: A reappraisal

K.J. Gergen

Editors'
Introduction

Theoretical Background

The background to this theoretical paper about the status of experimentation in social psychology was the so-called 'crisis of confidence' in social psychology that emerged in the early 1970s. From the end of World War II until the beginning of the 1970s social psychology developed rapidly, and in the 1960s it positively flourished. Much of this expansion took the form of theory-testing experimentation. Some of the most celebrated experiments in social psychology were conducted and reported in the 1960s. Examples include Aronson and Carlsmith's (1963) 'dissonance' study of the effects of severity of threat on children's liking for a toy, Latané and Darley's (1969) early experiments on bystander intervention, Milgram's initial research on obedience to authority (see chapter 16), and Stoner's (1961) discovery of what later came to be known as group polarization. In the early 1970s some commentators began to question the value of this outpouring of experimental research. Methodological critiques of experimentation had already been published; these included Orne's (1962, 1969) analyses of the role played by demand characteristics in experimental studies, and Rosenthal's (1966) work on experimenter expectancy effects. What was new in the 1970s was a more thoroughgoing critique of experimentation on the grounds that it lacked external validity (Tajfel, 1972), posed serious ethical issues (Kelman, 1972), and was incapable of producing knowledge that had lasting value (Gergen, 1973). This critical self-analysis and soul-searching came to be referred to as the 'crisis of confidence' in social psychology. The present reading can be regarded as representing the culmination of this wave of critical analysis of the use of experimentation in social psychology.

European Journal of Social Psychology (1978), 8:507–27.

Overview

The essence of Gergen's argument can be summarized as follows. Those who conduct experiments in social psychology do so in an attempt to reveal cause–effect relationships between independent (manipulated) and dependent (measured) variables. In doing so they necessarily isolate one or two variables from the rich context of everyday social interaction. Because everyday social reality is such that stimuli are only meaningful when they are located in their normal cultural and sequential context, the simplification involved in experimentation fails to capture these everyday meanings. Moreover, the meanings of social events change as a function of time, so the attempt to establish 'laws' of human social behaviour that are universally valid is doomed to fail. The result is that all reasonable hypotheses are likely to be valid, and that so-called 'critical' experiments designed to support one theory at the expense of another cannot be definitive. However, Gergen acknowledges that experimentation can serve useful functions.

Thesis

Let us examine each of Gergen's arguments more closely.

1   His first argument is that social events are 'culturally embedded.' In other words, the meaning of any stimulus event is dependent on the circumstances in which it occurs. A stimulus event is not simply one stimulus, but rather a configuration of co-occurring stimuli. The issue, then, is whether the experimental method is capable of capturing the complexity inherent in configurations of stimuli. Gergen accepts that the experimental method does allow one in principle to manipulate complex events, but he goes on to argue that the 'ideological orientation' of experimental social psychology is such that 'rigour' is favoured over 'reality,' with the result that stimuli are routinely disembedded from their cultural context. Note that one of the examples he mentions in passing is the manipulation of the presence or absence of weapons in a context in which one can aggress against someone who has provoked you (see the reading by Berkowitz and LePage, chapter 14). The result, according to Gergen, is that the 'normal' meaning of the stimulus is stripped away, and the way in which participants respond to such a stimulus in an experiment may be quite different from how they would react to it in everyday life. This line of argument is developed into the claim that the experimental context in which a stimulus is manipulated plays a crucial (but hidden) role in determining participants' reactions to the stimulus. The result is that the real task of an experimenter is to find or create a social context in the experiment that is appropriate to test a hypothesis concerning the effects of manipulating the key construct of theoretical interest.

2   Gergen's second argument is that social events are 'sequentially embedded'. By this he means that a stimulus not only occurs in a particular *cultural* context; it also occurs within a sequence of events, and its meaning depends importantly on *where* it occurs in this sequence. Although experiments are not in principle incapable of studying long sequences of events, Gergen argues that in practice they tend to focus on very short sequences (see

Cartwright, Chapter 1, for a similar criticism). The result, according to Gergen, is that social psychology can tell us little about the unfolding of things or processes such as family relationships, careers, ageing or extended negotiations.

3 Gergen's third argument is that social events are 'openly competitive'. In other words, the *strength* of a response to a stimulus is dependent on the context in which it occurs. Other stimuli are also present, and these compete with the stimulus for the participant's attention, thought, feeling or action. Thus one result of studying the effects of manipulating stimuli in experimental situations, according to Gergen, is that we have little idea of how much power they have to elicit the same effects in everyday life, where a greater number of competing stimuli are present.

4 Gergen's fourth argument is that social events are 'final common pathways'. By this he means that they are multiply determined: how someone acts in a particular social situation depends on a large number of co-occurring psychological factors. Disentangling this web of influences on social behaviour is almost impossible, so that when we think we have manipulated one psychological factor in a relatively 'pure' manner, it is very likely that we have manipulated two or more simultaneously. In short, the psychological causes of social behaviour are naturally confounded with each other. The result, according to Gergen, is that we are confronted with experimental findings that are explained by one group of researchers as reflecting the influence of construct X, and by another group of researchers as reflecting the influence of construct Y, and it is almost impossible to choose between these explanations. This means that precise tracing of causation is impossible.

5 Gergen's fifth argument is that social events are 'complexly determined'. The particular point he makes here concerns the difficulty of manipulating more than three experimental variables at a time. Practical, conceptual and statistical problems arise when one attempts to conduct highly complex experiments, in which four or more factors are manipulated simultaneously. And yet in everyday life one's behaviour may well be determined by the joint effects of four or more factors.

6 Gergen's sixth argument is that social behaviour is subject to change over time. If social psychology is intended to reveal the 'laws' of social behaviour, and yet social behaviour itself is subject to the influence of history, how can we hope to establish such laws? In other words, a causal relationship observed in, say, 1959 may not be found in 1999, simply due to the intervening change of circumstances. Gergen illustrates this argument by the use of a figure (Figure 4.1) illustrating possible causal paths linking the similarity of a person (*O*) with attraction to that person exhibited by another person (*P*), via a set of intervening psychological processes. The point of this figure is to show that the relationship between similarity and attraction is one that can involve different kinds of similarity and different kinds of attraction, and can work via different mediating processes. Gergen asserts that many aspects of this figure are subject to change over time and culture.

Conclusions

Gergen's conclusions are that (1) all 'reasonable' hypotheses are likely to be valid; (2) the 'critical' experiment is expendable; and (3) experiments are only useful for explicating 'biosocial relationships' (where there are grounds for thinking that the relationships are more stable), heightening our awareness of phenomena that we might otherwise take for granted, enhancing the impact of theoretical ideas, and helping to determine the value of social policy reforms.

Commentary

Gergen's article constitutes a sustained critique of the usefulness of experimentation in social psychology. It was written in an era when experimentation, and above all laboratory experimentation, was the dominant methodology used in social psychology. Today there is a greater variety of methods used than in the 1970s, including more quasi-experiments conducted in natural settings, although laboratory experiments do still dominate. Thus some aspects of his critique are less relevant now than they were in the 1970s – perhaps even as a result of his critique. Manipulating a variable in a natural or 'field' setting helps to overcome the kinds of objection voiced by Gergen in his first, second and third arguments. This is not to say that quasi-experiments are a flawless solution to the kinds of problem discussed by Gergen. As soon as one departs from random assignment of participants to experimental conditions, the ability to draw causal inferences is weakened, and it is the non-randomness of assignment to conditions that distinguishes a quasi-experiment from a true one. Other aspects of Gergen's critique are just as applicable now as they were in the 1970s. For example, doubts are still expressed about the ability to devise 'crucial experiments' that help one to determine which of two (or more) theoretical perspectives is correct (for example, Tetlock and Levi, 1982; Tetlock and Manstead, 1985); relatedly, some commentators continue to question the ability of experimentation to establish either the truth or falsity of a given theory (Greenwald et al., 1986; McGuire, 1983); and few present-day social psychologists would take serious issue with the notion that the processes and effects they are researching are at least partly determined by cultural factors that are specific to a particular time or place (cf. Smith and Bond, 1993; Triandis, 1994). Readers interested in a recent expansion of the arguments presented by Gergen in the present article should consult Gergen (1994).

In summary, Gergen's article serves as a useful reminder that the simple-minded application of experimental techniques to research complex social psychological phenomena runs the risk of arriving at conclusions that are at best only temporarily correct. Fortunately, the three decades since Gergen's paper was published have witnessed the development of a richer range of methodologies in social psychology. Although the laboratory experiment has by no means vanished, it is now properly regarded as one of a range of research methods available to social psychologists (see Judd, 1995). Moreover, the ideology accompanying the use of experimentation in social psychology has changed. Instead of treating experiments as ways of revealing 'eternal truths' about social behaviour, most social psychologists would now accept that experiments are ways of identifying the conditions under which particular hypotheses can be supported. When used sensitively and especially when used in combination with other methodologies, experiments still have a crucial role to play in social psychology.

FURTHER READING

Gergen, K.J. (1973). Social psychology as history. *Journal of Personality and Social Psychology*, 26, 309–20. The original statement of Gergen's thesis that social psychological knowledge is subject to change over time.

Schlenker, B. (1974). Social psychology and science. *Journal of Personality and Social Psychology*, 29, 1–15. A rebuttal of Gergen's thesis and a defence of social psychology's 'scientific' status.

REFERENCES

Aronson, E. and Carlsmith, J.M. (1963). Effect of the severity of threat on the devaluation of forbidden behavior. *Journal of Abnormal and Social Psychology*, 66, 584–8.

Gergen, K.J. (1994). *Toward transformation in social knowledge* (2nd edn). Beverly Hills, CA: Sage.

Greenwald, A.G., Pratkanis, A.R., Leippe, M.R. and Baumgardner, M.H. (1986). Under what conditions does theory obstruct research progress? *Psychological Review*, 93, 216–29.

Judd, C.M. (1995). Methodology. In A.S.R. Manstead and M. Hewstone (eds), *Blackwell Encyclopedia of Social Psychology* (pp. 385–8). Oxford: Blackwell.

Kelman, H.C. (1972). The rights of the subject in social research: An analysis in terms of relative power and legitimacy. *American Psychologist*, 27, 989–1016.

Latané, B. and Darley, J.M. (1969). Bystander 'apathy'. *American Scientist*, 57, 244–68.

McGuire, W.J. (1983). A contextualist theory of knowledge: Its implications for innovation and reform in psychological research. In L. Berkowitz (ed.), *Advances in Experimental Social Psychology* (vol. 16, pp. 1–47). New York: Academic Press.

Orne, M.T. (1962). On the social psychology of the social psychology experiment: With particular reference to demand characteristics and their implications. *American Psychologist*, 17, 776–83.

Orne, M.T. (1969). Demand characteristics and the concept of quasi-controls. In R. Rosenthal and R.L. Rosnon (eds), *Artifact in Behavioral Research* (pp. 143–79). New York: Academic Press.

Rosenthal, R. (1966). *Experimenter Effects in Behavioral Research*. New York: Appleton-Century-Crofts.

Smith, P.B. and Bond, M.H. (1993). *Social Psychology Across Cultures: Analysis and Perspectives*. Hemel Hempstead: Harvester-Wheatsheaf.

Stoner, J.A.F. (1961). A comparison of individual and group decisions involving risk. Unpublished master's thesis, Massachusetts Institute of Technology, Cambridge, MA.

Tajfel, H. (1972). Experiments in a vacuum. In J. Israel and H. Tajfel (eds), *The Context of Social Psychology: A Critical Assessment* (pp. 69–119). London: Academic Press.

Tetlock, P.E. and Levi, A. (1982). Attribution bias: On the inconclusiveness of the cognition–motivation debate. *Journal of Experimental Social Psychology*, 18, 68–88.

Tetlock, P.E. and Manstead, A.S.R. (1985). Impression management versus intrapsychic explanations in social psychology: A useful dichotomy? *Psychological Review*, 92, 59–77.

Triandis, H.C. (1994). *Culture and Social Behavior*. New York: McGraw-Hill.

Introduction

- - - - -
Primary
Reading
- - - - - - - -

During the past three decades the practice of social psychology has become unmistakably identified with the experimental method. For many this development has been welcomed and much effort has been devoted to sustaining its hegemony. In contrast to the earlier methodologies of social psychologists, the merits of the experimental approach have been readily apparent. Through experimentation one could move from sheer speculation to the level of empirically grounded theory. No longer was it necessary to rely on the wholly unreliable accounts of a single observer, nor was the scientist fettered by correlational techniques and their shaky grasp of causal sequence. Through experimentation, it seemed possible to test ideas against reality and to accumulate a repository of fundamental knowledge. Inroads could also be made into the control of social phenomena. In addition experimentation ensured that social psychologists could lay claim to the respectability increasingly enjoyed by their colleagues in the more traditional areas of psychology (e.g. sensory, learning, and physiological). Social psychology could finally link itself securely with the logical positivist orientation to scientific conduct (Koch, 1959).

The results of this line of development are widely apparent. The percentage of experimental studies appearing in the *Journal of Personality and Social Psychology*, the most prestigious voice in the field, increased from approximately 30 per cent in 1949 to 83 per cent in 1959, and then to 87 per cent in 1969 (Higbee and Wells, 1972). The *Journal of Experimental Social Psychology* and the *European Journal of Social Psychology* are commonly viewed as competitors in respectability. Their contributions are almost entirely experimental. Even in the more peripheral journals such as the *Journal of Research in Personality* and the newer *Journal of Applied Social Psychology*, the vast majority of the present contributions rely on experimentation. Simulation methodologies are rarely employed in these journals; survey research is almost exclusively limited to the field of sociology and political science (Fried, Gumper and Allen, 1973); and in Weick's (1968) review of observational methodology in social psychology, only 15 per cent of the 300 references are taken from the four major journals of the field and less than half of this group from the five-year period prior to publication of the review. The one elite organization within the field is aptly named the *Society for Experimental Social Psychology*. Within psychology the pursuit of social understanding has become virtually synonymous with the experimental method.

Criticisms of the experimental approach have emerged over the years. Classic is Orne's (1962) discussion of demand characteristics within the laboratory setting. Closely related is Rosenthal's (1966) extensive research on experimenter bias. However, the primary effect of this work has been to enhance experimental rigour. Numerous critics have called attention to the artificiality of the laboratory setting and to our inability to generalize from laboratory experiments to conventional settings (Kelman, 1972; McGuire, 1967; Tajfel, 1972; Harré and Secord, 1972; Bickman and Henchey, 1972). Such criticisms have given rise to a plethora of experiments in field settings, but as McGuire (1973) has argued the field experiment has operated as a "tactical evasion" of more basic problems. The ethical suppositions and implications of experimentation have also been seriously questioned (cf. Kelman, 1968) and Jourard and Kormann (1968) as well as Harré and Secord (1972) have argued that experimentation is limited to the study of superficial and highly defensive relationships among virtual strangers. Hampden-Turner (1970) has further taken experimental research to task for the misleading picture it paints of human motives and action. Yet, in spite of the emerging doubts, the experimental tradition has continued unabated. To be sure, greater sensitivity to potential biases and to ethical improprieties has been generated. And doubting graduate students may have paused fitfully before pushing on with an experimental thesis that would ensure passage to a secure professional niche. However, with the lack of convincing alternatives to experimentation, in combination with immense institutional inertia, business has continued more or less as usual.

Perhaps it is futile to raise the tattered colours and once again lay siege to the bastion of tradition. Yet, in light of the crisis-like atmosphere currently pervading the field (cf. Israel and Tajfel, 1972; Armistead, 1974; Elms, 1975), the moment may be propitious for a reassessment of the enterprise. While a recounting of the earlier criticisms does not seem particularly fruitful, renewed perspective may be gained by evaluating the experimental paradigm against the crucible of social life as commonly observed. That is, when paramount features of social existence are brought into focus, what increment in understanding may we anticipate in the employment of the experimental paradigm? Is experimentation an adequate means of generating knowledge of ongoing social behaviour? Our initial concern will be with the distinct features of the experimental method. We shall then turn to a consideration of experimentation within the range of techniques commonly used to test hypotheses about the relationship among variables. Our concern in this case will be with the utility of hypothesis testing within the context of historical change. The concluding section of the paper will elaborate on the specific ends which experimentation might effectively serve. Experimentation may be an invaluable technique under certain circumscribed conditions. However, the continued presumption that experimentation is the single best means by which we can attain knowledge of social behaviour seems both mistaken and of injurious consequence to the field and to those who look to the profession for enhancement of understanding.

Experimentation in Contemporary Context

Our initial task is to determine the sensitivity of the experiment to major features of social life. To what extent does experimental knowledge accurately map the contours of contemporary conduct? This question presumes, of course, that one has a preliminary grasp of the major aspects of such conduct. Unfortunately no such assurances can be provided. However, our ability to survive in the contemporary world does suggest that we are not wholly ignorant on such matters, and that as an initial approximation it would not be unwise to make use of an explicated form of common knowledge. The present treatment will be selective, and it is possible that an alternative treatment of social life might yield a more satisfactory appraisal of experimental knowledge. However, should such an account emerge, special effort must be given to discrediting the following lines of argument.

Social events as culturally imbedded

Common observation informs us that behavioural events typically occur within and are intimately related to a highly complex network of contingencies. That is, few stimulus events considered independently have the capacity to elicit predictable social behaviour; our response to most stimuli seems to depend on a host of attendant circumstances. For example, a clenched fist has little inherent stimulus value. Responses to the fist alone would be extremely varied and difficult to predict. However, as we add additional features to the situation response variability is typically decreased. When we know the age, the sex, the economic, marital, educational and ethnic characteristics of the person whose fist is in question, when we know about what others are present in the situation, the surrounding physical circumstances, and the events preceding the raising of the fist, we are able more accurately to predict responses to the stimulus. In another sense we may say that it is only by taking into account the range of attendant circumstances that the stimulus gains "meaning" for members of the culture. If the fist is that of a child of three in response to his mother's admonishment in the privacy of their own home, the response has far different social significance than if the fist is that of a thirty year old Puerto Rican on a street in Spanish Harlem. In effect, social stimuli are typically imbedded in broader circumstances, and reactions to the stimulus complex depend importantly on the cultural meanings which they evoke.

The experimental method is not fundamentally incapable of capturing the effects of complex stimulus configurations. However, in this case one must distinguish between the method and its ideological framework. While the method itself may permit the manipulation of complex sets of events, the ideological orientation currently pervading the discipline strongly favours rigour over reality. That is, the ideal experimenter delimits his or her concerns to independently delineated variables. The rigorous experiment is one which "disimbeds" the stimulus from its surroundings, and examines its independent effects on a given behaviour. One may examine the effects of noise level on helping, jury size on the harshness of the verdict, communicator credibility on attitude change, the presence of weapons on aggression, and so on. To the extent that a particular stimulus may be decomposed into more discrete units, the research may be denigrated and further studies mounted in an attempt to form a more precise statement regarding necessary and sufficient conditions. For example, if crowding is one's independent variable, and crowds tend to generate a higher noise level and greater heat, the rigorous experimenter will attempt to control these latter factors. Crowding is thus disimbedded so that its effects may be ascertained independent of noise level, heat and other "extraneous" factors. Although the logic of this practice is compelling, profound difficulties emerge as a result.

The initial difficulty is no stranger to the social psychological literature and need not be belaboured (cf. Tajfel, 1972; McGuire, 1973). In the attempt to isolate a given stimulus from the complex in which it is normally imbedded, its meaning within the normative cultural framework is often obscured or destroyed. When subjects are exposed to an event out of its normal context they may be forced into reactions that are unique to the situation and have little or no relationship to their behaviour in the normal setting. In more dramatic terms, Harré (1974) has termed the experimentalist "tragically deceived" and has concluded that "experiments are largely worthless, except as descriptions of the odd way people carry on in trying to make social sense of the impoverished environment of laboratories" (p. 146).

In addition to this unsettling problem, a concern with the imbedded character of social events raises additional issues of equal significance. Within the current ideological framework, the formulation of an hypothesis concerning the relationship between two or more isolated variables (along with an explanatory rationale) is sufficient grounds for mounting an empirical test. If we believe communicator credibility, forced compliance or crowding influence a given behaviour, and we can develop a theoretical rationale for such effects, we may immediately submit our ideas to the crucible of experimental test. However, in the facile employment of experiments to test isolated relationships among variables, account is seldom taken of the actual circumstances surrounding the manipulation of the stimulus, circumstances which may be essential to its effects. In spite of the fact that the experimental ideology encourages the investigator to think of variables in isolated form, the experiment itself provides a context in which the stimulus is actually imbedded and which may play an integral role in determining its effects. In testing communicator credibility effects, for example, one typically ensures that the subject must attend to the message and is not angered by doing so, that the message is relevant to the subject's realm of interest or knowledge and does not personally offend him or her, that the subject is in no way threatened by the presence (or absence) of the communicator, and so on. Such circumstances are wholly obscured in the concentration on the disimbedded stimulus, and yet may be absolutely essential to the effects of communicator credibility. What passes for knowledge within the discipline may thus rest on an immense number of unstated assumptions and obscured conditions. Knowledge, in the form of independent statements of relationship among variables, may be wholly misleading.

To extend the argument further, in the attempt to isolate particular variables for experimental test, an aggressive insensitivity to limiting or boundary conditions is invited. Consideration of a stimulus as it may be imbedded in various circumstances typically reveals that it may evoke a wide range of reactions depending on the character of these circumstances. Thus, if a broad analysis were to be made of wide-ranging cultural circumstances, the investigator would typically find numerous negations of his or her hypothesis. The preliminary location of such negations would eliminate the need for test of the initial hypothesis. To take only one example, Brehm and his colleagues (cf. Brehm, 1966; Wicklund, 1974) have carried out an extended set of experiments attempting to demonstrate that people in general react negatively to reductions in their freedom, and under such conditions strive to re-establish their initial set of behaviour options. In concentrating on the pure test of the simple reactance hypothesis, preliminary attention to the broad cultural patterns in which such tendencies may be enmeshed was disregarded. Yet, there are numerous instances in which people have readily relinquished their freedom and have pressed toward increasing controls over their own behaviour (cf. Müller, 1963; Weinstein and Platt, 1969). If research had commenced with a careful consideration of the cultural circumstances in which its occurrences are imbedded, it is unlikely that experimental tests of the general reactance hypothesis would have been conducted.

It might be countered that the success of the experimental demonstration is sufficient grounds to justify the effort. It is appropriate to rely on the results of the "general test" until further experimental evidence contradicts the initial assumption. This rebuttal has little merit. At the outset it would be a myopic and self-deceived science that failed to admit evidence collected on less than experimental grounds. More importantly, the success of the "general test" is not obstructed by countervening circumstance because in the subtle and unspoken decisions concerning the choice of experimental context, the content of the situation and measures employed, such deterrents can be obscured. In this sense, it is not so much that hypotheses are tested as that the experimenter searches for (or is aware of) the appropriate social context in which the validity of what is purported to be a general hypothesis can be demonstrated. As McGuire (1973) has put it, we have learned to be "finders of situations in which our hypotheses can be demonstrated as tautologically true" (p. 449). If one were to commence with a consideration of the extended culture and its patterned complexity, testing unbridled hypotheses about general reactions to cognitive dissonance, imbalance, group pressures, social attraction, bystanders in an emergency, inequity, aggression and so on would seldom occur.

Social events as sequentially imbedded

In addition to their linkages to the broader social context at any given time, most social events appear as integral parts of sequences occurring over time. The exchange of smiles at a first meeting is of a far different character than that occurring after a bitter fight, primarily because the sequence in which an event is imbedded is of utmost importance in understanding its social significance. In effect, the major parameters of relevance to any given behaviour are likely to depend on where it falls within a given sequence. Let us consider the experimental sequence within this light.

In the application of fundamental standards of rigour, the experimentalist attempts to ensure that variations in the dependent variables can be traced unequivocally to variations in one or more independent variables, each of which can be isolated independently or considered in combination with others. Normally this entails limiting oneself to very brief behavioural sequences, as the greater the interval separating the manipulation of the independent variable and the assessment of the dependent variable, the greater the difficulty in interpreting one's data. As the period intervening between the onset of the stimulus conditions and the assessment of the effects is increased, the number of uncontrolled processes or extraneous factors that can intrude to cloud the chain of causality responsible for the results is also increased. For this same reason most research in social psychology takes pains to ensure that after exposure to the major manipulation subjects do not speak with anyone whose behaviour is not standardized. It is partly out of the same interest in rigour that the psychology of group process has floundered so during the past two decades (cf. Steiner, 1974), and well-trained social psychologists often avoid research on programmes of social change. In both cases it has proved impossible to trace causal connections accurately among variables.

With such intensive concentration on brief sequences, extended patterns of social interaction are virtually non-existent in the social psychological literature. In spite of the immense importance of such phenomena, our texts have almost nothing to say about the social psychology of family relationships, the development of intimacy, professionalism, career trajectories, the ageing process, or the development of extended negotiations or armed conflict.[1] All would require an analysis of interaction patterns across extended periods. In the same way, experimentation too often commits itself to the dangerous assumption that initial reactions to a given stimulus are valid predictors of reactions to the same stimulus on subsequent occasions. For example, an immense amount of experimental research has shown that increases in similarity produce increases in attraction (cf. Clore and Baldridge, 1968; Byrne, 1969, 1971; Lamberth and Craig, 1970). In the interests of ruling out extraneous variables almost all of this research has utilized a stranger's attitude protocol as stimulus. Yet, as Kirckhoff and Davis (1962) have shown, similarity may have little predictive value at later points in a relationship. In the same way our reactions to another's inconsistency, inequity, positive regard, opinion statements, non-verbal cues or leadership tendencies may be far different when encountered for the first time in a brief relationship than when imbedded in long-term interaction sequences. Because long-term relationships embody numerous confounds, "late-stage" phenomena are not amenable to precise experimentation and thus may vanish from consideration.

Social events as openly competitive

We have already seen that the function form relating any two variables may be highly dependent on the specific context in which the variables are examined. Over and above this problem, it may be ventured that the magnitude of response produced by a given stimulus depends importantly on the array of simultaneously occurring stimuli. In particular, the potency of any given stimulus to elicit a response (at either a psychological or a behavioural level) is clearly related to the potency of its competitors at that moment. Thus, for example, whether a male's smile elicits a similar response in the female is likely to depend on what other factors demand psychological engagement. If an infant is crying or a jealous lover is looking on, the smile may have little effect. Let us consider the psychological experiment in the light of this self-evident surmise.

Experimentation is primarily designed to assess whether or not a given variable has *any* discernible effects on a specified behaviour. However, because of the isolated circumstances of the normal experiment, we are left ignorant concerning the power of any independent variable in comparison with its competitors in the normal circumstances of daily life. For example, in spite of the several hundred dissonance experiments, it is not at all clear what importance dissonance reduction has in contemporary society. Given the immense amount of inconsistency to which people seem generally exposed each day, it is possible that the psychology of dissonance reduction is primarily limited to the more intellectually prone college student who cannot otherwise escape its presence in the experiment. Or, as Lubek[2] has suggested, dissonance may only be a problem for the privileged class, those able to afford the luxury of an ordered world in which their decisions are important in controlling their destiny. In broader terms, the experimentalist may have little to say concerning the major problems of the day, and what he or she does have to offer may be grossly misleading.

Several counter-arguments to this thesis may be posed and each deserves attention. First, it may be ventured that experiments enable us to plot the relationship between a specified set of variables, independent of competing circumstances. In effect, they allow us to glimpse the *pure* relationship between the variables, uncontaminated by competing factors. Unfortunately this argument proves of little merit. For one, if social psychology is to be concerned with normally recurring patterns of social behaviour, then concentrating on behaviour in the uncontaminated setting is of little predictive value. If our essential task is that of understanding behaviour in naturally contaminated settings, it is not clear that findings in the pure condition will prove generalizable. Cronbach's (1975) discussion of the inability of experimenters to export basic "laws" of perception and learning from the laboratory into the real world should be sufficiently sobering.

In addition to our inability to generalize from the "pure" case, the argument that the traditional experiment provides an uncontaminated estimate of a variable's effects is ill-considered at the outset. Experimental settings are also composed of a complex variable array, and those effects which do emerge in any given experiment are inextricably linked to the particular character of this array. Research on experimenter effects in psychological research (cf. Rosenthal and Rosnow, 1969) has already informed us of the immense influence of the experimenter on research findings. We are now well aware that we cannot discuss experimental results as if the experimenter were absent from the scene. However, this research only scratches the surface. Experimental results may also depend on the fact that the research is conducted within the trusted confines of the university, that the aim of research is scientific knowledge, that the circumstances are short-lived and non-recurring, that one will not be held responsible for his or her behaviour once outside the confines of the experiment, and so on. A unique composite of stimulus features is apparent within any given experiment, and in no way can the effects of a given variable be demonstrated independent of such supporting conditions.

Field experiments provide one important palliative for this condition. In such circumstances the independent variable must compete on the open market place. However, this singular advantage of the field experiment does not compensate for the other substantial problems with which we are here concerned.

Social events as final common pathways

If our attempt is to understand social life as it naturally occurs, we must further be sensitive to the confounded psychological basis of most social acts. It seems clear that social events are typically influenced by a number of simultaneously occurring psychological factors. In this sense, any given social act may be viewed as "the final common pathway" for a confluence of interacting psychological states. To return to our simple case, the male's smile may evoke simultaneous feelings of excitement, sensual pleasure, anxiety and repulsion in the female. The response evoked by the smile will depend on the confluence of these various psychological states.

If this surmise is accurate, severe problems emerge. For the experimentalist, understanding behaviour requires a delineation of both the independent and interactive effects of isolated antecedents. The chief advantage of the experiment is that it purportedly allows for a precise tracing of causal sequence, from the antecedent stimuli through the intervening processes to the behaviour of interest. The promise primarily hinges on the capacity of the experimenter to single out specific variables and manipulate them independently while all other factors are either controlled or held constant. Unfortunately, this promise relies on the assumption that discrete events in the "real" world are linked in one-to-one fashion with particulate experiences or processes internal to the organism. The guiding ideal is possibly Weberian in origin; in it, the relationships between variations in a given stimulus are mapped to alterations in experience via a mathematical formulation (Weber, 1834). The experimentalist seldom approximates this goal, of course, and typically we settle for establishing two (and sometimes three) points along a stimulus continuum of unknown parameters. In this way we attempt to create states of high and low dissonance arousal, fear, communicator credibility, crowding, perceived intentionality, self-esteem, task effort and so on. Or, in the more rudimentary case, we compare the individual's behaviour when alone versus with others, when explanations are available for his or her actions or not, and so on.

This approach seems quite reasonable until we begin to examine the typical trajectory of research interests in the field. In the normal case initial hypotheses linking conceptually distinct variables are proposed and experimental results almost uncannily provide support for the propositions. Dissonance arousal is said to result in X, crowding in Y, and group discussion in Z. Once the formulation gains interest the argument is invariably made that the initial manipulation of independent variables did not properly alter the specific internal mechanism, state or process. The dissonance manipulation in reality manipulated self-observation, the crowding manipulation inadvertently altered the ambient temperature, and the group discussion engendered riskier decisions for a variety of compounded reasons. The alternative explanations are explored and support is again forthcoming; further critics note the impurity of these manipulations and attempt further purifications; successful alternatives are discovered, and over time the battle for explanatory prominence becomes, in Bem and McConnell's (1970) words, just "a matter of taste".

One major conclusion suggested by this common pattern is that wherever precise manipulation is paramount, the research enterprise is destined for the shoals of ennui. In dealing with human beings in a social setting it is virtually impossible to manipulate any variable at the psychological level in isolation of all others. Even the most elemental variations in an independent variable have the capacity to elicit a host of intervening reactions. While increasing shock is often used to increase fear, it may also affect generalized arousal, hostility towards the experimenter, feelings of obligation, desire for escape, desire for nurturance, and a host of other factors. Similarly, increasing the amount of material reward, often used to manipulate motivation, may alter feelings of generalized arousal, sentiments towards the experimenter, desire to please the experimenter, feelings of obligation towards the experimenter, relief, and so on. In addition to all the reactions specific to a given stimulus, additional confounds stem from the self-reflexive capacities of the human subject. At all times the subject may remove himself or herself from the immediate press of events to conceptualize himself or herself as a respondent. A person's reactions to the cognition of his or her own being in the situation may depend on a host of additional factors, including personal values, self-estimate, philosophical predilections and so on. In sum, it is virtually impossible to manipulate any variable in simple degree or amount. *Real-world variations in quantity inevitably become psychological variations in quality.* The assumption that experiments allow precise tracing of causal sequence dwindles into whimsy.

Social events as complexly determined

The preceding argument depended on the acceptance of psychological constructs into one's theoretical network. Of course, we need not so accept them. Reasonably reliable theories can be developed without recourse to intervening variables. We may develop a theory of attitude change which includes communicator credibility, one-sided vs. two-sided communication, and recency and primacy as predictor variables, for example, without reference to underlying psychological processes. From this standpoint, we might anticipate the development of theories composed of a wide variety of predictor variables which account for both the independent and interactive effects of these variables on the behaviour in question. Attitude change research in the Hovland tradition, in fact, begins to approximate this end. So too does the spate of research on help-giving in emergencies. On the basis of the available literature one can begin to construct a model in which such factors as the number of bystanders, the characteristics of the victim, the salience of the helping norm, the sex of the bystander and so on are all taken into account as they combine to determine helping behaviour in any given situation. Such an approach is demanded by the common observation that behaviour in most situations is determined not by one factor but by a complex set of interrelated factors.

From this perspective, the psychological experiment proves highly problematic. In social psychology, experiments employing more than three or four independent variables are very rare. Because of the extreme difficulties in experimental execution, location of large samples and interpretation of results, few investigators venture into the wilderness of multi-factor manipulation.[3] As Thorngate (1976) has shown, even with our increased sophistication in experimental technique, the size of multi-factor experimental designs has levelled off during the past five years. Even if optimistic in our estimate of expansion over the next decade, it is difficult to imagine experimental designs employing more than six independent variables. These pragmatic limits in experimental design place significant restrictions on our capacity to generate knowledge via this means. Several of these limitations have been extensively discussed by Thorngate (1976). As he points out, experiments place an upper limit on the number and types of function forms which can be used to capture events in nature. If the state of nature is sufficiently complex that high-order interactions among variables are most prevalent, knowledge accumulated through experimentation will always remain a crude approximation to its subject matter. This also means that highly complex explanations (involving large numbers of variables) cannot adequately be tested through experimental means. The explanation might be tested piece-meal, but never would the investigator be able to explore all possible interactions within the design.[4]

Such pragmatic limitations become especially onerous in the light of arguments emerging from other areas of the field. As McGuire has pointed out in his 1969 review of attitude research, the number of factors operating to enhance or impede change is immense, and the potential interactions among these factors truly formidable. Mischel (1973) has reached a similar conclusion in his discussion of personality and social behaviour. Likewise, Cronbach (1975) has shown how the delimitation of variables in experimentation conceals higher-order interactions which contribute to bloated main effects, erroneous lower-order interactions, and null effects where true effects actually exist.

In general it may be ventured that the search for higher-order interactions is presumed by the serious application of the experimental method. In order to accumulate knowledge in the experimental tradition, the solid demonstration of a main effect is ample reason to commence searching for factors that enhance, reduce or reverse the effect. The demonstration of first-order interaction is sufficient to trigger a search for second-order interactions, and so on. However, because of pragmatic limitations it is clear that the attempt to construct understanding in this way rapidly reaches an upper limit.

In sum, we find that in significant degree the social psychological experiment is interposed between the investigator and the phenomena he or she hopes to understand. Rather than elucidating the phenomena the experiment more often serves as a fun-house mirror in which reality is served up in distorted or ludicrous form. Such need not be the case, and later we shall consider several potential solutions to these dilemmas. Such indulgence must be postponed, however, for consideration of an additional issue of some importance. The argument in this case concerns not only the experiment, but the more general attempt to accumulate social knowledge via the hypothetico-deductive process.

Experimentation in Historical Context

In the main, social psychology is concerned with the exploration of the lawful aspects of interpersonal behaviour. However, it is also clear that the lawful properties of human relations are subject to continuous modification (Gergen, 1973). Thus, laws or principles of social behaviour developed and supported at one point in time do not necessarily retain their validity. To the extent that natural, social or subjective circumstances are altered, empirical findings may fluctuate. Theoretical statements resting on such a shifting data base may thus be of circumscribed validity across time. When we view the common practice of testing hypotheses in this perspective, fundamental difficulties emerge. Such difficulties are relevant not only to the experimental method, but to the entire range of techniques utilized for purposes of hypothesis testing. In the light of existing controversy over this general line of thinking (cf. Schlenker, 1974; Manis, 1975; Cronbach, 1975), careful elaboration of the problem is required.

To elucidate, let us consider a more or less established principle in contemporary social psychology, one for which there is immense experimental support and for which the claims of transhistorical validity could most convincingly be made. This proposition, found in virtually all the major texts of the field, is that attraction toward another is a positive function of O's similarity to P. At least 50 separate studies now support this general proposition (cf. discussions by Newcomb, 1961; Byrne, 1971; Berscheid and Walster, 1969). To be sure, there are conditions under which such results fail to emerge or may be reversed (cf. Mettee and Wilkins, 1972; Senn, 1971; Taylor and Mettee, 1971; Novak and Lerner, 1968), but few could doubt that over wide-ranging social and behavioural conditions, similarity does breed attraction.

For purposes of analysis let us further break the proposition down into independent, intervening and dependent variables and consider each in more detail. In the case of the independent variable, interpersonal similarity, it is initially clear that there may be many different types of similarity, and that not all types may have the same relationship with attraction. At a minimum, one might wish to distinguish between similarity in opinions and in personality. Most of the data supporting the general proposition have indeed been generated in the former area, and doubts have been cast about the generality of the proposition in the latter case (cf. Lipetz et al., 1970). However, for purposes of inquiry, further distinctions may be useful between political opinions and those concerning values and morality. There may also be a virtual infinity of personality dimensions, along with innumerable differences in physical appearance along which one may be judged similar or dissimilar. For convenience, these distinctions are portrayed in graphic form in figure 4.1.

Let us further expand the model to consider a range of intervening variables or processes that might link one or more types of similarity with resulting attraction. For one, another's similarity provides confirmation of one's own perceptions or beliefs; it may also suggest that the other will provide positive payoffs on further occasions; another's similarity can also relieve feelings of isolation or loneliness, or it may ease the course of interaction and thus make one feel more comfortable with the other. Another's similarity may also guarantee one's safety (criticisms are unlikely), or one may be attracted to a similar other as a by-product of attraction to self (the similar other being closer to self on a generalization gradient). Similarity may also function as a secondary stimulus within the classical conditioning paradigm and simply lend itself to attraction on an automatic basis. All of these intervening mechanisms have been added to figure 4.1.

However, such an analysis would be altogether biased without considering as well a number of processes that might engender a *negative* relationship between similarity and attraction. For example, as Fromkin has shown in a number of studies (1970, 1972), there may be a prevalent desire for uniqueness, such that the presence of someone who is similar could evoke a negative reaction. Another's similarity might further imply a constricted set of learning experiences; if the other is similar to self then one can learn little that is new. The presence of a similar other might also suggest stronger competition for scarce resources, or engender self-consciousness, a state that Duval and Wicklund (1972) contend is negative in character. Finally, a similar other may simply be more boring. Each of these various processes or tendencies should also be taken into account (see figure 4.1).

In turning to the dependent variable, social attraction, analytic differentiation is also required. There is little reason to suspect that feelings of admiration, sympathy, gratitude and so on all operate in the same way (Marlowe and Gergen, 1968). Thus, we might wish to consider the relationship between varying types of similarity and varying qualities of attraction. For example, we might admire another whose qualities were the same as our own, feel anticipatory gratitude for the rewards we expect to receive from them, or feel increased sympathy with their positive disposition (Stotland, 1969). By the same token, we might

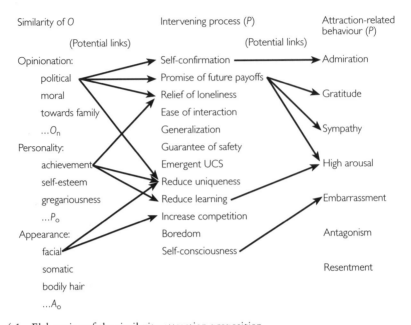

Similarity of *O*   Intervening process (*P*)   Attraction-related
                                                                            behaviour (*P*)

(Potential links)   (Potential links)

Opinionation: Self-confirmation ——————————→ Admiration
    political   Promise of future payoffs
    moral   Relief of loneliness   Gratitude
    towards family   Ease of interaction
    ...O_n Generalization   Sympathy
Personality: Guarantee of safety
    achievement   Emergent UCS   High arousal
    self-esteem   Reduce uniqueness
    gregariousness   Reduce learning   Embarrassment
    ...P_o Increase competition
Appearance: Boredom   Antagonism
    facial   Self-consciousness
    somatic   Resentment
    bodily hair
    ...A_o

Figure 4.1   Elaboration of the similarity-attraction proposition

Entries in each category are intended as examples, and not to be exhaustive. Virtually all linkages are possible between entities.

experience a low level of general arousal in anticipation of reduced learning, or an embarrassed antagonism in the case of enhanced self-consciousness. The formulation in figure 4.1 reflects these minimal distinctions.

Having glimpsed a variety of distinctions that may all bear on the validity of the general similarity–attraction proposition, we can consider the types of alteration we may anticipate as a function of changes in the social, physical or subjective context over time. Three types of alteration are of cardinal significance:

I   Alterations in entity frequency

Each entity in each sector of our model is subject to variations in its frequency of occurrence in society. For example, whether strong political opinionation is present in a culture depends on the historical climate. Where democracy prevails and differing parties compete for scarce positions, political opinionation may be highly prevalent; at other times or in other places, political opinionation may play a very modest role in social life. In the same way, whether strong needs for self-esteem or uniqueness exist is also primarily a matter of whether the society provides the necessary learning experiences. For example, in traditional Japanese culture needs for uniqueness did not seem to prevail among the common people (Benedict, 1946). Similarly, desires for uniqueness may change in our own society as patterns of family life are altered and the society becomes more or less homogeneous. Likewise, feelings of empathy, admiration, boredom and so on may also fluctuate in their relevance over time. Principles of behaviour developed at one point in time may thus be irrelevant at later periods in history. There may simply be no particulars for which the general principle holds true.

2   Alterations in independent–intervening variable bonds

More importantly, we find that the articulation between the independent variables and intervening processes is subject to fluctuation over time. Whether a given type of similarity elicits feelings of self-esteem, whether it promises rewards for the future, whether it bodes ill for one's desire for stimulation or information, all seem highly dependent on the prevailing context of experience. Certainly there is little reason to suspect genetically preferred connections between varying types of similarity and varying types of internal processes. Form this standpoint it is clear that virtually any type of similarity has the capacity to elicit, trigger or stimulate any type of intervening process. As indicated by the arrows in figure 4.1, depending on the learning experiences of the individual, prevalent beliefs or values, or structural constraints, political similarity could have strong consequences for self-esteem, or none at all. It could also indicate the likelihood of future rewards or it could play into one's needs for uniqueness. All such bonds are reasonable and variations in the type and strength of the various bonds can well be expected within any given culture.

3   Alterations in intervening–dependent variable bonds

In the same way that marked variation may be anticipated between independent and intervening variables, the relationships between intervening processes and dependent variables are also subject to the vicissitudes of history. For example, in the case of the linkage between anticipation of positive payoffs and gratitude, it is not at all clear that one's reaction will be positive. Gratitude is not always enhanced when one expects to be showered with positive outcomes; indeed, gifts, aid or help can often evoke hostility (Gergen and Gergen, 1971). In cultures such as Japan such reactions to gifts may be exceedingly complex (cf. Befu, 1966; Benedict, 1946). Similarly one may feel a lack of gratitude for another who has boosted his or her esteem; many people within our own culture view esteem enhancement as synonymous with pride or egotism. Uniqueness may not always be a congenial state as well, and there may be important historical periods (e.g. during World War II in the US) in which finding oneself in a unique political position could be extremely threatening. In sum, a myriad of differing connections between internal process and resulting effect are both reasonable and probable. Which connections exist and in what degree are matters of historical concern.

Before elaborating on the implication of these various types of change, it is important to note that almost all contemporary research and theory in social psychology is subject to such analysis. Not only may the prevalence of tendencies to reduce inconsistency, achieve balance, or attribute casuality wax and wane over time, but so may the prevalence of opposing tendencies to create inconsistency, to negate balance, and to view behaviour as environmentally rather than willfully determined. Likewise, the relationship between variables such as demands for obedience and obedient behaviour (Milgram, 1963), aggressive attack and aggressive response (Geen, 1968; Gentry, 1970), a leader's task capabilities and willingness to follow (Hollander, 1964), and so on is subject to alteration in strength and prevalence within society. And for each of these relationships there are several good reasons to suspect a function form opposite in direction from that now accepted as lawful. Over time, as the bonds among the variables are moulded anew, such tendencies could well increase in strength and/or prevalence.

It is additionally important to consider the possibility that these various alterations may fluctuate over very brief periods of time. Thus far we have viewed relations among variables much as one would a personality trait: as relatively enduring but subject to slow transitions or modifications over the years. However, it is also quite possible that such relations are subject to momentary fluctuations and thus approximate situationally induced states. For example, in examining one's own experience it should be possible to verify the existence of virtually all the bonds relating independent variables with intervening processes in figure 4.1. We may carry with us the potential for all such relationships. Depending on the situational cues or constraints, one or more of the bonds may become activated. Thus, if the individual participates in an experiment where self-esteem is threatened, the bond between similarity and esteem may become relevant; in a situation threatening one with boredom, stimulus needs might become more salient. To the extent that such momentary fluctuations can be documented, the problems stemming from the following arguments reach staggering proportions.

Having specified the major types of alteration within and between the various components of our model, the prospects and limitations of social psychological experiments, along with ancillary techniques, become apparent. The following conclusions are especially cogent:

1   All reasonable hypotheses are likely to be valid. Given the fluctuations within and between entities in the model, there is no reasonable hypothesis about social activity that is not likely to contain truth value for at least some persons at some time. Placing hypotheses under experimental test is thus primarily a challenge to the experimenter's skill in discerning the proper time, location and population in which the support for the hypothesis may be generated. The results of such tests seldom tell us anything we did not already know to be possible. Not only does this argument question the utility of our primary stock in trade, it further implies that for every hypothesis occupying the literature of the field, the contradiction is also valid. Such implications are indeed disturbing, as they suggest that all that has passed in our texts and from our podia as knowledge is no more accurate than its negation. Matters may indeed be more critical, as it is possible that the number of persons and situations for which the negation is valid may be more prevalent than the instances in which the particular theories may be confirmed. In the case of the more stimulating theories of the field, those which predict the non-obvious, there is ample reason to believe this is so. Yet, so long as the experiment is the chief instrument for gaining knowledge we shall not be able to escape this dilemma. As we have seen, the experiment tells us only that a particular hypothesis has demonstrable truth value. It does not inform us of the proportion of the population, or the range of instances, in which the hypothesis is valid.

2   The "critical experiment" is expendable. Traditionally the experiment has played a key role in ruling between competing hypotheses. It is commonly assumed that the experiment can be used as the crucible in which the validity of alternative or competing explanations may be determined. Such thinking continues to pervade contemporary social psychology. The past decade has witnessed, for example, an exhausting number of attempts to displace the cognitive dissonance formulation by demonstrating alternative explanations for its supporting evidence. Chapanis and Chapanis (1964), Bem (1967), Janis and Gilmore (1965), Silverman (1964) and many others have contributed to this colloquy. Similarly, numerous demonstrations have been made of alternatives to initial equity theory findings (cf. Lawler, 1968; Gergen, Morse and Bode, 1974), demonstrations of risky shift (cf. Cartwright, 1971; Pruitt, 1971) and so on. From the present standpoint there is little to be gained from such efforts. To the extent that a given stimulus may elicit a variety of different processes or internal reactions, and the strength and prevalence of such bonds are subject to historical fluctuation, critical tests contain little information value. When perfectly executed, they tell us only that some other process *could*

account for the observed patterns of behaviour at the present time. Given the premise that most reasonable hypotheses are likely to be valid at some time or place, and that most behaviour represents a final common pathway for many antecedent processes, such demonstrations may be viewed as unproductive.

The Critical Employment of Experimentation

The foregoing arguments strongly suggest that a continued commitment to the experimental paradigm will eventuate in a psychology that is both myopic in its vision and irrelevant to the continuously emerging character of social conduct. This is by no means to argue for a termination of the paradigm, but rather for the adoption of more critical standards in its application. In no way do I wish to see the death of the experimental enterprise, but rather its transfiguration. While the wholesale employment of experiments to test all manner of delimited hypotheses is virtually a dead-end, experimentation can productively be employed in several ways. Most important would appear to be the following:

1   Explicating bio-social relationships. Due to the relative stability and simplicity of the biological system (as contrasted with the vicissitudes of social history), experimental inquiry into its various relationships to social behaviour would seem reasonable. An understanding of the impact of biological process on social behaviour (e.g., behaviour genetics, generalized arousal, specific motivational states), the effects of social factors on biological process (e.g., perception of emotion, socialization of hunger, psychosomatics), and interdependencies between biological and social factors would seem much enhanced through continued experimentation. To be sure, many of these inter-relationships can be altered by time and circumstance; for example, affective, motivational and genetic contributions to behaviour can be wholly submerged by strong cultural norms. However, in contrast to the plasticity of the social arena, in which virtually any relationship between variables is possible, the biological system would seem to furnish an enduring backdrop for the shadow-show of mores, style and custom.

2   Experimentation for alteration of consciousness. It has been argued that most social psychological experiments primarily furnish us with an indication of what is possible in social life. Since common experience also furnishes us with a vast repository of knowledge concerning what is possible, most experiments do little more than validate some facet of common knowledge. Continuation of such efforts hardly seems merited. However, upon occasion the experiment can be used to unsettle our common understanding of "the way things are". They may generate a constructive self-consciousness, an enhanced awareness of various inequities or irrationalities built into our institutionalized ways of viewing things, or an increased caution before commitment. Some excellent examples of experimentation in the service of such "consciousness raising" would include Asch's (1956) research on conformity, Milgram's (1963) initial study on obedience to authority, the early work of Festinger (1957) on cognitive dissonance, Deutsch's classic (1969) research on conflict resolution, Darley and Latané's (1970) early research on bystander intervention, and initial demonstrations of causal attribution and perceptual defence. Such research has played a vital role in sensitizing us to little-considered possibilities in social life. Although these studies have been extremely valuable in their sensitizing function, we can be far less sanguine about their sequelae. In each case, hundreds of additional studies have been spawned: conceptual replications, attempts to find alternative explanations for the initial studies, and attempts to isolate additional factors that supposedly

round out our understanding of the phenomenon. Each of these latter pursuits presumes the possibility of constructing transhistorically valid and comprehensive principles of social behaviour on the basis of accumulated experimentation. As we have seen, such an assumption is indeed problematic. These classic studies contribute virtually nothing to such a theory, and the confluence of processes permitting the findings to emerge is subject to the tides of history. In their sensitization function, the classic experiments share the positive alerting function of various events of current history. Like Mai Lai, Watergate or political assassination, they stimulate widespread reassessment of our condition, our potential or the future. The experimental social psychologist is in a favourable, if not critical position, however, as he or she may create the event which stimulates the dialectic. In this sense, the experimentalist's task is not so much to reflect the character of contemporary behaviour as to *create* it.

3   Increasing theoretical impact. As argued elsewhere (Gergen, 1973) and as implied in the foregoing, there is little to be gained in attempting through experimentation to validate a series of general laws of social behaviour. With intelligence, all general theories of social behaviour (e.g., behaviourism, phenomenology, field theory, etc.) could probably be extended or elaborated to account for virtually all social phenomena. As we have also seen, there is little way of selecting among such theories on empirical grounds. This is not to say that general theories have no place in the field. They may have immense value in generating coherency, synthesizing disparate facts, sensitizing us to various factors affecting our lives, and demonstrating the shortcomings of conventional truth. However, these functions are not generally served by generating experimental proofs. Experimental data have neither enhanced nor detracted significantly from the contributions of Darwin, Marx, Durkehim, Freud, Parsons, Goffman, Lewin, Skinner or Heider. This is not to argue that experimental data are irrelevant to the impact or acceptance of such theories. Certainly in the case of Lewin, Skinner and Heider, experimental data have increased our concern for the widespread implications of the theorizing. However, where general theory is concerned, enhancement of viewpoint may indeed be the primary function of experimentation. While the formal testing of theories seems a chimerical goal, the occasional use of experiments to demonstrate the viability of a viewpoint ensures that we remain in a healthy state of conceptual conflict.

4   Experimentation in the service of social reform. A vital role may finally be played by experiments in testing the effects of varying social policies. Campbell (1969) has outlined a variety of ways in which various social reforms may be treated as natural experiments and the effects systematically documented. Such experimentation might be employed on both the national level (as in the case of new tax reforms or presidential pleas for energy conservation) as well as on the local scene (as in the case of alterations in local traffic regulations or school busing). The same logic applies, of course, in the pretesting of various reforms. As Rivlin (1973) concludes in her discussion of problems and prospects in this domain, social experiments in areas such as performance contracting, negative income tax and compensatory education have been highly enlightening and may engender far wiser legislation than otherwise. Riecken and Boruch (1974) have pinpointed additional cases in which experimentation may be utilized in social intervention. If we view such investigations in historical perspective, however, it must be concluded that experimentation may not yield answers of long-term validity. Simply because Programme A is superior to B at t^1, we cannot assume that it will remain so; with changing social conditions, the opposite results might also emerge. Thus, where social experimentation is concerned we must be prepared for periodic reassessment of competing policy alternatives.

It would be appropriate to complete this analysis with a strong endorsement of McGuire's (1973) exhortation to a broad liberalization of methodology in social psychology. Experimentation does not provide a solid foundation on which to build social knowledge. However, in the light of the present arguments, it would appear an auspicious time for a serious shift of our attentions to the area of methodology. Our major methods of inquiry have remained essentially unchanged over the past three decades and its seems a propitious moment to turn our attention from the "what" of social life to the "how" of knowing. Not only do we require better means of understanding naturally occurring behaviour, embedded in historical sequence, but we must develop ways of regenerating knowledge as the character of social conduct emerges anew.

NOTES

This article is based on an invited address to Division 8 at the 1975 meetings of the American Psychological Association in Chicago, Illinois. I wish to thank Curt Banks, Michael Basseches, Donald Campbell, Uriel Foa, Mary Gergen, Robert Helmreich, Clyde Hendricks, Ian Lubek, Serge Moscovici, Franz Samelson, Paul Secord, Philip Shaver, Siegfried Streufert, Karl Weick, and Ricardo Zuniga for their valuable commentary on an earlier draft of this paper. Special appreciation is also expressed to Robert Pages for making the facilities of the Laboratoire de Psychologie Sociale, Université de Paris VII, available for completing the final manuscript.

[1] Refreshing exceptions to the general case do exist. Both Levinger and Snoek (1972) and Altman and Taylor (1973) have developed models of growth in intimacy, and Osgood's (1962) GRIT model for reducing international tensions has fruitful implications for problems of sequence.

[2] Personal communication from Ian Lubek.

[3] Not the least of these difficulties is ensuring that each independent variable can be manipulated with just enough efficacy that subjects are aware of it, but not so much that it will obscure the effects of variables competing for attention. In addition, with multiple variables it is very likely that manipulation cannot occur independently; variations in one variable often interact with variations in others, thus raising extremely difficult problems of interpretation.

[4] Various research designs (e.g., Latin squares, latticed designs, multivariate analysis of variance) can be used to off-set the difficulties of large numbers of variables. However, none of these alternatives fully alleviates the problems described here. Cronbach's (1975) words provide the most onerous warning. "Once we attend to interactions, we enter a hall of mirrors that extends to infinity. However far we carry our analysis – to third order or fifth order or any other – untested interactions of still higher order can be envisioned."

REFERENCES

Altman, I. and Taylor D. (1973). *Social Penetration*. Holt, Rinehart and Winston, New York.

Armistead, N. (ed.) (1974). *Reconstructing Social Psychology*. Penguin Books, Middlesex.

Asch, S. (1956). "Studies of independence and conformity: A minority of one against a unanimous majority", *Psychological Monographs*, 70, Whole No. 416.

Befu, H. (1966). "Gift giving and social reciprocity in Japan", *France–Asia*, 188, 161–77.

Bem, D.J. (1967). "Self-perception, An alternative interpretation of cognitive dissonance phenomena", *Psychological Review*, 74, 183–200.

Bem, D.J. and McConnell, H.K. (1970). "Testing the self-perception explanation of dissonance phenomena: On the salience of premanipulation attitudes", *Journal of Personality and Social Psychology*, 14, 23–31.

Benedict, R. (1946). *The Chrysanthemum and the Sword*. Houghton Mifflin, New York.

Berscheid, E. and Walster, E. (1969). *Interpersonal Attraction*. Addison-Wesley, Reading, Mass.

Bickman, L. and Henchey, T. (1972). *Beyond the Laboratory: Field Research in Social Psychology*. McGraw-Hill, New York.

Brehm, J.W. (1966). *A Theory of Psychological Reactance*. Academic Press, New York.

Bryne, D. (1969). Attitudes and attraction. In Berkowitz, L. (ed.), *Advances in Experimental Social Psychology*, vol. 4. Academic Press, New York.

Byrne, D. (1971). *The Attraction Paradigm*. Academic Press, New York.

Campbell, D.T. (1969). "Reform as experiments", *American Psychologist*, 24, 409–29.

Cartwright, D. (1971). "Risk taking by individuals and groups: An assessment of research employing choice dilemmas", *Journal of Personality and Social Psychology*, 20, 361–78.

Chapanis, N. and Chapanis, A. (1964). 'Cognitive dissonance: Five years later,' *Psychological Bulletin*, 61, 1–22.

Clore, G.L. and Baldridge, B. (1968). "Interpersonal attraction: The role of agreement and topic interest", *Journal of Personality and Social Psychology*, 9, 340–6.

Cronbach, L.J. (1975). 'Beyond the two disciplines in scientific psychology', *American Psychologist*, 30, 116–27.

Darley, J. and Latané, B. (1970). *The Unresponsive Bystander: Why Doesn't He Help?* Appleton-Century-Crofts, New York.

Deutsch, M. (1969). "Socially relevant science: Reflections on some studies of interpersonal conflict", *American Psychologist*, 24, 1076–92.

Duval, S. and Wicklund, R.A. (1972). *A Theory of Objective Self-awareness*. Academic Press, New York.

Elms, A.C. (1975). "The crisis in confidence in social psychology", *American Psychologist*, 30, 967–76.

Festinger, L.A. (1957). *A Theory of Cognitive Dissonance*. Row, Peterson, Evanston, Illinois.

Fried, S.B., Gumper, D.C. and Allen, J.C. (1973). "Ten years of social psychology: Is there a growing commitment to field research?", *American Psychologist*, 28, 155–6.

Fromkin, H.L. (1970). "Effects of experimentally aroused feelings of undistinctiveness upon valuation of scarce and novel experiences", *Journal of Personality and Social Psychology*, 16, 521–9.

Fromkin, H.L. (1972). "Feelings of interpersonal undistinctiveness: An unpleasant affective state", *Journal of Experimental Research in Personality*, 6, 178–85.

Geen, R.G. (1968). "Effects of frustration, attack and prior training in aggressiveness upon aggressive behaviour", *Journal of Personality and Social Psychology*, 9, 316–21.

Gentry, W.D. (1970). "Effects of frustration, attack and prior aggressive training on overt aggression and vascular processes", *Journal of Personality and Social Psychology*, 16, 718–25.

Gergen, K.J. (1973). "Social psychology as history", *Journal of Personality and Social Psychology*, 26, 309–20.

Gergen, K.J. and Gergen, M.M. (1971). "Understanding foreign assistance through public opinion", *Yearbook of World Affairs*, Vol. 25. pp. 87–103. Institute of World Affairs, London.

Gergen, K.J., Morse, S.J. and Bode, K. (1974). "Overpaid or overworked: Cognitive and behavioural reactions to inequitable payment", *Journal of Applied Social Psychology*, 4, 259–74.

Hampden-Turner, C. (1970). *Radical Man*. Schenkman, Cambridge, Mass.

Harré, R. (1974). "Some remarks on 'rule' as a scientific concept". In Mischel, T. (ed.), *Understanding Other Persons*. Blackwell, Oxford.

Harré, R. and Secord, P. (1972). *The Explanation of Social Behaviour*. Blackwell, Oxford.

Higbee, K.L. and Wells, M.G. (1972). "Some research trends in social psychology during the 1960s", *American Psychologist*, 27, 963–6.

Hollander, E.P. (1964). *Leaders, Groups and Influence*. Oxford University Press, New York.

Israel, J. and Tajfel, H. (eds) (1972). *The Context of Social Psychology: A Critical Assessment*. Academic Press, London.

Janis, I.J. and Gilmore, J.B. (1965). "The influence of incentive conditions on the success of role playing in modifying attitudes", *Journal of Personality and Social Psychology*, 1, 17–27.

Jourard, S.M. and Kormann, L. (1968). "Getting to know the experimenter and its effect on psychological test performance", *Journal of Humanistic Psychology*, 8, 155–60.

Kelman, H.C. (1968). *A Time to Speak*. Jossey Bass, San Francisco.

Kelman, H.C. (1972). "The rights of the subject in social research: An analysis in terms of relative power and legitimacy", *American Psychologist*, 27, 989–1016.

Kerckhoff, A. and Davis, K.E. (1962). "Value consensus and need complementarity in mate selection", *American Sociological Review*, 27, 295–303.

Koch, S. (1959). "Epilogue". In Koch, S. (ed.), *Psychology: A Study of a Science*, vol. III, pp. 729–88. McGraw-Hill, New York.

Lamberth, J. and Craig, L. (1970). "Differential magnitude of reward and magnitude shifts using attitudinal stimuli", *Journal of Experimental Research in Personality*, 4, 281–5.

Lawler, E.E. (1968). "Effects of hourly overpayment on productivity and work quality", *Journal of Personality and Social Psychology*, 10, 306–14.

Levinger, G. and Snoek, J.D. (1972). *Attraction in Relationships: A New Look at Interpersonal Attraction*. General Learning Press, Morristown, N.J.

Lipetz, M.E., Cohen, I.H., Dowrin, J. and Rogers, L.S. (1970). "Need complementarity, marital stability and material satisfaction". In Gergen, K. and Marlowe, D. (eds), *Personality and Social Behaviour*, pp. 201–12. Addison-Wesley, Reading, Mass.

Manis, M. (1975). "Comment on Gergen"s "Social Psychology as History", *Personality and Social Psychology Bulletin*, 1, 450–5.

Marlowe, D. and Gergen, K.J. (1968). "Personality and social interaction". In Lindzey, G. and Aronson, E. (eds), *The Handbook of Social Psychology*, 2nd edn, vol. 3, pp. 590–665. Addison-Wesley, Reading, Mass.

McGuire, W.J. (1967). "Some impending reorientations in social psychology", *Journal of Experimental Social Psychology*, 3, 124–39.

McGuire, W.J. (1973). "The yin and yang of progress in social psychology", *Journal of Personality and Social Psychology*, 26, 446–56.

McGuire, W.J. (1969). "The nature of attitudes and attitude change". In Lindsey, G. and Aronson, E. (eds), *Handbook of Social Psychology*, 2nd edn, vol. 3, pp. 136–314. Addison-Wesley, Reading, Mass.

Mettee, D.R. and Wilkins, P.C. (1972). "When similarity 'hurts': Effects of perceived ability and a humorous blunder on interpersonal attraction", *Journal of Personality and Social Psychology*, 22, 246–58.

Milgram, S. (1963). "Behavioral study of obedience", *Journal of Abnormal and Social Psychology*, 67, 371–8.

Mischel, W. (1973). "Toward a cognitive social learning reconceptualization of personality", *Psychological Review*, 80, 252–83.

Müller, H.J. (1963). *Freedom in the Western World*. Harper Row, New York.

Newcomb, T. (1961). *The Acquaintance Process*. Holt, Rinehart and Winston, New York.

Novak, D.W. and Lerner, M.J. (1968). "Rejection as a consequence of perceived similarity", *Journal of Personality and Social Psychology*, 9, 147–52.

Orne, M.T. (1962). "On the social psychology of the psychological experiment: With particular reference to demand characteristics and their implications", *American Psychologist*, 17, 776–83.

Osgood, C.E. (1962). *An Alternative to War or Surrender*. University of Illinois Press, Urbana, Ill.

Pruitt, I.G. (1971). "Choice shifts in group discussion: An introductory review", *Journal of Personality and Social Psychology*, 3, 339–60.

Riecken, H.W. and Boruch, R.F. (eds) (1974). *Social Experimentation*. Academic Press, New York.

Rivlin, A.M. (1973). "Social experiments: The promise and the problems", *Evaluation*, 1, 13–24.

Rosenthal, R. (1966). *Experimenter Effects in Behavioural Research*. Appleton-Century-Crofts, New York.

Rosenthal, R. and Rosnow, R.L. (1969). *Artifact in Behavioral Research*. Academic Press, New York.

Schlenker, B.R. (1974). "Social psychology and science", *Journal of Personality and Social Psychology*, 29, 1–15.

Senn, D.J. (1971). "Attraction as a function of similarity–dissimilarity in task performance", *Journal of Personality and Social Psychology*, 18, 120–3.

Silverman, I. (1964). "Self-esteem and differential responsiveness to success and failure", *Journal of Abnormal and Social Psychology*, 69, 115–19.

Steiner, I. (1974). "Whatever happened to the group in social psychology", *Journal of Experimental Social Psychology*, 10, 94–108.

Stotland, E. (1969). "Exploratory investigations of empathy". In Berkowitz, L. (ed.), *Advances in Experimental Social Psychology*, vol. IV. Academic Press, New York.

Tajfel, H. (1972). "Experiments in a vacuum". In Israel, J. and Tajfel, H. (eds), *The Context of Social Psychology: A Critical Assessment*. Academic Press, London.

Taylor, S.E. and Mettee, D.R. (1971). "When similarity breeds contempt", *Journal of Personality and Social Psychology*, 20, 75–81.

Thorngate, W. (1976). "Possible limits on a science of man". In Strickland, L., Aboud, F. and Gergen, K.J. (eds), *Social Psychology in Transition*. Plenum, New York.

Weber, E.H. (1834). *De pulsu, resorptiones, auditu et tactu: Annotationes anatomicales et physiologicales*. Koehler, Leipzig.

Weick, K.E. (1968). "Systematic observational methods". In Lindzey, G. and Aronson, E. (eds), *Handbook of Social Psychology*, vol. II. Addison-Wesley, Reading, Mass.

Weinstein, G. and Platt, G. (1969). *The Wish to be Free*. University of California Press, Berkeley, Calif.

Wicklund, R. (1974). *Freedom and Reactance*. Wiley, New York.

Part II
Construction of the Social World

5 Basic Concepts and Approaches in Social Cognition

Forming impressions of personality

S.E. Asch

Theoretical Background

There are several justifications for including Asch's (1946) article in this volume. First, it is a true 'classic', the oldest article by some length that we include in this collection, which also proved a turning point in the literature. Second, Asch provided a method, albeit a very simple one, for studying how impressions were formed; and it was a method that was to be copied many times in subsequent studies. Third, it is instructive for students to see how research has changed, say from 1946 to 1996, in terms of the scope of questions we ask, and can ask, the methods we use, the inferential statistics computed, and even the style in which the article is written.

Asch proposed two alternative models of how we might form impressions of another person. According to the first model (since termed the 'algebraic' model; see Anderson, 1981), each trait produces its particular impression, and these individual impressions are combined into a summary evaluation that is nothing more than the sum of several independent impressions. According to the second, 'configural' model, we form an impression of the entire person, and traits are perceived in relation to each other. Thus, for example, if we first learn that a new lecturer is 'warm' or 'cold', we may later judge his or her ironic sense of humour as 'humorous' or 'sarcastic', respectively (see Kelley, 1950). The algebraic and configural models represent elemental and holistic approaches to social cognition (see Fiske and Taylor, 1991) and although Asch championed the holistic approach (see also Asch and Zukier, 1984; Zanna and Hamilton, 1977), Anderson (1981) in particular fought the opposite corner.

In this article Asch reviews a series of ten studies based on 1,000 participants. To be consistent with our other summaries, we focus on the first three experiments, using our standard set of subheadings. These experiments on 'central and peripheral characteristics' investigate the consequences of manipulating the presence or absence of traits thought to be either 'central' (affecting inferences about the presence of other traits) or 'peripheral' (having

Journal of Abnormal and Social Psychology (1946), 41:258–90.

little effect on other trait ratings) in a stimulus list supposedly describing another person on ratings of what people think that person will be like.

EXPERIMENT I

Hypotheses

Two competing hypotheses are tested. On the one hand (the algebraic or elemental prediction), two identical lists of stimulus traits (with the exception that one includes the trait 'warm' and the other includes 'cold') may produce identical ratings on all inferred traits (except the addition of warm or cold, respectively). On the other hand (the configural or holistic prediction), the choice of central trait will affect inferences concerning other traits and impart a general positive or negative impression.

Design

The design is simple – one-factor, between-subjects – comparing impressions in group A ('warm') and group B ('cold').

Method

The experimenter read aloud a list of seven traits, said to belong to a particular person. The lists were identical except that the fourth term was either 'warm' or 'cold'. Subjects were asked to form an impression of the person described, write a few sentences about him, and then complete a checklist of adjective pairs, indicating which one they thought described the person.

Results

Asch relies on the sentences written to provide 'evidence of the actual character of the impressions', and the checklist ratings for comparisons between groups assigned to different conditions. It is important to note that the presentation of results is entirely *descriptive* and therefore provides only suggestive support for any hypothesis. Were the study done today, peer-reviewers and the editor would insist, for example, that the open-ended descriptions be rated by two independent judges, who were blind to the conditions from which the descriptions were drawn; or that these materials should be content-analysed in some objective manner. The checklist ratings would have to be analysed with some form of parametric statistics (e.g., between-samples t-test, or one-way analysis of variance; it is not clear whether Asch did compute statistics, but not report them, since he does refer to a 'significant change').

These criticisms notwithstanding, the results do provide quite strong support for the second (Asch's configural) hypothesis. The more objective checklist ratings reveal that several of the eighteen traits in the list were assigned with different frequencies as a function of whether the 'central' trait in the list was 'warm' or 'cold' (see table 5.2). For example, someone described as warm (vs. cold) is much more likely to be described, on the basis of inference only, as also 'generous', 'happy', 'good-natured' and so on. But not all the traits in the list are affected in this way. For example, warm/cold has little impact on 'reliable', 'good-looking' or 'honest'. Asch interprets the written sketches about the person as indicating that the variable warm–cold produced a transformation in the meaning of some characteristics. Some subjects were also asked to rank-order the seven terms in their list of stimulus words in order of their importance for determining their overall impression. These rankings (see table 5.3) indicate that quite a few subjects considered warm or cold to be very important in this respect, although a high number also ranked cold least important.

EXPERIMENT II

The second study sought to demonstrate further the centrality of the warm–cold variable for total impression by *omitting* it from the stimulus lists and comparing responses of a new set of subjects (see 'Total', column 3 in table 5.2) with those of the first experiment. The average impression formed appears to be more neutral than either the 'warm' or the 'cold' impressions, although Asch reports that this is a statistical artifact brought about by averaging responses of subjects who tended to be clearly positive or negative in their evaluations. For this second experiment, the traits warm–cold were added to the checklist. When Asch divided subjects into those who ticked warm or cold (see columns 5 and 6, table 5.2), then their overall impressions were comparable (especially for warm) to those of subjects in the first experiment, whose stimulus list had included warm or cold. Asch interprets these results in terms of subjects inferring that the person is warm or cold when this is not explicitly stated, and then proceeding to infer qualities associated with someone who is warm or cold.

EXPERIMENT III

Having, he argued, demonstrated that the warm–cold variable is central, Asch then took another variable that he predicted would be peripheral in its impact on other traits. Now the two stimulus lists were presented to two groups of subjects, but with the fourth term being either 'polite' or 'blunt' (as opposed to warm or cold). The last two columns of table 5.2 reveal that the polite–blunt manipulation had much less impact on the inference of other traits than did warm–cold. However, there were still a number of clear differences; for example, a polite person was seen as more 'good-natured', 'humorous' and 'popular' and, somewhat implausibly, as less 'altruistic'.

Discussion

The later experiments in this article reveal that central traits are not always central, for example when the content of the words in the stimulus list changes (see experiment IV), and that the 'meaning' of any given trait is determined by its relation to other traits (experiment V). Later research by Wishner (1960) gave a rather different account of why traits such as 'warm' and 'cold' affect some, but not all, inferences concerning other traits. Wishner found that the impact of presented traits on inferences about other traits depended on their prior associations with those traits – that is, whether the traits were related by means of an 'implicit personality theory' of which traits 'go together' (see Zebrowitz, 1990, for more details). Asch's method also allowed for the study of order effects in information presented (primacy and recency effects; see experiments VI and VII), and exploration of the paradox that the same trait can mean different things in two different people (see experiment X).

In short, this classic study reveals a number of fascinating insights about traits, their importance across situations and perceivers, and how we integrate them to form an impression. This fascination with what exactly is conveyed by trait information is still evident in contemporary social psychology (e.g. Rothbart and Park, 1986). More recent research has also revealed a less schismatic and more flexible approach to impression formation than is conveyed by the opposition of elemental versus holistic (Ostrom, 1977). According to circumstances, including motivation and information load, social perceivers can be either elemental *or* holistic. Above all perhaps, Asch's research provided a compelling demonstration of the human tendency to 'go beyond the information given' (see Bruner, 1973). This is one of the cornerstones of research in social cognition.

FURTHER READING

Asch, S. and Zukier, H. (1984). Thinking about persons. *Journal of Personality and Social Psychology*, 46, 1230–40. In this paper Asch turns, nearly forty years on, to the question of how people may process information conveyed by inconsistent combinations of traits.

Fiske, S.T. and Neuberg, S.L. (1990). A continuum of impression formation, from category-based to individuating processes: Influences of information and motivation on attention and interpretation. In M.P. Zanna (ed.), *Advances in Experimental Social Psychology* (vol. 23, pp. 1–74). New York: Academic Press. A highly influential recent paper showing the continuing importance of impression-formation processes.

Zebrowitz, L.A. (1990). *Social Perception*. Milton Keynes: Open University Press. A detailed but very clear overview of the whole field, with one complete chapter devoted to impression formation.

REFERENCES

Anderson, N.H. (1981). *Foundations of information integration theory*. New York: Academic Press.

Bruner, J.S. (1973). *Beyond the Information Given: Studies in the Psychology of Knowing* (ed. J.M. Anglin). New York: Norton.

Fiske, S.T. and Taylor, S.E. (1991). *Social Cognition* (2nd edn). New York: McGraw-Hill.

Kelley, H.H. (1950). The warm–cold variable in first impressions of persons. *Journal of Personality*, 18, 431–9.

Ostrom, T.M. (1977). Between-theory and within-theory conflict in explaining context effects in impression formation. *Journal of Experimental Social Psychology*, 13, 492–503.

Rothbart, M. and Park, B. (1986). On the confirmability and disconfirmability of trait concepts. *Journal of Personality and Social Psychology*, 50, 131–42.

Wishner, J. (1960). Reanalysis of 'Impressions of personality'. *Psychological Review*, 67, 96–112.

Zanna, M.P. and Hamilton, D.L. (1977). Further evidence for meaning change in impression formation. *Journal of Experimental Social Psychology*, 13, 224–38.

- - - - -
Primary
Reading
- - - - - - - -

We look at a person and immediately a certain impression of his character forms itself in us. A glance, a few spoken words are sufficient to tell us a story about a highly complex matter. We know that such impressions form with remarkable rapidity and with great ease. Subsequent observation may enrich or upset our first view, but we can no more prevent its rapid growth than we can avoid perceiving a given visual object or hearing a melody. We also know that this process, though often imperfect, is also at times extraordinarily sensitive.

This remarkable capacity we possess to understand something of the character of another person, to form a conception of him as a human being, as a center of life and striving, with particular characteristics forming a distinct individuality, is a precondition of social life. In what manner are these impressions established? Are there lawful principles regulating their formation?

One particular problem commands our attention. Each person confronts us with a large number of diverse characteristics. This man is courageous, intelligent, with a ready sense of humor, quick in his movements, but he is also serious, energetic, patient under stress, not to mention his politeness and punctuality. These characteristics and many others enter into the formation of our view. Yet our impression is from the start unified; it is the impression of *one* person. We ask: How do the several characteristics function together to produce an impression of one person? What principles regulate this process?

We have mentioned earlier that the impression of a person grows quickly and easily. Yet our minds falter when we face the far simpler task of mastering a series of disconnected numbers or words. We have apparently no need to commit to memory by repeated drill the various characteristics we observe in a person, nor do some of his traits exert an observable retroactive inhibition upon our grasp of the others. Indeed, they seem to support each other. And it is quite hard to forget our view of a person once it has formed. Similarly, we do not easily confuse the half of one person with the half of another. It should be of interest to the psychologist that the far more complex task of grasping the nature of a person is so much less difficult.

There are a number of theoretical possibilities for describing the process of forming an impression, of which the major ones are the following:

(1) A trait is realized in its particular quality. The next trait is similarly realized, etc. Each trait produces its particular impression. The total impression of the person is the sum of the several independent impressions. If a person possesses traits a, b, c, d, e, then the impression of him may be expressed as:

$$\text{I. Impression} = a + b + c + d + e$$

Few if any psychologists would at the present time apply this formulation strictly. It would, however, be an error to deny its importance for the present problem. That it controls in considerable degree many of the procedures for arriving at a scientific, objective view of a person (e.g., by means of questionnaires, rating scales) is evident. But more pertinent to our present discussion is the modified form in which Proposition I is applied to the actual forming of an impression. Some psychologists assume, in addition to the factors of Proposition I, the operation of a "general impression." The latter is conceived as an affective force possessing a plus or minus direction which shifts the evaluation of the several traits in its direction. We may represent this process as follows:

Ia. Impression=

To the sum of the traits there is now added another factor, the general impression.

(2) The second view asserts that we form an impression of the entire person. We see a person as consisting not of these and those independent traits (or of the sum of mutually modified traits), but we try to get at the root of the personality. This would involve that the traits are perceived in relation to each other, in their proper place within the given personality. We may express the final impression as:

II. Impression=

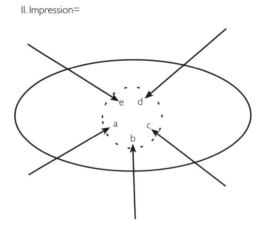

It may appear that psychologists generally hold to some form of the latter formulation. The frequent reference to the unity of the person, or to his "integration," implying that these qualities are also present in the impression, point in this direction. The generality of these expressions is, however, not suitable to exact treatment. Terms such as unity of the person, while pointing to a problem, do not solve it. If we wish to become clear about the unity in persons, or in the impression of persons, we must ask in what sense there is such unity, and in what manner we come to observe it. Secondly, these terms are often applied interchangeably to Propositions II and I*a*. It is therefore important to state at this point a distinction between them.

For Proposition II, the general impression is not a factor added to the particular traits, but rather the perception of a particular form of relation between the traits, a conception which is wholly missing in I*a*. Further, Proposition I*a* conceives the process in terms of an imposed affective shift in the evaluation of separate traits, whereas Proposition II deals in the first instance with processes between the traits each of which has a cognitive content.

Perhaps the central difference between the two propositions becomes clearest when the accuracy of the impression becomes an issue. It is implicit in Proposition II that the process it describes is for the subject a necessary one if he is to focus on a person with maximum clarity. On the other hand, Proposition I*a* permits a radically different interpretation. It has been asserted that the general impression "colors" the particular characteristics, the effect being to *blur* the clarity with which the latter are perceived. In consequence the conclusion is drawn that the general impression is a source of error which should be supplanted by the attitude of judging each trait in isolation, as described in Proposition I. This is the doctrine of the "halo effect" (9).

With the latter remarks, which we introduced only for purposes of illustration, we have passed beyond the scope of the present report. It must be made clear that we shall here deal with certain processes involved in the forming of an impression, a problem logically distinct from the actual relation of traits within a person. To be sure, the manner in which impression is formed contains, as we shall see, definite assumptions concerning the structure of personal traits. The validity of such assumptions must, however, be established in independent investigation.

The issues we shall consider have been largely neglected in investigation. Perhaps the main reason has been a one-sided stress on the subjectivity of personal judgments. The preoccupation with emotional factors and distortions of judgment has had two main consequences for the course investigation has taken. First, it has induced a certain lack of perspective which has diverted interest from the study of those processes which do not involve subjective distortions as the most decisive factor. Secondly, there has been a tendency to neglect the fact that emotions too have a cognitive side, that something must be perceived and discriminated in order that it may be loved or hated. On the other hand, the approach of the more careful studies in this region has centered mainly on questions of validity in the final product of judgment. Neither of the main approaches has dealt explicitly with the process of forming an impression. Yet no argument should be needed to support the statement that our view of a person necessarily involves a certain orientation to, and ordering of, objectively given, observable characteristics. It is this aspect of the problem that we propose to study.

Forming a unified impression: procedure

The plan followed in the experiments to be reported was to read to the subject a number of discrete characteristics, said to belong to a person, with the instruction to describe the impression he formed. The subjects were all college students, most of whom were women.[1] They were mostly beginners in psychology. Though they expressed genuine interest in the tasks, the subjects were not aware of the nature of the problem until it was explained to them. We illustrate our procedure with one concrete instance. The following list of terms was read: *energetic–assured–talkative–cold–ironical–inquisitive–persuasive*. The reading of the list was preceded by the following instructions:

I shall read to you a number of characteristics that belong to a particular person. Please listen to them carefully and try to form an impression of the kind of person described. You will later be asked to give a brief characterization of the person in just a few sentences. I will read the list slowly and will repeat it once.

The list was read with an interval of approximately five seconds between the terms. When the first reading was completed, the experimenter said, "I will now read the list again," and proceeded to do so. We reproduce below a few typical sketches written by subjects after they heard read the list of terms:

He seems to be the kind of person who would make a great impression upon others at a first meeting. However as time went by, his acquaintances would easily come to see through the mask. Underneath would be revealed his arrogance and selfishness.

He is the type of person you meet all too often: sure of himself, talks too much, always trying to bring you around to his way of thinking, and with not much feeling for the other fellow.

He impresses people as being more capable than he really is. He is popular and never ill at ease. Easily becomes the center of attraction at any gathering. He is likely to be a jack-of-all-trades. Although his interests are varied, he is not necessarily well-versed in any of them. He possesses a sense of humor. His presence stimulates enthusiasm and very often he does arrive at a position of importance.

Possibly he does not have any deep feeling. He would tend to be an opportunist. Likely to succeed in things he intends to do. He has perhaps married a wife who would help him in his purpose. He tends to be skeptical.

The following preliminary points are to be noted:

1   When a task of this kind is given, a normal adult is capable of responding to the instruction by forming a unified impression. Though he hears a sequence of discrete terms, his resulting impression is not discrete. In some manner he shapes the separate qualities into a single, consistent view. All subjects in the following experiments, of whom there were over 1,000, fulfilled the task in the manner described. No one proceeded by reproducing the given list of terms, as one would in a rote memory experiment; nor did any of the subjects reply merely with synonyms of the given terms.
2   The characteristics seem to reach out beyond the merely given terms of the description. Starting from the bare terms, the final account is completed and rounded. Reference is made to characters and situations which are apparently not directly mentioned in the list, but which are inferred from it.
3   The accounts of the subjects diverge from each other in important respects. This will not be surprising in view of the variable content of the terms employed, which permits a considerable freedom in interpretation and weighting.

In the experiments to be reported the subjects were given a group of traits on the basis of which they formed an impression. In view of the fact that we possess no principles in this region to help in their systematic construction, it was necessary to invent groupings of traits. In this we were guided by an informal sense of what traits were consistent with each other.

The procedure here employed is clearly different from the everyday situation in which we follow the concrete actions of an actual person. We have chosen to work with weak, incipient impressions, based on abbreviated descriptions of personal qualities. Nevertheless, this procedure has some merit for purposes of investigation, especially in observing the change of impressions, and is, we hope to show, relevant to more natural judgment.

More detailed features of the procedure will be described subsequently in connection with the actual experiments. We shall now inquire into some of the factors that determine the content and alteration of such impressions.

I. Central and Peripheral Characteristics

A. Variation of a central quality

Observation suggests that not all qualities have the same weight in establishing the view of a person. Some are felt to be basic, others secondary. In the following experiments we sought for a demonstration of this process in the course of the formation of an impression.

Experiment I

Two groups, A and B, heard read a list of character-qualities, identical save for one term. The list follows:

A   intelligent–skillful–industrious–*warm*–determined–practical–cautious

B   intelligent–skillful–industrious–*cold*–determined–practical–cautious

Group A heard the person described as "warm"; Group B, as "cold."

Technique

The instructions were as described above. Following the reading, each subject wrote a brief sketch.

The sketches furnish concrete evidence of the impressions formed. Their exact analysis involves, however, serious technical difficulties. It seemed, therefore, desirable to add a somewhat simpler procedure for the determination of the content of the impression and for the purpose of group comparisons. To this end we constructed a check list consisting of pairs of traits, mostly opposites. From each pair of terms in this list, which the reader will find

Table 5.1   Check list I

1	Generous–ungenerous	7	Popular–unpopular	13	Frivolous–serious
2	Shrewd–wise	8	Unreliable–reliable	14	Restrained–talkative
3	Unhappy–happy	9	Important–insignificant	15	Self-centered–altruistic
4	Irritable–good-natured	10	Ruthless–humane	16	Imaginative–hard-headed
5	Humorous–humorless	11	Good-looking–unattractive	17	Strong–weak
6	Sociable–unsociable	12	Persistent–unstable	18	Dishonest–honest

reproduced in table 5.1, the subject was instructed to select the one that was most in accordance with the view he had formed. Terms were included which were quite different from those appearing in the basic list, but which could be related to them. Of necessity we were guided in the selection of terms for the check list (as well as for the experimental lists) by an informal sense of what was fitting or relevant. Some of the terms were taken from written sketches of subjects in preliminary experiments. In the examination of results we shall rely upon the written sketches for evidence of the actual character of the impressions, and we shall supplement these with the quantitative results from the check list.

There were 90 subjects in Group A (comprising four separate classroom groups), 76 subjects in Group B (comprising four separate classroom groups).

Results

Are the impressions of Groups A and B identical, with the exception that one has the added quality of "warm," the other of "cold"? This is one possible outcome. Another possibility is that the differentiating quality imparts a general plus or minus direction to the resulting impression. We shall see that neither of these formulations accurately describes the results.

We note first that the characteristic "warm–cold" produces striking and consistent differences of impression. In general, the A-impressions are far more positive than the B-impressions. We cite a few representative examples:

Series A ("warm")
A person who believes certain things to be right, wants others to see his point, would be sincere in an argument and would like to see his point won.

A scientist performing experiments and persevering after many setbacks. He is driven by the desire to accomplish something that would be of benefit.

Series B ("cold")
A very ambitious and talented person who would not let anyone or anything stand in the way of achieving his goal. Wants his own way, he is determined not to give in, no matter what happens.

A rather snobbish person who feels that his success and intelligence set him apart from the run-of-the-mill individual. Calculating and unsympathetic.

This trend is fully confirmed in the check-list choices. In table 5.2 we report the frequency (in terms of percentages) with which each term in the check list was selected. For the sake of brevity of presentation we state the results for the positive term in each pair; the reader may determine the percentage of choices for the other term in each pair by subtracting the given figure from 100. To illustrate, under Condition A of the present experiment, 91 per cent of the subjects chose the designation "generous"; the remaining 9 per cent selected the designation "ungenerous." Occasionally, a subject would not state a choice for a particular pair. Therefore, the number of cases on which the figures are based is not always identical; however, the fluctuations were minor, with the exception of the category "good-looking–unattractive," which a larger proportion of subjects failed to answer.

We find:

1   There are extreme reversals between Groups A and B in the choice of fitting characteristics. Certain qualities are preponderantly assigned to the "warm" person, while the opposing

Table 5.2   Choice of fitting qualities (percentages)

		Experiment I		Experiment II			Experiment III	
		"Warm" N = 90	"Cold" N = 76	Total N = 56	"Warm" N = 23	"Cold" N = 33	"Polite" N = 20	"Blunt" N = 26
1	Generous	91	8	55	87	33	56	58
2	Wise	65	25	49	73	33	30	50
3	Happy	90	34	71	91	58	75	65
4	Good-natured	94	17	69	91	55	87	56
5	Humorous	77	13	36	76	12	71	48
6	Sociable	91	38	71	91	55	83	68
7	Popular	84	28	57	83	39	94	56
8	Reliable	94	99	96	96	97	95	100
9	Important	88	99	88	87	88	94	96
10	Humane	86	31	64	91	45	59	77
11	Good-looking	77	69	58	71	53	93	79
12	Persistent	100	97	98	96	100	100	100
13	Serious	100	99	96	91	100	100	100
14	Restrained	77	89	82	67	94	82	77
15	Altruistic	69	18	44	68	27	29	46
16	Imaginative	51	19	24	45	9	33	31
17	Strong	98	95	95	94	96	100	100
18	Honest	98	94	95	100	92	87	100

    qualities are equally prominent in the "cold" person. This holds for the qualities of (1) generosity, (2) shrewdness, (3) happiness, (4) irritability, (5) humor, (6) sociability, (7) popularity, (10) ruthlessness, (15) self-centeredness, (16) imaginativeness.

2   There is another group of qualities which is *not* affected by the transition from "warm" to "cold," or only slightly affected. These are: (8) reliability, (9) importance, (11) physical attractiveness, (12) persistence, (13) seriousness, (14) restraint, (17) strength, (18) honesty.

    These results show that a change in one character-quality has produced a widespread change in the entire impression. Further, the written sketches show that the terms "warm–cold" did not simply add a new quality, but to some extent transformed the other characteristics. With this point we shall deal more explicitly in the experiments to follow.

    That such transformations take place is also a matter of everyday experience. If a man is intelligent, this has an effect on the way in which we perceive his playfulness, happiness, friendliness. At the same time, this extensive change does not function indiscriminately. The "warm" person is not seen more favorably in all respects. There is a range of qualities, among them a number that are basic, which are not touched by the distinction between "warm" and "cold." Both remain equally honest, strong, serious, reliable, etc.

    The latter result is of interest with reference to one possible interpretation of the findings. It might be supposed that the category "warm–cold" aroused a "mental set" or established a halo tending toward a consistently plus or minus evaluation. We observe here that this trend did not work in an indiscriminate manner, but was decisively limited at certain points. If we assume that the process of mutual influence took place in terms of the actual character of the qualities in question, it is not surprising that some will, by virtue of their content, remain unchanged.[2]

The following will show that the subjects generally felt the qualities "warm–cold" to be of primary importance. We asked the subjects in certain of the groups to rank the terms of Lists A and B in order of their importance for determining their impression. Table 5.3, containing the distribution of rankings of "warm–cold," shows that these qualities ranked comparatively high. At the same time a considerable number of subjects relegated "cold" to the lowest position. That the rankings are not higher is due to the fact that the lists contained other central traits.

These data, as well as the ranking of the other traits not here reproduced, point to the following conclusions:

1   The given characteristics do not all have the same weight for the subject. He assigns to some a higher importance than to others.
2   The weight of a given characteristic varies – within limits – from subject to subject.

Certain limitations of the check-list procedure need to be considered: (1) The subject's reactions are forced into an appearance of discreteness which they do not actually possess, as the written sketches show; (2) the check list requires the subject to choose between extreme characteristics, which he might prefer to avoid; (3) the quantitative data describe group trends; they do not represent adequately the form of the individual impression. Generally the individual responses exhibit much stronger trends in a consistently positive or negative direction. For these reasons we employ the check-list results primarily for the purpose of comparing group trends under different conditions. For this purpose the procedure is quite adequate.

B. Omission of a central quality

That the category "warm–cold" is significant for the total impression may be demonstrated also by omitting it from the series. This we do in the following experiment.

Experiment II

The procedure was identical with that of Experiment I, except that the terms "warm" and "cold" were omitted from the list read to the subject (intelligent–skillful–industrious–determined–practical–cautious). Also the check list was identical with that of Experiment I, save that "warm–cold" was added as the last pair. There were three groups, consisting of a total of 56 subjects.

Under these conditions the selection of fitting characteristics shows a significant change. The distribution of choices for the total group (see table 5.2, column labeled "Total") now falls between the "warm" and "cold" variations of Experiment I. It appears that a more neutral impression has formed.

The total group results are, however, largely a statistical artifact. An examination of the

Table 5.3 Rankings of "warm" and "cold": Experiment I

Rank	"Warm"		"Cold"	
	N	Percentage	N	Percentage
1	6	14	12	27
2	15	35	8	21
3	4	10	1	2
4	4	10	2	5
5	4	10	3	7
6	3	7	2	5
7	6	14	13	33
	42	100	41	100

check-list choices of the subjects quickly revealed strong and consistent individual differences. They tended to be consistently positive or negative in their evaluations. It will be recalled that the terms "warm–cold" were added to the check list. This permitted us to subdivide the total group according to whether they judged the described person on the check list as "warm" or "cold." Of the entire group, 23 subjects (or 41 per cent) fell into the "warm" category. Our next step was to study the distribution of choices in the two subgroups. The results are clear: the two subgroups diverge consistently in the direction of the "warm" and the "cold" groups, respectively, of Experiment I. (See table 5.2.) This is especially the case with the two "warm" series, which are virtually identical.

It is of interest that the omission of a term from the experimental list did not function entirely as an omission. Instead, the subjects inferred the corresponding quality in either the positive or negative direction. While not entirely conclusive, the results suggest that a full impression of a person cannot remain indifferent to a category as fundamental as the one in question, and that a trend is set up to include it in the impression on the basis of the given data. In later experiments too we have found a strong trend to reach out toward evaluations which were not contained in the original description.

C. Variation of a peripheral quality

Would a change of *any* character-quality produce an effect as strong as that observed above? "Warm" and "cold" seem to be of special importance for our conception of a person. This was, in fact, the reason for selecting them for study. If there are central qualities, upon which the content of other qualities depends, and dependent qualities which are secondarily determined, it should be possible to distinguish them objectively. On this assumption the addition or omission of peripheral qualities should have smaller effects than those observed in Experiment I. We turn to this question in the following experiment.

Experiment III

The following lists were read, each to a different group:

A   intelligent–skillful–industrious–*polite*–determined–practical–cautious

B   intelligent–skillful–industrious–*blunt*–determined–practical–cautious

The A group contained 20, the B group 26 subjects.

The changes introduced into the selection of fitting characteristics in the transition from "polite" to "blunt" were far weaker than those found in Experiment I (see table 5.2). There is further evidence that the subjects themselves regarded these characteristics as relatively peripheral, especially the characteristic "polite." If we may take the rankings as an index, then we may conclude that a change in a peripheral trait produces a weaker effect on the total impression than does a change in a central trait (see table 5.4). (Though the changes produced are weaker than those of Experiment I, they are nevertheless substantial. Possibly this is a consequence of the thinness of the impression, which responds easily to slight changes.)

D. Transformation from a central to a peripheral quality

The preceding experiments have demonstrated a process of discrimination between central and peripheral qualities. We ask: Are certain qualities constantly central? Or is their functional value, too, dependent on the other characteristics?

Experiment IV

We selected for observation the quality "warm," which was demonstrated to exert a powerful effect on the total impression (Experiments I and II). The effect of the term was studied in the following two series:

A   obedient–weak–shallow–*warm*–unambitious–vain

B   vain–shrewd–unscrupulous–*warm*–shallow–envious

Immediately "warm" drops as a significant characteristic in relation to the others, as the distribution of rankings appearing in table 5.5 shows. (Compare table 5.3 of Experiment I.)

Table 5.4   Rankings of "polite" and "blunt": Experiment III

	A: "Polite"		B: "Blunt"	
Rank	*N*	*Percentage*	*N*	*Percentage*
1	0	0	0	0
2	0	0	4	15
3	0	0	3	12
4	2	10	5	19
5	3	16	6	23
6	4	21	1	4
7	10	53	7	27
	19	100	26	100

Table 5.5 Rankings of "warm" and "cold": Experiment IV

| | "Warm" | | | | "Cold" | |
| | Series A | | Series B | | Series C | |
Rank	N	Percentage	N	Percentage	N	Percentage
1	1	4	0	0	1	5
2	0	0	0	0	0	0
3	2	9	1	5	3	15
4	6	27	4	19	2	10
5	7	30	4	19	1	5
6	7	30	12	57	2	10
7	—	—	—	—	11	55
	23	100	21	100	20	100

More enlightening are the subjects' comments. In Series A the quality "warm" is now seen as wholly dependent, dominated by others far more decisive.

I think the warmth within this person is a warmth emanating from a follower to a leader.

The term "warm" strikes one as being a dog-like affection rather than a bright friendliness. It is passive and without strength.

His submissiveness may lead people to think he is kind and warm.

A more extreme transformation is observed in Series B. In most instances the warmth of this person is felt to lack sincerity, as appears in the following protocols:

I assumed the person to appear warm rather than really to be warm.

He was warm only when it worked in with his scheme to get others over to his side. His warmth is not sincere.

A similar change was also observed in the content of "cold" in a further variation. The subject heard List B of Experiment I followed by Series C below, the task being to state whether the term "cold" had the same meaning in both lists.

C   intelligent–skillful–sincere–*cold*–conscientious–helpful–modest

All subjects reported a difference. The quality "cold" became peripheral for all in Series C. The following are representative comments:

The coldness of 1 (Experiment I) borders on ruthlessness; 2 analyses coldly to differentiate between right and wrong.

1 is cold inwardly and outwardly, while 2 is cold only superficially.

1: cold means lack of sympathy and understanding; 2: cold means somewhat formal in manner.

Coldness was the foremost characteristic of 1. In 2 it seemed not very important, a quality that would disappear after you came to know him.

That "cold" was transformed in the present series into a peripheral quality is also confirmed by the rankings reported in table 5.5.

We conclude that a quality, central in one person, may undergo a change of content in another person, and become subsidiary. When central, the quality has a different content and weight than when it is subsidiary.

Here we observe directly a process of grouping in the course of which the content of a trait changes in relation to its surroundings. Secondly, we observe that the functional value of a trait, too – whether, for example, it becomes central or not – is a consequence of its relation to the set of surrounding traits. At the same time we are able to see more clearly the distinction between central and peripheral traits. It is inadequate to say that a central trait is more important, contributes more quantitatively to, or is more highly correlated with, the final impression than a peripheral trait. The latter formulations are true, but they fail to consider the qualitative process of mutual determination between traits, namely, that a central trait determines the content and the functional place of peripheral traits within the entire impression. In Series A, for example, the quality "warm" does not control the meaning of "weak," but is controlled by it.

The evidence may seem to support the conclusion that the same quality which is central in one impression becomes peripheral in another. Such an interpretation would, however, contain an ambiguity. While we may speak of relativity in the functional value of a trait within a person, in a deeper sense we have here the opposite of relativity. For the sense of "warm" (or "cold") of Experiment I has not suffered a change of evaluation under the present conditions. Quite the contrary; the terms in question change precisely because the subject does not see the possibility of finding in this person the same warmth he values so highly when he does meet it (correspondingly for coldness).

Experiment V

The preceding experiments have shown that the characteristics forming the basis of an impression do not contribute each a fixed, independent meaning, but that their content is itself partly a function of the environment of the other characteristics, of their mutual relations. We propose now to investigate more directly the manner in which the content of a given characteristic may undergo change.

Lists A and B were read to two separate groups (including 38 and 41 subjects respectively). The first three terms of the two lists are opposites; the final two terms are identical.

A   kind–wise–honest–*calm–strong*

B   cruel–shrewd–unscrupulous–*calm–strong*

The instructions were to write down synonyms for the given terms. The instructions read: "Suppose you had to describe this person in the same manner, but without using the terms you heard, what other terms would you use?" We are concerned with the synonyms given to the two final terms.

In table 5.6 we list those synonyms of "calm" which occurred with different frequencies in the two groups. It will be seen that terms appear in one group which are not at all to be found in the other; further, some terms appear with considerably different frequencies under the two conditions. These do not, however, include the total group of synonyms; many scattered terms occurred equally in both groups.

We may conclude that the quality "calm" did not, at least in some cases, function as an independent, fixed trait, but that its content was determined by its relation to the other terms. As a consequence, the quality "calm" was not the same under the two experimental conditions. In Series A it possessed an aspect of gentleness, while a grimmer side became prominent in Series B.[3]

Essentially the same may be said of the final term, "strong." Again, some synonyms appear exclusively in one or the other groups, and in the expected directions. Among these are:

Series A: fearless–helpful–just–forceful–courageous–reliable

Series B: ruthless–overbearing–overpowering–hard–inflexible–unbending–dominant

The data of table 5.6 provide evidence of a tendency in the described direction, but its strength is probably underestimated. We have already mentioned that certain synonyms appeared frequently in both series. But it is not to be concluded that they therefore carried the same meaning. Doubtless the same terms were at times applied in the two groups with different meanings, precisely because the subjects were under the control of the factor being investigated. To mention one example: the term "quiet" often occurred as a synonym of "calm" in both groups, but the subjects may have intended a different meaning in the two cases. For this reason table 5.6 may not reveal the full extent of the change introduced by the factor of embedding.

The preceding experiments permit the following conclusions:

1   There is a process of discrimination between central and peripheral traits. All traits do not have the same rank and value in the final impression. The change of a central trait may

Table 5.6   Synonyms of "calm": Experiment V

	"Kind" series	"Cruel" series
Serene	18	3
Cold, frigid, icy, cool, calculating, shrewd, nervy, scheming, conscienceless	0	20
Soothing, peaceful, gentle, tolerant, good-natured, mild-mannered	11	0
Poised, reserved, restful, unexcitable, unshakable	18	7
Deliberate, silent, unperturbed, masterful, impassive, collected, confident, relaxed, emotionless, steady, impassive, composed	11	26

completely alter the impression, while the change of a peripheral trait has a far weaker effect (Experiments I, II, and III).

2   Both the cognitive content of a trait and its functional value are determined in relation to its surroundings (Experiment IV).

3   Some traits determine both the content and the function of other traits. The former we call central, the latter peripheral (Experiment IV).

II. The Factor of Direction

If impressions of the kind here investigated are a summation of the effects of the separate characteristics, then an identical set of characteristics should produce a constant result. Is it possible to alter the impression without changing the particular characteristic? We investigate this question below.

Experiment VI

The following series are read, each to a different group:

A   intelligent–industrious–impulsive–critical–stubborn–envious

B   envious–stubborn–critical–impulsive–industrious–intelligent

There were 34 subjects in Group A, 24 in Group B.

The two series are identical with regard to their members, differing only in the order of succession of the latter. More particularly, Series A opens with qualities of high merit (intelligent–industrious), proceeds to qualities that permit of a better or poorer evaluation (impulsive–critical–stubborn), and closes with a dubious quality (envious). This order is reversed in Series B.

A considerable difference develops between the two groups taken as a whole. The impression produced by A is predominantly that of an able person who possesses certain shortcomings which do not, however, overshadow his merits. On the other hand, B impresses the majority as a "problem," whose abilities are hampered by his serious difficulties. Further, some of the qualities (e.g., impulsiveness, criticalness) are interpreted in a positive way under Condition A, while they take on, under Condition B, a negative color. This trend is not observed in all subjects, but it is found in the majority. A few illustrative extracts follow:

Series A
A person who knows what he wants and goes after it. He is impatient at people who are less gifted, and ambitious with those who stand in his way.

Is a forceful person, has his own convictions and is usually right about things. Is self-centered and desires his own way.

The person is intelligent and fortunately he puts his intelligence to work. That he is stubborn and impulsive may be due to the fact that he knows what he is saying and what he means and will not therefore give in easily to someone else's idea which he disagrees with.

Series B
This person's good qualities such as industry and intelligence are bound to be restricted by jealousy and stubbornness. The person is emotional. He is unsuccessful because he is weak and allows his bad points to cover up his good ones.

This individual is probably maladjusted because he is envious and impulsive.

In order to observe more directly the transition in question, the writer proceeded as follows. A new group (N = 24) heard Series B, wrote the free sketch, and immediately thereafter wrote the sketch in response to Series A. They were also asked to comment on the relation between the two impressions. Under these conditions, with the transition occurring in the same subjects, 14 out of 24 claimed that their impression suffered a change, while the remaining 10 subjects reported no change. Some of the latter asserted that they had waited until the entire series was read before deciding upon their impression. The following are a few comments of the changing group:

You read the list in a different order and thereby caused a different type of person to come to mind. This one is smarter, more likeable, a go-getter, lively, headstrong, and with a will of his own; he goes after what he wants.

The first individual seems to show his envy and criticism more than the second one.

Table 5.7 Choice of fitting qualities (percentages)

		Experiment VI		Experiment VII	
		Intelligent → Envious (N = 34)	Envious → Intelligent (N = 24)	Intelligent → Evasive (N = 46)	Evasive → Intelligent (N = 53)
1	Generous	24	10	42	23
2	Wise	18	17	35	19
3	Happy	32	5	51	49
4	Good-natured	18	0	54	37
5	Humorous	52	21	53	29
6	Sociable	56	27	50	48
7	Popular	35	14	44	39
8	Reliable	84	91	96	94
9	Important	85	90	77	89
10	Humane	36	21	49	46
11	Good-looking	74	35	59	53
12	Persistent	82	87	94	100
13	Serious	97	100	44	100
14	Restrained	64	9	91	91
15	Altruistic	6	5	32	25
16	Imaginative	26	14	37	16
17	Strong	94	73	74	96
18	Honest	80	79	66	81

This man does not seem so bad as the first one. Somehow, he seems more intelligent, with his critical attitude helping that characteristic of intelligence, and he seems to be industrious, perhaps because he is envious and wants to get ahead.

The check-list data appearing in table 5.7 furnish quantitative support for the conclusions drawn from the written sketches.

Under the given conditions the terms, the elements of the description, are identical, but the resulting impressions frequently are not the same. Further, the relations of the terms to one another have not been disturbed, as they may have been in Experiments I and II, with the addition and omission of parts. How can we understand the resulting difference?

The accounts of the subjects suggest that the first terms set up in most subjects a *direction* which then exerts a continuous effect on the latter terms. When the subject hears the first term, a broad, uncrystallized but directed impression is born. The next characteristic comes not as a separate item, but is related to the established direction. Quickly the view formed acquires a certain stability, so that later characteristics are fitted – if conditions permit[4] – to the given direction.

Here we observe a factor of primacy guiding the development of an impression. This factor is not, however, to be understood in the sense of Ebbinghaus, but rather in a structural sense. It is not the sheer temporal position of the item which is important as much as the functional relation of its content to the content of the items following it.[5]

Some further evidence with regard to this point is provided by the data with regard to ranking. We reproduce in table 5.8 the rankings of the characteristic "envious" under the two conditions.

Experiment VII

It seemed desirable to repeat the preceding experiment with a new series. As before, we reversed the succession of terms. Unlike the preceding series, there is no gradual change in the merit of the given characteristics, but rather the abrupt introduction at the end (or at the beginning) of a highly dubious trait. The series were:

A   intelligent–skillful–industrious–determined–practical–cautious–evasive

Table 5.8   Ranking of "envious": Experiment VI

Rank	Intelligent → Envious		Envious → Intelligent	
	N	*Percentage*	*N*	*Percentage*
1	5	15	7	29
2	4	11	4	17
3	5	15	5	21
4	3	9	2	8
5	4	11	2	8
6	13	39	4	17
	34	100	24	100

B   evasive–cautious–practical–determined–industrious–skillful–intelligent

While the results are, for reasons to be described, less clear than in the experiment preceding, there is still a definite tendency for A to produce a more favorable impression with greater frequency. We report below the more extreme protocols in each series.

Series A

He seems to be a man of very excellent character, though it is not unusual for one person to have all of those good qualities.

A scientist in an applied field, who does not like to discuss his work before it is completed. Retiring and careful – but brilliant. Works alone, does not like to be annoyed with questions. A very dynamic man.

A normal, intelligent person, who sounds as if he would be a good citizen, and of value to all who know him.

He seems to have at least two traits which are not consistent with the rest of his personality. Being *cautious* and *evasive* contradicts his positive qualities. Altogether, he is a most unattractive person – the two above-mentioned traits overbalancing the others.

Series B

This is a man who has had to work for everything he wanted – therefore he is evasive, cautious and practical. He is naturally intelligent, but his struggles have made him hard.

He is out for himself, is very capable but tends to use his skill for his own benefit.

He is so determined to succeed that he relies on any means, making use of his cunning and evasive powers.

Questioning disclosed that, under the given conditions, the quality "evasive" produced unusual difficulty. Most subjects in both groups felt a contradiction between it and the series as a whole. In response to the question, "Were there any characteristics that did not fit with the others?" 11 out of 27 in Group A mentioned "evasive" while it was mentioned by 11 out of a total of 30 in Group B.

It is of interest to observe how this crucial term was dealt with by individual subjects. Some in Group A felt unable to reconcile it with the view they had formed; consequently they relegated it to a subsidiary position and, in the most extreme cases, completely excluded it. Others reported the opposite effect: the final term completely undid their impression and forced a new view. The following comments are illustrative:

Series A

I put this characteristic in the background and said it may be a dependent characteristic of the person, which does not dominate his personality, and does not influence his actions to a large extent.

I excluded it because the other characteristics which fitted together so well were so much more predominant. In my first impression it was left out completely.

It changed my entire idea of the person – changing his attitude toward others, the type of position he'd be likely to hold, the amount of happiness he'd have – and it gave a certain amount of change of character (even for traits not mentioned), and a tendency to think of the person as somewhat sneaky or sly.

Similar reactions occur in Group B, but with changed frequencies.

The importance of the order of impressions of a person in daily experience is a matter of general observation and is perhaps related to the process under investigation. It may be the basis for the importance attached to first impressions. It is a matter of general experience that we may have a "wrong slant" on a person, because certain characteristics first observed are given a central position when they are actually subsidiary, or vice versa.

Experiment VIII

We studied the factor of direction in yet another way. Series A of Experiment VI was divided in two parts and presented to a new group as a description of two persons. The new series were:

A   intelligent–industrious–impulsive

B   critical–stubborn–envious

Procedure
(1) Series A was read to this group (Group 1), followed by the written sketch and the check list. (2) The subjects were instructed that they would hear a new group of terms describing a second person. Series B was read and the usual information was obtained. (3) Upon completion of the second task the subjects were informed that the two lists described a single person. They were instructed to form an impression corresponding to the entire list of terms. Certain questions were subsequently asked concerning the last step which will be described below. A control group (Group 2) responded only to the entire list of six terms (as in Series A of Experiment VI), and answered some of the final questions.

We are concerned mainly to see how Group 1 dealt with the final task, the establishing of an impression based on the two smaller series. That Lists A and B were widely different will be clear in the check-list results of table 5.9.

Most subjects of Group 1 expressed astonishment at the final information (of Step 3) and showed some reluctance to proceed. In response to the question, "Did you experience difficulty in forming an impression on the basis of the six terms," the majority of Group 1 (32 out of 52) replied in the affirmative. The reasons given were highly uniform: the two sets of traits seemed entirely contradictory.

I had seen the two sets of characteristics as opposing each other. It was hard to envision all these contradictory traits in one person.

The person seemed to be a mass of contradictions.

He seemed a dual personality. There are two directions in this person.

On the other hand, only a minority in Group 2 (9 out of 24) report any difficulty. Further, the reasons given by the latter are entirely different from those of Group 1. These subjects speak in very general terms, as:

Table 5.9 Choice of fitting qualities: Experiment VIII (percentages)

		Intelligent–industrious–impulsive (N = 52)	Critical–stubborn–envious (N = 52)
1	Generous	87	6
2	Wise	48	3
3	Happy	84	0
4	Good-natured	74	3
5	Humorous	87	12
6	Sociable	89	24
7	Popular	94	9
8	Reliable	85	47
9	Important	90	24
10	Humane	87	19
11	Good-looking	81	36
12	Persistent	85	67
13	Serious	87	83
14	Restrained	16	37
15	Altruistic	66	0
16	Imaginative	65	15
17	Strong	94	50
18	Honest	100	58

These characteristics are possessed by everyone in some degree or other. The terms do not give an inclusive picture.

Only two subjects in Group 2 mention contradiction between traits as a source of difficulty.

The formation of the complete impression proceeds differently in the two groups. Series A and B are at first referred, in Group 1, to entirely different persons. Each is completed in its direction, and the fact that they come successively seems to enhance the contrast between them. It is therefore difficult for them to enter the new impression. Some subjects are unable to reconcile the two directions completely; in consequence their divergence becomes the paramount fact, as the following protocols illustrate:

The directions reacted on each other and were modified, so that the pull in each direction is now less strong. This gives a Jekyll and Hyde appearance to this person.

I applied A to the business half of the man – as he appeared and acted during working hours. B I referred to the man's social life.

The independent development of A and B is on the other hand prevented in Group 2, where they function from the start as parts of one description.[6]

This conclusion is in general confirmed by the following observation. To the question: "Did you proceed by combining the two earlier impressions or by forming a new impression?" the following responses are obtained: (a) 33 of 52 subjects answer that they formed a new impression, different from either A or B; 12 subjects speak of combining the two impressions, while 7 subjects assert that they resorted to both procedures. The following are typical responses in the first subgroup:

> I couldn't combine the personalities of A and B. I formed an entirely new impression.

> I can conceive of the two sets of characteristics in one person, but I cannot conceive of my impressions of them as belonging to one person.

> As I have set down the impressions, one is exactly the opposite of the other. But I can fit the six characteristics to one person.

That the terms of Series A and B often suffered considerable change when they were viewed as part of one series becomes evident in the replies to another question. The subjects were asked, "Did the terms of the series A and B retain for you their first meaning or did they change?" Most subjects describe a change in one or more of the traits, of which the following are representative:

> In A *impulsive* grew out of imaginativeness; now it has more the quality of hastiness.

> *Industriousness* becomes more self-centered.

> *Critical* is now not a derisive but rather a constructive activity.

> *Stubborn* had an entirely personal meaning; now it refers to being set in one's ideas.

The tenor of most replies is well represented by the following comment:

> When the two came together, a modification occurred as well as a limiting boundary to the qualities to which each was referred.

III. Strongly Simplified Impressions

To a marked degree the impressions here examined possess a strongly unified character. At the same time they lack the nuances and discriminations that a full-fledged understanding of another person provides. Therefore they can be easily dominated by a single direction. We propose now to observe in a more direct and extreme manner the formation of a global impression.

Experiment IX

We select from the series of Experiment I three terms: *intelligent–skillful–warm* – all referring to strong positive characteristics. These form the basis of judgment. The results appear in table 5.10.

There develops a one-directed impression, far stronger than any observed in the preceding experiments. The written sketches, too, are unanimously enthusiastic. The impression also develops effortlessly.

Table 5.10   Choice of fitting qualities: Experiment IX (percentages)

		Intelligent– skillful–warm (N = 34)	Warm (N = 22)	Gold (N = 33)
1	Generous	100	100	12
2	Wise	97	95	11
3	Happy	100	100	10
4	Good-natured	100	100	8
5	Humorous	100	100	12
6	Sociable	100	100	9
7	Popular	100	100	6
8	Reliable	100	100	87
9	Important	84	68	54
10	Humane	97	100	17
11	Good-looking	72	95	57
12	Persistent	100	78	97
13	Serious	100	68	97
14	Restrained	66	41	97
15	Altruistic	97	91	3
16	Imaginative	82	95	9
17	Strong	97	74	87
18	Honest	100	100	81

Negative characteristics hardly intrude. That this fails to happen raises a problem. Many negative qualities could quite understandably be living together with those given. But the subjects do not as a rule complete them in this direction. This, indeed, they seem to avoid.

Experiment IXa

The next step was to observe an impression based on a single trait. There are two groups; one group is instructed to select from the check list those characteristics which belong to a "warm" person, the second group those belonging to a "cold" person. The results appear in table 5.10.

In order to show more clearly the range of qualities affected by the given terms we constructed a second check list (Check list II) to which the subjects were to respond in the manner already described. The results are reported in table 5.11.

A remarkably wide range of qualities is embraced in the dimension "warm–cold." It has reference to temperamental characteristics (e.g., optimism, humor, happiness), to basic relations to the group (e.g., generosity, sociability, popularity), to strength of character (e.g., persistence, honesty). It even includes a reference to physical characteristics, evident in the virtually unanimous characterizations of the warm person as short, stout, and ruddy, and in the opposed characterizations of the cold person.

The differences between "warm" and "cold" are now even more considerable than those observed in Experiment I. No qualities remain untouched. But even under these extreme

Table 5.11 Check list II: Choice of fitting qualities: Experiment IXa (percentages)

		Warm (N = 22)	Cold (N = 33)		Warm (N = 22)	Cold (N = 33)
1	Emotional	100	12	Unemotional	0	88
2	Practical	40	73	Theoretical	60	27
3	Optimistic	95	17	Pessimistic	5	83
4	Informal	95	0	Formal	5	100
5	Cheerful	100	18	Sad	0	82
6	Short	91	8	Tall	9	92
7	Modest	86	9	Proud	14	91
8	Imaginative	95	28	Unimaginative	5	72
9	Thin	15	93	Stout	85	7
10	Intelligent	81	96	Unintelligent	19	4
11	Brave	91	74	Cowardly	9	26
12	Pale	15	97	Ruddy	85	3

conditions the characterizations do not become indiscriminately positive or negative. "Warm" stands for very positive qualities, but it also carries the sense of a certain easy-goingness, of a lack of restraint and persistence, qualities which are eminently present in "cold." A simplified impression is not to be simply identified with a failure to make distinctions or qualifications. Rather, what we find is that in a global view the distinctions are drawn bluntly.

The consistent tendency for the distribution of choices to be less extreme in Experiment I requires the revision of an earlier formulation. We have said that central qualities determine the content and functional value of peripheral qualities. It can now be seen that the central characteristics, while imposing their direction upon the total impression, were themselves affected by the surrounding characteristics.

Upon the conclusion of the experiments, the subjects were asked to state the reason for their choice of one predominant direction in their characterizations. All agreed that they felt such a tendency. Some cannot explain it, saying, in the words of one subject: "I do not know the reason; only that this is the way it 'hit' me at the moment"; or: "I did not consciously mean to choose the positive traits." Most subjects, however, are explicit in stating that the given traits seemed to require completion in one direction. The following statements are representative:

> These qualities initiate other qualities. A man who is warm would be friendly, consequently happy. If he is intelligent, he would be honest.

> The given characteristics, though very general, were good characteristics. Therefore other good characteristics seemed to belong. When, for example, I think of a person as warm, I mean that he couldn't be ugly.

This was the tenor of most statements. A few show factors at work of a somewhat different kind, of interest to the student of personality, as:

> I naturally picked the best trait because I *hoped* the person would be that way.

I went in the positive direction because *I* should like to be all those things.

It is of interest for the theory of our problem that there are terms which simultaneously contain implications for wide regions of the person. Many terms denoting personal characteristics show the same property. They do not observe a strict division of labor, each pointing neatly to one specific characteristic; rather, each sweeps over a wide area and affects it in a definite manner.[7]

Some would say that this is a semantic problem. To do so would be, however, to beg the question by disposing of the psychological process that gives rise to the semantic problem. What requires explanation is how a term, and a highly "subjective" one at that, refers so consistently to so wide a region of personal qualities. It seems similarly unfruitful to call these judgments stereotypes. The meaning of stereotype is itself badly in need of psychological clarification. Indeed, in the light of our observations, a stereotype appears (in a first approximation) to be a central quality belonging to an extremely simplified impression.

We propose that there is, under the given conditions, a tendency to grasp the characteristics in their most outspoken, most unqualified sense, and on that basis to complete the impression. The subject aims at a clear view; he therefore takes the given terms in their most complete sense. (What is said here with regard to the present experiment seems to apply also to the preceding experiments. In each case the subject's impression is a blunt, definite characterization. It lacks depth but not definiteness. Even when the view is of a mediocre character, it is outspokenly so.) The comments of the subjects are in agreement with the present interpretation.

IV. Similarity and Difference of Impressions

The preceding discussion has definite consequences for the perception of identity and difference between the characteristics of different persons. Of these the most significant for theory is the proposition that a given trait in two different persons may not be the same trait, and, contrariwise, that two different traits may be functionally identical in two different persons. We turn now to an investigation of some conditions which determine similarity and difference between personal qualities.

Experiment X

I. The group has before it Sets 1, 2, 3, and 4 with instructions to state (1) which of the other three sets most resembles Set 1, and (2) which most resembles Set 2.

Set 1	*Set 2*	*Set 3*	*Set 4*
Quick	Quick	Slow	Slow
Skillful	Clumsy	Skillful	Clumsy
Helpful	Helpful	Helpful	Helpful

One quality – "helpful" – remains constant in all sets. The other two qualities appear in their positive form in Set 1, and are changed to their opposites singly and together in the three other sets.

Table 5.12   Resemblance of sets: Experiment X

Set	Set 1 resembles		Set 2 resembles	
	N	Percentage	N	Percentage
1	0	0	7	9
2	10	13	0	0
3	68	87	5	6
4	0	0	66	85
	78	100	78	100

A remarkable uniformity appears in the findings, reported in table 5.12.

Set 1 is equated with Set 3 in 87 per cent of the cases, while its similarity to Set 2 is reported in only 13 per cent of the cases. Similarly, Set 2 is asserted to resemble Set 4 in 85 per cent of the cases, while the resemblance to Set 1 drops to 9 per cent.

The choice of similar sets cannot in this case be determined merely on the basis of the number of "identical elements," for on this criterion Sets 2 and 3 are equally similar to 1, while Sets 1 and 4 are equally similar to 2. What factors may be said to determine the decisions with regard to similarity and difference?

We come somewhat closer to an answer in the replies to the following question: "Which characteristics in the other sets resemble most closely (*a*) 'quick' of Set 1? (*b*) 'quick' of Set 2? (*c*) 'helpful' of Set 1? (*d*) 'helpful' of Set 2?" The results appear in table 5.13.

We see that qualities which, abstractly taken, are identical, are infrequently equated, while qualities which are abstractly opposed are equated with greater frequency. For example, the quality "quick" of Sets 1 and 2 is matched in only 22 and 25 per cent of the cases, respectively, while "quick" of Set 1 is, in 32 per cent of the cases, matched with "slow" of Set 3, and "quick" of Set 2 with "slow" of Set 4 in 51 per cent of the cases.[8]

At this point the reports of the subjects become very helpful. They were requested at the conclusion to state in writing whether the quality "quick" in Sets 1 and 2 was identical or different, together with their reasons, and similarly to compare the quality "slow" in Sets 3 and 4. The written accounts permit of certain conclusions, which are stated below.

(1)   *The content of the quality changes with a change in its environment.* The protocols below, which are typical, will show that the "quicks" of Sets 1 and 2 are phenomenally different, and similarly for the "slows" of Sets 3 and 4.

The quickness of 1 is one of assurance, of smoothness of movement; that of 2 is a forced quickness, in an effort to be helpful.

1 is fast in a smooth, easy-flowing way; the other (2) is quick in a bustling way – the kind that rushes up immediately at your request and tips over the lamps.

3 takes his time in a deliberate way; 4 would like to work quickly, but cannot – there is something painful in his slowness.

Table 5.13 Resemblance of qualities: Experiment X

"Quick" of Set 1 resembles

	N	Percentage
"Quick" of Set 2	11	22
"Helpful" of Set 2	1	2
"Slow" of Set 3	16	32
"Skillful" of Set 3	21	42
"Helpful" of Set 3	1	2
	50	100

"Quick" of Set 2 resembles

	N	Percentage
"Quick" of Set 1	10	24
"Slow" of Set 4	21	51
"Clumsy" of Set 4	7	17
"Slow" of Set 3	2	5
"Helpful" of Set 3	1	3
	41	100

"Helpful" of Set 1 resembles

	N	Percentage
"Helpful" of Set 2	7	15
"Helpful" of Set 4	2	4
"Helpful" of Set 3	33	68
"Skillful" of Set 3	6	13
	48	100

"Helpful" of Set 2 resembles

	N	Percentage
"Helpful" of Set 1	5	11
"Quick" of Set 1	2	4
"Slow" of Set 4	2	4
"Helpful" of Set 4	30	65
"Clumsy" of Set 4	4	9
"Slow" of Set 3	3	7
	46	100

3 is slow in a methodical, sure way, aiming toward perfection; in 4 it implies a certain heaviness, torpor.

(2) *The dynamic sources of the quality are relationally determined.* In the protocols we observe a process of mutual determination between traits. They are grasped as not simply contiguous to one another but in dynamic relation, in which one is determined by, or springs from, the other.

1 is quick because he is skillful; 2 is clumsy because he is so fast.

Great skill gave rise to the speed of 1, whereas 2 is clumsy because he does everything so quickly.

The quality slow is, in person 3, something deliberately cultivated, in order to attain a higher order of skill.

In 3 slowness indicates care, pride in work well-done. Slowness in 4 indicates sluggishness, poor motor coordination, some physical retardation.

Speed and skill are not connected as are speed and clumsiness. Without exception, "quick" is perceived to spring from skill (skillful → quick); but the vector in Set 2 is reversed, "clumsy" becoming a consequence of speed (clumsy ← quick). While Sets 1 and 3 are identical with regard to the vectors, Set 2 is not equivalent to 4, the slowness and clumsiness of 4 being sensed as part of a single process, such as sluggishness and general retardation (slow ⇌ clumsy).

(3) *Dynamic consequences are grasped in the interaction of qualities.* "Quick" and "skillful" (as well as "slow" and "skillful") are felt as cooperating, whereas "quick" and "clumsy" cancel one another.

2 drops everything fast. He is fast but accomplishes nothing. The clumsy man might be better off if he were slow.

The second person is futile; he is quick to come to your aid and also quick to get in your way and under your hair.

1 can afford to be quick; 2 would be far better off if he took things more slowly.[9]

In the light of these comments, which are representative, we are able to formulate the prevailing direction of the relations within the sets.

In Sets 1 and 3 the prevailing structure may be represented as:

"Quick–slow" derive their concrete character from the quality "skillful"; these in turn stand in a relation of harmony to "helpful," in the sense that they form a proper basis for it and make it possible.

In Sets 2 and 4 the characteristic structures are as follows:

But now these stand in a relation of inherent contradiction to the quality "helpful," the fulfillment of which they negate.

Our results contain a proportion of cases (see tables 5.12 and 5.13) that are contrary to the described general trend. These do equate the characteristic of 1 and 2 and of 3 and 4. They require explanation. It is especially important to decide whether the disagreements are capricious or whether they have an understandable basis. As a rule we find in these cases that the given quality is viewed in a narrower, more limited way. For example, these subjects view "quick" of Sets 1 and 2 in terms of sheer tempo, deliberately excluding for the moment considerations of fitness. The following protocols are illustrative:

> These persons' reactions to stimuli are both quick, even though the results of their actions are in opposite directions.

> They are both quick, but they differ in the success of their actions.

> The two terms are basically the same, for both would execute their tasks with their individual maximum speed.

II.   The reader will readily think of other sets of characteristics involving similar processes. In view of the fact that such analyses have not been previously reported, we select for brief description a few additional examples.

The task was to state whether the term "aggressive" was alike or different in Sets 1 and 2, and 3 and 4, respectively. This example will be of particular interest to psychologists, in view of current discussions of aggressiveness.

Set 1	*Set 2*	*Set 3*	*Set 4*
Active	Lazy	Weak	Strong
Helpful	Unhelpful	Sensitive	Self-centered
Aggressive	*Aggressive*	*Aggressive*	*Aggressive*

Nineteen out of 20 subjects judge the term to be different in Sets 1 and 2; 17 out of 20 judge it to be different in Sets 3 and 4. Some representative reports follow:

The aggressiveness of 1 is friendly, open, and forceful; 2 will be aggressive when something offends him.

The aggressiveness of 1 is an expression of confidence in his abilities, of his strength of will and mind; in 2 it is a defensive measure to cover sensitivity.

3 will be aggressive to try to hide his weakness. The aggressiveness of 4 is a natural result of his strength and self-centeredness.

4 is aggressive because he has needs to be satisfied and wishes nothing to stand in his way; 3 has the aggressiveness of self-pity and indecision.

In nearly all cases the sources of aggression and its objects are sensed to be different. In consequence, the form it takes and its very psychological content become different in the series compared.

Substantially the same results are observed in another group in the comparison of "unaggressive" in Sets 1 and 2 below.

Set 1	*Set 2*
Active	Weak
Helpful	Sensitive
Unaggressive	*Unaggressive*

Twenty-eight out of 30 subjects call "unaggressive" different in the two series. Some of their reasons follow:

Unaggressive in 1 might mean that he does not push or force his way into things. In the second case it may mean meekness or fear of people.

1 does not care to be aggressive; 2 lacks the stamina for it.

2 does not fight back at the world nor try to rise above his weaknesses.

The word "aggressive" must have the same connotations in both cases; otherwise why not use different terms to express different things?

III.   The second and third terms in Sets 1 and 2 below were compared, respectively.

Set 1	*Set 2*
Intelligent	Impulsive
Critical	*Critical*
Stubborn	*Stubborn*

All subjects in a group of 31 judged the term "critical" to be different in the two sets; while 19 (or 61 per cent) judged "stubborn" as different. A few of the remarks follow:

Critical:
1 is critical because he is intelligent; 2 because he is impulsive.

The intelligent individual is critical in a constructive manner; the impulsive one probably hurls criticism unthinkingly.

The intelligent person may be critical in a completely impersonal way; 2 may be critical of people, their actions, their dress, etc.

Stubborn:
The stubbornness of an intelligent person is more likely to be based on reason and it can be affected by reasoning.

The intelligent person might be stubborn about important things, things that mean something to him, that he knows something about; whereas an impulsive person might be stubborn just to be contrary.

An intelligent person may be stubborn because he has a reason for it and thinks it's the best thing to do, while an impulsive person may be stubborn because at the moment he *feels* like it.

Some representative statements defending the identity of "stubborn" in the two series follow:

Stubbornness to me is the same in any language. Of course, an intelligent person may have a better reason for being stubborn than an impulsive one, but that does not necessarily change the degree of stubbornness.

Both refuse to admit to anything that does not coincide with their opinion.

In my opinion there is only one kind of stubbornness – an unswerving desire either to do or not to do a certain thing.

IV.   In the following series the second and third terms were to be compared:

Set 1	Set 2
Warm	Cold
Witty	Witty
Persuasive	Persuasive

Twenty-seven of 30 subjects judged "persuasive" as different; all judged "witty" to be different. A few of the comments follow:

Witty:
1 laughs with the audience; 2 is either laughing at or trying to make others laugh at some one. 2 is satirical, not humorous.

1 has a jolly and happy-go-lucky wit. 2 will use wit as one uses a bow and arrow – with precision. He will have a target which will not be missed.

The wit of the warm person touches the heart. The cold person's wit is touched with irony.

Persuasive:

1 is persuasive in trying to help others; 2 in trying to help himself.

2 may persuade through fear.

2 would be detached in his arguments; 1 would appeal more to the inner emotional being of others.

V.   The term "gay" was compared in the following series:

Set 2	*Set 2*
Gay	Gay
Intelligent	Stupid
Industrious	Lazy

Twenty-seven of 30 subjects call "gay" different. Some representative reasons follow:

They may both be equally gay, but the former is different. The stupid person can be gay over serious, sad matters, while the intelligent person is gay with reason.

The first person's gaiety comes from fullness of life; 2 is gay because he knows no better.

1 knows when to be gay and when not to be.

The gaiety of 1 is active and energetic; the gaiety of 2 is passive.

The intelligent person is gay in an intelligent way.

They are the same – gaiety has no relation to intelligence and industriousness.

The foregoing observations describe a process of relational determination of character-qualities. A given quality derives its full concrete content from its place within the system formed by the relations of the qualities. Some qualities are seen as a dynamic outgrowth of determining qualities. Qualities are seen to stand in a relation of harmony or contradiction to others within the system. These processes set requirements for the comparison of impressions. Identical qualities in different structures may cease to be identical: the vectors out of which they grow may alter, with the consequence that their very content undergoes radical change. In the extreme case, the same quality in two persons will have different, even opposed, meanings, while two opposed qualities will have the same function within their respective structures.

Discussion

I

The investigations here reported have their starting-point in one problem and converge on one basic conclusion. In different ways the observations have demonstrated that forming an impression is an organized process; that characteristics are perceived in their dynamic relations; that central qualities are discovered, leading to the distinction between them and peripheral qualities; that relations of harmony and contradiction are observed. To know a person is to have a grasp of a particular structure.

Before proceeding it may be helpful to note two preliminary points. First: For the sake of convenience of expression we speak in this discussion of forming an impression of a person, though our observations are restricted entirely to impressions based on descriptive materials. We do not intend to imply that observations of actual persons would not involve other processes which we have failed to find under the present conditions; we are certain that they would (see pp. 108–9ff). But we see no reason to doubt that the basic features we were able to observe are also present in the judgment of actual persons. Secondly: We have not dealt in this investigation with the role of individual differences, of which the most obvious would be the effect of the subject's own personal qualities on the nature of his impression. Though the issue of individual differences is unquestionably important, it seemed desirable to turn first to those processes which hold generally, despite individual differences. A proper study of individual differences can best be pursued when a minimum theoretical clarification has been reached.

Let us briefly reformulate the main points in the procedure of our subjects:

1   There is an attempt to form an impression of the *entire* person. The subject can see the person only as a unit;[10] he cannot form an impression of one-half or of one-quarter of the person. This is the case even when the factual basis is meager; the impression then strives to become complete, reaching out toward other compatible qualities. The subject seeks to reach the core of the person *through* the trait or traits.

2   As soon as two or more traits are understood to belong to one person, they cease to exist as isolated traits, and come into immediate dynamic interaction.[11] The subject perceives not this *and* that quality, but the two entering into a particular relation. There takes place a process of organization in the course of which the traits order themselves into a structure. It may be said that the traits lead an intensely social life, striving to join each other in a closely organized system. The representation in us of the character of another person possesses in a striking sense certain of the qualities of a system.

3   In the course of this process some characteristics are discovered to be central. The whole system of relations determines which will become central. These set the direction for the further view of the person and for the concretization of the dependent traits. As a rule the several traits do not have equal weight. And it is not until we have found the center that we experience the assurance of having come near to an understanding of the person.

4   The single trait possesses the property of a part in a whole. A change in a single trait may alter not that aspect alone, but many others – at times all. As soon as we isolate a trait we not only lose the distinctive organization of the person; the trait itself becomes abstract. The trait develops its full content and weight only when it finds its place within the whole impression.

5   Each trait is a trait of the entire person. It refers to a characteristic form of action or attitude which belongs to the person as a whole. In this sense we may speak of traits as possessing the properties of Ehrenfels-qualities. Traits are not to be considered as referring to different regions of the personality, on the analogy of geographical regions which border on another.

6   Each trait functions as a *representative* of the person. We do not experience anonymous traits the particular organization of which constitutes the identity of the person. Rather the entire person speaks through each of his qualities, though not with the same clearness.

7   In the process of mutual interaction the concrete character of each trait is developed in accordance with the dynamic requirements set for it by its environment. There is involved an understanding of necessary consequences following from certain given characteristics for others. The envy of a proud man is, for example, seen to have a different basis from the envy of a modest man.

8   On this basis consistencies and contradictions are discovered. Certain qualities are seen to cooperate; others to negate each other. But we are not content simply to note inconsistencies or to let them sit where they are. The contradiction is puzzling, and prompts us to look more deeply. Disturbing factors arouse a trend to maintain the unity of the impression, to search for the most sensible way in which the characteristics could exist together,[12] or to decide that we have not found the key to the person. We feel that proper understanding would eliminate, not the presence of inner tensions and inconsistencies, but of sheer contradiction. (It may be relevant to point out that the very sense of one trait being in contradiction to others would not arise if we were not oriented to the entire person. Without the assumption of a unitary person there would be just different traits.)

9   It follows that the content and functional value of a trait changes with the given context. This statement expresses for our problem a principle formulated in gestalt theory with regard to the identity of parts in different structures (8, 10). A trait central in one person may be seen as secondary in another. Or a quality which is now referred to the person may in another case be referred to outer conditions. (In the extreme case a quality may be neglected, because it does not touch what is important in the person.)

We conclude that the formation and change of impressions consist of specific processes of organization. Further, it seems probable that these processes are not specific to impressions of persons alone. It is a task for future investigation to determine whether processes of this order are at work in other important regions of psychology, such as in forming the view of a group, or of the relations between one person and another.

II

It may be of interest to relate the assumptions underlying the naive procedure of our subjects to certain customary formulations. (1) It should now be clear that the subjects express certain definite assumptions concerning the structure of a personality. The gaining of an impression is for them not a process of fixing each trait in isolation and noting its meaning. If they proceeded in this way the traits would remain abstract, lacking just the content and function which makes them living traits. In effect our subjects are in glaring disagreement with the elementaristic thesis which assumes independent traits (or traits connected only in a statistical sense) of constant content. (2) At the same time the procedure of our subjects departs from another customary formulation. It is equally far from the observed facts to describe the process as the forming of a homogeneous, undifferentiated "general impression." The unity perceived by the observer contains groupings the parts of which are in more intimate connection with each other than they are with parts of other groupings.[13] Discrimination of different aspects of the person and distinctions of a functional order are essential parts of the process. We may even distinguish different degrees of unity in persons. Increasing clearness in understanding another depends on the increased articulation of these distinctions. But in the process these continue to have the properties of parts in a single structure.

If we may for the purpose of discussion assume that the naive procedure is based on a sound conception of the structure of personality, it would by no means follow that it is therefore free from misconceptions and distortions. But in that case the nature of errors in judgment would have to be understood in a particular way. It would be necessary to derive the errors from characteristics of the organizational processes in judgment. The present investigation is not without some hints for this problem. It points to the danger of forcing the subject to judge artificially isolated traits – a procedure almost universally followed in rating studies – and to the necessity of providing optimal conditions for judging the place and weight of a characteristic within the person (unless of course the judgment of isolated traits is required by the particular problem). Under such conditions we might discover an improvement in the quality of judgment and in agreement between judges. At the same time this investigation contains some suggestions for the study of errors in factors such as oversimplification leading to "too good" an impression, viewing a trait outside its context or in an inappropriate context.

III

Returning to the main theoretical conceptions described earlier (see pp. 73–75) it is necessary to mention a variant of Proposition I, which we have failed so far to consider and in relation to which we will be able to state more precisely a central feature of Proposition II. It would be a possible hypothesis that in the course of forming an impression each trait interacts with one or more of the others, and that the total impression is the summation of these effects. The impression would accordingly be derived from the separate interaction of the components, which might be represented as follows:

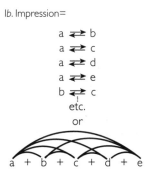

I*b*. Impression=

$$a \rightleftarrows b$$
$$a \rightleftarrows c$$
$$a \rightleftarrows d$$
$$a \rightleftarrows e$$
$$b \rightleftarrows c$$
etc.

or

It is important to note that this formulation is in a fundamental regard different from Proposition II. The latter proposition asserts that each trait is seen to stand in a particular relation to the others as part of a complete view. The entire view possesses the formal properties of a structure, the form of which cannot be derived from the summation of the individual relations.[14] In the same manner that the content of each of a pair of traits can be determined fully only by reference to their mutual relation, so the content of each relation can be determined fully only with reference to the structure of relations of which it is a part. This we may illustrate with the example of a geometrical figure such as a pyramid, each part of which (e.g., the vertex) implicitly refers to the entire figure. We would propose that this is the basis for the discovery of central and peripheral traits and for assertions such as that a given person is "integrated," restricted, etc.

On the other hand, the notion of structure is denied in all propositions of the form I, including I*b*. In the latter, an assumption is made concerning the interaction of qualities, which has the effect of altering the character of the *elements*. Once we have taken account of this change, we have in the final formulation again a sum of (now changed) elements:

$$\text{I}b. \quad \text{Impression} = \bar{a} + \bar{b} + \bar{c} + \bar{d} + \bar{e}$$

In still another regard there is a difference between Propositions II and I*b*. This has to do with the nature of the interaction between the traits. In terms of Proposition II the character of interaction is determined by the particular qualities that enter into the relation (e.g., "warm–witty" or "cold–witty"). It is doubtful however whether a theory which refuses to admit relational processes in the formation of a whole impression would admit the same relational processes in the interaction of one trait with another.

In view of the fact that Proposition I*b* has not, as far as we know, been explicitly formulated with reference to the present problem, it becomes necessary to do so here, and especially to state the process of interaction in such a manner as to be consistent with it. This we might do best by applying certain current conceptions. We could speak of traits as "conditioned verbal reactions," each of which possesses a particular "strength" and range of generalization. Interaction between traits would accordingly be assimilated to the schema of differential conditioning to single stimuli and to stimuli in combination, perhaps after the manner of the recent treatment of "stimulus configurations" by Hull (4, 5).[15]

How consistent would this interpretation be with the observations we have reported? It seems to us that there are grave difficulties in the way of such an interpretation. In so far as the terms of conditioning are at all intelligible with reference to our problem, the process of interaction can be understood only as a quantitative increase or diminution in a response. This is not, however, the essential characteristic of interaction as we have observed it, which consists in a change of content and function. The gaiety of an intelligent man is not more or less than the gaiety of a stupid man; it is different in quality. Further, the conditioning account seems to contain no principle that would make clear the particular direction interaction takes.

Here we may mention a more general point. We have referred earlier to the comparative ease with which complex situations in another person are perceived. If traits were perceived separately, we would expect to encounter the same difficulties in forming a view of a person that we meet in learning a list of unrelated words. That we are able to encompass the entire person in one sweep seems to be due to the structured character of the impression.[16] In terms of an interaction theory of component elements, the difficulty in surveying a person should be even greater than in the formulation of Proposition I, since the former must deal with the elements of the latter plus a large number of added factors.

IV

In order to retain a necessary distinction between the process of forming an impression and the actual organization of traits in a person, we have spoken as if nothing were known of the latter. While we cannot deal with the latter problem, one investigation is of particular relevance to the present discussion. We refer to the famous investigation of Hartshorne and May (3), who studied in a variety of situations the tendencies in groups of children to act honestly in such widely varied matters as copying, returning of money, correcting one's school work, etc. The relations between the actions of children in the different situations were studied by means of statistical correlations. These were generally low. On the basis of these results the important conclusion was drawn that qualities such as honesty are not consistent characteristics of the child but specific habits acquired in particular situations, that "neither deceit, nor its opposite, honesty, are unified character traits, but rather specific functions of life situations." Having accepted this conclusion, equally fundamental consequences were drawn for character education of children.

Abstracting from the many things that might be said about this work, we point out only that its conclusion is not proven because of the failure to consider the structural character of personality traits. As G.W. Allport (1, pp. 250ff) has pointed out, we may not assume that a particular act, say the clandestine change by a pupil of an answer on a school test, has the same psychological meaning in all cases.[17] Once this point is realized, its consequences for the thesis of Hartshorne and May become quite threatening. Let us consider a few of the possibilities in the situation, which would be classified as follows by Hartshorne and May:

Honest
1   The child wants to alter his answer on a test but fears he will be caught.
2   He does not change because he is indifferent to the grade.

Dishonest
1   The child changes his answer because he is devoted to his teacher and anxious not to lose her regard.
2   He cannot restrain the impulse to change the wrong answer into the answer he now knows to be correct.

Psychologically, none of these acts are correctly classified. Further, two of these are classified in precisely the wrong way. The child who wishes to cheat but is afraid does not belong in the honest category, while the child who cannot bear to leave the wrong answer uncorrected does not necessarily deserve to be called dishonest. We do not intend to say that the psychological significance of the reactions was as a rule misinterpreted; for the sake of illustration we have chosen admittedly extreme examples. But the failure to consider the psychological content introduces a serious doubt concerning the conclusions reached by Hartshorne and May.

V

A far richer field for the observation of the processes here considered would be the impressions formed of actual people. Concrete experience with persons possesses a substantial quality and produces a host of effects which have no room for growth in the ephemeral impressions of this investigation. The fact that we are ourselves changed by living people, that we observe them in movement and growth, introduces factors and forces of a new order. In comparison with these, momentary impressions based on descriptions, or even the full view of the person at a given moment, are only partial aspects of a broader process.

In such investigation some of the problems we have considered would reappear and might gain a larger application. Other problems, which were of necessity excluded from the present investigation, could be clarified in such an approach. We mention one which is of particular importance. It was a constant feature of our procedure to provide the subject with the traits of a person; but in actual observation the discovery of the traits in a person is a vital part of the process of establishing an impression. Since observation gives us only concrete acts and qualities, the application of a trait to a person becomes itself a problem. Is characterization by a trait, for example, a statistical generalization from a number of instances? Or is it the consequence of discovering a quality within the setting of the entire impression, which may therefore be reached in a single instance? In the latter case, repeated observation would provide not simply additional instances for a statistical conclusion, but rather a check on the genuineness of the earlier observation, as well as a clarification of its limiting conditions. Proceeding in this manner, it should be possible to decide whether the discovery of a trait itself involves processes of a structural nature. Only direct investigation based on the observation of persons can furnish answers to these questions.

In still another regard did our investigation limit the range of observation. In the views formed of living persons past experience plays a great role. The impression itself has a history and continuity as it extends over considerable periods of time, while factors of motivation become important in determining its stability and resistance to change.

Even within the limits of the present study factors of past experience were highly important. When the subject formed a view on the basis of the given description, he as a rule referred to a contemporary, at no time to characters that may have lived in the past; he located the person in this country, never in other countries. Further, experiments we have not here reported showed unmistakably that an identical series of traits produced distinct impressions depending on whether we identified the person as a man or woman, as a child or adult. Distinctions of this order clearly depend on a definite kind of knowledge obtained in the past. Indeed, the very possibility of grasping the meaning of a trait presupposes that it had been observed and understood.

That experience enters in these instances as a necessary factor seems clear, but the statement would be misleading if we did not add that the possibility of such experience itself presupposes a capacity to observe and realize the qualities and dynamic relations here described. The assertion that the properties of the impression depend on past experience can only mean that these were once directly perceived. In this connection we may refer to certain observations of Köhler (6, pp. 234ff) concerning our understanding of feelings in others which we have not observed in ourselves, or in the absence of relevant previous experiences. In his comprehensive discussion of the question, G.W. Allport (1, pp. 533ff) has equally stressed the importance of direct perception of a given structure in others, of our capacity for perceiving in others dynamic tendencies.

Nor do we consider it adequate to assert that in the present investigation our subjects were merely reproducing past observations of qualities and of the ways in which they modify each other. When the subject selected a certain trait as central (or when he deposed a once central trait to a minor role within a new context) it is by no means clear that he was guided by specific, acquired rules prescribing which traits will be central in each of a great number of constellations. It seems more in accordance with the evidence to suppose that the system of the traits itself points to a necessary center. And as we have mentioned earlier, the interaction between two traits already presupposes that we have discovered — whether in the past or in the present — the forces that work between them. Given the quality "quick" we cannot unequivocally infer the quality "skillful";[18] but given "quick–skillful" we try to see how one grows out of the other. We then discover a certain constancy in the relation between them, which is not that of a constant habitual connection.

While an appeal to past experience cannot supplant the direct grasping of qualities and processes, the role of past experience is undoubtedly great where impressions of actual people extending over a long period are concerned. Here the important question for theory is whether the factors of past experience involve dynamic processes of the same order that we find at work in the momentary impression, or whether these are predominantly of the nature of associative bonds. It seems to us a useful hypothesis that when we relate a person's past to his present we are again relying essentially on the comprehension of dynamic processes.

NOTES

The present investigation was begun in 1943 when the writer was a Fellow of the John Simon Guggenheim Memorial Foundation.

1   The writer wishes to express his gratitude to the following colleagues for their help in the performance of these experiments in their classes: Drs. B.F. Riess, L. Welch, V.J. McGill, and A. Goldenson of Hunter College; Drs. M. Blum and A. Mintz of the College of the City of New York; Dr. Lois Adams, Mr. Michael Newman, and Mr. Herbert Newman of Brooklyn College.

2   This by no means excludes the possibility that the nuances of strength, honesty, etc., do change in relation to "warm–cold."

3   In an earlier investigation the writer (2) has dealt with basically the same question though in a very different context. It was there shown that certain phenomena of judgment, which appeared to be due to changes of evaluation, were produced by a shift in the frame of reference.

4   For an instance in which the given conditions may destroy the established direction, see p. 89.

5   In accordance with this interpretation the effect of primacy should be abolished — or reversed — if it does not stand in a fitting relation to the succeeding qualities, or if a certain quality stands out as central despite its position. The latter was clearly the case for the quality "warm–cold" in Experiment I (see table 5.1) which, though occupying a middle position, ranked comparatively high.

The distinction between the two senses of primacy could be studied experimentally by comparing the recall of an identical series of character-qualities in two groups, one of which reads them as a discrete list of terms, the other as a set of characteristics describing a person.

6   The procedure of "successive impressions" here employed might be extended to the study of the effect of early upon later impressions. For example, the impression resulting from the sequence (A) + (B) might be compared with the reverse sequence (B) + (A), and each of these with the sequence (A + B) or (B + A).

7   On the basis of the last findings an objection might be advanced against our earlier account of the distinction between central and peripheral traits. If, as has just been shown, "warm" refers to such a wide range of qualities, then the force of the demonstration (see Experiment I) that it exerts a great effect on the final impression seems to be endangered. Is it to be wondered at that this quality, which

is single only in a linguistic sense, but psychologically plural, should be so effective? And should not be distinction be drawn rather between qualities which contain many other qualities and qualities – such as "politeness" – that are much more specific in range?

The objection presupposes that a quantitatively larger number of qualities will exert a greater effect than a smaller number. But this assumption is precisely what needs to be explained. Why does not the more inclusive term provide a greater number of occasions for being affected by other terms? What the assertion fails to face is that there is a particular direction of forces.

[8] In a forthcoming publication the writer will deal with theoretically similar issues in the context of a problem in social psychology. This will be the report of an investigation of changes in the content of identical social assertions when they function as part of different frames of reference.

[9] Parallel experiments in which the last term of the sets was changed to "not helpful" gave results essentially identical with above.

[10] To be sure, we do often react to people in a more narrow manner, as when we have dealings with the ticket-collector or bank teller. It cannot, however, be said that in such instances we are primarily oriented to the other as a person. The moment our special attitude would give way to a genuine interest in the other, the point stated above would fully apply.

[11] We cannot say on the basis of our observations whether exceptions to this statement occur, e.g., whether some traits may be seen as accidental, having no relation to the rest of the person. It seems more likely that even insignificant traits are seen as part of the person.

[12] Indeed, the perception of such contradiction, or of the failure of a trait to fit to the others, may be of fundamental importance for gaining a proper view. It may point to a critical region in the person, in which things are not as they should be.

[13] If we may assume that the situation in the observed person corresponds to this view, an important conclusion follows for method, namely, that we can study characteristics of persons without an exhaustive knowledge of the entire person.

[14] For a basic treatment of the concept of structure the reader is referred to M. Wertheimer (10).

[15] Proceeding in the same manner, it would be possible to restate some of our observations in terms such as the following: (1) the distinction between central and peripheral traits would be referred to a difference between conditioned reactions of greater and lesser strengths; (2) the change from a central to a peripheral trait could be explained by the displacement of a response by other, stronger responses; (3) the factor of direction might be dealt with in terms of changes in the temporal appearance of stimuli; (4) strongly unified impressions could be an expression of highly generalized reactions; etc. Such formulations would, however, fail to deal adequately with the central feature of our findings, namely, changes in the quality of traits and the organized form of the impression.

[16] It should not, however, be concluded that our views of persons are crystal clear. In fact, they lack the precision with which we grasp a mathematical theorem. We rarely feel that we have exhausted our understanding of another person. This has partly to do with the fact that the person is in constant change.

[17] See also discussion by D.W. MacKinnon (7, pp. 26ff).

[18] That it is at times difficult to infer qualities on the basis of central traits is due to such factors as the lability of the person, the degree to which the actions of a person are directed by a single center, as well as situational forces.

REFERENCES

1   Allport, G.W. *Personality: a psychological interpretation*. New York: Holt, 1937.

2   Asch, S.E. Studies in the principles of judgments and attitudes: II. Determination of judgments by group and by ego standards. *J. soc. Psychol.*, 1940, 12, 433–65.

3   Hartshorne, H., and May, M.A. Vol. I, *Studies in deceit*, 1928; Vol. II, *Studies in service and self-control*, 1939; Vol. III (with F.K. Shuttleworth), *Studies in the organization of character*, 1930.

4   Hull, C.L. *Principles of behavior*. New York: Appleton-Century, 1943.

5   Hull, C.L. The discrimination of stimulus configurations and the hypothesis of afferent neural interaction. *Psychol. Rev.*, 1945, 52, 133–42.

6   Köhler, W. *Gestalt psychology*. New York: Liveright, 1929.

7   MacKinnon, D.W. The structure of personality. In Hunt, J. McV. (ed.), *Personality and the behavior disorders*, Vol. I. New York: Ronald Press, 1944.

8   Ternus, J. Experimentelle Untersuchungen über phänomenale Identität. *Psych. Forsch.*, 1926, 7, 81–136.

9   Thorndike, E.L. A constant error in psychological rating. *J. appl. Psychol.*, 1920, 4, 25–9.

10 Wertheimer, M. *Productive thinking*. New York: Harper, 1946.

A hypothesis-confirming bias in labeling effects

J.M. Darley and P.H. Gross

- - - - -
Editors'
Introduction
- - - - - - - -

Theoretical Background

Social scientists have long been interested in what Merton (1948) first described as the 'self-fulfilling prophecy': perceivers, who hold a particular belief about another person, then behave towards that person in such a way that their initial expectancy is confirmed or 'fulfilled'. Research on this topic has a number of important applications outside the laboratory (e.g. teacher–pupil expectations and interactions in the classroom) and continues to be actively researched (see Jussim, 1986, for a review).

Clearly, social interaction can form the basis for self-fulfilling prophecies, including the maintenance of negative stereotypes of members of other groups. Darley and Gross did not deny the importance of this effect (which they termed a 'behavioral confirmation effect'), but asked whether a similar confirmation effect might occur in the absence of any interaction (a 'cognitive confirmation effect'). According to this view, without ever interacting with another person we could perceive that our expectations about him or her were confirmed, simply by interpreting his or her behaviour selectively, explaining it in a particular way, or selectively remembering (or forgetting) some details. Generally, though, behavioural and cognitive confirmation will tend to work in tandem to produce self-fulfilling prophecies.

This study looks at whether such cognitive confirmation effects exist and how they might be cognitively mediated. Darley and Gross propose that there are two stages in the expectancy-confirmation process. In the first stage, when perceivers are unsure whether their expectancy provides a valid basis for decisions about an individual, they should – and quite often do – proceed cautiously, scientifically, treating their expectancies 'as hypotheses' to be tested, not 'as

Journal of Personality and Social Psychology (1983), 44:20–33.

truths' to be accepted. If questioned at this stage, before they have observed any behaviour on the part of the other person, perceivers have no behavioural evidence to confirm their view and should respond accordingly. In the second stage, perceivers *are* given the opportunity to observe the behaviour of another person who has been labelled in some significant way. Now they can test their hypotheses against the behavioural evidence. While this hypothesis testing could, and should, be objective, if perceivers merely seek to confirm their initial view then they will somehow find supporting evidence, even when it does not actually exist. The authors see this 'opportunity to observe' as critical for the expectancy-confirmation process, because it both provides observers with what they think is valid evidence and allows them to feel, or claim, that they have made an 'unbiased' judgement (see Leyens et al., 1992, for a further development of this reasoning). The goal of this study was to test this two-process model by comparing judgements made by groups of subjects who had merely been given different expectancies about another person (by means of a label), and other subjects who first formed the expectancy and then observed the other person's performance.

Hypotheses

Two hypotheses are tested, the first of which entails two predictions:

1(a)　Perceivers given only an expectancy would be reluctant to evaluate the other person's ability on this basis.

1(b)　Perceivers given an expectancy and the opportunity to observe the other person's performance would make expectancy-confirming evaluations.

2　　The expectancy-plus-observation perceivers would report 'evidence' from identical observations of performance consistent with their expectancy.

Design

The experimental design was a two-factor, between-subjects design: 2 (expectancy: positive/negative) × 2 (performance: performance/no performance). Thus there were four experimental conditions, and two levels of each independent variable. There was also a performance-only (no expectancy) control condition. Thus there were five conditions in all, and subjects were randomly assigned to each condition, with the qualification that roughly equal numbers of males and females should occur in each condition.

Method

Subjects viewed a videotape of a fourth-grade (9-year-old) female child called 'Hannah' and read a short 'fact sheet' about her. For the experimental subjects, the videotape background was manipulated to create either a positive (higher socioeconomic status – SES) or negative (lower SES) expectancy, which was supported by the information in the fact sheet. Half of the subjects assigned each expectancy were then shown a second video of Hannah completing an achievement test; and the remaining subjects were not shown a second video. Control-subjects viewed only the second video, with no prior expectancy about Hannah's performance. The second video was carefully made to be rather uninformative about Hannah's abilities. All subjects then rated Hannah's achievement and academic skills, various checks on the experimental manipulations, and their suspicions about the study.

Results

Ability-level ratings

A 2×2 analysis of variance (ANOVA) was computed to compare subjects' ratings of Hannah's ability in each of three academic areas. The liberal arts, reading and mathematics ability levels were indices based on three, four and two items respectively. Strictly speaking, before combining each set of items into an index some check on their internal consistency should have been computed. For each separate index the interaction of expectancy × performance was reliable. Further tests showed that, consistent with hypothesis 1(a), there was little difference in the ability ratings as a function of expectancy for the no-performance subjects (i.e. those who saw only the first video), although there was a small effect in the case of the liberal arts index. Consistent with hypothesis 1(b), for subjects who did view the second video, every index showed a strong effect of expectancy, with higher ability ratings made by subjects with a positive expectancy. As the authors note, the 'fan-shaped' interaction shown in figure 5.1 is consistent with hypothesis 1, and the two-stage model of the confirmation process.

Manipulation checks

It was important to check that all subjects (and not just those who saw the second video) reported Hannah's SES to be consistent with their assigned expectancy; this was the case for all subjects. There were apparently no differences across conditions in ratings of Hannah's attractiveness, or the usefulness of SES information for predicting ability (but no analyses are reported). For control subjects, who viewed the second video without an expectancy, Hannah's performance was, as intended, seen as ambiguous (had it been too obviously good or bad, there would have been little room for bias to operate; see table 5.14).

Judgements of the performance

Three additional analyses of variance were computed only for those subjects who viewed the second, performance video, and these compared perceptions of the performance by subjects with positive versus negative expectancies *who viewed exactly the same videotape*. Subjects who held a positive expectancy of Hannah rated the test as more difficult (i.e. they indirectly rated her as more able). They also showed a non-significant tendency to estimate that she answered more problems correctly (interestingly, they did not claim this for the difficult problems, thus showing a constrained kind of bias). When asked to report in their own words which performance information was most relevant for judging Hannah's ability, subjects who held a positive expectancy reported a greater number of positive relative to negative behaviours. Overall these results confirm hypothesis 2.

Supplementary academic measures

The authors predicted that subjects shown only the first video would more often tick the box marked 'insufficient information' to make a judgement. This was indeed the case. Further analyses are consistent with the claim that subjects who viewed the second video felt that Hannah's test performance was a reasonable basis on which to make their judgements. Finally, ratings on twenty 'traits or skills' were analysed by grouping the twenty items into five trait dimensions (work habits, motivation, sociability, maturity and cognitive skills) and analysing each dimension separately. Only one dimension, work habits, showed the predicted expectancy × performance interaction. The most prominent effect here, shown on all four remaining measures, is a main effect of expectancy: subjects who held a positive expectancy rated Hannah more highly on each measure than subjects who held a negative expectancy, *whether they watched the second video or not*. As the authors acknowledge, these data argue against their two-stage model, at least for some kinds of judgement, although it is probably true that most of the time stereotypes consist of some one-stage and some two-stage inferences.

Discussion

The results provide broad support for both hypotheses and present a more detailed picture of the expectancy-confirmation process than we had previously had. It is striking that rather implicit expectancies (e.g. background cues in a videotape) had such strong effects, but one should note that the expectancies were more explicit in the 'fact sheet' given to each subject after watching the first video. None the less, the results are all the more impressive in view of the author's reporting that 'each participant was further admonished to be *as accurate and objective as possible* when evaluating their selected pupil' (italics added; see 'Instructions' section, below).

The research provides support for the two-stage process of expectancy confirmation (but only for ability judgements), which shows that at least some of the time perceivers might be more reluctant to apply their stereotypes than we fear. However, the facility with which they do apply these stereotypes to observed behaviour, and the biased manner in which they test their stereotypes, gives little cause for satisfaction (see also the reading by Snyder and Uranowitz, chapter 6). It is not clear from this research what cognitive mediators do underlie expectancy effects, but the results for selective recall and selective weighting of evidence are suggestive (see Jussim, 1991, for a recent attempt to further unpick expectancy effects; and Snyder and Cantor, 1979, for evidence of how we test hypotheses about other people).

FURTHER READING

Jussim, L. (1986). Self-fulfilling prophecies: A theoretical and integrative review. *Psychological Review*, 93, 429–45. A very detailed review of the occurrence of self-fulfilling prophecies, with special attention paid to educational settings.

Snyder, M. and Cantor, N. (1979). Testing hypotheses about other people: The use of historical knowledge. *Journal of Experimental Social Psychology*, 15, 330–42. This study reveals some of the subtle processes that come into play when people test their hypotheses about others; for instance, the means of testing tends to lead to false confirmation of the hypothesis.

REFERENCES

Jussim, L. (1991). Social perception and social reality: A reflection-construction model. *Psychological Review*, 98, 54–73.

Leyens, J.-P., Yzerbyt, V.Y. and Schadron, G. (1992). The social judgeability approach to stereotypes. In W. Stroebe and M. Hewstone (Eds.), *European review of social psychology* (3, 91–120). Chichester: J. Wiley.

Primary Reading

The expectancy-confirmation process is an important link in the chain leading from social perception to social action (Darley and Fazio, 1980; Rosenthal and Jacobson, 1968 ; Snyder and Swann, 1978a). As research has demonstrated, two processes leading to the confirmation of a perceiver's beliefs about another can be identified. The first, called a "behavioral confirmation effect" (Snyder and Swann, 1978b), is consistent with Merton's (1948) description of the "self-fulfilling prophecy." In this process, perceivers' behaviors toward the individual for whom they hold an expectancy channel the course of the interaction such that expectancy-confirming behaviors are elicited from the other individual (Rosenthal, 1974; Snyder, Tanke, and Berscheid, 1977). The second process leads to what we may call a "cognitive confirmation effect." We use this term to refer to expectancy-confirmation effects that occur in the absence of any interaction between the perceiver and the target person. In these cases, perceivers simply selectively interpret, attribute, or recall aspects of the target person's actions in ways that are consistent with their expectations (Duncan, 1976; Kelley, 1950; Langer and Abelson, 1974). Thus, perceivers with different expectancies about another may witness an identical action sequence and still emerge with their divergent expectancies "confirmed."

The focus of the present article is on the mediation of cognitive confirmation effects. We suggest that there are at least two different processes that bring about the cognitive confirmation of expectancies. The key to separating these processes lies in recognizing that people distinguish between the kinds of information that create conceptions of other people. Perceivers may define a continuum, one end of which involves information that is seen as a valid and sufficient basis for judgements about another; at the other end is evidence that is seen as a weak or invalid basis for those judgements.

As an example of valid information, consider a teacher who receives the results of a standardized test indicating that a particular pupil has high ability. The expectancies this information creates about the child are assumed to reflect the child's actual capabilities and are probably quite automatically applied. At the other end of the continuum, and of primary interest to this article, is expectancy-creating information that most perceivers would regard as incomplete with respect to an individual's abilities or dispositions. Many of our social stereo-types fall into this category. For example, racial or social-class categories are regarded by most of us as an insufficient evidential basis for conclusive judgements of another's dispositions or capabilities. In this case, we suspect that perceivers are highly resistant to automatically applying their expectancies to a target person. A teacher, for example, would be extremely hesitant to conclude that a black child had low ability unless that child supplied direct behavioral evidence validating the application of the label.

The end of the continuum defining information that is seen as insufficient evidence for social judgements is of interest because we find what appears to be a paradox in the literature dealing with social stereotypes. Some recent investigations of the influence of stereotypes on social judgements have demonstrated a "fading" of stereotypic attributions (e.g. Karlins, Coffman, and Walters, 1969; Locksley, Borgida, Brekke, and Hepburn, 1980). For example, investigators have noted participants' increasing unwillingness to make stereotypic trait ascriptions (Brigham, 1971). Moreover, Quattrone and Jones (1980) demonstrate that although people may make stereotype-based judgements about a social group, they are unwilling to use category-based information to predict the behavior of any one member of that group.

Given this resistance to the utilization of expectancies when the social labels establishing them are not seen as valid guides for judgements, one might expect an elimination of the expectancy-confirmation bias. That is, perceivers would not unjustly assume the truth of a stereotype; they would instead require that evidence substantiating the accuracy of that stereotype be provided. This leads to the prediction that, ultimately, judgements about the target person will reflect the actual evidence produced by his or her behavior, unbiased by the perceivers' initial expectancies. Unfortunately, this conclusion stands in contradiction to the bulk of the self-fulfilling prophecy literature in which one finds that confirmation effects are often produced when racial, ethnic, or other negative social labels are implicated – exactly those cases in which one expects perceivers to refrain from using category-based information (e.g. Foster, Schmidt, and Sabatino, 1976; Rist, 1970; Rosenhan, 1973; Word, Zanna, and Cooper, 1974). We suggest that this apparent contradiction can be resolved if the following two-stage expectancy-confirmation process is assumed: Initially, when perceivers have reason to suspect that the information that establishes an expectancy is not diagnostically valid for determining certain of the target person's dispositions or capabilities, they will refrain from using that information to come to diagnostic conclusions. The expectancies function not as truths about the target person but rather as hypotheses about the likely dispositions of that person. If perceivers were asked for judgements at this point in the process, without any behavioral evidence to confirm their predictions, they would not report evaluations based on their expectancies. They would instead report that either they did not have sufficient informa-tion or they would make judgements consistent with normative expectations about the general population.

The second stage occurs when perceivers are given the opportunity to observe the actions of the labeled other. They then can test their hypotheses against relevant behavioral evidence. The initiation of a hypothesis-testing process would seem to be an unbiased approach for deriving a valid basis for judgements about another. If, however, individuals test their hypothesis using a "confirming strategy" – as has often been demonstrated – a tendency to find evidence supporting the hypothesis being tested would be expected (Snyder and Cantor, 1979; Snyder and Swann, 1978b). A number of mechanisms operating in the service of a hypothesis-confirming strategy may contribute to this result. First, the search for evidence may involve selective attention to information that is consistent with expectations and a consequent tendency to recall expectancy-consistent information when making final evaluations (Zadny and Gerard, 1974). Second, a hypothesis-confirming strategy may affect how information attended to during a performance will be weighted. Typically, expectancy-consistent information has inferential impact, whereas inconsistent information has insufficient influence in social-decision tasks (Nisbett and Ross, 1980). In fact, a recent study by Lord, Ross, and Lepper (1979) indicates that even when expectancy-inconsistent information is brought to the attention of the perceiver, it may be regarded as flawed evidence and therefore given minimal weight in the evaluation process. Third, it is also possible for inconsistent actions to be attributed to situational factors and thereby be attributionally discounted (Regan, Strauss, and Fazio, 1974). Finally, apparently inconsistent behavior may be reinterpreted as a manifestation of dispositions that are consistent with the initial expectancy (Hayden and Mischel, 1976).

Given the operation of all of these biasing mechanisms, an expectancy-confirmation effect could arise even when the target person's behavior does not objectively confirm the perceiver's expectancies. Nonetheless, the opportunity to observe the diagnostically relevant information is critical to the process because it provides what perceivers consider to be valid evidence, and thus, they can feel that they have made an "unbiased" judgment.

In the present study, we attempted to find evidence of this two-stage expectancy-confirmation process. To do this, perceivers were given information that would induce them to categorize an elementary school child as belonging to a high- or low-socioeconomic-status (SES) class (cf. Cooper, Baron, and Lowe, 1975). Consistent with the two-stage model, we predicted that perceivers given only this demographic information about the child would be reluctant to provide label-consistent ability evaluations. Another group of evaluators were given the identical demographic information about the child (high or low SES) and were then shown a performance sequence that provided ability-relevant information about the child. Owing to the hypothesis-confirming bias, it was predicted that these individuals would find evidence in the identical performance sequence to support their opposing hypotheses and would thus report widely different judgements of the child's ability. Moreover, we expected these perceivers to mislocate the source of their evidence from their own expectancies to the "objective" evidence provided by the performance sequence.

Method

As part of a study on "teach evaluation methods," students viewed a videotape of a fourth-grade female child and were asked to evaluate her academic capabilities. Variation in the videotape determined the four experimental conditions. The first segment provided demographic information about the child and was used to establish either positive or negative expectations for the child's academic potential. Half of the participants viewed a sequence that depicted the child in an urban, low-income area (negative expectancy); the other half were shown the same child in a middle-class, suburban setting (positive expectancy).

Orthogonal to this manipulation was the performance variable. Half of the participants from each expectancy condition were shown a second tape segment in which the child responded to achievement-test problems (performance). The tape was constructed to be inconsistent and relatively uninformative about the child's abilities. The remaining participants were not shown this segment (no performance).

The design was thus a 2 × 2 factorial one, with two levels of expectancy (positive and negative) and two levels of performance (performance and no performance). In addition, a fifth group of participants viewed the performance tape but were not given prior information about the child's background (performance only). Their evaluations were used to determine if the performance tape was, as intended, an ambiguous display of the child's academic capabilities.

All viewers then completed an evaluation form on which they rated the child's overall achievement and academic skill level. Additional questions about the child's performance and manipulation checks were included. After completing their evaluation form, participants were given a questionnaire designed to probe their suspiciousness about the experiment. Finally, participants were debriefed, thanked, and paid.

Subjects

Seventy (30 male and 40 female) Princeton University undergraduates volunteered for a study on "teacher evaluation and referral" for which they were paid $2.50 for a 1-hour session. Participants were randomly assigned to one of five (four experimental and one control) conditions, with an attempt made to have an equal number of men and women in each condition. None of the students in the study reported having any formal teacher training; two students had informal teaching experience, both at the high school level. Only three of the original subjects were eliminated from the study because of suspiciousness about the experimental procedures.

Instructions

The experimenter introduced herself as a research assistant for a federal agency interested in testing new educational procedures. Students were told that their participation would be useful for determining the reliability of a new evaluation form teachers would use when referring pupils to special programs (these included remedial classes and programs for gifted students). To test the completeness and scorability of the evaluation form, subjects, acting as teachers, were asked to provide an academic evaluation of a selected child on this specially designed form. The experimenter emphasized that all evaluations would be anonymous and confidential and asked participants not to place their names anywhere on the form. She also requested that they replace the form in its envelope and seal it when they were finished. Each participant was further admonished to be as accurate and objective as possible when evaluating their selected pupil.

The research assistant then went on to explain that a videotape file of elementary school children had been prepared for a previous study (numerous videotape reels were on shelves in front of the subject). Participants would be selecting one child from this sample to observe and evaluate. It was made clear that this "randomly selected sample of children includes some who perform well above their grade level, some who would benefit from remedial programs, and some at all levels between these extremes." To select a child from this file, participants drew a number corresponding to a videotape reel. The experimenter, who had been blind to condition until this point, placed the tape on a television monitor and gave the participant a fact sheet appropriate to the child they selected.

The participant actually selected one of five prepared tapes (corresponding to the four experimental and one control conditions). In all conditions, the child observed was a nine-year-old female Caucasian named Hannah, who was a fourth grader attending a public elementary school. The information about the child's name, grade, and so forth appeared on the fact sheet and was reiterated in the narration of the tape.

Demographic expectancy manipulation

To establish either positive or negative expectancies about Hannah's ability, participants viewed a tape of Hannah that contained environmental cues indicating either a high or low socioeconomic background. Each tape included 4 minutes devoted to scenes of Hannah playing in a playground (filmed at a distance to prevent clear perception of her physical attractiveness) and 2 minutes devoted to scenes of her neighborhood and school. The tapes were filmed at two different locations.

In the negative-expectancy condition, subjects viewed Hannah playing in a stark fenced-in school yard. The scences from her neighborhood showed an urban setting of run-down two-family homes. The school she attended was depicted as a three-story brick structure set close to the street, with an adjacent asphalt school yard. The fact sheet given to participants included the following information about Hannah's parents: Both parents had only a high school education; her father was employed as a meat packer; her mother was a seamstress who worked at home.

In the positive-expectancy condition, Hannah was seen playing in a tree-lined park. The scenes from her neighborhood showed a suburban setting of five- and six-bedroom homes set on landscaped grounds. Her school was depicted as a sprawling modern structure, with adjacent playing fields and a shaded playground. Further, Hannah's fact sheet indicated that both her parents were college graduates. Her father's occupation was listed as an attorney, her mother's as a free-lance writer.

The performance manipulation

Two groups were asked to evaluate Hannah's academic ability immediately after viewing one or the other expectancy tape (no performance); two other groups were given the opportunity to observe Hannah in a test situation (performance).

Subjects in the performance conditions observed a second 12-minute tape sequence in which Hannah responded to 25 achievement-test problems. This portion of the tape was identical for both performance groups. The problems were modified versions of items selected from an achievement-test battery and included problems from the mathematics computation, mathematics concepts, reading, science, and social studies subtests. The grade level for the problems ranged from the second to the sixth grade. Participants were told that the test included "easy, moderate, and difficult problems." The problems were given orally to Hannah by a male tester who held up the possible solutions on cards. The sequence was filmed from behind the child so the viewer was able to see the cards held by the tester but not Hannah's face.

Hannah's performance was prearranged to present an inconsistent picture of her abilities. She answered both easy and difficult questions correctly as well as incorrectly. She appeared to be fairly verbal, motivated, and attentive on some portions of the tape and unresponsive and distracted on other portions of the tape. The tester provided little feedback about Hannah's performance. After each problem, he recorded Hannah's response and went on to the next problem.

To determine what information the tape provided about Hannah's ability in the absence of a priori expectancies, a group of participants, given the same cover story as subjects in the other conditions, were shown only the performance tape. These subjects were given no information about the child other than her name, age, grade, address, and the school she attended.

Dependent measures

After reviewing the tape, participants were given an evaluation form to complete. The form contained the following sections:

Ability measures

Nine curriculum areas forming three broad categories were listed. Included in this section were reading (reading comprehension, reading ability, writing, language ability), mathematics (mathematical concepts, mathematical computation), and liberal arts (science, general knowledge, social studies). Each curriculum area was followed by a scale extending from kindergarten to the sixth-grade, ninth-month grade level, with points labeled at 3-month intervals. Subjects were instructed to indicate the grade level that represented the child's ability in each of these areas. For subsequent analyses, mean ratings of items within these three categories were used, and grade levels were converted to a scale with months represented as fractions of a year (i.e., third grade, sixth month would equal 3.5).

Performance measures

Participants in the performance conditions were asked to estimate the number of easy, moderate, and difficult problems the child answered correctly and report the overall grade level of the test administered to the child. In an open-ended question, participants were asked to report the "information they found most useful in determining the child's capabilities."

Supplementary academic measures

Twenty traits or skills, followed by exemplars of classroom behaviors characterizing both the positive and negative ends of each of these traits, were listed. Subjects were asked to check the point on a 9-point scale that would best characterize the child on the dimension. Next to each scale, a box labeled "insufficient information" was also provided. Subjects were instructed to check this box rather than a scale value if they felt they had not been given sufficient information to rate the child on a given dimension.

These 20 items were selected to form five clusters: work habits (organization, task orientation, dependability, attention, thoroughness), motivation (involvement, motivation, achievement orientation), sociability (popularity, verbal behavior, cooperation), emotional maturity (confidence, maturity, mood, disposition), and cognitive skill (articulation, creativity, learning capability, logical reasoning). Mean ratings of items within these five categories were used in subsequent analysis.

Manipulation checks

In the last part of the booklet, subjects were asked to rate the child's "attractiveness" and the "usefulness of socioeconomic information as an indicator of a child's academic ability." The final open-ended question asked subjects to report the child's socioeconomic level.

Suspiciousness probe

Finally, participants filled out a questionnaire assessing, for the agency, "how they had been treated during the experimental session." This was designed to probe their suspiciousness about the experimental procedures and purpose of the study. Following this, participants were thoroughly debriefed and paid.

Results

Ability-level ratings

Our primary hypothesis was that expectancy-confirmation effects occur only when perceivers feel they have definitive evidence relevant to their expectations. Specifically, we predicted that subjects who viewed only the positive- or negative-expectancy tape segment (no performance) would show little, if any, signs of expectancy confirmation in their ratings of the child's ability level, whereas subjects who viewed both the expectancy segment and the test segment (performance) would show considerable signs of expectancy confirmation. As a test of this hypothesis, a 2 (positive vs. negative) × 2 (performance vs. no performance) analysis of variance (ANOVA) was performed on ability-level ratings.

As shown in figure 5.1, the results support our predictions. The ANOVA interaction term was significant for each index: liberal arts, $F(1, 56) = 6.67$, $p < .02$; reading $F(1, 56) = 5.73$, $p < .03$; and mathematics $F(1, 56) = 9.87$, $p < .01$. Although a main effect for expectancy emerged for each of the three indexes – liberal arts, $F(1, 56) = 19.24$, $p < .01$; reading, $F(1, 56) = 32.98$, $p < .001$; and mathematics, $F(1, 56) = 19.78$, $p < .001$ – Newman-Keuls tests revealed that the subjects in the no-performance conditions did not rate the child's ability level as differing much in either direction from her known school grade. On only one of the indexes (liberal arts) did the no-performance–positive-expectancy subjects rate the child significantly higher than the negative-expectancy subjects ($p < .05$). In the two performance conditions, however, positive-expectancy subjects made reliably higher ratings on all three indexes ($p < .05$ in all cases). The fanshaped interaction of figure 5.1 is consistent with the hypothesized two-stage confirmation process in which subjects first reserve judgment – if that judgment is based on only demographic indicators – but then allow their judgment about an ability to be biased in the direction of hypothesis confirmation.[1]

Manipulation checks

The manipulation checks indicate that the above results were not artifactually produced. First, the expectancy manipulation was as successful for subjects who viewed the child's test perform-

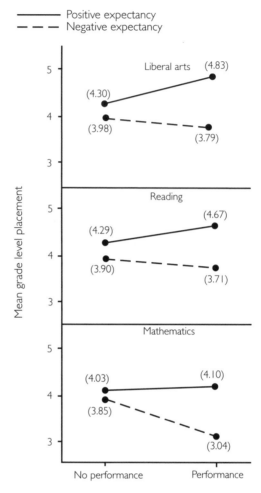

Figure 5.1   Mean grade-level placements on the liberal arts, reading, and mathematics indices for experimental conditions

ance as for those who did not. Without exception, positive-expectancy subjects reported the child's socioeconomic status as upper middle or upper class, and negative-expectancy subjects reported the child's socioeconomic status as lower middle or lower class. Second, analyses of ratings of the child's attractiveness and the usefulness of socioeconomic information for predicting ability yielded no differences across groups. The latter result is especially important in indicating that those who had seen the child's test performance did not regard the demographic information as any more diagnostic than those who had not seen it. Thus, the greater impact of induced expectancies in the performance conditions was not attributable to greater confidence in an implicit theory of the social-class–ability relation. Moreover, mean ratings of the usefulness of socioeconomic information (for all groups) were just below the midpoint toward the "not useful" end of the scale.

Finally, as can be seen in table 5.14, ability ratings of the performance-only group indicate that the performance segment was, as intended, an ambiguous display of Hannah's capabilities.

We hoped that evaluations of the child's ability would tend to be variable, reflecting the inconsistencies in the child's performance; however, mean estimates would be expected to fall close to the child's given grade level. As the data in table 5.14 indicate, ratings on the three curriculum indexes do show considerable variability, and the perceivers do use the child's grade level as an anchor for their judgments. The mathematics ratings were somewhat lower and less variable than the others, indicating that her performance in this area may have been poorer and more consistent.[2] (This will be discussed at a later point.)

Judgments of the performance

If performance subjects were no less aware of, or impressed by, the relevance of the expectancy information, it follows that they found support for their divergent hypotheses in the child's performance. Measures from the academic evaluation form indicate several ways in which perceivers obtained support for their diverse hypotheses. (All of these were measures of the subjects' perception of the performance and therefore were taken only from the groups that witnessed the test sequence. Recall that all of these subjects witnessed the identical performance tape.)

Test difficulty
Performance on a test is a joint function of the test taker's ability (and other personal factors) and the difficulty of the test. Therefore, one way of justifying a high-ability inference from an inconsistent test performance is to perceive the test as being very difficult. Conversely, one way of rationalizing a low-ability inference from the same performance would be to perceive the test as easy. This happened: Subjects in the positive-expectancy condition rated the test as significantly more difficult (M grade $= 4.8$) than did those in the negative-expectancy condition (M grade $= 3.9$), $t(2.8) = 2.69$, $p < .02$.

Problems correct
Subjects also estimated the number of problems the child answered correctly within each of the problem categories: very difficult, moderately difficult, and easy.

A repeated measures analysis of variance revealed a marginally reliable tendency for subjects with positive expectancies to estimate that the child correctly answered a higher percentage of

Table 5.14 Mean grade-level placements on curriculum areas by performance control group

Index	M	Grade level	SD
Liberal arts	4.0	3rd grade, 9th month	.505
Reading	3.8	4th grade	.581
Mathematics	3.5	3rd grade, 6th month	.238

$n = 10$.

problems, $F(1, 28) = 3.94$, $p < .06$. Follow-up analyses revealed that subjects with positive expectancies estimated that the child correctly answered more of the easy ($M = 94\%$ vs. 79%) and moderately difficult ($M = 69\%$ vs. 53%) problems than did subjects with negative expectancies, $t(28) = 2.55$ and 2.21, respectively, $ps < .05$. Expectancy did not affect estimates of answers to difficult problems ($M = 37\%$ vs. 36%). The overall pattern suggests a bias to report more instances of expectancy-consistent than expectancy-inconsistent test responses.

Reporting relevant behaviors

Subjects had been asked to report, in an open-ended format, the performance information "most relevant for determining the child's capabilities." We expected that subjects anticipating a good performance would report more instances of positive behaviors than those expecting a poor performance. For each subject, we computed a positivity index by subtracting the number of negative instances from the number of positive instances. Consistent with predictions, positive-expectancy subjects reported a significantly greater number of positive behaviors relative to negative ones as being relevant in their judgments than did negative-expectancy subjects, $t(28) = 34.65$, $p < .001$.

To summarize the performance judgments, positive- and negative-expectancy subjects, although agreeing that the performance provided information that was sufficient to estimate the child's capabilities, disagreed on how difficult the test was, how many problems the child answered correctly, and how many of her test behaviors reflected either positively or negatively on her achievement level. On every measure, positive-expectancy subjects made interpretations more favorable to the child than did negative-expectancy subjects.

Supplementary academic measures

Information sufficiency

Recall that subjects reporting on these measures were allowed to check a scale value or a box labeled insufficient information. We believed that the no-performance subjects who had only demographic-based expectancies to rely on would display a greater reluctance to evaluate the child and that this reluctance would lead to more frequent use of the insufficient information answer. A 2×2 analysis of variance on these data yielded only a main effect for performance, $F(1, 56) = 12.86$, $p < .001$, such that no-performance subjects chose this option more often ($M = 43\%$ of the items) than subjects who viewed the test sequence ($M = 22\%$ of the items). A one-way analysis of variance, comparing the no-performance, performance, and performance-only conditions yielded a reliable effect, $F(2, 67) = 12.41$, $p < .001$. Moreover, comparing these means (via Duncan's test), we find that the performance-witnessing groups were not significantly different from each other, whereas both were significantly different from the no-performance groups ($p < .01$). Thus, the difference found between performance and no-performance groups on the use of the insufficient information option did not seem to depend on the fact that the mere quantity of evidence provided to performance subjects was greater (two tape segments) than that given to no-performance subjects (one tape segment). The performance-only subjects, who also saw only one tape segment, did not differ from performance subjects on this measure. The difference is better attributed to the greater perceived diagnostic utility of the performance segment. Performance subjects apparently felt that the child's test performance provided sufficient diagnostic information on which to base their evaluations.

Table 5.15   Mean ratings on trait measures for experimental groups

Condition	Dependent measure				
	Work habits	Motivation	Sociability	Maturity	Cognitive skills
Positive, performance	5.21$_a$	5.16$_a$	5.25$_a$	5.33$_{a,b}$	4.73$_a$
Positive, no-performance	4.92$_{a,b}$	5.31$_a$	4.82$_{a,b}$	5.65$_b$	5.55$_b$
Negative, no-performance	5.13$_a$	4.80$_{a,b}$	4.38$_b$	4.67$_a$	4.83$_a$
Negative, performance	4.36$_b$	4.11$_b$	4.58$_{a,b}$	4.77$_{a,b}$	4.12$_a$

$n = 15$ per condition. The higher the number, the more positive the evaluation. Letter subscripts indicate vertical comparisons of cell means by Duncan's multiple-range test. Means that do not share a common subscript are significantly different from each other at the .05 level.

Trait measures

A 2 (expectancy) × 2 (performance) analysis of variance was performed on ratings for each of the five trait dimensions. Because participants were given the option of not checking a scale value on these measures, missing values were given a score of 5, which, on a 9-point scale, represents the neutral point.[3] These data are presented in table 5.15.

Consistent with our findings for the curriculum indexes, a significant interaction emerged for the work habits index such that individuals expecting the child to perform well rated her more positively after viewing the performance tape whereas those expecting her to perform poorly rated her more negatively after viewing the performance tape, $F(1, 56) = 5.15, p < .03$. The predicted interaction effect was not obtained for the motivation, sociability, emotional maturity, or cognitive skill measures. For each of these measures, we found a main effect for expectancy, with the positive-expectancy groups rating the child significantly higher than the negative-expectancy groups, $F(1, 56) = 6.99, 4.57, 5.76$, and 5.84, respectively, $ps < .05$. In addition, there was a significant effect for performance on the cognitive skill index, with the performance groups showing lower ratings than the no-performance groups, $F(1, 56) = 7.73$, $p < .05$. These data indicate that certain expectancy-consistent judgments may not require a two-stage process. Although it may be necessary to provide performance information to obtain judgments of a child's ability level, judgments about other dispositional characteristics may be made without this information.

Discussion

Unlike many previous studies demonstrating expectancy-confirmation effects, the expectancies in the present study were not created by information that most people would regard as definitively establishing their validity. They were not created by objective test results, expert judgments, or other authoritative information. Instead, the expectancies were conveyed by such cues as the child's clothes, the bleakness of the playground on which she played, or the high- or low-status character of her parents' occupations.

We suggested that perceivers would realize that expectancies created by this information do not form a completely valid basis for some of the evaluations they were asked to make. The results indicate that this is so: Perceivers who were given only demographic information about the child demonstrated a resistance to making expectancy-consistent attributions on the ability indexes. Their estimations of the child's ability level tended to cluster closely around the one concrete fact they had at their disposal: the child's grade in school. When given the opportunity to avoid making dispositional attributions altogether, nearly half of the time these perceivers chose that option.

In contrast, a marked expectancy-confirmation effect was evident for those perceivers who evaluated the child after witnessing an ability-relevant performance. Those who believed the child came from a high socioeconomic class reported that her performance indicated a high ability level, whereas those who believed the child came from a low socioeconomic class reported that the identical performance indicated a substantially lower level of ability.

This pattern of results suggests that when the diagnostic validity of a perceiver's expectations is suspect, expectancies function as hypotheses, and the task of evaluating an individual for whom one has an expectancy is a hypothesis-testing process. Expectancy confirmation, then, does not always result from an automatic inference process. Instead, it occurs as the end product of an active process in which perceivers examine the labeled individual's behavior for evidence relevant to their hypothesis.[4]

As is apparent from our data, the hypothesis-testing strategy that perceivers use has a bias (as Snyder and Cantor, 1979, have suggested) toward confirmation of the hypothesis being tested. The literature suggests a number of related mechanisms that can contribute to this effect (see Nisbett and Ross, 1980, for a review). We do have evidence to suggest what some of these mechanisms may have been in our study. First, there seems to be a selective recall of evidence: Perceivers who expected the child to do well reported the child as having answered more easy and more moderately difficult problems correctly than those expecting the child to do poorly. Second, there seems to be a selective weighting of the evidence such that hypothesis-consistent behaviors are regarded as more "typical" of the child's true capabilities. When people were asked to report what evidence they found most useful in determining their evaluations, they reported only those test items on which the child's performance was consistent with their initial expectations. Third, perceivers appeared to develop auxiliary hypotheses that would render apparently inconsistent behavior consistent with their hypotheses. These auxiliary hypotheses did not seem to be revised assessments of the actor but rather assessments of situational factors that could account for discrepancies in the actor's behavior. For instance, we found that persons who expected a good performance decided that the test given to the child was very difficult, a conclusion that would account for instances of otherwise inconsistent poor performance; whereas persons who expected a poor performance reported that the test was easy, which would account for inconsistent good performance. Finally, we found evidence in the open-ended reports of some participants to suggest that the meaning given to the child's behaviors was often consistent with the perceivers' initial hypotheses. For example, a low-SES Hannah was reported to have "difficulty accepting new information," whereas a high-SES Hannah was reported to have the "ability to apply what she knows to unfamiliar problems."

Implicit in these data is the conclusion that perceivers seem to be aware that witnessing a particular test performance does not give them automatic access to an individual's underlying ability. Many other factors, such as luck, task difficulty, or lack of motivation, may intervene

(Darley and Goethals, 1980; Weiner et al., 1971). Therefore, the meaning of a person's performance is susceptible to multiple interpretations that can be consistent with, and even supportive of, opposing hypotheses about that person's ability.

Thus far, we have treated information as creating expectancies that are either valid and automatically applied to others or weak and only hypothesis generating. It is more likely that any item of information about a person generates some certainties and some hypotheses, depending on the domain to which it is applied. In the present study, the demographic information seems to have this character of creating both certainties and hypotheses. On the supplemental measures related to school achievement – specifically, on measures of motivation, sociability, and emotional maturity – a simple main effect was obtained such that people who saw the child as coming from a high socioeconomic background judged her more positively, and those who did not see the performance had as extreme ratings as those who did. (But keep in mind that individuals had the opportunity not to rate the child on these measures and that, overall, many more people from the no-performance conditions chose not to rate.) Apparently, some individuals felt that demographic data alone were sufficient evidence on which to base an evaluation of, for example, a child's likely achievement orientation. Thus, the addition of performance information was not necessary for a conclusive judgment in this area. In general, our social categories do trigger expectancies for a constellation of dispositions and behaviors, and for some of these, it may not be necessary to rely on performance evidence to feel certain that one's expectations are accurate.

The validity of demographic evidence

From another perspective, one could ask whether demographic information does not warrant correspondent inferences of ability. Certainly, numerous studies show correlations between social class and school performance (Dreger and Miller, 1960; Kennedy, VanDeReit, and White, 1963; Lesser, Fifer, and Clark, 1965). From this perspective, the differential judgments of people who witnessed the same test with different demographically produced expectancies was less evidence of bias than it was of an understanding of the true workings of the world. Two things can be said about this: First, part of the general argument of those concerned with self-fulfilling prophecies is that the present process is exactly how the link between social class and academic performance comes about. Second, the data from our no-performance perceivers indicate that people regard the question of what exists in the world as a separate question from that addressed in the present study. Base-rate information (i.e., estimates of the frequencies with which an attribute or capability level occurs in a social group) represents probabilistic statements about a class of individuals, which may not be applicable to every member of the class. Thus, regardless of what an individual perceives the actual base rates to be, rating any one member of the class requires a higher standard of evidence. When one child's ability is being considered, demographic information does not appear to meet the perceiver's criteria for a valid predictor; performance information, on the other hand, clearly does.

There is yet another way to pose the validity question, and that is to consider the use of demographic evidence when perceivers formulate a working hypothesis. From an information-processing perspective, hypothesis formulation serves a useful function: It allows one to make better use of subsequent evidence. The rub, or course, is that once a hypothesis is formulated, regardless of our judgments of the validity of the evidence on which it is based, our cognitive mechanisms are biased toward its eventual confirmation. Thus, when asking whether the final judgments of the perceiver accurately reflect what exists in the world, we should not obscure an important point: how those judgments come about. To clarify further, the "judgmental bias" in the present study does not refer to the indiscriminate use of category-based information, or to the (in)accuracy of final judgments, but to the processes that determine what those judgments will be.

An alternative explanation

An alternative explanation for the general pattern of results reported here is possible. The individuals who witnessed only the demographic information may have actually made ability inferences but chosen not to report them. Their failure to report their evaluations may have been due to fears that the experimenter would regard the inferences as unjustified. However, in the experiment we minimized the possible cause for this concern by demonstrating to the participants that their responses would be anonymous. The experimenter was not present while the participant filled out the dependent-measures form and did not return until he or she deposited the questionnaire in an anonymity-guaranteeing location. Furthermore, on the final questionnaire, participants were asked if they were sufficiently assured of the anonymity of their responses, and all of them replied affirmatively.

It is, of course, still possible to make a generalized version of the same point: The perceiver's resistance to using the demographic information could, at least in part, be motivated by the awareness that their behavior was under scrutiny by others. This does not necessarily diminish the interest in the phenomenon. In the real world, people who make judgments frequently know their judgments may be public. Teachers classifying students, clinicians diagnosing clients, and employers selecting new personnel are all aware that their actions may be scrutinized by others. Thus, whether this awareness is based on personal knowledge, social pressures, or internalized social desirability concerns, both the processes that bring about those judgments and the consequences in terms of judgmental bias are likely to be the same.

The present study finds results that at first glance seem contradictory to results of some other studies. One thinks particularly of the work of Locksley et al. (1980) and that of Kahneman and Tversky (1973). In the Locksley et al. study, the direction of the interaction appears to be the reverse of that obtained here. A strong stereotype effect in trait ratings is found with category-membership information (gender labels) or when nondiagnostic information accompanies the category label. This stereotype effect disappears with diagnostic information. However, consider the differences in the type of information given to perceivers in the present study and that given to perceivers in the correspondent conditions of the Locksley et al. study. The perceivers in the present study who were reluctant to apply stereotypes (the no-performance conditions) received nondiagnostic case information, as do some in the Locksley et al. study. However, perceivers in the present study observe the child they will rate and are given a fair amount of family data – information that would certainly distinguish the child from others in her social group. The diagnostic information used by Locksley et al. consists of information that could be applied to almost any person and may not have created an individuated impression of the person to be rated. The two conditions, then, are not identical, and comparing them leads us to the following possibility: Stereotype effects persist with information that does not distinguish the target from the target's social category, whereas dilution effects (nonstereotypic judgments) appear when case information successfully creates an individuated impression of the target. Recent studies by Quattrone and Jones (1980) and Locksley, Hepburn, and Ortiz (in press) support this conclusion.

In comparing other conditions of the Locksley et al. (1980) and the present study, differences in the type of information given to perceivers produces discrepant results. The diagnostic information given to perceivers in the Locksley et al. study consists of a single behavioral exemplar that confirms or disconfirms a gender-based trait expectancy. A dilution effect is found only with a disconfirming behavior sample. In contrast, the diagnostic test sequence in the present study contains both confirming and disconfirming behavioral evidence. Furthermore, we know from supplementary measures that perceivers found the expectancy-consistent portions more diagnostically informative than the inconsistent portions. Therefore, with a source of multiple information – with many information elements that serve to confirm expectancies – a confirmation effect is not surprising. Had the performance tape in the present study provided only compelling disconfirming evidence, we suspect a dilution effect might have been found here as well.

Discrepancies between this work and that of Kahneman and Tversky (1973) can be addressed as well. In Kahneman and Tversky's studies, individuals are asked to predict a target person's occupational-category membership from a brief personality description. Predictions are overwhelmingly based on the degree to which the personality information "fits" with an occupational stereotype (i.e., a representativeness effect). This appears inconsistent with the stereotype-resisting judgments of the perceivers in our study who received no performance information. However, the demographic information given to our no-performance perceivers, although it does allow for a judgment of fit to a social category, does not provide information for a judgment on an ability dimension. The condition, then, is similar to Kahneman and Tversky's Experiment 3 in which the personality description is uninformative with regard to the target person's profession (i.e., it contains no occupation-relevant personality traits). In their study, occupational-category predictions were essentially random. That is, they were based neither on prior probabilities nor on similarity. This is essentially the same effect we find for no-performance perceivers in the present study. Apparently, the representativeness effect (or an expectancy effect) depends on the provision of information that allows for a similarity match to the categories perceivers are asked to judge.

Further, the no-performance conditions in the present study are not identical to Kahneman and Tversky's (1973) null-description condition. In that condition, subjects are given no information whatsoever about the target – neither individuating information nor category-relevant information. Here a strong base-rate effect emerges. Although this might cause one to predict a strong stereotype effect in the present no-performance conditions, our earlier point about individuating information may explain why it is not obtained. No-performance perceivers may lack relevant case information, but they do have a significant amount of individuating target information; apparently, this significantly alters the framework for prediction.

We might summarize as follows: Representativeness and expectancy effects are found when relevant case data are provided so that individuals can determine the target person's fit to a category. Base-rate effects (and nonobservationally based stereotypic judgments) are found when neither case data nor individuating information is given. Finally, assume that three conditions are met: individuating information is given, information about base rates is withheld, and a priori expectancies are not relied on because they may not be applicable to a particular target. Then, without relevant case data, a judgment of fit is precluded, attenuating a representativeness or a biased confirmation effect. In these circumstances, judgments are made at the scale midpoint or the chance level. We find this latter effect in both Kahneman and Tversky's (1973) uninformed condition and in the no-performance conditions of the present study.

A final point is relevant to both of the studies reviewed above. Predicting ability from social-class information may not be equivalent to predicting personality traits from gender labels or occupational membership. The nature of the prediction required (ability rather than personality characteristics) may cause individuals to regard social-class information as at the invalid end of the continuum we have defined. But an individual's gender or occupation, on the other hand, may be regarded as valid information on which to base an inference about personality. Related to this point is that the standards of evidence required for different stereotype-confirming judgments may be different. Automatic assumptions about personality may be made from occupation or gender label, and thus, stereotype effects are obtained with this information alone, or with minimal additional information. To make judgments of a low-SES child's ability, perceivers require more information and, specifically, criterion-relevant information. Thus, stereotypic judgments are not found with only category or nondiagnostic information but are found only when a sufficient amount of apparently confirming diagnostic information is provided.

Limits to the confirmation process

The present study finds results consistent with those of many other studies. For instance, Swann and Snyder (1980) found that target individuals labeled as dull witted were still seen as dull witted even after the perceivers had witnessed a sequence in which these target individuals outperformed those labeled as bright, a situation in which a cognitive confirmation effect triumphed over apparently strongly disconfirming evidence. Nonetheless, we suspect that there are limits to the cognitive confirmation process.

We can suggest several variables, some of which we have mentioned, that may determine whether a confirmation or a disconfirmation effect is found. First, there is the clarity of the disconfirming evidence. In the domain of abilities, in spite of the above example, a sustained high-level performance is compelling evidence for high ability. I may perceive another as a slow runner, but if I see him or her do several successive 4-minute miles, my expectancy must change. When this occurs, it is possible that a contrast effect will take place in which the significance of the disconfirming behavior will be exaggerated and the initial expectancy reversed. Intuitively, no such unambiguous evidence exists in the personality realm, where even compelling positive behavior can be attributed to negative underlying motives or dispositions. Second, the strength with which the initial expectancy or hypothesis is held may produce conflicting effects. "Strength of expectancy" is an ambiguous phrase. It may refer to one's degree of commitment to an expectancy of a fixed level, or it may refer to the extremity of the expectancy. In the first instance, the stronger the commitment to the expectancy, the more resistant it would be to disconfirmation. However, the more extreme the expectancy, the more evidence there is that potentially disconfirms it. Finally, the perceiver's motivation may play a role. Under certain circumstances, an individual may prefer to see his or her expectancy confirmed; in other situations he or she may have a preference for the disconfirmation of the same expectancy. All of these suggestions, of course, require empirical testing.

A Final Comment

The self-fulfilling prophecy and the expectancy-confirmation effect have been of interest to psychologists partially because of the social policy implications of the research. However, in many of the research studies that document the effect, the specific and limited character of the material that creates the expectancies is lost, and we talk as if any material that creates expectancies is automatically accepted as valid by the perceiver. The image of the perceiver that emerges is one of an individual who takes his or her stereotypes and prejudices for granted and indiscriminantly applies them to members of the class he or she has stereotyped without any consideration of the unjustness of such a proceeding. The present study suggests that this is an oversimplification that in turn does some injustice to the perceiver. There are times when perceivers resist regarding their expectancies as truths and instead treat them as hypotheses to be confirmed or disconfirmed by relevant evidence. Perceivers in the present study did not make the error of reporting stereotypic judgments without sufficient evidence to warrant their conclusions. They engaged in an extremely rational strategy of evaluating the behavioral evidence when it was available and refraining from judgment when it was not. It was the strategy perceivers employed to analyze the evidence that led them to regard their hypotheses as confirmed even when the objective evidence did not warrant that conclusion. The error the perceivers make, then, is in assuming that the behavioral evidence they have derived is valid and unbiased. Future research could profitably address the question of the conditions under which this general confirmation strategy can be reversed or eliminated. In the meantime, however, the image of the perceiver as a hypothesis tester is certainly more appealing than that of a stereotype-applying bigot, even though the end result of both processes, sadly enough, may be quite similar.

NOTES

The authors are grateful for the insightful comments of Nancy Cantor, Ron Comer, Joel Cooper, E.E. Jones, Charles Lord, Mark Zanna, and the members of the Princeton Social Psychology Research Seminar. Robin Akert, Kristin Boggiano, Paul Bree, Kay Ferdinandsen, Hannah McChesney, and Frederick Rhodewalt ably assisted in creating the stimulus materials.

[1] We also analyzed this data by pooling across the three ability measures. As one would expect, because this increases the number of observations, the significance levels are improved, although the basic interactional pattern ($p = .002$) remains the same. Again, post hoc comparisons reveal that the two performance conditions are reliably different ($p < .01$), whereas the two no-performance groups do not differ reliably.

[2] An F_{max} test of the difference between several variances indicates no difference between the variances of the liberal arts and reading indexes. The variance of the mathematics index is, however, significantly different from that of the liberal arts index, $F_{max}(9, 9) = 5.92, p < .05$, and shows a marginally significant difference from that of the reading index.

[3] Analyses of these data require a decision about how to treat the responses of subjects who checked the "not enough information to rate" alternative. The means presented in table 5.15 are calculated by assigning a score of 5 to missing scale values. This assumes that the nonresponding subjects would have checked the scale midpoint if forced to respond. Another way of dealing with the same issue is to insert the cell-mean score for each such subject. Using this procedure, the pattern of results is essentially unchanged. The same effects emerged as significant.

[4] In the experimental paradigm in which expectancy effects are typically demonstrated, perceivers are always provided with the opportunity to observe or interact with the labeled target person. By using this research design, one cannot conclusively determine whether the resulting expectancy effect was due to differential perceptions of that target person, as most researchers suggest, or if subjects had simply based their evaluations on the information provided by the label and had ignored the performance. By including conditions in the present study in which some perceivers are not provided with performance information, it becomes possible to distinguish between expectancy effects arising from a nonobservationally based inference process and those arising from expectancy-guided search processes.

REFERENCES

Brigham, J.C. Ethnic stereotypes. *Psychological Bulletin*, 1971, 76, 15–38.

Cooper, H.M., Baron, R.M., and Lowe, C.A. The importance of race and social class information in the formation of expectancies about academic performance. *Journal of Educational Psychology*, 1975, 67, 312–19.

Darely, J.M., and Fazio, R.H. Expectancy confirmation processes arising in the social interaction sequence. *American Psychologist*, 1980, 35, 867–81.

Darley, J.M., and Goethals, G.R. People's analyses of the causes of ability-linked performances. In L. Berkowitz (ed.), *Advances in experimental social psychology* (vol. 13). New York: Academic Press, 1980.

Dreger, R.M., and Miller, S.K. Comparative psychological studies of Negroes and whites in the United States. *Psychological Bulletin*, 1960, 57, 361–402.

Duncan, B.L. Differential social perception and attribution of intergroup violence: Testing the lower limits of stereotyping of blacks. *Journal of Personality and Social Psychology*, 1976, 34, 590–8.

Foster, G., Schmidt, C., and Sabatino, D. Teacher expectancies and the label "learning disabilities." *Journal of Learning Disabilities*, 1976, 9, 111–14.

Hayden, T., and Mischel, W. Maintaining trait consistency in the resolution of behavioral inconsistency: The wolf in sheep's clothing? *Journal of Personality*, 1976, 44, 109–32.

Kahneman, D., and Tversky, A. On the psychology of prediction. *Psychological Review*, 1973, 80, 237–51.

Karlins, M., Coffman, T.L., and Walters, G. On the fading of social stereotypes: Studies in three generations of college students. *Journal of Personality and Social Psychology*, 1969, 13, 1–16.

Kelley, H.H. The warm–cold variable in first impressions of persons. *Journal of Personality*, 1950, 18, 431–9.

Kennedy, W.A., VanDeReit, V., and White, J.C. A normative sample of intelligence and achievement of Negro elementary school children in the southeastern United States. *Monographs of the Society for Research in Child Development*, 1963, 28, 13–112.

Langer, E.J., and Abelson, R.P. A patient by any other name . . . : Clinician group differences in labeling bias. *Journal of Consulting and Clinical Psychology*, 1974, 42, 4–9.

Lesser, G.S., Fifer, G., and Clark, D.H. Mental abilities of children from different social class and cultural groups. *Monographs of the Society for Research in Child Development*, 1965, 30, 1–115.

Locksley, A., Borgida, E., Brekke, N., and Hepburn, C. Sex stereotypes and social judgment. *Journal of Personality and Social Psychology*, 1980, 39, 821–31.

Locksley, A., Hepburn, C., and Ortiz, V. Social stereotypes and judgments of individuals: An instance of the base-rate fallacy. *Journal of Experimental Social Psychology*, in press.

Lord, C., Ross, L., and Lepper, M.E. Biased assimilation and attitude polarization: The effects of prior theories on subsequently considered evidence. *Journal of Personality and Social Psychology*, 1979, 37, 2098–109.

Merton, R.K. The self-fulfilling prophecy. *Antioch Review*, 1948, 8, 193–210.

Nisbett, R., and Ross, L. *Human inference: Strategies and shortcomings of social judgment*. Englewood Cliffs, N.J.: Prentice-Hall, 1980.

Quattrone, G.A., and Jones, E.E. The perception of variability within in-groups and out-groups: Implications for the law of small numbers. *Journal of Personality and Social Psychology*, 1980, *38*, 141–52.

Regan, D.T., Strauss,, E., and Fazio, R. Liking and the attribution process. *Journal of Experimental Social Psychology*, 1974, *10*, 385–97.

Rist, R.C. Student social class and teacher expectations: The self-fulfilling prophecy in ghetto education. *Harvard Educational Review*, 1970, *40*, 411–51.

Rosenhan, D.L. On being sane in insane places. *Science*, 1973, *179*, 250–8.

Rosenthal, R. *On the social psychology of self-fulfilling prophecy: Further evidence for Pygmalion effects and their mediating mechanisms*. New York: MSS Modular Publications, Module 53, 1974.

Rosenthal, R., and Jacobson, L. *Pygmalion in the classroom*. New York: Holt, Rinehart & Winston, 1968.

Snyder, M., and Cantor, N. Testing hypotheses about other people: The use of historical knowledge. *Journal of Experimental Social Psychology*, 1979, *15*, 330–42.

Snyder, M., and Swann, W.B. Behavioral confirmation in social interaction: From social perception to social reality. *Journal of Experimental Social Psychology*, 1978, *14*, 148–62. (a)

Snyder, M., and Swann, W.B. Hypothesis-testing processes in social interaction. *Journal of Personality and Social Psychology*, 1978, *36*, 1202–12. (b)

Snyder, M., Tanke, E.D., and Berscheid, E. Social perception and interpersonal behavior: On the self-fulfilling nature of social stereotypes. *Journal of Personality and Social Psychology*, 1977, *35*, 656–66.

Swann, W.B., and Snyder, M. On translating beliefs into action: Theories of ability and their application in an instructional setting. *Journal of Personality and Social Psychology*, 1980, *6*, 879–88.

Weiner, B., et al. *Perceiving the causes of success and failure*. Morristown, N.J.: General Learning Press, 1971.

Word, C.O., Zanna, M.P., and Cooper, J. The nonverbal mediation of self-fulfilling prophecies in interracial interaction. *Journal of Experimental Social Psychology*, 1974, *10*, 109–20.

Zadny, J., and Gerard, H.B. Attributed intentions and informational selectivity. *Journal of Experimental Social Psychology*, 1974, *10*, 34–52.

6 Processing Social Information for Judgements and Decisions

Cognitive representation of personality impressions: Organizational processes in first impression formation

D.L. Hamilton, L.B. Katz and V.O. Leirer

Editors'
Introduction

Theoretical Background

The study of social aspects of memory has long been of interest to psychologists (Bartlett, 1932) and remains a core topic within social cognition, often called 'person memory' (see Wyer and Carlston, 1994). This article by Hamilton, Katz and Leirer illustrates how instructions to perform a more social task (e.g. being asked to form an impression of someone) can result in better recall of information than explicit instructions to memorize. The results are counter-intuitive and thus all the more interesting.

Hamilton and colleagues define an impression as 'the perceiver's *cognitive representation* of another person'. This definition opens up for enquiry the cognitive processes underlying social tasks such as how we form impressions of other people, and also paves the way for a new methodology, one that leans heavily on cognitive psychology. This methodology sees impression formation as more than the process of deciding whether we 'like' another person; it can also include how we encode information about him or her, and how we organize and represent that information in our memory.

The three studies in this paper compare the memory performance of perceivers asked to form an impression and perceivers asked to remember. Hamilton and colleagues suggest that impression-formation subjects will take a more active role in developing a coherent picture of the target person, relating items to each other as they seek to organize the information presented. Memory subjects, in contrast, focus on accurate recall of each individual item in a list and do not need to organize the information coherently. These different processes should result in better memory in the impression-formation than the memory task. The studies also investigate the role of distinctive information in forming an impression, whether a distinctive item (compared with a non-distinctive one) improves or worsens recall of other items in the list, and whether this effect varies across impression-formation and memory conditions. In this study distinctive items are negative behaviours – such as '[he] insulted his secretary without

Journal of Personality and Social Psychology (1980), 39:1050–63.

provocation' – in a series of common, everyday behaviours. The authors suggest that a distinctive item could lead to more associations being formed with other items, thus improving recall; or it could interfere, especially with other items close to it in the list.

Hypotheses

All three experiments test three hypotheses:

1 Subjects asked to form an impression of a person described by a series of items will recall more of those items than will subjects instructed to remember as many of the items as they can.
2 The presence of a distinctive item in the list will facilitate recall of other items in the impression-formation condition, but may decrease recall of these items in the memory condition.
3 Impression-formation subjects should be more accurate than memory subjects in stating where, in the sequence of items processed, the distinctive item occurred.

EXPERIMENTS 1 AND 2

Because experiments 1 and 2 are so similar, Hamilton et al. report them simultaneously.

Design

The design of primary interest in this research was, in each study, a two-factor, between-subjects design: 2 (processing set: impression formation vs. memory) × 2 (middle item: distinctive vs. non-distinctive). Thus there were four major experimental conditions, and two levels of each independent variable. As the authors make clear, the design is, in fact, more complex, because it includes a 'replications' factor for the distinctive or non-distinctive item located in the middle of the list of items presented. This means simply that across subjects there were two alternatives for the distinctive and non-distinctive middle item. This factor was not expected to have a significant effect, nor did it, so it does not occur in the analyses and we can treat the design as a more simple 2 × 2. It should be noted that the sample sizes in these studies were very low (only four subjects per cell), which limits the power of later analyses, especially to detect significant interactions.

Method

Subjects were asked to read fifteen short sentences, describing common behaviours, and either to form an impression of the person described or to try to remember the exact wording of items. Subjects were then briefly distracted before being asked to complete various recall measures. The middle item (serial position eight) was varied, to be either distinctive (highly negative) or non-distinctive (neutral). No pre-testing of distinctive vs. non-distinctive items is reported. As the authors later acknowledge, there are many ways to operationalize this variable and the chosen manipulation may not have worked as they intended.

Results

Free recall

The number of items recalled by each subject (excluding the middle item in the list) was analysed using analysis of variance (ANOVA). This analysis revealed strong support for hypothesis 1 in both studies: impression-formation subjects recalled significantly more items than did memory condition subjects (see figure 6.1). If, as predicted, the distinctive item had different effects in the two processing conditions, there should have been a significant Processing set × Middle item interaction. This effect was, however, non-significant in both studies, thus disconfirming hypothesis 2. The authors also analysed the percentage of subjects in each condition who correctly recalled the middle item (see table 6.1). In experiment 1 recall was more accurate for the distinctive item than the neutral item, in both processing conditions. In experiment 2 results were unreliable.

Before–after discrimination task

After the free recall, subjects were given another sheet of paper, with the item presented in the middle of the list shown at the top of a page (as a 'cue'), and a scrambled list of the other fourteen items below it. They were asked to indicate whether each item had come before or after the cued item in the sequence of sentences. The data are shown in figure 6.2. Only in experiment 2 was hypothesis 3 confirmed statistically: subjects in the impression-formation–distinctive-item condition made fewest errors.

EXPERIMENT 3

A third, comparable experiment was carried out to vary the effect of manipulating the sequential position of the distinctive item, and including some new ratings of the stimulus person. The authors predicted that the sequential position of this item would have little impact on recall in the impression-formation condition, but in the memory condition it would worsen recall when it occurred early (as opposed to late) in the list. The authors again demonstrated greater recall in the impression-formation than the memory tasks (hypothesis 1), but failed to support hypothesis 2 (see figure 6.3). The distinctive item was recalled by most subjects if they were given an impression-formation task, but not if given the memory task (table 6.2). This significant effect is viewed as indirect evidence of the authors' proposal that subjects in the impression-formation condition engage in more cognitive activity aimed at integrating the items in the list than do memory subjects.

One final twist in this experiment is noteworthy. The authors got subjects to perform their assigned tasks *twice*. As they point out, the recall task is a surprise the first time around for impression-formation subjects; but not the second time. They might change their strategy, perhaps trying to recall on the second task. Equally, the person-rating task is a surprise for the memory subjects on the first, but not the second, task. They might change their strategy too, perhaps trying to form an impression of the person. Figure 6.4 shows that, indeed, results were quite different on the first and second stimulus sets. From the data, it appears that impression-formation subjects maintained their (successful) strategy, and memory subjects adopted an impression-formation strategy on the second set, leading to an improvement in their performance. Thus on the second set there is no appreciable difference as a function of processing instructions: in effect, all the subjects may be processing the information in the same way.

Discussion

These experiments only consistently support hypothesis 1. But they do so very strongly, and illustrate neatly the social dimension of cognition. With hindsight, given the authors' interest in 'organizational processes' (see the title), it may seem surprising that they did not measure *organization* in recall at all. But it was only after this paper was published that social psychologists began to use newer, more sophisticated cognitive measures. Later studies by the authors and others did, however, use such measures of how impressions are organized in memory. These studies, anticipated in the final paragraph of this article, showed that subjects forming an impression organize their memories into 'clusters' representing different categories of information (e.g. abilities, interests, characteristics), whereas memory subjects did not do this to the same extent (see Hamilton, 1981; Hamilton et al., 1989, 1980). Other social-cognition research has also uncovered interesting findings by looking beyond the *amount* of information recalled to how that information is *organized* (see Hewstone et al., 1994; Ostrom et al., 1981; Srull, 1981).

FURTHER READING

Hamilton, D.L., Driscoll, D.M. and Worth, L.T. (1989). Cognitive organization of impressions: Effects of incongruency in complex representations. *Journal of Personality and Social Psychology*, 57, 925–39. A later paper by Hamilton and colleagues that develops the earlier one reprinted here.

Srull, T.K. (1981). Person memory: Some tests of associative storage and retrieval models. *Journal of Experimental Psychology: Human Learning and Memory*, 7, 440–63. A detailed study of memory for information about different persons, making good use of a variety of measures of memory and techniques for their analysis.

Wyer, R.S. Jr and Carlston, D.E. (1994). The cognitive representation of persons and events. In R.S. Wyer Jr and T.K. Srull (eds), *Handbook of Social Cognition* (2nd edn, vol. 1, pp. 41–98). Hillsdale, NJ: Erlbaum. An authoritative review of memory for information about persons, groups and social events, and also of general theories of social memory.

REFERENCES

Bartlett, F.C. (1932). *Remembering: A Study in Experimental and Social Psychology*. Cambridge: Cambridge University Press.

Hamilton, D.L. (1981). Organizational processes in impression formation. In E.T. Higgins, C.P. Herman and M. Zanna (eds), *Social Cognition: The Ontario Symposium* (vol. 1, pp. 135–60). Hillsdale, NJ: Erlbaum.

Hamilton, D.L., Katz, L.B. and Leirer, V.O. (1980). Organizational processes in impression formation. In R. Hastie, T.M. Ostrom, E.B. Ebbesen, R.S. Wyer, D.L. Hamilton and D.E. Carlston (eds), *Person Memory: The Cognitive Basis of Social Perception* (pp. 121–53). Hillsdale, NJ: Erlbaum.

Hewstone, M., Macrae, C.N., Griffiths, R., Milne, A. and Brown, R.J. (1994). Cognitive models of stereotype change: (5) Measurement, development and consequences of subtyping. *Journal of Experimental Social Psychology* 30, 505–26.

Ostrom, T.M., Pryor, J.B. and Simpson, D.D. (1981). The organization of social information. In E.T. Higgins, C.P. Herman and M. Zanna (eds), *Social Cognition: The Ontario Symposium* (vol. 1, pp. 3–38). Hillsdale, NJ: Erlbaum.

- - - - -
Primary
Reading
- - - - - - - -

For the last 15 years, the experimental study of impression formation processes has focused on testing and evaluating various models of information integration. The aim of this research has been to formulate, in precise and quantifiable terms, the relation between global judgments of a stimulus person and the collections of items of information on which they are based. The degree of precision achieved by some of these models has been impressive (e.g., Anderson, 1974).

Although this research literature has been informative regarding the effectiveness of various combinatory rules in predicting judgment responses, it has become apparent that this approach to studying the impression formation process is somewhat limited. One reason for the incompleteness of this approach is that these models shed relatively little light on the actual cognitive processes mediating the formation of first impressions. That is, it is not presumed that the mathematical operations specified in a combinatory rule represent cognitive operations performed by the perceiver. There is, then, a need for research focusing on the cognitive processes actually engaged in during the impression formation process.

A second respect in which information integration models are limiting as an approach to studying impression formation is reflected in the dependent variables used in these studies. Typically, the dependent variable is a judgment on a single scale, most frequently a judgment of one's "liking" for a stimulus person. Although such a response measure is an appropriate dependent variable for evaluating the predictive utility of various combinatory rules, a single evaluative judgment fails to adequately assess all that we typically mean when we speak of our impression of another person.

In the present article we shall adopt an alternative orientation. In the research reported here, we define an impression as the perceiver's *cognitive representation* of another person and focus our inquiry on the cognitive processes involved in the development of that representation from the stimulus information available to the perceiver. According to this view, forming an impression is an active process in which the perceiver imposes an organization on the information available about a target person in an effort to develop a coherent representation of him/her. That is, as the perceiver acquires items of information about the target person, the encoded information becomes organized and represented in memory in terms of a cognitive structure that represents the perceiver's accumulated knowledge (including both acquired information and inferences drawn from it) about the target person. It is this cognitive representation (and not the informational facts taken separately) that constitutes the basis for the perceiver's subsequent judgments about the person (Jaccard and Fishbein, 1975; Lingle, Geva, Ostrom, Leippe, and Baumgardner, 1979). By studying the way in which perceivers acquire collections of discrete items of information and represent them in a coherent cognitive representation of a person, we should be able to gain some understanding of the organizational processes by which these memory structures emerge.

To provide a context for the discussion to follow, consider an experiment in which subjects are instructed to form an impression of a person on the basis of a serially presented list of descriptive facts (e.g., descriptions of behaviors). According to the above argument, the subjects would take an active role in evolving a coherent representation of the target person's personality from whatever information items they were given. In doing so, it is likely that the subjects would organize the serially presented information in terms of certain cognitive structures (e.g., implicit personality theories, cognitive schemas, prototypes) that they brought with them to the experiment. As part of accomplishing this organization, subjects would engage in a process of relating each new information item they came on to others that had preceded it in the list (and perhaps to an already emerging impression). This process of relating items of information to each other would lead to the formation of associations among their representations in memory and would result in a progressively expanding structure as more facts about the target person are processed. Recent research in cognitive psychology has shown that such organizational, integrative activity facilitates later retrieval of stimulus information (cf. Bransford and Johnson, 1973; Smith, Adams, and Schorr, 1978).

For purposes of comparison, suppose the same list of descriptive facts is presented to subjects in the context of a memory experiment, with instructions to try to remember as many of the behavior descriptions as they can. In this case there would be no need for subjects to impose a coherent organization on the information contained in the list, since the task's emphasis would be on accuracy in the recall of individual items. Consequently, subjects should devote less cognitive effort toward interrelating the items and be more likely to engage in other strategies, such as the rehearsal of each item as it appeared in the serial sequence. Whatever organization emerged in memory would be due in large part to characteristics of the stimulus sequence, reflecting, for example, the extent to which items were contemporaneously rehearsed.

In each of the experiments reported in this article, we make use of this distinction between impression formation and memory tasks. If the argument developed above is correct, then we would expect that the greater number of interitem associations developed by impression formation subjects would facilitate recall of the stimulus items. The hypothesis that subjects instructed to form an impression of a person described by a series of items would recall more of those items than would subjects instructed to remember as many of the items as they can was tested in each of these experiments.

In addition to the effects of this "processing set" manipulation, the present research examined the role of distinctive information in forming an impression. In the process of organizing the information available about the target person, a highly distinctive item might well serve as a focal point around which the emerging impression can be structured. We might therefore expect a distinctive item to enter into more associative relationships with other items than would the less distinctive items. Such an effect would then be expected to increase recall in the presence of a distinctive item.

The literature on memory processes, on the other hand, suggests somewhat different consequences of the presence of a distinctive item in a serially presented list. Although it is known that the probability of recall of the distinctive item is much higher than that for nondistinctive items, evidence also suggests that recall of items near the distinctive item in the serial list may be somewhat depressed (cf. Wallace, 1965). This latter finding suggests some degree of interference in the recall of other items by the distinctive item. Thus, we hypothesized that the presence of a distinctive item in the stimulus list would facilitate recall of the other items in the impression formation condition, but that in the memory condition it would, if anything, result in decreased recall.

A second possible role of distinctive information in the impression formation process was also examined. If a coherent representation of a person emerges gradually as more and more information is incorporated into the developing impression, then subjects in this condition should be particularly aware of where, in the sequence of items received, the distinctive item had occurred. In contrast, if subjects in the memory condition attempt to learn the items individually, without considering the relations among their meanings, the position of the distinctive item in the stimulus sequence should be less apparent to them. This hypothesis was also tested in the experiments reported below.

Experiments 1 and 2

The first two experiments provided parallel tests of the above hypotheses and hence will be reported simultaneously.[1] In these experiments subjects read a series of 15 sentence predicates, each describing a particular behavior, for example, "took his dog for a walk in the park," "watched a movie on TV," and so forth. Half of the subjects were told that the study was concerned with processes involved in forming first impressions and were asked to form an impression of a person described by the series of statements. The other half of the subjects were told that the experiment was concerned with memory for verbal descriptions and were told to try to remember as many of the sentences as possible. The other manipulation was contained within the set of stimulus sentences. For half of the subjects, the middle item in the series of 15 statements was a highly distinctive behavior; for the other half the middle item was a common everyday behavior like the other items in the series.

Method

Subjects
The subjects in both studies were drawn from the student body of Southern Connecticut State University in New Haven, Connecticut. In Experiment 1 the subjects were 32 undergraduate students run in small groups in the social psychology laboratories at Yale University and were paid for their participation. Subjects in Experiment 2 were 32 master's level graduate students who were run in two groups as a part of their regular class sessions.

Design
The design of both experiments was a 2 (processing set: impression formation vs. memory) × 2 (middle item: distinctive vs. nondistinctive) × 2 (replications of middle item) analysis of variance (ANOVA). All three independent variables were between-groups factors. In both experiments there were four subjects in each of the eight cells of the design, with the exception that two subjects in Experiment 2 (each in a different cell of the design) failed

to follow instructions on the recall task, requiring omission of these subjects from those analyses.

Stimulus materials

The stimulus materials presented to the subjects consisted of a series of 15 sentence predicates, 14 of which described common, everyday behaviors (e.g., "read the evening newspaper," "cleaned up the house before company came," etc.). In addition to these items, one additional item was included in the eighth, or middle, position of the resulting 15-item sequence. To implement the distinctiveness manipulation, a highly distinctive negative behavior was used ("lost his temper and hit a neighbor he was arguing with" or "insulted his secretary without provocation"), and an additional neutral behavior was used in the middle position in the nondistinctive condition. Two replications of these middle-position items were used. Finally, two random orders of the 14 neutral context sentences were used, each order being presented to half of the subjects in each cell.

A comment regarding the manipulation of item distinctiveness is appropriate. There are many ways in which information can be distinctive, and the present operationalization reflects two properties commonly found in manipulations of distinctiveness in social psychological research. We wanted the distinctive items to stand out in relation to the common, everyday behaviors presented in the other items. The behaviors described in these items are nonnormative and hence are distinctive in the sense of unusualness or statistical infrequency. In addition, the behaviors described are negative in evaluation, whereas the other 14 items presented neutral or mildly desirable behaviors. Thus, the behaviors may also be seen as distinctive in the context of the other items in the stimulus set.

Procedure

Experiment 1 When all subjects for a given experimental session had arrived, each was handed a sheet giving general instructions that they were told to read to themselves while the experimenter read them aloud. The manipulation of processing set was implemented within these instructions. All participants in a given experimental session were administered the same instructional set; the order in which the impression and memory conditions were run was randomly determined in advance.

For subjects assigned to the impression formation condition, the instructions read as follows:

> The first part of this experiment is concerned with the way in which we form an impression of a person on the basis of his or her actions. In a few moments you will be shown a series of slides, each slide containing a single description of a person's behavior. Please read these sentences carefully, studying each one until the next slide appears on the screen. Do not be concerned with memorization – there are far too many individual items to remember. Try instead to form an overall impression of what the person who performed these various actions is like. At the end of the session, we will ask you a series of questions concerning the impression that you have formed of the person described in these sentences.

In contrast, the instructions for subjects in the memory condition read as follows:

> The first part of this experiment is concerned with the way in which we memorize verbal descriptions of action. In a few moments you will be shown a series of slides, each slide containing

a description of a particular behavior. Please read these sentences carefully, studying each one until the next slide appears on the screen. Try to remember the exact wording of each single description as accurately as you can. At the end of the session, we will ask you a series of questions pertaining to the information contained in these sentences.

As can be seen, an attempt was made to make the two sets of instructions as comparable as possible while still effectively manipulating the desired processing sets.

Each slide was shown for a period of 8 sec, controlled automatically by a timer in the slide projector. Each group saw 15 slides, the middle or 8th one being either a distinctive or a nondistinctive item. This manipulation, along with the processing set manipulation, created the 2×2 design of primary interest in this research. In each of these four cells, four replication sets were run, created by orthogonally combining the two replications of the "middle" items with the two different serial presentation orders of the 14 context sentences. The middle item and serial ordering given to each group were randomly determined in advance.

After the slides had been presented, subjects were given a distracting task of 5 minutes' duration to reduce their short term memory for the behavior descriptions. The dependent measures were administered immediately following the distracting task. When the dependent measures had been completed, the purpose of the experiment was explained, and any questions the subjects had were answered.

Experiment 2   The procedure and stimulus materials for Experiment 2 were essentially the same as those for Experiment 1, except that all materials were contained in booklets distributed at the start of a class session. To control exposure time for each behavior description, the experimenter sounded a bell at 8-sec intervals as a signal to turn to the next page of the booklet. The distracting task in this case lasted 15 min. Booklets for the different experimental conditions were distributed randomly throughout the two classes participating in the study. Thus, all conditions of the experiment were run simultaneously in both class sessions. The nature of the experiment and the hypotheses being tested were explained at the conclusion of the session.

Dependent measures

Free recall   Following the distracting task, all subjects were given a sheet on which they were instructed to list as many of the behavior descriptions as they could remember. Subjects were told not to worry about word-for-word accuracy but at the same time to come as close to each item's original wording as possible. Four minutes were allowed for completion of this free recall task, a time period that was sufficient in essentially all cases.

Before–after discrimination task   Following the free recall measure, subjects were given another sheet that presented, at the top of the page, the item that had appeared in the eighth or middle position in the series of 15 sentences the subjects had read. Below this item were listed the other 14 items, arranged in a scrambled order. The instructions informed the subject that the item at the top of the page had been the middle item in the series they had seen and that "some of the other sentences are listed below." For each of the other 14 items, they were asked to indicate whether it had come before or after this middle item in the stimulus sequence.

Confidence ratings   For each of the 14 judgments made in the before–after discrimination task, subjects were asked to rate their confidence in the correctness of their response for that item. Ratings were made on a 10-point scale, where 1 indicated "extremely unconfident" and 10 represented "extremely confident." These confidence data are available only for Experiment 1.

Results

The data from Experiments 1 and 2 were analyzed by a 2 (processing set: impression formation vs. memory) × 2 (item distinctiveness: distinctive vs. nondistinctive middle item) × 2 (Replications 1 and 2) ANOVA, all independent variables being between-groups factors.

Free recall

Impression versus memory set It was hypothesized that subjects given impression formation instructions would evidence better recall of the stimulus items than would subjects in the memory condition. To test this hypothesis, the number of items *other than the middle item* recalled by each subject was determined, and these scores were used in the ANOVA. The middle item was omitted from these recall scores due to expected differential recall of the distinctive and nondistinctive middle items. The criterion for accurate recall of an item was fairly liberal. As indicated in the recall instructions, word-for-word accuracy was not necessary (and, in fact, was infrequently achieved). If the subject's recall of an item contained the primary concept or meaning expressed in the behavior description, it was scored as accurate recall.

As is clearly evident in figure 6.1, in both Experiments 1 and 2 subjects given impression formation instructions recalled more items than did memory condition subjects. The main effect for the processing set manipulation was highly significant in both Experiment 1, $F(1, 24)$

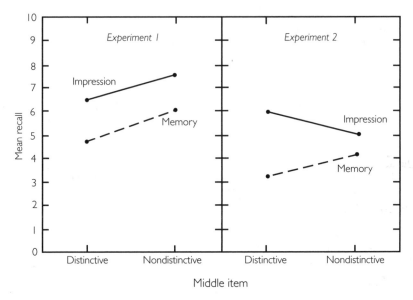

Figure 6.1 Mean number of items recalled in Experiments 1 and 2

= 7.57, $p < .02$, and Experiment 2, $F(1, 22) = 8.86$, $p < .01$. These results provide strong support for the hypothesis.

Effects of the distinctive item   It was hypothesized that the presence of a distinctive item would have a facilitating effect on recall in the impression formation condition and an interfering effect on recall in the memory condition. This hypothesis was tested by the interaction term of the ANOVA. The results of the two experiments differed somewhat and provided only weak support for the hypothesis. In Experiment 1 the interaction term did not approach significance, as indicated by the nearly parallel lines shown in the left panel of figure 6.1. Instead, a significant main effect for item distinctiveness, $F(1, 24) = 4.48$, $p < .05$, indicated that there was an interference effect due to the distinctive item in both the impression formation and memory conditions. The pattern of results obtained in Experiment 2 conformed more closely to the predicted findings, although the interaction term only weakly approached significance, $F(1, 22) = 2.52$, $p < .13$. Thus, although in both experiments the distinctive item tended to lower recall in the memory condition, its effects on recall in the impression formation condition were less consistent and inconclusive. In sum, the hypothesized effect of a distinctive item on free recall must be viewed with considerable caution.

Recall of middle item   Table 6.1 presents the percentage of subjects in each condition of Experiments 1 and 2 who recalled the middle item. In Experiment 1 the distinctive item was recalled by more subjects than was a nondistinctive middle item in both the impression formation and memory conditions ($p < .05$ and $p < .01$, respectively, by Fisher's exact probability test). In Experiment 2 this difference was evident only in the impression formation condition, although not significantly so ($p < .15$). The percentages shown for Experiment 2 suggest a possible interaction effect of the two independent variables on recall of the middle item. However, given the small sample sizes, a test of this interaction (cf. Langer and Abelson, 1972, pp. 28–9) was not significant.

Before–after discriminations
Accuracy   On the before–after discrimination task, subjects were asked to indicate, for each of the 14 context items, whether it came before or after the middle item in the stimulus sequence.

Table 6.1   Percentage of subjects who recalled key item: Experiments 1 and 2

	Middle item	
Processing set	*Distinctive*	*Nondistinctive*
Experiment 1		
Impression	87.5	25.0
Memory	100.0	25.0
Experiment 2		
Impression	71.4	28.6
Memory	37.5	28.6

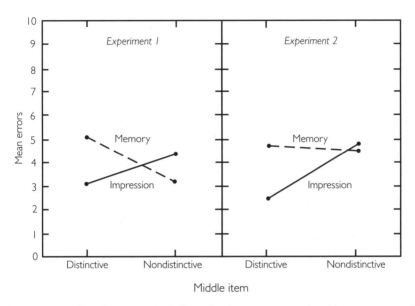

Figure 6.2   Mean number of errors on the before–after discrimination task in Experiments 1 and 2

It was predicted that subjects in the impression formation–distinctive item condition would make the fewest errors on this task. The hypothesis states that one cell of the design will differ significantly from the other three. To test this hypothesis, the number of errors made by each subject was determined and analyzed by an a priori contrast. As indicated in figure 6.2, the fewest errors in both experiments were made by subjects in the impression formation–distinctive item condition, as predicted. The a priori contrast for Experiment 1 was not significant, due to the unexpectedly (and unexplainably) high accuracy of subjects in the memory–nondistinctive item condition; because of this, the interaction term in the ANOVA was significant, $F(1, 24) = 7.24$, $p < .02$. In Experiment 2 the data fit the predicted pattern exactly, and the planned comparison was highly significant, $F(1, 24) = 7.16$, $p < .025$.

Confidence ratings   In Experiment 1 subjects rated their confidence in each of their before–after discrimination judgments. These ratings were summed across the 14 items for which the judgments were made. An ANOVA of these total confidence scores yielded no significant results.

Discussion

The first two experiments have provided clear evidence that subjects instructed to form an impression of a stimulus person on the basis of a series of behavior descriptions are subsequently able to recall more of those items than are subjects instructed to commit them to memory. This finding supports the view that forming an impression of a person inherently involves integration of the available items of information into some structural organization, that this process results in more extensively developed associations among those stimulus items, and that these associations ultimately facilitate later recall. In contrast, even though interitem associations may to some extent be formed in a memory task, such integration of items is not an inherent consequence of this task.

The role of a highly distinctive item in the formation of an impression or representation of a person remains unclear. The influence of the distinctive middle item on free recall differed somewhat in these two experiments and was not a powerful effect in either case. However, results of the before–after discrimination task indicated that impression formers in the distinctive item condition manifested the greatest degree of accuracy in both experiments; these subjects were able to accurately identify which items had preceded and which had followed the distinctive behavior description. These findings, although more suggestive than conclusive, are consistent with the view that in forming an impression, an attempt is made to relate each new piece of information to the others already processed and integrated into a continuously emerging representation of a person.

Experiment 3

In the first two studies, the key item whose distinctiveness was manipulated always occurred in the middle position of the stimulus sequence. The impact of a distinctive item may, however, differ depending on whether that item occurs relatively early, toward the middle, or relatively late in the stimulus sequence. In addition to providing a further test of the hypotheses investigated in the first two studies, Experiment 3 was designed to examine this possibility.

In both Experiments 1 and 2, recall performance of subjects in the memory condition was somewhat impaired when the stimulus list included a distinctive item. If this difference were due to the distinctive item disrupting rehearsal of other items in the list, then this effect should be greater when that item occurs early, rather than late, in the list, since in the latter case the preceding items would be well rehearsed before the disruptive influence occurs. Thus, varying the position of the distinctive item should result in differences in recall of the other items, with poorest recall when that item occurs early and improved recall as that item occurs later in the stimulus list.

In contrast, our assumptions about the impression formation process suggest an alternative outcome. In forming an impression, organization of information and formation of interitem associations should occur regardless of the distinctive item's position in the stimulus sequence. If so, then varying the position of the distinctive item should have little influence on recall of other items in the stimulus list.

In sum, several hypotheses were tested in Experiment 3. The two major hypotheses examined in Experiments 1 and 2 were tested again, namely (a) that subjects in the impression formation condition would recall more items than subjects in the memory condition and (b) that a distinctive item in the stimulus list would facilitate recall of impression formation subjects but impair recall for those in the memory condition. In addition, it was predicted (c) that the position of the distinctive item in the stimulus sequence would have little influence on recall in the impression formation condition, but in the memory condition it would impair recall more when it occurred early, as opposed to late, in the stimulus list.

Method

Subjects

The subjects in the experiment were 120 undergraduate students at the University of California at Santa Barbara (UCSB). All subjects received course credit for their participation. Subjects were run in small groups (1–6 persons) in the social psychology laboratories at UCSB.

Design

The major independent variables were processing set (impression formation vs. memory), key item (distinctive vs. nondistinctive), and position of key item (early, middle, late). There were 10 subjects in each cell of the resulting 2 × 2 × 3 design. In addition, two complete replication sets of both context sentences and key items (distinctive and nondistinctive) were constructed. In contrast to the previous experiments, in which each subject was presented with only one stimulus set, in this experiment two replications of the same stimulus condition were given to each subject. That is, subjects read a series of behavior descriptions, completed a filler task, and were administered the dependent measures, as in the previous studies. They were then given a second, totally different set of sentences, which represented a replication of the same stimulus condition they had received first, and after another filler task, completed the dependent measures with regard to this second stimulus sequence. Thus, in addition to the three major independent variables, there were two replication sets, and the order in which these sets were presented was counterbalanced.

To maintain comparability of the present analyses with those of the earlier studies and for substantive reasons to be indicated below, the primary results are based only on the first stimulus set that was presented to the subjects. Half of the subjects received Replication 1 first, and the other half received Replication 2 first. Thus, the design for the major analyses presented below was a 2 (processing set) × 2 (key item) × 3 (position of key item) × 2 (replication sets) ANOVA, with all factors being between-groups factors.

Stimulus materials

The stimulus sets presented to the subjects were similar to those used previously, although in this case the list consisted of 11, rather than 15, items. Two replications of 10 context sentences and of the distinctive and nondistinctive key items were developed. The position of the key item in the series of behavior descriptions was systematically varied. In the 11-item sequence, the key item occurred in either the 2nd, 6th (middle), or 10th position.

Procedure

The procedure for Experiment 3 was similar to that used in the previous experiments. The instructions administered to induce the impression formation versus memory processing set manipulation were essentially the same as those used in the first two studies. The stimulus sets, consisting of 11 sentence predicates, were presented in booklet form, one behavior description per page. Tape recorded instructions directed the subjects, at 8-sec intervals, to "turn to the next page." After a brief distracting task, subjects completed the dependent measures. At this point subjects were informed that they would be given a second set of behavior descriptions and were asked to perform the same tasks as they had just completed. The impression/memory instructions were readministered, and a second stimulus booklet was given. Each subject received a replication of the same Distinctiveness × Position of key item stimulus condition that he/she had received previously. The same dependent measures were administered following completion of the stimulus presentation. At the conclusion of this procedure, the purpose of the experiment was explained, and any questions the subjects had were answered.

Dependent measures

The dependent measures used in Experiment 1 were also used in Experiment 3: free recall, before–after discrimination task, and confidence ratings in the before–after judgments. On the before–after discrimination task, the key item identified in the instructions had, of course, actually occurred in either the 2nd, 6th, or 10th position in the 11-item sequence. Consequently, the instructions in this experiment simply identified the item as one of the phrases in the booklet (rather than as the "middle" item, as in the first two studies).

In addition, a series of other ratings was obtained in this study. The next page of the booklet had the following instructions at the top: "Consider that all of the sentences presented earlier described a single person. To what extent do you think you would like that person?" The first sentence of these instructions was necessary, since memory condition subjects presumably had not, up to this point, thought of the stimulus sentences as pertaining to the same person. This instruction led them to consider this possibility for the first time. These instructions were followed by two rating scales on which subjects indicated how much they would like the person and the extent to which they thought the series of sentences could describe a single person. Both of these ratings were made on 10-point scales with appropriate labels at the endpoints. The final page of the booklet contained 10 10-point trait rating scales. The 10 personality attributes to be rated were selected on the basis of the five factors reported by Norman (1963), two scales being included to represent each of the five factors.

Results and discussion

The presentation of the results will focus first on the analyses of the data obtained from the first stimulus replication to which the subjects responded. We will then turn to a consideration of some findings comparing results for the first and second stimulus sets.

Free recall

Impression versus memory set　The mean number of items recalled (excluding the key item) from the first stimulus set in each condition is shown in figure 6.3. As in the first two experiments, the main effect for processing set was significant, with greater recall evidenced by subjects in the impression formation than in the memory condition. Analysis of the data yielded a highly significant main effect, $F(1, 96) = 20.38$, $p < .01$. The mean number of items recalled by subjects in the impression formation condition was 5.50, compared to an average of 4.20 for the memory condition subjects. Thus, the major finding obtained in the first two experiments was replicated in Experiment 3.

Other effects　Experiment 3 provided another test of the hypothesis that the presence of a distinctive item in the stimulus list would facilitate recall of the other items in the impression formation condition, but would interfere with such recall in the memory condition. As in the first two studies, this hypothesis failed to receive statistical support (for the interaction of processing set and distinctiveness of the key item, $F < 1$).

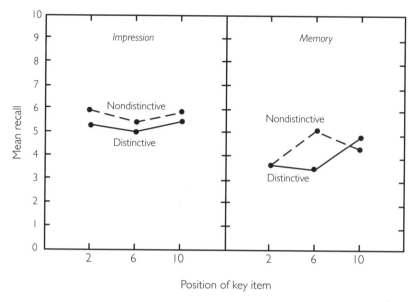

Figure 6.3 Mean number of items recalled in Experiment 3. (Data are from the first stimulus set only.)

It was hypothesized above that varying the position of the distinctive item would have differential effects in the impression formation and memory conditions. Although this manipulation was not expected to influence the recall performance of impression formation subjects, it was predicted that in the memory condition, performance would improve as the distinctive item occurred later in the stimulus sequence. Examination of the pattern of means in Figure 3 reveals some support for this hypothesis. However, the three-way interaction appropriate to testing the hypothesis was not statistically significant, $F(2, 96) = 1.25$, *ns*.

Recall of key item The percentage of subjects in the impression formation and memory conditions who recalled the key item (distinctive or nondistinctive) is shown in table 6.2. In the impression formation condition, the distinctive key item was recalled by significantly more subjects than was the nondistinctive key item, $\chi^2(1) = 8.30, p < .01$, but this difference did not occur in the memory condition. The interaction of processing set and distinctiveness on recall of the key item was highly significant ($Z = 2.66, p < .01$). The position in which the key item occurred had little influence on whether or not it was recalled.

Thus, the distinctive item was recalled by most subjects if they were given an impression formation set but not if given memory instructions. This pattern, which was also observed in Experiment 2 (though nonsignificantly so), has two interesting implications. First, the failure of memory condition subjects to recall the distinctive item suggests that this manipulation was ineffective in this condition. If so, then the weak evidence for the interfering effects of a distinctive item on recall of items is not surprising. Second, the fact that the distinctive item *was* recalled by most impression formation subjects suggests that this manipulation of distinctiveness may be context bound. That is, perhaps the negative behavior described in this item

Table 6.2 Percentage of subjects who recalled key item: Experiment 3

	Key item	
Processing set	*Distinctive*	*Nondistinctive*
Impression	76.7	40.0
Memory	43.3	53.3

was distinctive only when considered in the context of (i.e., in relation to) the neutral and mildly desirable behaviors described in the other items. If so, then this pattern of findings can be viewed as indirect evidence of the greater integrative activity hypothesized for impression formations, as compared to memory, condition subjects.

Before–after discriminations

Accuracy   The number of errors made on the before–after discrimination task was determined for each subject. Analysis of these data yielded a significant main effect due to position of the key item, $F(2, 96) = 8.84, p < .01$. Subjects made significantly fewer errors when the key item occurred in the second position, a result reflecting the salience of items occurring early in a stimulus sequence. In addition, the three-way Processing Set × Distinctiveness × Position of Key Item interaction was of borderline significance, $F(2, 96) = 3.03, p < .10$. This interaction was due primarily to the near perfect performance of impression formation subjects when a distinctive item occurred early in the list and the particularly poor performance of memory condition subjects when a nondistinctive item occurred late in the stimulus sequence.

In the first two studies, when the key item occurred in the middle position, superior performance was observed in the impression formation–distinctive item condition. This finding was not replicated in this experiment.

Confidence   For each before–after judgment, subjects rated their confidence in that judgment being correct. The average of each subject's confidence ratings was then determined. Subjects in the impression formation condition expressed greater confidence (M = 7.62) in the before–after judgments than did subjects in the memory condition (M = 6.76), $F(1, 96) = 4.48, p < .05$.

Ratings of stimulus persons

Subjects rated the stimulus person on a series of 10 trait scales, rated their liking for the person described by the sentences, and rated the extent to which the items could reasonably describe a single person. Two analyses were performed to examine the subjects' overall evaluative perceptions of the stimulus person. Each subject's ratings on the 10 trait scales were summed and used as a general measure of the evaluative character of the subject's inferences about the person. In addition, the liking ratings were analyzed as an indicator of the subject's personal affective reaction to the stimulus person. Neither of these analyses produced any substantively interesting findings. Other than one effect due to differences between replication sets, the only significant result was a main effect due to item distinctiveness: As one would expect, subjects gave less desirable trait ratings to the person described by a negative distinctive behavior. Finally, the analysis of ratings on the "single person" scale yielded no significant results.

Differences between first and second stimulus set data

The processing set manipulation used throughout this series of experiments leads subjects to expect that they will be performing different kinds of tasks. For subjects in the impression formation condition who expect to be asked about the target person's personality, the recall task comes as a surprise. Similarly, memory condition subjects, expecting that they will be asked to retrieve the stimulus information, do not anticipate having to make personality ratings. When another stimulus set is presented following completion of the dependent measures, all subjects have in common the knowledge of what tasks they will be asked to perform. Our intuition was that this difference between the first and second sets could have an important impact on how the stimulus descriptions were processed by the two groups of subjects. Impression formation subjects, knowing that they would have to recall the items, might alter their strategy in processing this information. Similarly, memory condition subjects, knowing that they would have to rate a stimulus person described by the items, might process the items with that task in mind. If these intuitions are correct, then the distinction between these two processing sets might be undermined for the second stimulus set.

In Experiment 3 this question was examined empirically by presenting subjects with two stimulus sets, the second one being a replication of the stimulus condition presented in the first set. The design of the experiment then becomes a 2 (processing set) $\times$ 2 (key item) $\times$ 3 (position of key item) $\times$ 2 (order of replications) $\times$ 2 (replication sets) design, with repeated measures on the last factor. The Order $\times$ Replication interaction in the ANOVA represents differences on a dependent measure as a function of having already completed a previous stimulus set. For several of the dependent measures, this interaction term was highly significant. Thus, it cannot be assumed that the data from the second stimulus set show the same pattern as in the first. It is for this reason that the presentation of the findings of this experiment has focused on results based only on the subjects' responses to the first stimulus set.

A detailed report of the findings from this analysis would be of tangential interest and hence will not be presented. However, one potentially interesting finding was obtained, though its interpretation must remain somewhat speculative. On the dependent variable of primary interest, free recall, the three-way Processing Set $\times$ Order $\times$ Replication interaction was highly significant, $F(1, 96) = 17.57, p < .01$. In effect, this result indicates that the difference between the impression and memory conditions differed for the two stimulus sets. The data from this analysis have been collapsed into first and second stimulus sets received (combining order and replication), and the mean number of items recalled by impression and memory subjects for each set is shown in figure 6.4. The left half of this figure shows the recall means reported earlier, indicating that in the first stimulus set they received, impression formation subjects recalled more items than did those in the memory condition. In their subsequent recall of items from the second stimulus set, however, the difference between these two groups was trivial. More specifically, subjects in the memory condition improved dramatically, whereas the performance of impression subjects was almost identical to their level of recall for the first stimulus set.

Although there may be several explanations for why recall performance in the memory group would improve while that of the impression subjects would remain stable, this pattern of results can be interpreted as consistent with the processes described in the Introduction to

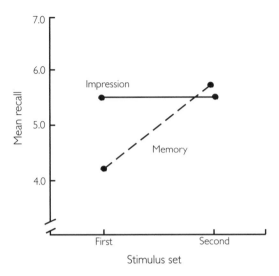

Figure 6.4   Mean number of items recalled for first and second stimulus sets in Experiment 3

this article. Specifically, we would suggest that in processing the information from the first stimulus set, the impression formation subjects developed associations among the items that facilitated recall, resulting in performance superior to that of the memory subjects, who may have used various other cognitive-processing tactics (e.g., rehearsal, memorization of key words, etc.) that result in interitem connections being formed to a lesser extent. However, after the dependent measures for the first stimulus set had been completed, and thus when the second set was presented, *all* subjects were aware that the questionnaire measures would require that they make ratings of a person described by these behavior descriptions. Consequently, in processing the items from the second (but not the first) stimulus set, memory subjects may have regarded the items as describing a common object – a person they would be asked to rate. In effect, the memory subjects may have been processing the stimulus information in much the same way as those in the impression formation group, thus producing more interitem associations than they had for the first stimulus set. This would result in the improved recall performance shown in figure 6.4. In the impression formation condition, on the other hand, the task requirements clearly included this integrative activity for both stimulus sets, resulting in a consistent level of performance.

General Discussion

The most consistent finding obtained in the three experiments reported above was the superior recall of impression formation subjects, as compared to those in the memory condition. The main effect for this processing set manipulation was highly significant in each experiment. These results provide strong support for the primary hypothesis underlying this research.

At first glance this finding may seem rather surprising. After all, memory condition subjects were told that the study was concerned with memory processes, instructions that strongly implied that they subsequently would be asked to remember the items presented to them. Impression formation subjects, on the other hand, were simply told to form an impression and hence had no "advance warning" that a recall task would be forthcoming. However, this result follows directly from the assumption we made at the outset – that the process of forming an impression inherently involves integrating the available information into an organized cognitive representation of the target person. Such organization of information would facilitate later retrieval of the individual descriptive items.

Even though we have interpreted this finding as reflecting differences between processing set conditions in information organization, other explanations cannot be ruled out. For example, the instructional manipulation may have induced impression formation subjects to attempt to comprehend the meaning of the items to a greater extent than memory condition subjects, who may have simply focused on retaining the exact wording of the items. The liberal criterion used in scoring recall (i.e., word-for-word accuracy was not necessary) may then have favored subjects in the impression condition. This explanation suggests that use of a more stringent recall criterion might reduce differences between these conditions in recall performance. Although this possibility cannot be totally dispelled, its viability is questioned by two observations. First, perfect word-for-word accuracy occurred relatively infrequently in the recall protocols; use of this criterion would result in low recall scores in both impression formation and memory conditions. Second, in Experiment 3 recall scores were also determined according to a criterion requiring closer (though not perfect) accuracy to the original wording than our more liberal criterion. Analysis of these data yielded results essentially identical to those reported above.

A number of theoretical perspectives can be adopted in thinking about the integrative, organizing process we have discussed. For example, a network model of memory (e.g., Anderson and Bower, 1973) might view the items as associated through their common linkages with a "person node" around which information about the target person is organized (see Hastie and Kumar, 1979, pp. 32–4, for an illustration of how such a model might be conceptualized). Alternatively, schema theory (cf. Rumelhart and Ortony, 1977) might conceive of the acquired information as organized into various schematic data structures. In this case items would be associated with each other through their being stored together in the same location in memory. The present experiments do not provide an empirical basis for evaluating the relative usefulness of these (or other) theoretical orientations. In either case, however, the resulting organization produces the consequence that recall of one item facilitates retrieval of other descriptive items with which it has come to be associated in memory. It is this organization that we believe is a natural consequence of the impression formation process.

In contrast to the impact of the processing set manipulation, the manipulation of item distinctiveness had surprisingly little effect on free recall performance. We had sought to use, as distinctive items, behaviors that were distinctive in their own right as infrequently occurring acts. Failure of memory subjects to differentially recall these items suggests that this manipulation was ineffective, at least in this condition. If so, then the lack of any systematic effect of distinctiveness on recall in the memory condition is understandable. We had also hypothesized that distinctive information would facilitate recall in the impression condition, but no support for this prediction was obtained. The fact that the distinctive items were to some extent evaluatively inconsistent with the context in which they were embedded may have prevented these items from serving as a focal point for the organization of information, as we expected. Perhaps the use of items of information that are distinctive but not evaluatively inconsistent with other items would have produced results providing stronger support for the hypothesis.

Although the distinctive item had little effect on recall of other stimulus items, the probability of recall was consistently higher for a distinctive than for a nondistinctive key item in the impression formation condition. Similar results have been reported by Hastie and Kumar (1979). Such findings indicate that distinctive information about a person is more likely to be retained and incorporated in the perceiver's cognitive representation of the person.

The results of these experiments provide encouraging support for the general perspective underlying the present approach to understanding impression development. Nevertheless, it is clear that a number of questions remain that will need to be addressed in future research. For example, given the sizable and consistent difference in recall performance of subjects in the impression formation and memory conditions, it becomes important to determine where, in the processing of information, the memory and impression formation processes diverge. Intuitively, it seems probable that a large part of the organizational activity involved in impression development occurs during the encoding of information into memory. However, additional organizing processes may continue after information input has been completed and may even occur as a part of the retrieval process. This issue remains unresolved at the present time. Second, future studies will need to go beyond the present research in investigating the organization of information more directly, perhaps by applying methods that cognitive psychologists have developed for studying subjective organization to this topic. Finally, we need to determine the relationship of findings obtained in this approach to investigating conceptions of persons, using free recall and related tasks, to existing knowledge about impression formation, based largely on research using evaluative judgments. The linkages between how information becomes organized and stored in a cognitive representation of a person and the nature of the perceiver's judgments about that person, both of which are based on the same information, is an unresolved issue that will require attention.

NOTES

This research was supported by National Institute of Mental Health Grant 29418 to the first author. The authors express their appreciation to Julie Cho-Polizzi, Terrence Rose, and William Trochim for their assistance in the collection and analysis of the data. They are also grateful to Terrence Rose for his helpful comments on an earlier version of the manuscript.

[1] In both of these studies, additional experimental conditions proved to be uninformative, and discussion of their results would be irrelevant for present purposes. Hence, in the interests of brevity and ease of presentation, only the overlapping portions of these experiments are reported here.

REFERENCES

Anderson, J.R., and Bower, G.H. *Human associative memory*. Washington, DC: Winston, 1973.

Anderson, N.H. Information integration theory: A brief survey. In D. Krantz, R.C. Atkinson, R.D. Luce, and P. Suppes (eds), *Contemporary developments in mathematical psychology* (vol. 2). San Francisco: Freeman, 1974.

Bransford, J.D., and Johnson, M.K. Considerations of some problems of comprehension. In W.G. Chase (ed.), *Visual information processing*. New York: Academic Press, 1973.

Hastie, R., and Kumar, P.A. Person memory: Personality traits as organizing principles in memory for behaviors. *Journal of Personality and Social Psychology*, 1979, 37, 25–38.

Jaccard, J.J., and Fishbein, M. Inferential beliefs and order effects in personality impression formation. *Journal of Personality and Social Psychology*, 1975, 31, 1031–41.

Langer, E.J., and Abelson, R.P. The semantics of asking a favor: How to succeed in getting help without really dying. *Journal of Personality and Social Psychology*, 1972, 24, 26–32.

Lingle, J.H., Geva, N., Ostrom, T.M., Leippe, M.R., and Baumgardner, M.H. Thematic effects of person judgments on impression organization. *Journal of Personality and Social Psychology*, 1979, 37, 674–87.

Norman, W.T. Toward an adequate taxonomy of personality attributes: Replicated factor structure in peer nomination personality ratings. *Journal of Abnormal and Social Psychology*, 1963, 66, 574–83.

Rumelhart, D.E., and Ortony, A. The representation of knowledge in memory. In R.C. Anderson, R.J. Spiro, and W.E. Montague (eds), *Schooling and the acquisition of knowledge*. Hillsdale, NJ: Erlbaum, 1977.

Smith, E.E., Adams, N., and Schorr, D. Fact retrieval and the paradox of interference. *Cognitive Psychology*, 1978, 10, 438–64.

Wallace, W.P. Review of the historical, empirical, and theoretical status of the von Restorff phenomenon. *Psychological Bulletin*, 1965, 63, 410–24.

Reconstructing the past: Some cognitive consequences of person perception

M. Snyder and S.W. Uranowitz

- - - - -
Editors'
Introduction
- - - - - - - -

Theoretical Background

The theory and methods of social cognition have contributed greatly to our understanding of how social stereotypes function (see Hamilton, 1981; Macrae et al., 1996). This article by Snyder and Uranowitz deals with one of the cognitive processes by which, in principle, stereotypes can be maintained (see also the reading by Darley and Gross, chapter 5). But it also shows how carefully hypotheses have to be tested.

One of the most important contributions of the social cognition perspective on stereotyping was to view stereotypes as a kind of 'schema', in terms of which information about other persons is processed. A schema is an abstract knowledge structure, stored in memory, that specifies the defining features and relevant attributes of a stimulus domain, and the interrelations among those attributes (Fiske and Taylor, 1991). If stereotypes are viewed as a type of schema, then the activation of a group stereotype should have the same general effects as the activation of any schema. Thus a great deal of research has investigated how stereotypes influence information processing in a 'top-down' fashion. According to schema theory, the activation of a schema of a social group should influence what aspects of the available information are attended to, how that information is encoded and interpreted, and what information will be available for later

Journal of Personality and Social Psychology (1978), 36:941–50.

retrieval from memory. Of particular importance, information that fits our stereotypic expectations would appear more likely to enter the information-processing system, where it is stored and represented within the organized structure of a stereotypic schema.

Snyder and Uranowitz were interested in the 'reconstructive process', whereby information retrieved from memory may be distorted in the direction of a stereotype activated *after* the information was presented. According to schema theory, people should use their knowledge structures when asked to decide whether a given piece of information has or has not been seen before. So Snyder and Uranowitz got subjects to read a short life history of a woman named Betty K. Either immediately after or one week after reading the story, subjects were told either that Betty K. was a lesbian, or that she was heterosexual. Another group of subjects was not told anything about her sexual preferences. Would the later knowledge of Betty K's sexual orientation have a retrospective effect on memory, causing subjects selectively to bring to mind some information, but to 'repress' other behaviours and incidents?

Hypothesis

This study tested the hypothesis that perceivers would 'reconstruct' the earlier-presented information to confirm the later-presented labels.

Design

The core experimental design was two-factor, between-subjects: 2 (sexual orientation of label: lesbian/heterosexual) × 2 (timing of label: immediate/delayed). Thus there were four main experimental conditions, two levels of each independent variable. There was also a no-label control condition (subjects learned nothing about Betty K.'s lifestyle). Finally, there were two 'fabrication conditions': in these latter conditions participants *who had not read the case history* were given the same set of questions as other subjects, but asked to answer which were most likely true in the case of an individual given only that her name was 'Betty K.' and she was living *either* a lesbian *or* a heterosexual lifestyle. Thus there were seven different conditions in all.

Method

Subjects all read exactly the same case history about the life of a woman ('Betty K.') and were asked to form an impression of her. The story was cleverly written so that it could fit with either image of Betty K. Subjects in the four experimental conditions learned after the case history that Betty K. was living either a lesbian or a heterosexual lifestyle; approximately half these subjects learned this information immediately after reading the case history, and the remaining subjects learned it one week later. At the second session, one week later, recognition memory was assessed with thirty-six multiple-choice questions. A fifth group of subjects read the case history, but learned nothing about Betty K's lifestyle, and then completed the same recognition test. The sixth and seventh groups of subjects read no case history, but then indicated which of the thirty-six answers were likely to be true for either a lesbian or a heterosexual Betty K., respectively.

Results

Of the thirty-six multiple-choice items, seventeen contained response alternatives relevant to the lesbian/heterosexual stereotype (according to a panel of seven 'judges' who had no access to the case history). Only these seventeen 'critical' items are used in the analyses, which showed interesting effects of the label but not of its presentation time (immediate/delayed).

Manipulation check

Footnote 12 in the article reveals that the final item in the memory questionnaire was a check on Betty K.'s sexual lifestyle. Since all subjects in the experimental conditions responded correctly, the label manipulation was clearly successful.

Impact of stereotypes on reconstruction

A 2 × 2 analysis of variance (ANOVA) revealed an effect of the label on how stereotypically subjects responded (see top line of table 6.3). Subjects who learned that Betty K. was living a lesbian lifestyle reconstructed the events of her life in a manner that reflected stereotyped beliefs to a greater extent than did subjects who learned she was living a heterosexual lifestyle. Surprisingly, this effect held whether subjects were given the label either immediately or one week later. A planned comparison (comparing columns 1 and 2 with column 5 in table 6.3) also showed that the answers of lesbian-label subjects were more stereotypical than those of subjects who received no information.

'Lesbian errors' and 'heterosexual errors'

Subjects in the lesbian-label condition made more recognition errors that indicated impending lesbianism in the events of the life history than did subjects in the heterosexual-label condition (similarly, heterosexual-label subjects made more 'heterosexual errors'). Thus when subjects erred in answering questions, their errors reflected their recently acquired assumptions about Betty K.'s sexual preference.

'Lesbian accuracy' and 'heterosexual accuracy'

Those subjects who had read the heterosexual label for Betty K. were significantly more likely to be accurate on label-consistent (i.e. heterosexual) items than were subjects assigned the lesbian label.

Reconstruction or fabrication?

To try to rule out the possibility that answers reflected guessing or fabrication, the authors had assigned some subjects to complete the questions without seeing the case history, but having been told that Betty K. was lesbian or heterosexual. As the last two columns of table 6.3 show, subjects in these two conditions did not give reliably different answers. Apparently, the label itself – in the absence of the case history – is not sufficient to generate the stereotypically biased pattern of responding.

Discussion

Fascinating as these results are, and clever as the design appears to be, Snyder and Uranowitz's claim to have demonstrated a reconstructive bias has been challenged on methodological grounds. Although memory researchers acknowledge that recognition measures are the most sensitive tests of what information subjects have seen before or not (see Srull, 1984), they are easily contaminated by response biases. Subjects may *guess* which items they have seen before or not, and they tend to guess more in the direction of schema-consistent than inconsistent items, whenever they are not perfectly sure about the information (see Stangor and McMillan, 1992).

Bellezza and Bower (1981) therefore replicated the Betty K. study, including measures of both accuracy of memory retrieval and response bias (using a signal-detection-theory approach). They found no effects of the label on recognition. There was, however, a response-bias effect: when unsure, subjects were likely to guess in the direction of the label (stereotype) they had received (see also Clark and Woll, 1981).

Despite these qualifications further Betty K. investigations using different measures (free recall and retrospective interpretation) do point to a reconstructive bias (see Snyder, 1984). Social perceivers are apparently very adept at interpreting almost any information in line with their activated stereotype, and this is a process by which stereotypes could be maintained.

FURTHER READING

Bellezza, F.S. and Bower, G.H. (1981). Person stereotypes and memory for people. *Journal of Personality and Social Psychology*, 41, 856–65. An important follow-up study which shows why recognition-memory data must be analyzed with controls to rule out the effects of guessing.
Snyder, M. (1984). When belief creates reality. In L. Berkowitz (ed.), *Advances in Experimental Social Psychology* (vol. 18, pp. 247–305). New York: Academic Press. A fascinating overview of Snyder's many studies in this domain, which sets the original 'Betty K.' study in a wider context.

REFERENCES

Clark, L.F. and Woll, S.B. (1981). Stereotype biases: A reconstructive analysis of their role in reconstructive memory. *Journal of Personality and Social Psychology*, 41, 1064–72.
Fiske, S.T. and Taylor, S.E. (1991). *Social Cognition* (2nd edn). New York: McGraw-Hill.
Hamilton, D.L. (ed.) (1981). *Cognitive Processes in Stereotyping and Intergroup Behavior*. Hillsdale, NJ: Erlbaum.

Macrae, C.N., Stangor, C. and Hewstone, M. (eds) (1996). *Stereotypes and Stereotyping*. New York: Guilford.
Srull, T.K. (1984). Methodological techniques for the study of person memory and social cognition. In R.S. Wyer Jr and T.K. Srull (eds), *Handbook of Social Cognition* (vol. 2, pp. 1–72). Hillsdale, NJ: Erlbaum.
Stangor, C. and McMillan, D. (1992). Memory for expectancy-congruent and expectancy-incongruent information: A review of the social and social developmental literature. *Psychological Bulletin*, 111, 42–61.

We do not first see, then define,
we define first and then see.

Walter Lippmann

With few exceptions, most students of person perception have endorsed the view that individuals construct images of other people in ways that serve to stabilize, make predictable, and make manageable their view of the social world (e.g., Heider, 1958; Jones and Davis, 1965; Kelley, 1972). To the extent that we attribute stable traits and enduring dispositions to other people, we may feel better able to understand their actions and to predict their future behavior. Moreover, we may use these beliefs to guide our behavioral interactions with them.

Primary
Reading

Much as we may prefer to live in a stable and predictable social world, events can and do lead us to change even the most firmly entrenched impressions of other individuals. Often, we are confronted with evidence so credible that it forces a new interpretation of a person's characteristic nature. Having known Mike since childhood, we may just now learn that he is a psychopathic confidence artist, a silver-tongued swindler, well-versed in the arts of deception, fraud, and manipulation. This information may precipitate a review of our past interactions with Mike in search of events that provide further evidence consistent with our new knowledge about him. Having now labeled him as a con artist, it may be all too easy to selectively bring to mind a variety of behaviors and incidents that may have been insufficient in and of themselves to warrant such an interpretation but that, in the light of our current knowledge, do seem to support an inference of psychopathic criminality. Mike's personal life history thus may be selectively rewritten to support our current interpretations of his character.

Such processes of *reconstruction* of past events may be a rich source of evidence with which to bolster present beliefs. In continuing and long-term social relationships, individuals may have access to extensive historical information about those with whom they have had extended interaction. When new information precipitates a shift in beliefs, knowledge of past events may serve as fertile ground for reconstructive processes that bolster and augment current impressions about another individual.

Memory researchers have long emphasized the role of active constructive processes in remembering (e.g., Bartlett, 1932; Bower, 1976; Bransford, Barclay, and Franks, 1972; Gauld and Stephenson, 1967; Loftus, 1975; Loftus and Palmer, 1974; Mandler and Johnson, 1977; Spiro, 1976). According to this viewpoint, we do not remember an event by activating or "replaying" some fixed memory trace. Rather, we construct a schematic representation of our past experience by piecing together remembered bits and pieces with new facts that we (knowingly or unknowingly) supply to flesh out or augment our emerging knowledge of the past. In particular, much attention has focused on the role of thematic information in memory for stories and narratives. However, researchers have been more successful in demonstrating the role of themes presented at a narrative's *outset* in encoding and organizational processes. There has been less attention devoted to uncovering the role of thematic information presented *after* narratives in retrieval and retrospective reconstructive processes of the type with which we are concerned (e.g., Bransford and Johnson, 1972; Dooling and Christiaansen, 1977; Dooling and Mullett, 1973; Thorndyke, 1977). Moreover, conspicuously neglected within this tradition is the process of greatest interest to students of person perception and social cognition: reconstruction precipitated by, and in support of, newly acquired beliefs about another individual. From the social psychologist's viewpoint, this reconstructive process is of particular importance when it is guided by social stereotypes.

Social stereotypes are a special case of interpersonal knowledge. Stereotypes are usually simple, overgeneralized, and widely accepted. However, stereotypes are often highly inaccurate. Nonetheless, stereotypes can and do influence information processing such that new evidence that confirms these stereotypes is more easily noticed and more easily stored in memory than is nonconfirming evidence (e.g., Berman and Kenny, 1976; Cantor and Mischel, 1977; Chapman and Chapman, 1967, 1969; Zadny and Gerard, 1974; Cohen, note 1; Hamilton, note 2; Rothbart, note 3). Clearly, stereotypes exert *prospective* or "before-the-facts" influences on the encoding and storage of later-learned social information. By contrast, little or nothing is known about the *retrospective* or "after-the-facts" influence of stereotypes on attempts to remember previously learned events. For, to the extent that individuals selectively retrieve information that bolsters current stereotypic interpretations about another person, reconstructive processes may serve to perpetuate acceptance of widely held but essentially inaccurate social stereotypes (cf. Ross, Lepper, and Hubbard, 1975).

To probe reconstructive processes in person perception, we conducted the following investigation of the impact of new stereotype-based beliefs about another person on recognition memory for past events consistent and inconsistent with those new beliefs. Individuals read identical life histories that were later followed by information that induced different interpretations of the main character. We assessed the extent to which individuals reconstructed the factual information of the life history to confirm and support these new interpretations.

Method

Participants

Two hundred twelve male and female undergraduates enrolled in introductory psychology courses at the University of Minnesota participated in this investigation for course credit.

Procedure

Participants first read an extensive case history narrative about the life of a woman. Although all participants read the identical case history, some participants *later* learned that the woman was currently living a lesbian life-style (lesbian label), other participants learned that she was living a heterosexual life-style (heterosexual label), and still others learned nothing about her current life-style (no label). Some participants received this labeling information immediately after reading the case history (immediate label), and others learned of her sexuality 1 week after reading the case history (delayed label). The effects of these manipulations on recognition memory for factual information about the woman's life were measured 1 week after the participants had read the case history.

Case history

When participants arrived at the experimental room, they learned that in order to investigate "the way individuals form impressions of other people," they would be reading a story about one individual's life, with only "names and places . . . changed to conceal the person's identity." They were "to form a complete impression of the person" in anticipation of answering "questions about your reactions to this person" at a later session.

Participants then read a 746-word narrative about events in the life of a woman named Betty K. The case history followed Betty K. from birth through childhood, education, and choice of profession. It provided information about the climate of her early home life, her relationship with her parents, her social life in high school and in college, and so on. We carefully constructed Betty K.'s life history to "fit" either the lesbian or the heterosexual outcome; for example, although she never had a steady boyfriend in high school, she did go out on dates. The case history also contained information outside the domain of sexuality; for example, names of her friends, schools, and towns in which she lived.[1] After reading the case history, participants were instructed "to spend a few minutes thinking about your impressions of this person. Go over the story in your mind, to work out your overall impression of this person."

Although all participants had read the identical case history, some participants later learned new facts that constituted the retrospective labeling manipulation. Participants in the lesbian label conditions ($n = 60$) learned that "during her senior year, Betty met a lesbian who introduced her to homosexual activity. Betty felt exhilarated and that she had finally found herself, and went on to a successful medical career living with her lesbian mate. She found life in general very satisfying." Participants in the heterosexual label conditions ($n = 60$) learned that "during her senior year, Betty met a man who introduced her to sexual activity. Betty felt exhilarated and that she had finally found herself. She married this man and went on to a successful medical career living with her husband. She found life in general very satisfying." Orthogonal to the label manipulation, participants in the immediate label conditions ($n = 62$) received this labeling information immediately after reading the case history; those in the delayed label conditions ($n = 58$) learned of Betty's sexual life-style 1 week after reading the case history but before the memory assessment. Participants in the no-label condition ($n = 30$) learned nothing about Betty K.'s current sexual life-style.

Memory measure

One week after they had read the case history, participants were instructed to remember as accurately as possible factual details of Betty K.'s life history.[2] Recognition memory measures were obtained from answers to 36 multiple-choice questions that dealt with factual information in the case history. Each multiple-choice question had four possible answers: The first three provided possible substantive information; the fourth alternative was to be used if the participant believed that no relevant information had been provided in the case history. Some questions concerned Betty K.'s attitudes toward males and females, her dating habits in high school and college, and her relationship with her parents. These items probed memory for factual material within domains thought to be relevant to sexual preference; for example:

In high school, Betty
(a)   occasionally dated men.
(b)   never went out with men.
(c)   went steady.
(d)   No information provided.

Other questions bore no possible relationship to her sexuality; for example, names of her friends, schools, and towns in which she lived. These items made possible an assessment of memory for information outside the domain of beliefs about sexuality; for example:

The name of Betty's high school guidance counselor was
(a)   Mrs. Pennington.
(b)   Mrs. Griffin.
(c)   Mrs. Lincoln.
(d)   No information provided.

In all cases, participants believed that they were being tested for *accuracy* of memory for *factual* information contained in the case history that they had read the previous week.

Fabrication comparison conditions

In two comparison conditions, participants *who had never read the case history* were asked to answer the 36 multiple-choice questions as best they could, simply given the one fact that a specific individual named Betty K. currently was living a lesbian life-style (lesbian fabrication condition, $n = 30$) or a heterosexual life-style (heterosexual fabrication condition, $n = 30$). These individuals knew that each question referred to factual information in an actual case history. It was their task to identify the answers most likely to have been true of the specific individual named Betty K. Thus, it was *not* their task to demonstrate their abstract knowledge of general stereotypes about female sexuality, but rather to identify concrete facts in the actual life of one specific person. For it was our intent, in these comparison conditions, to create circumstances that resembled the experimental conditions in all respects save exposure to the case history. Thus, by contrast with the experimental conditions, which permitted an assessment of the differential influence of the heterosexual and lesbian labels on recognition memory, the fabrication comparison conditions permitted an assessment of the differential influence of information about Betty K.'s sexual life-style in the *absence* of any actual memory for the factual events in her life history.

Results

Sets of "stereotyped lesbian" and "stereotyped heterosexual" answers to the multiple-choice questions were constructed by a panel of seven undergraduate rater–judges. They were asked to indicate, for each question, which response alternatives tended to indicate impending lesbianism, which alternatives tended to indicate impending heterosexuality, and which alternatives were "neutral" regarding sexuality, assuming the existence of general cultural stereotypes. Rater–judges had no access to the case history itself. They were specifically instructed to ignore both the accuracy of these stereotypes and their own personal beliefs in that domain. It was their task to demonstrate the extent of their *knowledge* of general stereotypes but *not* to demonstrate the extent of their *endorsement* of these stereotyped conceptions.[3] Response alterna-tives that were judged by the majority (four or more) of the rater–judges as stereotypically lesbian were assigned a rating of 3. Those response alternatives judged as stereotypically heterosexual by the majority were assigned a rating of 1. Response alternatives that the majority of the rater–judges categorized as "neutral" were assigned a rating of 2. According to the rater–judges, 17 of the 36 questionnaire items contained response alternatives relevant to stereotyped images of lesbian and heterosexual women.[4] For example, according to the stere-otype identified by the rater–judges, the lesbian woman had an abusive father, never had a steady boyfriend, never dated men, and was rather unattractive. By contrast, the stereotyped image of the heterosexual woman dictated that she had a tranquil childhood, often dated men, had a steady boyfriend in high school, and was rather attractive.[5]

With this information about preconceptions of female sexuality in hand, it was then possible for us to assess the extent to which participants had reconstructed Betty K.'s life history in support of their current beliefs about her sexual orientation. The rater–judges' stereotypes were used to construct separate but related measures that assessed the influence of current lesbian and heterosexual labels on answers to questions about previously learned factual information.

Impact of stereotypes on reconstruction

We first constructed, for each participant, a measure of the extent to which his or her answers to the 17 critical items (that had been identified by the rater–judges) reflected stereotyped beliefs about sexuality. This stereotype score could range from 1.00 (all answers indicated stereotypic heterosexuality) to 3.00 (all answers were stereotypically lesbian) for each partici-pant.[6] This measure, the means for which are displayed in the first row of table 6.3, provides clear evidence of the influence of contemporary information about Betty K.'s sexuality on answers to factual questions about previously learned events in her life. A 2 (lesbian label–heterosexual label) $\times$ 2 (immediate label–delayed label) unweighted-means analysis of variance yielded a highly reliable main effect of the experimental label manipulation, $F(1, 116) = 10.34$ $p < .002$.

Participants who learned that Betty K. was living a lesbian life-style reconstructed the events of her life in a manner that reflected stereotyped beliefs about lesbians ($M = 2.22$) to a greater extent than did participants who learned that she was living a heterosexual life-style ($M = 2.12$). A planned comparison also revealed that the pattern of answers of participants who learned that Betty K. was currently living a lesbian life-style was more stereotypically lesbian than that of participants in the no-label condition, $F(1, 145) = 8.27$, $p < .005$.[7] However, participants who learned that Betty K. was living a heterosexual life-style did not differ, on this measure, from participants in the no-label condition, $F(1, 145) = .784$, *ns*.

Stereotype scores were *not* noticeably affected by the timing of the information about Betty K.'s current sexual life-style, $F(1, 116) = .32$, *ns*. Whether participants learned this information immediately after reading the case history narrative or 1 week later, they manifested the same pattern of reconstruction of the events of Betty K.'s life history.

Our analysis of the stereotype scores suggests that our participants reconstructed Betty K.'s past in ways that bolstered and supported their current stereotyped interpretations of her sexual life-style. However, two processes may underlie our measure of the extent to which partici-pants' answers reflected stereotyped beliefs about sexuality: (a) differential *error* of recognition

Table 6.3   Reconstruction of the life history narrative

| Response type | Lesbian label | | Heterosexual label | | No label (n = 30) | Lesbian fabrication (n = 30) | Heterosexual fabrication (n = 30) |
	Immediate outcome (n = 31)	Delayed outcome (n = 29)	Immediate outcome (n = 31)	Delayed outcome (n = 29)			
Stereotype score[a]							
M	2.20	2.24	2.12	2.11	2.15	2.21	2.17
SD	.15	.23	.16	.17	.17	.26	.23
Lesbian errors[b]							
M	.541	.546	.401	.415	.515	.507	.462
SD	.219	.213	.242	.198	.205	.178	.137
Heterosexual errors[c]							
M	.186	.195	.287	.275	.234	.254	.269
SD	.175	.184	.165	.222	.170	.124	.100
Lesbian accuracy[d]							
M	.302	.336	.308	.294	.315	.416	.452
SD	.087	.114	.127	.101	.101	.189	.202
Heterosexual accuracy[e]							
M	.237	.236	.326	.333	.253	.244	.259
SD	.101	.114	.123	.071	.099	.167	.199

[a] Range = 1.00 to 3.00. Higher means indicate a more stereotypically lesbian response pattern to the 17 relevant multiple-choice questions.
[b] Higher means indicate greater mean proportion of "lesbian errors." according to the rater–judges' stereotype.
[c] Higher means indicate greater mean proportion of "heterosexual errors," according to the rater–judges' stereotype.
[d] Higher means indicate greater mean proportion of "lesbian accuracy."
[e] Higher means indicate greater mean proportion of "heterosexual accuracy."

and (b) differential *accuracy* of recognition. We next constructed measures of the separate contributions of each of these processes to reconstruction.

"Lesbian errors" and "heterosexual errors"

We assessed the nature of our participants' errors of recognition by means of two error ratios computed for each participant. Once again, guided by the sets of stereotyped lesbian and stereotyped heterosexual answers generated by the rater–judges, we calculated for each participant (a) the proportion of total errors that indicated (according to the stereotype) impending lesbianism in the details of the story of Betty K.'s life and (b) the proportion of total errors that indicated (according to the stereotype) impending heterosexuality.[8] Means for these measures are presented in the second and third rows of table 6.3.

It is clear that recognition errors were systematically influenced by the application of labels concerning Betty K.'s sexuality. A 2 (lesbian–heterosexual label) × 2 (immediate label–delayed label) unweighted-means analysis of variance revealed that participants in the lesbian label conditions showed a greater mean proportion of recognition errors that indicated impending lesbianism in the events of the life history ($M = .543$) than did participants who had read the identical story in the heterosexual label conditions ($M = .408$), $F(1, 116) = 11.44$, $p < .001$. Similarly, participants in the heterosexual label conditions showed a higher mean proportion of recognition errors classified as "heterosexual errors" based upon the stereotype generated by the rater–judges ($M = .281$) than did participants in the lesbian label conditions ($M = .190$), $F(1, 116) = 7.03$, $p < .01$.

Participants in the no-label condition showed the following pattern of errors: They made more "lesbian errors" than did participants in the heterosexual label conditions, contrast $F(1, 145) = 4.84$, $p < .05$, but neither more nor fewer than did participants in the lesbian label conditions, contrast $F(1, 145) < 1$, *ns*. By contrast, their proportion of heterosexual errors fell midway between that of the lesbian label and heterosexual label conditions, but did not differ reliably from either proportion, contrast $F(1, 145) = 1.12$, *ns* and $F(1, 145) = 1.31$, *ns*.

Once again, there were no reliable effects of the timing of the outcome manipulation: The patterning of lesbian errors and heterosexual errors was no different whether participants learned about Betty K.'s sexual life-style immediately after reading the facts of her life or 1 week later ($Fs < 1$).

"Lesbian accuracy" and "heterosexual accuracy"

Clearly, when participants erred, the nature of their errors reflected stereotyped beliefs about sexuality. But what of the nature of our participants' *accurate* answers to the 17 critical items? Were participants who learned that Betty K. was leading a lesbian life-style particularly accurate on those items for which the factually correct answer was also stereotypically lesbian (according to the rater–judges)? Similarly, were participants in the heterosexual label conditions particularly accurate on those items for which the factually correct answers happened to be stereotypically heterosexual? To answer these questions, we calculated for each participant (a) the proportion of his or her accurate answers to the 17 critical items that were stereotypically lesbian and (b) the proportion of his or her accurate answers to the 17 critical items that were stereotypically heterosexual.[9] Means for these measures of "lesbian accuracy" and "heterosexual accuracy" are presented in the fourth and fifth rows of Table 6.3.

Accuracy of recognition was systematically influenced by the application of labels concerning Betty K.'s sexuality, although this effect manifested itself only on the heterosexual accuracy measure. For participants in the heterosexual label conditions, a greater mean proportion of their correct answers to the 17 critical items was composed of answers to questions for which the factually correct answer had been identified (by the rater–judges) as stereotypically heterosexual ($M = .330$) than was the case for participants in the lesbian label conditions ($M = .237$), $F(1, 116) = 23.91$, $p < .000005$. Participants in the heterosexual label conditions also had higher mean proportions of heterosexual accuracy than did participants in the no-label condition, contrast $F(1, 145) = 10.97$, $p < .005$, who did not differ from those in the lesbian label conditions ($F < 1$). However, participants in the lesbian label and heterosexual label conditions did not differ on the proportion of their correct answers for which the correct answer was stereotypically lesbian ($F < 1$). For neither measure was there any reliable influence of the timing manipulation ($Fs < 1$).[10]

Reconstruction or fabrication?

Are these results the outcome of genuine reconstructive processes or, perhaps, the product of simple guesswork or fabrication of plausible answers based upon simple stereotypes about sexuality? An examination of the results of the fabrication conditions suggests that knowledge of Betty K.'s sexual life-style in and of itself was not sufficient to generate the differential pattern of reconstruction committed by participants who had first read the story and then learned of her sexual life-style. Recall that in the fabrication conditions, participants were given the questionnaire without ever having read the story of Betty K.'s life and were asked to answer the questions as best they could, simply given the fact that Betty K. was now living a lesbian life-style (lesbian fabrication condition) or a heterosexual life-style (heterosexual fabrication condition).[11]

In the fabrication conditions, knowledge of different sexual life-styles in no way whatsoever produced the same differential pattern of answers to the questionnaire items as that found in the experimental (story) conditions. That is, participants who knew only Betty K.'s sexual life-style did not manifest the same differential pattern of "fabrication" as the differential "reconstruction" that characterized the answers of participants in the experimental conditions (see table 6.3). Whether we examined the fabricators' mean stereotype scores, their mean proportions of lesbian errors, their mean proportions of heterosexual errors, their mean proportions of lesbian accuracy, or their mean proportions of heterosexual accuracy, participants in the lesbian fabrication condition and in the heterosexual fabrication condition simply did not generate reliably differing patterns of answers to the questions about the facts of Betty K.'s life (all Fs < 1, ns). Participants in the two fabrication conditions apparently were unwilling to fabricate a life history for a lesbian Betty K. that differed reliably from that for a heterosexual Betty K. *in the absence of any factual knowledge of her past.*

Apparently, it was only for participants who had actually read the facts of Betty K.'s life that new knowledge of her sexual life-style influenced reconstruction of the events of her life. Moreover, there is ample evidence that participants who had read the case history did have considerable memory for the facts in the story. They were substantially more accurate in their answers to the 17 critical stereotype items and the 18 neutral items[12] (identified by the rater–judges) than were individuals in the fabrication conditions, $F(1, 203) = 220.23, p < .001$, and $F(1, 203) = 141.23, p < .001$, respectively. Participants who had read the case history were factually correct, on the average, 10.71 times on the 17 critical items and 9.26 times on the 18 neutral items; fabricators were factually correct, on the average, only 5.58 times on the critical items and only 4.85 times on the neutral items. Overall, it appears that the differential errors and distortions made by participants in the experimental conditions occurred only in the presence of some knowledge of the actual events of Betty K.'s life and could not be generated by the simple use of stereotypes to generate plausible answers in the absence of any factual memory.[13]

Discussion

Of what consequence are our impressions of other people? Our empirical research suggests that current beliefs can and do exert powerful channeling effects on attempts to remember the past. Our participants first read an extensive life history about a woman. They later learned new information about her sexual life-style. This new knowledge then influenced their answers to factual questions about the events of her life. Participants reconstructed the events of this woman's life in ways that supported and bolstered their current stereotyped interpretations of her sexuality. When participants erred in answering questions about Betty K.'s life, their errors reflected their newly learned beliefs about her sexual life-style. Participants in the lesbian label conditions were particularly likely to commit lesbian errors; those in the heterosexual label conditions were particularly likely to commit heterosexual errors. There is also some evidence, albeit mixed, that participants were better able to accurately identify those facts of Betty K.'s life that confirmed stereotyped beliefs about sexuality. Participants in the heterosexual label conditions were particularly likely to manifest heterosexual accuracy; there was, however, no corresponding tendency for those in the lesbian label conditions to excel in lesbian accuracy.

In our experiment, the effects of new information did not differ as a function of the timing manipulation. Whether participants learned of Betty K.'s sexual life-style immediately or 1 week later, that information precipitated the same pattern of reconstruction that bolstered their new knowledge. Preconceived knowledge may exert its effects only in the context of active attempts to retrieve previously learned information. Perhaps, when asked to remember the facts of Betty K.'s life history, participants in the immediate label condition *first* retrieved the global information about her life-style and then used preconceptions about sexuality to guide further reconstructive processes. If so, at the time of retrieval, these participants were functionally in the same position as participants in the delayed label condition, who just then had learned about Betty K.'s sexual life-style. Accordingly, it becomes easier to understand why there were no differences in reconstruction as a function of the timing of the new information about Betty K.'s sexual life-style. However, this interpretation must remain tentative. For, other researchers have reported inconsistent effects of the timing of new information: Dooling and Christiaansen (1977) have reported greater reconstructive error in their equivalent of our immediate label condition; Loftus, Miller, and Burns (1978) have reported greater reconstructive error in their equivalent of our delayed label condition.

Our findings also place important limits on the distortions that can be induced by preconceived beliefs. Participants in the fabrication conditions were unwilling to differentially generate answers based upon knowledge of Betty K.'s sexual orientation in the absence of any substantive information about specific events of her life. It was only in the context of some memory for the facts of Betty K.'s life (and there is little doubt that participants who had read the case history *did* have considerable factual knowledge about Betty K.'s past) that stereotypes about sexuality influenced our participants' reconstruction of her history. The message seems clear: People will not indiscriminately use labels and stereotypes in their attempt to understand specific individuals. Rather, labels and the preexisting knowledge bases associated with them must interact with genuine memory in the reconstructive process.

The consequences of reconstructive processes are not without social import. Our investigation may provide confirmation for the process of retrospective reinterpretation that sociological labeling theorists (e.g., Schur, 1971) have suggested might be exploited to rationalize current labels of deviance:

> The subject reinterprets the individual's past behavior in the light of the new information concerning his . . . deviance . . . The subjects indicate that they reviewed their past interactions

with the individual in question, searching for subtle cues and nuances of behavior which might give further evidence of the alleged deviance. This retrospective reading generally provided the subjects with just such evidence to support the conclusion that "this is what was going on all the time." (Kitsuse, 1962, p. 253)

But most importantly of all, our investigation of reconstructive processes in person perception sensitizes us to the powerful, but often unnoticed, consequences of our beliefs about other people. In our quest to see others as stable and predictable creatures, we may cognitively create a world in which erroneous inferences about others can perpetuate themselves. It is perhaps for these reasons that so many widely held but essentially inaccurate stereotypes (including those concerning sexuality) are stubbornly resistant to change.

NOTES

This research and the preparation of this manuscript were supported in part by a grant in aid of research from the Graduate School of the University of Minnesota and by National Science Foundation Grants SOC 75-13872 and BNS 77-11346 to Mark Snyder. Portions of this research were presented at the annual meeting of the Western Psychological Association in Seattle, Washington, April 1977. We appreciate the helpful advice and constructive commentary of Eugene Borgida, Gordon Bower, Nancy Cantor, Herbert Clark, E.E. Jones, Elizabeth Loftus, and Ellen Markman.

[1] Copies of the experimental materials (the case history narrative and the memory questionnaire) may be obtained by writing to the authors.

[2] Two participants did not return for the second session and therefore could not complete the memory measures.

[3] It should be clear to the reader that the task of the rater–judges is critically and fundamentally different from that of participants in the fabrication conditions. Rater–judges reported general knowledge about what other people believe to be true about abstract classes of individuals who share a common sexual orientation. By contrast, fabricator-participants reported specific inferences about what they personally believed to be the true facts in an actual life history of one concrete individual.

[4] Of these 17 critical items, there were 4 cases for which the factually correct alternative was stereotypically lesbian, 5 cases for which the correct alternative was stereotypically heterosexual, 3 cases for which the correct alternative was categorized as "neutral" by the rater–judges, and 5 cases for which the correct alternative was "d" (no information provided).

[5] To the best of our knowledge and that of researchers in the field of human sexuality (e.g., Gagnon and Simon, 1973; Katchadourian and Lunde, 1975; Klaich, 1974; Martin and Lyon, 1972; Money and Ehrhardt, 1972; Riess, Safer, and Yotive, 1974), there is no factual basis for any of the 17 critical items that reflected stereotyped beliefs about heterosexual and lesbian women. For, "the state of knowledge as of the present does not permit any hypotheses (many psychodynamic claims to the contrary) that will predict with certainty which biographical conditions will ensure that an anatomically normal boy or girl will become erotically homosexual, bisexual or heterosexual" (Money and Ehrhardt, 1972, p. 235).

[6] To calculate the stereotype score, each participant's answers to the 17 critical questions were examined, and a mean of the rater–judges' stereotype ratings for each participant's "non-d" responses (that is, those questions for which the participant indicated one of the three factual answers was correct) was computed. Thus, if a participant responded with a "d" (no information provided) for 4 of the 17 critical questions, then his or her stereotype score was the mean of the ratings for the 13 "non-d" responses.

[7] Planned comparisons involving the no-label condition were calculated using the method for factorial designs with a control group described by Himmelfarb (1975, pp. 364–5).

[8] For example, if the correct answer to a question had been assigned a "heterosexual" rating of 1 by the panel of rater–judges, any other answer given by participants was classified as a "lesbian error" if it had been assigned a rating of 2 or 3 by the panel.

[9] Consider the case of a participant who was accurate on 12 of the stereotype items. If 3 of these 12 correct items were ones for which the correct answer had also been identified as stereotypically lesbian by the rater–judges and 2 of these correct answers were on items for which the correct answer was stereotypically heterosexual, this participant would be assigned a "lesbian accuracy" score of .25 (3 out of 12) and a "heterosexual accuracy" score of .167 (2 out of 12).

[10] We also calculated, for each participant (a) the proportion of the four critical items for which the factually correct answer was stereotypically lesbian that he or she answered correctly and (b) the proportion of the five critical items for which the factually correct answer was stereotypically heterosexual that he or she answered correctly. The results for these measures corroborate those of the "lesbian accuracy" and "heterosexual accuracy" measures reported in the text. Participants in the heterosexual label conditions correctly answered a greater mean proportion of the five heterosexual–critical items (M = .700) than did participants in the lesbian label conditions (M = .513), $F(1, 116) = 18.60, p < .00004$. Participants in the heterosexual label conditions also correctly answered a greater mean proportion of these items than did those in the no-label condition (M = .573), contrast $F(1, 145) = 5.80, p < .01$, who did not differ from those in the lesbian label conditions, contrast $F(1, 145) < 1.34$, *ns*. However, participants in the lesbian label and heterosexual label conditions did not differ on the mean proportion of the four lesbian–critical items answered correctly ($F < 1$). For neither measure was there any reliable influence of the timing manipulation ($Fs < 1$).

[11] The answers of fabricators would be rather uninformative if they chose response option "d" (no information provided) with substantially greater frequency than did participants in the experimental conditions. This is not the case. If anything, for the 17 critical items, participants in the fabrication conditions used "d" less frequently (M = 4.58) than did their counterparts in the experimental conditions (M = 8.18), $F(1, 203) = 20.42, p < .001$, who were presumably in a better position to endorse "d" when that option was, in fact, correct. Indeed, for those 12 of the 17 critical items for which the correct answer was *not* "d," fabricators used "d" as often (M = 3.62) as did participants who had read the story (M = 3.19), $F(1, 203) < 1$, *ns*.

[12] The last (i.e. 36th) question of the memory measure concerned Betty K.'s current sexual life-style. It served as a check on the adequacy of the labeling manipulation. No participant in any of the experimental label conditions affirmed the "wrong" sexual life-style in answering this question.

[13] Examination of memory test performance also indicates that the effects of the label manipulation on our measures of reconstruction cannot be attributed to differences in overall retention. Mean numbers of correct answers for the 17 critical stereotype items and the 18 neutral items, respectively, are: immediate–lesbian = 10.32, 9.74; immediate–heterosexual = 10.68, 8.39; delayed–lesbian = 10.55, 8.93; delayed–heterosexual = 10.75, 9.76; no label = 11.27, 9.50. Analyses of variance revealed neither reliable label nor reliable timing effects ($Fs < 1$). Accordingly, it is not retention in and of itself that accounts for the influence of labels on reconstruction, but rather the *nature* of accuracy and error in the experimental label conditions.

REFERENCE NOTES

1   Cohen, C. Cognitive basis of stereotyping. Paper presented at the meeting of the American Psychological Association, San Francisco, August 1977.

2   Hamilton, D.L. Illusory correlation as a basis for social stereotypes. Paper presented at the meeting of the American Psychological Association, San Francisco, August 1977.

3   Rothbart, M. Stereotype formation and maintenance. Paper presented at the meeting of the American Psychological Association, San Francisco, August 1977.

REFERENCES

Bartlett, F.C. *Remembering: A study in experimental and social psychology*. Cambridge, England: Cambridge University Press, 1932.

Berman, J.S., and Kenny, D.A. Correlational bias in observer ratings. *Journal of Personality and Social Psychology*, 1976, *34*, 263–73.

Bower, G. Experiments on story understanding and recall. *Quarterly Journal of Experimental Psychology*, 1976, *28*, 511–34.

Bransford, J.D., and Johnson, M.K. Contextual prerequisites for understanding: Some investigations of comprehension and recall. *Journal of Verbal Learning and Verbal Behavior*, 1972, *11*, 717–26.

Bransford, J.D., Barclay, J.R., and Franks, J.J. Sentence memory: A constructive versus interpretive approach. *Cognitive Psychology*, 1972, *3*, 193–209.

Cantor, N., and Mischel, W. Traits as prototypes: Effects on recognition memory. *Journal of Personality and Social Psychology*, 1977, *35*, 38–48.

Chapman, L.J., and Chapman J.P. The genesis of popular but erroneous psychodiagnostic observations. *Journal of Abnormal Psychology*, 1967, *72*, 193–204.

Chapman, L.J., and Chapman, J.P. Illusory correlation as an obstacle to the use of valid psychodiagnostic signs. *Journal of Abnormal Psychology*, 1969, *74*, 271–80.

Dooling, D.J., and Christiaansen, R.E. Episodic and semantic aspects of memory for prose. *Journal of Experimental Psychology: Human Learning and Memory*, 1977, *3*, 428–36.

Dooling, D.J., and Mullett, R.L. Locus of thematic effects in the retention of prose. *Journal of Experimental Psychology*, 1973, *97*, 404–6.

Gagnon, J.H., and Simon, W. *Sexual conduct: The social sources of human sexuality*. Chicago: Aldine, 1973.

Gauld, A., and Stephenson, G.M. Some experiments relating to Bartlett's theory of remembering. *British Journal of Psychology*, 1967, *58*, 39–49.

Heider, F. *The psychology of interpersonal relations*. New York: Wiley, 1958.

Himmelfarb, S. What do you do when the control group doesn't fit into the factorial design? *Psychological Bulletin*, 1975, *82*, 363–8.

Jones, E.E., and Davis, K.E. From acts to dispositions: The attribution process in person perception. In L. Berkowitz (ed.), *Advances in experimental social psychology* (vol. 2). New York: Academic Press, 1965.

Katchadourian, H.A., and Lunde, D.T. *Fundamentals of human sexuality* (2nd edn). New York: Holt, Rinehart & Winston, 1975.

Kelley, H.H. Attribution in social interaction. In E.E. Jones et al. (eds), *Attribution: Perceiving the causes of behavior*. Morristown, NJ: General Learning Press, 1972.

Kitsuse, J.I. Societal reactions to deviant behavior: Problems of theory and method. *Social Problems*, 1962, *9*, 247–56.

Klaich, D. *Woman and woman: Attitudes towards lesbianism*. New York: Simon & Schuster, 1974.

Loftus, E.F. Leading questions and the eyewitness report. *Cognitive Psychology*, 1975, *7*, 560–72.

Loftus, E.F., and Palmer, J. Reconstruction of automobile destruction. *Journal of Verbal Learning and Verbal Behavior*, 1974, *13*, 585–9.

Loftus, E.F., Miller, D.G., and Burns, H.J. Semantic integration of verbal information into a visual memory. *Journal of Experimental Psychology: Human Learning and Memory*, 1978, *4*, 19–31.

Mandler, J.M., and Johnson, N.S. Remembrance of things parsed: Story structure and recall. *Cognitive Psychology*, 1977, *9*, 111–51.

Martin, D., and Lyon, P. *Lesbian/woman*. San Francisco: Glide, 1972.

Money, J., and Ehrhardt, A.A. *Man and woman: Boy and girl*. Baltimore, MD: Johns Hopkins University Press, 1972.

Riess B.F., Safer, J., and Yotive, W. Psychological test data on female homosexuality: A review of the literature. *Journal of Homosexuality*, 1974, *1*, 71–85.

Ross, L., Lepper, M.R., and Hubbard, M. Perseverance in self-perception and social perception: Biased attributional processes in the debriefing paradigm. *Journal of Personality and Social Psychology*, 1975, *32*, 880–92.

Schur, E.M. *Labeling deviant behavior: Its sociological implications*. New York: Harper & Row, 1971.

Spiro, R.J. Remembering information from text: Theoretical and empirical issues concerning the state of schema reconstruction hypothesis. In R.C. Anderson, R.J. Spiro, and W.E. Montague (eds), *Schooling and the acquisition of knowledge*. Hillsdale, NJ: Erlbaum, 1976.

Thorndyke, P.W. Cognitive structures in comprehension and memory of narrative discourse. *Cognitive Psychology*, 1977, *9*, 77–110.

Zadny, J., and Gerard, H.B. Attributed intentions and informational selectivity. *Journal of Experimental Social Psychology*, 1974, *10*, 34–52.

7 Attribution Theory: Basic Issues and Applications

Videotape and the attribution process: Reversing actors' and observers' points of view

M.D. Storms

Editors'
Introduction

Theoretical Background

> *O wad some Pow'r the giftie gie us*
> *To see oursels as others see us!*
>
> Robert Burns, *To a Louse*

One of the best-known biases in causal attribution refers to the different ways in which 'actors' (those performing the behaviour) and 'observers' (those watching the behaviour) explain the same behaviour. According to Jones and Nisbett (1972) actors tend to attribute their actions to the situation, whereas observers tend to attribute the same actions to stable personal dispositions (for a comprehensive critique and review, see Watson, 1982).

This article provides an ingenious and elegant test of the simple idea that any such differences between the attributions of actors and observers are due to the fact that they have 'different points of view' (the observer watches the actor, and tends therefore to give more personal, dispositional attributions; the actor, however, focuses on the situation in which he or she is acting and tends therefore to give more situational attributions). If point of view is crucial to the actor–observer effect, then surely by changing people's point of view, one can change their attributions? This is precisely what Storms tried to do.

His study provides a nice example of the application of new technology to the practical solution of old problems. When the Scottish poet Robert Burns (1759–96) was writing, and for a long time afterwards, it was inconceivable that we could 'see ourselves as others see us'. But the advent of the videotape recorder provided a simple, fast and relatively cheap means of showing participants how they appeared to others. Storms's experiment used videotapes taken from various camera angles to vary the attentional focus of actors and observers, and to see whether presentation of a new visual orientation would change the way actors and observers attribute, or explain, behaviour in the course of a social interaction. More specifically, actors

Journal of Personality and Social Psychology (1973), 27:165–75.

(who typically attribute behaviour in terms of the situation), shown a video from the point of view of the observer, would see themselves and ought to make more personal attributions. Observers (who typically give personal attributions), shown a video from the point of view of the actor, would see another aspect of the actor's situation and ought to make more situational attributions.

Hypothesis

The hypothesis tested is whether actors' and observers' attributions can be altered, even reversed, by changing their visual orientations.

Design

The core experimental design was a two-factor, between-subjects design: 2 (role: actor/observer) × 2 (videotape orientation: same/new). Thus there were four experimental conditions, two levels of each independent variable. Subjects were randomly assigned to one level of each of the two independent variables. In addition there was a control condition in which no videotape was shown.

Method

Volunteer subjects who were not previously acquainted came to the laboratory in groups of four and were randomly assigned either to take part in a brief conversation with another stranger (i.e. two 'actors') or to watch the conversation (i.e. two 'observers'). The videotape apparatus was used to create three orientation conditions. In the *no-videotape* condition, two actors simply interacted, watched by two observers. In the *same-orientation* condition, all four subjects watched the interaction later on video, but they saw a replay of their original orientations (i.e. there were actor–same-orientation and observer–same-orientation subjects). In the *new-orientation* condition, the videotape reversed both the actors' and the observers' original orientations (i.e. actors saw a video of themselves: actor–new orientation; and observers saw a video of the other participant with whom the actor they had previously observed had interacted: observer–new orientation). Thus the three orientation conditions yielded two control conditions (actor–no-video and observer–no-video) and four experimental conditions. Each experimental session yielded one subject in each of the four experimental conditions: actor–same-orientation; observer–same-orientation; actor–new-orientation; and observer–new-orientation. At the end of each session all subjects completed a questionnaire including measures of dispositional and situational attribution, and behaviour ratings.

Results

The main dependent measures of attribution asked subjects to describe their own (or their matched actor's) behaviour along four dimensions and, for each one, to indicate how much the behaviour was caused by personal characteristics, and how much by the situation (separate ratings on nine-point scales). These last two questions provide the most direct assessment of attributions, on which we focus here. Storms created an index of attribution, summed over all four behaviours, by calculating dispositional minus situational attributions. Higher scores on this index denote more dispositional (and less situational) attributions. Storms also took a more indirect measure of dispositional attribution – whether subjects generalized their attributions from the short social interaction to their judgements of their own (or their matched actor's) behaviour in general. The actual method of analysis is not stated, but presumably Storms computed a 2×2 analysis of variance and then tested the differences between certain theoretically interesting means (see footnote 1). The main results (see table 7.1) can be presented under the following subheadings.

Testing the actor–observer difference

To test the hypothesis that actors give more situational and observers more dispositional attributions, Storms compared actors' and observers' mean dispositional–situational scores in the two conditions where participants received no new information (i.e. no videotape and same orientation). In the same-orientation condition (where one might have expected any effect to be *more* pronounced, since subjects saw again exactly the same perspective), this index was indeed significantly lower for actors than observers (i.e. actors were less dispositional and more situational). But the difference was not significant in what might be regarded as the baseline condition (no videotape). Generally, using the videotape to repeat subjects' original orientation had little effect on either actors' or observers' attributions.

Can we change attributions by changing orientations?

The highly reliable interaction between Role $\times$ Videotape orientation reflects the predicted reversal of actors' and observers' attributions after viewing a new perspective: actors become more dispositional (and less situational); observers become more situational (and less dispositional). The main hypothesis is thus supported, but further analyses show that it is situational attributions, not dispositional ones, that are altered by the change of orientation. There was additional, albeit statistically weaker, support for the main hypothesis from the more indirect measure of attribution (generalization; see table 7.2).

Discussion

Although Storms's study supports the hypothesis that one can change attributions by changing people's orientations or perspectives, it is, in fact, limited as a true test of Jones and Nisbett's hypothesis. They assert that actors tend to attribute their actions to the situation, whereas observers tend to attribute the same actions to stable personal dispositions. This implies that actors' attributions are more situational than dispositional, and that observers' attributions are more dispositional than situational. The data in table 7.1 show that the prediction for observers is correct; but not that for actors. All subjects, whatever their role, tended to give more dispositional than situational attributions. This is actually an example of a different attributional bias, the 'fundamental attribution error' (Ross, 1977), which refers to the tendency to overestimate personal causes and underestimate situational ones.

But this study was important in demonstrating the effect of salience on attribution, and that persons or situations could be manipulated in order to increase or decrease their apparent causal role (see McArthur and Post, 1977; Taylor and Fiske, 1978). Beyond that, this study demonstrates why actor–observer differences are important in many relationships, such as teacher–pupil, husband–wife, doctor–patient and coach–athlete.

FURTHER READING

McArthur, L.Z. and Post, D.L. (1977). Figural emphasis and person perception. *Journal of Experimental Social Psychology*, 13, 520–35. This study shows neatly that making a person appear more salient makes his or her behaviour seem more dispositionally, and less situationally, caused.

Taylor, S.E. and Fiske, S.T. (1978). Salience, attention and attribution: Top of the head phenomena. In L. Berkowitz (ed.), *Advances in Experimental Social Psychology* (vol. 11, pp. 250–89). New York: Academic Press. A review of the authors' many studies showing that manipulations of salience – for example by use of bright lights or distinctive appearance – can impact on causal attributions.

Watson, D. (1982). The actor and the observer: How are their perceptions of causality divergent? *Psychological Bulletin*, 92, 682–700. A rather technical review that explains exactly what is implied by the actor–observer hypothesis and what, in practice, is typically found.

REFERENCES

Jones, E.E. and Nisbett, R.E. (1972). The actor and the observer: Divergent perceptions of the causes of behaviour. In E.E. Jones, D.E. Kanouse, H.H. Kelley, R.E. Nisbett, S. Valins and B. Weiner (eds), *Attribution: Perceiving the Causes of Behaviour* (pp. 79–94). Morristown, NJ: General Learning Press.

Ross, L. (1977). The intuitive psychologist and his shortcomings: Distortions in the attribution process. In L. Berkowitz (ed.), *Advances in Experimental Social Psychology* (vol. 10, pp. 173–220). New York: Academic Press.

When an individual observes a behavior and attempts to understand its causes, he is concerned with the relative importance of personal dispositions of the actor and the surrounding social and environmental context. Both an observer who wishes to explain another's behavior and an actor who tries to understand his own behavior attempt to make the appropriate causal attributions. There is reason to believe, however, that actors and observers do not always arrive at the same explanation of the actor's behavior. Jones and Nisbett (1971) have argued that when actors seek to explain their own behavior, they are inclined to give considerable weight to external, environmental (i.e. situational) causes. Observers, on the other hand, place considerably more emphasis on internal, personal (i.e. dispositional) causes of the actor's behavior.

Several studies (Jones and Harris, 1967; Jones, Rock, Shaver, Goethals, and Ward, 1968; McArthur, 1970, 1972; Nisbett, Caputo, Legant, and Marecek, 1973) have been cited in

Primary Reading

support of this general proposition, and Jones and Nisbett have discussed a variety of factors which might lead to such attributional differences between actors and observers. These factors include (a) differences in information about the event, behavior, and context which is *available* to actors and observers and (b) differences in how information is *processed* by actors and observers. Actors may have private information about some aspects of the event, including their own feelings and the historical context in which the event transpires, while observers may have more complete information about the behavior itself. Furthermore, in the interests of controlling events and predicting the future, actors may attend more to situational variables in an event, and observers may attend more to variations in the actor's behavior.

The present study examines a fundamental difference between actors and observers which may lead, in turn, to some of the information differences postulated by Jones and Nisbett (1971). Perhaps the most obvious difference between actors and observers is that they have, quite literally, different points of view. Actors cannot see themselves act; physically they cannot observe much of their own behavior. They may watch the antecedents of their own behavior, or its consequences, or both. But they do not normally view the behavior itself. In addition to the physical difficulty of watching oneself, there are temporal restrictions which contribute to a lack of self-observation. There may not be enough time or mental capacity to contemplate past behavior, monitor present behavior, and plan future behavior all at once. Finally, there are motivational reasons for avoiding an excess of self-observation. In the interest of acting unself-consciously and maintaining control over the immediate events taking place, the actor may learn that it is dysfunctional to be overly concerned with his own present and past behavior. Instead, it is reasonable to assume that most actors focus on the situation in which they find themselves. They look at, attend to, and think about various changing aspects of the environment in which and to which they must respond.

While the actor is watching the situation in which he finds himself, the observer is probably watching the actor. It is usually interesting and often important to watch the behavior of other people. Consequently, observers are often visually oriented toward the actor. Although an observer can take his eyes off the actor and view other aspects of the situation, he probably sees less of the situation than the actor does. As with actors, the observer's scope is also limited by time. Observers cannot simultaneously watch the actor and observe as much of the situation as the actor can. Moreover, observers may find it more efficient in terms of controlling and predicting the ongoing event to concentrate on the actor's behavior rather than on the actor's situation. Finally, the actor is, after all, part of the observer's situation. For the same reasons that an actor focuses on his own situation, the observer focuses on the behavior of the actor, which is part of his (the observer's) situation.

Thus, we postulate that there is a simple difference between actors and observers. Actors watch their environment (which includes the behavior of other people) more than they watch their own behavior. Observers watch the behavior of the actor more than they watch the actor's situation.

If it is true that attributions are largely influenced by point of view, it should be possible to change the way actors and observers interpret a behavior by changing their visual orientations.

A test of this hypothesis requires some means of changing actors' and observers' orientations. Fortunately, modern technology provides a simple and interesting means to accomplish this change – namely, the use of videotape. Videotapes of an event, taken from various camera angles, can be replayed to actors and observers to redirect their attention to other aspects of the event. Of particular interest is the case in which videotape presents a new visual orientation, that is, when actors are shown a tape of their own behavior from the observer's perspective and when observers are shown a tape of some key aspect of the actor's situation from the actor's perspective. Such reorientation should affect actors and observers so as to weaken (or even reverse) their original attributional biases. Actors who see themselves should make more dispositional attributions about their own behavior. Observers who see another aspect of the actor's situation should become more situational in attributing the actor's behavior.

Thus, the question to be answered by this study is whether actors' and observers' attributions can be significantly influenced, perhaps even reversed, by changing their visual orientation toward an event. The implications of such a question may go beyond immediate theoretical concerns. Discrepancies between actors' and observers' perceptions and interpretations of behavior are of paramount concern to therapists, group relations consultants, and T-group trainers. Often such practitioners must attempt to bridge the interpretational gap between actor and observer, patient and therapist, and individual and group.

Method

Overview

The hypothesis was tested in an experiment that featured a simple interpersonal event, namely a brief getting-acquainted conversation between two strangers (actors). In addition, two other subjects (observers) were told to watch the conversation but not to participate in it.

Videotape replays of the conversation provided the experimental manipulation. The design made it possible to compare the effects of three orientation conditions: (a) one in which no visual reorientation was attempted (no videotape), (b) one in which videotape was used simply to repeat the subject's original orientations (same orientation), and (c) one in which videotape reversed the orientation of actor and observer (new orientation). In one set of conditions, actors and observers saw a videotape from essentially the same orientation as they had had in "real life." Actors saw a videotape replay of the other participant with whom they were conversing (actor–same orientation), and observers saw a videotape of the same actor they had been observing and about whom they would later answer questions (observer–same orientation). In another set of conditions, actors and observers received an entirely new orientation on videotape. Actors saw a videotape of themselves in the conversation (actor–new orientation), and observers saw a videotape of the other participant with whom their target actor had been conversing (observer–new orientation). In addition, a set of actors and observers were run with no videotape replay.

Subjects

One hundred and twenty Yale undergraduate male volunteers participated in 30 groups of 4. Subjects were solicited by sign-up sheets which specified that people who volunteered for the same session should not be previously acquainted.

Procedure

When each group of four subjects arrived at the experiment, they were told,

> This is a study in an area of social psychology called "interpersonal dynamics." More specifically, I'm interested in what I call "getting acquainted" – that is, what happens when two strangers meet for the first time and initiate their first conversation. Two of you in this study will be having a short, first conversation with each other. In addition, this study calls for two observers.

Subjects were randomly assigned to the role of actor (actually referred to as participant in the script) or observer. Two subjects were assigned to be actors and to have a getting-acquainted conversation together. Each of the remaining two observer subjects was assigned to observe his matched actor during the conversation.

The experimenter then mentioned,

> There is one thing I would like to add to the procedure today. I've gotten hold of some videotape equipment and I will be taping your conversation. My thought was that it might be useful to you in answering the questionnaires to see the conversation replayed on tape.

Subjects were then seated in the experimental room as shown in figure 7.1. Actors sat at one end of the table, across from each other, with one camera focused on each. Observers sat at the other end of the table, diagonally across from and facing their matched actors. The experimenter reiterated that the conversation would last about 5 minutes, that the actors could talk about anything they wished, perhaps starting with their names and where they lived, and that observers should silently watch their matched actors.

After adjusting the equipment, the experimenter signaled to the participants to begin their conversation. Five minutes later, he asked them to stop and wait silently while the tapes were rewound. At this point, the experimental manipulation was performed. A random number table was consulted to determine whether the session would be a control session, in which case the subject would not see any tape, or an experimental session. If an experimental session was indicated, the experimenter continued, "I'm afraid only one camera was working very well and

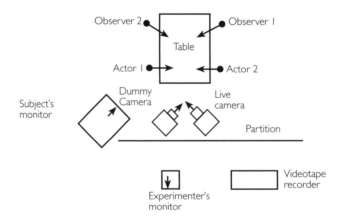

Figure 7.1　Setup of the experimental room

the other one is just too poor to see anything. So we'll only be able to see one of you on the videotape." Experimental subjects were always shown the tape of Actor 1.

Thus one actor, Actor 2, saw a tape of the same participant he had just seen in real life (Actor 1) and was the actor–same orientation subject. The other actor, Actor 1, viewed the tape of himself and was the actor–new orientation subject. Similarly, one observer, Observer 1, saw a tape of the same actor he had been observing in the conversation (Actor 1) and was the observer–same orientation subject. The other observer, Observer 2, saw a tape of the participant whom he had not been observing previously (Actor 1) and was the observer–new orientation subject. Thus each experimental session yielded one subject in each of the four experimental cells.

If a control session was indicated, the experimenter said the following instead: "I'm afraid this is lousy equipment. It just didn't take a good enough picture to be worth our while looking at it. So we'll just skip the tapes and go on to the questionnaire." These no-videotape control sessions produced two actor–no-videotape subjects and two observer–no-videotape subjects.

At this point, for control subjects, and after the videotape replay for experimental subjects, the experimenter introduced the questionnaire, stressing that it was confidential and that the subjects would not see each other's responses. When the subjects completed the questions, they were debriefed. At this time, the experimenter raised the issue of experimental deception, but no subject indicated suspicion that the videotape had been a deliberate manipulation or even an essential part of the experiment.

Measures

On the postexperimental questionnaire, actor subjects answered mostly questions about themselves, and observer subjects answered questions about their matched actor. After a few introductory filler items, a page of instructions and the key dependent measures of attribution were presented. The instructions informed subjects that in the next part of the questionnaire they would be asked to describe their own (their matched actor's) behavior along four standard dimensions: friendliness, talkativeness, nervousness, and dominance. Then, for each of the four behaviors, subjects were to indicate how much influence they thought the following two factors had in causing that behavior:

> (A) *Personal characteristics about yourself* (your matched participant): How important were your (his) personality, traits, character, personal style, attitudes, mood, and so on in causing you (him) to behave the way you (he) did?
> (B) *Characteristics of the situation*: How important were such factors as being in an experiment, the "getting acquainted" situation, the topic of conversation, the way the other participant behaved and so on the causing you (him) to behave the way you (he) did?

Thus, on each of the next four pages, three questions were presented. The first asked about the perceived level of behavior on one of the four dimensions, for example, "To what extent did you (your matched participant) behave in a friendly, warm manner?" The question was followed by a 9-point scale labeled extremely friendly (9) to extremely unfriendly (1). Presented next were the two attribution questions: "How important were *personal characteristics* about you (your matched participant) in causing you (him) to behave that way?" and "How important were *characteristics of the situation* in causing you (him) to behave that way?" Each of these questions was followed by a 9-point scale labeled extremely important (9) to extremely unimportant (1).

These last two questions, repeated over the four behavioral dimensions, provided the principal and most direct measure of subjects' attributions. These four dimensions were not selected on the basis of any particular theoretical or empirical considerations, but simply because it was anticipated that subjects would manifest behaviors along each of these dimensions and that subjects would be able to make judgments about them. Since the hypothesis was concerned with the relative strength of dispositional versus situational attributions and made no distinctions among the four behavioral dimensions, the appropriate measure was the difference between perceived importance of personal characteristics and perceived importance of situational characteristics in causing the actor's behavior, summed over all four behaviors. This difference score was referred to as the dispositional–situational index. A higher value on this index indicated that a subjects' attributions were relatively more dispositional and less situational. It is important to note this dual meaning of the dispositional–situational index. When an effect is described as "relatively more dispositional," it is equally valid to say "relatively less situational."

A second, less direct measure of the subjects' attributions appeared later in the questionnaire. The subjects were asked to report their estimates of the actor's level of behavior in *general* on each of the four behavioral dimensions, for example, "How friendly a person are you (is your matched participant) in general?" Responses were made on a scale from very friendly (9) to very unfriendly (1). It was then possible to compare these answers to the subjects' previous answers about the actor's level of behavior in the conversation. If a subject had perceived that the actor's behavior in the conversation was due to a stable personal disposition, then the subject would likely have predicted that the actor behaved the same way in general. Thus, dispositional attributions would lead to a low discrepancy between the subject's perception of the actor's behavior in the conversation and his behavior in general. On the other hand, if the subject had thought that the actor's behavior was caused by the situation, he would more likely have reported that the actor behaved differently in general. Thus, situational attributions would lead to greater discrepancy between the subjects' perceptions of the actor's present and general levels of behavior. The simplest measure of this discrepancy was the absolute value of the difference between the present level-of-behavior scores and the general level-of-behavior scores, summed over all four behaviors. This measure was referred to as the present-behavior–general-behavior index. The higher the value of this discrepancy index, the more a subject made situational (or the less he made dispositional) attributions.

The remainder of the questionnaire contained items not directly related to present concerns.

Results

Dispositional versus situational attributions for behavior

The main hypothesis of the present study concerns the effects of videotape reorientation on actors' and observers' causal attributions of the actor's behavior. Before considering the effects of reorientation, however, it is helpful to examine the evidence pertinent to the original Jones and Nisbett (1971) hypothesis that actors are characteristically inclined to attribute causality to aspects of the situation, while observers tend to attribute causality to the actor's disposition.

Evidence for this proposition is found in two conditions of the present experiment: the no-videotape cells in which the subjects did not receive any videotape replay, and the same-orientation cells in which the videotape merely repeated the subjects' original visual perspectives.

The relevant data are presented in table 7.1. The key dependent measure, the total dispositional–situational index, reflects the relative strength of dispositional and situational attributions; a higher value on this index indicates relatively more dispositional (less situational) attributing. A comparison of the dispositional–situational means for actors and observers in the no-videotape and same-orientation cells reveals that, in both of these conditions, actors attributed relatively more to situational causes than did observers ($p < .12, p < .05$, respectively).[1] It is further noted from these data that a videotape which merely repeated the subjects' original orientation had little effect on either actors or observers. Dispositional–situational scores for actors in the same-orientation condition did not differ from those for actors in the no-videotape condition ($q = 1.79$, *ns*), and scores for observers in the two conditions were also similar ($q = 1$, *ns*). Thus, under conditions of no videotape and under conditions of repeated videotape orientation, the subject's role as actor or observer was an important determinant of attributions. Actors attributed their own behavior relatively more to situational causes, and observers attributed the behavior relatively more to dispositional causes.

The main hypothesis of the present study can be examined with the data presented in the last column of table 7.1. It was anticipated that actors who saw themselves on videotape would become relatively less situational (more dispositional) in attributions of their own behavior, while observers who saw a videotape of the other participant with whom the actor had been conversing would become relatively more situational (less dispositional) in their attributions of the actor's behavior. Since opposite effects of videotape reorientation were predicted for actors and observers, the hypothesis was properly tested by the interaction between subjects' roles (actor or observer) and videotape orientation. The predicted Role × Videotape orientation interaction was obtained at beyond the .001 level of confidence ($F = 9.72, df = 2/114, p < .001$). Neither the main effect for role, nor the main effect for videotape orientation, was significant.

Table 7.1 Dispositional, situational, and dispositional minus situational attribution scores totaled over all four behaviors

Attribution	Same orientation	No videotape	New orientation
Actors' attributions of own behavior			
Dispositional	26.10	27.35	27.50
Situational	25.95	25.10	20.70
Dispositional–situational	.15[a]	2.25[ab]	6.80[c]
Observers' attributions of matched actor's behavior			
Dispositional	27.10	27.30	25.75
Situational	22.20	22.50	24.15
Dispositional–situational	4.90[bc]	4.80[bc]	1.60[ab]

Dispositional–situational means not sharing the same superscript are significantly different at the .05 level or beyond by Newman-Keuls tests.

The interaction reflected a complete reversal of the relative perspectives of actor and observer in the new-orientation condition. In the same-orientation and no-videotape conditions, the actors' attributions were more situational than the observers'. In the new-orientation condition, in contrast, the actors were relatively more dispositional than the observers. This reversed effect was significant in itself ($p < .05$).

Examing the simple dispositional and situational scores also presented in table 7.1, it is apparent that reorientation had a stronger influence on the subjects' evaluation of situational factors than on their evaluation of dispositional factors. The array of means for attributions to dispositional causes was in the direction of the predicted interaction, but the effect did not reach significance ($F = 1.38$, $df = 2/114$, ns). The situational attribution scores showed the expected reverse pattern, and the interaction was significant ($F = 5.78$, $df = 2/114$, $p < .005$)

The hypothesis is thus strongly supported. Visual orientation has a powerful influence on the attributions of actors and observers. Indeed, the data in table 7.1 suggest the strongest possible conclusion: Under some circumstances actual role as actor or observer is unimportant, and visual orientation is totally determinative of attributions.

Two other aspects of the dispositional–situational data are noteworthy. (a) Repetition on videotape of essentially the same information which had been presented in real life had little effect on either the actors or the observers. Actors in the same-orientation condition were only slightly and nonsignificantly more situational than no-videotape actors, and same-orientation observers were only slightly and nonsignificantly more dispositional than no-videotape observers. (b) The predicted experimental effects were not obtained with equal strength for all four of the behaviors on which the total dispositional–situational index was based.

The fact that videotape in the same-orientation cells had little effect on the subject's attributions suggests that mere repetition of information and the addition of time to review the event did not affect the subject's perceptions of the event. The subjects appear to have absorbed all relevant data about the event during its real-life occurrence. Of course, one would not necessarily expect this to be true of all events. If the episode were more complex or of longer duration, subjects could easily miss important information in vivo. A videotape replay would fill in these informational gaps and could, quite possibly, produce different attributions.

The most noteworthy difference among the four behavioral dimensions was the failure of the dominance dimension to contribute to the experimental effects. Considering each behavioral dimension separately, the Role × Videotape orientation interaction was significant for friendliness, talkativeness, and nervousness, each at the .025 level of confidence, but was trivial for dominance ($F < 1$). Comments by subjects during the debriefing suggest a possible reason for the failure of dominance to contribute to the experimental effects. Subjects complained that dominance was a difficult dimension on which to judge people in the context of a simple, 5-minute getting-acquainted conversation. While friendliness, talkativeness, and nervousness are dimensions with concrete behavioral counterparts (such as smiling, talking, and fidgeting), apparently dominance is a more abstract dimension and requires a higher order of inference.

When the dominance question was excluded from the analysis, each of the experimental effects was strengthened. Across the remaining three dimensions, the interaction test of videotape reorientation was strengthened from an F of 9.72 to an F of 13.89 ($df = 2/114$, $p < .001$). Tests for the Jones and Nisbett (1971) hypothesis were also strengthened; the contrast between actors and observers in the no-videotape condition was significant at the .05 level, and the contrast between actors and observers in the same-orientation conditions was significant at the .01 level.

Perceived level of behavior and perceived discrepancy from general behavior

In addition to the two attribution questions, the subjects also answered questions about the perceived level of behavior on each dimension. Past experiments in this area have typically created a specific, standardized behavior for subjects to attribute. The present experiment, with its unstructured conversations, did not furnish all subjects with the same behavior. This flexibility was desirable, in that it provided a more general test of the attribution hypotheses over several, naturally occurring behaviors. But it also created the possibility that perceptions of the perceived level or intensity of behavior could differ among experimental conditions and thus account for the different attributions. This does not appear to have been the case, however. There were two ways of calculating perceived level of behavior: (a) by taking the direct value from the 9-point scale for each level-of-behavior response and (b) since the scales were bipolar (for example, 9 = very friendly to 1 = very unfriendly), by taking the deviation of the subject's response from the midpoint of the scale (5). Neither of these measures yielded significant comparisons between any cells in the experiment, either for each behavior considered separately or for all four behaviors totaled. Furthermore, the overall correlations between the total dispositional–situational measure of attributions and the two measures of perceived level of behavior were trivial and nonsignificant ($r = -.049$, for the direct score; $r = -.021$, for the score of deviation from midpoint). Thus, it is apparent that differences in perceived level of behavior could not account for the attribution differences.

Since there were no significant differences in perceived level of behavior, it is meaningful to examine the second measure of subjects' attributions, the present-behavior–general-behavior discrepancy scores. This index reflected the absolute difference between the subjects' perceptions of the actor's *present behavior* (in the conversation) and the actor's *general behavior*, summed over all four behaviors. A small discrepancy would indicate that a subject expected the actor's present behavior to generalize and was thus making a dispositional attribution. A greater discrepancy would indicate less generalization of the actor's behavior and thus a situational attribution.

The results of the present-behavior–general-behavior discrepancy measure, presented in table 7.2, corroborated the findings on the dispositional–situational measure of attributions. The effects of videotape reorientation, as tested in the Role × Videotape orientation interaction, reached significance at $p < .05$, ($F = 3.38$, $df = 2/144$). Again, neither the main effect for role nor the main effect for orientation was significant. Although the direction of differences

Table 7.2 Present behavior minus general behavior discrepancy scores summed over all four behaviors

Subjects	Same orientation	No videotape	New orientation
Actors	7.15	5.00	4.25
Observers	5.45	4.90	5.90

between the actors and observers in the various conditions was as expected, none of the individual comparisons between cells reached significance on the present-behavior–general-behavior measure, even with the exclusion of the dominance dimension. It appears that the results for the present-behavior–general behavior measure followed the same pattern as, but were generally weaker than, the results for the dispositional–situational measure. The two measures were, incidentally, significantly correlated (overall $r = .361$, $p < .01$).

Discussion

The present study demonstrates that visual orientation has a powerful influence on the inferences made by actors and observers about the causes of the actor's behavior. When videotape was not presented and subjects were left to assume their own orientations, or when videotape reproduced subjects' original orientations, actors attributed their behavior relatively more to situational causes than did observers. This finding supports the Jones and Nisbett (1971) hypothesis that actors' attributions are typically more situational than observers'. But under conditions of reorientation, when subjects saw a new point of view on videotape, the attributional differences between actors and observers were exactly reversed. Reoriented, self-viewing actors attributed their behaviors relatively less to situational causes than did observers. This effect was obtained on two very different measures of attribution across a variety of behavioral dimensions in an unstructured situation.

Mechanisms of videotape reorientation

Two important issues arise concerning the possible mechanisms by which video orientation affected attributions. The first issue, one crucial to any laboratory social psychology experiment, concerns experimenter demand characteristics. Demand characteristics could have influenced the results of the present study if the hypotheses had been communicated to subjects either by the experimenter's behavior or by the fact the subjects viewed only one videotape. Both of these possibilities depend on subjects' developing the expectation that videotape had importance for how they should respond. The possibility of communicating the hypotheses was avoided by leading subjects to believe that videotape was not an essential part of the experiment and that the experimenter had wanted to show both tapes but could not, due to circumstances beyond his control. During debriefing, subjects were questioned on their reactions to this hoax; they reported no suspicion that the videotape breakdown had been intentional or important. Moreover, if subjects had been responding to the attribution questions out of desire to support the experimenter's hypotheses, it is unlikely they could have produced the results of the indirect present-behavior–general-behavior measure. This index was derived from the absolute value of the difference between the four level-of-behavior questions and the four general-behavior questions. These questions were widely separated in the questionnaire, and subjects would have had to perform a rather elaborate calculus to produce these results deliberately. Thus, it does not seem likely that the reorientation effects can be accounted for by experimenter demand characteristics.

The second issue involves the possible mechanisms by which videotape caused the predicted attributions. This study was designed to demonstrate that a global manipulation (visual orientation) affects actors' and observers' attributions of the actor's behavior. The study was not designed to separate out the many possible mechanisms by which this might occur. However, some informed speculation is possible.

Jones and Nisbett (1971) proposed several factors that contribute to attributional differences between actors and observers, including differences in the information available about an event and differences in how that information is processed. These two categories are not mutually exclusive, and videotape orientation may have affected aspects of both information availability and information processing. When actors or observers saw a videotape of an event from a different point of view, they may have received some totally new information. The actor may have realized, for the first time, some new aspects of his own behavior; the observer may have seen new aspects of the situation or of the other participant. These new facts could have contributed to changes in subjects' inferences about the cause of behavior. Second, the salience of already available information may have changed for reoriented subjects. Changes in the salience of information have been shown to affect people's perceptions of the reasons for their behavior. For example, Kiesler, Nisbett, and Zanna (1969) found that subjects tended to adopt as explanations of their own behavior motives that were made salient by a confederate. Similarly, subjects in the present study might have formulated their attributions about the actor's behavior on the basis of potential causes which had just been made salient by the videotape. Finally, videotape reorientation may have produced new response sets for subjects. Actors who viewed themselves on tape may have been put into a "self-discovery" frame of mind and thus led to think about their own personality as revealed in their behavior. Similarly, observers who saw a videotape from the actor's point of view may have developed an "empathic" set, imagining themselves to be in the actor's shoes.

It is also of interest to consider the exact nature of the attributional changes evoked by videotape. Changes on the key dependent variable, the dispositional–situational index, were accounted for mostly by changed evaluations of situational causes. Actors assigned a great deal of causality to the situation unless videotape forced them to look away from the situation and toward their own behavior. Observers originally assigned less causality to the situation unless videotape impressed situational factors on them. Differences in attribution to dispositional causes, although in the expected direction, were much weaker than these differences in attribution to situational causes. It may be that the relatively greater amount of change on the situational dimension reflects people's general way of viewing the role of dispositions in causing behavior. People may characteristically assign fixed and fairly high importance to personal responsibility for behavior. Consequently, they may be left with only one means of modifying their relative assignment of causality and responsibility, namely by varying their evaluations of the situation. In line with this possibility, there may have been a ceiling effect for dispositional attributions in the present study; the overall mean importance assigned to dispositional causes equaled nearly 7 out of a possible 9 scale points. Subjects were thus left with little room to express enhanced dispositional influences.

Up to this point, discussion has been limited to information-related variables which may be modified by video exposure and may in turn affect attributions. Undoubtedly, motivational variables, such as the need to maintain self-esteem and particular self-concepts, could also be affected by videotape observations. One might expect the self-viewing actors in particular to be influenced by such motivations. It is important to note, however, that the present findings were obtained in a situation which was, in many respects, low-key. The behaviors elicited in the getting-acquainted conversations were routine and probably not highly relevant to actors' self-concepts, the interaction between subjects was fairly unemotional, and actors and observers did not have the opportunity to discuss their potentially opposing views of the actor's behavior. It is therefore important to consider whether the present findings would generalize to situations where actors and observers are more emotionally involved, such as in psychotherapy and T groups. There is reason to believe that the present findings have some applicability to the use of videotape even in such emotionally charged settings.

Videotape in therapy and T groups

There has been a recent and dramatic increase in the application of videotape feedback in therapy and human relations training. Alger and Hogan (1966a) asserted that "videotape recording represents a technological breakthrough with the kind of significance for psychiatry that the microscope has had for biology" (p. 1). In clinical practice, videotape is frequently used to increase a patient's knowledge of his own behavior (cf. Bailey and Sowder, 1970; Holzman, 1969), and this apparently leads to therapeutic gain. Reivich and Geertsma (1968) reported increased accuracy in patients' knowledge of their own behavior after videotape self-observation. They measured the disparity between a patient's self-ratings on clinical scales and the ratings given him by psychiatric nurses. After videotape self-observation, the ratings of the actor patient came to agree more with the ratings of the observer nurses. Alderfer and Lodahl (1971) found that videotape playback in T groups increased subjects' "openness." Openness was defined as willingness to explore the internal meaning of and accept personal responsibility for an attitude or behavior. Finally, case studies in marital therapy (Alger and Hogan, 1966a; Kagan, Krathwohl, and Miller, 1963) have reported that one or both marriage partners are more willing to assume the blame for a poor relationship after seeing themselves on videotape.

On the other hand, some negative consequences of self-observation have also been reported. For instance, Carrere (1954) used videotape to show alcoholics how they behaved when intoxicated, but he found it necessary to edit the more shocking scenes. The full presentation of their behavior when drunk was too stressful for many of his patients. Parades, Ludwig, Hassenfeld, and Cornelison (1969) similarly reported the lowering of alcoholic patients' self-esteem after viewing their own drunken behavior on tape. Leitenberg, Agras, Thompson, and Wright (1968) gave behavioral feedback (although not video) to phobic patients undergoing behavior modification. These authors found that feedback to patients about successful progress speeds their cure, but information about temporary setbacks interferes with the therapy. Finally, Geertsma and Reivich (1965) reported that some self-viewing depressive patients become more depressed, some schizophrenic patients engage in more bizarre behavior, and some neurotics show an increase in the symptoms characteristic of their particular disorder.

Research to date on the use of videotape in therapy is insufficient to indicate how and with whom it is a beneficial therapy adjunct. It may be possible, however, to apply the findings and the theoretical framework of the present study to the issue of videotape use in therapy. The present study demonstrates that self-observation can change the causal interpretation a person gives to his own behavior. The self-viewing actor (and possibly the self-viewing patient) is more likely to accept personal, dispositional responsibility for his behavior and is less likely to deflect responsibility to the situation.

This attributional consequence of self-observation may help to account for some of the effects of videotape in therapy. For example, the increased openness of T group participants after self-observation may reflect a tendency for each group member to assume more personal, dispositional responsibility for his behavior in the group. Similarly, in marital therapy, the husband or wife who sees himself or herself on videotape may realize for the first time his or her own behavioral contribution to the marital conflict and may be more willing to place a dispositional blame on himself or herself. Finally, the reported increase in agreement between a patient's clinical self-ratings after videotape self-observation and the ratings of observing psychiatric nurses closely parallels the present findings. Self-observation increases an individual's dispositional attributions, thus bringing him more in agreement with the observer's built-in bias for dispositional attributions.

It seems likely that this increase in dispositionality of a patient's attributions would prove to be sometimes therapeutic and sometimes distherapeutic. Successful therapy no doubt usually involves making a patient aware of his own behavior and convincing him to accept personal responsibility for that behavior. Self-observation apparently aids this process and, to that extent, should be therapeutic. However, two potentially negative outcomes of this process might be suggested. First, in becoming more dispositional about their own behavior, individuals who see themselves on videotape may actually underestimate real and viable situational explanations for their behavior. Actors in the present study who saw their own behavior on videotape had a higher mean for dispositional attributions and a lower mean for situational attributions than any other group of subjects. This suggests the possibility that self-viewing actors may have been "undersituational" in attributing their own behavior. That is, videotape may have reoriented these actors so much that they perceived situational causes for their behavior to be even less important than did others who viewed them. And if, as Jones and Nisbett (1971) have suggested, observers are themselves inclined to underattribute to the situation, this poses a disturbing possibility for therapy. Ironically, the therapist and the self-viewing patient could reach complete agreement about the patient's behavior, yet this agreement could result from a mutual underestimation of the importance of the patient's situation in causing his behavior. This collaborative illusion between patient and therapist could be especially harmful if the patient blames himself for behavior that is in fact due to some aspect of his environment.

Past research on attribution processes has uncovered another area where attributions to the self can have distherapeutic results. Storms and Nisbett (1970) and Valins and Nisbett (1971) have suggested that negative self-labeling which results from attributing uncomplimentary behaviors to dispositions within oneself often lead to a loss of self-esteem and an actual increase in the pathological behavior. For example, insomniacs who attribute their sleeplessness to some negative state within themselves may increase their anxiety and thus aggravate their original condition. Storms and Nisbett proposed that such exacerbation may result whenever self-attributions of a negative disposition increase the individual's anxiety and when anxiety is an irritant to the pathology, such as in impotence, stuttering, and other neurotic conditions. This exacerbation phenomenon may be occurring in some of the therapy cases where negative results have followed the use of videotapes. The finding that self-observation lowers the self-esteem of alcoholic patients might be an instance of this. An alcoholic patient who sees a tape of his own drunken behavior may become quite upset and depressed about himself. Such a traumatic experience may only increase the likelihood that the patient will drink to excess. Whenever a pathology is caused or influenced by a poor self-concept, self-observation of extremely uncomplimentary behavior may serve to retard therapeutic progress.

Research on attribution processes may help to create a theoretical framework for the area of videotape self-observation in therapy settings. The present study suggests that self-observation increases an individual's dispositional attributions of his own behavior and that this brings interpretation of his behavior more in line with an observer's interpretation. In most cases, this should be advantageous to the therapy process, but in certain cases self-attributions could lead to an exacerbation of the original pathology. Therapists would therefore be well advised to look critically at the potential consequences of self-observation. It seems especially important to consider whether a personal, dispositional attribution of the pathological behavior aids the patient to become aware of his problem and to deal with it, or whether self-attribution increases the patient's anxiety to the point of exacerbating his problem.

NOTES

The research for this article was performed as part of the author's PhD dissertation submitted to the Department of Psychology, Yale University. The author wishes to express his appreciation to Richard E. Nisbett, who served as advisor for the thesis and who has contributed many helpful criticisms of the present article.

[1] These comparisons, and all two-cell comparisons in the present study, are based on the q statistic from the Newman-Keuls procedure for testing differences among several means (see Winer, 1962). The degrees of freedom, taken from the overall analysis of variance, equal 114; n equals 20 per cell. The Newman-Keuls is a more stringent test than the usual two-tailed t-test.

REFERENCES

Alderfer, C.P., and Lodahl, T.M. A quasi experiment on the use of experiential methods in the classroom. *Journal of Applied Behavioral Science*, 1971, 7, 43–69.

Alger, I., and Hogan, P. The use of videotape recordings in conjoint marital therapy. Paper presented at the meeting of the American Psychoanalytic Association, Atlantic City, NJ, May 1966. (a)

Alger, I., and Hogan, P. Videotape: Its use and significance in psychotherapy. Paper presented at the meeting of the Society of Medical Psychoanalysts, New York Academy of Medicine, New York, September 1966. (b)

Bailey, K.G., and Sowder, W.T. Audiotape and videotape self-confrontation in psychotherapy. *Psychological Bulletin*, 1970, 74, 127–37.

Carrere, M.J. Le psychochoc cinématographique. *Annales Médico-Psychologiques*, 1954, 112, 240–5.

Geertsma, R.H., and Reivich, R.S. Repetitive self-observation by videotape playback. *Journal of Nervous and Mental Disease*, 1965, 141, 29–41.

Holzman, P.S. On hearing and seeing oneself. *Journal of Nervous and Mental Disease*, 1969, 148, 198–209.

Jones, E.E., and Harris, V.A. The attribution of attitudes. *Journal of Exprimental Social Psychology*, 1967, 3, 1–24.

Jones, E.E., and Nisbett, R.E. *The actor and the observer: Divergent perceptions of the causes of behavior.* Morristown, NJ: General Learning Press, 1971.

Jones, E.E., Rock, L., Shaver, K.G., Goethals, G.R., and Ward, L.M. Pattern of performance and ability attribution: An unexpected primacy effect. *Journal of Personality and Social Psychology*, 1968, 10, 317–40.

Kagan, N., Krathwohl, D.R., and Miller, R. Stimulated recall in therapy using videotape: A case study. *Journal of Counseling Psychology*, 1963, 10, 237–43.

Kiesler, C.A., Nisbett, R.E., and Zanna, M.P. On inferring one's beliefs from one's behavior. *Journal of Personality and Social Psychology*, 1969, 11, 321–7.

Leitenberg, H., Agras, W.S., Thompson, L.E., and Wright, D.E. Feedback in behavior modification: An experimental analysis of two cases. *Journal of Applied Behavioral Analysis*, 1968, *1*, 131–7.

McArthur, L. Appropriateness of the behavior and consensus and distinctiveness information as determinants of actors' and observers' attributions. Unpublished manuscript, Yale University, 1970.

McArthur, L.A. The how and what of why: Some determinants and consequences of causal attribution. *Journal of Personality and Social Psychology*, 1972, *22*, 171–93.

Nisbett, R.E., Caputo, G.C., Legant, P., and Marecek, J. Behavior as seen by the actor and as seen by the observer. *Journal of Personality and Social Psychology*, 1973, *27*, 154–64.

Parades, A., Ludwig, K.D., Hassenfeld, I.N., and Cornelison, F.S. A clinical study of alcoholics using audio-visual self-image feedback. *Journal of Nervous and Mental Disease*, 1969, *148*, 449–56.

Reivich, R.S., and Geertsma, R.H. Experiences with videotape self-observation by psychiatric in-patients. *Journal of Kansas Medical Society*, 1968, 69, 39–44.

Storms, M.D., and Nisbett, R.E. Insomnia and the attribution process. *Journal of Personality and Social Psychology*, 1970, *16*, 319–28.

Valins, S., and Nisbett, R.E. *Some implications of attribution process for the development and treatment of emotional disorders*. Morristown. NJ. General Learning Press, 1971.

Winer, B.J. *Statistical principles in experimental design*. New York: McGraw-Hill, 1962.

Attributions and behavior in marital interaction

T.N. Bradbury and F.D. Fincham

- - - - -
Editors'
Introduction
- - - - - - - -

Theoretical Background

The vast majority of studies on causal attribution have been carried out in the laboratory, using rather artificial stimuli and focusing on intrapersonal processes. This study is representative of a new, more dynamic perspective that examines attributions of people involved in long-term relationships (such as marriage), and investigates how attributions relate to behaviour. While extending attribution theory, this kind of research also provides a detailed analysis of intrapersonal processes that is lacking in most observational studies of interpersonal behaviour in marriage. It thus builds a bridge between the areas of causal attribution, interpersonal communication and close relationships (see chapters 7, 11 and 12 in the textbook, and the reading by Noller, chapter 11 in this *Reader*).

Previous work had demonstrated that partners unhappy with their marriage ('dissatisfied spouses') make different kinds of attribution for events in their marriage to those made by partners content with their marriage ('satisfied spouses'; see, e.g., Holtzworth-Munroe and Jacobson, 1985). Most importantly, dissatisfied spouses tend to give explanations for events that increase the impact of negative events and lessen the impact of positive events – a vicious cycle (see Bradbury and Fincham, 1990). In this way attributions could be the cause of marital distress, or help to maintain it once the relationship had reached that stage.

This research asks the next, logical question: are attributions in marriage related to behav-

Journal of Personality and Social Psychology (1992), 63:613–28.

iours in marriage? And it also asks whether the same relationship between attributions and behaviour is found in both 'distressed' and 'non-distressed' marriages, and whether attributions of cause and responsibility are both related to interpersonal behaviour. Some other studies, reviewed by the authors, hint at these relationships, but their data are open to alternative interpretations. The two studies reported were carefully designed to rule out alternative explanations of the data by, for example, observing behaviour in interaction directly, including a variety of attributional measures (attributions of cause and responsibility), sampling a range of (dis)satisfied spouses, and by controlling for the effects of marital satisfaction.

Hypotheses

Both studies address two main hypotheses:

1   Spouses' attributions for marriage problems will be related to their behaviours when trying to resolve those problems; there will be an association between negative partner-attributions and negative behaviours (i.e. ones that impede problem solving).
2   There will be a stronger association between attributions and behaviours for distressed than non-distressed spouses, especially in the case of wives (who are often more concerned with the socioemotional aspects of relationships than are husbands).

A third hypothesis is also mentioned:

3   The relationship between responsibility attributions and behaviour will be stronger than that between causal attributions and behaviour.

STUDY I

Design

The study was correlational, assessing the association between types of attribution and problem-solving behaviour.

Method

Couples participating in the study (selected from replies to an advertisement) came to the laboratory and completed a questionnaire including independent measures of marital satisfaction, an inventory of marital problems, and both causal and responsibility attributions for two marital problems. An index of causal attributions was created by summing responses assessing the locus, globality and stability of attributions across both marital problems. Higher scores on the index indicate that the cause of the problem is located in the partner, and is seen as global and stable (i.e. a negative pattern of attribution for marital problems). An index of responsibility attributions was created in the same way, by summing responses assessing blame, intention and motivation. Higher scores on this index denote that the partner is seen as to blame for the problem, and that his or her contribution is intentional and motivated by selfish concerns (i.e. again a negative pattern of attribution). These attributional indices were generally reliable, except in the case of causal attributions made by husbands.

Each couple was then asked to try to resolve a problem that they had both listed, during which period they were videotaped. These videotapes were later coded by two independent coders to create scores on a reliable index of 'problem-resolution behaviour'.

Results

Preliminary correlational analyses

As in previous studies, higher levels of marital distress were related to negative patterns of causal and responsibility attributions. Poorer problem-solving skills were also more likely to be shown by both distressed husbands and wives.

Attributions and behaviour

The correlations between attributions and the 'composite behavioral index' are shown in the bottom lines of the separate results for husbands and wives (see table 7.3, top and bottom half, respectively). Both husbands' and wives' responsibility attributions were significantly related to behaviour, but only wives' causal attributions showed this association. To examine the relationship between attributions and problem-solving behaviours, while controlling for marital satisfaction, the authors computed partial correlations between attributions and behaviours, while statistically controlling for marital satisfaction scores. The only significant partial correlation was between wives' responsibility attributions and problem-solving skills.

Moderating effects of marital satisfaction

The authors also computed analyses, separately for husbands and wives, to assess whether the association between attributions and behaviours was different for distressed and non-distressed spouses (classified according to whether scores were above or below 100 on the marital-adjustment test). This analysis tested whether marital satisfaction 'moderated' the association between attributions and behaviours. The relationship between attributions and behaviour was only moderated by satisfaction in the case of responsibility attributions for wives: as predicted, the association was stronger among (and indeed only significant for) distressed wives.

STUDY 2

A further study was carried out, using similar methodology, but designed to pay more attention to attributions in relation to interpersonal *exchanges* of behaviour, and to provide a more fine-grained analysis of behaviour. In addition to the main hypotheses, it was also predicted that spouses making maladaptive attributions would be: (a) more likely to engage in explicit discussion of the conflict; (b) more inclined to reciprocate the partner's negative behaviour; and (c) less inclined to respond to the partner's negative behaviour by either avoiding it or responding positively. A sophisticated 'lag-sequential' analysis was computed on the behavioral data to assess the likelihood that a behaviour by one spouse would be followed by a specified behaviour by the partner (e.g. negative behaviour by a husband would be followed by negative behaviour by the wife). This analysis, which controls for the overall rate at which the partner displayed the specified behaviour, allowed the authors to determine whether the behaviour by the spouse tended to increase the likelihood that the partner would display a particular behaviour.

Results again revealed a significant association between negative patterns of attribution and negative behaviours, especially for wives (see table 7.4). Bradbury and Fincham took the analysis a stage further in this study, by then analyzing the association between attributions and sequences of behaviour. There are few such links for husbands, but more in the case of wives (see table 7.5). In particular wives' tendency towards negative reciprocity (reacting to husbands' negative behaviour with their own negative behaviour) was greater, to the extent that wives viewed their marital problems as caused by the husband, and by global and stable factors (i.e. causal attributions); and they viewed their husbands as blameworthy, acting intentionally and with selfish motivation (i.e. responsibility attributions). These associations remain significant after controlling for marital satisfaction. Moderational analyses again highlighted the association between maladaptive attributions and negative reciprocal behaviour for distressed wives only.

Discussion

The two studies yielded partial support for both the main hypotheses. Hypothesis 1, relating maladaptive attributions to negative behaviour, was supported for wives only in study 1, but for husbands and wives in study 2 (except in the case of sequences of behaviour, where the association was found only for wives). Hypothesis 2, regarding a stronger association between attributions and behaviours for distressed than non-distressed spouses (especially for wives) also received some support in both studies; but the link between attributions and behaviour was not limited exclusively to distressed wives. These results support the key role of attributions in marriage, but complex issues surround the ambitious aim of exploring this role, and these are cautiously examined by the authors. There was also some support for the third hypothesis mentioned, that there would be a stronger relationship between responsibility (vs. causal) attributions and behaviour. This view is supported in study 1, but study 2 shows consistent associations between causal attributions and behaviours as well. Overall, this and continuing research attests to the important role of attributions in marriage (see Bradbury et al., 1996; Fincham, 1994; Miller and Bradbury, 1995).

FURTHER READING

Bradbury, T.N. and Fincham, F.D. (1990). Attributions in marriage: Review and critique. *Psychological Bulletin*, 107, 3–33. A complete picture of when and how attributions affect marital functioning.

Holtzworth-Munroe, A. and Jacobson, N.S. (1985). Causal attributions of married couples: When do they search for causes? What do they conclude when they do? *Journal of Personality and Social Psychology*, 48, 1398–1412. This study is of interest for its analysis of indirect, or unsolicited, 'attributional thoughts' made by distressed and non-distressed couples.

REFERENCES

Bradbury, T.N., Beach, S.R.H., Fincham, F.D. and Nelson, G.M. (1996). Attributions and behaviour in functional and dysfunctional marriages. *Journal of Consulting and Clinical Psychology*, 64, 569–76.
Fincham, F.D. (1994). Cognition in marriage: Current status and future challenges. *Applied and Preventive Psychology*, 3, 185–98.
Miller, G.E. and Bradbury, T.N. (1995). Refining the association between attributions and behaviour in marital interaction. *Journal of Family Psychology*, 9, 196–208.

Observational studies of interpersonal behavior in marriage indicate that dissatisfied couples, compared with satisfied couples, show higher rates of negative behavior, more reciprocation of negative behavior, and a greater degree of behavioral stereotypy or rigidity (for reviews see Christensen, 1987; Weiss and Heyman, 1990). Although these studies have illuminated important aspects of marital interaction, the behavioral model that guides them has been criticized for limiting the understanding of marital dysfunction. For example, within this framework, little consideration is given explicitly to spouses' prior experiences in the relationship, to their expectations and goals for the marriage, and to the process by which behavior and satisfaction come to be related (e.g., see Bradbury and Fincham, 1989; Margolin, 1983). In an effort to provide a more complete account of marital dysfunction, investigators have shifted their attention to intrapersonal factors that may influence marital satisfaction and interpersonal behavior.

A common focus of research in this developing literature is the attributions or explanations that spouses make for events that occur in their marriage. According to these studies, dissatisfied spouses, compared with satisfied spouses, offer attributions that accentuate the impact of negative events and diminish the impact of positive events. For example, a happily married wife might ascribe her husband's lack of interest in sex to pressures on him at work, whereas a distressed wife might attribute this same behavior to her husband's lack of love for her. Moreover, a satisfied husband might attribute an unexpected gift from his wife to her wanting to do something special for him, whereas a dissatisfied husband might view the same act as an attempt on her part to justify spending money on herself. This association between attributions and marital satisfaction, which appears to be quite robust (see Bradbury and Fincham, 1990), is viewed as important because attributions may initiate or maintain marital distress; recent longitudinal studies lend support to this possibility (Fincham and Bradbury, 1987, 1991b).[1]

Despite the progress made toward understanding spouses' attributions, fundamental questions remain regarding their actual impact in marriage. Indeed, a primary reason for studying attributions in marriage – that they might provide an explanation for why satisfied and dissatisfied couples differ in their behavior – has received only scant attention. The purpose of the present research, therefore, is to determine whether spouses' attributions for events in their

Primary
Reading

marriage are related to the behaviors they exhibit when interacting with their partner. A second purpose is to determine whether the association between attributions and behavior differs across distressed and nondistressed marriages. Investigation of these issues was motivated in part by the need to examine attributions in relation to observational data rather than self-report data, thus providing an assessment of their importance in marriage that is not confounded by common method variance. Before describing the present studies in greater detail, we first review conceptual and empirical work that bears on the interplay of attributions and behavior in marriage.

Attributions and Marital Behavior: Theory and Research

A common assumption of attribution models in social psychology is that an individual's attributions will affect his or her subsequent behavior (e.g., Heider, 1958; Kelley, 1973). For example, Heider (1944, p. 367). Noted that "our reaction to a disagreeable experience . . . is greatly influenced by the attribution to a source, which we may see in another person, in the workings of chance, or in ourselves. . . . When an injury is attributed to a personal agent, it is more likely to lead to an aggressive reaction." This notion is basic also to applications of attribution models, particularly in the area of marriage and close relationships (e.g., Baucom and Epstein, 1990; Bugental, 1987; Dodge, Pettit, McClaskey, and Brown, 1986; Kelley et al., 1983; Rusbult, Johnson, and Morrow, 1986; Weiss, 1984). The proposed association between attributions and marital behavior is perhaps stated most explicitly in the contextual model of marriage (Bradbury and Fincham, 1987, 1988, 1991a); hence, we examine this model in greater detail.

A view from the contextual model

Following Raush, Barry, Hertel, and Swain's (1974, p. 11) observation that "an act can seldom be independent of the context of other events in which it is embedded," the contextual model emphasizes that behaviors exchanged in an interaction can mean different things, depending on other events occurring in the interaction. According to this model, when one spouse behaves, the partner attends to and perceives that behavior, assigns some meaning to it, and then exhibits a behavior of his or her own. The events that intervene between the observable behavior of the spouse and the observable behavior of the partner are referred to as the partner's *processing stage*, which is assumed to occur rapidly and without much conscious awareness. An interaction can be viewed as comprising many such sequences of spouse's behavior → partner's processing → partner's behavior → spouse's processing → spouse's behavior, and so forth. The processing stage itself is hypothesized to be influenced by the nature of the stimulus behavior and many other factors, including momentary or transient thoughts and emotions experienced by the individual and by his or her relatively stable psychological characteristics, such as personality, chronic mood state, attitudes and beliefs about relationships, memories of prior events in the relationship, degree of satisfaction with the marriage, and so on. This framework expands the behavioral model of interaction beyond its exclusive emphasis on behavior and satisfaction by incorporating a variety of affective and cognitive constructs and in so doing seeks to permit broader examination of the relationships among intrapersonal phenomena and the interpersonal behaviors that spouses exhibit.

An important contributor to the meaning that spouses assign to partner behavior is the attribution or explanation made for that behavior. As Kelley and Thibaut (1978, p. 209) noted, "Interdependent persons have strong interests in explaining one another's behavior. Each wants to know what the other person is really like in order to know what can be expected of him in the future and under what conditions his behavior will change." The motivation to explain, predict, and modify interpersonal events is heightened when they are negative, important, and self-relevant (Weiner, 1985b), and in the domain of marriage, this typically involves negative behaviors exhibited by the partner and associated relationship difficulties encountered by the couple. The attributions offered by spouses for such events are assumed to derive from an accumulation of experiences in interaction with the partner, and in subsequent situations when the negative behavior or difficulty occurs it is likely to be understood or interpreted in terms consistent with that attribution.

The behavior that a spouse exhibits in these situations will depend in part on the attribution that he or she has made and, although the behavioral response can take many forms (e.g., clarification of own point of view, rejection of the partner's position, expression of support or optimism), it is expected that adaptive or benign attributions will give rise to behaviors that promote the resolution of the difficulty, whereas maladaptive attributions will lead to behaviors that allow the difficulty to persist. The predicted association between attributions and behavior follows from the view that if a spouse makes a maladaptive attribution for a marital difficulty (e.g., "We don't spend much time together because you insist on staying up all night watching TV!") then that spouse will tend to express emotions that discourage problem solving (e.g., anger, contempt), to convince the partner that this explanation is the correct one and that he or she is at fault for the problem (which may lead to defensiveness by the partner and further anger by the spouse) or to persuade the partner to somehow change his or her behavior (e.g., by inducing guilt: 'Sometimes I think you would rather watch TV than be with me"). In contrast, an attribution by the spouse that does not implicate the partner directly ("We don't spend much time together because we can't get our schedules in synch – you come home late and want to relax in front of the TV, and I have to be in bed early so I can get up and go off to work in the morning") may lead the spouse to exhibit behaviors that have a different emotional tone and to identify more fruitful solutions (e.g., "I'm really worried that we're not spending enough time together – do you think your boss would let you come to work a few hours early every now and then?").

Thus, even though attributions are not expected to determine a spouse's behavior entirely, the contextual model does predict an association between the degree to which a spouse's attributions for relationship difficulties are maladaptive and his or her tendency to engage in behaviors that hinder resolution of such difficulties. A pattern of maladaptive attributions followed by negative behavior and the perpetuation rather than resolution of marital difficulties may contribute to confirmation of the attribution, further exchanges of negative behavior, and declines in marital satisfaction over time. The validity of this supposition, which is consistent with the aforementioned longitudinal data relating maladaptive attributions to decreases in marital quality (Fincham and Bradbury, 1987, 1991a), rests to a large degree on whether there is a link between attributions and behavior in marital interaction. The nature of this link and its operation in distressed and nondistressed marriages is the focus of the present research.

Review and analysis of prior research

An association between attributions and behavior in marital interaction appears plausible, yet only a few studies have addressed this issue. In an experimental study, Fincham and Bradbury (1988) found that a group of dissatisfied spouses exhibited higher rates of negative behavior when they were led to believe that their partner was responsible for writing a negative description of them, relative to a group of dissatisfied spouses led to believe that their partner was not responsible for writing the negative description. Spouses' attributions for conflicts in hypothetical marriages were assessed by Doherty (1982), who reported that the tendency of wives to infer negative intent on the part of the portrayed character covaried with the amount of verbal criticism they displayed in interaction with their husbands. Fincham and O'Leary (1983) asked spouses to make attributions for hypothetical positive and negative marital events and to report their likely affective and behavioral responses to those events, and found that attributions were related to affective reactions for positive events. A subsequent study by Fincham, Beach, and Nelson (1987) indicated that spouses' attributions were related to their reported affective and behavioral responses, but only when the attribution judgments concerned the partner's accountability for their actions. Related results were presented by Sillars (1985), who found that the degree to which spouses blamed their partner covaried with more negative behavior and less positive behavior in interaction. Finally, Miller, Lefcourt, Holmes, Ware, and Saleh (1986) determined that spouses who reported a relatively external locus of control for marital outcomes were less engaged in a discussion of hypothetical conflicts and produced solutions to those conflicts that were of lower quality (for a detailed review of these studies see Bradbury and Fincham, 1990).

These studies indicate that attributions may indeed be related to behavior in marital interaction in the manner specified by the contextual model. However, rival interpretations for these data limit the conclusions that can be drawn from them and, at the same time, point to methodological refinements that need to be implemented in future research. These include (a) the need to observe behavior in interaction rather than to rely on spouses' self-reports of their behavior, as the latter are subject to distortion and may overestimate the association between attributions and behavior because of common method variance; (b) the need to measure not only causal attributions, which pertain to who or what caused some marital event, but also responsibility attributions, which pertain to accountability and blameworthiness, as both sorts reflect important attributional phenomena in marriage (Bradbury and Fincham, 1990; Shaver and Drown, 1985; see the Conceptualization of Attributions section); (c) the need to study spouses who represent the full range of marital satisfaction so that results are potentially generalizable to all couples; and (d) the need to control for the effects of marital satisfaction to demonstrate that the association between attributions and behavior is not an artifact of their shared variance with satisfaction.

Overview of the Present Research

Hypotheses

Two studies incorporating these refinements were conducted to test the proposition that attributions are related to behavior in marital interaction. On the basis of the contextual model outlined earlier, we hypothesized that spouses' attributions for problems occurring in their marriage would be related to behaviors they exhibited when attempting to resolve those problems such that attributions portraying the partner in a negative light would covary with behaviors that interfere with problem solving. Any associations between attributions and behavior were expected to remain after controlling for the effects of marital satisfaction, which might otherwise inflate these associations.

A second purpose of these studies was to determine whether the association between attributions and behavior is different at different levels of marital satisfaction. A testable hypothesis in this case begins with an examination of the basic role assigned to attributions in most attribution models. Specifically, if an attribution enables the perceiver to understand and modify unpleasant or undesirable circumstances, then a person who is experiencing circumstances of this sort should be especially inclined to engage in attributional activity. The resulting attribution is likely to be relatively well developed, and it should guide how the individual behaves to alter the difficulty. In contrast, the attribution made by an individual contending with a less challenging situation is likely to be less well developed and less critical for resolving the problem at hand and, as a consequence, may have a weaker effect on the behaviors enacted to resolve the problem. Applied to the study of marriage, this analysis gives rise to the hypothesis that the attributions made by spouses in distressed marriages will be more predictive of behavior than will be the attributions made by the spouses in nondistressed marriages.

An important extension of this line of reasoning is that the tendency to engage in meaningful attributional analysis for marital difficulties will be great not only for those individuals who are in distressed marriages, but also for women, who are often more strongly oriented than men to the socioemotional dimension of close relationships (see Worell, 1988). The relative importance that women accord their relationships is likely to contribute to their motivation for developing informative attributions about problems that arise in those relationships, and in turn, those attributions should be more predictive of behaviors enacted to alleviate such problems, compared with the attributions made by men. Thus, the second hypothesis can be made more specific: A stronger association between attributions and behavior is expected for distressed than nondistressed spouses, especially in the case of wives.

Conceptualization of attributions

Finally, two important considerations arise when examining the association between attributions and behavior. The first concerns the relationship events for which attributions are made. Although it is possible to assess attributions for discrete partner behaviors in interaction, this approach rests on the questionable assumption that attributions are typically elicited by such stimuli (see Eiser, 1983), and data indicate that spouses may not make attributions for behaviors at this level of specificity (Camper, Jacobson, Holtzworth-Munroe, and Schmaling, 1988). The present studies therefore focus instead on the attributions that spouses make for current marital difficulties, which, according to the literature on marital therapy, are a common stimulus for attributional activity (e.g., Baucom and Epstein, 1990). If a reliable association is obtained between attributions and behavior at this level of analysis, subsequent studies will be justified in investigating the molecular process by which attributions lead to specific behaviors in interaction.

The second consideration involves the types of attributions that are studied in relation to behavior. The earliest studies of attributions in marriage evolved from the learned helplessness formulation of depression and, accordingly, emphasized differences between distressed and nondistressed spouses in how they perceived the *causes* of relationship events (e.g., Fincham and O'Leary, 1983). However, recent theoretical developments recognize that this formulation neglects the interpersonal context of attributions, and the domain of marital attributions has therefore expanded to include attributions of *responsibility* (see Fincham and Bradbury, 1991a; Shaver, 1985). Whereas causal attributions concern the factors that produce an event or behavior, responsibility attributions involve an individual's accountability to another person for some misdeed, and they rest on such judgments as whether the individual behaved intentionally and with selfish motivation. Attributions of responsibility are thought to presuppose, or follow from, attributions of cause (i.e., if someone did not cause something, he or she probably will not be held responsible for it; Fincham and Jaspars, 1980) and, as a consequence, the two classes of attributions are expected to covary. Although this covariation implies that causal and responsibility attributions may be comparable in their relations to behavior, the inherently interpersonal nature of responsibility attributions suggests that they will be more consistently related to behavior than will causal attributions. This expectation is consistent with studies reviewed earlier, which showed that judgments of accountability and blame were predictive of marital behavior (Fincham et al., 1987; Sillars, 1985).

Study I

Method

Subjects

Subjects were recruited through advertisements in local media inviting "couples from all walks of life" to participate in a research project on marriage. Interested couples were mailed a description of the study, a demographics questionnaire, and a 6-item measure of marital satisfaction (Norton, 1983). Of the approximately 225 respondents (about 85% of whom reported relatively high levels of marital quality), couples were considered for participation if they were married, living together, had completed at least the 10th grade of high school, and were not receiving marital counseling. Use of these criteria ensured that all couples defined their relationship in similar (i.e., legally sanctioned) terms, that spouses within a couple had frequent contact with each other, that subjects could read and understand the questionnaires, and that couples were not seeking therapy to make major changes in their relationship. The full range of marital satisfaction scores was sampled when selecting couples for participation to represent all levels of satisfaction about equally.

The 47 couples who participated in the study had been married an average of 8.5 years (SD = 6.8), had 1.8 children (SD = 1.4; mode = 2), and had a median income between $25,000 and $30,000. Husbands averaged 32.6 years of age (SD = 7.4) and 14.0 years of formal education (SD = 2.3), and obtained a mean score of 101.3 (SD = 28.7) on the Marital Adjustment Test (MAT; Locke and Wallace, 1959). Wives averaged 30.7 years of age (SD = 6.8) and 13.7 years of education (SD = 2.2), and obtained a mean score of 101.5 (SD = 30.1) on the MAT. On the basis of the normative data presented by Crane, Allgood, Larson, and Griffin (1990), it was determined that 57% of the subjects scored within one standard deviation of the standardization mean; this suggests that most spouses in the sample scored in the mildly dissatisfied to mildly satisfied range of marital functioning.

Procedure

Couples meeting the screening criteria were contacted by telephone and all agreed to partici-pate in a laboratory session. During this session spouses independently completed a consent form, a demographics questionnaire, a measure of marital satisfaction (the MAT), and an instrument to assess the degree to which they experienced a number of common marital problems (the Inventory of Marital Problems). The experimenter examined the responses of both spouses on the latter form and summed, for each topic, the husband's and wife's independent ratings of the degree to which each topic was experienced as a difficulty in the marriage. Spouses were then instructed individually to make causal and responsibility attribu-tion ratings for the topic yielding the highest summed value. The experimenter also identified for each spouse a second topic that the spouse rated as being a difficulty in the marriage and instructed him or her to make attribution ratings for this problem. Unlike the first topic, the second topic was not necessarily the same for both spouses because spouses sometimes disagreed on what topics were problems in the marriage. Subjects were then reunited, seated facing each other, and instructed to "try to work toward a mutually agreeable solution" to the one problem they both viewed as presenting difficulties for them. The experimenter left the room, prepared the cameras and videocassette recorder for taping, and signaled the couple to begin their discussion. The couples were signaled to end their discussion after 15 min had elapsed. Couples were then debriefed and paid $30 for their participation. Videotapes of the interactions were later coded for the problem-solving behaviors that spouses exhibited.

Questionnaires

MAT Marital satisfaction was assessed with the 15-item MAT, an internally consistent (split half reliability = .90) and widely used index of marital satisfaction that discriminates between nondistressed spouses and spouses with documented marital problems (Locke and Wallace, 1959). Scores on the MAT can range from 2 to 158.

Inventory of Marital Problems The topic for the 15-min discussion was derived from spouses' ratings of 19 issues (e.g., in laws, sex, trust, and finances) that are common problems in marriage (Geiss and O'Leary, 1981). Spouses rated on 11-point scales the extent to which each item was a source of difficulty or disagreement in their marriage ($1 = not\ a\ problem$, $11 = major\ problem$).

Attributions for marital problems Spouses made causal and responsibility attributions for each of two issues that they had identified on the Inventory of Marital Problems as presenting major difficulties for them. To assess causal attributions, which pertain to the factors that produce an event (in this case a marital problem), spouses were asked to write what they considered to be the major cause of each problem. They then rated on 7-point scales the extent to which this cause (a) rests in the partner (locus: "To what extent does the cause of the difficulty rest in your spouse?" $1 = not\ at\ all$, $7 = totally$); (b) affects only the specific problem versus other areas of the marriage (globality: "Is this cause something that just affects this difficulty or does it affect other areas of your marriage?" $1 = affects\ only\ this\ area$, $7 = affects\ all\ areas$); and (c) is likely to be absent versus present when the problem occurs in the future (stability: "In the future when this difficulty arises, will the cause again be present?" $1 = will\ never\ again\ be\ present$, $7 = will\ always\ be\ present$). As in prior studies, a composite measure of causal attribution was formed to reduce the ratio of variables to subjects and to provide a more stable attribution index. This strategy was also indicated because the hypotheses under consideration did not relate to specific attribution dimensions. To form the composite measure, the six causal judgments (2 problems × 3 dimensions) were summed. Higher scores on the index represent the extent to which the respondent locates the cause of the problem in the partner and perceives the cause to be stable and global. (Coefficient alpha: for wives = .77; for husbands = .45.)

Spouses also made three responsibility attribution judgments, which pertain to the partner's accountability or answerability for producing some event, by indicating on 7-point scales the extent to which (a) the partner deserves to be blamed for the problem (blame: "To what extent do you blame your spouse for this difficulty?" 1 = *not at all*, 7 = *totally*): (b) the partner's contribution to the problem is intentional (intent: "When your spouse does things that contribute to this difficulty, are they planned – done 'on purpose' – or are they unplanned – NOT done 'on purpose'?" 1 = *planned*, 7 = *unplanned*); and (c) the problem reflects the partner's selfish concerns (motivation: "To what extent does this difficulty reflect your spouse's selfish concerns?" 1 = *not at all*, 7 = *totally*). A composite measure of responsibility attributions was formed by summing the six responsibility judgments; higher scores on this index represent the extent to which the partner's contribution to the problem is motivated by selfish concerns, intentional, and worthy of blame. (Coefficient alpha: for wives = .84; for husbands = .82.)

Behavioral coding

On the basis of discussions by behavioral marital therapists concerning the skills that couples need to solve their problems (Jacobson and Margolin, 1979; Stuart, 1980), a coding system was devised to assess the quality of each spouse's approach to solving the problem under discussion. Two trained research assistants independently coded all videotapes by making 5-point ratings on nine dimensions; the behaviors of husbands and wives were coded in separate viewings of the videotapes. There was little variance on one dimension ("extent to which the problem is denied versus accepted"), and coders could not agree reliably on a second dimension ("degree to which the spouse is disengaged versus engaged"), and hence both were dropped from further analysis.

Pearson product–moment correlations between observer ratings on the remaining seven dimensions were significant (all $ps < .001$) and ranged from .70 to .93 for husbands, median $r(45) = .81$, and from .66 to .93 for wives, median $r(45) = .75$. A final set of codes was derived from resolving disagreements between the two coders, and the internal consistency among the ratings made across the seven dimensions was examined. Examination of coefficient alpha indicated that two additional codes should be dropped ("degree to which the spouse is concerned with existing problems or with solutions to those problems" and "number of solutions proposed"), which resulted in a final composite for problem resolution behavior that was reliable for husbands (coefficient alpha = .74) and for wives (coefficient alpha = .82). Higher scores on this variable reflect problem-solving behavior of greater quality or skill. The five dimensions included in this final composite were the degree to which the spouse denies versus acknowledges his or her own contribution to the problem; the spouse focuses unconstructively on the history of the problem versus constructively on the present and future; solutions are abandoned versus pursued and explored; the spouse adopts a nonnegotiative versus negotiative approach to solving the problem; and the spouse fails to consider, versus considers, the partner's views and opinions. The median correlation among these dimensions was $r(45) = .38$ for husbands and $r(45) = .52$ for wives.

Results and discussion

Preliminary analyses

Preliminary analyses indicated that poorer problem-solving skills were more likely to be demonstrated by maritally distressed husbands, $r(45) = .26$, $p < .05$, and wives, $r(45) = .49$, $p < .001$. Replicating prior studies, higher levels of marital distress were also related to maladaptive causal attributions – that is, to greater tendencies toward attributing marital problems to the partner and to global and stable causes; for husbands, $r(45) = -.50$, $p < .001$; for wives, $r(45) = -.61$, $p < .001$ – and to maladaptive responsibility attributions – that is, to greater tendencies toward seeing the partner as worthy of blame for the problem and behaving intentionally and with selfish motivation when contributing to the problem; for husbands, $r(45) = -.45$, $p < .001$; for wives, $r(45) = -.62$, $p < .001$. Although causal and responsibility attributions were correlated; for husbands, $r(45) = .52$, $p < .001$; for wives, $r(45) = .73$, $p < .001$, factor analyses have shown that these two classes of attributions load on separate factors (Fincham and Bradbury, 1992); accordingly, the two indices were retained to examine their separate associations with marital behavior.

Attributions and behavior

Correlations between attributions and the composite variable representing problem-solving behavior were significant for wives' causal attributions and for husbands' and wives' responsibility attributions. These results are shown in the last rows of table 7.3. Because these associations might be inflated because of variance that attributions and behavior share with marital satisfaction, they were recomputed with marital satisfaction statistically controlled. Resulting partial correlations revealed that the relation between poor problem-solving skills and maladaptive attributions remained significant for wives' responsibility attributions. These results are shown also in the bottom rows of table 7.3.

Analyses were undertaken next to determine whether the association between wives' responsibility attributions and their problem-solving behavior was specific to one behavioral category or whether it generalized across behavioral categories. Correlations computed between wives' responsibility attributions and the five behavioral categories, before and after partialing marital satisfaction from the associations, are shown in table 7.3. The partial correlations indicate that the association does not appear to be restricted to one behavioral category, as benign responsibility attributions were related to wives' tendencies to acknowledge their own contribution to the problem, to focus constructively on the problem, to adopt a negotiative stance in the discussion, and to consider the husband's point of view. Husband's benign responsibility attributions were related to a tendency to focus constructively on the problem. In contrast, all partial correlations involving husbands' and wives' causal attributions were nonsignificant.

Moderating effects of marital satisfaction

A final set of analyses was conducted, separately for husbands and wives, to determine whether the association between attributions and problem-solving behavior would differ across levels of marital satisfaction. Groups of distressed and nondistressed subjects were first formed, using the standard cutoff score of 100 on the MAT to determine group assignment. This resulted in distressed groups of 21 subjects (MAT scores for husbands: $M = 74.2$, $SD = 17.8$; for wives: $M = 72.1$, $SD = 16.3$) and nondistressed groups of 26 subjects (for husbands: $M = 123.3$, $SD =$

Table 7.3 Correlations and partial correlations (controlling for marital satisfaction) between attributions and behavioral coding: Study 1

Behavior	Causal attribution composite		Responsibility attribution composite	
	r	*Partial* r	r	*Partial* r
Husband				
Acknowledges own contribution to problem	−.12	−.09	−.19	−.16
Focuses constructively on problem	−.11	.00	−.36**	−.30*
Pursues and explores solutions	−.22	−.11	−.20	−.10
Adopts a negotiative approach	−.26*	−.20	−.19	−.12
Considers partner's point of view	−.13	−.07	.01	.08
Composite behavioral index	−.24	−.13	−.26*	−.17
Wife				
Acknowledges own contribution to problem	−.25*	−.05	−.40**	−.25*
Focuses constructively on problem	−.39**	−.18	−.49***	−.32*
Pursues and explores solutions	−.07	.02	−.08	.01
Adopts a negotiative approach	−.37**	−.13	−.51***	−.32*
Considers partner's point of view	−.32*	.05	−.58***	−.35**
Composite behavioral index	−.34**	−.08	−.51***	−.30*

$N = 47$ couples. Higher attribution scores reflect attributions that are relatively maladaptive. Higher behavior scores reflect problem-solving behaviors of greater quality or skill.
*$p < .05$.
**$p < .01$.
***$p < .001$.

11.9; for wives: $M = 125.2, SD = 11.9$). These groups differed significantly on MAT scores; for husbands, $t(45) = -11.28, p < .001$; for wives, $t(45) = -12.95, p < .001$. Following recommendations by Baron and Kenny (1986) for investigating the moderating effects of one variable on the relation between two others, we computed regression equations in which problem-solving behavior was predicted from marital satisfaction group (1 = *distressed*, 2 = *nondistressed*), one of the attribution composites, and the Group × Attribution interaction term. A significant contribution to the equation by the interaction term (after marital satisfaction group and the attribution composite have been entered) can be interpreted to indicate that the association between attributions and behavior is moderated by marital satisfaction group.

Results supported the hypothesis that the association between attributions and behavior would be strongest among distressed wives, and, consistent with expectations, this finding emerged for responsibility attributions, for the interaction term, $t(45) = 1.95, p < .01$. Specifically, the relation between maladaptive responsibility attributions and poorer problem solving was stronger among distressed wives, $r(19) = -.47, p < .05$, than nondistressed wives, $r(24) = -.07$, *ns*. Follow-up analyses, using as dependent measures the separate behavioral categories rather than the composite problem-solving index, yielded an association between responsibility attributions and the extent to which wives acknowledged their own contribution to the problem; for the interaction term $t(45) = 2.50$, $p < .05$. The association between responsibility attributions and this behavior was stronger among distressed wives, $r(19) = -.47$, $p < .05$, than nondistressed wives, $r(24) = .15$, *ns*. There were no significant Group × Attribution interactions for causal attributions, and the interaction terms in parallel analyses comparing distressed and nondistressed husbands were not significant.

Conclusion

In addition to replicating the relation between marital satisfaction and behavior, and between marital satisfaction and attributions, Study 1 provides support for the hypothesis that maladaptive attributions are related to less effective or skillful problem-solving behavior in marital interaction. This association was confined largely to wives' responsibility attributions. Examination of the moderating effects of marital satisfaction revealed further that maladaptive responsibility attributions were related more strongly to behavior among distressed than nondistressed wives. This finding indicates that knowledge of distressed wives' responsibility attributions permits greater prediction of problem-solving behavior than does knowledge of nondistressed wives' responsibility attributions.

Although these results are in accordance with hypotheses and with prior findings, the observational coding may have been cast at too gross a level to detect behaviors that would relate to husbands' causal and responsibility attributions and to wives' causal attributions. That is, coders were required to make global or molar ratings that captured the interaction as a whole, rather than specific or molecular judgments about discrete behavioral acts (for a discussion of this distinction see Cairns and Green, 1979). The contextual model assumes, in contrast, that attributions will influence spouses' specific responses to discrete partner behaviors; it is therefore necessary to measure behavior at a finer level of analysis before concluding that attributions and behavior are unrelated for husbands or that causal attributions and behavior are unrelated for husbands and wives.

An additional shortcoming of Study 1 is that it focuses solely on the intrapersonal association between attributions and behavior. This also contrasts with the contextual model, which emphasizes attributions in relation to interpersonal exchanges of behavior. More important, as a result of its intrapersonal focus, an assumption of Study 1 is that the association between a spouses' attributions and behavior does not vary as a function of the partner behavior to which he or she was responding. This may be an untenable assumption because, for example, a spouse's maladaptive attribution might be more likely to guide his or her behavior after a negative partner behavior than after a positive partner behavior. Such an expectation is based on the notion, outlined in the introduction, that negative or threatening events are especially likely to prompt attributional activity and to require a behavioral response that permits the attributor to exercise some degree of control over the interaction.

To examine attributions in relation to interpersonal behavior, and to address the possibility that the association between attributions and behavior might vary as a function of antecedent partner behavior, a second study was conducted in which each individual speaking turn in the interaction was coded for the problem-solving behavior that spouses exhibited. The sequential patterns or dependencies among these behaviors were derived and analyzed in relation to husbands' and wives' attributions.

Study 2

Study 2 was conducted to investigate the degree to which spouses' causal and responsibility attributions for marital problems were related to the avoidant, positive, and negative behaviors they exhibited in a problem-solving discussion. For behavioral rates, we hypothesized that spouses making maladaptive attributions would be less likely to avoid explicit discussion of the conflict (i.e., they would be more likely to engage the problem at hand) and would exhibit relatively high rates of negative behavior and relatively low rates of positive behavior. For behavioral sequences, we hypothesized that spouses making maladaptive attributions would be more inclined to respond to the partner's behavior with negative behavior and less inclined to respond to the partner's behavior with avoidant and positive behavior. Our hypothesis for behavioral sequences was cast at this relatively general level because there is little relevant research to guide hypotheses about the relative strength of associations between attributions and specific sequences of behavior. Nevertheless, because of the prominence accorded to negative reciprocity sequences in marital interaction (see Gottman, 1979; Rusbult, Verette, Whitney, Slovik, and Lipkus, 1991; Weiss and Heyman, 1990), we were particularly interested in examining whether the reciprocating spouse's maladaptive attributions would predict the likelihood of him or her responding to a negative partner behavior with a negative behavior of his or her own. Finally, marital satisfaction was expected to moderate these associations, such that attributions and behavior would be related more strongly among distressed than nondistressed spouses, especially among wives.

Method

Subjects
Subjects were recruited through advertisements in local newspapers and, to sample the full range of marital quality in a more efficient manner than in Study 1, we also recruited subjects seeking marital therapy from a local clinic. The 40 couples (29 from the community and 11 seeking therapy) selected to participate had been married an average of 6.5 years ($SD = 6.7$), had 1.5 children ($SD = 1.4$; mode $= 1$), and had a median family income of approximately $22,500. Husbands averaged 31.5 years of age ($SD = 7.3$) and 14.4 years of formal education ($SD = 3.4$) and obtained a mean score of 99.4 ($SD = 22.7$) on the MAT. Wives averaged 30.3 years of age ($SD = 6.8$) and 14.0 years of formal education ($SD = 3.1$) and obtained a mean score of 92.1 ($SD = 29.0$) on the MAT. On the basis of the normative data presented by Crane et al. (1990), 68% of the subjects scored within one standard deviation of the standardization mean; as in Study 1 this indicates that most spouses in the sample were mildly dissatisfied to mildly satisfied with their marriage.

Procedure and questionnaires
On arrival at the laboratory, spouses were separated and asked to complete a consent form, a demographics questionnaire, the MAT, the Inventory of Marital Problems, and, for two marital difficulties identified from responses on the Inventory, the measure of Attributions for Marital Problems (see Study 1 for a description of these instruments). The procedures used to identify two difficulties as stimuli for the attribution ratings and one difficulty as the topic for the conversation were identical to those used in Study 1. After completing these measures spouses

were reunited and instructed to work toward a mutually agreeable solution to the primary marital problem identified by the experimenter. Couples were signaled to end their discussion after 15 min had elapsed, at which point they were debriefed and paid $30. Videotapes of the interactions were later coded for the problem-solving behaviors that spouses exhibited. Internal consistency analyses indicated that, for the causal attribution index, coefficient alpha was .65 for wives and .61 for husbands; for the responsibility attribution index, coefficient alpha was .68 for wives and .76 for husbands.

Behavioral coding

Verbatim transcripts of the interactions were prepared and divided into individual speaking turns ($M = 187.8$ speaking turns per couple, $SD = 64.8$), and trained coders used the transcripts and videotapes to assign one of seven codes to each turn. These codes, which comprised the Verbal Tactics Coding Scheme (see Sillars, 1981), were reduced as recommended by Sillars to three summary codes in the following manner: Behaviors reflecting denial of the problem or shifting of the discussion away from the problem were coded as *avoidant*, behaviors reflecting hostility or rejection of the partner's views were coded as *negative*, and behaviors reflecting empathy for the partner and neutral or positive information about the problem were coded as *positive*. Coders were also allowed to assign an *other* code to behaviors, but to reduce the number of significance tests conducted, and to circumvent the problem of ipsative data that results from the analysis of proportions, these codes were omitted from analysis. Coders were instructed to make a global evaluation of each speaking turn, attending to the verbal and nonverbal components of the behavior. Independent coding of 20% of the videotapes revealed that coders were reliable (coefficient kappa = .84).

To control for variation across spouses in their number of speaking turns, we divided the number of times each of the three codes was emitted by each spouse in the interaction by their number of speaking turns. To stabilize variance of these proportions, they were then subjected to an arcsine transformation (see Kleinbaum and Kupper, 1978).

To examine the sequential patterning of the three classes of behavior between husbands and wives in the interaction, we performed lag sequential analysis on the behavioral data (see Sackett, 1979, for a discussion of lag sequential analysis, and see Allison and Liker, 1982, for a description of the z score computation used here). This procedure yields z scores that represent the likelihood that a behavior by one spouse will be followed by a specified behavior by the partner, controlling for the base rate with which the partner exhibits that behavior. (See Bradbury and Fincham, 1991b, and Sackett, 1979, for details on why the resulting values are z scores.) Thus, for example, this procedure generates values reflecting the likelihood that the wife will respond to the husband's negative behavior with her own negative behavior, taking into account her general tendency to exhibit negative behavior in the interaction.

Although lag sequential analysis permits investigation of contingencies between behaviors that are separated by several speaking turns, only immediate (i.e., Lag 1) contingencies between behaviors were investigated in the present study. This focus was adopted because, in its present form, the contextual model makes no specific predictions about the association between a spouse's attributions and behavior beyond the immediately preceding partner behavior and because investigation of longer sequences of behavior (even with relatively few behavioral categories) generates a high number of nonindependent statistical tests. Application of lag sequential analysis produced nine z scores for husbands when they responded to their partner and nine z scores for wives when they responded to their partner, as each spouse could respond to each of three partner behaviors with any one of their own three behaviors.

Results and discussion

Preliminary analyses

With lower levels of marital satisfaction, husbands tended to exhibit more avoidant behaviors, $r(38) = -.28$, $p < .05$; more negative behaviors, $r(38) = -.37$, $p < .01$; and fewer positive behaviors, $r(38) = .43$, $p < .005$. Although corresponding correlations for wives were in the expected direction, their marital satisfaction was unrelated to their avoidant, $r(38) = -.07$, *ns*; negative, $r(38) = -.12$, *ns*; and positive, $r(38) = .13$, *ns*, behaviors. The latter finding is unexpected, particularly in view of the significant results for husbands with these behaviors and the significant results for husbands and wives in Study 1. Although a nonsignificant association between behavior and satisfaction has been obtained in previous studies (see Baucom and Adams, 1987), an explanation for this finding is not immediately apparent.

Higher levels of marital distress were related to maladaptive causal attributions – that is, to greater tendencies to attribute marital problems to the partner and to global and stable causes for wives, $r(38) = -.39$, $p < .01$, but not for husbands, $r(38) = -.20$, *ns*. Higher levels of distress were related to maladaptive responsibility attributions – specifically, to greater tendencies to see the partner as blameworthy for the problems and as behaving intentionally and with selfish motivation when contributing to the problems; for husbands, $r(38) = -.45$, $p < .005$; for wives, $r(38) = -.32$, $p < .05$. These findings are consistent with existing research, as responsibility attributions tend to relate more reliably than causal attributions to marital satisfaction (see Bradbury and Fincham, 1990). Causal and responsibility attributions were related for husbands, $r(38) = .61$, $p < .001$, and for wives, $r(38) = .78$, $p < .001$, and as in Study 1, they were retained for examination of their separate associations with marital behavior.

Attributions and behavioral rates

Partial correlations were computed between the attribution composites and the three behavior categories, with marital satisfaction statistically controlled. The results of these analyses, shown in table 7.4, indicate first that husbands and wives were more likely to exhibit negative behavior to the extent that they attributed their marital problems to their partner and to global and stable causes. Husbands' and wives' rates of negative behavior were also greater to the extent that the partner was viewed as blameworthy, behaving intentionally, and selfishly motivated. Second, wives exhibited less positive behavior to the extent that they made unfavorable causal and responsibility attributions. Finally, all partial correlations between rates of avoidant behavior and attributions were nonsignificant.

The relation between husbands' and wives' maladaptive attributions and their higher rates of negative behavior is consistent with expectations and supports the contention made following Study 1, that a relatively molecular level of coding would afford a more powerful test of the association between attributions and behavior. These findings are also noteworthy because they were obtained despite nonsignificant associations between husbands' marital satisfaction and causal attributions and between wives' marital satisfaction and their rates of negative behavior. Indeed it is surprising that significant prediction of wives' negative behavior was possible from their causal and responsibility attributions, but not from their marital satisfaction.

Table 7.4 Correlations and partial correlations (controlling for marital satisfaction) between attributions and behavioral rates: Study 2

Behavior	Causal attribution composite		Responsibility attribution composite	
	r	Partial r	r	Partial r
	Husband			
Avoidant	−.14	−.21	−.08	−.23
Negative	.32*	.27*	.54****	.45***
Positive	−.15	−.08	−.40**	−.25
	Wife			
Avoidant	.09	.07	−.10	−.13
Negative	.61****	.62****	.60****	.59****
Positive	−.55****	−.55****	−.46***	−.44***

$N = 40$ couples. Higher attribution scores reflect attributions that are relatively maladaptive.
*$p < .05$.
**$p < .01$.
***$p < .005$.
****$p < .001$.

Attributions and behavioral sequences

Correlations were computed next between the attribution composites and the z scores derived from lag sequential analysis, before and after statistically controlling for marital satisfaction. These analyses, presented in table 7.5, reveal several significant associations between both classes of attributions and several sorts of behavioral responses to partner behavior for wives, and few such associations for husbands. Perhaps the most notable of these results involves the wives' negative responses to the husbands' negative behavior (i.e., husband negative → wife negative in table 7.5). The present findings indicate that this tendency toward negative reciprocity, viewed by many as the hallmark of marital discord, is greater to the extent that wives (a) view their marital problems as caused by the husband and by global and stable factors and (b) view their husband as blameworthy and acting intentionally and with selfish motivation when contributing to marital problems. Most important, these associations remain after controlling for marital satisfaction.

In addition to showing that wives will reciprocate negative behavior to the extent that they make maladaptive attributions, the partial correlations in table 7.5 reveal that wives' tendency to respond to a negative behavior with other than a negative behavior is also related to their attributions. Specifically, wives making relatively benign responsibility attributions tend to respond to a negative behavior with an avoidant behavior or with a positive behavior, relative to wives making maladaptive responsibility attributions.

Wives' responding to husbands' avoidant behavior with a positive behavior of their own was also related to their causal and responsibility attributions. Specifically, wives' tendency to

Table 7.5 Correlations and partial correlations (controlling for marital satisfaction) between attributions and *z* scores representing Lag 1 sequential dependencies among husband and wife behaviors: Study 2

Behavior sequence	Causal attribution composite		Responsibility attribution composite	
	r	*Partial* r	r	*Partial* r
Wife				
H avoidant → W avoidant	.22	.30*	.05	.11
H avoidant → W negative	−.14	−.09	−.31*	−.27
H avoidant → W positive	.34*	.29*	.44***	.40**
H negative → W avoidant	−.19	−.16	−.41**	−.39*
H negative → W negative	.45***	.59****	.32*	.41*
H negative → W positive	−.16	−.21	−.40*	−.45***
H positive → W avoidant	−.05	−.11	.08	.05
H positive → W negative	−.10	−.07	−.29	−.28
H positive → W positive	−.31*	−.24	−.38**	−.33*
Husband				
W avoidant → H avoidant	−.25	−.23	−.16	−.12
W avoidant → H negative	−.03	.00	−.18	−.12
W avoidant → H positive	.06	.04	.28*	.27*
W negative → H avoidant	−.00	.06	−.17	−.05
W negative → H negative	−.05	−.09	.17	.10
W negative → H positive	−.01	.00	−.11	−.08
W positive → H avoidant	.26	.23	.14	.08
W positive → H negative	−.04	−.04	−.11	−.13
W positive → H positive	−.29*	−.24	−.34*	−.22

N = 40 couples. Higher attribution scores reflect attributions that are relatively maladaptive. Degrees of freedom vary slightly across values because not all spouses exhibited all classes of behavior in sufficient numbers for lag sequential analysis. H = husband; W = wife.
*$p < .05$.
**$p < .01$.
***$p < .005$.
****$p < .001$.

exhibit positive behavior following an avoidant partner behavior was greater to the extent that they make maladaptive causal and responsibility attributions. This may suggest a strategy on the part of those wives holding such attributions to use positive behavior to bring their retreating husbands back into the conflict, perhaps only to express at a later point their negative impressions of his role in the problem. Wives also tended to respond to an avoidant behavior with an avoidant behavior of their own to the extent that they make relatively maladaptive causal attributions. We can speculate that this reflects a tendency to "let the husband off the hook" and to follow him as he takes the discussion away from the problem under discussion, perhaps in response to recognizing that the husband's desire to withdraw results from her critical view of his contribution to the conflict.

In addition, wives appear to reciprocate positive behavior to the extent that they make benign or adaptive responsibility attributions. Together with the significant results obtained for wives' rates of positive behavior (see previous section) and for their positive responses to husbands' avoidant and negative behaviors, this association is noteworthy because it indicates that attributions are related not only to the negative behaviors that are often highlighted in analyses of marital interaction, but also to behaviors reflecting empathy and consideration of the partner's views.[2]

Moderating effects of marital satisfaction

As in Study 1, we sought to determine whether the relation between attributions and behaviors differed across levels of marital satisfaction. A cutoff score of 100 on the MAT was used again to determine group assignment, resulting in distressed groups of 19 subjects (MAT scores for husbands: $M = 79.6$, $SD = 14.1$; for wives: $M = 66.0$, $SD = 17.4$) and nondistressed groups of 21 subjects (husbands: $M = 117.2$, $SD = 11.0$; wives: $M = 116.6$, $SD = 11.0$). These groups differed significantly on MAT scores; for husbands, $t(38) = -9.47$, $p < .001$; for wives, $t(38) = -10.88$ $p < .001$. The possible moderating effects of marital satisfaction were again examined by determining, with regression equations, whether the Marital satisfaction group × Attribution composite term was a significant predictor of the behavioral variable in question, beyond the effects of marital satisfaction group and the attribution composite.

Behavioral rates   The Marital satisfaction group × Causal attribution interaction term was a significant predictor of avoidant behavior among husbands, $t(38) = 1.71$, $p < .05$. Examination of corresponding within-group correlations indicated that distressed husbands were less likely to avoid discussion of the problem to the extent that they made maladaptive causal attributions, $r(17) = -.44$, $p < .05$, whereas this relation was nonsignificant for nondistressed husbands, $r(19) = .06$, *ns*. This indicates that distressed husbands, but not nondistressed husbands, pursued discussion of the problem rather than avoided it to the degree that they located the cause of the problem in their spouse and saw it as temporally stable and globally influential in the marriage. Remaining interaction effects for husbands were not significant.

For wives, a significant interaction between marital satisfaction group and responsibility attributions was obtained in the prediction of positive behaviors, $t(38) = -1.69$, $p < .05$. The corresponding correlations indicated that nondistressed wives were more likely to exhibit positive behaviors to the extent that they made less maladaptive responsibility attributions, $r(17) = -.59$, $p < .005$, whereas this association was nonsignificant for distressed wives, $r(19) = -.18$, *ns*. Thus, relatively benign responsibility attributions covaried with higher rates of positive behavior for nondistressed wives, but no such covariation was found among distressed wives. Remaining interaction effects for wives were not significant.

Behavioral sequences   Marital satisfaction moderated the association between husbands' attributions and their responses to avoidant partner behavior and between wives' attributions and their responses to negative partner behavior (see table 7.6). Specifically, to the extent that they make relatively maladaptive causal attributions, distressed husbands are *more* likely to respond to their partner's avoidant behavior with a positive behavior of their own. This distinguishes

Table 7.6   Significant moderating effects of marital satisfaction on associations between attributions and behavior sequences: Study 2

Attribution and behavior sequence	Marital satisfaction group × Attribution interaction		Marital satisfaction group	
	B	*t*	*Distressed* r	*Nondistressed* r
	Husbands			
Causal attributions with				
W avoidant → H positive	−.17	−2.37*	.46†	−.29
W avoidant → H avoidant	.44	3.03**	−.55††	.28
	Wives			
Causal attributions with				
H negative → W negative	−.55	−4.23***	.63†††	.37
Responsibility attributions with				
H negative → W negative	−.44	−2.19*	.54†	.21

N = 19 distressed couples and 21 nondistressed couples. Higher attribution scores reflect attributions that are relatively maladaptive. Degrees of freedom vary slightly across values because not all spouses exhibited all classes of behavior in sufficient numbers for lag sequential analysis. H = husband; W = wife.
For B: *$p < .05$. **$p < .005$. ***$p < .001$.
For r: †$p < .05$. ††$p < .01$. †††$p < .005$.

them from nondistressed husbands, whose causal attributions are unrelated to their positive responses to avoidant behavior.[3] In addition, to the extent that they make maladaptive causal attributions, distressed husbands are *less* likely to respond to their wive's avoidant behavior with an avoidant behavior of their own. This also distinguishes them from nondistressed husbands, whose causal attributions are unrelated to their tendency to reciprocate avoidant behavior. The remaining moderating analyses for husbands were not significant.

The reason for this pattern of results is not clear, but one possibility is that the behavioral sequence involving husbands' positive behavior is a cause of maladaptive attributions, whereas the sequence involving husbands' failure to reciprocate avoidant behavior is a consequence of maladaptive attributions. Specifically, if we assume that husbands are especially motivated to keep their level of emotional arousal at a manageable level because it is "harmful, unpleasant, and undesirable" for them (Gottman and Levenson, 1986, p. 44), then they may behave in ways that allow them to minimize their involvement in conflict. One behavioral strategy that may reflect this need and accomplish this goal would involve responding to their wife's avoidant behavior with a positive behavior. Over time, however, the tendency for the wife to avoid conflict and for the husband to reward inadvertently this avoidance may result in their failure to resolve that conflict. When asked to provide an attribution for why this problem exists in the marriage, the husband may reflect on the events in their interactions and assert that "it's all because of my wife – she doesn't seem to want to do anything to change it." This attribution, which is maladaptive in part because it does not acknowledge the husband's own role in the failure to resolve the problem, may contribute in turn to the husband's subsequent tendency to not allow his wife to avoid the problem ("this problem is her fault and it really bothers me that we haven't solved it. . . . I'm not going to let her get off the hook this time").

Although this explanation goes far beyond the data we have presented here, it does mesh well with recent speculation that distressed husbands seek to escape high levels of affective arousal and that couples are conditioned to repeat those sequences of behavior that restore calm in interaction (Gottman and Levenson, 1986). It also provides a starting point for understanding the interactional precursors to spouse's attributions, an issue that has remained largely unaddressed in the marital attribution literature.

Turning to the results for wives, table 7.6 shows that their attributions appeared to be especially important when responding to the negative behavior of their husbands. To the extent that they made relatively maladaptive attributions of either type, distressed wives were more likely to reciprocate their husbands' negative behavior. Distressed and nondistressed wives differ in this regard, as nondistressed wives' responsibility attributions were unrelated to their tendency to reciprocate negative behavior. This suggests that the association between wives' maladaptive responsibility attributions and their reciprocation of negative behavior (see table 7.5) is limited to maritally distressed wives. This finding is noteworthy because it shows that the general deficit in problem solving that covaries with maladaptive attributions (in Study 1) can be specified as a predisposition toward negative reciprocity (in Study 2). The remaining moderating analyses for wives were not significant.

Conclusion

In this study, husbands' and wives' causal and responsibility attributions were related to the rates at which they exhibited negative behavior, and wives' causal and responsibility attributions were related to the rates at which they exhibited positive behavior. With the data from Study 1, these results lend greater support to the hypothesis that attributions for marital problems are related to the behaviors that spouses exhibit in problem-solving discussions. More important, Study 2 demonstrates that spouses' attributions are related to the behavioral responses they make to specific partner behaviors. These data are among the first to address the role of spouses' attributions at an interpersonal level of analysis, and they are consistent with the possibility that attributions contribute to behavioral responding in marital interaction.

The associations between attributions and behavior were qualified in important ways when examined within distressed and nondistressed groups. Fox example, among distressed husbands (but not among nondistressed husbands), maladaptive attributions were related to a decreased tendency to reciprocate wives' avoidant behavior and to an increased tendency to respond to wives' avoidant behavior with a positive behavior. Among wives, the tendency to reciprocate negative behavior was related significantly to maladaptive attributions in the distressed group but not in the nondistressed group. This latter finding is consistent with predictions and adds to a growing literature that indicates that distressed wives, possibly in response to their disengaged and withdrawn husbands, are particularly likely to exhibit and reciprocate negative behavior (e.g., Floyd and Markman, 1983). The present findings extend this literature by suggesting that this pattern of behavior is especially characteristic of those distressed wives who view the causes of marital problems as stable, global, and located within the partner, and who believe that the partner is acting intentionally, with selfish motivation, and in a blameworthy manner when contributing to those problems.

General Discussion

Rationale and results of the studies

Research on marital interaction has yielded considerable insight into behavioral differences between distressed and nondistressed couples, and in recent years, investigation of intrapersonal factors in marriage has shown that distressed and nondistressed couples display differences also in the attributions they make for events in their relationship. Examination of the interplay between behavior and attributions in this domain is important because, on one hand, the determinants of marital interaction patterns are largely unspecified and, on the other hand, the impact of attributions on interpersonal processes in marriage is not well understood. The present studies were designed to combine these two lines of research by determining whether spouses' attributions were related to their behavior in interaction and whether the association between attributions and behavior was different in distressed and nondistressed marriages.

The first hypothesis, that maladaptive attributions for marital problems would covary with behaviors that interfered with the resolution of such problems, received partial support in both studies. In Study 1, wives making relatively maladaptive responsibility attributions tended to exhibit a variety of behaviors likely to hinder effective problem solving, and in Study 2, husbands and wives making relatively maladaptive causal and responsibility attributions tended to exhibit higher rates of interpersonally hostile and rejecting behaviors. Sequences of behavior were also examined in Study 2, which showed that wives making relatively maladaptive causal and responsibility attributions were more likely to reciprocate their husband's negative behavior. Wives making relatively maladaptive responsibility attributions were also less likely to reciprocate the husband's empathic and supportive behaviors. In each case these results were significant after controlling for marital satisfaction.

The second hypothesis, that the association between attributions and behavior would be greater among distressed spouses and particularly among distressed wives, also received some support. In Study 1 the association between relatively maladaptive responsibility attributions and poorer problem-solving behaviors was significant for distressed wives but not for nondistressed wives. This finding was extended to behavioral sequences in Study 2, where it was found that the maladaptive causal and responsibility attributions of distressed wives covaried significantly with their tendency to reciprocate negative partner behaviors; these associations were not significant for nondistressed wives. The significant associations in Study 2 between attributions and behavior were not limited entirely, however, to distressed wives. For example, distressed husbands, but not nondistressed husbands, were less likely to avoid discussion of the problem to the extent they made relatively maladaptive causal attributions, and nondistressed wives, but not distressed wives, were found to exhibit more positive behaviors to the extent that they made relatively benign responsibility attributions.

These findings extend the largely independent literatures on interaction and attributions in marriage by suggesting that the behaviors that spouses exhibit in conversations with their partner may be due, in part, to the attributions they have formed for their marital difficulties. With marital satisfaction statistically controlled, it appears that the degree to which a spouse is generally constructive or counterproductive in resolving a conflict may depend on the extent to which he or she tends to hold benevolent or malevolent explanations for marital conflicts. Moreover, the degree of covariation between attributions and behavior appears to differ in happy and unhappy marriages so that, for example, critical or hostile behavior is more predictable from attributions in the case of distressed wives compared with nondistressed wives. We might expect that a spouse's consistent tendency to attribute marital problems to the partner, and, accordingly, to exhibit more negative behavior, would contribute to the perpetuation of those problems and, over time, to declines in marital satisfaction.

To our knowledge these data are the first to relate spouses' causal and responsibility attributions to rates and sequences of behavior in interaction. These findings build on prior research on attributions and behavior in marriage and lend support to formulations of marriage that emphasize the role of intrapersonal variables in interpersonal behavior and marital dysfunction. We now turn to a discussion of the limitations of the present studies before considering their implications for theory and research.

Limitations and qualifications

Although promising, interpretation of these studies is qualified by a number of factors. First, the results might be influenced by important unmeasured variables. Most prominent in this regard are depression, which is known to be more prevalent among maritally distressed than nondistressed spouses (Beach, Sandeen, and O'Leary, 1990), and a number of cognitive variables that are likely to correlate with attributions (e.g., maladaptive beliefs and assumptions about marriage); factors such as these should be examined directly in future studies. Second, a number of points can be raised about the assessment of attributions: (a) spouses were asked to make attributions for two problems and then to discuss only one of them, which may underestimate the relation between attributions and behavior but may also assume greater cross-situational consistency among spouses' attributions than actually exists (cf. Baucom, Sayers, and Duhe, 1989); (b) the attribution ratings that were solicited in response to specific questions may differ from those that would be obtained from unstructured, open-ended responses; (c) coefficient alpha obtained for some of the attribution composites, especially husbands' causal attributions, attenuates correlations with other variables, thus emphasizing the need for more reliable assessment of attributions for marital difficulties; and (d) administration of the attribution questionnaire before the interaction may have influenced the interaction and altered the association between attributions and behavior, suggesting that future studies should consider manipulating the order of the attribution and behavior assessments.

Third, although the topics identified for discussion were major marital problems for all couples, distressed couples may have discussed issues that were more serious or difficult than those discussed by nondistressed couples. This factor, which is a greater threat to the validity of the second purpose of the studies than the first (in which the effects of satisfaction were partialed from associations between attributions and behavior), should be controlled in future studies. Fourth, the present findings are based on couples who had been married for about 7 years and may not generalize to couples at different stages in their marriage (e.g., newlyweds, long-term marriages). Finally, the cross-sectional design used here does not permit statements to be made about the causal relations between attributions and behavior.[4]

Implications for theory

Although the present studies address a fundamental assumption of attribution models (i.e., that an individual's attributions affect his or her social behavior), they were designed for the more specific purpose of examining the widely held view that attributions influence behavior in functional and dysfunctional relationships. According to the contextual model of marriage that guided these studies (Bradbury and Fincham, 1987, 1988, 1991a), spouses attend to, perceive, and assign meaning to behavior exhibited by the partner and, as a function of this processing and the factors that influence it, they then exhibit a behavioral response of their own. Taken together, Studies 1 and 2 indicate that one likely component of the processing stage, spouses' attributions for marital problems and the partner's role in them, does account for variation in behavioral responding. The studies indicate further that (a) this link remains intact after controlling for marital satisfaction, which can be understood in terms of the contextual model as a stable intraindividual factor that influences the processing stage, and (b) the strength of the link between a spouse's attribution and his or her behavior appears to vary as a function of the partner behavior that he or she is processing.

In addition to lending support to basic assertions of the contextual model, the present data help to identify a number of issues in need of further study. First, important questions remain regarding the most appropriate conception of attributions in the model. Although it seems plausible to assume that spouses do not make attributions anew for each partner behavior in the rapidly unfolding course of interaction, the mechanism by which existing attributions are activated and acted on in interpersonal settings is unknown. One possibility is that the negative affect associated with marital distress renders maladaptive attributions chronically active and accessible, so that when negative events are encountered the distressed spouse interprets them automatically in terms of that explanation and behaves accordingly. This possibility is consistent with the significant moderating analyses reported here, and within the contextual model, this would be an example of the more general process whereby an enduring affective state (i.e., marital distress) influences how partner behavior is processed by the spouse to produce a behavioral response by the spouse. One means of exploring this hypothesis is to induce a positive emotional state in distressed and nondistressed spouses before a problem-solving discussion and to examine the relative impact of the manipulation on attributions and behavioral exchanges.

A second issue raised by these studies concerns the contributions of causal and responsibility attributions to behavior in interaction. The contextual model, drawing on models of attribution that propose that responsibility attributions presuppose or follow from causal attributions (see Fincham and Jaspars, 1980), assumes that the relatively affectively laden responsibility attributions will bear a more consistent relation with marital behavior compared with causal attributions. Prior studies (Fincham, Beach and Nelson, 1987; Sillars, 1985) and the results of Study 1 do lend support to this position, but the consistent associations between causal attributions and the behavioral rates and sequences examined in Study 2 indicate that it would be premature to assume that causal judgments are an unnecessary component of the processing stage in the contextual model and that they are less important than responsibility attributions for understanding marital interaction.[5]

If further studies corroborate the utility of retaining both causal and responsibility attributions in the contextual model and indicate that both make contributions to marital behavior, then the question of how these attributions operate in the processing stage will need to be addressed directly. One possibility is that certain partner behaviors differentially activate causal judgments (e.g., concerning the causal locus of the problem: "Things have gotten better between us since I changed jobs, don't you think?") or responsibility judgments (e.g., concerning the degree to which contributions to the problem are intentional: "Why do you insist on aggravating me when I am talking to my friends on the telephone?") which, depending on the relative distribution of such partner behaviors in an interaction, could lead to different associations between the two classes of attribution and behavior. Regardless of the accuracy of this proposition, the data presented here suggest that causal attributions may indeed play an important role in how spouses process and respond to partner behavior, but additional data are necessary to make more specific statements about the nature of the processing stage.

A third issue highlighted by these studies is that further refinement of the contextual model should acknowledge the possibility that husbands and wives differ in their processing of partner behavior. In its original formulation the contextual model assumed that the processing of partner behavior was the same for husbands and wives, and in this regard the model is similar to most psychological models of overt behavior in marital interaction, such as Gottman's (1979) structural model, in that it does not assign separate and unique roles and qualities to husbands and wives. However, the results of the present studies tend to be more reliable for wives than for husbands,[6] and overall, they depict husbands whose behavior is more predictable from marital quality than from attributions (cf. table 7.5) and wives whose behavior seems to covary somewhat closely with the inferences they make for marital problems. This may reflect a more differentiated and sensitive capacity among women to interpret and respond to partner behavior (e.g., husbands base their behavior on global sentiment toward the marriage, whereas wives base their behavior on global sentiment as well as their explanations for partner behavior), but far more research and theoretical development are required on this subject before such a characterization of processing can be held with confidence (see Peplau, 1983).

Implications for research

These studies help to clarify our understanding of existing research on marriage. For example, with regard to research on marital interaction, the present findings indicate that the degree to which spouses make maladaptive attributions may account in part for why distressed spouses tend to exhibit and reciprocate negative partner behavior (e.g., Gottman, 1979), why distressed spouses are especially reactive to negative partner behavior (e.g., Jacobson, Waldron, and Moore, 1980), and why distressed wives are especially prone to these behavioral tendencies (e.g., Floyd and Markman, 1983). With regard to research on attributions, these findings lend ecological validity to the experimentally obtained relation between attributions and behavior (Fincham and Bradbury, 1988) and suggest that maladaptive attributions may predict declines in marital quality over time (e.g., Fincham and Bradbury, 1987) because of their association with less positive behavior and more negative behavior in interaction; the degree to which attributional tendencies precede rather than follow from marital interaction is an important topic for future research.

Several new lines of research are also suggested by the present results. First, it would be valuable to compare attributions in the manner they are assessed here with attributions made "on-line" for each partner behavior in interaction. A high degree of redundancy between these two modes of measurement would suggest that attributions are best understood as stable and traitlike variables, whereas low redundancy would suggest they are more situational and statelike in nature. It is possible also that attributions for negative events will be traitlike for distressed couples but statelike for happy couples (see Baucom et al., 1989). Second, in view of theoretical links proposed between attributions and specific affects in social psychology (e.g., Weiner, 1985b) and empirical studies relating the expression of specific affects with declines in marital satisfaction (Gottman and Krokoff, 1989), it would be useful to determine whether attributions are related to specific affects in interaction and whether certain attributions are differentially predictive of affective expressions (e.g., viewing the causes of marital problems as stable and global may predict sadness, whereas viewing the partner as behaving intentionally and selfishly when contributing to problems may predict anger). Finally, these studies indicate that variation in attributions across spouses relates to variation in overt behavior. A more powerful test of the attribution–behavior association could be undertaken by examining the degree to which behavior is a function of variation in attributions within spouses over time.

Conclusion

Although interactional differences between distressed and nondistressed couples are well documented, surprisingly little is known about the factors that contribute to these differences. The two studies presented here indicate that spouses' behaviors in interaction are related to the attributions they make for marital problems. In addition to extending the interaction literature, these studies are noteworthy because, unlike many marital attribution studies, they relate spouses' attributions to important aspects of marriage in a manner unconfounded by common method variance. Further development of theory and research in this domain appears necessary because "very few studies have addressed the intricate connections between overt and covert classes of events within interaction" and because "the interface between overt behaviors and their interpretive antecedents and consequences defines a very important area for future research" (McClintock, 1983, p. 108).

NOTES

Thomas N. Bradbury was supported in this research by National Research Service Award MH 09740-01 from the National Institute of Mental Health and by National Science Foundation Grant BNS 88-13052. Frank D. Fincham was supported in this research by National Institute of Mental Health Grant MH 44078-01.
    We thank Susan Campbell, Andrew Christensen, Cathy Cohan, Ben Karney, Anne Peplau, and Bernard Weiner for their helpful comments on an earlier version of this article.

[1] For brevity, we use the term *maladaptive* to characterize attributions that, compared with *adaptive* or *benign* attributions, exaggerate the destructive aspects of negative partner behavior or minimize the constructive aspects of positive partner behavior. No causal effect of attributions on the quality of marriage is intended.

[2] We examined the relations between individual attribution dimensions and the likelihood of various behavioral sequences, with marital satisfaction controlled. For wives, significant associations were obtained across all dimensions. For husbands, significant findings emerged only on the dimension of intent; for example, to the extent they believed that their partner was contributing intentionally to the marital difficulty, they were less likely to reciprocate positive behavior, partial $r(37) = -.27, p < .05$, and more likely to reciprocate negative behavior, partial $r(37) = .35, p < .05$.

[3] Similar but nonsignificant results were found for this behavior sequence and responsibility attributions, $t(38) = 1.42$, *ns*. For distressed husbands, relatively maladaptive responsibility attributions correlated with an increased tendency to respond to avoidant behaviors with positive behaviors, $r(17) = .53, p < .05$; nondistressed husbands showed no such tendency, $r(19) = .07$, *ns*.

[4] It is possible that significant results were obtained in the comparisons of distressed and nondistressed subjects because these groups differed in the degree of variability in their satisfaction, attribution, or behavior scores. To test this possibility, a series of F tests for variance were computed for all variables analyzed in the two studies, for husbands and wives. (With these tests, F values were generated for a given variable by dividing the larger sample variance by the smaller sample variance with $df = 1, 45$ in Study 1 and $df = 1, 38$ in Study 2.) The majority (71%) of these tests were not significant ($p > .05$), and none of the tests were significant for marital satisfaction. The tests reaching statistical significance suggested that nondistressed couples were more variable than distressed couples; these differences were comparable for husbands and wives and did not bear any systematic relation to the significant moderating effects reported in the two studies.

[5] Fisher's r-to-z transformations showed that, in Study 1, partial correlations were stronger for responsibility attributions than causal attributions for focusing constructively on the problem (husbands: $z = 2.07, p < .05$) and for considering the partner's point of view (wives: $z = 2.76; p < .01$). Remaining comparisons in Study 1 and all such comparisons in Study 2 were nonsignificant.

[6] Fisher's r-to-z transformations were used to compare the partial correlations between attributions and behavior for husbands and wives. In table 7.3, the association between responsibility attributions and consideration of the partner's point of view was greater for wives than for husbands ($z = 2.96, p < .005$). In table 7.4, the association between causal attributions and negative behavior ($z = 2.80, p < .01$) and between causal attributions and positive behavior ($z = 3.36, p < .001$) was greater for wives than for husbands. In table 7.5, for causal attributions, associations were greater for wives than for husbands with the avoidant → avoidant sequence ($z = 3.40, p < .001$) and the negative → negative sequence ($z = 4.80, p < .0001$). For responsibility attributions, associations were greater for wives than for husbands with the negative → avoidant ($z = 2.26, p < .05$), negative → negative ($z = 2.10, p < .05$), and negative → positive ($z = 2.53, p < .05$) sequences. Thus, in no case was the association between attributions and behavior greater for husbands than for wives. Remaining comparisons in the tables were nonsignificant.

REFERENCES

Allison, P., and Liker, J. (1982). Analyzing sequential categorical data on dyadic interaction: A comment on Gottman. *Psychological Bulletin*, 91, 393–403.

Baron, R.M., and Kenny, D.A. (1986). The moderator–mediator variable distinction in social psychological research: Conceptual, strategic and statistical considerations. *Journal of Personality and Social Psychology*, 51, 1173–82.

Baucom, D.H., and Adams, A.N. (1987). Assessing communication in marital interaction. In K.D. O'Leary (ed.), *Assessment of marital discord* (pp. 139–81). Hillsdale, NJ: Erlbaum.

Baucom, D.H., and Epstein, N. (1990). *Cognitive-behavioral marital therapy*. New York: Brunner/Mazel.

Baucom, D.H., Sayers, S.L., and Duhe, A. (1989). Attributional style and attributional patterns among married couples. *Journal of Personality and Social Psychology*, 56, 596–607.

Beach, S.R., Sandeen, E.E., and O'Leary, K.D. (1990). *Depression in marriage*. New York: Guilford Press.

Bradbury, T.N., and Fincham F.D. (1987). Affect and cognition in close relationships: Towards an integrative model. *Cognition and Emotion*, 1, 59–87.

Bradbury, T.N., and Fincham, F.D. (1988). Individual difference variables in close relationships: A contextual model of marriage as an integrative framework. *Journal of Personality and Social Psychology*, 54, 713–21.

Bradbury, T.N., and Fincham, F.D. (1989). Behavior and satisfaction in marriage: Prospective mediating processes. *Review of Personality and Social Psychology*, 10, 119–43.

Bradbury, T.N., and Fincham, F.D. (1990). Attributions in marriage: Review and critique. *Psychological Bulletin*, 107, 3–33.

Bradbury, T.N., and Fincham, F.D. (1991a). A contextual model for advancing the study of marital interaction. In G.J.O. Fletcher and F.D. Fincham (eds), *Cognition in close relationships* (pp. 127–47). Hillsdale, NJ: Erlbaum.

Bradbury, T.N., and Fincham, F.D. (1991b). The analysis of sequence in social interaction. In D.G. Gilbert and J.J. Conley (eds) *Personality, social skills, and psychopathology* (pp. 257–89). New York: Plenum Press.

Bugental, D.B. (1987). Attributions as moderator variables within social interactional systems. *Journal of Social and Clinical Psychology*, 5, 469–84.

Cairns, R.B., and Green, J.A. (1979). How to assess personality and social patterns: Observations or ratings? In R.B. Cairns (ed.), *The analysis of social interactions: Methods, issues, and illustrations* (pp. 209–26). Hillsdale, NJ: Erlbaum.

Camper, P.M., Jacobson, N.S., Holtzworth-Munroe, A., and Schmaling K.B. (1988). Causal attributions for interactional behaviors in married couples. *Cognitive Therapy and Research*, 12, 195–209.

Christensen, A. (1987). Assessment of behavior. In K.D. O'Leary (ed.), *Assessment of marital discord* (pp. 13–57). Hillsdale, NJ: Erlbaum.

Crane, D.R., Allgood, S.M., Larson, J.H., and Griffin, W. (1990). Assessing marital quality with distressed and nondistressed couples: A comparison and equivalency table for three frequently used measures. *Journal of Marriage and the Family*, 52, 87–93.

Dodge, K.A., Pettit, G., McClaskey, C.L., and Brown, M.M. (1986). Social competence in children. *Monographs of the Society for Research in Child Development*, 51(2, Serial No. 213).

Doherty, W.J. (1982). Attribution style and negative problem-solving style in marriage. *Family Relations*, 31, 201–5.

Eiser, J.R. (1983). From attributions to behavior. In M. Hewstone (ed.), *Attribution theory: Social and functional extensions* (pp. 160–9). Oxford, England: Blackwell.

Fincham. F.D., and Bradbury, T.N. (1987). The impact of attributions in marriage: A longitudinal analysis. *Journal of Personality and Social Psychology*, 53, 510–17.

Fincham, F.D., and Bradbury, T.N. (1988). The impact of attributions in marriage: An experimental analysis. *Journal of Social and Clinical Psychology*, 7, 122–30.

Fincham, F.D., and Bradbury, T.N. (1991a). Cognition in marriage: A program of research on attributions. In W.H. Jones and D. Perlman (eds) *Advances in personal relationships* (vol. 2, pp. 159–203). London: Kingsley.

Fincham, F.D., and Bradbury, T.N. (1991b). Marital satisfaction, depression, and attributions: A longitudinal analysis. Manuscript submitted for publication.

Fincham, F.D., and Bradbury, T.N. (1992). Assessing attributions in marriage: The Relationship Attribution Measure. *Journal of Personality and Social Psychology*, 62, 457–68.

Fincham, F.D., and Jaspars, J. (1980). Attribution of responsibility: From man the scientist to man as lawyer. In L. Berkowitz (ed.), *Advances in experimental social psychology* (vol. 13, pp. 81–138). San Diego, CA: Academic Press.

Fincham, F.D., and O'Leary, K.D. (1983). Causal inferences for spouse behavior in maritally distressed and nondistressed couples. *Journal of Social and Clinical Psychology*, 1, 42–57.

Fincham, F.D., Beach, S.R., and Nelson, G. (1987). Attribution processes in distressed and nondistressed couples: 3. Causal and responsibility attributions for spouse behavior. *Cognitive Therapy and Research*, 11, 71–86.

Floyd, F.J., and Markman, H.J. (1983). Observational biases in spouse observation: Toward a cognitive/behavioral model of marriage. *Journal of Consulting and Clinical Psychology*, 51, 450–7.

Geiss, S.K., and O'Leary, K.D. (1981). Therapist ratings of frequency and severity of marital problems: Implications for research. *Journal of Marital and Family Therapy*, 7, 515–20.

Gottman, J.M. (1979). *Marital interaction: Experimental investigations*. San Diego, CA: Academic Press.

Gottman, J.M., and Krokoff, L.J. (1989). Marital interaction and satisfaction: A longitudinal view. *Journal of Consulting and Clinical Psychology*, 57, 47–52.

Gottman, J.M., and Levenson, R.L. (1986). Assessing the role of emotion in marriage. *Behavioral Assessment*, 8, 31–48.

Heider, F. (1944), Social perception and phenomenal causality. *Psychological Review*, 51, 358–74.

Heider, F. (1958). *The psychology of interpersonal relations*. New York: Wiley.

Jacobson, N.S., and Margolin, G. (1979). *Marital therapy: Strategies based on social learning and behavior exchange principles*. New York: Brunner/Mazel.

Jacobson, N.S., Waldron, H., and Moore, D. (1980). Toward a behavioral profile of marital distress. *Journal of Consulting and Clinical Psychology*, 48, 696–703.

Kelley, H.H. (1973). The process of causal attribution. *American Psychologist*, 28, 107–28.

Kelley, H.H., and Thibaut, J.W. (1978). *Interpersonal relations: A theory of interdependence*. New York: Wiley.

Kelley, H.H., Berscheid, E., Christensen, A., Harvey. J.H., Huston, T.L., Levinger, G., McClintock, E., Peplau, L.A., and Peterson, D.R. (eds) (1983). *Close relationships*. San Francisco: Freeman.

Kleinbaum, D.G., and Kupper, L.L. (1978). *Applied regression analysis and other multivariable methods*. North Scituate. MA: Duxbury.

Locke, H., and Wallace, K. (1959). Short marital-adjustment and prediction tests: Their reliability and validity. *Marriage and Family Living*, 21, 251–5.

Margolin, G. (1983). An interactional model for the assessment of marital relationships. *Behavioral Assessment*, 5, 103–27.

McClintock, E. (1983). Interaction. In H.H. Kelley, E. Berscheid, A. Christensen, J.H. Harvey, T.L. Huston, G. Levinger, E. McClintock, L.A. Peplau, and D.R. Peterson (eds). *Close relationships* (pp. 68–109). San Francisco: Freeman.

Miller, P.C., Lefcourt, H.M., Holmes, J.G., Ware E.E., and Saleh, W.E. (1986). Marital locus of control and marital problem solving. *Journal of Personality and Social Psychology*, 51, 161–9.

Norton, R. (1983). Measuring marital quality: A critical look at the dependent variable. *Journal of Marriage and the Family*, 45, 141–51.

Peplau, L.A. (1983). Roles and gender. In H.H. Kelley. E. Berscheid. A. Christensen, J.H. Harvey, T.L. Huston, G. Levinger, E. McClintock, L.A. Peplau, D.R. Peterson (eds), *Close relationships* (pp. 220–64). San Francisco: Freeman.

Raush, H.L., Barry, W.A., Hertel, R.K., and Swain, M.A. (1974). *Communication, conflict, and marriage*. San Francisco: Jossey-Bass.

Rusbult, C., Johnson, D.J., and Morrow, G.D. (1986). Impact of couple patterns of problem solving on distress and nondistress in dating relationships. *Journal of Personality and Social Psychology*, 50, 744–53.

Rusbult, C.E., Verette, J., Whitney, G.A., Slovik, L.F., and Lipkus, I. (1991). Accommodation processes in close relationships: Theory and preliminary empirical evidence. *Journal of Personality and Social Psychology*, 60, 53–78.

Sackett, G.P. (1979). The lag sequential analysis of contingency and cyclicity in behavioral interaction research. In J.D. Osofsky (ed.), *Handbook of infant development* (pp. 623–49). New York: Wiley.

Shaver, K. (1985). *The attribution of blame: Causality, responsibility, and blameworthiness*. New York: Springer-Verlag.

Shaver, K., and Drown, D. (1985). On causality, responsibility, and self-blame: A theoretical note. *Journal of Personality and Social Psychology*, 50, 697–702.

Sillars, A.L. (1981). Attributions and interpersonal conflict resolution. In J.H. Harvey, W. Ickes, and R.F. Kidd (eds), *New directions in attribution research* (vol. 3, pp. 279–305). Hillsdale, NJ: Erlbaum.

Sillars, A.L. (1985). Interpersonal perception in relationships. In W. Ickes (ed.), *Compatible and incompatible relationships* (pp. 277–305). New York: Springer-Verlag.

Stuart, R.B. (1980). *Helping couples change*. New York: Guilford Press.

Weiner, B. (1985a). An attributional theory of achievement motivation and emotion. *Psychological Review*, 92, 548–73.

Weiner, B. (1985b). "Spontaneous" causal thinking. *Psychological Bulletin*, 97, 74–84.

Weiss, R.L. (1984). Cognitive and behavioral measures of marital interaction. In K. Hahlweg and N.S. Jacobson (eds) *Marital interaction: Analysis and modification* (pp. 232–52). New York: Guilford Press.

Weiss, R.L., and Heyman, R.E. (1990). Observation of marital interaction. In F.D. Fincham and T.N. Bradbury (eds), *The psychology of marriage* (pp. 87–117). New York: Guilford Press.

Worell, J. (1988). Women's satisfaction in close relationships. *Clinical Psychology Review*, 8, 477–98.

8 Attitudes: Structure, Measurement and Functions

Empirical validation of affect, behavior, and cognition as distinct components of attitude
S.J. Breckler

Theoretical Background

As noted by the author in his introduction to this paper, the distinction between thinking (cognition), feeling (affect) and behaving (conation) is one that has its roots in ancient Greek philosophy. Since the 1960s this tripartite distinction has often been used by attitude theorists to refer to the different ways in which people can express their evaluative response to an attitude object (see Eagly and Chaiken, 1993, Ch. 1). According to this view, an attitude is an evaluative response to an individual, a group, a concept or a thing. This evaluative response can be expressed cognitively, for example in the form of thoughts or beliefs about the attitude object. The evaluative response can also be expressed affectively, for example in the form of feelings or emotions about the attitude object. Finally, the evaluative response can be expressed behaviourally, for example in the form of intentions to behave or actual behaviour towards the attitude object.

The idea underlying this 'tripartite' distinction is that the three components of attitude are usually reasonably correlated with one another. After all, if someone has positive thoughts about an attitude object, one would expect this person also to have positive feelings about the object, and to be inclined to behave in a positive way towards the object. However, this need not always be the case. Consider attitudes to visiting the dentist for a check-up. Most people believe that this is a sensible course of action that is good for their health and well-being, but these positive thoughts about going for a dental check-up are not always accompanied by positive feelings. Similarly, the positive thoughts are not always accompanied by positive behavioural inclinations. Why should this be the case?

One answer to this question emphasizes the different origins of thoughts, feelings and action tendencies; here the argument is that we acquire thoughts, feelings and action tendencies by different means, with the result that they can vary in their positivity or negativity. Another sort of answer to this question stresses the notion that human beings consist of

Journal of Personality and Social Psychology (1984), 47:1191–205.

independent and only partly overlapping subsystems, one cognitive, another affective and a third behavioural. Whichever view one adopts, there are grounds for thinking that cognitive, affective and behavioural measures of attitude to an object will not overlap completely, and will therefore have *discriminant validity*.

The goal of the research reported in this paper was to provide a strong test of the tripartite model of attitude. Breckler proposes five criteria that need to be satisfied in order to have a strong test, and then argues that previous studies have at best only fulfilled-two-and-a-half of these.

Hypothesis

The hypothesis under test in this research is that cognitive, affective and behavioural measures of evaluative responses to an attitude object will be sufficiently empirically distinct to uphold the tripartite model of attitude. For reasons given below, Breckler expected that the first of the two studies would provide better support for this prediction than the second.

Design

Two studies are reported in this paper. Both are correlational in nature. In Study 1, Breckler takes both verbal (i.e. self-report) and non-verbal measures of cognitive, affective and behavioural responses to snakes. These measures were taken in the presence of a live (caged) snake. Study 2 is a replication of Study 1, except that only verbal measures of the three components of attitude were taken, and no snake was present at the time of measurement. This second study was conducted in order to provide a better comparison with previous studies of this issue, which tended to collect verbal measures of attitudinal responses to symbolic (i.e. not physically present) attitude objects. Both studies are designed to test the idea that a three-factor structure provides a better description of the data than does a one-factor structure, but Breckler expected that the use of only verbal measures of responses to a symbolic attitude object would result in less discrimination between the three components in Study 2.

Method

A key feature of the methodology is the use of 'covariance structure analysis', a statistical method for analysing the relationships between hypothetical (or 'latent') variables: affect, behaviour and cognition. These latent variables are represented by the three circles shown in Figure 8.2. Each latent variable is derived from a number of observed (or 'measured') variables. Each measured variable is represented by a box in Figure 8.2, which shows the predicted three-factor structure. Figure 8.3 shows a rival, one-factor model, in which all of the measured variables load on one common factor. The LISREL statistical program used by Breckler to perform the covariance structure analysis offers a way of comparing these two models and telling the researcher which one provides a better fit with the data. In Study 1 subjects provided four measures of affective responses to snakes, one of which (heart rate) was non-verbal; three measures of behavioural responses to snakes, two of which were non-verbal; and three measures of cognitive responses to snakes. In Study 2 subjects provided only verbal measures of each construct, without a snake being present.

Results

The main findings of Study 1 can be found in Table 8.2. The upper half of this table shows the 'factor loadings' of the measured variables on the three latent variables. If the measured variable is a good index of the underlying, latent variable, then the factor loading for that measured variable should be high. The factor loadings in Table 8.2 are all reasonably high, with the exception of heart rate. It can be concluded that the measured variables are tapping different underlying constructs. The lower half of this table shows the correlations between the three latent variables, ranging from .378 to .701. Even the strongest of these correlations (that between behaviour and cognition) shows that the two constructs only have about 50 per cent of shared variance (or statistical overlap). Another important result from Study 1 is reported in the last paragraph of the Results section: here the three-factor model is compared with the one-factor model, and is found to provide a much better fit with the data.

The results from Study 2 are broadly consistent with those from Study 1. The main findings are shown in Table 8.4. Again, we see that the measured variables load highly on the latent variables; this time there are no exceptions. However, the interfactor correlations in the lower part of Table 8.4 show that the correlations between the latent variables were higher than was the case in Study 1, ranging from .814 to .862. This shows, as expected, that when you only take verbal measures of the three components of attitude, the components are less easily distinguished from each other. Finally, in the last paragraph of the Results section of Study 2, we are told that the three-factor model provided a better fit with the data than did the one-factor model, although this time the difference between the two models was less striking.

Discussion

This research provides good evidence for the discriminant validity of the cognitive, affective and behavioural measures of attitudes to snakes. In other words, it is possible to distinguish between these components of attitude empirically, as well as conceptually. The differences between the findings of Study 1 and Study 2 are also informative: if one only uses verbal measures to assess the three components, and in the absence of the attitude object, the components are less discriminable. However, the fact that there were two differences between Studies 1 and 2 (verbal measures only, and attitude object not physically present) means that it is impossible to know whether the weaker discrimination between the three components is due to the exclusive use of verbal measures or to the absence of the attitude object.

A further limitation of the research is the fact that it is only concerned with attitudes to one object, snakes, and (as Breckler himself admits) there are grounds for thinking that these attitudes may be more likely than others to exhibit some degree of discrepancy between the different components of attitude. One may 'know' that a given snake is harmless (especially if it is caged), but at the same time 'feel' anxious in the presence of the snake and be disinclined to approach it. Recent research has tended to focus more specifically on the distinction between the cognitive and affective components of attitude, and this research confirms Breckler's conclusion that these components are often empirically discriminable, although the strength of the correlation between cognitive and affective measures of attitude does vary across attitude objects (see Crites et al., 1994).

FURTHER READING

Breckler, S.J. and Wiggins, E.C. (1989). Affect versus evaluation in the structure of attitudes. *Journal of Experimental Social Psychology*, 25, 253–71. This paper focuses on the distinction between affective and cognitive aspects of attitudes, and shows that affect can be a stronger predictor of behaviour than cognition.

Eagly, A.H., Mladinic, A. and Otto, S. (1994). Cognitive and affective bases of attitudes toward social groups and social policies. *Journal of Experimental Social Psychology*, 30, 113–37. The research reported in this paper makes creative use of an open-ended response methodology to assess the distinction between cognitive and affective components of attitude.

REFERENCES

Crites, S.J., Jr, Fabrigar, L.R. and Petty, R.E. (1994). Measuring the affective and cognitive properties of attitudes: Conceptual and methodological issues. *Personality and Social Psychology Bulletin*, 20, 619–34.

Eagly, A.H. and Chaiken, S. (1993). *The Psychology of Attitudes*. Fort Worth, TX: Harcourt Brace Jovanovich.

- - - - -
Primary
Reading
- - - - - - - -

In discussions of the attitude concept, it is very common to identify three attitude components: affect, behavior, and cognition. The present concern is with the validity of this tripartite model of attitude structure.

Figure 8.1 suggests a useful way for conceptualizing the tripartite model. Attitude is defined as a response to an antecedent stimulus or attitude object. The stimulus may or may not be observable, and can best be thought of as an independent or exogenous variable. Affect, behavior, and cognition are three hypothetical, unobservable classes of response to that stimulus.

In the present view, affect refers to an emotional response, a gut reaction, or sympathetic nervous activity. One can measure it by monitoring physiological responses (e.g., heart rate, galvanic skin response) or by collecting verbal reports of feelings or mood. Behavior includes overt actions, behavioral intentions, and verbal statements regarding behavior. Beliefs, knowledge structures, perceptual responses, and thoughts constitute the cognitive component.

A core assumption underlying the attitude concept is that the three attitude components vary on a common evaluative continuum (cf. Allport, 1935). Affect can vary from pleasurable (feeling good, happy) to unpleasurable (feeling bad, unhappy). Behavior can range from favorable and supportive (e.g., keeping, protecting) to unfavorable and hostile (e.g., discarding,

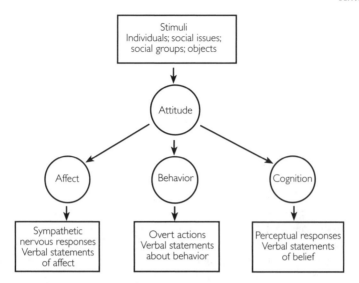

Figure 8.1 The tripartite model of attitude structure (after Rosenberg and Hovland, 1960)

destroying). Likewise, cognitions or thoughts may vary from favorable to unfavorable (e.g., supporting versus derogating arguments).

History of the Tripartite Model

The affect–behavior–cognition distinction is an old one. The trichotomy of feeling, acting, and knowing as three facets of human experience can be traced to the Greek philosophers (McGuire, 1969) and was considered in some of the earliest social psychological writings (e.g., Bogardus, 1920; McDougall, 1908; see Allport, 1954, and Hilgard, 1980, for broad reviews). Interestingly, the concept of attitude was not formally explicated in terms of the tripartite model until the late 1940s, when Smith (1947) distinguished among affective, cognitive, and policy orientation (conative) aspects of attitude (see also Chein, 1951; Kramer, 1949; Krech and Crutchfield, 1948).

By 1960, the tripartite model began to play a central role in major treatments of attitude theory and attitude change (Insko and Schopler, 1967; Katz and Stotland, 1959; Rosenberg, Hovland, McGuire, Abelson, and Brehm, 1960). The model's impact is also evidenced by its inclusion in introductory social psychology textbooks (e.g., Baron and Byrne, 1977; Krech, Crutchfield, and Ballachey, 1962; Lambert and Lambert, 1973; Newcomb, Turner, and Converse, 1965; Secord and Backman, 1964; Shaver, 1977; Worchel and Cooper, 1979; Wrightsman and Deaux, 1981), often without reference to original sources. Special topic books on attitude theory typically emphasize the tripartite model, and most include reproductions of Rosenberg and Hovland's (1960, Figure 1) schematization (Ajzen and Fishbein, 1980; Oskamp, 1977; Rajecki, 1982; Triandis, 1971; Zimbardo, Ebbesen, and Maslach, 1977).

Despite the tripartite model's acceptance by textbook writers, the multicomponent view appears to have had little impact on attitude researchers. Ostrom (1968) concluded that "the bulk of attitude research and, consequently, the theory developed to understand the attitude change process, continues to focus primarily on affect to the detriment of understanding the other characteristics of attitude" (p. 27).

Theoretical Underpinnings of the Tripartite Model

Several theoretical traditions lend support to the three-component view. One approach is to analyze the tripartite model in terms of each component's distinguishing antecedents (cf. Greenwald, 1968b; Insko and Schopler, 1967; Triandis, 1971). Action tendencies may develop through processes of instrumental learning (e.g., past reinforcement for a particular response to an attitude object). Cognitions can develop through previous exposure to communications or educational materials. And affect (or emotion) may be the product of classical conditioning – that is, the past pairing of an attitude object with an affective stimulus.

According to this view, not all attitude components are built up through cognitive processes. Attitudinal affect may not have verbal or cognitive antecedents. Many behaviors and action tendencies may also be established through nonverbal or noncognitive mechanisms. Thus the three components of attitude are distinguishable in terms of their developmental roots.

Recently, Greenwald (1982) suggested the utility of analyzing the person in terms of distinguishable and only partly overlapping or communicating subsystems (an approach called personalysis). According to this view, one's verbal response system may only partly overlap with, say, one's bodily response system. Therefore, "inconsistent truths can be communicated simultaneously by verbal and nonverbal systems of the same person" (Greenwald, 1982, p. 161). To the extent that each attitude component resides in a different subsystem, personalysis suggests a basis for distinguishing among affect, behavior, and cognition as three separable attitude components.

It is ordinarily assumed that affect, behavior, and cognition display some degree of positive correlation. For example, consistency among the components is implied by Allport's (1935) definition of attitude as being "organized through experience." Consistency might be expected because all three components represent the experience of a single individual. Also, the distinguishing antecedents of affect, behavior, and cognition can be satisfied by the same learning situation (Greenwald, 1968b), thereby producing triadic consistency. People may also be motivated or strive to maintain consistency in their attitudinal responses, especially when all measures derive from one's cognitive representation of attitude (cf. Festinger, 1957; Heider, 1958; McGuire, 1966).

High intercomponent correlations do not necessarily follow from the tripartite view. For example, affect, behavior, and cognition can sometimes be the products of very different learning situations (Greenwald, 1968b). Even if they are produced by the same learning conditions, the three components may be "coded" differently, which implies that they can operate in partial, or even complete, independence (Greenwald, 1982; Zajonc, 1980).

Requirements for a Strong Test of the Tripartite Model

Five conditions are essential for making a strong test of the tripartite model's validity. These conditions follow from general principles of construct validation (Cronbach and Meehl, 1955) and from the tripartite model's theoretical basis.

1   Both verbal and nonverbal measures of affect and behavior are required. The three attitude components may be built up through processes other than cognitive ones (Greenwald, 1968b). Thus one's cognitive system cannot be assumed to have complete access to emotional and behavioral experience. Intercomponent correlations are also likely to be overestimated when all three components are indexed solely by verbal report measures (Greenwald, 1982). Nonverbal measures might include physiological responses of affect and recordings of overt behavior.

2   Dependent measures of affect, behavior, and cognition must take the form of *responses* to an attitude object. Each of the three attitude components represents alternative classes of response. If the attitude object is not physically present, then one can respond only to a symbolic or mental representation of the object. Because such responses are (presumably) mediated by one's cognitive system, observed measures may assess primarily the cognitive component, and may therefore produce inflated estimates of intercomponent consistencies.

3   Multiple, independent measurements of affect, behavior, and cognition are needed. The three attitude components are hypothetical, unobservable constructs. They are represented by observable measures. No single measure can be assumed to capture the full nature of an unobservable construct. In the tradition of classical test theory (Lord and Novick, 1968), composite measures can produce a better (truer) assessment of the hypothetical construct because, across measures that share little or no common method variance, measurement errors cancel out. When the multiple measurements are not independent, however, measurement error may accumulate, which produces a distorted picture of the construct.

4   A confirmatory, rather than exploratory, approach to validation should be used. This approach requires an a priori method for classifying measures of affect, behavior, and cognition. The confirmatory approach is easily accomplished with confirmatory factor analysis models or, more generally, with covariance structure analysis (Bentler, 1980; Joreskog and Sorbom, 1981; Long, 1983b). One advantage to this approach is that it provides a formal, statistical means for evaluating a model's goodness of fit. It also allows a comparison among competing theoretical models. An exploratory approach (e.g., common factor analysis; Rummel, 1970) is often associated with ambiguities inherent in the subjective, post hoc interpretation of factors.

5   All dependent measures must be scaled on a common evaluative continuum. Attitude is defined in terms of evaluation (Allport, 1935), and it therefore follows that all dependent measures should reflect an evaluative disposition (response) toward the attitude object.

Empirical Support for the Tripartite Model

The principal objectives in tests of the tripartite model have been to determine the degree to which components are correlated and the extent to which they diverge as separable components of attitude. The earliest tests were concerned with the correspondence between pairs of components (e.g., Harding, Kutner, Proshansky, and Chein, 1954; Rosenberg, 1956) or with the multifaceted nature of individual components (e.g., Scott, 1969; Triandis, 1967). In only four studies have researchers examined all three attitude components with the stated goal of testing the tripartite model's validity (Kothandapani, 1971; Mann, 1959; Ostrom, 1969; Woodmansee and Cook, 1967).

Mann (1959) examined the relation among cognitive, affective, and behavioral aspects of racial prejudice. The observed pattern of correlations did not support the tripartite model.

However, the measures of affect, behavior, and cognition were not scaled on a common evaluative continuum, and the attitude measures did not logically follow from a definition of attitude components. This study also relied on an exploratory evaluation of correlations.

Woodsmansee and Cook (1967) also examined dimensions of racial attitudes. Instead of finding support for three attitude components, they found a large number of "content defined" dimensions. However, measures were not classified as ones of affect, behavior, or cognition; all measures took the form of verbal reports; and an exploratory, rather than confirmatory, approach to validation was used.

The two strongest tests of the tripartite model were by Ostrom (1969), who examined attitudes toward the church, and by Kothandapani (1971), who examined attitudes toward birth control. Both investigators used a multitrait–multimethod approach to assess convergent and discriminant validity (cf. Campbell and Fiske, 1959), and in so doing met two and a half of the five conditions just outlined. That is, they used multiple measurements, scaled their dependent variables on an evaluative continuum, and used a quasi-confirmatory approach to validation. It is called *quasi-confirmatory* because although the multiple measures were identified on a priori grounds as ones of affect, behavior, or cognition, the procedures used to evaluate the multitrait–multimethod correlation matrix were somewhat subjective.

Since publication of the Ostrom (1969) and Kothandapani (1971) studies, several investigators have reevaluated those data, using more formal statistical methods (Bagozzi, 1978; Breckler, 1983). For example, Bagozzi (1978) reanalyzed both sets of data using an early version of the LISREL computer program (Joreskog and Van Thillo, 1972). For Ostrom's data, Bagozzi's conclusions agreed with Ostrom's: Discriminant validity was demonstrated, but very little unique variance was associated with each component. Bagozzi's reanalysis of Kothandapani's data led to conclusions different from Kothandapani's: He found no statistical support for the discriminant validity of the tripartite model. Breckler (1983) performed a similar reanalysis; with Ostrom's data it indicated statistical support for the tripartite model, but the components were very highly correlated (from .94 to .98). The reanalysis of Kothandapani's data indicated moderate intercomponent correlations, but the tripartite model was statistically rejected.

Present Purpose

One may conclude from the foregoing analysis that no previous studies have provided clear, strong support for the tripartite model of attitude structure. The present purpose was to evaluate the model's validity in light of the conditions set forth earlier.

In two studies the affective, behavioral, and cognitive components of attitudes toward snakes were examined. Study 1 satisfied the five conditions needed for a strong test of the tripartite model. Study 2 was a replication of Study 1, with the exceptions that (a) all attitude measures took the form of verbal self-reports, and (b) the attitude object was not physically present while subjects responded to questions. To the extent that the latter two conditions produce an overestimation of intercomponent consistencies, correlations among components should be higher in Study 2 than in Study 1.

Study 1

As noted earlier, in a strong test of the tripartite model, one should use (a) verbal as well as nonverbal measures of affect and behavior; (b) dependent measures of affect, behavior, and cognition in the form of responses to an attitude object; (c) multiple, independent measures of affect, behavior, and cognition; (d) a confirmatory, rather than exploratory, approach to validation; and (e) dependent measures scaled on a common evaluative continuum.

The attitude domain of *snakes* was selected for the present study because (a) the attitude object can be (literally) placed in the presence of subjects (so that subjects can respond to the actual object, rather than a symbolic or mental representation of it); (b) there are relatively obvious and easy-to-collect measures of affective and behavioral responses to snakes; (c) an extremely negative attitude toward snakes (i.e., a phobia) may be characterized by independence between the behavioral and cognitive components (Coleman, 1976), affording the possibility of estimating a lower bound for the intercomponent correlations, and (d) understanding the interrelations among affect, behavior, and cognition in the context of a phobia may have useful clinical applications (cf. Bandura, Blanchard, and Ritter, 1969).

Method

Two theoretical models
In the terminology of factor analysis (Rummel, 1970), the tripartite model corresponds to a three-factor solution. It is an empirical problem to determine the magnitude of intercomponent correlations. An alternative, competing model corresponds to a one-factor solution. In the one-factor model, measures of each attitude component are assumed to represent only a single, underlying construct (viz., attitude), with no differentiation among attitude components. The one-factor model is both a theoretically and a statistically competing model. Theoretically, it is a simpler, more parsimonious model of attitude. Statistically, it is equivalent to a three-factor model with the constraints that (a) each measured variable loads on one and only one factor, and (b) all intercomponent correlations are fixed to 1.0.

The tripartite model is supported when the three-factor model provides a better account for the observed correlations than does the one-factor model. To the extent that intercomponent correlations are high, the one-factor and three-factor models will converge.

Evaluating goodness of fit
Covariance structure analysis (cf. Long, 1983b), carried out with the LISREL V (Joreskog and Sorbom, 1981) computer program, was used to evaluate the tripartite model. Covariance structure analysis allows the specification of relations among unobserved, hypothetical constructs (referred to as *latent variables*). Each latent variable is associated with (represented by) one or more observable *measured variables*. The three attitude components are latent variables. The attitude scales used to measure the components are measured variables.

Figure 8.2 shows a structural diagram that corresponds to the tripartite model of attitude. This special case of covariance structure models can be recognized as confirmatory factor analysis (cf. Long, 1983a). Three latent variables (affect, behavior, and cognition) are indicated in circles. Nine measured variables (X_1 through X_9) are indicated in boxes. (By convention, latent variables are always enclosed in circles and measured variables are always enclosed in boxes.) Each path connecting a latent variable to a measured variable represents a factor loading. It is significant that a given measured variable loads on one latent variable and not on the others. The εs represent the unique variances associated with each measured variable (that is, variance not shared with the common factor). The three double-headed curved paths that interconnect affect, behavior, and cognition represent the correlations among those three latent

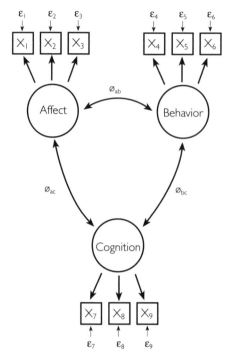

Figure 8.2   Structural representation of the tripartite model of attitude

variables. They correspond to interfactor correlations in an oblique factor analysis (Rummel, 1970).

The competing, one-factor model is shown in figure 8.3. Here there is only one latent variable, and every measured variable is assumed to load on it. One could specify an alternative (and equivalent) representation of the one-factor model in figure 8.2 by fixing each of the three interfactor correlations to 1.0.

The covariance structure approach to model fitting is a confirmatory one. The investigator specifies the form of the model to be fit. Input to the computer program (e.g., LISREL) consists of a sample variance–covariance matrix. A maximum likelihood procedure is used to estimate all of the model's unknown parameters. A chi-square (χ^2) statistic indicates whether the model is a plausible representation of the data. Unlike traditional statistical procedures, a nonsignificant χ^2 indicates a relatively good fit.

Caution must be exercised when using the chi-square statistic to evaluate a model's goodness of fit. The statistic tends to increase with increasing sample size. Most models will therefore be rejected with large samples. A model may also provide a good representation of the data, even though the chi-square statistic leads to rejection of the model. Therefore, other statistics must be used along with the chi-square statistic to help evaluate a model's goodness of fit.

Bentler and Bonett (1980) have described several such additional statistics. With one, the normed fit index (Δ), one makes a comparison between a given model and its corresponding "null" model, which represents a restricted case in which the variables are assumed to be

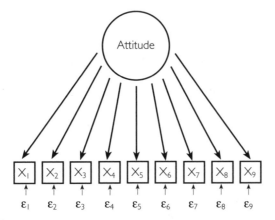

Figure 8.3 Structural representation of a one-factor model of attitude

mutually independent (i.e., a model in which there is no inherent structure among the correlations). This statistic can range in value from 0 to 1. A value greater than .9 generally indicates a good fit (Bentler and Bonett, 1980, p. 600).

With a second statistic, the incremental fit index (Δ_{inc}), one makes a comparison between two hierarchical models relative to a common null model. Two models are hierarchical when one of them contains all of the parameters of the other plus some other parameters. The incremental fit index therefore allows a comparison between the competing one-factor and three-factor models. This index is large when the less restricted model (e.g., a three-factor model) provides a substantially better fit than the more restricted model (e.g., a one-factor model).

Subjects
Subjects were 138 undergraduates who participated in fulfillment of a course requirement. Subjects were recruited for a study on "attitude structure," and were informed only after arrival at the laboratory that the study involved snakes.

Summary of measured variables
Ten measures were used to estimate the structural models of figures 8.2 and 8.3. There were four measures of affect, and three measures each of behavior and cognition. These measures are introduced here and then described in detail in the next sections.

Affect measures   The four measures of affect were taken while the subject was in the presence of a live snake. The measures were heart rate (HR), an adjective checklist measure of positive mood (MACL+), an adjective checklist measure of negative mood (MACL−), and a Thurstone equal-appearing interval measure of affect (Thurstone affect; Thurstone and Chave, 1929).

Behavior measures   The three measures of behavior were a Thurstone equal-appearing interval measure of behavior (Thurstone behavior), the average distance to which the subject would be willing to approach a variety of pictured snakes (distance), and the extent of contact in which the subject was willing to engage with a live snake (action sequence).

Cognition measures   The three measures of cognition were a Thurstone equal-appearing interval measure of belief (Thurstone cognition), ratings of snakes on scales representing the evaluative dimension of the semantic differential (SD), and the net proportion of favorable-to-snake listed thoughts given in the presence of a snake (listed thoughts).

Measures of the affective component

Thurstone affect   This scale included 16 statements such as "I feel anxious," "I feel tense," and "I feel happy." This measure was calculated as the median Thurstone scale value of checked items.

MACL+ and MACL−   These two measures of affect were derived from the Mood Adjective Check-List (MACL; Nowlis, 1965). One calculates the measure of positive affect (MACL+) by summing responses to nine adjectives representing the Surgency, Elation, and Social Affection scales: *carefree, elated, affectionate, playful, overjoyed, kindly, witty, pleased*, and *warmhearted*. One calculates the measure of negative affect (MACL−) by summing responses to nine adjectives representing the Anxiety, Sadness, and Aggression scales: *angry, tense, regretful, defiant, fearful, sad, rebellious, jittery*, and *sorry*.

Heart rate   The fourth measure of affect was derived from heart-rate measurements. Each subject's pulse rate was recorded four separate times during the course of the experimental session. Each of the four heart-rate measurements involved recording the subject's pulse (beats per minute) for a period of 3 min. Twelve recordings were made, each separated by 15 s. The highest and lowest recordings were discarded, and the remaining 10 recordings were averaged to produce a single heart-rate measurement. This procedure was repeated four times during the experimental session, thereby producing four measurements of heart rate. The four heart-rate measurements were standardized in relation to their overall mean. One of the four heart-rate measurements was taken while the subject was in the presence of a live snake. The heart-rate measure of affect was the z score corresponding to the latter measurement. Thus the other three measurements served as baselines.

Measures of the behavioral component

Thurstone behavior   This scale included 14 statements such as "I scream whenever I see a snake" and "I like to handle snakes." This measure was calculated as the median Thurstone scale value of checked items.

Action sequence   A second measure of behavior was an overt action sequence. Subjects were asked to engage in a series of actions that brought them into increasingly closer physical contact with a live snake. When this measure was taken, the snake was in its cage on the table in front of the subject. The investigator said, "For the next part of the study, I'd like to find out whether you would be willing to do a variety of things involving the snake. I'm not going to ask you to do anything that would make you feel uncomfortable. If what I ask would make you feel at all uneasy, just say so and I won't ask you to do it. First, would you prefer that I take the snake away or leave it here for the rest of the experiment? If you would really prefer that I take it away, just say so." The subject's response was noted, but regardless of the reply the snake remained in the cage on the table. The experimenter then said, "The next question is whether it is alright with you if I take the snake out of the cage? I'll hold on to it, but if that would make you feel even slightly uncomfortable, just say so." If the subject agreed to the request, the snake was removed from its cage and held by the investigator in the subject's presence. If the subject declined, the snake was left in its cage. The experimenter then said, "Will you touch the snake while I hold it? If you really prefer not to, please let me know." If the subject agreed, the experimenter held out the snake for petting. Finally, the experimenter said, "Will you hold the snake by yourself? If you don't want to, just say so." The experimenter waited for a reply, but placed the snake back in the cage regardless of the answer. There were four steps in this action sequence (allow snake to stay, remove snake from cage, pet snake, hold snake). The score for this measure was the number of actions agreed to by the subject. Its value ranges from 0 to 4.

Distance   The third measure of behavior was a preferred distance measure. Subjects were shown 12 color slides of snakes that varied in size, color, dangerousness, and so on. The slides were projected on a screen placed to the subject's front and right. Subjects were instructed to "imagine as if each snake is a real live snake, and that it is sitting right there where the screen is, just as it is shown in the picture." Subjects were then asked to indicate "the closest you would be willing to get to each snake, if it was a real live snake." Subjects indicated the distance by pointing to the corresponding physical location along a numbered line that hung perpendicularly from the projection screen. The line was numbered in integers from 1 to 50 at intervals of 8.5 cm. The subject was told to "indicate the number that corresponds to the closest you would stand if the snake was right where the screen is. For example, if you would get right next to it, or even touch it, you can indicate a zero or one. If the closest you would get is where you are right now, you would indicate a 36 or 37 [the subject's location]. If the closest you would get is even further, you can go back to 50. If you would stay past that, you can just say 'more than 50.'" After these instructions, the lights were dimmed and the slides were displayed one at a time. The ordering of slides was different for each subject. The 12 color slides were a subset of Blackhawk Films' set of "Snakes of the Eastern United States." The scale value for this measure was the average of the 12 distances.

Measures of the cognitive component

Thurstone cognition   This scale included 14 statements such as "Snakes are soft and smooth," "Snakes control the rodent population," and "Snakes will attack anything that moves." This measure was calculated as the median Thurstone scale value of checked items.

Semantic differential (SD)[1]   Subjects rated snakes on each of these six bipolar scales representing the evaluative dimension of the semantic differential (Osgood, Suci, and Tannenbaum, 1957); good/bad, friendly/unfriendly, kind/cruel, clean/dirty, beautiful/ugly, and important/unimportant. The scale value for this measure was the mean rating (larger numbers attached to the more favorable pole) across all six scales.

Listed thoughts   The listed thoughts (cognitive response) procedure (Greenwald, 1968a; Petty, Ostrom, and Brock, 1981) required subjects to list all of their thoughts while they were in the presence of the snake. After listing their thoughts, subjects were instructed to indicate which of them were favorable toward snakes and which were unfavorable. This measure was the difference between proportion of favorable and unfavorable thoughts (net positive thoughts). The proportions were first converted via an arcsin transformation (Winer, 1971) before their differences were calculated.

Procedure[2]

The verbal report measures were contained in a booklet that each subject completed while a live, caged snake was in their presence. The snake was a juvenile corn snake, and was placed on the table approximately 60 cm in front of the subject. The booklet included (a) the MACL and Thurstone measures of affect, (b) the listed thoughts, semantic differential, and Thurstone measures of cognition, and (c) the Thurstone measure of behavior. The booklet also included a single-item self-rating scale and several background questions.

Booklet format   The booklet was divided into three sections. The first section included the two affect scales and the listed thoughts procedure (the latter measure consisted of four pages). The ordering of these three measures was counterbalanced across subjects. These measures always appeared first because they depended most on initial spontaneous responses to the snake's presence and to avoid contamination from the other self-report scales. The second section included the semantic differential scale, the Thurstone measure of cognition, and the Thurstone measure of behavior. The ordering of these three scales was counterbalanced across subjects. The third section consisted of a single page that included a single-item self-rating scale and various background questions (e.g., the subject's age, sex, college major).

Sequence and distance measures   When the subject had completed the booklet, the experimenter delivered the instructions for the action sequence measure. After the last step in that sequence had been completed, the experimenter removed the caged snake from the subject's presence. The experimenter then delivered the instructions for the preferred distance measure. Subjects were then debriefed, requested not to mention details of the study to other potential participants, and asked to complete a general evaluation of their experience in the experiment. No subject indicated prior knowledge regarding the use of a snake in the study.

Results

The analyses reported here are limited to ones that are of concern in validating the tripartite model. Correlations among the measured variables are in table 8.1. (The signs associated with correlations for the MACL– and distance measures have been reversed, so that all expected directions of correlation would be positive.)

The LISREL V computer program (Joreskog and Sorbom, 1981) was used to estimate the unknown parameters for both the one-factor and three-factor models (figures 8.2 and 8.3). Table 8.2 contains the LISREL estimates for the three-factor model's unknown parameters. The $\chi^2(32, N = 138) = 37.51$, $p > .20$, and the normed fit index $\Delta = .92$. These results strongly support the three-component classification both in terms of statistical criteria and relative fit. Examination of the factor loadings (table 8.2) indicates that all measured variables loaded highly on their respective factors, with the single exception of heart rate.[3] Finally, the three attitude components were only moderately correlated ($.38 < r < .71$).

The three-factor model was also compared to the one-factor model. For the one-factor model, $\chi^2(35, N = 138) = 113.45$, $p < .01$, and $\Delta = .74$. Thus the one-factor model was statistically rejected and its relative fit was poor. The difference between the one-factor and three-factor models yielded $\chi^2(3, N = 138) = 75.94$, $p < .01$, and $\Delta_{inc} = .172$. These results indicate a very substantial improvement of the three-factor model over the one-factor model, lending further support for the tripartite model's validity.

Table 8.1   Correlation matrix for evaluating tripartite model (Study 1)

Measures	1	2	3	4	5	6	7	8	9	10
Affective										
1. Thurstone affect	–									
2. MACL+	45	–								
3. MACL–[a]	50	13	–							
4. Heart-rate	17	04	04	–						
Behavioral										
5. Action sequence	35	25	37	02	–					
6. Distance[a]	23	26	15	–07	52	–				
7. Thurstone behavior	38	26	28	03	66	50	–			
Cognitive										
8. Thurstone cognition	18	13	21	05	29	27	33	–		
9. Semantic differential	30	23	29	05	45	47	58	61	–	
10. Listed thoughts	30	17	28	–01	38	25	44	36	55	–

Decimal points are omitted; $n = 138$. MACL = Mood Adjective Check List.
[a] Signs are reversed.

Table 8.2   LISREL estimates for unknown parameters of three-factor model (data from Study 1)

Parameter	Estimate	Standard error
	Factor loadings	
Affect		
Thurstone affect	.920 (.153)	.099 (.140)
MACL+	.474 (.775)	.091 (.102)
MACL–	.543 (.705)	.092 (.099)
Heart rate	.164 (.973)	.092 (.118)
Behavior		
Action sequence	.769 (.409)	.078 (.069)
Distance	.627 (.607)	.083 (.083)
Thurstone behavior	.846 (.284)	.076 (.066)
Cognition		
Thurstone cognition	.638 (.592)	.082 (.081)
Semantic differential	.947 (.103)	.076 (.080)
Listed thoughts	.591 (.651)	.083 (.086)
	Interfactor correlations	
Affect/behavior	.495	.087
Affect/cognition	.378	.089
Behavior/cognition	.701	.063

MACL = Mood Adjective Check List. Values in parentheses are unique variances. One can calculate approximate T values by dividing an estimate by its standard error.

Discussion

The results from Study 1 provide strong support for the tripartite model. When conditions suitable for a rigorous test of the tripartite model were met, affect, behavior, and cognition emerged as three distinct components of attitude. The generality of this conclusion is limited, however, to the single attitude domain of snakes.

The attitude domain of snakes was purposely selected as one that had a strong a priori likelihood of allowing independence among attitude components. Many responses to snakes may be controlled reflexively, with little or no cognitive mediation. One's cognitive system may therefore produce responses that are different from, or independent of, those produced by other response systems (Greenwald, 1982).

Relative independence of attitude components should be expected when responses to an object are mediated by multiple response systems. For example, allergic reactions may control affective and behavioral responses, independently of one's cognitive response system. Thus one may (cognitively) like dogs very much, but nevertheless avoid them or have adverse physiological reactions in their presence because of an allergy.

Less independence is expected when measures of the three attitude components derive from, or are largely mediated by, a single response system. The exclusive use of paper-and-pencil measures is one example of responses mainly under control of one's verbal knowledge system. In some attitude domains subjects can only respond to a cognitive representation, and so responses are necessarily controlled by that single response system. Abstract attitude objects – for example, love, peace, God, religion – are of this sort. Responding to a mental or symbolic representation of the attitude object, rather than to the actual object, may likewise produce high intercomponent correlations.

Study 2

The major point of departure between Study 1 and past tests of the tripartite model was the inclusion of nonverbal measures of affect and behavior, and the real presence of an attitude object to which subjects could respond. A second study was done in order to evaluate the extent to which these two conditions were important in producing the obtained results. Study 2 was a verbal report analogue of Study 1. Instead of using a real, live snake, subjects were asked to imagine one was present. All of the nonverbal measures were translated into a verbal report format.

Method

Subjects
Subjects were 105 undergraduates who participated in fulfillment of a course requirement. Subjects were recruited for a study on "attitude structure" and were informed only after arrival at the laboratory that the study involved snakes.

Measures of affective component
The MACL (which produces two scores: MACL+ and MACL−) and the Thurstone affect scales were administered. Subjects were instructed to imagine they were in the presence of a live

snake. Other than this modification in instructions, these measures were the same as in Study 1.

Measures of the cognitive component

The Thurstone measure of belief and the semantic differential scales were administered just as in Study 1. The listed thoughts measure was modified in that subjects were asked to think about snakes (because one was not present). In all other respects, these three measures were the same as in Study 1.

Measures of the behavioral component

The Thurstone measure of behavior was administered just as in Study 1. The action sequence and distance measures were represented in the form of behavioral intention (BI) scales. There were two measures of behavioral intention: one mapped on to the action sequence, and the other mapped on to the distance measure.

BI: Action sequence   Subjects were instructed to rate the likelihood of their (a) staying in the same room with a live, caged snake, (b) letting someone else hold a live snake while in their presence, (c) touching a live snake while someone else holds it, and (d) holding a live snake. The four actions correspond directly to the four action-sequence steps of Study 1. The likelihood ratings were scored from −3 (*very unlikely*) to 3 (*very likely*). The four ratings were summed to produce a single score.

BI: Distance   Subjects were instructed to rate the likelihood of their getting close to or touching (a) a small snake, (b) a dangerous snake, (c) a harmless snake, and (d) a large snake. The likelihood ratings were scored from −3 (*very unlikely*) to 3 (*very likely*). The four ratings were summed to produce a single score.

Procedure[4]

Subjects were scheduled in groups of 3 to 10 for a session that lasted under 1 hour. The study was conducted in a large classroom. The experimenter distributed booklets containing all measures and instructed subjects to complete the questionnaire at their own pace.

The booklet was divided into three sections. The first section included the two affect scales (MACL and Thurstone) and the listed thoughts procedure. The ordering of these measures was counterbalanced across subjects. These measures appeared first in order to avoid contamination from the other scales. The second section included measures of behavior and behavioral intention. The ordering of these scales was counterbalanced across subjects. The third section of the booklet consisted of a single-item self-rating scale along with background questions (e.g., subject's age, sex, college major).

Results

Correlations among the measured variables involved in testing the tripartite model are in table 8.3. (As in Study 1, the signs associated with correlations for the MACL− measure have been reversed, so that all expected directions of correlation would be positive.)

As in the previous analyses, LISREL V (Joreskog and Sorbom, 1981) was used to estimate the unknown parameters for both the one-factor and three-factor models. Table 8.4 contains the LISREL estimates for the three-factor model; $\chi^2(24, N = 105) = 42.29, p < .05$, and $\Delta = .94$. Thus the tripartite model was statistically rejected but nevertheless provided a good relative fit.

Table 8.3   Correlation matrix for testing tripartite model (Study 2)

Measure	1	2	3	4	5	6	7	8	9
Affective									
1. Thurstone mood	–								
2. MACL+	57	–							
3. MACL–[a]	54	42	–						
Behavioral									
4. Distance (BI)	57	43	58	–					
5. Action sequence (BI)	57	44	67	82	–				
6. Thurstone behavior	58	42	63	77	85	–			
Cognitive									
7. Thurstone cognition	33	22	40	45	42	49	–		
8. Semantic differential	60	46	60	71	70	72	69	–	
9. Listed thoughts	62	48	51	65	61	63	44	69	–

Decimal points are omitted, $n = 105$. MACL = Mood Adjective Check List. BI = behavioral intention.
[a] signs are reversed.

Table 8.4   LISREL Estimates for unknown parameters of three-factor model (data from Study 2)

Parameter	Estimate	Standard error
	Factor loadings	
Affect		
Thurstone affect	.758 (.426)	.089 (.077)
MACL+	.608 (.631)	.095 (.097)
MACL–	.760 (.423)	.089 (.077)
Behavior		
Action sequence (BI)	.931 (.133)	.075 (.032)
Distance (BI)	.872 (.240)	.079 (.042)
Thurstone behavior	.901 (.188)	.077 (.036)
Cognition		
Thurstone cognition	.694 (.519)	.088 (.078)
Semantic differential	.962 (.075)	.076 (.048)
Listed thoughts	.735 (.459)	.086 (.071)
	Interfactor correlations	
Affect/behavior	.862	.048
Affect/cognition	.823	.056
Behavior/cognition	.814	.043

MACL = Mood Adjective Check List. BI = behavioral intention. Values in parentheses are unique variances. One can calculate approximate T values by dividing an estimate by its standard error.

Examination of the factor loadings (table 8.4) indicated that all measured variables loaded significantly on their respective factors. Finally, the intercomponent correlations were relatively high ($.81 < r < .87$).

The one-factor model was also evaluated: $\chi^2(27, N = 105) = 84.25$, $p < .05$, and $\Delta = .88$. Thus the one-factor model was rejected, and its relative fit was marginal. The difference between the one-factor and three-factor models yielded $\chi^2(3, N = 105) = 41.96$, $p < .05$, and $\Delta_{inc} = .06$. These results indicate a statistically significant improvement of the three-factor model over the one-factor model, but the magnitude of that difference was relatively small.

Discussion

The major objective in Study 2 was to evaluate the extent to which verbal report measures and the absence of the attitude object lead to an overestimate of correlations among affect, behavior, and cognition. The results from Study 2 confirmed that they do. The verbal report measures from Study 2 indicated discriminant validity for the three-component distinction. At the same time, the attitude components were observed to be more highly correlated in Study 2 (average $r = .83$) than in Study 1 (average $r = .55$).

One important aspect of Study 2 was that a real live snake was not present during the time subjects completed the questionnaire, as compared with Study 1, in which a snake was present while subjects responded to the scales. The correlation between the MACL+ and MACL− scales suggests how measures of actual affective states can differ from ones of expected or imagined affective states. In Study 1, in which subjects presumably answered on the basis of how they actually felt, the correlation was $-.13$ (*ns*). In contrast, the subjects in Study 2 answered on the basis of how they imagined they would feel, and the correlation was $-.42$ ($p < .01$). The latter correlation reflects a commonsense interpretation of affect, one that may not apply to affect that is produced in response to an actual affective stimulus.

The exclusive use of verbal report measures has been identified as one factor that can produce high intercomponent correlations. Consistency among components should also increase as one gains experience interacting with an attitude object. With increasing experience, one gains verbal knowledge of one's affective and overt behavioral reactions to the object. In support of this interpretation, recent research has indicated greater attitude–behavior consistency when the attitude has been formed on the basis of direct experience (Fazio and Zanna, 1978, 1981; Fazio, Zanna, and Cooper, 1978). The past experience predictions gain further support from additional analysis of the Study 2 data. Subjects were grouped on the basis of their past experience with snakes, and confirmatory factor analyses were conducted for each group separately. The behavior–cognition correlation was greater for subjects who had past experience ($r = .90$) than for those who had not ($r = .71$). These results should be interpreted as only suggestive, however, because they were based entirely on verbal report measures.

General Discussion

Summary of results

Study 1 indicated strong support for affect, behavior, and cognition as distinct attitude components. That is, the tripartite model was not rejected by the chi-square test, and its relative fit (the Δ index) was very good. Furthermore, the three-component model fit substantially better than the one-component model, indicating its discriminant validity. Study 2 suggested that the exclusive use of verbal report measures, and the physical absence of the attitude object, can produce increased (and presumably inflated) estimates of intercomponent correlations.

Future directions

Generalizing to other attitude domains

One limitation in the present studies was the focus on a single attitude domain. As noted previously, snakes were used in the present studies to allow for the possibility of low correlations among – and, therefore, discriminant validity of – the three attitude components. The conclusion in favor of the utility of distinguishing among affective, behavioral, and cognitive components of attitude can use support from similar validation studies in which other attitude objects are used.

Constructing a taxonomy of attitude domains

It would be desirable to construct a method for identifying, on a priori grounds, those attitude domains that should be associated with high versus low intercomponent consistency. Attitude domains in which respondents presumably have had extensive past experience (e.g., the church) are likely to be associated with very high intercomponent correlations. In comparison, attitude domains for which respondents are likely to have had minimal prior experience (e.g., snakes) should produce low intercomponent consistency. (See discussion of Study 2 for evidence supporting this prediction.)

Low intercomponent correlations might be expected for attitude objects in which responses are mediated by more than one response system. This might be the case for food preferences. One may like certain foods very much but nevertheless have intense allergies to them. Thus cognitive responses may be generally favorable, whereas affective responses indicate extreme aversion.

Intercomponent consistency may also be related to the abstractness versus concreteness of the attitude object. People respond to abstract attitude objects only at a conceptual or symbolic level. Therefore, most responses are likely to be mediated almost exclusively by one's verbal knowledge or cognitive systems. In contrast, responses to concrete attitude objects may be mediated by bodily control systems (e.g., reflexes, physiological reactions) in addition to one's verbal knowledge system.

Application to persuasion research

One of the major applications of the tripartite model is in the area of persuasion research (Rosenberg et al., 1960). One issue of concern is whether change in one component leads to change in other components. For example, in an attitude change campaign, one may concentrate on the cognitive component by using appeals based on information or logical arguments. The desired result is (a) to produce a corresponding change in other components (e.g., behavior), and (b) to produce a lasting change in attitude.

Most persuasion studies concentrate on changing only the cognitive component. One goal of that change is to bring about a corresponding change in the other attitude components. Such change might be expected if triadic consistency is assumed to reflect an equilibrium or steady state. It is not clear, however, that changing one attitude component is enough to produce changes in the other two. Triadic inconsistency may also be restored more simply by the cognitive component's moving back in a direction that is consistent with affect and behavior. This view is confirmed by analyses of the persistence of attitude change (Cook and Flay, 1978): Persuasion that initially changes behavior appears to persist longer than persuasion that produces only cognitive change.

Predicting overt behavior

One of the classic problems in social psychology is that of the attitude–behavior relationship. A substantial literature has been interpreted to indicate very little attitude–behavior correspondence (e.g., LaPiere, 1934; see Wicker, 1969, for a summary of this view). However, recent investigators have been critical of the past interpretations (e.g., Dillehay, 1973) and have turned their attention to producing conditions that ensure strong attitude–behavior correlations or strong behavior prediction (Ajzen and Fishbein, 1973, 1977; Fishbein and Ajzen, 1974; Wicker, 1971).

In the context of the tripartite model, the attitude–behavior problem is one of predicting the behavioral component of attitude from prior knowledge of other variables. In practice, the term *attitude* in "attitude–behavior relationship" sometimes refers to the cognitive component of attitude, and sometimes to the affective component of attitude, and only rarely to the entire three-component structure. Definitions of attitude that follow more clearly from conceptions of attitude components may aid the development of good behavioral prediction models. For example, alternative measures of the behavioral component should be better predictors of subsequent overt behavior than ones of the affective or cognitive components, because the former presumably share greater variance. This prediction has been confirmed in past evaluations of the tripartite model (Kothandapani, 1971; Ostrom, 1969), and in data connected with the present studies (Breckler, 1983).

Conclusion

The results from Studies 1 and 2 indicated that affect, behavior, and cognition are distinguishable components of attitude. Correlations among these three components were moderate, suggesting the practical importance of discriminating among them. Thus attitude researchers are advised either to measure each of the three components or to specify which of the three is of focal concern. To say a researcher is measuring "attitude" is ambiguous, because it does not specify which of the three components is being measured.

Before the present studies, only Ostrom (1969) and Kothandapani (1971) had attempted to validate the tripartite model. Given the model's prominent treatment in social psychology and attitude theory textbooks, it is surprising that so few researchers have investigated it. Perhaps this reflects a preoccupation in social psychology with determining *causation* (e.g., Cook and Campbell, 1979), rather than with the logically prior problem of identifying, measuring, and validating the theoretical constructs that participate in causal relations.

NOTES

This research was supported by a Graduate Alumni Research Award and a Herbert Toops Research Award (both to S.J. Breckler), and by NSF Grant BNS 82-17006 (to A.G. Greenwald). It is partly based on a doctoral dissertation completed in the social psychology program at Ohio State University. The article was written, in part, while the author was a National Institute of Mental Health Post-Doctoral Trainee in the Department of Psychology at Northwestern University. Dissertation committee members Thomas M. Ostrom and Robert C. MacCallum provided helpful feedback during all phases of the research. I am especially grateful to my advisor, Anthony G. Greenwald, and to Anthony R. Pratkanis, both of whom contributed in every way possible to this work. I also thank Thomas D. Cook, Harry C. Triandis, and three anonymous reviewers for commenting on an earlier draft of the manuscript.

[1] One might argue that the sematic differential is more a measure of affect than of cognition. Here it is considered a measure of cognition because (a) the label applied to the measurement technique itself (i.e., semantic diferential) identifies it as focusing on dimensions of meaning or perception, which are constructs that are clearly cognitive in nature; (b) the scales were administered in a way that made clear to subjects that they were to evaluate an attribute of the attitude object; and (c) such use can be distinguished from the present conception of affect, which has been operationally defined in terms of the subject's own emotional state. Thus the statement "Snakes are bad" is considered to reflect a cognitive response to snakes, whereas the statement "Snakes make me feel bad" (or even better, "I feel bad," said in the presence of a snake) is assumed to reflect an affective response. All of the cognitive measures are evaluatively laden; that is the hallmark of an attitude. That evaluative nature, however, is not to be confused with affect or mood as one of three evaluatively laden components of attitude.

[2] A more detailed description of the procedure, along with reproductions of all attitude scales, can be found in Breckler (1983).

[3] The pattern of factor loadings and correlations indicate that heart rate was not a good indicator of affect (nor any other attitude component). These results were unexpected (explanations can be found in Breckler, 1983). All reported analyses were repeated with the exclusion of heart rate. Those analyses produced the same pattern of results, and all interpretations were the same.

[4] Several aspects of Study 2 have been excluded from this report. The questionnaire booklet contained additional scales, including ones of past behavior, subjective norms, and good/bad ratings of behaviors. Subjects also participated in a second session that included additional attitude measures. The present analyses were concerned only with those parts of Study 2 that have relevance for the present evaluation of the tripartite model. See Breckler (1983) for a report of the other analyses.

REFERENCES

Ajzen, I., and Fishbein, M. (1973). Attitudinal and normative variables as predictors of specific behaviors. *Journal of Personality and Social Psychology*, 27, 41–57.

Ajzen, I., and Fishbein, M. (1977). Attitude–behavior relations: A theoretical analysis and review of empirical research. *Psychological Bulletin*, 84, 888–918.

Ajzen, I., and Fishbein, M. (1980). *Understanding attitudes and predicting social behavior*. Englewood Cliffs, NJ: Prentice-Hall.

Allport, G.W. (1935). Attitudes. In C. Murchison (ed.), *Handbook of social psychology* (pp. 798–844). Worcester, MA: Clark University Press.

Allport, G.W. (1954). The historical background of modern social psychology. In G. Lindzey (ed.), *Handbook of social psychology* (vol. 1, pp. 3–56). Cambridge, MA: Addison-Wesley.

Bagozzi, R.P. (1978). The construct validity of the affective, behavioral, and cognitive components of attitude by analysis of covariance structures. *Multivariate Behavioral Research*, 13, 9–31.

Bandura, A., Blanchard, E.B., and Ritter, B. (1969). Relative efficacy of desensitization and modeling approaches for inducing behavioral, affective, and attitudinal changes. *Journal of Personality and Social Psychology*, 13, 173–99.

Baron, R.A., and Byrne, D. (1977). *Social psychology: Understanding human interaction* (2nd edn). Boston: Allyn and Bacon.

Bentler, P.M. (1980). Multivariate analysis with latent variables: Causal modeling. In M.R. Rosenzweig and L.W. Porter (eds), *Annual review of psychology* (pp. 419–56). Palo Alto, CA: Annual Reviews, Inc.

Bentler, P.M., and Bonett, D.G. (1980). Significance tests and goodness of fit in the analysis of covariance structures. *Psychological Bulletin*, 88, 588–606.

Bogardus, E.S. (1920). *Essentials of social psychology*. Los Angeles: University of Southern California Press.

Breckler, S.J. (1983). Validation of affect, behavior, and cognition as distinct components of attitude. Unpublished doctoral dissertation, Ohio State University, Columbus.

Campbell, D.T., and Fiske, D.W. (1959). Convergent and discriminant validation by the multitrait–multimethod matrix. *Psychological Bulletin*, 56, 81–105.

Chein, I. (1951). Notes on a framework for the measurement of discrimination and prejudice. In M. Jahoda, M. Deutsch, and S.W. Cook (eds), *Research methods in social relations* (pp. 381–90). New York: Dryden Press.

Coleman, J.C. (1976). *Abnormal psychology and modern life* (5th edn). Glenview, IL: Scott, Foresman and Company.

Cook, T.D., and Campbell, D.T. (1979). *Quasi-experimentation*. Chicago: Rand-McNally.

Cook, T.D., and Flay, B.R. (1978). The persistence of experimentally induced attitude change. In L. Berkowitz (ed.), *Advances in experimental social psychology* (vol. 11, pp. 1–57). New York: Academic Press.

Cronbach, L.J., and Meehl, P.E. (1955). Construct validity in psychological tests. *Psychological Bulletin*, 52, 281–302.

Dillehay, R.C. (1973). On the irrelevance of the classical negative evidence concerning the effect of attitudes on behavior. *American Psychologist*, 28, 887–91.

Fazio, R.H., and Zanna, M.P. (1978). On the predictive validity of attitudes: The roles of direct experience and confidence. *Journal of Personality*, 46, 228–43.

Fazio, R.H., and Zanna, M.P. (1981). Direct experience and attitude–behavior consistency. In L. Berkowitz (ed.), *Advances in experimental social psychology* (vol. 14, pp. 161–202). New York: Academic Press.

Fazio, R.H., Zanna, M.P., and Cooper, J. (1978). Direct experience and attitude–behavior consistency: An information processing analysis. *Personality and Social Psychology Bulletin*, 4, 48–52.

Festinger, L. (1957). *A theory of cognitive dissonance*. Stanford, CA: Stanford University Press.

Fishbein, M., and Ajzen, I. (1974). Attitudes toward objects as predictors of single and multiple behavioral criteria. *Psychological Review*, 81, 59–74.

Greenwald, A.G. (1968a). Cognitive learning, cognitive response to persuasion, and attitude change. In A.G. Greenwald, T.C. Brock, and T.M. Ostrom (eds), *Psychological foundations of attitudes* (pp. 147–70). New York: Academic Press.

Greenwald, A.G. (1968b). On defining attitudes and attitude theory. In A.G. Greenwald, T.C. Brock, and T.M. Ostrom (eds), *Psychological foundations of attitudes* (pp. 361–88). New York: Academic Press.

Greenwald, A.G. (1982). Is anyone in charge? Personalysis versus the principle of personal unity. In J. Suls (ed.), *Psychological perspectives on the self* (vol. 1, pp. 151–81). Hillsdale, NJ: Erlbaum.

Harding, J., Kutner, B., Proshansky, H., and Chein, I. (1954). Prejudice and ethnic relations. In G. Lindzey (ed.), *Handbook of social psychology* (vol. 2, pp. 1021–61). Cambridge, MA: Addison-Wesley.

Heider, F. (1958). *The psychology of interpersonal relations*. New York: Wiley.

Hilgard, E.R. (1980). The trilogy of mind: Cognition, affection, and conation. *Journal of the History of the Behavioral Sciences*, 16, 107–17.

Insko, C.A., and Schopler, J. (1967). Triadic consistency: A statement of affective–cognitive–conative consistency. *Psychological Review*, 74, 361–76.

Joreskog, K.G., and Sorbom, D. (1981). *LISREL V*. Chicago: National Educational Resources.

Joreskog, K.G., and Van Thillo, M. (1972). *LISREL: A general computer program for estimating a linear structural equation system involving multiple indicators of unmeasured variables*. Educational Testing Service Research Bulletin No. 72–56.

Katz, D., and Stotland, E. (1959). A preliminary statement to a theory of attitude structure and change. In S. Koch (ed.), *Psychology: A study of a science* (vol. 3, pp. 423–75). New York: McGraw-Hill.

Kothandapani, V. (1971). Validation of feeling, belief, and intention to act as three components of attitude and their contribution to prediction of contraceptive behavior. *Journal of Personality and Social Psychology*, 19, 321–33.

Kramer, B.M. (1949). Dimensions of prejudice. *Journal of Psychology*, 27, 389–451.

Krech, D., and Crutchfield, R.S. (1948). *Theory and problems of social psychology*. New York: McGraw-Hill.

Krech, D., Crutchfield, R.S., and Ballachey, E.L. (1962). *Individual in society*. New York: McGraw-Hill.

Lambert, W.W., and Lambert, W.E. (1973). *Social psychology* (2nd edn). Englewood Cliffs, NJ: Prentice-Hall.

LaPiere, R.T. (1934). Attitudes versus actions. *Social Forces*, 13, 230–7.

Long, J.S. (1983a). *Confirmatory factor analysis*. Beverly Hills, CA: Sage.

Long, J.S. (1983b). *Covariance structure models: An introduction to LISREL*. Beverly Hills, CA: Sage.

Lord, F.M., and Novick, M.R. (1968). *Statistical theories of mental test scores*. Reading, MA: Addison-Wesley.

Mann, J.H. (1959). The relationship between cognitive, affective, and behavioral aspects of racial prejudice. *Journal of Social Psychology*, 49, 223–8.

McDougall, W. (1908). *An introduction to social psychology*. London: Methuen.

McGuire, W.J. (1966). The current status of cognitive consistency theories. In S. Feldman (ed.), *Cognitive consistency: Motivational antecedents and behavioral consequents* (pp. 1–46). New York: Academic Press.

McGuire, W.J. (1969). The nature of attitudes and attitude change. In G. Lindzey and E. Aronson (eds), *The handbook of social psychology* (2nd edn, vol. 3, pp. 136–314). Reading, MA: Addison-Wesley.

Newcomb, T.M., Turner, R.H., and Converse, P.E. (1965). *Social psychology*. New York: Holt, Rinehart and Winston.

Nowlis, V. (1965). Research with the Mood Adjective Check List. In S.S. Tomkins and C.E. Izard (eds), *Affect, cognition and personality* (pp. 352–89). New York: Springer.

Osgood, C.E., Suci, G.J., and Tannenbaum, P.H. (1957). *The measurement of meaning*. Urbana: University of Illinois Press.

Oskamp, S. (1977). *Attitudes and opinions*. Englewood Cliffs, NJ: Prentice-Hall.

Ostrom, T.M. (1968). The emergence of attitude theory: 1930–1950. In A.G. Greenwald, T.C. Brock, and T.M. Ostrom (eds), *Psychological foundations of attitudes* (pp. 1–32). New York: Academic Press.

Ostrom, T.M. (1969). The relationship between the affective, behavioral and cognitive components of attitude. *Journal of Experimental Social Psychology*, 5, 12–30.

Petty, R.E., Ostrom, T.M., and Brock, T.C. (eds) (1981). *Cognitive responses in persuasion*. Hillsdale, NJ: Erlbaum.

Rajecki, D.W. (1982). *Attitudes: Themes and advances*. Sunderland, MA: Sinauer.

Rosenberg, M.J. (1956). Cognitive structure and attitudinal affect. *Journal of Abnormal and Social Psychology*, 53, 367–72.

Rosenberg, M.J., and Hovland, C.I. (1960). Cognitive, affective, and behavioral components of attitude. In M.J. Rosenberg, C.I. Hovland, W.J. McGuire, R.P. Abelson, and J.W. Brehm (eds), *Attitude organization and change: An analysis of consistency among attitude components* (pp. 1–14). New Haven, CT: Yale University Press.

Rosenberg, M.J., Hovland, C.I., McGuire, W.J., Abelson, R.P., and Brehm, J.W. (eds) (1960). *Attitude organization and change: An analysis of consistency among attitude components*. New Haven, CT: Yale University Press.

Rummel, R.J. (1970). *Applied factor analysis*. Evanston, IL: Northwestern University Press.

Scott, W.A. (1969). Structure of natural cognitions. *Journal of Personality and Social Psychology*, 12, 261–78.

Secord, P.F., and Backman, C.W. (1964). *Social psychology*. New York: McGraw-Hill.

Shaver, K.G. (1977). *Principles of social psychology*. Cambridge, MA: Winthrop.

Smith, M.B. (1947). The personal setting of public opinions: A study of attitudes toward Russia. *Public Opinion Quarterly*, 11, 507–23.

Thurstone, L.L., and Chave, E.J. (1929). *The measurement of attitude*. Chicago: University of Chicago Press.

Triandis, H.C. (1967). Toward an analysis of the components of interpersonal attitudes. In C.W. Sherif and M. Sherif (eds), *Attitude, ego-involvement, and change* (pp. 227–70). New York: Wiley.

Triandis, H.C. (1971). *Attitude and attitude change*. New York: Wiley.

Wicker, A.W. (1969). Attitudes versus actions: The relationship of verbal and overt behavioral responses to attitude objects. *Journal of Social Issues*, 25, 41–78.

Wicker, A.W. (1971). An examination of the "other variables" explanation of attitude–behavior inconsistency. *Journal of Personality and Social Psychology*, 19, 18–30.

Winer, B.J. (1971). *Statistical principles in experimental design* (2nd edn). New York: McGraw-Hill.

Woodmansee, J.J., and Cook, S.W. (1967). Dimensions of verbal racial attitudes: Their identification and measurement. *Journal of Personality and Social Psychology*, 7, 240–50.

Worchel, S., and Cooper, J. (1979). *Understanding social psychology* (rev. edn). Homewood, IL: Dorsey.

Wrightsman, L.S., and Deaux, K. (1981). *Social psychology in the 80s* (3rd edn). Monterey, CA: Brooks/Cole.

Zajonc, R.B. (1980). Feeling and thinking: Preferences need no inferences. *American Psychologist*, 35, 151–75.

Zimbardo, P.G., Ebbesen, E.B., and Maslach, C. (1977). *Influencing attitudes and changing behavior* (2nd edn). Reading, MA: Addison-Wesley.

Prediction of goal-directed behavior: Attitudes, intentions, and perceived behavioral control

I. Ajzen and T.J. Madden

Theoretical Background

- - - - -
Editors'
Introduction
- - - - - - - -

At the time this article was published, social-psychological research on the attitude–behavior relationship was still dominated by the theory of reasoned action, which had been developed a decade earlier by Fishbein and Ajzen (1975). In this article, Ajzen and Madden present an extension of this theory, the theory of planned behavior, and also two studies which pitted the two models against each other. Although the theory of planned behavior had already been described in two earlier publications (Ajzen, 1985; Schifter and Ajzen, 1985), it is this article which made it popular, presumably because it provided empirical evidence of the superiority of the new model.

Journal of Experimental Social Psychology (1986), 22:453–74.

The theory of reasoned action predicts an individual's intention to perform a particular action and assumes that actual behaviour is a function of an individual's behavioural intention. Behavioural intentions are assumed to be determined by two factors: the attitude towards performing the behaviour and subjective norms. Although the theory of reasoned action had been successful in predicting a variety of behaviours, ranging from blood donations to smoking marijuana, it had been suggested that a model which solely relied on intentions to predict actions would do poorly in predicting behaviours over which the individual had only limited control (because they required skills, abilities, opportunities or the cooperation of others). To improve predictions of this kind of behaviour, a model must assess not only intentions but also the extent to which the individual is capable of exerting control over the behaviour in question.

In response to these criticisms, Ajzen modified the theory of reasoned action by adding perceived behavioural control as a third predictor. This control reflects the actor's beliefs about how easy or difficult performance of a given behaviour is likely to be, and is thus similar to Bandura's (1986) concept of self-efficacy. Perceived behavioural control is assumed to influence behaviour via behavioural intentions. The less people believe that they are able to perform a given behaviour, the less they should intend to perform it. In addition to the link to behaviour via intention, Ajzen and Madden suggest a direct link to behaviour, which has a different theoretical status from the indirect link and is assumed to emerge only under certain specified conditions. Whereas the link from perceived control to behaviour via intentions is causal, the direct link to behaviour is not. It is actual rather than perceived control which directly influences behaviour. For example, if a student's attendance at a lecture is dependent on the reliability of her or his car, attendance behaviour will be influenced by the car's actual rather than perceived reliability. Thus, measures of perceived control will improve the prediction of behaviour over and above the prediction based on intention only to the extent that perceived behavioural control is an accurate predictor of actual control over the behaviour.

STUDY I

Hypothesis

This study tests the hypothesis that a measure of perceived behavioural control will improve the prediction of behavioural intentions over a prediction which is based solely on attitudes towards the behaviour and subjective norms. The direct link to action was not expected to emerge because actual control in this situation was thought to be high.

Design

This was a field study, not an experiment, and used a longitudinal design.

Method

The study was conducted in the context of regular class meetings. Each of the three predictors of intentions (i.e. attitudes, subjective norms and perceived control) was assessed both directly and via the underlying beliefs. The two types of measure showed reasonable correlations. Intention was assessed by means of three questions on estimates of the likelihood of attending class. The behaviour to be predicted, class attendance, was measured in eight sessions by means of an attendance form. Thus, care was taken to assure that all variables were assessed with measures which were reliable.

Results

The two theories were tested by hierarchical regressions, a statistical procedure which assesses the independent contributions of each of the various theoretical variables to the prediction of intentions and of behaviour. For the first prediction of intentions, attitude and subjective norm were entered in the first step, and perceived behavioural control on the second. The first step constitutes a test of the theory of reasoned action. Both attitude and subjective norm made significant contributions to the prediction of intention, resulting in a multiple correlation of .55. This is consistent with both theories. However, consistent with the theory of planned behaviour, the introduction of perceived behavioural control into the regression equation resulted in a significant improvement of the multiple correlation, from .55 to .68.

A second regression analysis was conducted to test whether perceived behavioural control improved the prediction of behaviour over and above the prediction made on the basis of intention. This analysis entered intention in the first step and control in the second. Control was not found to make a significant contribution to the prediction of behaviour over and above a prediction based on intention.

STUDY 2

The second study pitted the two models against each other using 'getting an A' (the best grade) on a course as the behavioural goal, and making use of the fact that American students usually have three examinations for any given course spread equally throughout the semester or term. Attitudes, norms, perceived control and behavioural intentions were assessed twice, once before the first examination and a second time at the end of the semester, approximately one week before the final exams. It was assumed that the experience gained in taking two exams would increase students' accuracy of the control they perceived over their performance in these tests. (That this was a valid assumption was indicated by the fact that correlations between expected and received grades increased substantially over the two points in time.) It was expected that results during the first time of measurement would replicate the findings of study 1, with perceived behavioural control exerting only an indirect influence on behaviour (i.e. via intention), but that at the second measurement the direct link between perceived control and behaviour would emerge. Results were consistent with these predictions.

Discussion

Taken together, the findings of the study provide strong support for the new model. In each of the three tests of the theory, the inclusion of perceived control improved predictions of behavioural intentions over a prediction which was based solely on assessments of attitudes and norms. Furthermore, the second study supported the prediction that with increasing accuracy of control perceptions, perceived control becomes a direct predictor of behaviour. The direct link between perceived control and behaviour did not emerge in study 1, and this was explained in terms of the fact that class attendance is a behaviour over which individuals have nearly perfect control. However, it is worth noting that the superiority of the theory of planned behaviour over the theory of reasoned action is thought to be greatest where control over the behaviour in question is less than perfect. Thus there would seem to be a degree of inconsistency in the predictions relating to study 1. Presumably even class attendance is a behaviour over which students feel they have less than perfect control, which helps to account for the superiority of the theory of planned behaviour. However, the control is still large enough to rule out a direct link between perceived behavioural control and behaviour.

FURTHER READING

Ajzen, I. (1985). From intentions to actions: A theory of planned behavior. In J. Kuhl and J. Beckmann (eds), *Action Control: From Cognition to Behavior* (pp. 11–40). New York: Springer-Verlag. An extensive presentation of the theory of planned behavior.

Ajzen, I. (1988). *Attitudes, Personality, and Behavior*. Milton Keynes: Open University Press. A very readable account of the conditions under which attitudes (and personality traits) predict behaviour.

REFERENCES

Bandura, A. (1986). *Social Foundations of Thought and Action: A Cognitive Social Theory*. Englewood Cliffs, NJ: Prentice-Hall.

Fishbein, M. and Ajzen, I. (1975). *Belief, Attitude, Intention, and Behavior: An Introduction to Theory and Research*. Reading, MA: Addison-Wesley.

Schifter, D.E. and Ajzen, I. (1985). Intention, perceived control, and weight loss: An application of the theory of planned behavior. *Journal of Personality and Social Psychology*, 49, 843–51.

Primary
Reading

Much recent research on the attitude–behavior relation has been conducted within the framework of the "theory of reasoned action" (Ajzen and Fishbein, 1980; Fishbein and Ajzen, 1975). Considerable evidence in support of the theory has accumulated in a variety of experimental and naturalistic settings (see, e.g., Ajzen and Fishbein, 1980; Ajzen, Timko, and White, 1982; Bentler and Speckart, 1979, 1981; Fredricks and Dossett, 1983; Manstead, Proffitt, and Smart, 1983; Smetana and Adler, 1980). The behaviors involved have ranged from very simple strategy choices in laboratory games to actions of appreciable personal or social significance, such as having an abortion, smoking marijuana, and choosing among candidates in an election.

The constructs employed by the theory of reasoned action are fundamentally motivational in nature. According to the theory, the immediate antecedent of any behavior is the *intention* to perform the behavior in question. The stronger a person's intention, the more the person is expected to try, and hence the greater the likelihood that the behavior will actually be performed.

The theory of reasoned action specifies two conceptually independent determinants of intention. One is a personal factor termed *attitude toward the behavior* and refers to the degree to which a person has a favorable or unfavorable evaluation of the behavior in question. The second predictor of intention is *subjective norm*, a social factor; it refers to the perceived social pressure to perform or not to perform the behavior. Attitude and subjective norm, each weighted for its relative importance, are assumed jointly to determine behavioral intention. A diagram of this model is shown in figure 8.4.

The theory of reasoned action also deals with the antecedents of attitudes and subjective norms, antecedents which in the final analysis determine intentions and actions. At the most basic level of explanation, the theory postulates that behavior is a function of salient information, or beliefs relevant to the behavior. Two kinds of beliefs are distinguished, *behavioral beliefs* which are assumed to influence attitudes toward the behavior and *normative beliefs* which constitute the underlying determinants of subjective norms. Each behavioral belief links the behavior to a certain outcome, or to some other attribute such as the cost incurred by performing the behavior. The outcome's subjective value then contributes to the attitude toward the behavior in direct proportion to the strength of the belief, i.e., the subjective probability that performing the behavior will lead to the outcome under consideration. To obtain an estimate of attitude, belief strength is multiplied by outcome evaluation, and the resulting products are summed across all salient behavioral beliefs. Normative beliefs, on the other hand, are concerned with the likelihood that important referent individuals or groups would approve or disapprove of performing the behavior. The strength of each normative belief is multiplied by the person's motivation to comply with the referent in question, and an estimate of subjective norm is obtained by summing the resulting products across all salient referents.

Volitional control

In spite of the success achieved by the theory of reasoned action, some fundamental problems, related primarily to the theory's boundary conditions, remain unresolved. For the most part, these conditions have to do with the transition from verbal responses to actual behavior. A strong association between intention and behavior is dependent on three prerequisites. First,

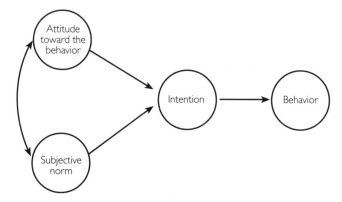

Figure 8.4   Theory of reasoned action

the measure of intention must correspond in its level of generality to the behavioral criterion (cf., Ajzen, 1982; Ajzen and Fishbein, 1977). Thus, to predict a specific behavior, such as attending the lectures of a given class on a regular basis, we must assess equally specific intentions, i.e., intentions to regularly attend the class lectures in question. A second requirement is that the intention must not have changed in the interval between the time at which it was assessed and the time at which the behavior is observed. The longer the time interval, the more likely is occurrence of unforeseen events that may change the intention. It follows that accuracy of prediction will usually vary inversely with the time interval between measurement of intention and observation of behavior.

Of greatest interest for present purposes, however, is the requirement that the behavior under consideration be under volitional control (see Fishbein and Ajzen, 1975). A behavior may be said to be *completely* under a person's control if the person can decide at will to perform it or not to perform it. Conversely, the more that performance of the behavior is contingent on the presence of appropriate opportunities or on possession of adequate resources (time, money, skills, cooperation of other people, etc.), the less the behavior is under volitional control.

At first glance, the problem of control may appear to apply to only a limited range of behaviors. Closer scrutiny reveals, however, that even very mundane activities, which can usually be executed (or not executed) at will, are sometimes subject to the influence of factors beyond one's control. Such a simple behavior as driving to the supermarket may be thwarted by mechanical trouble with the car. Behavioral control can thus best be viewed as a continuum. On one extreme are behaviors that encounter few if any problems of control, while on the other extreme are behaviors or behavioral events over which we have relatively little control. Most behaviors, of course, fall somewhere in between those extremes. People usually encounter few problems of control when trying to attend class lectures or read a book, but problems of control are more readily apparent when people try to overcome such powerful habits as smoking or drinking or when they set their sights on such difficult to attain goals as becoming a movie star. Viewed in this light it becomes clear that, strictly speaking, most intended behaviors are best considered *goals* whose attainment is subject to some degree of uncertainty. We can thus speak of behavior–goal units; and of intentions as plans of action in pursuit of behavioral goals (Ajzen, 1985).

A theory of planned behavior

The above discussion suggests that the theory of reasoned action, which relies on intention as the sole predictor of behavior, will be insufficient whenever control over the behavioral goal is incomplete. Many factors can interfere with control over intended behavior, some internal to the individual, others external. Examples of internal factors are skills, abilities, knowledge, and adequate planning; while examples of external factors are time, opportunity, and dependence of the behavior on the cooperation of other people. To ensure accurate prediction of behavior over which individuals have only limited control, we must not only assess intention but also obtain some estimate of the extent to which the individual is capable of exercising control over the behavior in question.

In an attempt to go beyond purely volitional action, Ajzen (1985; Schifter and Ajzen, 1985) has proposed a "theory of planned behavior" which extends the theory of reasoned action by including the concept of behavioral control. Psychologists are becoming increasingly interested in the role of control over desired behavior. The importance of *actual* control is self-evident: The resources and opportunities available to individuals must to some extent dictate the likelihood of behavioral achievement. To enable accurate prediction of behavior over which people have imperfect control, therefore, investigators have proposed assessing the presence of "facilitating factors" (Triandis, 1977), "the context of opportunity" (Sarver, 1983), "resources" (Liska, 1984), or "action control" (Kuhl, 1985). The importance of control over behavior has also been recognized by clinical psychologists attempting to help people overcome undesired habits, fears, or inhibitions (e.g., Kanfer and Hagerman, 1981).

Unfortunately, it is often very difficult if not impossible to secure an adequate measure of actual control in advance of observing the behavior. Many of the factors that can prevent execution of an intended action are accidental in nature and can, by definition, not be anticipated. In addition, our ability to identify requisite skills or other internal factors, and to assess them validly, is also quite limited. In short, we can usually not be sure that individuals in fact possess the requisite resources and that appropriate opportunities will present themselves unless and until an attempt is made to perform the behavior under consideration.

It is, however, possible to measure *perceived behavioral control*, the person's belief as to how easy or difficult performance of the behavior is likely to be. According to the theory of planned behavior, among the beliefs that ultimately determine intention and action is a set that deals with the presence or absence of requisite resources and opportunities. The more resources and opportunities individuals think they possess, and the fewer obstacles or impediments they anticipate, the greater should be their perceived control over the behavior. As in the case of behavioral and normative beliefs, it is possible to separate out these control beliefs and treat them as partly independent determinants of behavior. Just as beliefs concerning consequences of the behavior are viewed as determining attitudes, and normative beliefs are viewed as determining subjective norms, so beliefs about resources and opportunities may be viewed as underlying perceived behavioral control. These beliefs about behavioral control may be based in part on past experience with the behavior, but they will usually also be influenced by second-hand information about the behavior, by the experiences of acquaintances and friends, and by other factors that increase or reduce the perceived difficulty of performing the behavior in question.

The effect of *perceived* behavioral control on human judgment and behavior has also attracted the attention of many investigators (e.g., Averill, 1973; Janis and Rodin, 1979; Langer, 1983; Rothbaum, Weisz, and Snyder, 1982; Steiner, 1970). This interest has been stimulated in part by Rotter's (1966) work, whose internal–external locus of control scale, or some variant thereof, has been used repeatedly in attempts to predict a variety of different behaviors (see Lefcourt, 1982; Strickland, 1978). Most similar to the present use of perceived behavioral control, however, is Bandura's (1977, 1982) concept of self-efficacy beliefs. Bandura and his associates (e.g., Bandura, Adams, and Beyer, 1977; Bandura, Adams, Hardy, and Howells, 1980) have provided evidence showing that people's behavior is strongly influenced by their confidence in their ability to perform it (i.e., by perceived behavioral control). The theory of planned behavior places this construct within a more general framework of the relations among beliefs, attitudes, intentions, and behavior.

Two possible versions of the theory of planned behavior are presented schematically in figure 8.5. The first model, which does not include the broken link from perceived behavioral control to behavior, is based on the assumption that perceived behavioral control has

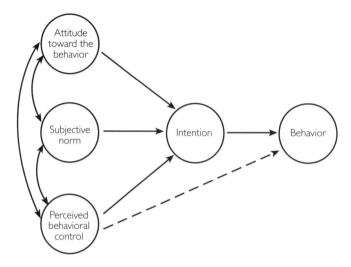

Figure 8.5   Theory of planned behavior: Version 1 without broken arrow, Version 2 with broken arrow

motivational implications for intentions. People who believe that they have neither the resources nor the opportunities to perform a certain behavior are unlikely to form strong behavioral intentions to engage in it even if they hold favorable attitudes toward the behavior and believe that important others would approve of their performing the behavior. We would thus expect an association between perceived behavioral control and intention that is not mediated by attitude and subjective norm. Consistent with these considerations, figure 8.5 shows perceived behavioral control to correlate with attitude and subjective norm and to exert an independent effect on behavioral intention.

This version of the theory of planned behavior assumes that the effect of perceived behavioral control on behavior is *completely* mediated by intention, and that intention in turn is the immediate antecedent of goal-directed behavior. In contrast, the second version considers the possibility of a direct link between perceived behavioral control and behavior. As noted earlier, in many instances, performance of a behavior will depend not only on motivation but also on adequate control over the behavior in question. It follows that perceived behavioral control can help predict goal attainment independent of behavioral intention to the extent that it reflects actual control with some degree of accuracy. In other words, according to the second version of the theory, perceived behavioral control can influence behavior indirectly, via intentions, and it can also be used to predict behavior directly because it may be considered a partial substitute for a measure of actual control. In line with this reasoning, the broken arrow in figure 8.5 shows a direct link between perceived behavioral control and behavior. Strictly speaking, of course, it is *actual* control that is expected to exert a direct influence on behavior, not perceived control. However, perceived behavioral control may often quite accurately reflect available resources and opportunities; that is, actual control may influence both perceived behavioral control and behavior. The relation between perceived behavioral control and behavior is thus to be understood in terms of the role of actual control as a determinant of human action.

The present article reports the first complete test of the theory of planned behavior in the form presented above. A general discussion of the question of control, and its relation to intentions and behavior, can be found in Ajzen (1985), but the model shown in figure 8.5 is presented here for the first time. Schifter and Ajzen (1985) reported a partial test of this model which focused on various personality factors that may moderate the effect of perceived behavioral control on behavior.

The research reported in the present article was designed to test the theory of planned behavior in a systematic fashion, with particular emphasis on the role of perceived control. The first version of the theory shown in figure 8.5 goes beyond the theory of reasoned action in that it proposes a direct causal effect of perceived behavioral control on intention, an effect not mediated by attitude or subjective norm. However, the effect need not be additive in nature. It could be argued instead that perceived behavioral control is a necessary, but not sufficient, condition for the formation of intention to perform a behavior. Besides believing that one *could* perform the behavior, one must also be inclined to do so for other reasons. These considerations imply the possibility that perceived behavioral control affects intention in interaction with attitude and subjective norm.

The second version of the theory of planned behavior assumes that attainment of behavioral goals is dependent not only on intention but also on behavioral control, an effect that can be examined in terms of the direct relation between perceived behavioral control and behavior. According to this version of the theory, we can expect a direct link between perceived behavioral control and behavior that is not mediated by intention. However, a strong effect of perceived behavioral control is expected only under two conditions. First, the behavior being predicted must not be under complete volitional control. When it is, then the concept of perceived behavioral control becomes largely irrelevant for prediction of behavior and the theory of planned behavior reduces to the theory of reasoned action (see Ajzen, 1985). Second, perceptions of behavioral control must reflect actual control in the situation with some degree of accuracy. When this is not the case, the measure of perceived behavioral control can add little to the prediction of behavior. Finally, the idea that both intention and control are necessary for performance of a behavior again suggests an interaction effect, such that the effect of intention on behavior depends on perceived behavior control.

Two experiments were conducted to explore these issues. The behavior examined in the first experiment, students' class attendance, poses few problems of control. The perceived ease or difficulty of attending class should influence intentions, but when it comes to carrying out those intentions, perceived behavioral control should add little further information of value for the prediction of actual attendance. The criterion in the second experiment was attainment of a behavioral goal, namely getting an "A" in a certain course, an event over which students have only limited behavioral control. In this situation, perceived control is expected to contribute to the prediction of intentions and, to the extent that it is realistic, also to the prediction of goal attainment. To examine the latter hypothesis, perceptions of behavioral control were assessed early as well as late in the semester. Since these perceptions should increase in accuracy as the semester progresses, their contribution to the prediction of goal attainment should be greater at the end as compared to the beginning of the semester.

It was noted earlier that perceived behavioral control is likely to reflect, among other factors, past performance of the target behavior. To rule out the possibility that the effect of perceived behavioral control is "nothing but" a self-prediction of future behavior based on past experience, measures of prior behavior were obtained in both experiments.

Experiment 1

Method

Respondents and procedure

Participants in the experiment were 169 undergraduate college students enrolled in an introductory social psychology class; 45 were males and 124 were females.[1] The investigation was fashioned after Fredricks and Dossett's (1983) study on attendance of class lectures, an activity highly familiar to college students. It can be assumed that beliefs, attitudes, intentions, and perceptions of control were quite well established prior to the initial period of behavioral observation and that the situation remained stable enough to prevent drastic changes in these variables over a short period of time.

The study was conducted in the context of regular class meetings. About 3 weeks into the fall semester, after the "add–drop" period had been concluded and enrollment had stabilized, an experimenter entered the class to solicit participation.[2] The study was described as a survey designed to discover why students attend, or fail to attend, class sessions. Attendance sheets would be passed around for several weeks and, whenever they were present, participants would be asked to sign their names. In addition, they would be required to complete a brief questionnaire during the course of the investigation which would deal with their personal views and expectations regarding class attendance. It was emphasized that all responses would be completely confidential. The class instructor and the experimenter both assured the students that the instructor had nothing to do with the study, that she would have no access to the attendance or questionnaire data, that the information obtained in the study would have no effect whatsoever on students' grades, and that all identifying information would be destroyed as soon as the data had been collected. The students were offered experimental credit for their participation and were given a full explanation at the conclusion of the investigation.

Attendance data was collected at 16 regular class sessions, 8 prior to administration of the questionnaire and 8 following administration. Two class meetings used for examinations, and the session at which the questionnaire was administered, were omitted. The number of sessions attended during the first and second 8-week periods served, respectively, as measures of prior and later behavior.[3]

Questionnaire

Much of the questionnaire was designed to obtain measures of the constructs contained in the theory of planned behavior. Since most items used a semantic differential format, the first page provided instructions concerning use of the 7-point scales. The next section assessed evaluations of 11 possible consequences of attending class regularly or of missing some sessions. These consequences were taken from Fredricks and Dossett (1983) and included such statements as "My learning more about the subject matter of this course" and "My falling behind in studying for this class." Each outcome was rated on a 7-point scale with endpoints labeled *extremely good* and *extremely bad*. At a later point in the questionnaire, belief strength associated with each of the possible outcomes was assessed by means of a 7-point probability scale. Thus, the statement, "My attending this class every session will result in my missing a lot of sleep" was rated on a scale ranging from *extremely likely* to *extremely unlikely*, as was the statement, "My being absent from this class will result in wasting money paid for tuition." The measure of belief strength with respect to each outcome was multiplied by the corresponding evaluation, and the sum over the 11 products served as a belief-based measure of attitude toward attending class.[4] The α coefficient of this scale was .61.

A more direct measure of attitude was obtained by means of a set of evaluative semantic differential scales. The concept, "My attending this class every session" was rated on 22 bipolar adjective scales selected from the evaluation, potency, and activity factors of the semantic differential (see Osgood, Suci, and Tannenbaum, 1975). The same set of scales was also used in the second experiment to be described later. Of course, only a subset of these scales was expected to tap an evaluative (attitude) dimension. Confirmatory factor analyses in both experiments, using LISREL VI (Joreskog and Sorbom, 1983), resulted in the selection of a set of eight evaluative scales: *rewarding–punishing, useful–useless, good–bad, harmful–beneficial, wise–foolish, happy–sad, sharp–dull,* and *attractive–unattractive.* The sum over these eight scales served as the measure of attitude; its α coefficient was found to be .86.

Subjective norms were also assessed in two ways. The first measure was based on normative beliefs concerning the expectations of five referents: instructor, parents, husband or wife (girlfriend or boyfriend), parents/relatives/children, and friends/peers/classmates. Respondents first indicated their motivations to comply with each referent on a 7-point scale ranging from *very much* to *not at all.* With respect to the instructor, for example, the statement rated was, "Generally speaking, how much do you want to do what the instructor of this course thinks you should do?" Later in the questionnaire, the strength of each normative belief (e.g., "The instructor thinks I should attend every session of this course") was assessed on a 7-point *extremely likely* to *extremely unlikely* scale. Each normative belief was multiplied by motivation to comply with the referent, and the sum of the products constituted the belief-based measure of subjective norm. Its internal consistency, as measured by coefficient α, was .84. The second measure assessed perceived social pressure in a more global fashion. Using the same 7-point scales, normative beliefs and motivations to comply were assessed with respect to "most people who are important to me," and the product of the two responses served as the second measure of subjective norm.

To develop measures of perceived behavioral control, a pilot study was conducted in which a sample of 24 college students was asked to list the factors that could prevent them from attending their classes. The following 10 frequently mentioned factors were selected for inclusion in the main study: conflicting events, sickness, family obligations, employment, being tired or listless, transportation problems, upsetting personal problems, oversleeping or forgetting, heavy load imposed by other classes, and failure to prepare class assignments. On a 7-point scale, respondents rated each factor's frequency of occurrence. The exact wording of the scale's endpoints depended on the factor involved. Thus, respondents judged the frequency of upcoming events that might conflict with class attendance on a scale ranging from *many events* to *none at all,* but the frequency of transportation problems on a *never–frequently* scale. Responses to all 10 items were summed to produce one measure of perceived behavioral control, with a reliability coefficient α of .73.

A second measure approached the issue directly by asking respondents to judge the degree to which they felt in control of attending all class sessions. Specifically, three questions were posed at separate points in the questionnaire: "How much control do you have over whether you do or do not attend this class every session?" (*complete control–very little control*), "For me to attend every session of this class is *easy–difficult*," and 'If I wanted to I could easily attend this class every session" (*extremely likely–extremely unlikely*). Confirmatory factor analysis revealed that these three items assessed a single underlying dimension,[5] and they were summed to produce the second indicator of perceived control, with an α coefficient of .74.

Finally, intentions were assessed by means of three questions that appeared at different points in the questionnaire and that dealt with the likelihood of attending every class session. The statements, "I intend to attend this class every session" and "I will try to attend this class every session" were rated on 7-point *extremely likely–extremely unlikely* scales; and the question, "How regularly do you intend to come to sessions of this class?" was rated on a 4-point scale that ranged from *every time* to *rarely.* Again using confirmatory factor analysis, these three items were found to form a unidimensional scale. The sum over the three responses served as the measure of intention, with a coefficient α of .69.

Results and discussion

Before turning to tests of the theory of planned behavior, it is of interest to examine the relations between the belief-based and the direct measures of attitude, subjective norm, and perceived behavioral control. According to the theory, beliefs provide the basis for the formation of attitudes, subjective norms, and perceptions of behavioral control. We would therefore expect to find appreciable correlations between the two types of measures. The results confirmed these expectations. The correlations were .51 for attitude, .47 for subjective norm, and .54 for perceived behavioral control, all significant beyond the .01 level.

Table 8.5 presents the results of hierarchical regression analyses for the prediction of intentions to attend class regularly and for actual class attendance.[6] The direct measures of attitude, subjective norm, and perceived behavioral control were used in the analyses shown in table 8.5, but the results obtained with the belief-based measures are virtually identical. For the prediction of intentions, attitude and subjective norm were entered on the first step, perceived behavioral control on the second step, and the interactions between these variables on the third step. The first step constitutes a test of the original theory of reasoned action. It can be seen that both attitude and subjective norm made significant contributions to the prediction of intention, resulting in a multiple correlation of .55.

However, consistent with the theory of planned behavior, the addition of perceived behavioral control greatly improved the model's predictive power ($F(3, 165) = 46.16, p < .01$). This finding indicates that the original theory of reasoned action, with its implication that perceived behavioral control can influence intention only indirectly via attitude or subjective norm, does not adequately account for the present data. Inspection of the results at the second step shows that each of the three independent variables (attitude, subjective norm, and perceived behavioral control) made a significant contribution to the prediction of intentions and that the multiple correlation increased from .55 to .68.

A second hierarchical regression analysis was conducted to examine whether perceived behavioral control was merely a reflection of past class attendance, or whether it provided information useful for the prediction of intentions that went beyond past behavior. In this analysis, past behavior (attendance during the eight class sessions prior to administration of the questionnaire) was entered on the first step, prior to all other independent variables. The results showed clearly that the role of perceived behavioral control went beyond any effect of past behavior; its regression coefficient in the prediction of intentions remained high (.28) and significant ($F(4, 164) = 19.57, p < .01$).

Table 8.5 Hierarchical regressions: Experiment 1 – class attendance

	r	b	R
Prediction of intentions			
Step 1 – Theory of reasoned action			
Attitude	.51	.44	
Subjective norm	.35	.21	.55
Step 2 – Theory of planned behavior			
Attitude	.51	.32	
Subjective norm	.35	.16	
Perceived behavioral control	.57	.44	.68
Prediction of behavior			
Step 1 – Theory of reasoned action			
Intention	.36	.36	.36
Step 2 – Theory of planned behavior			
Intention	.36	.30	
Perceived behavioral control	.28	.11*	.37

The increment in explained variance from Step 1 to Step 2 is significant ($p <$ .01) for the prediction of intentions and not significant for the prediction of behavior.

* Not significant; all other coefficients $p < .01$.

To test the possibility of interaction effects, perceived behavioral control was multiplied with attitude and with subjective norm, and the resulting product scores were entered into the hierarchical regression analysis after the basic variables.[7] Contrary to expectations, there was no evidence for significant interaction effects. The F ratio was less than 1 for the interaction between attitude and perceived behavioral control, and it was 1.61 (n.s.) for the subjective norm by perceived behavioral control interaction.

The lower part of table 8.5 shows the results of the hierarchical regression analysis for the prediction of behavior. In this analysis, intention was entered on the first step and perceived behavioral control on the second. Since the degree of *actual* control in this situation was thought to be relatively high, the addition of perceived control was expected to have little effect on predictive validity. The results of the analysis confirm this expectation. The regression coefficient of perceived behavioral control was not significant, and its inclusion in the prediction equation failed to raise the correlation with behavior appreciably. Intention alone had a correlation of .36 with behavior and the addition of perceived behavioral control resulted in a multiple correlation of .37.[8]

The possibility of an interaction effect was tested by entering the product of intention and perceived behavioral control on the third step of the hierarchical regression. The results again showed the interaction effect to be nonsignificant ($F = 1.52$).

In sum, the data presented thus far lend support to the first version of the theory of planned behavior (see figure 8.5). Perceived behavioral control had a strong effect on intentions to attend class, an effect not mediated by attitude and subjective norm, and not dependent on the influence of past behavior. This effect added to the prediction of intentions in a linear fashion; the interactions between perceived behavioral control and the other two predictors, attitude and subjective norm, were not significant. Contrary to the theory's second version, there was little evidence for a direct link between perceived behavioral control and actual class attendance, or for an interaction between control and intention. It should be recalled, however, that class attendance is relatively free of behavioral control problems and that for a behavior of this kind, perceived control over the behavior is not expected to add much predictability beyond intentions. The second experiment permits a comparison of this situation with one in which the behavioral goal is only partly under volitional control.

Experiment 2

Method

Respondents and procedure

Ninety undergraduate college students enrolled in three upper division business administration courses participated in Experiment 2; 34 were males and 56 were females.[9] Data were obtained in two waves. The first wave of data was collected approximately 3 weeks into the spring semester. Class instructors informed their students that they would be asked to participate in a survey of students' views and expectations with respect to getting an "A" in a particular course, that their participation was completely voluntary, and that their responses were confidential. Prior to distributing the questionnaire, the experimenter again assured the students that their responses would be completely confidential; that the instructor had nothing to do with the survey and would not see their responses; that their answers would have no effect whatsoever on the grades they received in the course; and that all identifying information would be destroyed as soon as data collection was completed.

To collect the data of the second wave, the same questionnaire was readministered toward the end of the semester, approximately one week prior to the final examination period. By this time, students had received considerable information concerning their performance in the course by means of feedback on class projects and examinations. This information was expected to have an impact on perceptions of control over receiving an "A" in the course and on related variables. The instructors' records were consulted to ascertain the actual grades students had obtained in the course under consideration.

Questionnaire

In a pilot study, 21 college students were asked to list (1) the advantages and disadvantages of getting an "A" in a particular course, (2) the people who might approve or disapprove of their getting an "A" in the course, and (3) the factors that might help or prevent them from getting an "A" in the course. Responses to these questions were used to develop belief items relevant, respectively, to the assessment of behavioral beliefs, normative beliefs, and control beliefs with respect to getting an "A."

The first page of the questionnaire provided instructions concerning use of the 7-point semantic-differential-type scales that would be encountered throughout. The next section assessed evaluations of 10 salient consequences of receiving an "A" in the course: getting a sense of personal accomplishment, being able to get a job or to go to graduate school, making friends feel awkward, creating expectations that would be hard to fulfill, working so hard that grades in other courses would suffer, having an opportunity to work with the course instructor in future semesters, recognition of efforts invested in the course, demonstrating thorough understanding of the course's subject matter, raising one's grade point average, and becoming overconfident with regard to the course's subject matter. Each consequence was rated on a 7-point *good–bad* scale. At a later point in the questionnaire, belief strength associated with each of the 10 possible outcomes was measured by means of a 7-point probability scale. For example, the statement, "My receiving an 'A' in this course will give me a feeling of personal accomplishment" was rated on a 7-point scale with endpoints labeled *likely* and *unlikely*. A belief-based measure of attitude toward receiving an "A" was calculated by summing over the 10 products of belief strength times the corresponding evaluation. The α coefficients of this measure in Waves 1 and 2 were .61 and .58, respectively.

As described in the method section of Experiment 1, a second, more direct measure of attitude was obtained by means of eight evaluative semantic differential scales selected on the basis of a confirmatory factor analysis. The concept rated in Experiment 2 was, "My receiving an 'A' in this course," and the scale's internal consistency, as indexed by coefficient α, was .78 in the first wave and .87 in the second.

Subjective norms were also assessed in two ways. The first measure was based on normative beliefs concerning the expectations of five referents: instructor, family, future employer, close friends, and classmates. On 7-point scales, respondents indicated their beliefs that each referent would *approve* or *disapprove* of their getting an "A" in the course. In a later section of the questionnaire, respondents expressed their motivations to comply with each referent on a 7-point scale ranging from *very much* to *not at all*. The sum over the five products of normative belief times motivation to comply constituted the belief-based measure of subjective norm, with α coefficients equal to .79 in Wave 1 and .81 in Wave 2.

The second measure was a direct indication of perceived social pressure. The statement, "If I received an 'A' in this course, most people who are important to me would" was rated on a 7-point *approve–disapprove* scale, and this score was multiplied by the response to the 7-point motivation to comply scale described above.

Two measures of perceived behavioral control over getting an "A" were constructed as follows. One was formed by summing over eight beliefs dealing with specific facilitating or inhibiting factors; other classes with demands on time and energy, involvement in extracurricular activities, the extent to which the subject matter of the course stimulates motivation, the nature of the assigned text and reading materials, the exams and other requirements of the course, the clarity and organization of the lectures, the student's skills and background, and availability of assistance by the instructor. Respondents stated their beliefs with respect to each factor on an appropriately labeled 7-point scale. To illustrate, the question, "How often do you get involved in extracurricular activities that might prevent you from getting an 'A' in this course?" was rated on a *frequently–never* scale; and the statement, "I have the skills and background needed to get an 'A' in this course" was rated on a scale that ranged from *likely* to *unlikely*. The internal consistency of the eight-item scale was .54 in Wave 1 and .62 in Wave 2.

A second measure of perceived behavioral control was obtained more directly by assessing the degree to which participants believed they had control over receiving an "A" in the course. The following five items addressing this issue were dispersed throughout the questionnaire: "It is mostly up to me whether or not I get an 'A' in this course" (*true–false*); "If I wanted to I could get an 'A' in this course" (*likely–unlikely*); "There is very little I can do to make sure that I get an 'A' in this course" (*agree–disagree*); "For me to get an 'A' in this course is" (*easy–difficult*); "How much control do you have over whether you do or do not get an 'A' in this course?" (*complete control–very little control*). Responses to these five items which, in a confirmatory factor analysis were found to form a unidimensional scale, were summed to obtain the second indicator of perceived behavioral control. The reliability of this measure, as assessed by coefficient α, was .69 in the first wave and .79 in the second.

The following three 7-point scales, appearing at different points in the questionnaire, were summed to obtain a measure of intention: "I am aiming at an 'A' in this course" (*definitely yes–definitely not*); "I will try my best to get an 'A' in this course" (*likely–unlikely*); and "I intend to get an 'A' in this course" (*likely–unlikely*). Confirmatory factor analysis revealed that these three items formed a unidimensional scale; and its reliability coefficient α was .82 in Wave 1 and .78 in Wave 2.

The final section of the questionnaire requested information about past academic performance. In the first wave only, respondents were asked to report their overall grade point averages, the number of graded courses they had taken in the past, and in how many of those courses they had received an "A." These questions were repeated for courses in the major field of studies. The last item in the questionnaires of both waves asked respondents to indicate what grades they expected to get in the present course.

Results and discussion

As in the first experiment, the belief-based and the relatively direct measures of attitude, subjective norm, and perceived behavioral control were found to correlate significantly. These correlations were, respectively, .47, .57, and .55 in Wave 1, and .58, .51, and .63 in Wave 2. Hierarchical regression analyses (using the direct measures of attitude, subjective norm, and perceived behavioral control) were performed to test the theoretical models.

Wave 1

Intentions to get an "A" and grades actually obtained served as dependent variables in the hierarchical regression analyses. Although obtaining a good grade in a course is associated with difficulties of control, perceptions of behavioral control were expected to be relatively inaccurate early in the semester. It was therefore expected that perceived behavioral control should influence intentions, but that it might add little to the prediction of grade attainment.

The major results of the hierarchical regressions of the first wave data are displayed in table 8.6. Looking at the findings for the first step, it can be seen that attitude, but not subjective norm, had a significant regression coefficient in the prediction of intentions. More important, and consistent with expectations, introduction of perceived behavioral control on the second step improved the prediction of intentions from .48 to .65 ($F(3, 86) = 29.40, p < .01$). As in Experiment 1, this effect was clearly additive, since introduction of interaction terms on the third step of the analysis failed to yield a significant improvement in the prediction of intentions ($F < 1$ for both, the interaction of perceived behavioral control with attitudes and with subjective norms).

Also consistent with the first experiment, the effect of perceived behavioral control on intention could not be explained in terms of prior experience with the behavioral goal. When past grade point average was entered into the analysis prior to any other variable, the regression

Table 8.6 Hierarchical regressions: Experiment 2, Wave 1 – grades

	r	b	R
Prediction of intentions			
Step 1 – Theory of reasoned action			
Attitude	.48	.48	
Subjective norm	.11*	−.02*	.48
Step 2 – Theory of planned behavior			
Attitude	.48	.50	
Subjective norm	.11	−.09*	
Perceived behavioral control	.44	.45	.65
Prediction of behavior			
Step 1 – Theory of reasoned action			
Intention	.26	.26	.26
Step 2 – Theory of planned behavior			
Intention	.26	.26	
Perceived behavioral control	.11*	−.01*	.26

The increment in explained variance from Step 1 to Step 2 is significant ($p <$ .01) for the prediction of intentions and not significant for the prediction of behavior.

* Not significant; all other coefficients $p < .01$.

coefficient of perceived behavioral control remained high (.40) and significant ($F(4, 85) = 24.98, p < .01$).

Table 8.6 also shows that the addition of perceived behavioral control did nothing to improve the prediction of attained grades obtained on the basis of intentions alone; the correlation remained .26. And again as in the first experiment, there was no evidence for an interaction between perceived behavioral control and intention ($F < 1$).[10]

To summarize briefly, the results of the first wave were quite similar to the findings of Experiment 1. In terms of its ability to account for variance in intentions, the theory of planned behavior was clearly superior to the theory of reasoned action. Moreover, perceived behavioral control was found to have a significant effect on intention, independent of attitude and subjective norm, and independent of prior behavior. In terms of predicting attained grades, however, perceived behavioral control was of no value. It appears that at the time of Wave 1, little information was available to permit accurate perceptions of control. Being relatively uninformed, these perceptions failed to correlate with actual grades attained. We would expect, however, that at the time of Wave 2, information relevant to the particular course taken will be reflected in perceptions of control (as well as intentions). If this expectation is correct, then we should observe increased importance of perceived behavioral control in analyses of the Wave 2 data.

Wave 2

Before turning to tests of the models, it is instructive to examine some of the changes that occurred between Waves 1 and 2. In the first wave, respondents on the average expected to receive a grade of 4.56 (5 = "A," 4 = "B," . . . 1 = "F"), i.e., a grade midway between an "A" and a "B." In fact, 50% expected to get an "A," 49% a "B," and only 1% a "C." At the time of Wave 2, respondents had significantly lowered their expectations to an average grade of 4.26 ($t(89) = 3.62, p < .01$); 38% now expected to get an "A," 48% a "B," and 14% a "C." (The average grade actually attained was a 3.76, midway between a "B" and a "BC.") Perhaps more important, the correlation between grade expectations in Waves 1 and 2 was only .30 ($p < .01$), indicating considerable changes at the individual level that went beyond the relatively small decline in average expectations. Examination of the correlations between expected grades and actual grades attained revealed that expectations had become considerably more accurate: The correlation was only .07 in Wave 1 but increased to .63 in Wave 2.

Table 8.7 presents the changes that were observed in the main constructs of the theory of planned behavior. Prior to conducting these analyses, each indicator was "normalized" so that scores would fall into a −3 to +3 range. The two indicators for each construct were then averaged. It can be seen that, at the time of Wave 1, participants had positive attitudes and subjective norms, moderately high expectations of control, and strong intentions to get an "A" in the course. At the time of Wave 2, subjective norms had remained virtually unchanged; and attitudes, although significantly lower, had also remained quite positive. Large and significant shifts, however, occurred in perceptions of control and in intentions. The students no longer believed that it was definitely under their control to get an "A," and they correspondingly lowered their intentions to try. Between-wave correlations are displayed in the last column of table 8.7. It can be seen that they were all of moderately high magnitude.

The results of hierarchical regression analyses for the second wave are displayed in table 8.8. In terms of predicting intentions, no appreciable differences between Waves 1 and 2 were expected, and none were found. As before, only attitudes and perceived behavioral control had significant regression coefficients, and the increased predictability of intentions (from .49 to .64) due to perceived behavioral control was highly significant ($F(3, 86) = 19.98, p < .01$). Also as in the first wave, there was no evidence for interactions between perceived behavioral control and attitude ($F = 1.06$, n.s.) or subjective norm ($F < 1$), nor was the effect of perceived behavioral control accounted for by past performance. When prior grade point average was statistically controlled by entering it on the first step, the regression coefficient of perceived behavioral control was still .38 ($F(4, 85) = 19.45, p < .01$).

The most interesting findings emerged with respect to the prediction of target behavior from the Wave 2 data. Since perceived behavioral control toward the end of the semester was expected to have become relatively accurate, reflecting actual control reasonably well, it was

Table 8.7   Changes in attitudes, subjective norms, perceived behavioral control, and intentions

| Construct | Means | | Degrees of freedom | t-value | Between-wave correlation |
	Wave 1	Wave 2			
Attitude	1.62	1.45	87	2.92*	.56*
Subjective norm	1.88	1.86	87	.44	.61*
Perceived control	1.02	.60	87	4.82*	.57*
Intention	2.09	1.29	88	5.91*	.51*

*$p < .01$.

Table 8.8 Hierarchical regressions: Experiment 2, Wave 2 – grades

	r	b	R
Prediction of intentions			
Step 1 – Theory of reasoned action			
Attitude	.48	.43	
Subjective norm	.30	.12*	.49
Step 2 – Theory of planned behavior			
Attitude	.48	.39	
Subjective norm	.30	.13*	
Perceived behavioral control	.45	.41	.64
Prediction of behavior			
Step 1 – Theory of reasoned action			
Intention	.39	.39	.39
Step 2 – Theory of planned behavior			
Intention	.39	.27	
Perceived behavioral control	.38	.26	.45

The increment in explained variance from Step 1 to Step 2 is significant ($p <$ .01) in each case.
* Not significant; all other coefficients $p < .01$.

expected to aid in the prediction of actual grade attained. The results of the relevant hierarchical regression analysis are shown in the lower part of table 8.8. The correlation between attained grades and intentions alone was .39. With the addition of perceived behavioral control on the second step, the correlation went up to .45, a significant improvement in predictive accuracy ($F(2, 87) = 11.19, p < .01$). This effect remained significant after controlling for past behavioral achievement. When prior grade point average was entered first, perceived behavioral control retained a significant ($F(3, 86) = 3.04, p < .05$) regression coefficient of .23. Finally, as in the previous analyses, perceived behavioral control did not interact significantly with intention in its effect on behavioral performance ($F < 1$).

Summarizing the results of the second wave, it can be said that the effects of perceived behavioral control were generally consistent with expectations. As in the first wave, perceived behavioral control influenced intentions beyond any mediating effects of attitude or subjective norm, and independent of prior performance. However, in contrast to the first wave, it also added significantly to the prediction of actual grades attained, and this contribution was not mediated by intentions, nor was it explained by the effect of prior performance on perceptions of behavioral control. The one finding that was again contrary to expectations was the absence of significant interactions between perceived behavioral control and any of the other independent variables.

Conclusions

Taken together, the two experiments reported in this article provide strong support for the proposed theory of planned behavior. Consistent with the theory's first version, addition of perceived behavioral control to the variables contained in Ajzen and Fishbein's (1980) theory of reasoned action greatly improved prediction of behavioral intentions in both experiments. This finding indicates that perception of control, like attitude toward the behavior and subjective norm, can have an important impact on a person's behavioral motivation. The more that attainment of a behavioral goal is viewed as being under volitional control, the stronger is the person's intention to try.

The second version of the theory of planned behavior also received some empirical support. After controlling for intentions, the relation between perceived behavioral control and target behavior was significant in the second wave of Experiment 2. Our interpretation of these results is that perceived behavioral control can indeed influence behavior independent of its effect on intention. This is likely to be the case, however, only under certain conditions. First, the behavior in question must at least in part be determined by factors beyond a person's control; and second, perceived behavioral control must be reasonably realistic. These two conditions were clearly met only in the second wave of Experiment 2. Getting an "A" in a course involves factors over which students have only partial control; and at the time of Wave 2, sufficient feedback had been provided to permit relatively accurate assessments of behavioral control.

It must be recalled at this point that we are not claiming a direct causal effect for perceived behavioral control. At the time of Wave 2, many students had little if any realistic chance of getting an "A" in the course. This lack of *actual* control, not perceptions of it, is assumed to prevent students from getting an "A" (if they indeed continue to try). Perceived behavioral control may in part reflect anticipated grades, and some of the specific control beliefs may constitute "rationalizations" or post hoc explanations for an inability to attain an intended grade. Nevertheless, to the extent that the measures of perceived behavioral control accurately reflect actual control in the situation, they permit us to improve prediction of goal attainment.

Contrary to intuition, perceived behavioral control interacted significantly neither with attitude or subjective norm in its effect on intentions nor with intention in its effect on target behavior. Although somewhat unexpected, the absence of significant interactions is not inconsistent with the results of past research. For example, Schifter and Ajzen (1985) examined the interaction between weight loss intentions and perceived behavioral control over body weight and found that the effect was weak and only marginally significant. Similarly, research on factors influencing task performance has usually found main effects of ability and motivation, but only weak and contradictory evidence for interactions between these variables (see Locke, Mento, and Katcher, 1978). Indeed, past research has shown that linear models will usually perform adequately even when interactions are known to be present in the data (cf., Slovic and Lichtenstein, 1971).

Even without entering into interactions, however, perceived behavioral control was found to be an important predictor beyond attitude, subjective norm, and intention, the variables contained in the original theory of reasoned action. Like attitudes and subjective norms, perceptions of behavioral control were shown to be related to an underlying set of salient beliefs. Although not considered in detail in this article, these beliefs provide useful information about the opportunities and resources that are viewed as important factors in performance of behaviors that are not completely under volitional control.

NOTES

We are grateful to Frank Callahan and Jacquelyn Twible for their assistance in collecting and analyzing the data, and to Bill Dillon for his helpful comments.

[1] Although women exhibited a somewhat higher attendance rate and expressed more favorable attitudes and intentions than did men, there were no systematic differences between the sexes in terms of the pattern of intercorrelations among the variables assessed in the present study. All analyses reported are therefore based on pooled data.

[2] We thank Linda Carli for permitting us to conduct the study in her class.

[3] Signatures on the questionnaires and attendance sheets were compared in a random sample of 25 participants. No apparent deceptions were discovered.

[4] This measure is derived from expectancy-value theory which assumes that attitude is a function of *all* salient beliefs about the attitude object. Consequently, no attempt was made to refine this measure by means of item analysis or to assure its unidimensionality by means of confirmatory factor analysis. For the same reason, all belief items were retained in the belief-based measures of subjective norm and perceived control, described below.

[5] In order to gain a degree of freedom, a restriction was imposed such that the λ's of two indicators were constrained to be equal.

[6] In addition to performing hierarchical regressions, the data in both studies were also analyzed by means of three-stage least-square procedures (White, 1978) and by means of LISREL (Joreskog and Sorbom, 1983). In these analyses, the direct and indirect measures served as different indicators of attitude, subjective norm, and perceived behavioral control. The results obtained were similar to those reported here. Hierarchical regressions were preferred because they permit relatively easy incorporation of interaction terms (see Cohen, 1978).

[7] The untransformed data were used to compute interaction terms in all analyses reported in this article. Although linear transformations will influence zero-order correlations of the product scores with other variables, the results of the hierarchical regression analysis remain unaffected by such transformations (see Cohen, 1978).

[8] The intention–behavior correlation in this study is low in comparison to the findings of other investigations that have examined behaviors under relatively high volitional control (see Ajzen, 1985; Ajzen and Fishbein, 1980). This may be due at least in part to the relatively poor reliability of the behavioral measure. The correlation between the first and the second sets of eight behavioral observations was only .46, and the α coefficient for the eight later observations which served as the criterion was .56.

[9] There were no significant differences between the sexes on any measure obtained in this study.

[10] Attempts were also made to rescore the measures of behavior so that they would correspond more closely to the questionnaire items which dealt with receiving an "A" in the course. Thus, past performance was redefined as the number (or proportion) of "A"s received in past courses, and performance in the present course was dichotomized into "received an A" versus "did not receive an A." Although the pattern of intercorrelations and the major findings remained the same, the restriction of range resulted in generally lower correlations. Similarly, past achievement in courses related only on the student's major field of study reduced the correlation with performance in the present course.

REFERENCES

Ajzen, I. (1982). On behaving in accordance with one's attitudes. In M.P. Zanna, E.T. Higgins, and C.P. Herman (eds), *Consistency in social behavior: The Ontario Symposium* (vol. 2, pp. 3–15). Hillsdale, NJ: Erlbaum.

Ajzen, I. (1985). From intentions to actions: A theory of planned behavior. In J. Kuhl and J. Beckman (eds), *Action-control: From cognition to behavior* (pp. 11–39). Heidelberg: Springer.

Ajzen, I., and Fishbein, M. (1977). Attitude–behavior relations: A theoretical analysis and review of empirical research. *Psychological Bulletin*, 84, 888–918.

Ajzen, I., and Fishbein, M. (1980). *Understanding attitudes and predicting social behavior*. Englewood-Cliffs, NJ: Prentice-Hall.

Ajzen, I., Timko, C., and White, J.B. (1982). Self-monitoring and the attitude–behavior relation. *Journal of Personality and Social Psychology*, 42, 426–35.

Averill, J.R. (1973). Personal control over aversive stimuli and its relationship to stress. *Psychological Bulletin*, 80, 286–303.

Bandura, A. (1977). Self-efficacy: Toward a unifying theory of behavioral change. *Psychological Review*, 84, 191–215.

Bandura, A. (1982). Self-efficacy mechanism in human agency. *American Psychologist*, 37, 122–47.

Bandura, A., Adams, N.E., and Beyer, J. (1977). Cognitive processes mediating behavioral change. *Journal of Personality and Social Psychology*, 35, 125–39.

Bandura, A., Adams, N.E., Hardy, A.B., and Howells, G.N. (1980). Tests of the generality of self-efficacy theory. *Cognitive Therapy and Research*, 4, 39–66.

Bentler, P.M., and Speckart, G. (1979). Models of attitude–behavior relations. *Psychological Review*, 86, 452–64.

Bentler, P.M., and Speckart, G. (1981). Attitudes "cause" behavior: A structural equation analysis. *Journal of Personality and Social Psychology*, 40, 226–38.

Cohen, J. (1978). Partialed products *are* interactions: Partialed powers *are* curve components. *Psychological Bulletin*, 85, 858–66.

Fishbein, M., and Ajzen, I. (1975). *Belief, attitude, intention, and behavior: An introduction to theory and research*. Reading, MA: Addison-Wesley.

Fredricks, A.J., and Dossett, K.L. (1983). Attitude–behavior relations: A comparison of the Fishbein–Ajzen and the Bentler–Speckart models. *Journal of Personality and Social Psychology*, 45, 501–12.

Janis, I.L., and Rodin, J. (1979). Attribution, control, and decision making: Social psychology and health care. In G.C. Stone, F. Cohen, and N.E. Adler (eds), *Health psychology – A handbook* (pp. 487–521). San Francisco: Jossey-Bass.

Joreskog, K.G., and Sorbom, D. (1983). *LISREL IV; Estimation of linear structural equation systems by maximum likelihood methods*. Chicago: National Educational Resources.

Kanfer, F.H., and Hagerman, S. (1981). The role of self-regulation. In L.P. Rehm (ed.), *Behavior therapy for depression: Present status and future direction* (pp. 143–79). New York: Academic Press.

Kuhl, J. (1985). Volitional aspect of achievement motivation and learned helplessness: Toward a comprehensive theory of action control. In B.A. Maher (ed.), *Progress in experimental personality research* (vol. 13, pp. 99–171). New York: Academic Press.

Langer, E.J. (1983). *The psychology of control*. Beverly Hills, CA: Sage.

Lefcourt, H.M. (1982). *Locus of control: Current trends in theory and research* (2nd edn). Hillsdale, NJ: Erlbaum.

Liska, A.E. (1984). A critical examination of the causal structure of the Fishbein/Ajzen attitude–behavior model. *Social Psychology Quarterly*, 47, 61–74.

Locke, E.E., Mento, A.J., and Katcher, B.L. (1978). The interaction of ability and motivation in performance: An exploration of the meaning of moderators. *Personnel Psychology*, 31, 269–80.

Manstead, A.S.R., Proffitt, C., and Smart, J.L. (1983). Predicting and understanding mothers' infant-feeding intentions and behavior: Testing the theory of reasoned action. *Journal of Personality and Social Psychology*, 44, 657–71.

Osgood, C.E., Suci, G.J., and Tannenbaum, P.H. (1957). *The measurement of meaning*. Urbana, IL: University of Illinois Press.

Rothbaum, F., Weisz, J.R., and Snyder, S.S. (1982). Changing the world and changing the self: A two-process model of perceived control. *Journal of Personality and Social Psychology*, 42, 5–37.

Rotter, J.B. (1966). Generalized expectancies for internal versus external control of reinforcement. *Psychological Monographs*, 80 (1, Whole No. 609).

Sarver, V.T., Jr (1983). Ajzen and Fishbein's "theory of reasoned action": A critical assessment. *Journal for the Theory of Social Behavior*, 13, 155–63.

Schifter, D.B., and Ajzen, I. (1985). Intention, perceived control, and weight loss: An application of the theory of planned behavior. *Journal of Personality and Social Psychology*, 49, 843–51.

Slovic, P., and Lichtenstein, S. (1971). Comparison of Bayesian and regression approaches to the study of information processing in judgment. *Organizational Behavior and Human Performance*, 6, 649–744.

Smetana, J.G., and Adler, N.E. (1980). Fishbein's value × expectancy model: An examination of some assumptions. *Personality and Social Psychology Bulletin*, 6, 89–96.

Speckart, G., and Bentler, P.M. (1982). Application of attitude–behavior models to varied content domains. *Academic Psychology Bulletin*, 4, 453–65.

Steiner, I.D. (1970). Perceived freedom. In L. Berkowitz (ed.), *Advances in experimental social psychology* (vol. 5, pp. 187–248). New York: Academic Press.

Strickland, B.R. (1978). Internal–external expectancies and health-related behavior. *Journal of Consulting and Clinical Psychology*, 46, 1192–211.

Triandis, H.C. (1977). *Interpersonal behavior*. Monterey, CA: Brooks/Cole.

White, K.J. (1978). A general computer program for econometric methods – SHAZAM. *Econometrica*, 46, 239–40.

9 Principles of Attitude Formation and Strategies of Attitude Change

Decision freedom as a determinant of the role of incentive magnitude in attitude change

D.E. Linder, J. Cooper and E.E. Jones

Editors'
Introduction

Theoretical Background

According to Popperian philosophy, progress in science results from a competition of ideas in which theorists try to disprove each other's theories, and to develop new theories or modify existing ones to account for discrepant findings. The controversy between dissonance and reinforcement or incentive theorists is one of the few examples in social psychology that follow this somewhat idealized pattern. On a methodological level, this controversy is over the issue of construct validity: that is, the question of which theoretical constructs were *really* manipulated in the various experiments.

In 1959 Festinger and Carlsmith reported a study supporting the predictions derived from Festinger's (1957) cognitive dissonance theory. The theory predicted that individuals who were induced to behave publicly in a manner inconsistent with their private attitudes were more likely to change their attitudes towards their public advocacy, if they received a small ($1) rather than a large ($20) reward. This finding, replicated by Cohen (1962), seemed to be inconsistent with the then dominant reinforcement or incentive ideas, which argued that greater rewards should lead to more attitude change.

Rosenberg (1965) challenged the conclusions drawn from the dissonance studies, arguing that the reward manipulation used in the Festinger and Carlsmith and the Cohen experiments varied not the construct 'dissonance' but 'evaluation apprehension'. He predicted that if evaluation apprehension were reduced, the positive relationship between magnitude of reward

Journal of Personality and Social Psychology (1967), 6:245–54.

and attitude change, predicted by incentive theories, would emerge. His findings appeared to support this hypothesis.

In the present paper, Linder and colleagues in turn challenged Rosenberg's conclusions, arguing (1) that he had inadvertently manipulated the construct 'freedom of choice' instead of 'evaluation apprehension', and (2) that his findings were consistent with a modified version of dissonance theory.

EXPERIMENT I

Hypotheses

Depending on subjects' 'freedom of choice' (i.e. their freedom to refuse the request of the experimenter), the relationship between magnitude of incentives on attitude change is either negative or positive. Under 'high choice' the dissonance-predicted negative relationship will be observed; under 'low choice' the incentive-predicted positive relationship will emerge.

Design

The experimental design was a post-test-only, two-factor, between-subjects design with an added control group: 2 (magnitude of incentive: high/low) × 2 (freedom of choice: high/low). Thus, there were four experimental conditions. The dependent variable was assessed only after subjects had been exposed to the experimental manipulations. A no-manipulation control group was added to assess the baseline attitude of subjects not exposed to any experimental manipulation.

Method

The study was a classic laboratory experiment using an elaborate experimental scenario or cover story to justify the experimental manipulations. Magnitude of incentive was manipulated by offering student subjects either $.50 or $2.50 for a counter-attitudinal essay. Freedom of choice was manipulated as follows: under high choice the experimenter emphasized subjects' rights to refuse compliance. Under low choice the experimenter acted as if, in volunteering, participation subjects had already committed themselves. Subjects were randomly assigned to the four experimental groups. By running the control group only after the main experiment, the rules of random allocation were violated with regard to the control group and the data of the control group were not included in the statistical analyis. The dependent variable was assessed on a seven-point numerical rating scale with the end points reflecting the extreme positions on the attitude issue. We note in passing that the fact that subjects in the high incentive condition were paid less than they were promised would now be in violation of the American Psychological Association's ethical rules for experiments, according to which promises about payment have to be kept.

Results

There were no manipulation checks. Subjects should have been asked to estimate the magnitude of the incentive and to indicate how free they felt to refuse the experimenter's request, to verify the success of the incentive and freedom-of-choice manipulations.

The study predicted an interaction of magnitude of incentive and freedom of choice on attitudes: that is, the impact of the reward manipulation was expected to depend on whether freedom of choice was high or low. The pattern of means supported predictions (table 9.1) and a two-factor analysis of variance on the attitude measure revealed a significant interaction (table 9.2). Additional statistical tests were conducted on the 'simple effects' to assess whether the impact of the incentive manipulation was significant both under high choice (dissonance effect) and under low choice (reinforcement). The dissonance effect (i.e. the difference between 2.96 and 1.64) was statistically significant, but the reinforcement effect (i.e. the difference between 1.66 and 2.34) was not.

EXPERIMENT 2

Since the relevance of the results of experiment 1 as a critique of the Rosenberg experiment rests on the claim that his way of removing evaluation apprehension in fact removed freedom of choice, experiment 2 was conducted as a close replication of the Rosenberg experiment, with the one exception that for half the subjects a condition of high freedom of choice was created by emphasizing that subjects should feel free to refuse the request of the second experimenter. In line with predictions, the introduction of high freedom of choice reversed the Rosenberg findings and resulted in the negative relationship between magnitude of incentives and attitude change that was predicted by dissonance theory.

Discussion

The results of Linder and colleagues support their hypothesis, thus allowing them to account for the inconsistencies between the results of Rosenberg, on the one hand, and of Festinger and Carlsmith and of Cohen, on the other. In demonstrating that counter-attitudinal advocacy resulted in dissonance if, and only if, subjects felt free to refuse the experimenter's demands, Linder and his colleagues also clarified dissonance theory. They thus continued a process (which had started with Brehm and Cohen, 1962), of identifying conditions that had to be met in order to produce the negative relationship between counter-attitudinal advocacy and attitude change. According to modern dissonance theory (e.g. Cooper and Fazio, 1984), which differs considerably from the theory proposed by Festinger in 1957, the dissonance effect occurs only when (1) subjects freely choose to engage in counter-attitudinal behaviour, (2) they feel committed to this behaviour, (3) the behaviour results in unwanted consequences, and (4) subjects feel personally responsible for these consequences.

FURTHER READING

Cooper, J. and Worchel, S. (1970). Role of undesired consequences in arousing cognitive dissonance. *Journal of Personality and Social Psychology*, 16, 199–206. Empirical study which demonstrates that the consequences of counter-attitudinal behaviour have to be negative to produce dissonance.

Cooper, J. and Fazio, R.H. (1984). A new look at dissonance theory. In L. Berkowitz (ed.), *Advances in Experimental Social Psychology* (vol. 17, pp. 229–66). San Diego, CA: Academic Press. This chapter reviews the theoretical modifications dissonance theory has undergone since the original formulation of Festinger (1957). It presents a reformulation of the theory which is widely accepted.

REFERENCES

Brehm, J.W. and Cohen, A.R. (1962). *Explorations in Cognitive Dissonance*. New York: Wiley.

Cohen, A.R. (1962). An experiment on small rewards for discrepant compliance and attitude change. In Brehm, J.W. and Cohen, A.R., *Explorations in Cognitive Dissonance* (pp. 75–7). New York: Wiley.

Festinger, L. (1957). *A Theory of Cognitive Dissonance*. Stanford, CA: Stanford University Press.

Festinger. L. and Carlsmith, J.M. (1959). Cognitive consequences of forced compliance. *Journal of Abnormal and Social Psychology*, 59, 203–10.

Rosenberg, M.J. (1965) When dissonance fails: On eliminating evaluation apprehension from attitude measurement. *Journal of Personality and Social Psychology*, 1, 28–42.

If a person can be induced to behave publicly in a manner that does not follow from his private attitudes, he will experience cognitive dissonance. The magnitude of dissonance will be greater when there are few reasons for complying than when there are many reasons (Festinger, 1957). This dissonance may be reduced by an accommodating change in private attitude if other ways of reducing dissonance are not available. Thus a person who has been induced to behave in a counterattitudinal fashion will change his private attitude more the less he has been rewarded for complying. Festinger and Carlsmith (1959) found support for this proposition in a study in which subjects were persuaded (for $1 or $20) to extol the attractiveness of a dull and tedious task for the benefit of the next subject. Also, Cohen (1962) found that Yale students who were induced to write essays in favor of the New Haven police later showed more positive attitudes the smaller the incentive they had been offered to write the essay.

Rosenberg (1965) has recently questioned the generality of this proposed relationship and has suggested that subjects in the Festinger and Carlsmith (1959) and the Cohen (1962) experiments must have considered the incentive excessive and, because of the "evaluation apprehension" that subjects in psychology experiments commonly feel, those in the high-incentive conditions may have interpreted the experiment as one testing their honesty and autonomy. To resist influence in the face of a substantial bribe, therefore, would cause the experimenter to evaluate them favorably. Alternatively, Rosenberg suggests that the subjects may have suspected deception in the high-incentive condition and angrily resisted confirming the perceived hypothesis. Either reaction might conceivably account for the obtained inverse

- - - - -
Primary
Reading
- - - - - - - -

relationship between incentive amount and degree of ultimate congruence between attitude and behavior.

Rosenberg proceeded to conduct an experiment loosely replicating Cohen's (1962), the major difference being that one experimenter provided the incentive for essay writing and another measured the subsequent attitude. The two tasks were presented to the subjects as unrelated, and thus there was presumably no chance for evaluation apprehension to affect the results. Rosenberg found that attitude and behavior were most congruent when subjects were offered $5 for writing essays and least in line when they were offered $.50. Rosenberg's results are clearly at variance with the apparent dissonance prediction and with the findings obtained by Cohen and by Festinger and Carlsmith. Instead, the results seem to favor a reinforcement position or, as Rosenberg would prefer, a theoretical position that considers the effects of reinforcement in the context of an affect–cognition consistency model. In Rosenberg's view, either the expectation or the receipt of reward strengthens and stabilizes the cognition associated with the counterattitudinal statement – the greater the reward, the greater the stabilizing effect. There is then a change in attitudinal affect in the interests of cognitive–affective consistency.

Nuttin (1964) carefully replicated Rosenberg's experiment and found that – even with evaluation apprehension removed in the same manner – inferred attitude change varied inversely with the amount of incentive offered. While Nuttin's results were of only borderline significance, they clearly offered more support for the dissonance proposition than for the counterproposition reflecting reinforcement theory. Aronson (1966) has criticized Rosenberg's reasoning and his conclusions on many different grounds. Perhaps his most telling criticism was that Rosenberg should have tried to reproduce the inverse incentive effects previously attributed to dissonance theory by adding conditions to his design in which the same experimenter called for the essay and measured the subsequent attitude. Aronson argued that there were many differences between the Cohen experiment and the Rosenberg replication, and to assume that his results reversed the dissonance proposition solely because evaluation apprehension was removed is unwarranted.

The fact remains that Rosenberg (1965) was able to obtain a positive relationship between amount of incentive and inferred attitude change, and the intriguing empirical and theoretical problem is how to account for the fact that both dissonance and reinforcement effects have been found within the forced-compliance paradigm. Carlsmith, Collins, and Helmreich (1966) have predicted and successfully produced these opposing effects in a context approximating the original Festinger and Carlsmith (1959) study. When the subject was induced to describe the task as attractive to the next "unsuspecting subject," the former's subsequent task-attractiveness ratings were more positive in low- than in high-incentive conditions. When the subject was instead asked to write an essay praising the task, portions of which might later be used by the experimenter, rated attractiveness varied directly with the amount of incentive offered. Carlsmith et al. argued that amount of incentive will relate directly to attitude change (a reinforcement effect) whenever the dissonance involved in a counterattitudinal act is minimal. The subject who complied in the essay-writing conditions of their experiment had a number of legitimate reasons for doing so, and the experimenter, the only person to read the essay, knew full well that the essay did not express the subject's private opinion. Dissonance should be much greater in the conditions requiring the subject to dupe another person like himself.

The Carlsmith et al. (1966) experiment is especially important because of the care with which it was conducted, the clear replication of the Festinger and Carlsmith (1959) results it provides, and the separate elicitation of both dissonance and reinforcement effects within the same general design. But while they may account for the Rosenberg reinforcement effect, Carlsmith et al. are left without any clear explanation for Cohen's (1962) results. After all, he required an essay rather than a deceitful confrontation with another subject and obtained dissonance rather than reinforcement effects. One could argue that attitudes toward the New Haven police are likely to be more central and important than attitudes toward a boring task, and thus a counterattitudinal essay is more inherently dissonant in the former case. Or, one could argue that the subjects in Cohen's experiment were not really assured anonymity (as in Carlsmith et al.'s). Nevertheless, the empirical discrepancies existing in the forced-compliance literature are not entirely reconciled by the Carlsmith et al. study.

The major focus of these studies has been the relationship between the amount of incentive offered and subsequent attitude change, but a clear prediction from dissonance theory cannot be made unless the subject makes his decision to comply *after* considering the incentive magnitude. The incentive must be one of the conditions potentially affecting the decision to comply rather than a reward for having already so decided.

Both Cohen (1962) and Rosenberg (1965) reported that they took care to assure subjects that the decision to write the essay was entirely their own. It may be argued, however, that Rosenberg's major alteration of Cohen's procedure, the separation of the compliant-behavior setting from the attitude-measurement setting to eliminate evaluation apprehension, reduced his subjects' freedom not to comply. When Rosenberg's subjects arrived for the experiment, they found him busily engaged and were given the option of waiting for "15 or 20 minutes" or, as an afterthought, participating in "another little experiment some graduate student in education is doing." Professing to know little about this other experiment except that it "has to do with attitudes" and "I gather they have some research funds," Rosenberg did not pressure the subject into a decision, but let him decide for himself whether he wanted to participate or wait. Having made the decision to participate, each subject further strengthened his commitment by walking to the location of the second experiment. The choice then offered by the second experimenter was considerably less than a free one. Being already effectively committed, the subject would be more likely to treat the subsequent monetary offering as a bonus for prior compliance than as one of the conditions to be considered in making a free choice.

If the preceding argument is correct, Rosenberg's findings cannot be compared with Cohen's because different conditions prevailed in the two experiments when the counterattitudinal essays were written. Rosenberg inadvertently made it difficult for subjects not to comply and found that degree of attitude change was positively related to incentive magnitude, in support of a reinforcement position or an affective–cognitive consistency model (Rosenberg, 1960). In contrast to this, Cohen's procedure presented the choice not to comply as a more viable alternative and found that attitude change was inversely related to incentive magnitude, in support of a derivation from dissonance theory. A meaningful resolution of these discrepant findings would be to show that the effects of incentive magnitude on attitude change are either direct or inverse, depending on the presence or absence of freedom not to comply. The first experiment to follow was conducted as a direct test of the role of such freedom to choose not to engage in counterattitudinal behavior.

Experiment I

Method

Attitude issue and subjects

At the time of the first experiment a rather heated controversy was raging in the state of North Carolina concerning the wisdom of a law that forbade Communists and Fifth Amendment pleaders from speaking at state-supported institutions. On the basis of informal opinion sampling, fortified by the plausible expectation that students deplore implied restrictions on their own freedom to listen, we assumed that college-student subjects would be strongly opposed to speaker-ban legislation. The issue thus seemed comparable to "the actions of the New Haven police" (Cohen, 1962) and to a ban on Ohio State's participation in the Rose Bowl (Rosenberg, 1965).

Fifty-five introductory psychology students at Duke University served as subjects in the experiment. Forty subjects (15 males and 25 females) were randomly assigned to four experimental conditions;[1] 13 were subsequently assigned to a control condition. All experimental subjects were asked to write a "forceful and convincing essay" in favor of the speaker-ban law. After writing the essay, each subject was asked to indicate his opinion about the speaker-ban law by checking a point on a 31-point scale comparable to Cohen's (1962) and Rosenberg's (1965) measure. The scale read, "In my opinion the Speaker Ban Law of North Carolina is . . . ," followed by 31 horizontal dots with seven labels ranging from "not justified at all" to "completely justified." Subjects in the control condition merely filled out the scale without having previously written a pro-speaker-ban essay.

Procedure and design

The basic procedure was closely modeled after that of Cohen (1962) except that the subjects were recruited from the introductory psychology course and came individually to the laboratory, rather than being approached in their dormitory rooms. The experimenter introduced himself as a graduate student in psychology. In the *free-decision* condition he immediately said, "I want to explain to you what this task is all about. I want to make it clear, though, that the decision to perform the task will be entirely your own." In the *no-choice* condition he merely said, "I want to explain to you what this task that you have volunteered for is all about." He then proceeded in both conditions to provide the following rationale for the essay-writing task:

> The Association of Private Colleges of the South-east, of which Duke is a member, is considering the adoption of a uniform speaker policy that would be binding on its member schools. Before they can decide what kind of policy to adopt, if indeed they decide to adopt one, they have undertaken a large scale research program in order to help them understand what the issues really are. This study is part of that program. The APCSE is working through the Department of Psychology here at Duke and through the departments of psychology at other private schools in the area because of the access which the department has to a wide cross-section of students such as yourself who must participate in psychological experiments and because of the number of graduate students that are available to conduct research. We have found, from past experience, that one of the best ways to get relevant arguments on both sides of the issue is to ask people to write essays favoring only one side. We think we know pretty much how you feel about the student's rights in

this matter. [Here the experimenter paused and waited for a comment that would confirm the subject's initial opinion opposing the speaker-ban law. Only one subject expressed a favoring opinion at this point; see footnote 1.] Nonetheless, what we need now are essays favoring the speaker ban.

At this point, the free-decision and no-choice conditions again diverged. In the free-decision condition the subjects were told that the APCSE was paying $.50 (low incentive) or $2.50 (high incentive) in addition to the standard experimental credit given to all subjects. The experimenter again stressed that the decision to write the essay was entirely up to the subject and that he would receive experimental credit in any case. In the no-choice condition the experimenter acted as if, naturally, the subject in volunteering for the experiment had committed himself to its requirements. He simply pointed out that the experiment involved writing a strong and forceful essay favoring the speaker-ban law. After the subject was handed a pencil and some paper, but before be began to write, the experimenter broke in: "Oh yes, I almost forgot to tell you. . . . The APCSE is paying all participants $.50 [or $2.50] for their time."

In all conditions subjects were paid, *before* they wrote the essay, the amount of money promised them. The experimenter then left the room and allowed the subject 20 minutes to complete his essay. When he returned, the experimenter collected the essay, administered the brief attitude scale, and interviewed the subject concerning his perceptions of the experiment. No subject indicated any suspicion regarding the true purpose of the experiment. The purpose was then explained to each in detail, and all deceptions were revealed. None of the subjects recalled having any doubts about the existence of the fictitious APCSE. Each subject was ultimately allowed to keep $1.50. Because they were made to realize that they were assigned by chance to the high-inducement condition, those who had initially received $2.50 were quite agreeable when asked to return $1 of their money. Subjects in the low-inducement condition were delighted to learn of their good fortune – that they would receive $1 more than they had bargained for.

Results

Before the results bearing on the central hypothesis are presented, it is of interest to note the difference in decision time in the two free-decision conditions. After the experimenter began to notice that *free-decision* subjects in the low-incentive condition took much longer to make up their minds about writing the essay than *free-decision* subjects in the high-incentive condition, he started to record decision times with a hidden stopwatch. The last seven subjects in the low-incentive condition took an average of 25.29 seconds to reach a decision; the comparable mean for the last seven subjects in the high-incentive condition was 11.00 seconds. In spite of the reduced n, this difference is significant ($p < .025$, U test). This evidence strongly suggests that there was greater predecisional conflict in the low-incentive condition, and thus the conditions are appropriate for testing the dissonance hypothesis: since predecisional conflict leads to postdecisional dissonance (Festinger, 1964), more dissonance and hence more attitude change should occur in the free-decision–low-incentive condition.

After establishing that the means for female and male subjects were nearly identical ($t = .18$). the posttreatment attitude scores were placed in a simple 2 (for Degree of decision freedom) × 2 (for Level of incentive) factorial design. The means for each condition are

Table 9.1   Attitude-scale means obtained in the five conditions: Experiment I

	Incentive	
	$.50	$2.50
No choice	1.66[a]	2.34
Free decision	2.96	1.64
Control[b]	1.71	

$n = 10$ under both incentives for free-choice and free-decision conditions. For the control condition, $n = 13$.

[a] The higher the number, the more the speaker-ban law was considered to be justified.

[b] Since subjects in the control condition were all run after the main experiment was completed, the mean for this condition is presented only as an estimate of student opinion toward the issue in the absence of dissonance or incentive effects. The data from the control condition were not included in the statistical analysis.

Table 9.2   Summary of analysis of variance: Experiment I

Source of variation	MS	F
Choice (A)	.90	<1
Incentive (B)	1.02	<1
A × B	10.00	8.70****
Error	1.15	
Low incentive vs. high incentive within free-decision conditions	8.71	7.57****
Low incentive vs. high incentive within no-choice conditions	2.31	2.01*

Two-way analysis of experimental conditions.

$*p < .20$, $df = 1/36$.

$****p < .01$, $df = 1/36$.

presented in table 9.1. Scale values could range from 1.0 (antispeaker ban) to 7.0 (prospeaker ban). Table 9.2 summarizes the analysis of variance and appropriate orthogonal comparisons. The prediction that the amount of inferred attitude change would relate positively to inducement level in the no-choice conditions and negatively in the free-decision conditions is clearly confirmed ($F_{1,36} = 8.70$; $p < .01$). The dissonance effect in the free-decision condition was itself significant; the reinforcement effect in the prior-commitment condition was not. The control subjects, who checked the scale without writing an essay, were about as much against the speaker ban as subjects in the conditions where little or no change was predicted.

In an effort to shed light on possible mechanisms underlying these findings, the essays themselves were examined. The average number of words per essay was 192.3, and there were no significant differences among the four conditions in essay length. The essays were evaluated in a manner similar to that described by Rosenberg (1965). Two independent raters, blind as to the subject's condition, rated the essays in terms of the degree of organization manifested and the degree of "intent to persuade." Each of these ratings was made in terms of a 5-point scale. The judges agreed or were 1 point discrepant in 72% of the organization ratings and 85% of the persuasiveness ratings. These percentages of agreement were comparable to those obtained by Rosenberg (1965), but two independent judges using 5-point rating scales should, by chance, be no more than 1 point discrepant on more than 50% of their ratings. When a more traditional estimate of the reliability of the ratings was calculated (Winer, 1962, pp.124ff), it was found that the reliability coefficient for the ratings of degree of organization was .54, and the coefficient for the ratings of persuasiveness was .55. These coefficients estimate the reliability of the ratings that result from averaging over the two judges. When these ratings were submitted to an analysis of variance, there were no differences among conditions in either organization or persuasiveness.

Since the reliability of the ratings discussed above was quite low, an attempt was made to obtain ratings of acceptable high reliability. Two varsity debate partners agreed to rate the essays. General criteria to be used in determining the ratings were discussed, but the ratings were made independently. Each essay was rated for the persuasiveness of the presentation on a 7-point scale. Sixty percent of these ratings were no more than 1 point discrepant; the reliability coefficient was .48. (The chance percentage for agreements or 1-point discrepancies is 39% when a 7-point scale is used by two independent judges.) There were again no differences among the conditions in the rating received. Also, no between-condition differences appeared on the ratings made by any individual judge.

Discussion

The major purpose of the present experiment was achieved: to show that dissonance and reinforcement effects can be obtained within the same forced-compliance paradigm by varying the degree to which the subject is committed to comply before learning about the monetary incentive. Subjects who commit themselves after weighing the unpleasantness of the essay-writing task against the amount of incentive offered show the effects predicted by dissonance theory. The decision-time data strongly suggest that the subjects do in fact consider the essay-writing task unpleasant. Subjects who are not free to decide against compliance and then learn about a financial "bonus" produce results in line with reinforcement theory (that which is associated with something of value itself takes on value) or in line with the more complex affective–cognitive consistency model espoused by Rosenberg.

The present study was stimulated by Rosenberg's (1965) experiment, but the relevance of the results to a critique of Rosenberg's conclusions rests on the claim that his way of removing evaluation apprehension precommitted the subject to an unpleasant task before he had a chance to weigh the incentive for compliance. If this criticism is valid, then it should be possible to reproduce Rosenberg's results by closely replicating his procedures, and to obtain the converse of these results (confirming the dissonance prediction) by insuring that the subject does not commit himself before being confronted with the incentive for compliance. A second experiment was planned in an attempt to do precisely this.

Experiment II

Method

Attitude issue

As we prepared to run the second experiment, certain paternalistic policies of the Duke University administration were being challenged by the undergraduates, and there was a movement toward liberalization of *in loco parentis* social regulations. It was assumed, therefore, that undergraduates who were induced to write forceful and convincing essays in support of strict enforcement of *in loco parentis* policies would be performing a counterattitudinal task.

Subjects

Fifty-nine male introductory psychology students volunteered to participate for experimental credit in a study described as an "Attitude Survey." The data of 50 of these students, who were randomly assigned to the four experimental conditions and the control condition, were used in the reported analysis. Six subjects were eliminated because they did not complete the experimental procedure. Usually, they chose to read or study while waiting for the first experimenter rather than go to the second experimenter. Another subject was eliminated because he was initially in favor of strict *in loco parentis* policies, and writing the essay would not have been counterattitudinal for him.

Only two subjects who had completed the procedure were eliminated from the analysis. The first of these was excluded when it was discovered during the final interview that he had misinterpreted the attitude questionnaire. The second was eliminated because he accurately perceived the true purpose of the experiment. Both subjects had been assigned to the *free-decision–high-incentive* condition. The results of the study are not changed if these two subjects are included in the analysis.

Procedure and design

The procedure was a close approximation to that used by Rosenberg (1965). All subjects reported to the office of the first experimenter (E_1) where they found E_1 engaged in conversation with another student and were told, "I'm sorry, but I'm running late on my schedule today, and I'll have to keep you waiting for about 15 or 20 minutes. Is that all right?" All subjects agreed to wait.

Each experimental subject was then told:

> Oh, I've just thought of something; while you're waiting you could participate in another little experiment that some graduate student in education is doing. This fellow called me the other day and said he needed volunteers in a hurry for some sort of study he's doing – I don't know what it's about exactly except that it has to do with attitudes and that's why he called me, because my research is in a similar area as you'll see later. Of course, he can't give you any credit but I gather thay have some research funds and they are paying people instead. So, if you care to do that, you can.

At this point, one-half of the experimental subjects (*prior-commitment* condition) were allowed to leave for the second experiment without further comment by E_1. Since it was believed that Rosenberg's procedure restricted subjects' freedom not to comply with the task of the "little experiment," it was decided to manipulate degree of choice by removing this restriction. Thus, for subjects in the *free decision* condition, after the subject had agreed to participate in the second experiment, E_1 added:

> All I told this fellow was that I would send him some subjects if it was convenient but that I couldn't obligate my subjects in any way. So, when you get up there, listen to what he has to say and feel free to decide from there.

All experimental subjects then reported to the second experimenter (E_2). To control for the effects of experimenter bias, E_2 was not informed whether the subject was in the prior-commitment condition or the free-decision condition. E_2 presented himself as a graduate student in the Department of Education and introduced the essay-writing task using a procedure that, as in Experiment I, very closely approximated Cohen's (1962).

Rather than the free-decision versus no-choice manipulation of Experiment I, E_2 began by saying to all subjects, "At the present time, Duke University is beginning to question the wisdom of assuming the role of 'substitute parent' to its students." From that point, the instructions paralleled those of Experiment I with the substitution of *in loco parentis* regulations for the speaker-ban law. After confirming that the subject held an opinion opposed to rigid *in loco parentis* regulations, E_2 concluded:

> What we need now are essays favoring a strict enforcement of *in loco parentis*. So, what we would like you to do – if you are willing[2] – is to write the strongest, most forceful and most convincing essay that you can in favor of a strict enforcement of the substitute parent concept here at Duke.

It was then explained that the sponsoring agency was offering either $.50 (*low-incentive* conditions) or $2.50 (*high-incentive* conditions) for participation in the study. When the subject agreed to write the essay, he was paid the money promised to him and then began the task.

After completing the essay and being thanked and dismissed by E_2 all experimental subjects returned to E_1's office. To introduce the dependent measure, E_1 explained:

> What I had wanted you to do was participate in a continuing study I carry on every semester as a sort of Gallup poll to keep a check on opinion patterns on different University issues. I'd like you to fill out this questionnaire as an objective indication of your opinions and when you've finished I'd like to chat for a while about various issues on campus. OK?

E_1 was not informed of the amount of money the subject had received, and in no case did he find out until after the subject had completed the dependent measure.

The dependent measure consisted of an eight-item questionnaire dealing with various university issues. The critical item read, "How justified is the University's policy of assuming parental responsibilities for its students?" and was accompanied by the familiar 31-point scale. When the subject had completed the questionnaire, E_1 put it aside (without looking at the responses) and began a structured interview that included probes for suspicion and checks on perceptions of the manipulations. When E_1 was satisfied that the subject had not perceived the true purpose of the experiment, he revealed the deceptions and explained the necessity for them. As in Experiment I, all experimental subjects agreed to accept $1.50 for their time.

Subjects assigned to the control condition also found E_1 engaged in conversation and were asked if they could return in 15 or 20 minutes. Upon their return they were treated exactly as experimental subjects.

These procedures resulted in five conditions: two levels of incentive magnitude under a condition of free decision, the same two levels under a condition of prior commitment, and the control condition.

Results

The mean attitude-scale scores on the critical item for each of the five conditions are presented in table 9.3. It can be seen that the results are very similar to those of Experiment I. The data were submitted to a one-way analysis of variance, summarized in table 9.4. The overall treatment effect was significant ($F_{4,45} = 4.02$; $p < .01$). The two comparisons reflecting the hypotheses of this study were also significant: Within the free-decision conditions a low incentive produced more inferred attitude change than a high incentive ($F_{1,45} = 6.82$; $p < .025$). Within the prior-commitment conditions this effect was reversed, and a high incentive produced more inferred attitude change than a low incentive ($F_{1,45} = 4.90$; $p < .05$). The position of the control group indicates that differences between the experimental conditions resulted from positive attitude change rather than a combination of positive and negative changes.

Once again we attempted to investigate the possibility that these effects were mediated by some aspect of the counterattitudinal performance. Two raters, working independently and without knowledge of the experimental conditions, rated each essay on 7-point scales for the extremity of attitudinal position advocated, the persuasiveness of the essay, and its degree of organization. The two raters agreed or were within 1 point of each other for 65% of the essays when estimating the attitudinal position, 60% when rating them for persuasiveness, and 52.5% when rating them for organization. The reliability coefficient for the estimated attitudinal position (Winer, 1962, pp. 124ff) was .67, the coefficient for the persuasiveness ratings was .51, and the coefficient for the organization ratings was .38. There were no

Table 9.3   Attitude-scale means obtained in the five conditions: Experiment II

| | *Incentive* | |
	$.50	*$2.50*
Prior commitment	2.68[a]	3.46
Free decision	3.64	2.72
Control	2.56	

$n = 10$ in all conditions.

[a] The higher the number, the more strict application of *in loco parentis* regulations was considered justified.

Table 9.4 Summary of analysis of variance: Experiment II

Source of variation[a]	MS	F
Treatment	2.49	4.02****
Error	.62	
Low incentive vs. high incentive free-decision conditions	4.23	6.82***
Low incentive vs. high incentive prior-commitment conditions	3.04	4.90**

One-way analysis of five conditions.
[a] The control condition differs significantly from both the prior-commitment–high-incentive and the free-decision–low-incentive conditions.
** $p < .05$, $df = 1/45$.
*** $p < .025$, $df = 1/45$.
**** $p < .01$, $df = 1/45$.

differences among conditions on any of these ratings. The essays were then rated for the persuasiveness of the presentation on a 7-point scale by the same varsity debaters as had rated the essays from Experiment I. The debaters agreed or were within 1 point of each other for 65% of the essays, and the reliability coefficient was a somewhat more acceptable .71. Again, however, there were no differences among conditions on these ratings, whether the judges' ratings were averaged or each judge's ratings were examined separately. In a final attempt to find a performance difference among the conditions the number of words in each essay was counted; the conditions were compared on this measure of performance and were found not to differ from one another.

Discussion

The results of Experiment II suport the argument that Rosenberg's (1965) procedure for the elimination of evaluation apprehension committed his subjects to perform the essay-writing task before they learned of the nature of the task and the amount of reward offered. The positive relationship between incentive magnitude and attitude change in the prior-commitment conditions of the present experiment replicates the no-choice results of Experiment I and the relationship found by Rosenberg (1965). It could be argued on this basis alone that such procedures as Rosenberg's have the same effect as allowing the subject no choice concerning performance of the counterattitudinal act. The argument becomes much more convincing, however, if it can be shown that appropriate alteration of Rosenberg's procedure, reducing the prior commitment of the subject, leads to an *inverse* relationship between incentive magnitude and attitude change. The free-decision conditions of Experiment II demonstrate precisely this point: when the subject does not feel that he has previously committed himself to performance of the counterattitudinal action requested by E_2, attitude change is an inverse function of incentive magnitude.

It should be noted here that a "balanced replication" (Aronson, 1966) of Rosenberg's (1965) study was required. Had Experiment II included only the free-decision conditions it would be possible to argue that our procedure was not successful in eliminating evaluation apprehension and that the results reflected once again the effect of this contaminant in research on forced compliance. The results of the prior-commitment conditions of Experiment II, however, counter this criticism. A persistent critic might still argue that the free-decision manipulation reintroduced evaluation apprehension. Perhaps the comment added to create the free-decision condition in some way increased the chances that subjects would see the experiments as related. However, the structured interview conducted by E_1 revealed no differential level of suspicion between the prior commitment and free-decision conditions. In the absence of a reliable and valid measure of evaluation apprehension, we can do no more than contend that our interview was sensitive enough to detect suspicion and that we found no indication of differential suspicion among the conditions.

The results of the two studies reported above imply that the discrepancy between Cohen's (1962) findings and the results of Rosenberg's (1965) experiment may indeed be resolved in the manner indicated earlier in this paper. For Cohen's subjects the decision not to comply was a viable alternative at the time they were confronted with the essay-writing task and offered an incentive of certain value. Under such conditions dissonance will be induced whenever the incentive is not large enough to justify performance of the task, and incentive magnitude will be inversely related to subsequent attitude change. However, if a subject's freedom not to comply has been restricted before he is confronted with the task and with a clear description of the incentive, dissonance cannot be induced by an incentive of insufficient magnitude. Under these conditions, the reinforcing properties of the incentives will lead to a positive relationship between incentive magnitude and attitude change. Although Rosenberg (1965) demonstrated such a relationship, his assertion that it may be obscured by failure to remove evaluation apprenhension seems no longer tenable. No attempt was made in the procedure of Experiment I to remove evaluation apprehension, and yet the results are very similar to the results of Experiment II.

Rosenberg (1966) has more recently advanced two additional hypotheses intended to resolve discrepancies in the forced-compliance literature. The first of these is that we must distinguish counterattitudinal actions that are simple and overt from those featuring the elaboration of a set of arguments. Supposedly a performance of the former kind (e.g., eating a disliked food) will lead to the inverse relationship between attitude change and incentive magnitude, while an act of the latter kind (e.g., writing a counterattitudinal essay) will result in a positive relationship. The second hypothesis is that we must distinguish between two kinds of counterattitudinal performances: (a) those carried out under instructions that lead the subject to believe his performance will be used to deceive others, and (b) those following from instructions to elaborate, for some reasonable and legitimate purpose, a set of arguments opposite to his private opinion. It is hypothesized that even if the actual task is the same, say essay writing, the first type of instruction will lead to an inverse relationship between incentive magnitude and attitude change, and the second type of instruction will lead to a positive relationship.

In the studies reported above the subject's task was presented with no hint that his performance would be used to deceive anyone, and the task in all cases was to elaborate a set of arguments opposite to his own opinion. It follows from the two hypotheses suggested by Rosenberg (1966) and presented above that we should not have been able to obtain the inverse relationship between incentive magnitude and attitude change using our procedures. However, in both experiments, we obtained the positive *and* the inverse relationship. We are forced to conclude that neither the "simple versus complex" hypothesis nor the "duplicity versus legitimate" hypothesis can account for the present results.

In place of these hypotheses we conclude that at least some of the discrepancies in the forced-compliance literature may be resolved by closer attention to the role of decision freedom at the time the incentive is offered. A barely sufficient incentive for making counterattitudinal statements *does* result in dissonance and subsequent attitude change if the subject feels he is quite free not to comply. When the freedom not to comply is removed or markedly decreased, on the other hand, attitude change is greater the greater the incentive for compliance.

NOTES

This experiment was facilitated by National Science Foundation Grant 8857. We are indebted to H.B. Gerard for his valuable suggestions.

[1] Two more experimental subjects were actually run whose data were not analyzed. One of these was obviously in favor of the speaker-ban law at the outset, and the other was the victim of experimenter error in presenting instructions.

[2] This vague statement of choice was given to all subjects in order to keep the instructions constant across experimental groups and to enable E_2 to remain "blind" as to the condition of each subject. It was assumed that the crucial manipulation of free decision versus prior commitment had already been accomplished by E_1.

REFERENCES

Aronson. E. The psychology of insufficient justification. In S. Feldman (ed.), *Cognitive consistency: Motivational antecedents and behavioral consequents* New York: Academic Press. 1966. Pp. 115–33.

Carlsmith. J.M., Collins, B.E., and Helmreich, R.L. Studies in forced compliance: I. The effect of pressure for compliance on attitude change produced by face-to-face role playing and anonymous essay writing. *Journal of Personality and Social Psychology.* 1966. 4. 1–13.

Cohen, A.R. An experiment on small rewards for discrepant compliance and attitude change. In J.W. Brehm and A.R. Cohen. *Explorations in cognitive dissonance.* New York: Wiley, 1962. Pp. 73–8.

Festinger, L. *A theory of cognitive dissonance.* Evanston. Ill.: Row, Peterson, 1957.

Festinger. L. *Conflict, decision, and dissonance. Stanford*: Stanford University Press, 1964.

Festinger, L., and Carlsmith, J.M. Cognitive consequences of forced compliance. *Journal of Abnormal and Social Psychology*, 1959, 58, 203–10.

Nuttin, J.M., Jr. Dissonant evidence about dissonance theory. Paper read at 2nd conference of experimental social psychologists in Europe, Frascati, Italy, 1964. (Mimeo)

Rosenberg, M.J. An analysis of affective–cognitive consistency. In C.I. Hovland and M.J. Rosenberg (eds), *Attitude organization and change.* New Haven: Yale University Press, 1960. Pp. 15–64.

Rosenberg, M.J. When dissonance fails: On eliminating evaluation apprehension from attitude measurement. *Jouurnal of Personality and Social Psychology*, 1965, *1*, 28–42.

Rosenberg, M.J. Some limits of dissonance: Toward a differentiated view of counter-attitudinal performance. In S. Feldman (ed.), *Cognitive consistency: Motivational antecedents and behavioral consequents.* New York: Academic Press, 1966. Pp. 135–70.

Winer, B.J. *Statistical principles in experimental design.* New York: McGraw-Hill, 1962.

Personal involvement as a determinant of argument-based persuasion

R.E. Petty, J.T. Cacioppo and R. Goldman

- - - - -
Editors'
Introduction
- - - - - - - -

Theoretical Background

This is a key study in the recent history of research on attitude change. As the authors explain in the introduction to the paper, until the 1980s the study of attitude change had been characterized by two general approaches. One approach emphasized the *arguments* contained in a persuasive communication. According to one version of this approach, persuasion results from attending to these arguments, understanding them, learning their content, and remembering their content (McGuire, 1969). This has been summarized as the 'message-learning' approach to attitude change (Petty and Cacioppo, 1981). Another version of the argument-centred approach to understanding attitude change focused less on attending to, understanding, learning and remembering the actual content of the message, and more on the way in which the message generated *thoughts* in the mind of the audience (Greenwald, 1968). This has been dubbed the 'cognitive response' approach to attitude change.

What these approaches have in common is their focus on arguments. Thus in a message intended to encourage smokers to quit smoking, the prime determinant of attitude change, according to these approaches, is the quality of the argumentation in the message. If it is powerful enough to attract attention, to be readily understood, to be learned, and to be remembered, it will (according to the message-learning approach) be effective in changing attitudes. If it is powerful enough to generate plenty of thoughts about the benefits of quitting smoking, and very few thoughts about the downside of quitting, it will (according to the cognitive-response approach) be effective in changing attitudes.

These argument-based approaches can be contrasted with a group of approaches that focus more on the *form* or *packaging* of the message than on its argumentation. For example, if the advocated position or product is associated with positive cues (e.g. cigarettes are shown being smoked by youthful, healthy, sports-playing and physically attractive persons), this may be more effective in bringing about attitude change in the advocated direction than a message without these associated cues. However, it is clear that the positivity or negativity of the cues has little to do with the argument content of the message. Indeed, simply associating an attitude object with positive or negative cues, in the absence of any argumentation, has been shown to result in attitude change, presumably by one of the low-effort attitude-change processes such as classical conditioning (Staats and Staats, 1958; Zanna et al., 1970) or identification (Kelman, 1958).

Petty and Cacioppo (1981; Cialdini et al., 1981) synthesized these two general approaches to understanding attitude change within one theoretical framework. They argued that there are two 'routes' to attitude change: a *central route*, resulting from careful consideration of the arguments contained in a message; and a *peripheral route*, resulting from simple association of

Journal of Personality and Social Psychology (1981), 41:847–55.

the advocated position or product with cues that are either positive or negative in nature. The key objective of the present study was to study what determines whether those who receive a persuasive communication adopt the central or the peripheral route. The variable selected for study is personal relevance of, or involvement in, the topic of the message. The authors argue that when the topic is high in personal relevance, attitude change will occur via the central route: receivers will scrutinize the arguments contained in the message and will change their attitudes as a function of the quality of these arguments. However, when the topic is low in personal relevance, attitude change will occur via the peripheral route: receivers will not process the argument content of the message, but will change their attitudes as a function of the quality of the cues associated with the advocated position. To test this rationale, the authors manipulated argument quality, source expertise, and personal relevance. Their reasoning would be supported if attitude change varied as a function of argument quality under high-relevance conditions, but as a function of source expertise under low-relevance conditions.

Hypothesis

The hypothesis is that under high-involvement conditions, thoughtful consideration of message content is the most important determinant of attitude change, but that under low-involvement conditions, peripheral cues determine attitude change.

Design

The basic design is a 2 (issue involvement: high versus low) × 2 (argument quality: strong versus weak) × 2 (source expertise: high versus low) factorial (i.e. every possible combination of the three factors is used, resulting in a total of eight conditions). The authors added a no-message control condition, at the suggestion of reviewers of the paper, two years after conducting the main experiment.

Method

The participants in this experiment were students who were told that their university was considering some changes in academic policy, and that as part of the evaluation process a number of statements about academic policy had been audiotaped. The participant's task was to listen to one of these taped statements and to rate it. The tape heard by all subjects advocated that all students should have to take a comprehensive examination in their major area of study before they could graduate. To manipulate personal involvement, half the participants were led to believe that the policy changes would be implemented next year, and the other half were led to believe that these changes would not be implemented for ten years. Thus high-involvement participants believed that they personally would be affected by the changes, whereas low-involvement participants believed that they personally would not be affected. To manipulate source expertise, half the participants were told that the tape they would hear was based on a report prepared by the 'Carnegie Commission on Education' (high expertise) while the other half were told that the tape was based on a report prepared by a local high school class (low expertise). Argument quality was manipulated by constructing messages based on eight arguments previously found to be either strong (i.e. elicited predominantly thoughts favorable to the advocacy) or weak (i.e. elicited predominantly thoughts unfavorable to the advocacy). After hearing the taped message, participants completed two measures of their own attitude to the issue of comprehensive examinations. These two measures were combined into a single index. Other ratings served as checks on the effectiveness of the three manipulations.

Results

The data were analysed using $2 \times 2 \times 2$ analyses of variance (ANOVA). Analysis of the manipulation check data showed that all three manipulations achieved the desired effects. The most important findings are the ones relating to the attitude ratings. Statistically speaking, the authors' hypothesis predicts two two-way interactions: one between involvement and argument quality, and one between involvement and source expertise. In other words, within the high-involvement condition participants should have had more positive attitudes to comprehensive exams when the argument quality was strong than when it was weak, but this difference should have been absent or at least weaker within the low-involvement condition. Similarly, within the low-involvement condition participants should have had more positive attitudes to comprehensive exams when the source expertise was high than when it was low, but this difference should have been absent or at least weaker within the high-involvement condition. As shown in Figure 9.1, both predictions are supported by the data (the first prediction is reflected in the bottom half of the figure, and the second in the top half). The ANOVA on the attitude ratings showed that both the predicted two-way interactions were statistically significant, and further analyses comparing means in the different conditions showed that the argument quality effect was only significant within the high-involvement condition, and that the source expertise effect was only significant within the low-involvement condition. The attitude data are also shown in Table 9.5, where the results from the no-message control group have been included. The two asterisks in Table 9.5 show the conditions under which attitudes to comprehensive exams differed from those of the control group; both conditions are ones in which argument quality was strong and involvement was high. Thus although attitudes to comprehensive exams within the low-involvement condition were more positive when source expertise was high than when it was low, the attitudes of the high expertise participants did not differ significantly from those of the no-message control participants.

Discussion

The results are strongly supportive of the authors' hypothesis. The quality of the source's argumentation only makes a difference to the receivers' attitudes if the receivers are involved enough in the issue to think carefully about what the source is saying; how much expertise the source has on the issue in question only makes a difference to receivers' attitudes if the receivers are uninvolved in the issue. This pattern of findings does indeed suggest that there are 'two routes' to persuasion, one more thoughtful, the other more superficial. In the Discussion section of their paper, the authors consider why it is that greater personal involvement results in argument quality being an important determinant of attitudes. They identify two factors, which they call *motivation* and *ability*. The motivational argument is straightforward: if the topic is one that is high in personal relevance, one should be more highly motivated to hold the 'right' opinion, and one will therefore scrutinize more carefully any information that is relevant to that opinion. One is therefore more responsive to the quality of the argumentation in the message. The ability argument is a bit more complicated: if the topic is one that is high in personal relevance, one may have a better developed cognitive framework (or 'schema') for thinking about it. Thus one is better able to think about information relating to the issue, and this enables one to be more responsive to the quality of the argumentation in the message. The authors conclude that the motivational explanation probably accounts for the findings in the present case, since there is no reason to think that the high- and low-involvement participants differed in how much they knew about the issue of comprehensive exams prior to the experiment. Indeed, involvement is now regarded as a factor influencing motivation (rather than ability) to process message content, although it is also generally recognized that involvement as manipulated in the present experiment is only one sense in which a receiver can be 'involved' in the content of a message (see Johnson and Eagly, 1989).

Subsequent research has been consistent with the theoretical reasoning that led the authors to conduct this experiment. Present-day research on persuasion is dominated by two theoretical models, the elaboration likelihood model (Petty and Cacioppo, 1986) and the heuristic–systematic model (Chaiken et al., 1989), both of which argue that there are two routes to persuasion, one thoughtful and the other more superficial (see Eagly and Chaiken, 1993, for a review).

Modern studies routinely make use of a measure known as 'thought-listing', in which participants are asked to write down all the thoughts they had while listening to or reading the message. This measure is taken in an attempt to identify the process mediating attitude change. In the present experiment, for example, one would expect to find that only within the high-involvement condition was attitude change mediated by careful thinking about the message, such that strong-argument-quality subjects had more positive attitudes and weak-argument-quality participants had less positive attitudes.

A further development since the present experiment was conducted is the notion that a 'peripheral cue', such as source expertise or attractiveness, may under certain circumstances have an effect on attitudes even when receivers are motivated to process the content of a message very carefully (cf. Chaiken and Maheswaran, 1994). One can imagine, for example, that the expertise or attractiveness of a source might influence how much effort one is prepared to invest in thinking about a message when it is moderately difficult to process the message, because of time pressure, competition from other stimuli, or the inherent complexity of the issue (cf. Petty and Cacioppo, 1986).

FURTHER READING

Eagly, A.H. and Chaiken, S. (1993). *The Psychology of Attitudes*. Fort Worth, TX: Harcourt Brace Jovanovich. Ch. 7 of this essential volume contains an overview of theory and research on the elaboration likelihood and heuristic–systematic models of persuasion.

Petty, R.E. and Cacioppo, J.T. (1984). The effects of involvement on responses to argument quantity and quality: Central and peripheral routes to persuasion. *Journal of Personality and Social Psychology*, 46, 69–81. A later study showing that a peripheral cue (in this case number of arguments) is more influential under low-involvement conditions, whereas argument quality is more influential under high-involvement conditions.

REFERENCES

Chaiken, S. and Mahesweran, D. (1994). Heuristic processing can bias systematic processing: Effects of source credibility, argument ambiguity, and task importance on attitude judgment. *Journal of Personality and Social Psychology*, 66, 460–73.

Chaiken, S., Liberman, A. and Eagly, A.H. (1989). Heuristic and systematic processing within and beyond the persuasion context. In J. Uleman and J. Bargh (eds), *Unintended Thought* (pp. 212–52). New York: Guilford Press.

Cialdini, R.B., Petty, R.E. and Cacioppo, J.T. (1981). Attitudes and attitude change. In M. Rosenzweig and L. Porter (eds), *Annual Review of Psychology* (vol. 32, pp. 357–404). Palo Alto, CA: Annual Reviews.

Greenwald, A.G. (1968). Cognitive learning, cognitive response to persuasion, and attitude change. In A.G. Greenwald, T.C. Brock and T.M. Ostrom (eds), *Psychological Foundations of Attitudes* (pp. 147–70). New York: Academic Press.

Johnson, B.T. and Eagly, A.H. (1989). The effects of involvement on persuasion: A meta-analysis. *Psychological Bulletin*, 106, 290–314.

Kelman, H.C. (1958). Compliance, identification, and internalization: Three processes of attitude change. *Journal of Conflict Resolution*, 2, 51–60.

McGuire, W.J. (1969). The nature of attitudes and attitude change. In G. Lindzey and E. Aronson (eds), *Handbook of Social Psychology* (vol. 3, pp. 136–314). New York: Random House.

Petty, R.E. and Cacioppo, J.T. (1981). *Attitudes and Persuasion: Classic and Contemporary Approaches*. Dubuque, IA: Wm. C. Brown.

Petty, R.E. and Cacioppo, J.T. (1986). *Communication and Persuasion: Central and Peripheral Routes to Attitude Change*. New York: Springer-Verlag.

Staats, A.W. and Staats, C.K. (1958). Attitudes established by classical conditioning. *Journal of Abnormal and Social Psychology*, 57, 37–40.

Zanna, M.P., Kiesler, C.A. and Pilkonis, P.A. (1970). Positive and negative attitudinal affect established by classical conditioning. *Journal of Personality and Social Psychology*, 14, 321–8.

- - - - -
Primary
Reading
- - - - - - - -

In a recent review of the numerous approaches to attitude change that have developed over the past 35 years, Petty and Cacioppo (1981) suggested that these many approaches could be seen as proposing two distinct routes to persuasion. One, called the *central route*, views attitude change as resulting from a diligent consideration of issue-relevant arguments. The approaches that fall under this route have emphasized such factors as the comprehension, learning, and retention of message arguments (e.g., Eagly, 1974; McGuire, 1968; Miller and Campbell, 1959); the self-generation of arguments (e.g., Cacioppo and Petty, 1979a; Greenwald, 1968; Tesser, 1978; Vinokur and Burnstein, 1974); and the combination and integration of issue-relevant arguments into an overall evaluative reaction (e.g., Anderson, 1971; Fishbein and Ajzen, 1975; Wyer, 1974).

In contrast to this focus on the arguments central to the issue under consideration, a second group of approaches to persuasion has developed that emphasizes a more *peripheral route* to attitude change (Petty and Cacioppo, 1981). Under this second view, attitudes change because the attitude object has been associated with either positive or negative "cues." The approaches that fall under this second route have emphasized associating the advocated position with such basic cues as food (e.g., Janis, Kaye, and Kirschner, 1965) and pain (e.g., Zanna, Kiesler, and Pilkonis, 1970) or more secondary cues such as credible (e.g., Kelman and Hovland, 1953), attractive (e.g., Mills and Harvey, 1972), and powerful (e.g., Kelman, 1961) sources. These cues may shape attitudes or allow a person to decide what attitudinal position to adopt without the need for engaging in any extensive issue-relevant thinking. Furthermore, these cues can presumably influence attitudes whether or not any issue-relevant arguments are presented or considered (e.g., Maddux and Rogers, 1980; Norman, 1976; Staats and Staats, 1958).

Enough research has now accumulated in support of both routes to persuasion to clearly indicate that both processes operate (Eagly and Himmelfarb, 1978). Attitude change is not determined exclusively by either issue-relevant argumentation or simple cue association. A profitable direction for current research, then, is to document the differing consequences of each route to persuasion (if any) and to indicate the variables that determine which route will be followed. For example, in a recent review of attitude-change research, Cialdini, Petty, and Cacioppo (1981) concluded that one consequence of the different routes to persuasion was that changes induced via the central route tended to be enduring and predictive of subsequent behavior, whereas changes induced via the peripheral route tended to be more ephemeral and less predictive of subsequent behavior (see also Chaiken, 1980; Cook and Flay, 1978). Our goal in the present study was to explore the conditions under which each route to persuasion would be taken.

Specifically, we hypothesized that when a persuasive communication was on a topic of high personal relevance, attitude change would be governed mostly by a thoughtful consideration of the issue-relevant arguments presented (central route). On the other hand, when a message was on a topic of low personal relevance, we hypothesized that peripheral features of the persuasion situation would be more potent. As Miller, Maruyama, Beaber, and Valone (1976) noted, "It may be irrational to scrutinize the plethora of counterattitudinal messages received daily. To the extent that one possesses only a limited amount of information processing time and capacity, such scrutiny would disengage the thought processes from the exigencies of daily life" (p. 623). Thus, persons must choose which stimuli should be scrutinized carefully and which are not worthy of extensive thought.[1]

Recent research has indicated that the level of personal involvement with an issue is one variable that influences the extent to which issue-relevant arguments will be considered. For example, Cialdini et al. (1976) found that subjects who expected to engage in a discussion with an opponent generated more supportive arguments in anticipation of the discussion when the attitude issue had high rather than low personal relevance. Also, Petty and Cacioppo (1979a, 1979b) have reported that subjects' message-relevant thoughts showed higher correlations with message acceptance when the issue was of high rather than low personal importance. Thus, the hypothesis that issue-relevant argumentation becomes a more important determinant of persuasion as the personal relevance of an issue increases has received some support (see review by Burnkrant and Sawyer, in press).

The complementing hypothesis – that peripheral cues in the persuasion situation become more important as the personal involvement with an issue decreases – has received less attention, although the available data are consistent with this view. For example, Johnson and Scileppi (1969) and Rhine and Severance (1970) found that a manipulation of source credibility was more impactful under low- than under high-involvement conditions. In the most directly relevant study on involvement and type of persuasion to date, Chaiken (1980) exposed subjects to a message containing either two or six arguments, from a likable or dislikable source, under either high- or low-involvement conditions. She found that the message manipulation had a greater impact on persuasion under high involvement but that the source manipulation had a greater impact on attitude under low involvement. Although these data are highly suggestive, they do not provide definitive support for the two routes to persuasion because the particular message manipulation employed by Chaiken (number of arguments) has the ability to serve as a simple cue much in the same way that a source manipulation (likable or dislikable source) can serve as a cue. In other words, even if subjects did no thinking about the message arguments at all, it is likely that they would have realized that the message they heard had either relatively few or relatively many arguments. A simple desire to identify with a side that has many rather than few arguments may have been sufficient to produce the differential persuasion for the two- and six-argument messages under the high-involvement conditions. Thus, both the source manipulation and the message manipulation may have provided simple cues for message acceptance, making a cognitive evaluation of the message content unnecessary. It is sufficient to propose that under low-involvement conditions, the source cue was more potent but that under high-involvement conditions, the message cue was more potent.

The study reported here was designed to provide a more direct test of the hypothesis that, under high-involvement conditions, a thoughtful evaluation of message content is the most important determinant of persuasion but that, under low-involvement conditions, peripheral cues in the situation are more impactful. In the present study, all subjects heard a counterattitudinal communication. In addition to manipulating the personal importance of the message, the quality of the arguments that subjects heard in support of the advocated position was varied, as was the expertise of the source of the communication. By manipulating the quality or cogency of the arguments used in the messages, but keeping the number of arguments in the communications constant, the ability of subjects to evaluate the advocacy on the basis of a simple message cue (length) was eliminated. For the manipulation of message cogency to have an impact on persuasion, communication recipients must actually think about the merits of the arguments presented. Of course the expertise of the source of the communication could still provide a simple cue for message acceptance. Our hypothesis was that under conditions of high personal involvement, persuasion would be affected more by the quality of the message arguments employed, but that under low-involvement conditions, persuasion would be tied more strongly to the expertise of the source.

Method

Procedure

One hundred forty-five male and female undergraduates at the University of Missouri participated in order to earn extra credit in an introductory psychology course. The design was a 2 (issue involvement: high or low) × 2 (argument quality: strong or weak) × 2 (source expertise: high or low) factorial. Subjects were tested in groups of 3 to 16 in cubicles designed so that no subject could have visual or verbal contact with any other subject. During any one session, it was possible to conduct all eight experimental conditions (if enough subjects were present).

The subjects were told that the University of Missouri was currently undergoing an academic reevaluation and that the new chancellor was seeking recommendations about policy changes to be instituted. To obtain a variety of opinions about the university and its future, the subjects were told that the chancellor had asked several individuals and groups to prepare policy statements. The subjects were further told that each of the policy statements had been recorded for possible broadcast on a campus radio station. The subjects were told that the psychology department was cooperating with the university administration in having the taped statements rated for broadcast quality.

After reading these background comments, the subjects heard one of the tape recordings over headphones. All of the tapes were made by the same male speaker and advocated that seniors be required to take a comprehensive exam in their major area as a prerequisite to graduation. After listening to the appropriate communication, subjects completed a dependent variable booklet and were then debriefed, thanked, and dismissed.

Independent variables

Personal involvement
In the background material that subjects read prior to message exposure, half were told that the chancellor was seeking recommendations about policy changes to be instituted the following year (high personal involvement), whereas the other half were told that the chancellor was seeking recommendations about changes that would take effect in 10 years (low personal involvement). Clearly then, in the high-involvement conditions, the subjects would be affected personally by the advocated change, whereas in the low-involvement conditions they would not.

Source expertise
Half of the subjects learned that the tape they would hear was based on a report prepared by a class at a local high school (low expertise), whereas the remaining subjects learned that the tape was based on a report prepared by the Carnegie Commission on Higher Education, which was chaired by a professor of education at Princeton University (high expertise). Of course all subjects actually heard the same speaker.

Argument quality
Even though all subjects heard a message advocating the institution of senior comprehensive exams, the arguments used in support of the message conclusion were varied. In brief, the strong version of the message provided persuasive evidence (statistics, data, etc.) in support of the exam (e.g., institution of the exams had led to a reversal in the declining scores on standardized achievement tests at other universities). In contrast, the weak version of the message relied more on quotations, personal opinion, and examples to support its position (e.g., a friend of the author's had to take a comprehensive exam and now had a prestigious academic position). The messages were equivalent in length, and each contained elaborations of eight arguments. The strong arguments were selected from a pool that elicited primarily favorable thoughts in a pretest, and the weak arguments were selected from a pool that elicited primarily counterarguments in a pretest. The specific arguments employed in this study were adapted

from the "strong" and "very weak" communications described by Petty, Harkins, and Williams (1980). Pretest ratings of the two messages indicated that they did not differ in the extent to which they were "difficult to understand," were "hard to follow," or possessed "complex structure."

Dependent variables

Subjects were told that because their personal views on the desirability of instituting a comprehensive exam might influence the way they rated the broadcast quality of the tapes, a measure of their own opinion was desired. Two measures of attitude were included. The first asked subjects to rate the concept "Comprehensive Exams" on four 9-point semantic differential scales (good/bad, beneficial/harmful, foolish/wise, and unfavorable/favorable). Next, on an 11-point scale anchored by 1-"do not agree at all," and 11-"agree completely," subjects rated the extent to which they agreed with the proposal requiring seniors to take a comprehensive exam before graduating. The subjects' responses to the two attitude measures were converted to standard scores and averaged for an index of attitude toward comprehensive exams. The within-cell correlation between the two measures was .75.

Subjects then responded to a number of additional items including measures designed to maintain the cover story (e.g., ratings of speaker voice quality, delivery, enthusiasm, etc.). With one exception, the ancillary measures produced no significant effects and will not be discussed further.[2]

Next, subjects responded to three questions designed to assess the effectiveness of the three experimental manipulations. Finally, subjects were given 4 min. to list as many of the arguments from the message as they could recall. Two judges, blind to the involvement and expertise manipulations, rated each argument listed for accuracy ($r = .92$). Similar statements of the same argument were counted only once. Disagreements between judges were resolved by consulting a third judge.

No-message control

Although the primary aim of the experiment was to assess how personal involvement would affect the relative importance of argument quality and source expertise in influencing subjects' postcommunication attitudes toward the topic, a no-message control condition was also conducted to assess absolute attitude change from a premessage baseline. An additional 18 undergraduates from the same subject pool were asked to participate in a "Survey of Campus Issues" study.[3] These control subjects gave their opinions on a number of different contemporary issues facing universities across the country. The fifth issue in each survey booklet concerned requiring seniors at the University of Missouri to pass a comprehensive exam in their major area as a prerequisite to graduation. The crucial issue was embedded in the context of many others to reduce the likelihood that subjects would spend an undue amount of time thinking about the issue, which could result in attitude polarization (see Tesser, 1978). Half of the surveys indicated that the exam requirement was being proposed for next year, and half of the surveys indicated that the exam requirement was being proposed to take effect in 10 years. Subjects recorded their attitudes on the issue on the same scales as those employed in the experimental conditions described previously. Since the manipulation of involvement in the control cells did not significantly affect the attitudes reported ($p > .20$), the data for these two conditions were combined.

Results

Experimental groups

Preliminary 2 (personal involvement) × 2 (source expertise) × 2 (argument quality) × 2 (sex of subject) analyses of variance on each dependent measure produced no significant main effects nor interactions involving sex. Thus, this factor was ignored in all subsequent analyses.

Manipulation checks
To assess the effectiveness of the message quality manipulation, subjects were asked: "How would you rate the quality of the arguments used by the speaker to support the position advocated?" On a scale where 1 indicated "not very good arguments," and 11 indicated "very good arguments," subjects hearing the strong arguments ($M = 8.9$) rated their quality as significantly higher than subjects hearing the weak arguments ($M = 4.5$), $F(1, 137) = 51.02$, $p < .001$. To assess the expertise manipulation, subjects were asked: "Regardless of how you felt about what the author had to say, how qualified did you think he was to speak on the topic?" On a scale where 1 indicated "not very qualified" and 11 indicated "very qualified," subjects hearing the high-expert speaker rated his qualifications as significantly higher ($M = 6.8$) than subjects hearing the low-expert speaker ($M = 5.7$), $F(1, 137) = 4.86$, $p < .03$. In addition, subjects hearing the strong arguments rated the speaker as more qualified ($M = 7.6$) than subjects hearing the weak arguments ($M = 4.9$), $F(1, 137) = 39.2$, $p < .001$. Finally, to assess the personal relevance manipulation, subjects were asked to rate 'How likely is it that the University of Missouri will institute comprehensive exams while you are a student here?" On a scale where 1 indicated "not very likely" and 11 indicated "very likely," subjects in the high-involvement conditions rated the likelihood as higher ($M = 5.5$) than subjects in the low-involvement conditions ($M = 2.7$), $F(1,137) = 5.12$, $p < .2$. In sum, all three independent variables were manipulated successfully.

Attitude and recall measures
A three-way analysis of variance (ANOVA) on the index of attitude toward comprehensive exams produced two main effects and two interactions. A main effect for the expertise manipulation revealed that subjects agreed with the communication more when the source had high expertise ($M = .21$) than when the source had high expertise ($M = -.21$), $F(1, 137) = 16.24$, $p < .001$. Also, a main effect for argument quality revealed that subjects agreed with the message more when it contained strong ($M = .36$) rather than weak arguments ($M = -.36$), $F(1, 137) = 20.35$, $p < .001$.

Of greater interest, however, were two interactions that qualified these two main effects. First, an Involvement × Expertise interaction, $F(1, 137) = 3.92$, $p < .05$, revealed that the expertise manipulation had a stronger effect under low personal-involvement conditions than under high (see top panel of figure 9.1). In fact, a Newman-Keuls analysis of this interaction revealed that a source of high expertise produced significantly more agreement than a source of low expertise *only* under the low-involvement conditions. A complementing Involvement ×

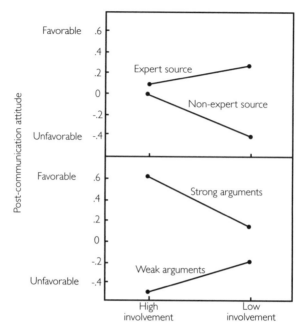

Figure 9.1 Top panel: interactive effect of involvement and source expertise on postcommunication attitudes. Bottom panel: interactive effect of involvement and argument quality on postcommunication attitudes

Argument quality interaction, $F(1, 137) = 6.05$, $p < .02$, demonstrated that the argument quality manipulation had a stronger effect under high personal-involvement conditions than under low (see bottom panel of figure 9.1). A Newman-Keuls analysis of this interaction revealed that the strong arguments produced significantly more agreement than the weak *only* under the high-involvement conditions.

An analysis of the argument recall score revealed that subjects recalled more of the strong ($M = 4.2$) than of the weak arguments ($M = 3.2$), $F(1, 137) = 14.93$, $p < .001$, but the personal involvement and expertise manipulations did not affect argument recall, and no interactions were obtained on this measure. Consistent with previous research, within-cell correlations failed to substantiate a relationship between argument learning and agreement for either the strong ($r = .05$) or weak ($r = -.09$) argument messages. When manipulations of argument quality are successful, it apparently has more to do with argument evaluation or elaboration than argument memorization (cf., Cacioppo and Petty, 1979b; Insko, Lind, and LaTour, 1976).

No-message control

In table 9.5, the attitude scores have been restandardized to include the no-message control data. This table also provides pair-wise comparisons of all eight experimental cells employing the Newman-Keuls test and a test of each experimental group with the control employing Dunnett's procedure (see Kirk, 1968).

Table 9.5   Standardized attitude scores for experimental and control subjects

| | High involvement | | Low involvement | | |
| | Expert source | Nonexpert source | Expert source | Nonexpert source | No-message control |
Arguments					
Strong	$.64_a$*	$.61_a$*	$.40_{a,b}$	$-.12_{a,b,c}$	$-.18$
Weak	$-.38_{b,c}$	$-.58_c$	$.25_{a,b}$	$-.64_c$	

Within the experimental cells, means without a common subscript are significantly different at the .05 level by the Newman-Keuls procedure.

* Experimental mean is significantly different from the control mean at the .05 level by Dunnett's test.

Consistent with the two-way interactions reported previously, the Newman-Keuls analysis revealed that under high involvement, argument quality affected attitudes but source expertise did not. Under low involvement, however, the reverse pattern tended to occur. Attitudes of subjects in the no-message control condition fell in between the attitudes of subjects in the experimental cells, suggesting that the significant differences among the various experimental conditions may have resulted from a combination of both persuasion and boomerang processes. The largest (though nonsignificant) boomerang effects occurred in the two cells where nonexpert sources presented weak arguments. It is interesting to speculate that under low involvement, the tendency toward boomerang was produced primarily by a rejection of the message source, whereas under high involvement, the tendency toward boomerang was produced primarily by a rejection of the message arguments. Two experimental groups showed significant persuasion in relation to the no-message control. This occurred when strong arguments, regardless of the source, were presented under high involvement. According to the present analysis, these are the two cells that should have resulted in the most favorable issue-relevant thinking.

Discussion

Previous research on persuasion has tended to characterize attitude change as resulting either from a thoughtful consideration of issue-relevant arguments or from associating various positive or negative cues with the attitude object. Furthermore, researchers favoring one process have tended to downplay the importance of the other. For example, in a recent paper, Fishbein and Ajzen (1981) have argued that:

> The general neglect of the information contained in a message . . . is probably the most serious problem in communication and persuasion research. We are convinced that the persuasiveness of a communication can be increased much more easily and dramatically by paying careful attention to its content . . . than by manipulation of credibility, attractiveness, . . . or any of the other myriad factors that have caught the fancy of investigators in the area of communication and persuasion. (p. 359)

The present study suggests that although the message content may be the most important determinant of persuasion under some circumstances, in other circumstances such noncontent manipulations as source credibility, attractiveness, and so forth, may be even *more* important. Specifically, in the present article, we have shown that when a persuasive message concerned an issue of high personal relevance, the effectiveness of the appeal was a function more of the cogency of the arguments presented in the message than of such peripheral cues as the expertise of the message source. On the other hand, when the message concerned an issue of relatively low personal relevance, effectiveness was a function more of peripheral cues than of the arguments presented. Interestingly, the long-standing tradition of persuasion researchers to employ messages that are low in personal relevance (cf. Hovland, 1959) may be responsible for the voluminous number of studies emphasizing the influence of noncontent factors in persuasion and relatively ignoring issue-relevant arguments. Importantly, the present data suggest that it would be equally inappropriate to overemphasize the influence of issue-relevant argumentation and ignore the role of peripheral cues. Each type of persuasion occurs in some instances, and the level of personal involvement with an issue appears to be one moderator of which type of persuasion occurs.

There are at least two reasons why an increase in involvement might be associated with an increase in the importance of message arguments in producing persuasion. First, as an issue increases in its personal implications for the message recipient, it becomes more important to form a reasoned and veridical opinion. An attitude based on a careful examination of issue-relevant arguments will likely prove to be more adaptive and will certainly be easier to defend if challenged in the future. If people are motivated to hold "correct" opinions on personally important issues, and a consideration of the arguments relevant to an issue enhances the likelihood of veridicality, then it follows that people will be more motivated to scrutinize the arguments presented when an issue has many personal consequences than when personal consequences are few. When an issue has few personal consequences, it is unlikely that people will be motivated to do the cognitive work necessary to evaluate an advocacy on the basis of its arguments. The cognitive consideration of arguments is difficult work and is presumably best undertaken when the personal consequences of an issue are high. When the personal importance of the issue is low, people may be motivated less by a desire to be correct than by a desire to minimize cognitive work (cf. McGuire's "lazy organism," 1969, p. 198) or to manage the impressions of others (cf. Cialdini, Levy, Herman, Kozlowski, and Petty, 1976).

In addition to this motivational factor, it might also be that people have a better developed schema or framework for thinking about things that are relevant to the self than things that are irrelevant (cf. Markus, 1977). Thus, a second reason why the processing of issue-relevant argumentation may be greater under high involvement than under low is that people have a greater *ability* to do so. If an issue has high personal consequences, it is likely that the person has done considerable thinking about the issue in the past and has a large structure of preexisting information that can be useful in evaluating new information. Thus, a person might find it easier to evaluate the cogency of an argument on a topic of high rather than low involvement. Of course in the present study, prior knowledge about the issue was identical for both high- and low-involvement groups, and thus the effect of involvement in the current study presumably hinged more on motivational than on ability factors. Nevertheless, it is still possible that when a person learns that a communication has high personal relevance, a self-schema is invoked, and this framework of self-relevant cognitions increases one's ability to evaluate the implications of the message arguments.

Our reasoning that a person's motives and abilities are typically different under high- and low-involvement conditions suggests that some manipulations should be effective under high but not low involvement, but other variables should show the reverse pattern. The present study provides an example of one variable of each type. In addition, some variables might have effects under both high and low involvement, but the effects might be quite different in each case. For example, in a study on the effects of using rhetorical questions on persuasion, Petty, Cacioppo, and Heesacker (1981) found that using rhetorical questions enhanced message-relevant processing under low-involvement conditions (when thinking about the message would ordinarily have been low) but disrupted message-relevant processing under high-involvement conditions (when thinking about the message would ordinarily have been high).

The realization that an independent variable may have different (and even opposite) effects, depending on the level of personal relevance of a message, may provide some insight into the conflicting pattern of results that is said to characterize much attitude research (Fishbein and Ajzen, 1972). It may well be that there are two distinct routes to persuasion and that these routes are characterized by different antecedents and consequents (Chaiken, 1980; Petty and Cacioppo, 1979b, 1981). If so, future work could profitably be aimed at uncovering moderators other than personal involvement of the route to persuasion. These moderators could be variables within the persuasion situation or within the message recipient. In general, we suspect that any variable that increases the likelihood that people will be motivated and able to engage in the difficult task of evaluating the message arguments increases the likelihood of the central route to persuasion. On the other hand, any variable that reduces a person's motivation and/or ability to think about the message content would make the peripheral route more likely. These moderator variables would, therefore, include such things as message repetition and distraction, the number of people responsible for message evaluation, an individual's "need for cognition," and others (cf. Cacioppo and Petty, 1979b, in press; Petty et al., 1976, 1980).

NOTES

The data reported here are based in part on a master's thesis conducted by the third author under the supervision of the first two authors. The advice of thesis committee members Russell Geen, Donald Granberg, and Larry Siegel is acknowledged with thanks. We also thank Stan Wilensky and Don Fry for providing access to the University of Missouri learning lab facilities. This research was supported by National Science Foundation Grant BNS 7913753, and portions of this article were presented at the annual meeting of the American Psychological Association, September 1979, in New York.

[1] The notion that people sometimes devote considerable cognitive effort to processing a stimulus and at other times cognitive effort is minimal can also be seen in the recent psychological distinctions between mindfulness versus mindlessness (Langer and Imber, 1980), deep versus shallow processing (Craik and Lockhart, 1972), controlled versus automatic processing (Schneider and Shiffrin, 1977), and systematic versus heuristic processing (Chaiken, 1980). The notion that there are different *kinds* of persuasion was apparent in Aristotle's *Rhetoric*, but achieved the most contemporary recognition in Kelman's three process view of persuasion. In Kelman's (1961) system, the type of persuasion is determined primarily by the source of the message (expert sources produce internalization, attractive sources produce identification, and powerful sources produce compliance). According to the central/peripheral distinction, the central route is followed when issue-relevant argumentation is responsible for inducing change

regardless of the message source. A person who changes simply because an expert, attractive, or powerful source endorses a particular position (without engaging in issue-relevant thought) would be following the peripheral route.

[2] On the measure of speaker voice quality, a significant main effect for issue importance (better voice quality with low than high importance), and argument quality (better voice quality with weak than strong arguments), and a three-way interaction (uninterpretable) appeared. Since this pattern of data did not follow the pattern found on the crucial attitude measure, and since the within-cell correlation between voice quality and agreement was small and not significant ($r = .04$), this measure will not be given further consideration.

[3] The no-message control attitude data were collected at the suggestion of the *Journal of Personality and Social Psychology* reviewers approximately 2 years after the data from the main experiment. As a check on the stability of students' attitudes toward comprehensive exams over this period, control subjects' responses on the 11-point Likert scale were compared with no-message control data on the same issue and scale collected in a pilot study that was conducted at about the same time as the main experiment reported here (the semantic differential measure was not collected in the earlier pilot study). A comparison of the two sets of control data collected about 2 years apart revealed no statistically significant difference ($p > .20$), suggesting that opinions on the issue over the intervening period were relatively stable. In any case, the statistical tests of the major hypotheses of interest in the present investigation could be and were conducted *excluding* the control data.

REFERENCES

Anderson, N.H. Integration theory and attitude change. *Psychological Review*, 1971, 78, 171–206.

Burnkrant, R.E., and Sawyer, A.G. Effects of involvement and message content on information processing intensity. In R. Harris (ed.), *Information processing research in advertising*. Hillsdale, NJ: Erlbaum, in press.

Cacioppo, J.T., and Petty, R.E. Attitudes and cognitive response: An electrophysiological approach. *Journal of Personality and Social Psychology*, 1979, 37, 2181–99. (a)

Cacioppo, J.T., and Petty, R.E. Effects of message repetition and position on cognitive responses, recall, and persuasion. *Journal of Personality and Social Psychology*, 1979, 37, 97–109. (b)

Cacioppo, J.T., and Petty, R.E. The need for cognition. *Journal of Personality and Social Psychology*, in press.

Chaiken, S. Heuristic versus systematic information processing and the use of source versus message cues in persuasion. *Journal of Personality and Social Psychology*, 1980, 39, 752–66.

Cialdini, R.B., Petty, R.E., and Cacioppo, J.T. Attitude and attitude change. In M. Rosenzweig and L. Porter (eds), *Annual Review of Psychology* (vol. 32). Palo Alto, CA: Annual Reviews, 1981.

Cialdini, R.B., Levy, A., Herman, P., Kozlowski, L., and Petty, R.E. Elastic shifts of opinion. Determinants of direction and durability. *Journal of Personality and Social Psychology*, 1976, 34, 663–72.

Cook, T.D., and Flay, B.R. The temporal persistence of experimentally induced attitude change: An evaluative review. In L. Berkowitz (ed.), *Advances in Experimental Social Psychology* (vol. 11). New York: Academic Press, 1978.

Craik, F.M., and Lockhart, R.S. Levels of processing: A framework for memory research. *Journal of Verbal Learning and Verbal Behavior*, 1972, 11, 671–84.

Eagly, A.H. Comprehensibility of persuasive arguments as a determinant of opinion change. *Journal of Personality and Social Psychology*, 1974, 29, 758–73.

Eagly, A.H., and Himmelfarb, S. Attitudes and opinions. In M. Rosenzweig and L. Porter (eds), *Annual Review of Psychology* (vol. 29). Palo Alto, CA: Annual Reviews, 1978.

Fishbein, M., and Ajzen, I. Attitudes and opinions. In M. Rosenzweig and L. Porter (eds), *Annual Review of Psychology* (vol. 23). Palo Alto, CA: Annual Reviews, 1972.

Fishbein, M., and Ajzen, I. *Belief, attitude, intention, and behavior: An introduction to theory and research.* Reading, MA: Addison-Wesley, 1975.

Fishbein, M., and Ajzen, I. Acceptance, yielding, and impact: Cognitive processes in persuasion. In R. Petty, T. Ostrom, and T. Brock (eds), *Cognitive responses in persuasion.* Hillsdale, NJ: Erlbaum, 1981.

Greenwald, A.G. Cognitive learning, cognitive response to persuasion, and attitude change. In A. Greenwald, T. Brock, and T. Ostrom (eds), *Psychological foundations of attitudes.* New York: Academic Press, 1968.

Hovland, C.I. Reconciling conflicting results derived from experimental and survey studies of attitude change. *American Psychologist,* 1959, *14,* 8–17.

Insko, C.A., Lind, E.A., and LaTour, S. Persuasion, recall, and thoughts. *Representative Research in Social Psychology,* 1976, 7, 66–78.

Janis, I.L., Kaye, D., and Kirschner, P. Facilitating effects of "eating while reading" on responsiveness to persuasive communications. *Journal of Personality and Social Psychology,* 1965, *1,* 181–6.

Johnson, H.H., and Scileppi, J.A. Effects of ego-involvement conditions on attitude change to high- and low-credibility communicators. *Journal of Personality and Social Psychology,* 1969, *13,* 31–6.

Kelman, H.C. Processes of opinion change. *Public Opinion Quarterly,* 1961, *25,* 57–78.

Kelman, H.C., and Hovland, C.I. Reinstatement of the communicator in delayed measurement of opinion change. *Journal of Abnormal and Social Psychology,* 1953, *48,* 327–35.

Kirk, R.E. *Experimental design: Procedures for the behavioral sciences.* Belmont, CA: Brooks/Cole, 1968.

Langer, E.J., and Imber, L. Role of mindlessness in the perception of deviance. *Journal of Personality and Social Psychology,* 1980, *39,* 360–7.

Maddux, J.E., and Rogers, R.W. Effects of source expertness, physical attractiveness, and supporting arguments on persuasion: A case of brains over beauty. *Journal of Personality and Social Psychology,* 1980, *38,* 235–44.

Markus, H. Self-schemata and processing information about the self. *Journal of Personality and Social Psychology,* 1977, *35,* 63–78.

McGuire, W.J. Personality and attitude change: An information processing theory. In A. Greenwald, T. Brock, and T. Ostrom (eds), *Psychological foundations of attitudes.* New York: Academic Press, 1968.

McGuire, W.J. The nature of attitudes and attitude change. In G. Lindzey and E. Aronson (eds), *The handbook of social psychology* (2nd edn). Vol. 3. Reading, MA: Addison-Wesley, 1969.

Miller, N., and Campbell, D.T. Recency and primacy in persuasion as a function of the timing of speeches and measurements. *Journal of Abnormal and Social Psychology,* 1959, *59,* 1–9.

Miller, N., Maruyama, G., Beaber, R., and Valone, K. Speed of speech and persuasion. *Journal of Personality and Social Psychology,* 1976, *34,* 615–25.

Mills, J., and Harvey, J. Opinion change as a function of when information about the communicator is received and whether he is attractive or expert. *Journal of Personality and Social Psychology,* 1972, *21,* 52–5.

Norman, R. When what is said is important: A comparison of expert and attractive sources. *Journal of Experimental Social Psychology,* 1976, *12,* 294–300.

Petty, R.E., and Cacioppo, J.T. Effects of forewarning of persuasive intent and involvement on cognitive responses and persuasion. *Personality and Social Psychology Bulletin,* 1979, *5,* 173–6. (a)

Petty, R.E., and Cacioppo, J.T. Issue-involvement can increase or decrease persuasion by enhancing message-relevant cognitive responses. *Journal of Personality and Social Psychology,* 1979, *37,* 1915–26. (b)

Petty, R.E., and Cacioppo, J.T. *Attitudes and persuasion: Classic and contemporary approaches.* Dubuque, IO: Wm. C. Brown, 1981.

Petty, R.E., Cacioppo, J.T., and Heesacker, M. The use of rhetorical questions in persuasion: A cognitive response analysis. *Journal of Personality and Social Psychology,* 1981, *40,* 432–40.

Petty, R.E., Harkins, S.G., and Williams, K.D. The effects of group diffusion of cognitive effort on attitudes: An information processing view. *Journal of Personality and Social Psychology,* 1980, *38,* 81–92.

Petty, R.E., Wells, G.L., and Brock, T.L. Distraction can enhance or reduce yielding to propaganda: Thought disruption versus effort justification. *Journal of Personality and Social Psychology*, 1976, *34*, 874–84.

Rhine, R.J., and Severance, L.J. Ego-involvement, discrepancy, source credibility, and attitude change. *Journal of Personality and Social Psychology*, 1970, *16*, 175–90.

Schneider, W., and Shiffrin, R.M. Controlled and automatic human information processing: I. Detection, search, and attention. *Psychological Review*, 1977, *84*, 1–66.

Staats, A.W., and Staats, C.K. Attitudes established by classical conditioning. *Journal of Abnormal and Social Psychology*, 1958, *57*, 37–40.

Tesser, A. Self-generated attitude change. *Advances in Experimental Social Psychology*, 1978, *11*, 289–338.

Vinokur, A., and Burnstein, E. The effects of partially shared persuasive arguments on group-induced shifts: A group problem-solving approach. *Journal of Personality and Social Psychology*, 1974, *29*, 305–15.

Wyer, R.S. *Cognitive organization and change: An information processing approach.* Potomac, MD: Erlbaum, 1974.

Zanna, M.P., Kiesler, C.A., and Pilkonis, P.A. Positive and negative attitudinal affect established by classical conditioning. *Journal of Personality and Social Psychology*, 1970, *14*, 321–8.

Part III
Emotion, Communication and Relationships

10   Emotion

Cognitive, social, and physiological determinants of emotional state

S. Schachter and J.E. Singer

Theoretical Background

Editors'
Introduction

The background to this paper lies in one of the oldest problems in psychology: what is the basis of human emotional experience? William James (1884) argued that emotional experience is the awareness of the bodily changes that are generated by perceiving an emotional stimulus. This implies that there should be as many different patterns of bodily changes as there are subjectively discriminable emotions. Cannon's (1927) review of the early research suggested that this is not the case, which led him to propose that the same 'visceral changes' can occur in different states. This provided one important basis for Schachter and Singer's study.

A second basis for their research was provided by Marañon's (1924) research on the effects of injecting subjects with adrenaline, a drug that mimics the activity of the autonomic nervous system. Marañon reported that most subjects did not report any emotion; those that did mention emotion reported that they felt 'as if' they were experiencing an emotion, suggesting that something was missing.

The third line of research that was crucial to the Schachter and Singer experiment was Schachter's own research (Schachter, 1959) on the effects of anxiety on affiliation. In a series of studies, he had found that subjects who are anxious and fearful about a forthcoming event prefer to wait in the company of others who are also waiting for that event, rather than waiting alone. He explained these findings by arguing that the anxious and fearful subjects were uncertain about the appropriateness of their emotional reactions, and preferred to wait with others so that they could compare their own feelings with those of others awaiting the same event, and thereby evaluate whether their own reactions were 'appropriate'. These three strands of research led Schachter and Singer to argue that physiological arousal by itself is not sufficient to generate subjective emotion and that the 'missing element' is cognitive in nature. Thus if you were to repeat Marañon's study, but this time provide subjects with cognitive cues

Psychological Review (1962), 69:379–99.

suggesting that an emotional interpretation of their feelings would be appropriate, they should experience emotion.

Hypotheses

The hypotheses are stated in the form of three 'propositions':

1   Subjects who are aroused but who do not know why they are aroused will interpret that arousal in terms of whatever plausible cognitive factors are available. Thus if the available cognitive factors imply happiness, subjects should feel happy: if they imply anger, they should feel angry, and so on – even if they are in precisely the same *physiological* state of arousal.
2   If subjects are aroused but have an appropriate, non-emotional explanation for their arousal, they will not become emotional, even if cognitive cues suggesting emotion are available.
3   If subjects are not aroused, they will not become emotional, even if cognitive cues suggesting emotion are available.

Design

Testing these hypotheses required the manipulation of three variables: physiological arousal; availability of a non-emotional explanation for the arousal; and availability of cognitive cues suggesting an emotional label for arousal. Note that the design used in this study is non-orthogonal, meaning that not every possible combination of each manipulation was implemented.

Method

The methods used by Schachter and Singer to carry out their study are ones that would almost certainly not be regarded as permissible today: they would be deemed ethically unacceptable. Physiological arousal was manipulated by the disguised administration of epinephrine (a synthetic form of adrenaline) to some subjects, and a placebo to others. Availability of a non-emotional explanation for the arousal was manipulated by telling some subjects (labelled as Epi Inf) injected with adrenaline to expect side-effects typical of adrenaline, others to expect side-effects atypical of adrenaline (Epi Mis), and giving a third group no information about side-effects (Epi Ign). Availability of cognitive cues suggestive of emotion was manipulated by means of a confederate who posed as a fellow subject. The idea (adopted from Schachter's earlier research on affiliation) was that subjects who were aroused but who did not know why they were aroused would be influenced by the apparent emotional state of the confederate. In one condition the confederate acted as if angry, in another as if euphoric. The real subject's emotion was assessed by means of self-report and by observing his or her behaviour.

Results

In one case it is made clear that the data (for initiation of acts in the Euphoria condition; see Table 10.3) were analyzed by means of X^2. In all other cases the data were presumably analyzed by using t-tests to make pair-wise comparisons of the means in the different conditions – although this is not made explicit in the paper. The results are presented by Schachter and Singer as supporting their hypotheses. There is no doubt that some aspects of the findings are supportive of the predictions. For example, the findings shown in Tables 10.2 and 10.4 support the second hypothesis: subjects who were aroused but correctly informed about the side-effects of the injection reported feeling less euphoric and less angry than did their counterparts who were either misinformed or uninformed about the side-effects. However, the findings do not provide compelling support for the first hypothesis. To be consistent with this hypothesis, the self-report means of subjects in the anger condition should have been on the negative side of the scale. Yet the means shown in Table 10.4 are all positive, suggesting that subjects exposed to the angry confederate did not actually feel angry, regardless of their physiological state and the availability of a non-emotional explanation for their arousal. Support for hypothesis 3 was weak: to be consistent with this hypothesis, participants in the placebo condition should not have reacted emotionally to the anger or euphoria settings, and should therefore have scored significantly lower on measures of emotion than participants who were aroused but incorrectly informed (or not informed at all) about the side-effects. Yet Tables 10.2 and 10.3 show that there was no difference within the Euphoria condition between placebo participants and those who were aroused but either misinformed or uninformed. Moreover, Table 10.4 shows that there was no difference within the Anger condition between pacebo participants and those who were uninformed (Epi Ign) with respect to self-report. Only in Table 10.5 is there clear support for hypothesis 3: here the placebo participants did differ from those who were aroused but uninformed, but did not differ from those who were aroused and correctly informed.

Discussion

Given that the unsupported first hypothesis was the most original proposition of Schachter and Singer's reasoning, it is somewhat surprising that their findings were so widely interpreted as providing good support for the hypotheses. Admittedly, Schachter and Singer offer several reasons for thinking that their results should not be taken at face value; for example, they argue that their subjects were simply unwilling to admit to feelings of anger, and that we should therefore attach more importance to the behavioural data. However, these data in the anger condition cannot be compared directly with those from the euphoria condition, because quite different aspects of behaviour were measured, thereby making a direct test of the first hypothesis impossible (see Manstead and Wagner, 1981, and Reisenzein, 1983, for analyses of the extent to which this study supports the crucial first hypothesis).

Despite these shortcomings, the Schachter and Singer experiment has been (and to some extent remains) enormously influential. It provides the cornerstone for what came to be known as Schachter's (1964) 'two-factor' theory of emotion, the two factors being physiological arousal and cognitive labelling. The proposition that emotion arises from the interaction between a coarse type of global physiological arousal and finely differentiated cognitions appealed greatly to social psychologists who were becoming increasingly interested in the role played by cognition, and the study was quickly seized on by attribution theorists (e.g. Nisbett and Valins, 1972), who regarded it as evidence that attributions made for arousal helped to shape emotion.

FURTHER READING

Dutton, D.G. and Aron, A.P. (1974). Some evidence for heightened sexual attraction under conditions of high anxiety. *Journal of Personality and Social Psychology*, 28, 510–17. An investigation of the extent to which naturally occurring arousal due to fear of heights can be 'misattributed' to an attractive other.

Valins, S. (1966). Cognitive effects of false heart rate feedback. *Journal of Personality and Social Psychology*, 4, 400–8. Here the Schachter and Singer logic is taken one step further: Valins claims that only the *perception* of arousal is needed to generate an emotional response, provided that a plausible cause for this arousal is present.

REFERENCES

Cannon, W.B. (1927). The James–Lange theory of emotion: A critical examination and an alternative theory. *American Journal of Psychology*, 39, 106–24.

James, W. (1884). What is an emotion? *Mind*, 9, 188–205.

Marañon, G. (1924). Contribution à l'étude de l'action émotive de l'adrénaline. *Revue Française d'Endocrinologie*, 2, 301–25.

Manstead, A.S.R. and Wagner, H.L. (1981). Arousal, cognition and emotion: An appraisal of two-factor theory. *Current Psychological Reviews*, 1, 35–54.

Nisbett, R.E. and Valins, S. (1972). Perceiving the causes of one's own behavior. In E.E. Jones, D.E. Kanouse, H.H. Kelley, R.E. Nisbett, S. Valins and B. Weiner (eds), *Attribution: Perceiving the Causes of Behavior* (pp. 63–78). Morristown, NJ: General Learning Press.

Reisenzein, R. (1983). The Schachter theory of emotion: Two decades later. *Psychological Bulletin*, 94, 239–64.

Schachter, S. (1959). *The Psychology of Affiliation*. Stanford, CA: Stanford University Press.

Schachter, S. (1964). The interaction of cognitive and physiological determinants of emotional state. In L. Berkowitz (ed.), *Advances in Experimental Social Psychology* (vol. 1, pp. 49–80). New York: Academic Press.

- - - - -
Primary
Reading
- - - - - - - -

The problem of which cues, internal or external, permit a person to label and identify his own emotional state has been with us since the days that James (1890) first tendered his doctrine that "the bodily changes follow directly the perception of the exciting fact, and that our feeling of the same changes as they occur *is* the emotion" (p. 449). Since we are aware of a variety of feeling and emotion states, it should follow from James' proposition that the various emotions will be accompanied by a variety of differentiable bodily states. Following James' pronouncement, a formidable number of studies were undertaken in search of the physiological differentiators of the emotions. The results, in these early days, were almost uniformly negative. All of the emotional states experimentally manipulated were characterized by a general pattern of excitation of the sympathetic nervous system but there appeared to be no clear-cut physiological discriminators of the various emotions. This pattern of results was so consistent from experiment to experiment that Cannon (1929) offered, as one of the crucial criticisms of the James–Lange theory, the fact that "the same visceral changes occur in very different emotional states and in non-emotional states" (p. 351).

More recent work, however, has given some indication that there may be differentiators. Ax (1953) and Schachter (1957) studied fear and anger. On a large number of indices both of these states were characterized by a similarly high level of autonomic activation but on several indices they did differ in the degree of activation. Wolf and Wolff (1947) studied a subject with a gastric fistula and were able to distinguish two patterns in the physiological responses of the stomach wall. It should be noted, though, that for many months they studied their subject during and following a great variety of moods and emotions and were able to distinguish only two patterns.

Whether or not there are physiological distinctions among the various emotional states must be considered an open question. Recent work might be taken to indicate that such differences are at best rather subtle and that the variety of emotion, mood, and feeling states are by no means matched by an equal variety of visceral patterns.

This rather ambiguous situation has led Ruckmick (1936), Hunt, Cole, and Reis (1958), Schachter (1959) and others to suggest that cognitive factors may be major determinants of emotional states. Granted a general pattern of sympathetic excitation as characteristic of emotional states, granted that there may be some differences in pattern from state to state, it is suggested that one labels, interprets, and identifies this stirred-up state in terms of the characteristics of the precipitating situation and one's apperceptive mass. This suggests, then, that an emotional state may be considered a function of a state of physiological arousal[1] and of a cognition appropriate to this state of arousal. The cognition, in a sense, exerts a steering function. Cognitions arising from the immediate situation as interpreted by past experience provide the framework within which one understands and labels his feelings. It is the cognition which determines whether the state of physiological arousal will be labeled as "anger," "joy," "fear," or whatever.

In order to examine the implications of this formulation let us consider the fashion in which these two elements, a state of physiological arousal and cognitive factors, would interact in a variety of situations. In most emotion inducing situations, of course, the two factors are completely interrelated. Imagine a man walking alone down a dark alley; a figure with a gun suddenly appears. The perception–cognition "figure with a gun" in some fashion initiates a state of physiological arousal; this state of arousal is interpreted in terms of knowledge about dark alleys and guns and the state of arousal is labeled "fear." Similarly a student who unexpectedly learns that he has made Phi Beta Kappa may experience a state of arousal which he will label "joy."

Let us now consider circumstances in which these two elements, the physiological and the cognitive, are, to some extent, independent. First, is the state of physiological arousal alone sufficient to induce an emotion? Best evidence indicates that it is not. Marañon (1924), in a fascinating study, (which was replicated by Cantril and Hunt, 1932, and Landis and Hunt, 1932) injected 210 of his patients with the sympathomimetic agent adrenalin and then simply asked them to introspect. Seventy-one percent of his subjects simply reported their physical symptoms with no emotional overtones; 29% of the subjects responded in an apparently emotional fashion. Of these the great majority described their feelings in a fashion that Marañon labeled "cold" or "as if" emotions, that is, they made statements such as "I feel *as if*

I were afraid" or "*as if* I were awaiting a great happiness." This is a sort of emotional "déjà vu" experience; these subjects are neither happy nor afraid, they feel "as if" they were. Finally a very few cases apparently reported a genuine emotional experience. However, in order to produce this reaction in most of these few cases, Marañon (1924) points out:

> One must suggest a memory with strong affective force but not so strong as to produce an emotion in the normal state. For example, in several cases we spoke to our patients before the injection of their sick children or dead parents and they responded calmly to this topic. The same topic presented later, during the adrenal commotion, was sufficient to trigger emotion. This adrenal commotion places the subject in a situation of 'affective imminence' (pp. 307–8).

Apparently, then, to produce a genuinely emotional reaction to adrenalin, Marañon was forced to provide such subjects with an appropriate cognition.

Though Marañon (1924) is not explicit on his procedure, it is clear that his subjects knew that they were receiving an injection and in all likelihood knew that they were receiving adrenalin and probably had some order of familiarity with its effects. In short, though they underwent the pattern of sympathetic discharge common to strong emotional states, at the same time they had a completely appropriate cognition or explanation as to why they felt this way. This, we would suggest, is the reason so few of Marañon's subjects reported any emotional experience.

Consider now a person in a state of physiological arousal for which no immediately explanatory or appropriate cognitions are available. Such a state could result were one covertly to inject a subject with adrenalin or, unknown to him, feed the subject a sympathomimetic drug such as ephedrine. Under such conditions a subject would be aware of palpitations, tremor, face flushing, and most of the battery of symptoms associated with a discharge of the sympathetic nervous system. In contrast to Marañon's (1924) subjects he would, at the same time, be utterly unaware of why he felt this way. What would be the consequence of such a state?

Schachter (1959) has suggested that precisely such a state would lead to the arousal of "evaluative needs" (Festinger, 1954), that is, pressures would act on an individual in such a state to understand and label his bodily feelings. His bodily state grossly resembles the condition in which it has been at times of emotional excitement. How would he label his present feelings? It is suggested, of course, that he will label his feelings in terms of his knowledge of the immediate situation.[2] Should he at the time be with a beautiful woman he might decide that he was wildly in love or sexually excited. Should he be at a gay party, he might, by comparing himself to others, decide that he was extremely happy and euphoric. Should he be arguing with his wife, he might explode in fury and hatred. Or, should the situation be completely inappropriate, he could decide that he was excited about something that had recently happened to him or, simply, that he was sick. In any case, it is our basic assumption that emotional states are a function of the interaction of such cognitive factors with a state of physiological arousal.

This line of thought, then, leads to the following propositions:

1   Given a state of physiological arousal for which an individual has no immediate explanation, he will "label" this state and describe his feelings in terms of the cognitions available to him. To the extent that cognitive factors are potent determiners of emotional states, it

could be anticipated that precisely the same state of physiological arousal could be labeled "joy" or "fury" or "jealousy" or any of a great diversity of emotional labels depending on the cognitive aspects of the situation.

2   Given a state of physiological arousal for which an individual has a completely appropriate explanation (e.g., "I feel this way because I have just received an injection of adrenalin") no evaluative needs will arise and the individual is unlikely to label his feelings in terms of the alternative cognitions available.

Finally, consider a condition in which emotion inducing cognitions are present but there is no state of physiological arousal. For example, an individual might be completely aware that he is in great danger but for some reason (drug or surgical) remain in a state of physiological quiescence. Does he experience the emotion "fear"? Our formulation of emotion as a joint function of a state of physiological arousal and an appropriate cognition, would, of course, suggest that he does not, which leads to our final proposition:

3   Given the same cognitive circumstances, the individual will react emotionally or describe his feelings as emotions only to the extent that he experiences a state of physiological arousal.[3]

Procedure

The experimental test of these propositions requires (a) the experimental manipulation of a state of physiological arousal, (b) the manipulation of the extent to which the subject has an appropriate or proper explanation of his bodily state, and (c) the creation of situations from which explanatory cognitions may be derived.

In order to satisfy the first two experimental requirements, the experiment was cast in the framework of a study of the effects of vitamin supplements on vision. As soon as a subject arrived, he was taken to a private room and told by the experimenter:

> In this experiment we would like to make various tests of your vision. We are particularly interested in how certain vitamin compounds and vitamin supplements affect the visual skills. In particular, we want to find out how the vitamin compound called 'Suproxin' affects your vision.
>
> What we would like to do, then, if we can get your permission, is to give you a small injection of Suproxin. The injection itself is mild and harmless; however, since some people do object to being injected we don't want to talk you into anything. Would you mind receiving a Suproxin injection?

If the subject agrees to the injection (and all but 1 of 185 subjects did) the experimenter continues with instructions we shall describe shortly, then leaves the room. In a few minutes a physician enters the room, briefly repeats the experimenter's instructions, takes the subject's pulse and then injects him with Suproxin.

Depending upon condition, the subject receives one of two forms of Suproxin – epinephrine or a placebo.

Epinephrine or adrenalin is a sympathomimetic drug whose effects, with minor exceptions, are almost a perfect mimicry of a discharge of the sympathetic nervous system. Shortly after injection systolic blood pressure increases markedly, heart rate increases somewhat, cutaneous blood flow decreases, while muscle and cerebral blood flow increase, blood sugar and lactic acid concentration increase, and respiration rate increases slightly. As far as the subject is concerned the major subjective symptoms are palpitation, tremor, and sometimes a feeling of flushing and accelerated breathing. With a subcutaneous injection (in the dosage administered to our subjects), such effects usually begin within 3–5 minutes of injection and last anywhere from 10 minutes to an hour. For most subjects these effects are dissipated within 15–20 minutes after injection.

Subjects receiving epinephrine received a subcutaneous injection of $1/2$ cubic centimeter of a $1:1000$ solution of Winthrop Laboratory's Suprarenin, a saline solution of epinephrine bitartrate.

Subjects in the placebo condition received a subcutaneous injection of $1/2$ cubic centimeter of saline solution. This is, of course, completely neutral material with no side effects at all.

Manipulating an appropriate explanation

By "appropriate" we refer to the extent to which the subject has an authoritative, unequivocal explanation of his bodily condition. Thus, a subject who had been informed by the physician that as a direct consequence of the injection he would feel palpitations, tremor, etc. would be considered to have a completely appropriate explanation. A subject who had been informed only that the injection would have no side effects would have no appropriate explanation of his state. This dimension of appropriateness was manipulated in three experimental conditions which shall be called: Epinephrine Informed (Epi Inf), Epinephrine Ignorant (Epi Ign), and Epinephrine Misinformed (Epi Mis).

Immediately after the subject had agreed to the injection and before the physician entered the room, the experimenter's spiel in each of these conditions went as follows:

Epinephrine informed

> I should also tell you that some of our subjects have experienced side effects from the Suproxin. These side effects are transitory, that is, they will only last for about 15 or 20 minutes. What will probably happen is that your hand will start to shake, your heart will start to pound, and your face may get warm and flushed. Again these are side effects lasting about 15 or 20 minutes.

While the physician was giving the injection, she told the subject that the injection was mild and harmless and repeated this description of the symptoms that the subject could expect as a consequence of the shot. In this condition, then, subjects have a completely appropriate explanation of their bodily state. They know precisely what they will feel and why.

Epinephrine ignorant

In this condition, when the subject agreed to the injection, the experimenter said nothing more relevant to side effects and simply left the room. While the physician was giving the injection, she told the subject that the injection was mild and harmless and would have no side effects. In this condition, then, the subject has no experimentally provided explanation for his bodily state.

Epinephrine misinformed

> I should also tell you that some of our subjects have experienced side effects from the Suproxin. These side effects are transitory, that is, they will only last for about 15 or 20 minutes. What will probably happen is that your feet will feel numb, you will have an itching sensation over parts of your body, and you may get a slight headache. Again these are side effects lasting 15 or 20 minutes.

And again, the physician repeated these symptoms while injecting the subject.

None of these symptoms, of course, are consequences of an injection of epinephrine and, in effect, these instructions provide the subject with a completely inappropriate explanation of his bodily feelings. This condition was introduced as a control condition of sorts. It seemed possible that the description of side effects in the Epi Inf condition might turn the subject introspective, self-examining, possibly slightly troubled. Differences on the dependent variable between the Epi Inf and Epi Ign conditions might, then, be due to such factors rather than to differences in appropriateness. The false symptoms in the Epi Mis condition should similarly turn the subject introspective, etc., but the instructions in this condition do not provide an appropriate explanation of the subject's state.

Subjects in all of the above conditions were injected with epinephrine. Finally, there was a placebo condition in which subjects, who were injected with saline solution, were given precisely the same treatment as subjects in the Epi Ign condition.

Producing an emotion inducing cognition

Our initial hypothesis has suggested that given a state of physiological arousal for which the individual has no adequate explanation, cognitive factors can lead the individual to describe his feelings with any of a diversity of emotional labels. In order to test this hypothesis, it was decided to manipulate emotional states which can be considered quite different – euphoria and anger.

There are, of course, many ways to induce such states. In our own program of research, we have concentrated on social determinants of emotional states and have been able to demonstrate in other studies that people do evaluate their own feelings by comparing themselves with others around them (Schachter, 1959; Wrightsman, 1960). In this experiment we have attempted again to manipulate emotional state by social means. In one set of conditions, the subject is placed together with a stooge who has been trained to act euphorically. In a second set of conditions the subject is with a stooge trained to act in an angry fashion.

Euphoria

Immediately[4] after the subject had been injected, the physician left the room and the experimenter returned with a stooge whom he introduced as another subject, then said:

> Both of you have had the Suproxin shot and you'll both be taking the same tests of vision. What I ask you to do now is just wait for 20 minutes. The reason for this is simply that we have to allow 20 minutes for the Suproxin to get from the injection site into the bloodstream. At the end of 20 minutes when we are certain that most of the Suproxin has been absorbed into the bloodstream, we'll begin the tests of vision.

The room in which this was said had been deliberately put into a state of mild disarray. As he was leaving, the experimenter apologetically added:

> The only other thing I should do is to apologize for the condition of the room. I just didn't have time to clean it up. So, if you need any scratch paper or rubber bands or pencils, help yourself. I'll be back in 20 minutes to begin the vision tests.

As soon as the experimenter had left, the stooge introduced himself again, made a series of standard icebreaker comments, and then launched his routine. For observation purposes, the stooge's act was broken into a series of standard units, demarcated by a change in activity or a standard comment. In sequence, the units of the stooge's routine were the following:

1. Stooge reaches for a piece of paper and starts doodling saying, "They said we could use this for scratch, didn't they?" He doodles a fish for some 30 seconds, then says:

2. "This scrap paper isn't even much good for doodling" and crumples paper and attempts to throw it into wastebasket in far corner of the room. He misses but this leads him into a "basketball game." He crumples up other sheets of paper, shoots a few baskets, says "Two points" occasionally. He gets up and does a jump shot saying, "The old jump shot is really on today."

3. If the subject has not joined in, the stooge throws a paper basketball to the subject saying, "Here, you try it."

4. Stooge continues his game saying, "The trouble with paper basketballs is that you don't really have any control."

5. Stooge continues basketball, then gives it up saying, "This is one of my good days. I feel like a kid again. I think I'll make a plane." He makes a paper airplane saying, "I guess I'll make one of the longer ones."

6. Stooge flies plane. Gets up and retrieves plane. Flies again, etc.

7. Stooge throws plant at subject.

8. Stooge, flying plane, says, "Even when I was a kid, I was never much good at this."

9. Stooge tears off part of plane saying, "Maybe this plane can't fly but at least it's good for something." He wads up paper and making a slingshot of a rubber band begins to shoot the paper.

10. Shooting, the stooge says, "They [paper ammunition] really go better if you make them long. They don't work right if you wad them up."

11. While shooting, stooge notices a sloppy pile of manila folders on a table. He builds a tower of these folders, then goes to the opposite end of the room to shoot at the tower.

12. He misses several times, then hits and cheers as the tower falls. He goes over to pick up the folders.

13. While picking up, he notices, behind a portable blackboard, a pair of hula hoops which have been covered with black tape with a few wires sticking out of the tape. He reaches for these, taking one for himself and putting the other aside but within reaching distance of the subject. The stooge tries the hula hoop, saying, "This isn't as easy as it looks."

14. Stooge twirls hoop wildly on arm, saying, "Hey, look at this – this is great."

15. Stooge replaces the hula hoop and sits down with his feet on the table. Shortly thereafter the experimenter returns to the room.

This routine was completely standard, though its pace, of course, varied depending upon the subject's reaction, the extent to which he entered into this bedlam and the extent to which he initiated activities of his own. The only variations from this standard routine were those forced by the subject. Should the subject originate some nonsense of his own and request the stooge to join in, he would do so. And, he would, of course, respond to any comments initiated by the subject.

Subjects in each of the three "appropriateness" conditions and in the placebo condition were submitted to this setup. The stooge, of course, never knew in which condition any particular subject fell.

Anger

Immediately after the injection, the experimenter brought a stooge into the subject's room, introduced the two and after explaining the necessity for a 20 minute delay for "the Suproxin to get from the injection site into the bloodstream" he continued, "We would like you to use these 20 minutes to answer these questionnaires." Then handing out the questionnaires, he concludes with, "I'll be back in 20 minutes to pick up the questionnaires and begin the tests of vision."

Before looking at the questionnaire, the stooge says to the subject,

> I really wanted to come for an experiment today, but I think it's unfair for them to give you shots. At least, they should have told us about the shots when they called us; you hate to refuse, once you're here already.

The questionnaires, five pages long, start off innocently requesting face sheet information and then grow increasingly personal and insulting. The stooge, sitting directly opposite the subject, paces his own answers so that at all times subject and stooge are working on the same question. At regular points in the questionnaire, the stooge makes a series of standardized comments about the questions. His comments start off innocently enough, grow increasingly querulous, and finally he ends up in a rage. In sequence, he makes the following comments.

1. Before answering any items, he leafs quickly through the questionnaire saying, "Boy, this is a long one."
2. Question 7 on the questionnaire requests, "List the foods that you would eat in a typical day." The stooge comments, "Oh for Pete's sake, what did I have for breakfast this morning?"
3. Question 9 asks, "Do you ever hear bells? ——— . How often? ——— ." The stooge remarks, "Look at Question 9. How ridiculous can you get? I hear bells every time I change classes."
4. Question 13 requests, "List the childhood diseases you have had and the age at which you had them" to which the stooge remarks, "I get annoyed at this childhood disease question. I can't remember what childhood diseases I had, and especially at what age. Can you?"
5. Question 17 asks "What is your father's average annual income?" and the stooge says, "This really irritates me. It's none of their business what my father makes. I'm leaving that blank."
6. Question 25 presents a long series of items such as "Does not bathe or wash regularly," "Seems to need psychiatric care," etc. and requests the respondent to write down for which member of his immediate family each item seems most applicable. The question specifically prohibits the answer "None" and each item must be answered. The stooge says, "I'll be damned if I'll fill out Number 25. 'Does not bathe or wash regularly' – that's a real insult." He then angrily crosses out the entire item.
7. Question 28 reads:
"How many times each week do you have sexual intercourse?" 0–1 ——— 2–3 ——— 4–6 ——— 7 and over———. The stooge bites out, "The hell with it! I don't have to tell them all this."
8. The stooge sits sullenly for a few moments then he rips up his questionnaire, crumples the pieces and hurls them to the floor, saying, "I'm not wasting any more time. I'm getting my books and leaving" and he stamps out of the room.

9. The questionnaire continues for eight more questions ending with: "With how many men (other than your father) has your mother had extramarital relationships?"
4 and under ——— : 5–9 ——— : 10 and over ———.

Subjects in the Epi Ign, Epi Inf and Placebo conditions were run through this "anger" inducing sequence. The stooge, again, did not know to which condition the subject had been assigned.

In summary, this is a seven condition experiment which, for two different emotional states, allows us (a) to evaluate the effects of "appropriateness" on emotional inducibility and (b) to begin to evaluate the effects of sympathetic activation on emotional inducibility. In schematic form the conditions are the following:

Euphoria	*Anger*
Epi Inf	Epi Inf
Epi Ign	Epi Ign
Epi Mis	Placebo
Placebo	

The Epi Mis condition was not run in the Anger sequence. This was originally conceived as a control condition and it was felt that its inclusion in the Euphoria conditions alone would suffice as a means of evaluating the possible artifactual effect of the Epi Inf instructions.

Measurement

Two types of measures of emotional state were obtained. Standardized observation through a one-way mirror was the technique used to assess the subject's behavior. To what extent did he act euphoric or angry? Such behavior can be considered in a way as a "semiprivate" index of mood, for as far as the subject was concerned, his emotional behavior could be known only to the other person in the room – presumably another student. The second type of measure was self-report in which, on a variety of scales, the subject indicated his mood of the moment. Such measures can be considered "public" indices of mood, for they would, of course, be available to the experimenter and his associates.

Observation

Euphoria

For each of the first 14 units of the stooge's standardized routine an observer kept a running chronicle of what the subject did and said. For each unit the observer coded the subject's behavior in one or more of the following categories:

Category 1: Joins in activity. If the subject entered into the stooge's activities, e.g., if he made or flew airplanes, threw paper basketballs, hula hooped, etc., his behavior was coded in this category.

Category 2: Initiates new activity. A subject was so coded if he gave indications of creative euphoria, that is, if, on his own, he initiated behavior outside of the stooge's routine. Instances of such behavior would be the subject who threw open the window and, laughing, hurled paper basketballs at passersby; or, the subject who jumped on a table and spun one hula hoop on his leg and the other on his neck.

Categories 3 and 4: Ignores or watches stooge. Subjects who paid flatly no attention to the stooge or who, with or without comment, simply watched the stooge without joining in his activity were coded in these categories.

For any particular unit of behavior, the subject's behavior was coded in one or more of these categories. To test reliability of coding two observers independently coded two experimental sessions. The observers agreed completely on the coding of 88% of the units.

Anger

For each of the units of stooge behavior, an observer recorded the subject's responses and coded them according to the following category scheme:

Category 1: Agrees. In response to the stooge the subject makes a comment indicating that he agrees with the stooge's standardized comment or that he, too, is irked by a particular item on the questionnaire. For example, a subject who responded to the stooge's comment on the "father's income" question by saying, "I don't like that kind of personal question either" would be so coded (scored +2).

Category 2: Disagrees. In response to the stooge's comment, the subject makes a comment which indicates that he disagrees with the stooge's meaning or mood; e.g., in response to the stooge's comment on the "father's income" question, such a subject might say, "Take it easy, they probably have a good reason for wanting the information" (scored −2).

Category 3: Neutral. A noncommittal or irrelevant response to the stooge's remark (scored 0).

Category 4: Initiates agreement or disagreement. With no instigation by the stooge, a subject, so coded, would have volunteered a remark indicating that he felt the same way or, alternatively, quite differently than the stooge. Examples would be "Boy I hate this kind of thing" or "I'm enjoying this" (scored +2 or −2).

Category 5: Watches. The subject makes no verbal response to the stooge's comment but simply looks directly at him (scored 0).

Category 6: Ignores. The subject makes no verbal response to the stooge's comment nor does he look at him; the subject, paying no attention at all to the stooge, simply works at his own questionnaire (scored −1).

A subject was scored in one or more of these categories for each unit of stooge behavior. To test reliability, two observers independently coded three experimental sessions. In order to get a behavioral index of anger, observation protocol was scored according to the values presented in parentheses after each of the above definitions of categories. In a unit-by-unit comparison, the two observers agreed completely on the scoring of 71% of the units jointly observed. The scores of the two observers differed by a value of 1 or less for 88% of the units coded and in not a single case did the two observers differ in the direction of their scoring of a unit.

Self-report of mood and physical condition

When the subject's session with the stooge was completed, the experimenter returned to the room, took pulses and said:

Before we proceed with the vision tests, there is one other kind of information which we must have. We have found, as you can probably imagine, that there are many things beside Suproxin that affect how well you see in our tests. How hungry you are, how tired you are, and even the mood you're in at the time – whether you feel happy or irritated at the time of testing will affect how well you see. To understand the data we collect on you, then, we must be able to figure out which effects are due to causes such as these and which are caused by Suproxin.

The only way we can get such information about your physical and emotional state is to have you tell us. I'll hand out these questionnaires and ask you to answer them as accurately as possible. Obviously, our data on the vision tests will only be as accurate as your description of your mental and physical state.

In keeping with this spiel, the questionnaire that the experimenter passed out contained a number of mock questions about hunger, fatigue, etc., as well as questions of more immediate relevance to the experiment. To measure mood or emotional state the following two were the crucial questions:

1. How irritated, angry or annoyed would you say you feel at present?

I don't feel at all irritated or angry	I feel a little irritated and angry	I feel quite irritated and angry	I feel very irritated and angry	I feel extremely irritated and angry
(0)	(1)	(2)	(3)	(4)

2. How good or happy would you say you feel at present?

I don't feel at all happy or good	I feel a little happy and good	I feel quite happy and good	I feel very happy and good	I feel extremely happy and good
(0)	(1)	(2)	(3)	(4)

To measure the physical effects of epinephrine and determine whether or not the injection had been successful in producing the necessary bodily state, the following questions were asked:

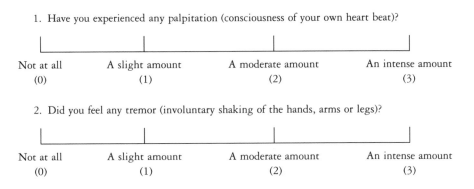

1. Have you experienced any palpitation (consciousness of your own heart beat)?

Not at all	A slight amount	A moderate amount	An intense amount
(0)	(1)	(2)	(3)

2. Did you feel any tremor (involuntary shaking of the hands, arms or legs)?

Not at all	A slight amount	A moderate amount	An intense amount
(0)	(1)	(2)	(3)

To measure possible effects of the instructions in the Epi Mis condition, the following questions were asked:

1. Did you feel any numbness in your feet?
2. Did you feel any itching sensation?
3. Did you experience any feeling of headache?

To all three of these questions was attached a four-point scale running from "Not at all" to "An intense amount."

In addition to these scales, the subjects were asked to answer two open-end questions on other physical or emotional sensations they may have experienced during the experimental session. A final measure of bodily state was pulse rate which was taken by the physician or the experimenter at two times – immediately before the injection and immediately after the session with the stooge.

When the subjects had completed these questionnaires, the experimenter announced that the experiment was over, explained the deception and its necessity in detail, answered any questions, and swore the subjects to secrecy. Finally, the subjects answered a brief questionnaire about their experiences, if any, with adrenalin and their previous knowledge or suspicion of the experimental setup. There was no indication that any of the subjects had known about the experiment beforehand but 11 subjects were so extremely suspicious of some crucial feature of the experiment that their data were automatically discarded.

Subjects

The subjects were all male, college students taking classes in introductory psychology at the University of Minnesota. Some 90% of the students in these classes volunteer for a subject pool for which they receive two extra points on their final exam for every hour that they serve as experimental subjects. For this study the records of all potential subjects were cleared with the Student Health Service in order to insure that no harmful effects would result from the injections.

Evaluation of the experimental design

The ideal test of our propositions would require circumstances which our experiment is far from realizing. First, the proposition that: "A state of physiological arousal for which an individual has no immediate explanation will lead him to label this state in terms of the cognitions available to him" obviously requires conditions under which the subject does not and cannot have a proper explanation of his bodily state. Though we toyed with such fantasies as ventilating the experimental room with vaporized adrenalin, reality forced us to rely on the disguised injection of Suproxin – a technique which was far from ideal, for no matter what the experimenter told them, some subjects would inevitably attribute their feelings to the injection. To the extent that subjects did so, differences between the several appropriateness conditions should be attenuated.

Second, the proposition that: "Given the same cognitive circumstances the individual will react emotionally only to the extent that he experiences a state of physiological arousal" requires for its ideal test the manipulation of states of physiological arousal and of physiological quiescence. Though there is no question that epinephrine effectively produces a state of arousal, there is also no question that a placebo does not prevent physiological arousal. To the extent that the experimental situation effectively produces sympathetic stimulation in placebo subjects, the proposition is difficult to test, for such a factor would attenuate differences between epinephrine and placebo subjects.

Both of these factors, then, can be expected to interfere with the test of our several propositions. In presenting the results of this study, we shall first present condition by condition results and then evaluate the effect of these two factors on experimental differences.

Results

Effects of the injections on bodily state

Let us examine first the success of the injections at producing the bodily state required to examine the propositions at test. Does the injection of epinephrine produce symptoms of sympathetic discharge as compared with the placebo injection? Relevant data are presented in table 10.1, where it can be immediately seen that on all items subjects who were in epinephrine conditions show considerably more evidence of sympathetic activation than do subjects in placebo conditions. In all epinephrine conditions pulse rate increases significantly when compared with the decrease characteristic of the placebo conditions. On the scales it is clear that epinephrine subjects experience considerably more palpitation and tremor than do placebo subjects. In all possible comparisons on these symptoms, the mean scores of subjects in any of the epinephrine conditions are greater than the corresponding scores in the placebo conditions at better than the .001 level of significance. Examination of the absolute values of these scores makes it quite clear that subjects in epinephrine conditions were, indeed, in a state of physiological arousal, while most subjects in placebo conditions were in a relative state of physiological quiescence.

The epinephrine injection, of course, did not work with equal effectiveness for all subjects; indeed for a few subjects it did not work at all. Such subjects reported almost no palpitation

Table 10.1   The effects of the injections on bodily state

| Condition | N | Pulse | | Self-rating of | | | | |
		Pre	Post	Palpitation	Tremor	Numbness	Itching	Headache
Euphoria								
Epi Inf	27	85.7	88.6	1.20	1.43	0	.16	.32
Epi Ign	26	84.6	85.6	1.83	1.76	.15	0	.55
Epi Mis	26	82.9	86.0	1.27	2.00	.06	.08	.23
Placebo	26	80.4	77.1	.29	.21	.09	0	.27
Anger								
Epi Inf	23	85.9	92.4	1.26	1.41	.17	0	.11
Epi Ign	23	85.0	96.8	1.44	1.78	0	.06	.21
Placebo	23	84.5	79.6	.59	.24	.14	.06	.06

or tremor, showed no increase in pulse and described no other relevant physical symptoms. Since for such subjects the necessary experimental conditions were not established, they were automatically excluded from the data and all further tabular presentations will not include such subjects. Table 10.1, however, does include the data of these subjects. There were four such subjects in euphoria conditions and one of them in anger conditions.

In order to evaluate further data on Epi Mis subjects it is necessary to note the results of the "numbness," "itching," and "headache" scales also presented in table 10.1. Clearly the subjects in the Epi Mis condition do not differ on these scales from subjects in any of the other experimental conditions.

Effects of the manipulations on emotional state

Euphoria

Self-report The effects of the several manipulations on emotional state in the euphoria conditions are presented in table 10.2. The scores recorded in this table are derived, for each subject, by subtracting the value of the point he checks on the irritation scale from the value of the point he checks on the happiness scale. Thus, if a subject were to check the point "I feel a little irritated and angry" on the irritation scale and the point "I feel very happy and good" on the happiness scale, his score would be +2. The higher the positive value, the happier and better the subject reports himself as feeling. Though we employ an index for expositional simplicity, it should be noted that the two components of the index each yield results completely consistent with those obtained by use of this index.

Let us examine first the effects of the appropriateness instructions. Comparison of the scores for the Epi Mis and Epi Inf conditions makes it immediately clear that the experimental differences are not due to artifacts resulting from the informed instructions. In both conditions the subject was warned to expect a variety of symptoms as a consequence of the injection. In the Epi Mis condition, where the symptoms were inappropriate to the subject's bodily state, the self-report score is almost twice that in the Epi Inf condition, where the symptoms were completely appropriate to the subject's bodily state. It is reasonable, then, to attribute differences between informed subjects and those in other conditions to differences in manipulated appropriateness rather than to artifacts such as introspectiveness or self-examination.

It is clear that, consistent with expectations, subjects were more susceptible to the stooge's mood and consequently more euphoric when they had no explanation of their own bodily states than when they did. The means of both the Epi Ign and Epi Mis conditions are considerably greater than the mean of the Epi Inf condition.

Table 10.2 Self-report of emotional state in the euphoria conditions

Condition	N	Self-report scales	Comparison	p[a]
Epi Inf	25	.98	Epi Inf vs. Epi Mis	<.01
Epi Ign	25	1.78	Epi Inf vs. Epi Ign	.02
Epi Mis	25	1.90	Placebo vs. Epi Mis.	*ns*
Placebo	26	1.61	Ign, or Inf	

All *p* values reported throughout paper are two-tailed.

It is of interest to note that Epi Mis subjects are somewhat more euphoric than are Epi Ign subjects. This pattern repeats itself in other data shortly to be presented. We would attribute this difference to differences in the appropriateness dimension. Though, as in the Epi Ign condition, a subject is not provided with an explanation of his bodily state, it is, of course, possible that he will provide one for himself which is not derived from his interaction with the stooge. Most reasonably he could decide for himself that he feels this way because of the injection. To the extent that he does so he should be less susceptible to the stooge. It seems probable that he would be less likely to hit on such an explanation in the Epi Mis condition than in the Epi Ign condition, for in the Epi Mis condition both the experimenter and the doctor have told him that the effects of the injection would be quite different from what he actually feels. The effect of such instructions is probably to make it more difficult for the subject himself to hit on the alternative explanation described above. There is some evidence to support this analysis. In open-end questions in which subjects described their own mood and state, 28% of the subjects in the Epi Ign condition made some connection between the injection and their bodily state compared with the 16% of subjects in the Epi Mis condition who did so. It could be considered, then, that these three conditions fall along a dimension of appropriateness, with the Epi Inf condition at one extreme and the Epi Mis condition at the other.

Comparing the placebo to the epinephrine conditions, we note a pattern which will repeat itself throughout the data. Placebo subjects are less euphoric than either Epi Mis or Epi Ign subjects but somewhat more euphoric than Epi Inf subjects. These differences are not, however, statistically significant. We shall consider the epinephrine–placebo comparisons in detail in a later section of this paper following the presentation of additional relevant data. For the moment, it is clear that, by self-report, manipulating appropriateness has had a very strong effect on euphoria.

Behavior   Let us next examine the extent to which the subject's behavior was affected by the experimental manipulations. To the extent that his mood has been affected, one should expect that the subject will join in the stooge's whirl of manic activity and initiate similar activities of his own. The relevant data are presented in table 10.3. The column labeled "Activity index" presents summary figures on the extent to which the subject joined in the stooge's activity. This is a weighted index which reflects both the nature of the activities in which the subject engaged and the amount of time he was active. The index was devised by assigning the following weights to the subject's activities: 5 – hula hooping; 4 – shooting with slingshot; 3 – paper airplanes; 2 – paper basketballs; 1 – doodling; 0 – does nothing. Pretest scaling on 15 college students ordered these activities with respect to the degree of euphoria they represented. Arbitrary weights were assigned so that the wilder the activity, the heavier the weight. These weights are multiplied by an estimate of the amount of time the subject spent in each activity, and the summed products make up the activity index for each subject. This index may be considered a measure of behavioral euphoria. It should be noted that the same between-condition relationships hold for the two components of this index as for the index itself.

The column labeled "Mean number of acts initiated" presents the data on the extent to which the subject deviates from the stooge's routine and initiates euphoric activities of his own.

On both behavioral indices, we find precisely the same pattern of relationships as those obtained with self-reports. Epi Mis subjects behave somewhat more euphorically than do Epi Ign subjects, who in turn behave more euphorically than do Epi Inf subjects. On all measures,

Table 10.3 Behavioral indications of emotional state in the euphoria conditions

Condition	N	Activity index	Mean number of acts initiated
Epi Inf	25	12.72	.20
Epi Ign	25	18.28	.56
Epi Mis	25	22.56	.84
Placebo	26	16.00	.54

	p *value*	
Comparison	Activity index	Initiates
Epi Inf vs. Epi Mis	.05	.03
Epi Inf vs. Epi Ign	*ns*	.08
Plac vs. Epi Mis, Ign, or Inf	*ns*	*ns*

ᵃTested by X^2 comparison of the proportion of subjects in each condition initiating new acts.

then, there is consistent evidence that a subject will take over the stooge's euphoric mood to the extent that he has no other explanation of his bodily state.

Again it should be noted that on these behavioral indices, Epi Ign and Epi Mis subjects are somewhat more euphoric than placebo subjects but not significantly so.

Anger

Self-report Before presenting data for the anger conditions, one point must be made about the anger manipulation. In the situation devised, anger, if manifested, is most likely to be directed at the experimenter and his annoyingly personal questionnaire. As we subsequently discovered, this was rather unfortunate, for the subjects, who had volunteered for the experiment for extra points on their final exam, simply refused to endanger these points by publicly blowing up, admitting their irritation to the experimenter's face or spoiling the questionnaire. Though as the reader will see, the subjects were quite willing to manifest anger when they were alone with the stooge, they hesitated to do so on material (self-ratings of mood and questionnaire) that the experimenter might see, and only after the purposes of the experiment had been revealed were many of these subjects willing to admit to the experimenter that they had been irked or irritated.

This experimentally unfortunate situation pretty much forces us to rely on the behavioral indices derived from observation of the subject's presumably private interaction with the stooge. We do, however, present data on the self-report scales in table 10.4. These figures are derived in the same way as the figures presented in table 10.2 for the euphoria conditions, that is, the value checked on the irritation scale is subtracted from the value checked on the happiness scale. Though, for the reasons stated above, the absolute magnitude of these figures (all positive) is relatively meaningless, we can, of course, compare condition means within the

Table 10.4   Self-report of emotional state in the anger conditions

Condition	N	Self-report scales	Comparison	p
Epi Inf	22	1.91	Epi Inf vs. Epi Ign	.08
Epi Ign	23	1.39	Placebo vs. Epi Ign or Inf	*ns*
Placebo	23	1.63		

set of anger conditions. With the happiness–irritation index employed, we should, of course, anticipate precisely the reverse results from those obtained in the euphoria conditions; that is, the Epi Inf subjects in the anger conditions should again be less susceptible to the stooge's mood and should, therefore, describe themselves as in a somewhat happier frame of mind than subjects in the Epi Ign condition. This is the case; the Epi Inf subjects average 1.91 on the self-report scales while the Epi Ign subjects average 1.39.

Evaluating the effects of the injections, we note again that, as anticipated, Epi Ign subjects are somewhat less happy than Placebo subjects but, once more, this is not a significant difference.

Behavior   The subject's responses to the stooge, during the period when both were filling out their questionnaires, were systematically coded to provide a behavioral index of anger. The coding scheme and the numerical values attached to each of the categories have been described in the methodology section. To arrive at an "Anger index" the numerical value assigned to a subject's responses to the stooge is summed together for the several units of stooge behavior. In the coding scheme used, a positive value to this index indicates that the subject agrees with the stooge's comment and is growing angry. A negative value indicates that the subject either disagrees with the stooge or ignores him.

The relevant data are presented in table 10.5. For this analysis, the stooge's routine has been divided into two phases – the first two units of his behavior (the "long" questionnaire and "What did I have for breakfast?") are considered essentially neutral revealing nothing of the stooge's mood; all of the following units are considered "angry" units, for they begin with an irritated remark about the "bells" question and end with the stooge's fury as he rips up his questionnaire and stomps out of the room. For the neutral units, agreement or disagreement with the stooge's remarks is, of course, meaningless as an index of mood and we should anticipate no difference between conditions. As can be seen in table 10.5, this is the case.

For the angry units, we must, of course, anticipate that subjects in the Epi Ign condition will be angrier than subjects in the Epi Inf condition. This is indeed the case. The Anger index for the Epi Ign condition is positive and large, indicating that these subjects have become angry, while in the Epi Inf condition the Anger index is slightly negative in value, indicating that these subjects have failed to catch the stooge's mood at all. It seems clear that providing the subject with an appropriate explanation of his bodily state greatly reduces his tendency to interpret his state in terms of the cognitions provided by the stooge's angry behavior.

Finally, on this behavioral index, it can be seen that subjects in the Epi Ign condition are significantly angrier than subjects in the Placebo condition. Behaviorally, at least, the injection of epinephrine appears to have led subjects to an angrier state than comparable subjects who received placebo shots.

Table 10.5 Behavioral indications of emotional state in the anger conditions

Condition	N	Neutral units	Anger units
Epi Inf	22	+.07	−.18
Epi Ign	23	+.30	+2.28
Placebo	22[a]	−.09	+.79

Comparison for anger units	P
Epi Inf vs. Epi Ign	<.01
Epi Ign vs. Placebo	<.05
Placebo vs. Epi Inf	*ns*

[a] For one subject in this condition the sound system went dead and the observer could not, of course, code his reactions.

Conformation of data to theoretical expectations

Now that the basic data of this study have been presented, let us examine closely the extent to which they conform to theoretical expectations. If our hypotheses are correct and if this experimental design provided a perfect test for these hypotheses, it should be anticipated that in the euphoria conditions the degree of experimentally produced euphoria should vary in the following fashion:

$$\text{Epi Mis} \geq \text{Epi Ign} > \text{Epi Inf} = \text{Placebo}$$

And in the anger conditions, anger should conform to the following pattern:

$$\text{Epi Ign} > \text{Epi Inf} = \text{Placebo}$$

In both sets of conditions, it is the case that emotional level in the Epi Mis and Epi Ign conditions is considerably greater than that achieved in the corresponding Epi Inf conditions. The results for the Placebo condition, however, are ambiguous, for consistently the Placebo subjects fall between the Epi Ign and the Epi Inf subjects. This is a particularly troubling pattern, for it makes it impossible to evaluate unequivocally the effects of the state of physiological arousal and indeed raises serious questions about our entire theoretical structure. Though the emotional level is consistently greater in the Epi Mis and Epi Ign conditions than in the Placebo condition, this difference is significant at acceptable probability levels only in the anger conditions.

In order to explore the problem further, let us examine the experimental factors identified earlier, which might have acted to restrain the emotional level in the Epi Ign and Epi Mis conditions. As was pointed out earlier, the ideal test of our first two hypotheses requires an experimental setup in which the subject has flatly no way of evaluating his state of physiological arousal other than by means of the experimentally provided cognitions. Had it been possible to physiologically produce a state of sympathetic activation by means other than injection, one could have approached this experimental ideal more closely than in the present setup. As it stands, however, there is always a reasonable alternative cognition available to the aroused subject – he feels the way he does because of the injection. To the extent that the subject seizes on such an explanation of his bodily state, we should expect that he will be uninfluenced by the stooge. Evidence presented in table 10.6 for the anger condition and in table 10.7 for the euphoria conditions indicates that this is, indeed, the case.

As mentioned earlier, some of the Epi Ign and Epi Mis subjects in their answers to the open-end questions clearly attributed their physical state to the injection, e.g., "the shot gave me the shivers." In tables 10.6 and 10.7 such subjects are labeled "Self-informed." In table 10.6 it can be seen that the self-informed subjects are considerably less angry than are the remaining subjects; indeed, they are not angry at all. With these self-informed subjects eliminated, the difference between the Epi Ign and the Placebo conditions is significant at the .01 level of significance.

Precisely the same pattern is evident in table 10.7 for the euphoria conditions. In both the Epi Mis and the Epi Ign conditions, the self-informed subjects have considerably lower activity indices than do the remaining subjects. Eliminating self-informed subjects, comparison of both of these conditions with the Placebo condition yields a difference significant at the .03 level of significance. It should be noted, too, that the self-informed subjects have much the same score on the activity index as do the experimental Epi Inf subjects (table 10.3).

It would appear, then, that the experimental procedure of injecting the subjects, by providing an alternative condition, has, to some extent, obscured the effects of epinephrine. When account is taken of this artifact, the evidence is good that the state of physiological arousal is a necessary component of an emotional experience, for when self-informed subjects are removed, epinephrine subjects give consistent indications of greater emotionality than do placebo subjects.

Let us examine next the fact that consistently the emotional level, both reported and behavioral, in Placebo conditions is greater than that in the Epi Inf conditions. Theoretically, of course, it should be expected that the two conditions will be equally low, for by assuming that emotional state is a joint function of a state of physiological arousal and of the appropriateness of a cognition we are, in effect, assuming a multiplicative function, so that if either component is at zero, emotional level is at zero. As noted earlier this expectation should hold if we can be sure that there is no sympathetic activation in the Placebo conditions. This assumption, of course, is completely unrealistic, for the injection of placebo does not prevent sympathetic activation. The experimental situations were fairly dramatic and certainly some of

Table 10.6   The effects of attributing bodily state to the injection on anger in the anger Epi Ign condition

Condition	N	Anger index	p
Self-informed subjects	3	−1.67	*ns*
Others	20	+2.88	*ns*
Self-informed vs. Others			.05

Table 10.7 The effects of attributing bodily state to the injection on euphoria in the euphoria Epi Ign and Epi Mis conditions

	Epi Ign		
	N	Activity Index	p
Self-informed subjects	8	11.63	*ns*
Others	17	21.14	*ns*
Self-informed vs. Others			.05

	Epi Mis		
	N	Activity Index	p
Self-informed subjects	5	12.40	*ns*
Others	20	25.10	*ns*
Self-informed vs. Others			.10

the placebo subjects gave indications of physiological arousal. If our general line of reasoning is correct, it should be anticipated that the emotional level of subjects who give indications of sympathetic activity will be greater than that of subjects who do not. The relevant evidence is presented in tables 10.8 and 10.9.

As an index of sympathetic activation we shall use the most direct and unequivocal measure available – change in pulse rate. It can be seen in table 10.1 that the predominant pattern in the Placebo condition is a decrease in pulse rate. We shall assume, therefore, that those subjects whose pulse increases or remains the same give indications of sympathetic activity while those subjects whose pulse decreases do not. In table 10.8, for the euphoria condition, it is immediately clear that subjects who give indications of sympathetic activity are considerably more euphoric than are subjects who show no sympathetic activity. This relationship is, of course, confounded by the fact that euphoric subjects are considerably more active than noneuphoric subjects – a factor which independent of mood could elevate pulse rate. However, no such factor operates in the anger condition where angry subjects are neither more active nor talkative than calm subjects. It can be seen in table 10.9 that Placebo subjects who show signs of sympathetic activation give indications of considerably more anger than do subjects who show no such signs. Conforming to expectations, sympathetic activation accompanies an increase in emotional level.

It should be noted, too, that the emotional levels of subjects showing no signs of sympathetic activity are quite comparable to the emotional level of subjects in the parallel Epi Inf conditions (see tables 10.3 and 10.5). The similarity of these sets of scores and their uniformly low level of indicated emotionality would certainly make it appear that both factors are essential to an emotional state. When either the level of sympathetic arousal is low or a completely appropriate cognition is available, the level of emotionality is low.

Table 10.8 Sympathetic activation and euphoria in the euphoria Placebo condition

Subjects whose:	N	Activity index	p
Pulse decreased	14	10.67	*ns*
Pulse increased or remained same	12	23.17	*ns*
Pulse decrease vs. pulse increase or same			.02

Table 10.9 Sympathetic activation and anger in anger placebo condition

Subjects whose:	N^a	Anger index	p
Pulse decreased	13	+0.15	*ns*
Pulse increased or remained same	8	+1.69	*ns*
Pulse decrease vs. pulse increase or same			.01

$^a N$ reduced by two cases owing to failure of sound system in one case and experimenter's failure to take pulse in another.

Discussion

Let us summarize the major findings of this experiment and examine the extent to which they support the propositions offered in the introduction of this paper. It has been suggested, first, that given a state of physiological arousal for which an individual has no explanation, he will label this state in terms of the cognitions available to him. This implies, of course, that by manipulating the cognitions of an individual in such a state we can manipulate his feelings in diverse directions. Experimental results support this proposition, for following the injection of epinephrine, those subjects who had no explanation for the bodily state thus produced, gave behavioral and self-report indications that they had been readily manipulable into the disparate feeling states of euphoria and anger.

From this first proposition, it must follow that given a state of physiological arousal for which the individual has a completely satisfactory explanation, he will not label this state in terms of the alternative cognitions available. Experimental evidence strongly supports this expectation. In those conditions in which subjects were injected with epinephrine and told precisely what they would feel and why, they proved relatively immune to any effects of the manipulated cognitions. In the anger condition, such subjects did not report or show anger; in the euphoria condition, such subjects reported themselves as far less happy than subjects with an identical bodily state but no adequate knowledge of why they felt the way they did.

Finally, it has been suggested that given constant cognitive circumstances, an individual will react emotionally only to the extent that he experiences a state of physiological arousal. Without taking account of experimental artifacts, the evidence in support of this proposition is consistent but tentative. When the effects of "self-informing" tendencies in epinephrine subjects and of "self-arousing" tendencies in placebo subjects are partialed out, the evidence strongly supports the proposition.

The pattern of data, then, falls neatly in line with theoretical expectations. However, the fact that we were forced, to some extent, to rely on internal analyses in order to partial out the effects of experimental artifacts inevitably makes our conclusions somewhat tentative. In order to further test these propositions on the interaction of cognitive and physiological determinants of emotional state, a series of additional experiments, published elsewhere, was designed to rule out or overcome the operation of these artifacts. In the first of these, Schachter and Wheeler (1962) extended the range of manipulated sympathetic activation by employing three experimental groups – epinephrine, placebo, and a group injected with the sympatholytic agent, chlorpromazine. Laughter at a slapstick movie was the dependent variable, and the evidence is good that amusement is a direct function of manipulated sympathetic activation.

In order to make the epinephrine–placebo comparison under conditions which would rule out the operation of any self-informing tendency, two experiments were conducted on rats. In one of these Singer (1961) demonstrated that under fear inducing conditions, manipulated by the simultaneous presentation of a loud bell, a buzzer, and a bright flashing light, rats injected with epinephrine were considerably more frightened than rats injected with a placebo. Epinephrine-injected rats defecated, urinated, and trembled more than did placebo-injected rats. In nonfear control conditions, there were no differences between epinephrine and placebo groups, neither group giving any indication of fear. In another study, Latané and Schachter (1962) demonstrated that rats injected with epinephrine were notably more capable of avoidance learning than were rats injected with a placebo. Using a modified Miller-Mowrer shuttlebox, these investigators found that during an experimental period involving 200 massed trials, 15 rats injected with epinephrine avoided shock an average of 101.2 trials while 15 placebo-injected rats averaged only 37.3 avoidances.

Taken together, this body of studies does give strong support to the propositions which generated these experimental tests. Given a state of sympathetic activation, for which no immediately appropriate explanation is available, human subjects can be readily manipulated into states of euphoria, anger, and amusement. Varying the intensity of sympathetic activation serves to vary the intensity of a variety of emotional states in both rats and human subjects.

Let us examine the implications of these findings and of this line of thought for problems in the general area of the physiology of the emotions. We have noted in the introduction that the numerous studies on physiological differentiators of emotional states have, viewed en masse, yielded quite inconclusive results. Most, though not all, of these studies have indicated no differences among the various emotional states. Since as human beings, rather than as scientists, we have no difficulty identifying, labeling, and distinguishing among our feelings, the results of these studies have long seemed rather puzzling and paradoxical. Perhaps because of this, there has been a persistent tendency to discount such results as due to ignorance or methodological inadequacy and to pay far more attention to the very few studies which demonstrate *some* sort of physiological differences among emotional states than to the very many studies which indicate no differences at all. It is conceivable, however, that these results should be taken at face value and that emotional states may, indeed, be generally characterized by a high level of sympathetic activation with few if any physiological distinguishers among the many emotional states. If this is correct, the findings of the present study may help to resolve the problem. Obviously this study does *not* rule out the possibility of physiological differences among the emotional states. It is the case, however, that given precisely the same state of epinephrine-induced sympathetic activation, we have, by means of cognitive manipulations, been able to produce in our subjects the very disparate states of euphoria and anger. It may indeed be the case that cognitive factors are major determiners of the emotional labels we apply to a common state of sympathetic arousal.

Let us ask next whether our results are specific to the state of sympathetic activation or if they are generalizable to other states of physiological arousal. It is clear that from our experiments proper, it is impossible to answer the question, for our studies have been concerned largely with the effects of an epinephrine created state of sympathetic arousal. We would suggest, however, that our conclusions are generalizable to almost any pronounced internal state for which no appropriate explanation is available. This suggestion receives some support from the experiences of Nowlis and Nowlis (1956) in their program of research on the effects of drugs on mood. In their work the Nowlises typically administer a drug to groups of four subjects who are physically in one another's presence and free to interact. The Nowlises describe some of their results with these groups as follows:

> At first we used the same drug for all 4 men. In those sessions seconal, when compared with placebo, increased the checking of such words as expansive, forceful, courageous, daring, elated, and impulsive. In our first statistical analysis we were confronted with the stubborn fact that when the same drug is given to all 4 men in a group, the N that has to be entered into the analysis is 1, not 4. This increases the cost of an already expensive experiment by a considerable factor, but it cannot be denied that the effects of these drugs may be and often are quite contagious. Our first attempted solution was to run tests on groups in which each man had a different drug during the same session, such as 1 on seconal, 1 on benzedrine, 1 on dramamine, and 1 on placebo. What does seconal do? Cooped up with, say, the egotistical benzedrine partner, the withdrawn, indifferent dramimine partner, and the slightly bored lactose man, the seconal subject reports that he is distractible, dizzy, drifting, glum, defiant, languid, sluggish, discouraged, dull, gloomy, lazy, and slow! This is not the report of mood that we got when all 4 men were on seconal. It thus appears that the moods of the partners do definitely influence the effect of seconal (p. 350).

It is not completely clear from this description whether this "contagion" of mood is more marked in drug than in placebo groups, but should this be the case, these results would certainly support the suggestion that our findings are generalizable to internal states other than that produced by an injection of epinephrine.

Finally, let us consider the implications of our formulation and data for alternative conceptualizations of emotion. Perhaps the most popular current conception of emotion is in terms of "activation theory" in the sense employed by Lindsley (1951) and Woodworth and Schlosberg (1958). As we understand this theory, it suggests that emotional states should be considered as at one end of a continuum of activation which is defined in terms of degree of autonomic arousal and of electroencephalographic measures of activation. The results of the experiment described in this paper do, of course, suggest that such a formulation is not completely adequate. It is possible to have very high degrees of activation without a subject either appearing to be or describing himself as "emotional." Cognitive factors appear to be indispensable elements in any formulation of emotion.

Summary

It is suggested that emotional states may be considered a function of a state of physiological arousal and of a cognition appropriate to this state of arousal. From this follows these propositions:

1 Given a state of physiological arousal for which an individual has no immediate explanation, he will label this state and describe his feelings in terms of the cognitions available to him. To the extent that cognitive factors are potent determiners of emotional states, it should be anticipated that precisely the same state of physiological arousal could be labeled "joy" or "fury" or "jealousy" or any of a great diversity of emotional labels depending on the cognitive aspects of the situation.
2 Given a state of physiological arousal for which an individual has a completely appropriate explanation, no evaluative needs will arise and the individual is unlikely to label his feelings in terms of the alternative cognitions available.
3 Given the same cognitive circumstances, the individual will react emotionally or describe his feelings as emotions only to the extent that he experiences a state of physiological arousal.

An experiment is described which, together with the results of other studies, supports these propositions.

NOTES

This experiment is part of a program of research on cognitive and physiological determinants of emotional state which is being conducted at the Department of Social Psychology at Columbia University under PHS Research Grant M-2584 from the National Institute of Mental Health, United States Public Health Service. This experiment was conducted at the Laboratory for Research in Social Relations at the University of Minnesota.

The authors wish to thank Jean Carlin and Ruth Hase, the physicians in the study, and Bibb Latané and Leonard Weller, who were the paid participants.

[1] Though our experiments are concerned exclusively with the physiological changes produced by the injection of adrenalin, which appear to be primarily the result of sympathetic excitation, the term "physiological arousal" is used in preference to the more specific "excitation of the sympathetic nervous system" because there are indications, to be discussed later, that this formulation is applicable to a variety of bodily states.

[2] This suggestion is not new, for several psychologists have suggested that situational factors should be considered the chief differentiators of the emotions. Hunt, Cole, and Reis (1958) probably make this point most explicitly in their study distinguishing among fear, anger, and sorrow in terms of situational characteristics.

[3] In his critique of the James–Lange theory of emotion, Cannon (1929) also makes the point that sympathectomized animals and patients do seem to manifest emotional behavior. This criticism is, of course, as applicable to the above proposition as it was to the James–Lange formulation. We shall discuss the issues involved in later papers.

[4] It was, of course, imperative that the sequence with the stooge begin before the subject felt his first symptoms, for otherwise the subject would be virtually forced to interpret his feelings in terms of events preceding the stooge's entrance. Pretests had indicated that, for most subjects, epinephrine-caused symptoms began within 3–5 minutes after injection. A deliberate attempt was made then to bring in the stooge within 1 minute after the subject's injection.

REFERENCES

Ax, A.F. Physiological differentiation of emotional states. *Psychosom. Med.*, 1953, *15*, 433–42.

Cannon, W.B. *Bodily changes in pain, hunger, fear and rage.* (2nd edn) New York: Appleton, 1929.

Cantril, H., and Hunt, W.A. Emotional effects produced by the injection of adrenalin. *Amer. J. Psychol.*, 1932, *44*, 300–7.

Festinger, L. A theory of social comparison processes. *Hum. Relat.*, 1954, *7*, 114–40.

Hunt, J.McV., Cole, M.W., and Reis, E.E. Situational cues distinguishing anger, fear, and sorrow. *Amer. J. Psychol.*, 1958, *71*, 136–51.

James, W. *The principles of psychology.* New York: Holt, 1890.

Landis, C., and Hunt, W.A. Adrenalin and emotion. *Psychol. Rev.*, 1932, *39*, 467–85.

Latané, B., and Schachter, S. Adrenalin and avoidance learning. *J. Comp. Physiol. Psychol.*, 1962, *65*, 369–72.

Lindsley, D.B. Emotion. In S.S. Stevens (ed.), *Handbook of experimental psychology.* New York: Wiley, 1951. Pp. 473–516.

Marañon, G. Contribution à l'étude de l'action émotive de l'adrénaline. *Rev. Française Endocrinol.*, 1924, *2*, 301–25.

Nowlis, V., and Nowlis, H.H. The description and analysis of mood. *Ann. N. Y. Acad. Sci.*, 1956, *65*, 345–55.

Ruckmick, C.A. *The psychology of feeling and emotion.* New York: McGraw-Hill, 1936.

Schachter, J. Pain, fear, and anger in hypertensives and normotensives: A psychophysiologic study. *Psychosom. Med.*, 1957, *19*, 17–29.

Schachter, S. *The psychology of affiliation.* Stanford, CA: Stanford University Press, 1959.

Schachter, S., and Wheeler, L. Epinephrine, chlorpromazine, and amusement. *J. Abnorm. Soc. Psychol.*, 1962, *65*, 121–8.

Singer, J.E. The effects of epinephrine, chlorpromazine and dibenzyline upon the fright responses of rats under stress and non-stress conditions. Unpublished doctoral dissertation, University of Minnesota, 1961.

Wolf, S., and Wolff, H.G. *Human gastric function.* New York: Oxford University Press, 1947.

Woodworth, R.S., and Schlosberg, H. *Experimental psychology.* New York: Holt, 1958.

Wrightsman, L.S. Effects of waiting with others on changes in level of felt anxiety. *J. Abnorm. Soc. Psychol.*, 1960, *61*, 216–22.

Constants across cultures in the face and emotion

P. Ekman and W.V. Friesen

Theoretical Background

Editors' Introduction

The extent to which facial expressions of emotion are universal across cultures or culture-specific is a research question of long-standing importance in the psychology of emotion. Those theorists who regard emotions as phenomena that are learned, much as language has to be learned, argue that there are important differences between cultures with regard to the way in which emotions are expressed, and/or with regard to the meanings that are attached to given expressions. Those theorists who regard emotions as phenomena with a strong inherited component argue that there are fundamental similarities across cultures with regard to both the way in which at least some emotions are expressed in the face and the way in which certain expressions are interpreted by others. Ekman and Friesen (1969) developed a theoretical framework in which they tried to reconcile these differing perspectives by arguing that although there is cultural variability with respect to (1) the kinds of stimulus that elicit certain emotions and (2) the rules governing the appropriateness of expressing one's emotions in public, there is universality with respect to the fundamental relationship between subjectively experienced emotion and facial expressive behaviour. That is, although there may well be variation across cultures with respect to what makes one feel afraid, and with respect to whether one is supposed or allowed to express one's fear in public, there is nevertheless a fundamental consistency across cultures in the way that one expresses the feeling of fear in the face. If one feels afraid, and providing there are no social rules leading one to hide the display of one's fear, then persons in all cultures will express fear the same way, and this expression will be recognized as an expression of fear by persons in all cultures. This is the 'hypothesized universal element' referred to by Ekman and Friesen in the introduction to the present paper.

A strong test of this argument requires researchers to examine the way in which facial expressions are made and interpreted in cultures that have had little contact with western print or electronic media. This is exactly what Ekman and Friesen did in the research reported in this paper. They had already made one attempt to study 'preliterate' cultures (Ekman et al., 1969), but the people who participated in that research were those who had had a reasonable amount of contact with westerners. Thus evidence of consistency across cultures could be interpreted as showing that members of preliterate cultures had 'learned' the rules of emotional expression adhered to by westerners. More convincing would be research on members of preliterate cultures who had had no (or at least minimal) contact with western culture. This was the primary objective of the present research.

Journal of Personality and Social Psychology (1971), 17:124–9.

Hypothesis

The hypothesis tested in this research is that members of a preliterate culture who were selected on the basis that they had had minimal contact with literate cultures would associate the same faces with certain emotions as do members of these literate cultures. More specifically, the hypothesis was that members of the preliterate culture would interpret a set of photographs depicting facial expressions in the same way as do most members of literate cultures. Note that the 'preliterate/literate' distinction made by the researchers actually has little to do with literacy per se; rather, it is a way of distinguishing between cultures that have a lot of visual contact with each other, through exposure to face-to-face interaction and shared media (i.e. literate cultures), and cultures that have little visual contact with other cultures (i.e. preliterate cultures). Of course, many preliterate cultures *do* have plenty of visual contact with other cultures; an important attribute of the culture studied by Ekman and Friesen was its relative geographical remoteness and consequent cultural isolation at the time the research was conducted.

Design

The main independent variable in this study was the emotion that had to be interpreted by the participants. Six emotions were used: happiness, anger, sadness, disgust, surprise and fear. Previous research in western cultures had shown that these six emotions are associated with distinctive facial expressions. Less central independent variables were the sex of the participant, the age of the participant (in the case of children), and the degree of contact he or she had had with western culture. The main dependent variable was the percentage of participants who 'correctly' classified the stimulus photographs.

Method

The research was conducted in the highlands of New Guinea, using as participants members of the Fore linguistic-cultural group. As explained by the authors, conducting research on how members of a preliterate culture interpret facial expressions poses special problems. Obviously, one cannot present a respondent with a photographed expression and a written list of emotion terms and ask him or her to select the appropriate term from this list. In pilot research, Ekman and Friesen had tried reading the list of emotion terms to participants, but this clearly places demands on short-term memory, and also has the disadvantage that each English emotion term has to be translated into a single term in the Fore language. To overcome this problem, the researchers prepared short stories describing situations in which the protagonist would experience an emotion. This story was read to the participants, and they were then asked to choose which of three (in the case of adults) or two (in the case of children) photographs depicted the face of the protagonist. Notice that some of the stories do explicitly mention the target emotion but others (surprise and disgust) do not. The photographs were ones in which the target emotion had been 'correctly' recognized by at least 70 per cent of respondents in literate cultures. Although it is not explicitly stated in the paper, the photographs all depicted

Caucasians. The 'correct' expression for a given story was presented along with two (for adults) or one (for children) 'incorrect' expressions. Rather than presenting each correct photograph with all possible combinations of incorrect photographs, the researchers selected combinations of photographs that included the most difficult ones to discriminate (e.g. anger from disgust, fear from surprise). The stories were told to participants by a bilingual member of their own culture. Ekman and Friesen report that these translators were carefully trained to ensure that they presented the stories in a standard way.

Results

The principal findings are reported in Tables 10.10 and 10.11. Table 10.10 shows the results for adult participants, Table 10.11 those for children. The results are expressed in terms of the percentage of respondents who selected the correct expression. To analyse the data, Ekman and Friesen conducted a series of binomial tests. These are non-parametric tests comparing the observed percentage correct with the percentage correct that would be expected by chance (i.e. 33 per cent for the adults, 50 per cent for the children). Table 10.10 shows that adults' correct choices were significantly above chance for all discriminations except those where 'fear' was the target and 'surprise' was one of the two incorrect expressions (last three rows of Table 10.10). Table 10.11 shows that children's correct choices were all significantly above chance, although they were not asked to choose between 'fear' and 'surprise' when 'fear' was the target emotion. Further analyses using *t*-tests found no significant differences between males and females (among either adults or children), between more westernized and less westernized participants, or between older and younger children.

Discussion

The results provide good support for the hypothesis. Faces that are judged by members of literate cultures as good exemplars of the six emotions studied here were associated with the same emotions by members of a remote, preliterate culture who had had little contact with westerners. Note that in the Discussion section of their paper, Ekman and Friesen briefly refer to another study in which Fore participants were asked to pose the faces they associated with certain emotions; these expressions were videotaped and shown to US college students, who 'accurately' judged the intended emotion. Although we are given no detailed information about this study (it is reported more fully in Ekman, 1972), the authors use it to reject the argument that the Fore participants in their main study were able to choose the correct photograph because they had learned to recognize the way in which westerners express emotions. Ekman and Friesen reason that it is unlikely that this learning would enable them to pose the 'western' expression, as well as recognize it in others. Other arguments for rejecting the 'learning' explanation are that neither degree of westernization nor sex of participant made a difference to the performance of the Fore adults, despite the fact that there were large differences (among males) in degree of westernization, and males had on average more contact with westerners than did females. The one aspect of the findings that did not support the hypothesis – the failure of Fore adults to discriminate fear from surprise, when fear was the target emotion – is explained by the authors as reflecting the fact that in Fore culture fearful events tend also to be surprising.

Thus the explanation preferred by Ekman and Friesen is the universalist one: particular facial expressions are universally associated with particular emotions. Notice that they are careful not to jump to the conclusion that this universality must reflect the influence of innate neural programmes: they also acknowledge that it might reflect the fact that humans in all cultures are exposed to a common set of learning experiences. Cross-cultural consistency in recognition of facial expression is nevertheless often regarded as evidence for the innateness of a facial affect programme that links subjective experience to facial displays. It is even seen by some as evidence for the innateness of facial display recognition. However, as Ekman (1989) acknowledges, there is as yet no definitive research ruling out a species-constant learning explanation.

Furthermore, there are grounds for questioning some aspects of the evidence for universality of facial display recognition. Russell (1994) has argued that this evidence is not as strong as it is sometimes claimed or assumed to be. Indeed, his review of the literature on this issue led him to conclude that there are systematic differences between western, non-western/literate, and non-western/illiterate judges with respect to how they label facial expressions of emotion. He also criticizes the methodology typically used in this research, including the methods used by Ekman and Friesen in the present study. Russell's (1994) review generated a lively debate with Ekman and Izard, who are advocates of the universalist position (see Ekman, 1994; Izard, 1994; Russell, 1995). Russell's criticisms of the methods used by Ekman and Friesen in the New Guinea research are strongly rejected by Ekman (1994). With regard to the general evidence on universality of facial expressions, Russell argues that there is more variation across cultures than would be predicted on the basis of a strictly universalist position, while Ekman and Izard argue that there is more consistency across cultures than would be expected on the basis of a culture-specific perspective. Meanwhile, the steady disappearance of cultures that are truly isolated from western influences makes it ever harder to conduct strong tests of the universalist hypothesis.

FURTHER READING

Boucher, J.D. and Carlson, G.E. (198). Recognition of facial expression in three cultures. *Journal of Cross-Cultural Psychology*, 11, 263–80. These researchers used a different method to the one used by Ekman and Friesen.

Russell, J.A. (1994). Is there universal recognition of emotion from facial expression? A review of the cross-cultural studies. *Psychological Bulletin*, 115, 102–41. A critical review of the cross-cultural research on this issue, focusing on methodological issues.

REFERENCES

Ekman, P. (1972). Universals and cultural differences in facial expressions of emotion. In J.K. Cole (ed.), *Nebraska Symposium on Motivation* (pp. 207–83). Lincoln, NE: University of Nebraska Press.

Ekman, P. (1989). The argument and evidence about universals in facial expressions of emotion. In H.L. Wagner and A.S.R. Manstead (eds), *Handbook of Social Psychophysiology* (pp. 143–64). Chichester: Wiley.

Ekman, P. (1994). Strong evidence for universals in facial expression: A reply to Russell's mistaken critique. *Psychological Bulletin*, 115, 268–87.

Ekman, P. and Friesen, W.V. (1969). The repertoire of nonverbal behavior – Categories, origins, usage and coding. *Semiotica*, 1, 49–98.

Ekman, P., Sorenson, E.R. and Friesen, W.V. (1969). Pan-cultural elements in facial displays of emotion. *Science*, 164, 86–8.

Izard, C.E. (1994). Innate and universal facial expressions: Evidence from developmental cross-cultural research. *Psychological Bulletin*, 115, 288–99.

Russell, J.A. (1995). Facial expressions of emotion: What lies beyond minimal universality? *Psychological Bulletin*, 118, 379–91.

Prolonged and at times heated controversy has failed to demonstrate whether facial behaviors associated with emotion are universal for man or specific to each culture. Darwin (1872) postulated universals in facial behavior on the basis of his evolutionary theory. Allport (1924), Asch (1952), and Tomkins (1962, 1963) have also postulated universals in emotional facial behavior, although each writer offered a different theoretical basis for his expectation. The culture-specific view, that facial behaviors become associated with emotion through culturally variable learning, received support from Klineberg's (1938) descriptions of how the facial behaviors described in Chinese literature differed from the facial behaviors associated with emotions in the Western world. More recently, Birdwhistell (1963) and LaBarre (1947) have argued against the possibility of any universals in emotional facial behavior, supplying numerous anecdotal examples of variations between cultures.

Ekman (1968) and Ekman and Friesen (1969) considered these contradictory viewpoints within a framework which distinguished between those elements of facial behavior that are universal and those that are culture specific. They hypothesized that the universals are to be found in the relationship between distinctive patterns of the facial muscles and particular emotions (happiness, sadness, anger, fear, surprise, disgust, interest). They suggested that cultural differences would be seen in some of the stimuli, which through learning become established as elicitors of particular emotions, in the rules for controlling facial behavior in particular social settings, and in many of the consequences of emotional arousal.

To demonstrate the hypothesized universal element, Ekman and Friesen (1969) conducted experiments in which they showed still photographs of faces to people from different cultures in order to determine whether the same facial behavior would be judged as the same emotion, regardless of the observers' culture. The faces were selected on the basis of their conformity to Ekman, Friesen, and Tomkins's (in press) a priori descriptions of facial muscles involved in each emotion. College-educated subjects in Brazil, the United States, Argentina, Chile, and Japan were found to identify the same faces with the same emotion words, as were members of two preliterate cultures who had extensive contact with Western cultures (the Sadong of Borneo and the Fore of New Guinea), although the latter results were not as strong (Ekman, Sorenson, and Friesen, 1969). Izard (1968, 1969), working independently with his own set of faces, obtained comparable results across seven other culture–language groups.

While these investigators interpreted their results as evidence of universals in facial behavior, their interpretation was open to argument; because all the cultures they compared

Primary Reading

had exposure to some of the same mass media portrayals of facial behavior, members of these cultures might have learned to recognize the same set of conventions, or become familiar with each other's different facial behavior.

To overcome this difficulty in the interpretation of previous results, it is necessary to demonstrate that cultures which have had minimal visual contact with literate cultures show similarity to these cultures in their interpretation of facial behavior. The purpose of this paper was to test the hypothesis that members of a preliterate culture who had been selected to insure maximum visual isolation from literate cultures will identify the same emotion concepts with the same faces as do members of literate Western and Eastern cultures.

Method

Subjects

Members of the Fore linguistic-cultural group of the South East Highlands of New Guinea were studied. Until 12 years ago, this was an isolated, Neolithic, material culture (Gajdusek, 1963; Sorenson and Gajdusek, 1966). While many of these people now have had extensive contact with missionaries, government workers, traders, and United States scientists, some have had little such contact. Only subjects who met criteria established to screen out all but those who had minimal opportunity to learn to imitate or recognize uniquely Western facial behaviors were recruited for this experiment. These criteria made it quite unlikely that subjects could have so completely learned some foreign set of facial expressions of emotion that their judgments would be no different from those of members of literate cultures. Those selected had seen no movies, neither spoke nor understood English or Pidgin, had not lived in any of the Western settlement or government towns, and had never worked for a Caucasian (according to their own report). One-hundred and eighty-nine adults and 130 children, male and female, met these criteria. This sample comprises about 3% of the members of this culture.

In addition to data gathered from these more visually isolated members of the South Fore, data were also collected on members of this culture who had had the most contact with Westerners. These subjects all spoke English, had seen movies, lived in a Western settlement or government town, and had attended a missionary or government school for more than 1 year. Twenty-three male adults, but no females, met these criteria.

Judgment Task

In a pilot study conducted 1 year earlier with members of this same culture, a number of different judgment tasks were tried. The least Westernized subjects could not be asked to select from a printed list of emotion terms the one that was appropriate for a photograph, since they could not read. When the list was repeated to them with each photograph, they seemed to have difficulty remembering the list. Further, doubts remained about whether the meaning of a particular emotion concept was adequately conveyed by translating a single English word into a single South Fore word. Asking the subject to make up his own story about the emotions shown in a picture was not much more successful, although the problems were different. Subjects regarded this as a very difficult task, repeated probes were necessary, and as the procedure became lengthy, subjects became reluctant.

To solve these problems, it was decided to employ a task similar to that developed by

Dashiell (1927) for use with young children.[1] Dashiell showed the child a group of three pictures simultaneously, read a story, and told the child to point to the picture in which the person's face showed the emotion described in the story. The advantages of this judgment task in a preliterate culture are that (a) the translator recounts well-rehearsed stories which can be recorded and checked for accurate translation; (b) the task involves no reading; (c) the subject does not have to remember a list of emotion terms; (d) the subject need not speak, but can point to give his answer; and (e) perfect translation of emotion words is not required since the story can help provide connotations.

Emotion Stories

With the exception of the stories for fear and surprise, those used in the present study were selected from those which had been most frequently given in the pilot study. Considerable care was taken to insure that each story selected was relevant to only one emotion within the Fore culture, and that members of the culture were agreed on what that emotion was. Since the stories told by the pilot subjects for fear and surprise did not meet these criteria, the authors composed stories for these emotions based on their experience within the culture. The stories used are given below:

> Happiness: His (her) friends have come, and he (she) is happy.
>> Sadness: His (her) child (mother) has died, and he (she) feels very sad.
>> Anger: He (she) is angry; or he (she) is angry, about to fight.
>> Surprise: He (she) is just now looking at something new and unexpected.
>> Disgust: He (she) is looking at something he (she) dislikes; or He (she) is looking at something which smells bad.
>> Fear: He (she) is sitting in his (her) house all alone, and there is no one else in the village. There is no knife, axe, or bow and arrow in the house. A wild pig is standing in the door of the house, and the man (woman) is looking at the pig and is very afraid of it. The pig has been standing in the doorway for a few minutes, and the person is looking at it very afraid, and the pig won't move away from the door, and he (she) is afraid the pig will bite him (her).[2]

Pictures and Emotions

The six emotions studied were those which had been found by more than one investigator to be discriminable within any one literate culture (cf. Ekman, Friesen, and Ellsworth, in press, for a review of findings). The photographs used to show the facial behavior for each of the six emotions had been judged by more than 70% of the observers in studies of more than one literate culture as showing that emotion. The sample included pictures of both posed and spontaneous behavior used by Ekman and Friesen (1968), Frijda (1968), Frois-Wittmann (1930), Izard (1968), Engen, Levy, and Schlosberg (1957), and Tomkins and McCarter (1964). A total of 40 pictures were used of 24 different stimulus persons, male and female, adult and child. The photographs were prepared as 3 × 5 inch prints, cropped to show only the face and neck.

Story-Photographs Trial

A single item consisted of an emotion story, a correct photograph, in which the facial behavior shown in the photograph was the same as that described in the story, and either one or two incorrect photograph(s). Adult subjects were given two incorrect pictures with each correct picture; children were given only one because of a shortage of copies of the stimuli.

Because of a limitation on the number of available photographs, and upon the subjects' time, not all of the possible pairings of correct and incorrect photographs were tested. Instead, the subjects were presented with some of the presumably more difficult discriminations among emotions. The emotion shown in at least one of the incorrect photographs was an emotion which past studies in literate cultures had found to be most often mistaken for the correct emotion. For example, when *anger* was the emotion described in the story, the incorrect choices included *disgust*, *fear*, or *sadness*, emotions which have been found to be often mistaken for anger. The age and sex of the stimulus persons shown in the correct and incorrect photographs were held constant within any trial.

No one subject was given all the emotion discriminations, because again the stimuli would have been too few and the task too long. Instead, subjects from different villages were required to make some of the same and some different discriminations. Subjects were shown from 6 to 12 sets of photographs, but no picture appeared in more than 1 of the sets shown to any one particular subject.[3] A subject's task included making at least three different emotion discriminations; the same story was told more than once, with differing correct and incorrect photographs, and often requiring discrimination among differing sets of emotions. For example, the anger story might have been read once with Anger Picture A, Sadness Picture B, and Fear Picture C; the same anger story might have been read again to the same subject, but now with Anger Picture D, Disgust Picture E, and Surprise Picture F.

Procedure

Two-person teams conducted the experiment. A member of the South Fore tribe recruited subjects, explained the task, and read the translated stories; a Caucasian recorded the subjects' responses. Three such teams operated at once within a village; one team with a male Caucasian worked with male adult subjects; the two others with female Caucasians worked with the female adult subjects and the children. In most instances, almost all members of a village participated in the experiment within less than 3 hours.

Considerable practice and explanation was given to the translators. They were told that there was no correct response and were discouraged from prompting. Repeated practice was given to insure that the translators always repeated the stories in the same way and resisted the temptation to embellish. Spot checks with tape recordings and back translations verified that this was successful. The Caucasians, who did know the correct responses, averted their faces from the view of the subject, looking down at their recording booklet, to reduce the probability of an unwitting experimenter bias effect. Data analysis did not reveal any systematic differences in the responses obtained with different translators.

Results

No differences between male and female subjects were expected, and no such differences had been found in the literate culture data. In this New Guinea group, however, the women were more reluctant to participate in the experiment, and were considered by most outsiders to have had less contact with Caucasians than the men. The number of correct responses for each subject was calculated separately for males and females and for adults and children. The *t* tests were not significant; the trend was in the direction of better performance by women and girls. The data revealed no systematic differences between male and female subjects in the discrimination of particular emotions, or in relation to the sex of the stimulus person shown on the photographs. In the subsequent analyses, data from males and females were combined.

Table 10.10 shows the results for the least Westernized adults for each emotion discrimination. Within each row, the percentage of subjects who gave the correct response for a particular discrimination between three emotions was calculated across all subjects shown that particular discrimination, regardless of whether the photographs used to represent the three emotions differed for individual subjects. Within each row, each subject contributed only one response, and thus the sum of responses was derived from independent subjects. However, the rows are not independent of each other. Data from a given subject appear in different rows, depending upon the particular discriminations he was asked to make. If a group of subjects was requested to discriminate the same emotion from the same two other emotions more than once, only one randomly chosen response was included in the table.

Table 10.10   Adult results

Emotion described in the story	Emotions shown in the two incorrect photographs	No. Ss	% choosing correct face
Happiness	Surprise, disgust	62	90**
	Surprise, sadness	57	93**
	Fear, anger	65	86**
	Disgust, anger	36	100**
Anger	Sadness, surprise	66	82**
	Disgust, surprise	31	87**
	Fear, sadness	31	87**
Sadness	Anger, fear	64	81**
	Anger, surprise	26	81**
	Anger, happiness	31	87**
	Anger, disgust	35	69*
	Disgust, surprise	35	77**
Disgust (smell story)	Sadness, surprise	65	77**
Disgust (dislike story)	Sadness, surprise	36	89**
Surprise	Fear, disgust	31	71*
	Happiness, anger	31	65*
Fear	Anger, disgust	92	64**
	Sadness, disgust	31	87**
	Anger, happiness	35	86**
	Disgust, happiness	26	85**
	Surprise, happiness	65	48
	Surprise, disgust	31	52
	Surprise, sadness	57	28[a]

*$p < .05$.
**$p < .01$.
[a]Subjects selected the surprise face (67%) at a significant level ($p < .01$, two-tailed test).

A binomial test of significance assuming chance performance to be one in three showed that the correct face was chosen at a significant level for all of the discriminations (rows) except that of fear from surprise. Twice, fear was not discriminated from surprise, and once surprise was chosen more often than fear, even though the story had been intended to describe fear. A binomial test assuming chance to be one in two (a more conservative test, justified if it was thought that within a set of three pictures, there may have been one which was obviously wrong) still yielded significant correct choices for all but the fear-from-surprise discriminations.

The results for the most Westernized male adults were almost exactly the same as those reported in table 10.10 for the least Westernized male and female adults. The number of correct responses for each subject was calculated; the *t* test showed no significant difference between the most and least Westernized subjects. Again, the only failure to select the correct picture occurred when fear was to be distinguished from surprise.

Table 10.11 shows the results for the children, tabulated and tested in similar fashion. The children selected the correct face for all of their discriminations. Through an oversight, the one discrimination which the adults could not make, fear from surprise, was not tried with the children. The percentages reported in table 10.11 are generally higher than those in table 10.10, but this is probably due to the fact that the children were given two photographs rather than three, and chance performance would be 50% rather than about 33%. Six- and 7-year-old children were compared with 14- and 15-year-olds, by the same procedures as described for comparing males and females. No significant differences or trends were noted.

Table 10.11   Results for children

Emotion described in the story	Emotion shown in the one *incorrect* photograph	No. Ss	% choosing the correct face
Happiness	Surprise	116	87*
	Sadness	25	96*
	Anger	25	100*
	Disgust	25	88*
Anger	Sadness	69	90*
Sadness	Anger	60	85*
	Surprise	33	76*
	Disgust	27	89*
	Fear	25	76*
Disgust (smell story)	Sadness	19	95*
Disgust (dislike story)	Sadness	27	78*
Surprise	Happiness	14	100*
	Disgust	14	100*
	Fear	19	95*
Fear	Sadness	25	92*
	Anger	25	88*
	Disgust	14	100*

*$p \leq .01$.

Discussion

The results for both adults and children clearly support our hypothesis that particular facial behaviors are universally associated with particular emotions. With but one exception, the faces judged in literate cultures as showing particular emotions were comparably judged by people from a preliterate culture who had minimal opportunity to have learned to recognize uniquely Western facial expressions. Further evidence was obtained in another experiment, in which the facial behavior of these New Guineans was accurately recognized by members of a literate culture. In that study, visually isolated members of the South Fore posed emotions, and college students in the United States accurately judged the emotion intended from their videotaped facial behavior. The evidence from both studies contradicts the view that all facial behavior associated with emotion is culture specific, and that posed facial behavior is a unique set of culture-bound conventions not understandable to members of another culture.[4]

The only way to dismiss the evidence from both the judgment and posing studies would be to claim that even these New Guineans who had not seen movies, who did not speak or understand English or Pidgin, who had never worked for a Caucasian, still had *some* contact with Westerners, sufficient contact for them to learn to recognize and simulate culture-specific, uniquely Western facial behaviors associated with each emotion. While these subjects had some contact with Westerners, this argument seems implausible for three reasons. First, the criteria for selecting these subjects makes it highly improbable that they had learned a "foreign" set of facial behaviors to such a degree that they could not only recognize them, but also display them as well as those to whom the behaviors were native. Second, contact with Caucasians did not seem to have much influence on the judgment of emotion, since the most Westernized subjects did no better than the least Westernized and, like the latter, failed to distinguish fear from surprise. Third, the women, who commonly have even less contact with Westerners than the men, did as well in recognizing emotions.

The hypothesis that there are constants across cultures in emotional facial behavior is further supported by Eibl-Eibesfeldt's (1970) films of facial behavior occurring within its natural context in a number of preliterate cultures. Evidence of constants in facial behavior and emotion across cultures is also consistent with early studies which showed many similarities between the facial behavior of blind and sighted children (Fulcher, 1942; Goodenough, 1932; Thompson, 1941). Universals in facial behavior associated with emotion can be explained from a number of nonexclusive viewpoints as being due to evolution, innate neural programs, or learning experiences common to human development regardless of culture (e.g., those of Allport, 1924; Asch, 1952; Darwin, 1872; Huber, 1931; Izard, 1969; Peiper, 1963; Tomkins, 1962, 1963). To evaluate the different viewpoints will require further research, particularly on early development.

The failure of the New Guinean adults to discriminate fear from surprise, while succeeding in discriminating surprise from fear, and fear from other emotions, suggests that cultures may not make *all* of the same distinctions among emotions, but does not detract from the main finding that most of the distinctions were made across cultures. Experience within a culture, the kinds of events which typically elicit particular emotions, may act to influence the ability to discriminate particular pairs of emotions. Fear faces may not have been distinguished from surprise faces, because in this culture fearful events are almost always also surprising; that is, the sudden appearance of a hostile member of another village, the unexpected meeting of a ghost or sorcerer, etc.

The growing body of evidence of a pan-cultural element in emotional facial behavior does not imply the absence of cultural differences in the face and emotion. Ekman (1968) and Ekman and Friesen (1969) have suggested that cultural differences will be manifest in the circumstances which elicit an emotion, in the action consequences of an emotion, and in the display rules which govern the management of facial behavior in particular social settings. Izard (1969) agrees with the view that there are cultural differences in the antecedent and consequent events, and has also found evidence suggesting differences in attitudes about particular emotions.

NOTES

The authors are indebted to E. Richard Sorenson, National Institute of Neurological Diseases and Blindness, for collaboration in planning the early stages of this research, and providing background material relevant to understanding of the Fore people. The authors are also grateful to Neville Hoffman, University of Western Australia, for his extraordinary ability to enlist cooperation from subjects and his many useful suggestions about the procedure. The research was supported by Grant AFOSR 1229–67 from the Advanced Research Projects Agency and Career Scientist Development Award 5-KO2-MH060 92 from the National Institute of Mental Health. Patricia Garlan and Robert Kleck provided editorial help on the preparation of this report.

[1] Carrol E. Izard brought Dashiell's procedure to our attention. This method has also been used in recent studies of referential communications (e.g., Rosenberg and Gordon, 1968).

[2] The fear story had to be long in order to eliminate possibilities for anger or surprise being associated with the story.

[3] The number of sets of photographs shown varied among villages, because a limited number of photographs were available in this field setting; the need to assure that the three pictures in any one set were comparable (in terms of the configuration of the mouth, the tilt of the head, and the age of the stimulus persons) restricted the number of sets which could be composed for some of the combinations.

[4] If posed behavior were simply a set of arbitrary conventions, it would be unlikely that the same conventions would be utilized in the cultures discussed here. That does not, however, imply that posed facial behavior is identical with spontaneous behavior. Ekman, Friesen, and Ellsworth (in press) have suggested that most posed behavior is similar in appearance to that spontaneous facial behavior which is of extreme intensity and unmodulated, although it may still differ in onset, duration, and decay time.

REFERENCES

Allport, F.H. *Social psychology.* Boston: Houghton Mifflin, 1924.

Asch, S.E. *Social psychology.* Englewood Cliffs, N.J.: Prentice-Hall, 1952.

Birdwhistell, R.L. The kinesic level in the investigation of the emotions. In P.H. Knapp (ed.), *Expression of the emotions in man.* New York: International Universities Press, 1963.

Darwin, C. *The expression of the emotions in man and animals.* London: Murray, 1872.

Dashiell, J.F. A new method of measuring reactions to facial expression of emotion. *Psychological Bulletin,* 1927, 24, 174–5.

Eibl-Eibesfeldt, I. *Ethology, the biology of behavior.* New York: Holt, Rinehart and Winston, 1970.

Ekman, P. Research findings on recognition and display of facial behavior in literate and nonliterate cultures. *Proceedings of the 76th Annual Convention of the American Psychological Association*, 1968, *3*, 727. (Summary)

Ekman, P., and Friesen, W.V. Nonverbal behavior in psychotherapy research. In J. Shlien (ed.), *Research in psychotherapy*. Vol. 3. Washington, D.C.: American Psychological Association, 1968.

Ekman, P., and Friesen, W.V. The repertoire of nonverbal behavior – Categories, origins, usage and coding. *Semiotica*, 1969, *1*, 49–98.

Ekman, P., Friesen, W.V., and Ellsworth, P. *Emotion in the human face: Guidelines for research and integration of findings*. New York: Pergamon Press, in press.

Ekman, P., Friesen, W.V., and Tomkins, S.S. Facial affect scoring technique: A first validity study. *Semiotica*, in press.

Ekman, P., Sorenson, E.R., and Friesen, W.V. Pan-cultural elements in facial displays of emotions. *Science*, 1969, *164*, 86–8.

Engen, T., Levy, N., and Schlosberg, H. A new series of facial expressions. *American Psychologist*, 1957, *12*, 264–6.

Frijda, N.H. Recognition of emotion. In L. Berkowitz (ed.), *Advances in experimental social psychology*. New York: Academic Press, 1968.

Frois-Wittmann, J. The judgment of facial expression. *Journal of Experimental Psychology*, 1930, *13*, 113–51.

Fulcher, J.S. 'Voluntary' facial expression in blind and seeing children. *Archives of Psychology*, 1942, *38*, 272.

Gajdusek, D.C. Kuru. *Transactions of the Royal Society of Tropical Medicine and Hygiene*, 1963, *57*, 151–69.

Goodenough, F.L. Expression of the emotions in a blind-deaf child. *Journal of Abnormal and Social Psychology*, 1932, *27*, 328–33.

Huber, E. *Evolution of facial musculature and facial expression*. Baltimore: Johns Hopkins Press, 1931.

Izard, C.E. Cross-cultural research findings on development in recognition of facial behavior. *Proceedings of the 76th Annual Convention of the American Psychological Association*, 1968, *3*, 727. (Summary)

Izard, C.E. The emotions and emotion constructs in personality and culture research. In R.B. Cattell (ed.), *Handbook of modern personality theory*. Chicago: Aldine Press, 1969.

Klineberg, O. Emotional expression in Chinese literature. *Journal of Abnormal and Social Psychology*, 1938, *33*, 517–20.

LaBarre, W. The cultural basis of emotions and gestures. *Journal of Personality*, 1947, *16*, 49–68.

Peiper, A. *Cerebral function in infancy and childhood*. New York: Consultants Bureau, 1963.

Rosenberg, S., and Gordon, A. Identification of facial expressions from affective descriptions: A probabilistic choice analysis of referential ambiguity. *Journal of Personality and Social Psychology*, 1968, *10*, 157–66.

Sorenson, E.R., and Gajdusek, D.C. The study of child behavior and development in primitive cultures. A research archive for ethnopediatric film investigations of styles in the patterning of the nervous system. *Pediatrics*, 1966, *37* (1, Pt. 2).

Thompson, J. Development of facial expression of emotion in blind and seeing children. *Archives of Psychology*, 1941, *37*, 264.

Tomkins, S.S. *Affect, imagery, consciousness*. Vol. 1. *The positive affects*. New York: Springer, 1962.

Tomkins, S.S. *Affect, imagery, consciousness*. Vol. 2. *The negative affects*. New York: Springer, 1963.

Tomkins, S.S., and McCarter, R. What and where are the primary affects? Some evidence for a theory. *Perceptual and Motor Skills*, 1964, *18*, 119–58.

11 Interpersonal Communication

Secondary baby talk: Judgments by institutionalized elderly and their caregivers

L.R. Caporael, M.P. Lukaszewski and G.H. Culbertson

Editors'
Introduction

Theoretical Background

This study is concerned with 'baby talk'. Baby talk is what we do when communicating with babies and small children: the pitch of our voices increases, and the intonation becomes more exaggerated, presumably in an attempt to simplify and clarify the communication. 'Secondary' baby talk is the same type of speech, but addressed to persons other than babies or small children. The specific concern of this study is with the use of secondary baby talk to address elderly people residing in institutions such as nursing homes. In her previous research, Caporael (1981) had found that baby talk is often used by caregivers when speaking to the elderly in institutional settings, and that this talk is not distinguishable from that used when speaking to 2-year-olds. However, she was surprised to find that when this secondary baby talk was content-filtered (i.e. the verbal content was electronically removed in such a way that non-verbal information was preserved) and presented to college students, it was judged quite positively. This stands in contrast to a general tendency to find secondary baby talk patronizing. The primary purpose of the present study was to have secondary baby talk judged both by the institutionalized elderly and by their caregivers. The authors expected that the judgements made by the elderly might vary as a function of their dependence on others for care: if you were truly dependent, you might find it reassuring and comforting to be addressed in this way. The authors also reasoned that how this baby talk was judged by caregivers might be related to their expectations about the competency of the elderly care receivers: caregivers with low expectations ought to rate baby talk more positively.

Hypotheses

Two hypotheses were tested in this study. First, with regard to the elderly judges, it was predicted that the more dependent on others they were, the more they would prefer baby talk

Journal of Personality and Social Psychology (1983), 44:746–54.

over other types of speech. Second, with regard to the caregiver judges, it was predicted that the lower their expectations of elderly people, the more they would think that the baby talk would be preferred by care receivers, and the more they would think that it would be effective in interactions with the elderly.

Design

The study is correlational in design. The investigators presented judges with pairs of recorded speech, drawn from three types of message: caregivers' talk to care receivers in baby talk; caregivers' talk to care receivers not in baby talk; and caregivers' talk to other caregivers in 'normal' adult speech. Participants made their judgements by choosing one type of speech from each pair. In order to have care receivers who varied in how dependent they were on others, the receivers were recruited from different kinds of nursing home, in the expectation that those residing in a 'skilled nursing facility' would be more dependent on others and therefore more inclined to make positive judgements of the baby talk. The correlations relevant to the authors' hypotheses are those between care receivers' positive judgements of baby talk and their dependency on others (hypothesis 1); and between caregivers' positive judgements of the use of baby talk and their expectations of elderly care receivers' abilities (hypothesis 2).

Method

The participants in the study were thirty-nine caregivers and sixty care receivers. They were recruited from three nursing homes, identified in the paper as A, B, and C. Nursing home A was the 'skilled' facility, whose residents generally needed a higher level of care. Because there was quite a lot of variation in mobility and mental and physical health within each institution, each resident was individually rated for his or her 'functional ability' by several caregivers. A care receiver's functional ability score was the mean of the ratings made by the different caregivers. These ratings also provided the basis for the caregivers' expectation scores regarding the functional ability of elderly care receivers. A caregiver's expectation score was the mean of the ratings she gave for the five or six care receivers she was asked to judge. Three kinds of caregiver speech were presented on audiotape (baby talk to care receivers, non-baby talk to care receivers, and 'normal' adult speech). Thirty taped messages were used as the stimuli in this study, one example of each speech type from each of ten caregivers. These tapes had been previously recorded in institutional settings and were carefully selected on the basis of pretests. The tapes were electronically filtered so that the verbal content could not be decoded. To make the judgement task manageable for the elderly care receivers, the messages were presented in pairs, and the elderly judges were asked to identify which one in each pair they preferred. Note that they were told that the study was concerned with talk in nursing homes, and the general instruction was to choose the voice that elderly people 'like you' prefer. Caregivers listened to the stimulus tape twice: first, they were asked to say which one in each pair of messages they thought would be better liked by care receivers; then they were asked to identify which one they thought would be more effective in dealing with care receivers.

Results

Table 11.2 shows the mean functional ability scores of the care receivers in the three institutions. High scores indicate less functional ability. As expected, residents of institution A had significantly higher scores than did those in the other two institutions, who did not differ significantly from each other. This helps to validate the functional ability measure. Preference for baby talk among care receivers was measured by counting the number of times they chose the baby talk message in preference to one of the other two types. Caregivers' judgements of baby talk were scored in a similar way. A further measure taken from each group reflected their preference for normal adult speech over non-baby-talk, when pairings of these two messages were presented. Two kinds of result support the authors' first hypothesis. First, care receivers' preference for baby talk was greater in institution A than in the other two institutions. Second, there was a significant correlation between care receivers' functional ability scores and their preference for baby talk. Figure 11.1 shows the results of simultaneously analysing the relationships between care receivers' preference for baby talk and (a) whether or not they lived in institution A and (b) their functional ability score. Although we are not told whether all paths of this model are significant, the results suggest that care receivers' preference for baby talk is a function of both the type of institution in which they reside and their personal functional ability score. By contrast, care receivers' preference for adult speech was not related to their functional ability. Turning to the authors' second hypothesis, table 11.3 shows the correlations between caregivers' expectancy scores and their judgements of the messages. Focusing on the overall expectancy scores, it can be seen that high expectancy scores (reflecting *lower* expectations of the elderly's abilities) were significantly related to judgements that the baby-talk messages would be both better liked by care receivers and more effective in dealing with them. Moreover, there was a tendency for low expectations of the elderly's abilities to be related to judgements that care receivers would like normal adult speech less than non-baby-talk speech addressed to care receivers, and that normal adult speech would be less effective than non-baby-talk speech in dealing with elderly care receivers.

Discussion

The findings clearly support the authors' idea that elderly care receivers' preference for baby talk would depend on their functional ability. Those who were more dependent on others made more positive judgements of baby talk. Those who were less dependent on others tended to prefer other kinds of talk. One way to interpret these findings is that baby talk denotes that the target of the message is perceived as needing to be cared for, and this perception is welcomed by those who actually are in need of care but may be resented by those who are more independent. These findings are echoed by those for the caregivers. Caregivers with low expectations of the elderly were more likely to predict that care receivers would prefer the baby talk, and were more likely to believe that the baby talk would be effective in dealing with care receivers. To the extent that caregivers' expectations of the elderly do not accurately reflect the elderly's abilities, we could interpret these findings as suggesting that caregivers' use of baby talk when addressing elderly care receivers is driven more by their own expectations than by the real needs of the receivers. In particular, there is a danger that the use of baby talk may communicate expectations to the receivers which then become self-fulfilling: being treated as if one is dependent on others may encourage one to become dependent on others (cf. Snyder et al., 1977). However, it is worth noting that the present study does not show that caregivers who have low expectations of care receivers also use more baby talk when they actually address elderly care receivers.

FURTHER READING

Ryan, E.B., Bartolucci, G., Giles, H. and Henwood, K. (1986). Psycholinguistic and social psychological components of communication by and with older adults. *Language and Communication*, 6, 1–22. The authors argue that the type of adjustments made when speaking to the elderly may be mediated by stereotypes concerning competence, but may also be a way of establishing social control.

Snyder, M., Tanke, E.D. and Berscheid, E. (1977). Social perception and interpersonal behavior: On the self-fulfilling nature of social stereotypes. *Journal of Personality and Social Psychology*, 35, 656–66. A classic experimental demonstration of the self-fulfilling prophecy.

REFERENCES

Caporael, L.R. (1981). The paralanguage of caregiving: Baby talk to the institutionalized aged. *Journal of Personality and Social Psychology*, 40, 876–84.

- - - - -
Primary
Reading
- - - - - - - -

Baby talk is one of a set of several speech registers that simplify, clarify, and add affect to language (Ferguson, 1977). Most research on the baby talk register has investigated primary baby talk, which is operationally defined as all speech addressed to 2- to 5-year-olds – regardless of tonal variations (Snow and Ferguson, 1997). Yet most of us are casually aware of, and occasionally offended by, what is colloquially known as baby talk in other contexts. This baby talk speech is called "secondary" or "displaced" baby talk (Ferguson, 1977). The vernacular identification of baby talk, and thereby its sociolinguistic significance, is not based on a taxonomy of linguistic co-ocurrence rules, nor on a catalog of contexts. Rather, the hallmark of baby talk is its high pitch and exaggerated intonation contour (Brown, 1977; Caporael, 1981; Garnica, 1977). The anecdotal and empirical evidence merely confirms the distinctive properties of a voice register that we intuitively identify: We know baby talk when we hear it.

Secondary baby talk is relevant for two research areas, although it has been extensively studied in neither. First, it is significant as a comparison register for research on the role of primary baby talk in language acquisition because a speaker is not trying to teach language in these secondary contexts. Second, it is significant for vocal nonverbal communication research because the affect and expectancies communicated in the voice can influence a listener's emotional and behavioral response (Harper, Wiens, and Matarazzo, 1978; Weitz, 1979).

Secondary baby talk is widely reported anecdotally. The high pitch-exaggerated intonation pattern was noted at least 2,000 years ago by Varro, a Roman grammarian, and extensive ethnographic research strongly suggests baby talk is universal among human languages

(Ferguson, 1964, 1977). Sachs (1977) argues that the vocal features are part of a human "species-specific" communication pattern, but it is also significant in interspecies communication with some animals – dogs, as any dog owner can verify, and chimpanzees (Premack, Woodruff, and Kennel, 1979). In communication between adults, baby talk can reinforce the speaker's own feeling of nurturance, communicate affection, indicate playful intimacy, suggest senility or sickness by signaling the childhood status of the adult, and provide a wealth of possibilities for irony, humor, and insult. Baby talk is as much a device for the political wit as it is for a concerned family member or a hospital staff person.

The use of baby talk to address elderly people in institutions is the only secondary use of baby talk that has been systematically studied. Caporael (1981; Culbertson and Caporael, reference note 1) conducted a field study and two judgment studies to empirically verify and describe caregivers' use of baby talk in an institutional setting. Three kinds of speech were distinguished and used in the judgment studies: baby talk, speech to the elderly that was not in baby talk, and speech between caregivers. The major conclusions were that baby talk was a significant feature in the elderly participants' language environment; baby talk to elderly adults was not distinguishable on the basis of vocal intonation from baby talk to 2-year-old children; and content-filtered baby talk messages with no information given about the identity of the target conveyed a comforting message (relative to adult speech and non-baby-talk speech) to college student judges. This last finding was surprising because most competent adults seem to interpret baby talk to adults as pejorative (Brown, 1977; Taylor, 1979). But it is possible that baby talk in caretaking settings is used to convey nurturance, and the attribution of the meaning is related to the listener's evaluation of its appropriateness. The college students' ratings of baby talk may reflect a positive affect fundamental to baby talk and/or an inference that the baby talk was speech to children and therefore appropriate.

One purpose of this study was to replicate and clarify the findings on judgments of baby talk by working with institutionalized elderly adults. In addition, we investigated the relationship between characteristics of the elderly and their judgments of baby talk. There are conflicting "pejorative" versus "nurturant" evaluations of baby talk to hospitalized and elderly patients (Brown, 1977; Ferguson, 1964, 1977; Taylor, 1979). Caporael (1981) suggested that elderly who are "truly dependent" may interpret baby talk as a reassurance of caretaking, implying that people's competence or functional ability is related to their evaluations of baby talk when they are the speech targets.

A second question was derived from previously observed variation in the use of baby talk within the institution (Caporael, 1981). The use of baby talk by different caregivers ranged from about 7% to 30% of all recorded speech production, but the caregivers' ratings of the dependent or likable attributes of care receivers were not correlated with caregivers' speech. An alternative hypothesis is that the caregivers themselves have a range of expectations about the competency of the elderly, and these expectancies govern the production of baby talk. The importance of expectancy effects in "real world" environments has already been demonstrated, and laboratory research indicates that tone of voice can be a potent medium for the transmission of expectations (Rosenthal, 1976; Rosenthal and Rubin, 1978). We examined the relationship between the expectancies of caregivers and their endorsements of speech that would be effective for interacting with the elderly and that elderly people would like. Because production data are difficult to obtain, endorsement was used as a substitute variable for production.

Aged care receivers and their caregivers at two health-related facilities and one skilled nursing home participated in the study. Each caregiver rated several residents in her facility on daily living activities, sensory and communication impairments, behavioral disruptions, and social functioning. The ratings were the basis for both care receivers' functional ability scores and caregivers' expectancy scores. Both care receivers and caregivers judged vocal nonverbal messages prepared from audiotapes of caregivers interacting with their co-workers and elderly residents. The stimulus tape, made unintelligible by rerecording through a low band-pass filter, consisted of caregiver speech to care receivers in baby talk, speech to them not in baby talk, and speech to other caregivers. The messages were presented as pair comparisons, and judges were asked to pick one of the pair. Care receivers judged which voice of the pair they liked better. At the two health-related facilities, but not at the skilled nursing home, care receivers also judged the stimuli on the dimensions of "soothing" and "irritating." All caregivers predicted which voice in the pair elderly people would like better and which voice would be most effective for interacting with the elderly.

We hypothesized that the lower a care receiver's functional ability, the more likely he or she would prefer baby talk to the other speech types. For caregivers, we hypothesized that lower expectancy of elderly people's ability would be related to endorsement of baby talk as more liked by elderly people and as more effective for interacting with them.

Hypotheses on the soothing and irritating qualities of the messages were less clear. Although almost any organism can indicate preference in a pair-comparison task, it is a far more difficult task to assess the relevance of a specific quality or to judge relative quantity. The redundant judgments of soothing and irritating were an attempt not only to identify subjective qualities of messages that would bear on the preference judgments but also to provide a check on the meaningfulness of "soothing" and "irritating" as descriptions of baby talk. The two dimensions should be inversely related to each other; soothing should be positively related to liking, whereas irritating should be negatively related to liking.

Method

Setting and participants

Three nursing homes, A, B, and C, participated in the study. Institution A was a skilled nursing facility that was part of a larger residential and hospital complex. Approximately 45 care receivers, ranging in age from 72 to 99 years, lived on the floor that was involved in the study. Institutions B and C were health-related facilities that provided care for elderly people who did not require extensive nursing but did need help with daily living activities. There were approximately 80 residents at B and 100 residents at C ranging in age from 62 to 100 years. In general, the residents at A had poorer health than residents at B and C, but care receivers at all three institutions varied widely in mobility, activity, talkativeness, physical health, and spells of confusion.

Participants in the study were 39 caregivers (12 in Institution A, 10 in B, and 17 in C) and 60 care receivers (20 at each institution). All caregivers worked on the day shift. With the help of the head nurse at each facility, a list was made of the elderly residents who would most likely be able to do the rating task. All the caregivers were given this list with the names randomly ordered and were asked to rank order the 10 people they knew best and could rate with the most confidence. The 20 residents in each institution who had the highest combined rankings were asked to participate in the research. Two residents, both in Institution A, were male, and 58 were female.

Procedures

Functional ability and caregiver expectation

Each caregiver independently rated five to six care receivers. The assignment of care receivers for rating was based on the caregivers' initial rankings of the elderly participants. Names of care receivers were distributed so that they could be rated as much as possible by the caregivers who knew them best. For each of the care receivers assigned to them, caregivers completed a functional inventory form adapted from an assessment instrument developed by the New York State Department of Mental Hygiene for use in determining appropriate placement of elderly people in long-term health care facilities (Schneider, 1980). Technical items on specific medical conditions were eliminated. The functional inventory consists of Guttman-type items specific to four general areas: daily living activities (e.g., personal grooming, ambulation), behavior problems (e.g., assaultive, hallucinates), social functioning (e.g., motivation, friendships), and sensory impairments (e.g., sight, communication). For each item, the caregiver indicated the statement that best described the care receiver, which resulted in a score from 1 to 6. The *functional ability* score for each care receiver was the mean of the functional inventory scores he or she received from the several caregivers who rated him or her.

The *expectation* score for each caregiver was the mean of the scores she assigned to the care receivers she rated. We assumed that any given rating was due in part to the real functional ability of the care receiver, and due in part to the caregiver's general tendency to rate care receivers as high or low, influenced to some degree by the caregiver's institutional experience. The procedure ensured an incontrovertible link between measuring functional ability and measuring an *expectation* of the functional ability of a category of people.

Audiotapes

Speech samples for judgments were taken from audiotapes recorded during field studies conducted in two nursing homes, Institution A and a West Coast facility. The same recording, coding, and reliability assessment procedures were used in both settings. Caregivers were equipped with wireless radio microphones that transmitted to a receiver setup that tape-recorded their conversations with each other, care receivers, staff, and visitors. All recording was done during lunchtime as the caregiver carried out her routine responsibilities, which included general supervision of the dining room, serving, and sometimes feeding.

The tapes were coded for three categories of speech: speech to other caregivers, assumed to be normal adult speech; speech to care receivers not in baby talk; and speech in baby talk. Thus, the first two speech types were identified on the basis of their target. Baby talk was identified impressionistically by two experienced field observers on the basis of its exaggerated intonation pattern. To assess the reliability, two naive judges independently rated 10-minute samples of each caregiver's speech. The samples chosen were those the experienced judges indicated had the most baby talk utterances. The experienced judges were considered as one judge for reliability assessment, and Cohen's kappa was calculated for the three pair-wise combinations of two naive and one experienced judge. The z score derived from kappa is an indirect but conservative and legitimate statistic for evaluating the observed agreement between judges' ratings on nominal scales (Hubert, 1977). Reliability figures from the West Coast institution have been previously reported (Caporael, 1981); at Institution A, observed agreement among the three combinations of judges was .72, .52, .52, and the associated z scores were 13.58, 9.28, and 8.66.

Stimulus tapes

The 30 messages used were four- to seven-word sentences, one sentence in each of the three speech registers, taken from the audiotapes of 10 caregivers. Fifteen of the messages were used in a previous study (Caporael, 1981), and the same method and criteria for selection were used for the other 15. In short, voice samples used were the first in the required register with no overlapping speech or interfering noise, roughly equated for sentence form (interrogative or declarative) across speech type. All the utterances were content filtered to make the speech unintelligible.

A check on the identification of the speech types was made by a paralinguistic expert who transcribed the unfiltered 30 messages and categorized them into the three speech registers. Twenty-two messages were correctly identified. Five confusion errors were misidentifications between adult speech and non-baby-talk speech, and three were between non-baby-talk speech and baby talk speech. There was no confusion between adult speech and baby talk.

Participants in a small pilot study objected strenuously to making ratings on a scale from 1 to 7, so it was decided to use pair comparisons for the judgment task. Because this would have made the task too long for most of the elderly judges, five stimulus tapes were prepared, which were counterbalanced for speaker, setting, and order of presentation. Although each stimulus tape contained all the message pairs, only the first 12 pairs were rated by the elderly judges. The messages from each caregiver speaker were arranged in two sets of the three possible pairings of the speech registers (i.e., XY, ZX, YZ), with one set having the reverse order of presentation for the message pairs, and the sets were ordered so that the same number of judgments of each speaker were made within each of the three institutions. Altogether each of 10 speakers was rated 24 times, and each of 60 care receivers rated 4 speakers.

Judgments

Each care receiver participated individually. The study was described as one concerned with talk in nursing homes. The graduate student experimenter explained that she was interested in "what kinds of voices elderly people like you like the best" and then described the comparison-judgment task. She answered questions and, if the care receiver wanted to describe the kind of voice she liked (most did), listened noncommitally. Two sample messages were played to demonstrate the sound of content-filtered voices. The experimenter played the stimulus tape, stopping between pairs while the care receiver indicated a preference for the first or second message. She responded as minimally as possible to commentary during the ratings. In each setting, four care receivers judged the first 12 messages of each of five tapes.

At Institutions B and C, the care receivers rated the stimulus tape three times, judging which voices they liked best, which was the most soothing, and which was the most irritating. The order of presentation of the three dimensions was counterbalanced among care receivers.

The caregivers were run in small groups, and the presentation of the rapes was not completely balanced across subjects. This was not a major concern because all the caregivers rated all 30 messages on a tape. The instructions to caregivers were to choose the voice in the pair that elderly residents would probably like. The tape was replayed, and the caregivers were asked to identify the voice that would be most effective for interacting with the residents.

The judgments could have been partitioned for scoring in a number of ways. Our primary interest was on the ratings of baby-talk speech. Two-thirds of the comparisons judged by a participant included a baby talk comparison. The number of times a person indicated a preference for baby talk was the "score" for baby talk choices. In the case of care receivers, who rated only the first 12 messages on a tape, this score could range from 0 to 8, and for caregivers who rated all 30 messages, from 0 to 20. For the remaining messages, the number of times adult speech was chosen over non-baby-talk was the score for adult speech. This procedure produces two non-overlapping variables.

Results

Functional inventory scale

Item scores were weighted to correct for an unequal number of alternatives for different items. Subscale scores were summed to produce an overall scale score. The functional ability score (FA) for each care receiver was the mean of the ratings assigned by the four to six caregivers. The expectation score (EXP) for each caregiver was the mean of the ratings she assigned to the care receivers she rated. High FA scores indicate low functional ability and high EXP scores indicate low expectation.

Initial analyses examined the integrity of the functional inventory because significant deletions had been made when it was adapted for use. Table 11.1 reports the correlations between the overall score and the subscale scores. Correlations above the diagonal are for care receiver FA scores, and correlations below the diagonal are for caregiver EXP scores. Over the three institutions, the subscales were strongly correlated with the overall scale score and with each other. Neither age nor length of stay in the institution was correlated with functional ability. Additionally, the correlation between age and length of institutional stay was nonsignificant.

If the functional inventory is a valid indicator of functional status, it should distinguish between the skilled nursing facility and the health care facilities. Planned contrasts were undertaken on the functional ability scores across institutions. Table 11.2 shows the means for the three institutions for the total scores and subscores on the functional inventory. For the total FA scores, the A versus B and C contrast (i.e., skilled nursing vs. health care) accounted for 98.5% of the between-institution variance, $F(1, 57) = 39.56$, $p < .001$. The results were similar for the Daily Living Activities subscale, $F(1, 57) = 71.14$, $p < .001$; the Behavioral Disruptiveness subscale, $F(1, 57) = 12.16$, $p < .001$; and the Social Functioning subscale, $F(1, 57) = 17.63$, $p < .001$. The latter subscale also differentiated between Institutions B and C, $F(1, 57) = 4.81$, $p < .05$. The Sensory Communication Impairments subscale was not significant for

Table 11.1   Subscale correlations for care receiver functional ability scores (above diagonal) and caregiver expectancy scores (below diagonal)

Measure	1	2	3	4	5
1 Overall score		.87	.71	.74	.87
2 Daily Living Activities	.87		.52	.44	.60
3 Sensory Communication Impairments	.74	.50		.38	.51
4 Behavioral Disruptiveness	.78	.51	.52		.74
5 Social Functioning	.86	.62	.62	.61	

For all correlations, $p < .002$.

Table 11.2   Mean functional ability scores

Institution	DL	SC	BD	Soc	Overall score
A	34.98	23.19	26.62	26.46	111.25
B	21.40	21.24	22.31	18.63	83.57
C	20.11	21.23	23.65	22.26	87.24

$n = 20$ for each institution. DL = Daily Living Activities, SC = Sensory Communication Impairments, BD = Behavioral Disruptiveness, Soc = Social Functioning. High scores indicate low functional ability.

any of the contrasts, but this is not surprising because the task precluded the participation of elderly persons with sensory or communication handicaps.

We concluded that the functional inventory was an adequate measure of functional status.

Judgments by the elderly

Although the selection procedures were designed to maximize the likelihood that residents who could do the task participated in the study, a screening rule was adopted a priori to remove subjects who seemed unable to do the task. Participants were eliminated prior to any analysis if they selected the same position, either the first or the second message, for all 12 choices. For the remaining subjects, the number of baby talk choices was counted for each care receiver. For "liking," the only dimension on which all elderly participants made judgments, data were obtained from 48 residents (16, 13, and 19 for Institutions A, B, and C, respectively).

The mean score for elderly residents for preference for baby talk was 3.73, which is not significantly different from 4.0 ($t = 1.14$). There is therefore no evidence that overall the elderly residents liked or disliked the baby talk voice tone compared to the other two voices. Likewise, there was no evidence that adult speech was preferred to non-baby-talk speech.

The liking scores for baby talk were further analyzed across institutions. The mean baby talk liking score at the skilled nursing facility was 4.56, whereas the mean at the health care facilities was only 3.31. The A versus B and C contrast ($F = 6.81$, $p < .05$) accounted for 97% of the between-institutions variance. The B versus C contrast was nonsignificant ($F < 1.0$).

The Pearson correlation coefficient between FA and liking for baby talk speech was .42, $p < .002$, indicating a relationship between overall functional ability and preference for baby talk speech.

It is clear that both low functional ability and skilled nursing residency predict liking for baby talk on the same order of magnitude (FA predicts 18% of the liking variance whereas institution predicts 13%). Moreover, these two predictors are highly colinear, as well they should be because FA was designed to measure the relevant differences between the two kinds of institutions. A simple causal model that FA causes both liking for baby talk and institutional assignment – whereas type of institution has an independent effect on liking for baby talk (figure 11.1) – yields .34 as the estimate of the path coefficient from FA to liking for baby talk and .15 as the estimate for institution to liking. Of course other models, including reciprocal causation between FA and institution, would be consistent with the data and would yield somewhat different estimates of path coefficients. But it is unlikely that any reasonable model would yield a negligible path coefficient from FA to liking.

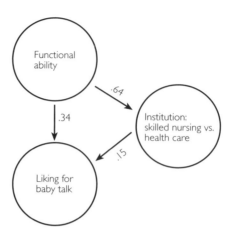

Figure 11.1   Path coefficients for functional ability, institution, and liking for baby talk

One would expect, because of the correlation between total scale and subscale scores, that preference for baby talk would be related to each of the subscales similarly to the way it is related to the total scale. The expected similarity held for the Social Functioning ($r = .42, p < .01$), Behavioral Disruptiveness ($r = .37, p < .01$), and Daily Living Activities subscales ($r = .34, p < .02$) but not for the Sensory Communication Impairments ($r = .22, p < .14$) subscale. The pattern of correlations suggests that the instrument measures a global construct of functional status that is related to judgments of baby talk speech.

Correlations were also calculated between functional inventory scores and preference for adult speech over non-baby-talk speech. None of the correlations approached significance.

It appears that institutionalized elderly people are able to respond to the distinctive features of baby talk and to indicate a preference that is predictable from their functional ability. But it is not possible to predict a preference for adult speech as compared to non-baby-talk speech, perhaps because the small range of possible scores was insensitive to variations in preferences or, alternatively, because of an absence of distinctive features between these two speech types. The subtlety of the variations is suggested by the confusion errors made by the paralinguistic expert who transcribed the messages.

Residents at Institutions B and C rated the speech samples for "irritating" and "soothing" as well as for "liking." It was predicted that judgments of irritating and soothing should be inversely related, that judgments of soothing and a liking for baby talk should be positively related, and that judgments of irritating and a liking for baby talk should be negatively related. For the latter two predictions, the correlations were in the right direction but nonsignificant. There was no suggestion of a negative correlation between "irritating" and "soothing" ($r = .03$).

The lack of the predicted relationships for judgments of soothing and irritating suggests that these are not meaningful dimensions for the judgments of speech by elderly people.

Judgments by the caregivers

For each caregiver, the number of baby talk choices (of 20 possible) and the number of adult speech choices (of 10 possible) were counted for predicted liking and predicted effectiveness. Pearson correlation coefficients between each judged dimension and the caregivers' expectation scores were used to test the prediction that the lower a caregiver's expectation of elderly people is, the more likely she is to predict that elderly people prefer baby talk and to endorse baby talk as a more effective speech register. Table 11.3 shows the correlations between the four judgments and the overall expectancy scores and the subscales scores.

Given that caregiver expectation scores include variance due to actual functional ability and to expectations built up within institutions, the consistent pattern of results suggests a robust phenomena even though many of the significant correlations are low. Overall expectancy was positively related to both predicted liking and predicted effectiveness of baby talk and was inversely related to the predicted effectiveness of adult speech. Predicted liking for adult speech versus non-baby-talk fails to reach a conventional significance level but shows a trend ($r = -.22$, $p = .09$). Although the subscales of the functional inventory are intercorrelated and there was no reason to expect any particular subscale to emerge as especially important for caregivers' judgments of speech, the Social Functioning subscale had the most reliable and consistent relationship to the ratings. Caregivers with a low expectation of elderly people's behavior in a social sphere were more likely to judge baby talk as the most effective for interacting with the elderly and as the most likely to be preferred by the elderly. Likewise, low social expectations of the elderly were related to predicting that the elderly would prefer non-baby-talk to adult speech.

General Discussion

The results show a consistent pattern that qualifies and extends previous research on speech to the institutionalized elderly. The most important qualification is on the preference for baby talk speech. College-student judges (Caporael, 1981) rated baby talk speech more positively than they rated speech to the elderly that was not in baby talk or speech among caregivers. But the students were not asked to make their judgments in the context of any particular speech target. The institutionalized elderly, on the other hand, did not unequivocally prefer baby talk speech. Rather, it was the residents with lower functional ability scores that tended to prefer baby talk speech.

The findings indicate that elderly people who are functioning at a lower level, and who need a significant amount of attention in their day-to-day living, respond positively to baby talk

Table 11.3 Correlations between caregivers' expectancy scores and message judgments

Judgment	Overall score	DL	SC	BD	Soc
Baby talk					
Predicted liking	.27*	.17	.30*	−.02	.46**
Effectiveness	.37**	.17	.42**	.13	.57**
Adult speech					
Predicted liking	−.22	−.18	−.08	−.03	−.39**
Effectiveness	−.40**	−.42**	−.31*	−.10	−.41**

$n = 37$ for all correlations. DL = Daily Living Activities, SC = Sensory Communication Impairments, BD = Behavioral Disruptiveness, Soc = Social Functioning.
*$p < .05$.
**$p < .01$.

messages, perhaps simply because this is the way their caregivers talk or possibly because baby talk communicates reassurance and nurturance. For adults at a higher level of functioning, other speech is more likely to be preferred. The baby talk speech register may be perceived by high-functioning adults as denoting a need for caretaking that is unsuitable for their functional status. More generally, it is clear that whether baby talk communicates pejorative or nurturant affect is in the ear of the target and not just any listener.

The relationships between caregivers' expectations and endorsements of speech registers were quite regular. Caregivers with low expectations of elderly people were more likely to predict that baby talk would be liked by elderly people and would be more effective in interactions with them. The opposite pattern was found for adult speech – caregivers with low expectations predicted that adult speech would not be liked and would not be effective with the elderly.

Thus, the previously observed variation in the use of baby talk, which does not appear to be a "fine-tuning" of speech to match the characteristics of the elderly (Caporael, 1981), may be explained by variations in caregiver expectation. The critical link for this hypothesis is the relationship between the endorsements of speech registers and the proportions of baby talk speech produced by caregivers. Given that voice is an effective channel for communicating expectancy, it seems likely that this relationship would obtain.[1] If so, the use of baby talk would not be genuinely communicative in the sense that communication refers to people responding to the moment-to-moment characteristics or behavior of each other. This is not to say that baby talk is inappropriate to the speech environment of the institutionalized elderly. To the extent that in any conversation a caregiver's expectation is congruent with a care receiver's functional ability, a communication match could occur. It is entirely possible that caregivers choose to interact with elderly people most likely to meet their expectations of the aged. On the other hand, caregivers' expectation could created self-fulfilling prophecies for the elderly, influencing their functional status. This hypothesis suggests not only that some caregivers would promote dependency, as shown in Barton, Baltes, and Orzech (1980), but also that other caregivers may promote independence or at least be less active in promoting dependency. In any event, measurable differences in caregiver expectancy does permit under-taking quasi-experimental approaches for investigating the relationships among expectation, the channels for communicating expectation, and health care outcomes. From an immediate policy perspective, it may be desirable to train caregivers to be sensitive to characteristics of the aged related to a preference for baby talk speech, that is, to actually use baby talk as a fine-tuning communication to the elderly rather than solely as a sociolinguistic register.

The expectancy scores on the subscales are interesting because they suggest the aspects of the aged to which caregiver expectations may be most responsive. One would expect the subscales to show a relationship to endorsements similar to the overall score, that is, that there is some global expectation of elderly people's functioning. This does not appear to be the case. Rather, caregivers' expectation of elderly people's social functioning was a stronger predictor than was overall expectancy score. A weaker, but nevertheless significant, correlational pattern was also found between caregivers' endorsements and their expectation of sensory-communication abilities.

It may be that the variations in caregiver expectancy operate through a social stereotype of the elderly. The subscales evincing the systematic relationships to speech endorsements are those that would be consistent with a common stereotype and be of a level of generality that would be sensitive to individual bias. The social functioning questions were concerned with independence and adaptation to declining capacities, and the sensory-communication questions were concerned with deficiencies in these areas. The Sensory Communication Impairments subscale did not discriminate between levels of institution or relate to elderly judges' preferences, largely because participants with severe sensory-communication disabilities were excluded a priori from the study, yet caregivers demonstrated a systematic pattern of speech endorsements related to expectations on this subscale. The two subscales are suggestive of a common social stereotype of institutionalized elderly people characterized by incipient deafness, failing vision, and loss of independence. The subscales that were *not* significantly correlated with speech endorsements appear to have items at a level of behavioral specificity (e.g., needing to be fed, having hallucinations, being verbally abusive) that would not be included in a stereotypic characterization.

This conceptualization is related to research by Brewer, Dull, and Lui (1981), which demonstrated that elderly people are perceived in terms of meaningful subcategories or prototypes (e.g., elder statesman and senior citizen) associated with distinctive physical, behavioral, and personality attributes. These prototypes play an important role in the recall and evaluation of information about specific people. Although little research has been done on individual variations in prototypes (Mervis and Rosch, 1981), we suggest that prototypes, perhaps influenced by institutional experience, are a "third variable" in the relationship between caregiver expectancy and endorsement of speech registers.

In summary, the research reported here indicates that a caregiver's use of speech appropriate to the care receiver may be related to her expectation of elderly people in general, but the positive interpretations of the speech register by the elderly person is related to his or her functional status.

NOTES

This research was supported by National Institute on Aging Grant AG 02559 to the first author. We are grateful to the health facility administrators, staff, and residents who allowed us to conduct this research; to Nancy Nielsen, Prasad Vukkadala, Candace Ray, and Marianne Haggerty, who were research assistants; to Melvin Hoffman, English Department, State University of New York at Buffalo, for his paralinguistic transcription; and to Marilynn Brewer and Robyn Dawes for their critical comments.
[1] Data on production were available for only 10 caregivers, an insufficient number to allow for an adequate test of the relationship. The correlation between expectancy and proportion of speech in baby talk was in the right direction but failed to attain significance.

REFERENCE NOTE

1 Culbertson, G.H., and Caporael, L.R. Complexity and content in baby talk and non-baby-talk messages to institutionalized elderly adults. Manuscript submitted for publication, 1982.

REFERENCES

Barton, E.M., Baltes, M.M., and Orzech, M.J. Etiology of dependence in older nursing home residents during morning care: The role of staff behavior. *Journal of Personality and Social Psychology*, 1980, *38*, 423–31.

Brewer, M.B., Dull, V., and Lui L. Perceptions of the elderly: Stereotypes as prototypes. *Journal of Personality and Social Psychology*, 1981, *41*, 656–70.

Brown, R. Introduction. In C.E. Snow and C.A. Ferguson (eds), *Talking to children: Language input and acquisition*. New York: Cambridge University Press, 1977.

Caporael, L.R. The paralanguage of caregiving: Baby talk to the institutionalized aged. *Journal of Personality and Social Psychology*, 1981, *40*, 876–84.

Ferguson, C.A. Baby talk in six languages. *American Anthropologist*, 1964, *66*, 103–14.

Ferguson, C.A. Baby talk as a simplified register. In C.E. Snow and C.A. Ferguson (eds), *Talking to children: Language input and acquisition*. New York: Cambridge University Press, 1977.

Garnica, O.D. Some prosodic and paralinguistic features of speech to young children. In C.E. Snow and C.A. Ferguson (eds), *Talking to children: Language input and acquisition*. New York: Cambridge University Press, 1977.

Harper, R.G., Wiens, A.N., and Matarazzo, J.D. *Non-verbal communication: The state of the art*. New York: Wiley, 1978.

Hubert, L. Kappa revisited. *Psychological Bulletin*, 1977, *84*, 289–97.

Mervis, C.B., and Rosch, E. Categorization of natural objects. *Annual Review of Psychology*, 1981, *32*, 89–115.

Premack, D., Woodruff, G., and Kennel, K. Paper-marking test for chimpanzee: Simple control for social cues. *Science*, 1979, *202*, 903–5.

Rosenthal, R. *Experimenter effects in behavioral research* (rev. edn). New York: Irvington, 1976.

Rosenthal, R., and Rubin, D.B. Interpersonal expectancy effects: The first 345 studies. *Behavioral and Brain Sciences*, 1978, *3*, 377–415.

Sachs, J. The adaptive significance of linguistic input to prelinguistic infants. In C.E. Snow and C.A. Ferguson (eds.), *Talking to children: Language input and acquisition*. New York: Cambridge University Press, 1977.

Schneider, D. *Patient/client assessment in New York State, Volume II: Sourcebook of patient assessment instruments*. Troy, NY: Schneider and Associates, 1980.

Snow, C.E., and Ferguson, C.A. (eds). *Talking to children: Language input and acquisition*. New York: Cambridge University Press, 1977.

Taylor, S.E. Hospital patient behavior: Reactance, helplessness or control? *Journal of Social Issues*, 1979, *35*, 156–84.

Weitz, S. *Nonverbal communication: Readings with commentary* (2nd edn). New York: Oxford University Press, 1979.

Channel consistency and inconsistency in the communications of married couples

P. Noller

- - - - -
Editors'
Introduction
- - - - - - - -

Theoretical Background

This paper grew out of an interest in the applicability of certain ideas concerning inconsistency between communication channels to the study of marital communication. A communication channel in this context refers to visual, vocal or verbal behaviour. Visual behaviour refers to anything that can be seen. Vocal behaviour typically refers to the way in which things are said, as opposed to what is said. Verbal behaviour refers to what is said. Obviously, it is possible to

Journal of Personality and Social Psychology (1982), 43:732–41.

say something negative in a positive tone of voice, or with a smile on one's face. These would be examples of channel discrepancies: in the first case a verbal–vocal discrepancy, and in the second case, a verbal–visual discrepancy.

Interest in communication discrepancies grew in the 1960s and 1970s. Bateson and his colleagues (Bateson et al., 1956) developed a theory of schizophrenia centred on the notion of communication discrepancies, and much social-psychological research in the area of non-verbal communication focused on the notion that non-verbal cues are more informative about an individual's state than is what he or she actually says. Especially relevant to the concerns of the present experiment was a line of research developed by Bugental (e.g., Bugental et al., 1971) in which disturbed mother–child relationships were found to be characterized by greater discrepancy between communication channels.

Noller's intention in conducting the present experiment was to examine the extent to which this notion of inconsistency between communication channels could be used to study communication between marital partners. Are unhappily married couples characterized by communication styles different to those of happily married couples? If so, do these two communication styles differ with respect to channel consistency?

Hypotheses

No hypotheses were formally tested in this experiment. However, it is clear that the author expected that the communication behaviour of the couples who participated in this study would vary as a function of the degree of marital adjustment. In particular, she had reason to expect that couples low in marital adjustment would exhibit more inconsistency between communication channels than would couples high in marital adjustment.

Design

The basic design of this experiment is a 3 (marital adjustment: high, medium, or low) × 4 (channel: verbal, vocal, visual or total) × 2 (sex of participant: male or female) factorial, which means that all possible combinations of these three factors are included. An unusual feature of this experiment is that the unit of analysis is a marital couple, not an individual participant. This is entirely appropriate, since the behaviour of husbands and wives when communicating with each other is probably at least partly dependent on the marital partner. Marital adjustment is treated as a 'between-subjects' factor (meaning that couples fell into just one of the three levels of this factor), whereas both channel and sex are treated as 'within-subjects' factors (meaning that a given couple produced communications in all four channels, and from both males – i.e. the husband – and females – i.e. the wife).

Method

Forty-eight married couples participated in the experiment. They were divided into three marital adjustment groups (high, moderate and low) on the basis of their scores on the Marital

Adjustment Test, a widely used measure. They also completed two other questionnaires, one of which (the Areas of Change Questionnaire) assesses the extent to which one partner wishes to see changes in his or her spouse's behaviour. Each couple was then invited to discuss with each other any issues that had been raised by the questionnaires. The idea was that completing the questionnaires would make participants focus on their marriages, and lead them to want to discuss the marital relationship. These discussions were openly videotaped for subsequent scoring.

The videotaped discussions were scored by a trained coder who was blind to the couple's marital adjustment level. Steps were taken to establish that the coder's scores were (1) internally consistent, and (2) consistent with the scores made by an independent coder. The results reported in Table 11.4 show that these consistencies were satisfactory. Four types of coding were made, one for each of the following channels: (1) verbal, made on the basis of a transcript of what was said; (2) visual, made on the basis of a videotape without soundtrack; (3) vocal, made on the basis of a soundtrack without video; (4) total, made on the basis of all information contained on the videotape. Within each channel, each 'thought unit' (roughly corresponding to a speaker turn in a conversation) was scored as positive, neutral or negative. Thus each participant had twelve scores, reflecting the percentage of positive, neutral and negative 'thought units' in each of the four channels of communication. Finally, each participant was given two 'discrepancy' scores, one reflecting the comparison between the visual channel and the verbal channel, the other the comparison between the visual channel and the vocal channel. The 'direction' of any discrepancy (e.g. positive visual/negative verbal vs. negative visual/positive verbal) was also taken into account.

Results

The results are analysed using a series of mixed-model analyses of variance (ANOVAs). The first set of analyses concern what are called 'single channel scores', and assess the degree to which marital adjustment, sex and communication channel influenced the percentage of positive, neutral and negative communications made. The relevant means are shown in Table 11.6, and the results of the ANOVAs in Table 11.5. Positive messages were used more by high- and moderate-marital-adjustment couples than by low-adjustment couples, and were used less in the verbal channel than in the other three. Neutral messages were sent less by low-adjustment couples than by the other two groups. Neutral messages were also sent more often by males than by females, especially within the low adjustment group (see Figure 11.2, upper panel). Negative messages were used more by low-adjustment couples than by the moderate- and high-adjustment couples, and more in the vocal and total channels than in the verbal and visual ones. Females made more negative communications than males did, especially within the low adjustment group (see Figure 11.2, lower panel). Finally, the tendency for low-adjustment couples to make more negative communications was apparent in all communication channels except the visual one (see Figure 11.3).

The second set of analyses concern the discrepancy scores. Mean discrepancy scores are shown in Table 11.8, and the results of the ANOVA are shown in Table 11.7. Note that in this ANOVA the channel factor was replaced by two factors, type of discrepancy (i.e. visual/verbal or visual/vocal) and direction of discrepancy (i.e. more positive in visual channel than other channel or less positive in visual channel than other channel). Consistent with expectations, low-adjustment couples sent more discrepant communications than did moderate- or high-adjustment couples. Furthermore, females sent more discrepant communications than males did. Discrepancies were more likely to involve positivity in the visual channel and negativity in the vocal channel than any of the other possible combinations. Especially interesting are the results depicted in Figure 11.4: these show that the differences between levels of marital adjustment with regard to discrepancies between channels were limited to communications in which the visual channel was more positive than the other channel.

Follow-up analyses checked on two issues. First, how were communications involving positive visual messages but negative vocal or verbal messages coded when all cues were available? The answer is that they were more likely to be coded as positive than negative, but only when the sender was male. Second, to what extent was the finding that females (especially in the low-adjustment group) were more likely than males to send positive visual and negative verbal or vocal communications simply the result of the higher rate of positive visual behaviour in females? Clearly, if females are more positive than males in their visual behaviour, there is a greater chance for them to make more discrepancies of the positive visual/negative verbal or vocal type. To put this point simply, if women smiled all the time, then every time they said something negative, or in a negative tone of voice, this would count as a discrepancy of this type. The 'analysis to test for chance effects' reported in the paper found that if one controls statistically for the higher level of positive visual behaviour in females, then sex differences in type of discrepant communications disappear, suggesting that these differences are indeed the result of the higher rate of positive visual behaviour in females.

Discussion

The findings are consistent with the general expectation that couples differing in marital adjustment levels are characterized by different communication styles. Not surprisingly, there was less positivity and more negativity in the communications between low-adjustment couples. The results of the analysis of discrepancies between communication channels are especially interesting. Low-adjustment couples were more likely than moderate- or high-adjustment couples to send communications characterized by positive visual behaviour but negative words and/or tone of voice. Given that communication channel discrepancy has also been found by other researchers examining 'troubled' relationships, the question is whether a discrepant communication style is a cause of relationship difficulties or the result of problems in the relationship. Both possibilities seem plausible. If one or both partners in a relationship habitually send(s) ambiguous messages, this can result in misunderstandings and thereby generate conflict and resentment in the relationship. Equally, if the relationship is problematic, this may give rise to conflicting attitudes and emotions towards the partner, thereby resulting in a greater number of discrepant communications.

It is almost certainly inappropriate to pose this as an 'either–or' question. Obviously, some individual communication styles will make it more difficult for individuals to enter into or maintain a close relationship (see Check el al., 1985; Manstead and Edwards, 1992). However, it is equally obvious that even those who are highly 'skilled' in their communication style can and do encounter problems in their close relationships, so it would be a mistake to regard all relationship problems as arising from deficient communication in one or both partners. Communication discrepancies may reflect troubled relationships; but these discrepancies may then, in turn, make it more difficult for a couple to resolve the problem in their relationship.

Interesting though Noller's results are, we should not automatically assume that communication channel discrepancy is the hallmark of a troubled marital relationship. In follow-up research Noller (1985) found that when she focused only on *negative* communications, there was no relationship between marital adjustment and channel discrepancy. Instead, low-marital-adjustment couples were characterized by the intensity of the negativity in their communications. Subsequent research has shown that happily and unhappily married couples differ in several respects in the way that they communicate with each other (Noller and Fitzpatrick, 1988). Negative reciprocity, whereby a negative remark made by one partner is followed by a negative remark made by the other, appears to be especially damaging to the future of a relationship (Levenson and Gottman, 1985).

FURTHER READING

Noller, P. (1985). Negative communications in marriage. *Journal of Social and Personal Relationships*, 2, 289–301. A follow-up paper to the present article, analysing the same data in a different way, and arriving at somewhat different conclusions. It is shown that (irrespective of gender or marital satisfaction level), the most common way in which negative messages are sent between spouses is with a smile.

Noller, P. and Fitzpatrick, M.A. (eds) (1988). *Perspectives on Marital Interaction.* Clevedon: Multilingual Matters. A collection of chapters focusing on marital communication. Especially relevant are chs 3, 7 and 8.

REFERENCES

Bateson, G., Jackson, D.D., Haley, J. and Weakland, J. (1956). Toward a theory of schizophrenia. *Behavioral Science*, 1, 363–8.

Bugental, D.E., Love, L.R., Kaswan, J.W. and April, C. (1971). Verbal–nonverbal conflict in parental messages to normal and disturbed children. *Journal of Abnormal Psychology*, 77, 6–10.

Check, V.P., Perlman, D. and Malamuth, N.M. (1985). Loneliness and aggressive behavior. *Journal of Social and Personal Relationships*. 2, 243–54.

Levenson, R.W. and Gottman, J. (1985). Physiological and affective predictors of change in relationship satisfaction. *Journal of Personality and Social Psychology*, 49, 85–94.

Manstead, A.S.R. and Edwards, R. (1992). Communicative aspects of children's emotional competence. In K.T. Strongman (ed.), *International Review of Studies on Emotion* (vol. 2, pp. 167–95). Chichester: Wiley.

- - - - -
Primary
Reading
- - - - - - - -

Interest in channel inconsistency (discrepancies between the verbal and nonverbal components of a message or between the various nonverbal channels) has come in recent years from three separate areas: clinical psychology and psychiatry, with the work on the double-bind theory of schizphrenia (Bateson, Jackson, Haley, and Weakland, 1956); counseling, with its emphasis on congruence in the counselor (Rogers, 1957; Truax and Carkhuff, 1967) and confrontation of lack of congruence in the client (Alger and Hogan, 1967); and social psychology, with a large range of experiments (e.g., Argyle, Alkema, and Gilmour, 1972; Bugental, 1974; DePaulo and Rosenthal, 1979; Ekman and Friesen, 1974; Mehrabian, 1971).

Research findings have included the relative importance of nonverbal cues to verbal cues (Argyle, Salter, Nicholson, Williams, and Burgess, 1970; Fraser, 1976), the primacy of visual cues (Mehrabian and Ferris, 1967; Zaidel and Mehrabian, 1969), and the greater likelihood of communication with conflicting channels in disturbed mother–child relationships (Bugental, Love, Kaswan, and April, 1971).

There is also evidence that messages with conflicting channels are coded differently depending on the sex of both sender and receiver, and to some extent, the age of the receiver (Bugental, Kaswan, and Love, 1970). For instance, where there was positivity in the visual channel and negativity in the auditory channel, a woman's smile was ignored, whereas a man's smile was seen as counteracting the negative message and turning the message into a joke (or tease), at least in this study by Bugental and her colleagues.

This article examines the encoding of married couples from three marital adjustment groups in an interaction situation. The idea was to examine different relationships between channels, particularly differences in the occurrence of discrepancies related to marital adjustment level and sex.

Method

Subjects and procedure

The subjects were 48 married couples used in previous studies (Noller, 1980a, 1980b, 1981). Each couple was seen individually and each member of the dyad was asked to fill in three questionnaires, independently of the spouse: (a) a demographic questionnaire asking for personal details, (b) the short Marital Adjustment Test (Locke and Wallace, 1959), and (c) the Areas of Change Questionnaire (Weiss, Hops, and Patterson, 1973), a questionnaire measuring the amount of change that a person would like to see in his or her spouse over a number of behaviors.

Subjects were divided into three groups on the basis of scores on the Marital Adjustment Test – those couples where both members scored 120 or above were assigned to the high marital adjustment group, couples where at least one member scored 95 or less were assigned to the low marital adjustment group, and all other couples were assigned to the moderate marital adjustment group.[1]

When subjects had completed the questionnaires, they were asked to discuss with their spouses any issues that had been raised for them by this task. It was hoped that this task would make subjects aware of issues in their marriages and motivate them to discuss the issues. Subjects were asked to be honest in their discussions but were told that they need not reveal their actual answers to the questions unless they wished to. This task seemed to be fairly arousing for most couples, whatever their level of marital adjustment, and the questionnaires provided a worthwhile basis for discussion.

The fact that their discussion was to be videotaped was revealed to subjects at this time, but they were assured that they would be able to see the videotape later in the session and could refuse permission for the tape to be used for research purposes if they wished. After asking the couple to continue the discussion until she returned (in exactly 10 minutes) the experimenter switched on the equipment and left the room.

Coding

A verbatim transcript of each couple's discussion was made and the script was divided into "thought units" (Gottman, Notarius, and Markman, reference note 1), which were basically speaker turns. All coding of units was carried out by a trained coder who was blind to the aims of the study and to the marital adjustment level of the couples. Each thought unit was coded four times by the trained coder, once for each channel. (See definitions following.) Coding was carried out over a 9-month period, and all codings of one channel were completed before codings of another channel were commenced.

Intrarater reliability was computed by comparing the coder's ratings of the same tape on two different occasions. The coder recoded tapes of two couples selected at random after all other coding for that channel had been completed. Cohen's kappa (K; Fleiss, 1975) was calculated as a measure of association between the two ratings on positive and negative items. Results can be seen in table 11.4. The percentage of agreement between the coder's ratings for each type of message for each channel were also calculated, with the mean percentage agreement being 78.5%.

Interrater reliability was computed by comparing the experimenter's ratings of the tapes of two couples with the coder's ratings of the same tapes. Again, Cohen's kappa (K) was calculated (see table 11.4). The percentage of agreement between the ratings of the two coders for each type of message for each channel was also calculated, with the mean percentage agreement being 79.8%.

The four codings carried out were:

1   Verbal channel: Each thought unit was coded as positive, neutral, or negative using only the words as they appeared on paper, with no reference to nonverbal behavior.
2   Visual channel: Each thought unit was coded as positive, neutral, or negative using only the information from the visual channel. To achieve this, a separate videotape was made without sound and unit numbers were added to the sound track. This procedure enabled the units to be coded without reference to the script.
3   Vocal channel: Each thought unit was coded as positive, neutral, or negative using only the vocal channel of the sound track. This included verbal content plus any paralinguistic modification.

Table 11.4   Measures of inter- and intrarater reliability between ratings of positive and negative

	Channel							
	Verbal		Visual		Vocal		Total	
Sex of encoder	Inter-	Intra-	Inter-	Intra-	Inter-	Intra-	Inter-	Intra-
Male	.92	.94	.92	.88	.86	.84	.89	.82
Female	.92	.92	.86	.86	.90	.84	.75	.80

4   Total channel: Each thought unit was coded as positive, neutral, or negative using the total information available from the videotape.

Categories used by Raush and his colleagues (Raush, Barry, Hertel, and Swain, 1974) for cognitive (neutral), affiliative (positive), and coercive (negative) items, along with the content categories from the Couple's Interaction Scoring System (Gottman et al., reference note 1; C.I.S.S.) were used for the verbal coding. The affect codes from the C.I.S.S. were used for coding the nonverbal channels.

In terms of verbal categories, units such as "There's not enough happiness in the marriage" or "You never talk to me about anything interesting" were coded negative. Units such as "Which one's that?" or "I'm going to see your mother tomorrow" or "Which friends would you like to see more?" were coded neutral. Units such as "I'm very happy with your appearance" or "I feel very happy with you at the moment" or "You're beaut with the way you help with the house" were coded as positive. In terms of nonverbal categories, behaviors such as frowns, scowls, angry tones, and so on were coded as negative, whereas smiles, grins, expressions of surprise, and so on were coded as positive. Neutral nonverbal behaviors involved an absence of positive or negative characteristics.

Scoring

Two separate sets of scores were calculated at this stage for each subject.

Single channel scores

Each subject was given 12 scores that were, for each of the four channels, the percentage of thought units that were coded positive, neutral, and negative.

Discrepancies

Each subject was given two scores in this category, with each score representing a comparison between the visual channel and one other channel (verbal or vocal). A discrepancy was scored when one channel was coded positive and the other channel was coded negative. Scores were also calculated separately for each direction. For example, a positive visual and negative verbal score (+ −) was calculated separately from a negative visual and positive verbal score (− +). The scores were calculated as a percentage of thought units.

Results

For all results, measures of magnitude of effect (Cohen, 1969; Friedman, 1968) are included with probability levels.

Single Channel Scores

Three 3-way analyses of variance were carried out, one for each type of message. Marital adjustment level was treated as a between-subjects independent variable for this analysis, whereas sex (since the subjects were actually couples in interaction) and channel were treated as within-subjects variables.

Results of *F* tests are presented in table 11.5; means for each cell can be seen in table 11.6.

Positive messages

Positive messages were used more by high and moderate marital adjustment subjects and were used less in the verbal channel than in other channels (Newman-Keuls, $p < .01$).

Neutral messages

Neutral messages were used less by low marital adjustment subjects than other subjects and were used by males more than by females.

The interaction of marital adjustment level and sex showed that although the males generally used more neutral messages than females, the difference between the males and females was particularly large for the low marital adjustment group (see figure 11.2(a)).

The interaction of marital adjustment level and channel showed that although the low marital adjustment subjects tended to have a lower percentage of neutral messages than did other subjects, this was not true for the visual channel.

Negative messages

Low marital adjustment subjects used more negative messages than either of the other groups, and there were fewer negatives in the verbal and visual channels than in the vocal and total channels (Newman-Keuls, $p < .05$). There were more negative messages for females than males, with the difference between the males and the females being greater for the low marital adjustment group than for other groups (see figure 11.2(b)).

Table 11.5   Results for analyses of variance on positive, neutral, and negative units

	Results			
Effect	df	F	p<	*Magnitude (η)*
	Positive units			
Marital adjustment	2, 39	5.356	.01	.464
Channel	3, 117	131.526	.001	.878
	Neutral units			
Marital adjustment	2, 39	6.518	.01	.557
Sex	1, 39	21.304	.001	1.48[a]
Channel	3, 117	1142.725	.001	.983
Marital adjustment × Sex	2, 39	3.86	.03	.406
Marital adjustment × Channel	6, 117	3.43	.005	.387
	Negative units			
Marital adjustment	2, 39	14.721	.001	.556
Sex	1, 39	7.302	.01	.865[a]
Channel	3, 117	14.01	.001	.514
Marital adjustment × Channel	6, 117	3.69	.01	.399
Marital adjustment × Sex	2, 39	6.77	.01	.508

[a] Effect magnitude given is *d*, rather than η.

Table 11.6 Mean single channel scores for males and females at three levels of marital adjustment

Sex	Channel			
	Verbal	*Visual*	*Vocal*	*Total*
High marital adjustment				
Male				
+	7.5	30.1	21.7	31.1
0	89.1	60.0	66.8	62.9
−	3.5	8.2	11.5	8.1
Female				
+	9.8	35.3	25.3	29.3
0	87.2	53.6	66.3	59.3
−	3.0	9.7	9.2	10.1
Moderate marital adjustment				
Male				
+	3.9	29.9	22.3	26.8
0	86.4	53.6	58.9	56.0
−	9.8	15.5	19.5	15.2
Female				
+	6.9	34.2	22.7	33.2
0	83.4	50.5	58.1	51.4
−	9.7	15.1	19.3	16.2
Low marital adjustment				
Male				
+	4.6	25.6	16.7	22.6
0	79.9	59.7	60.4	53.1
−	15.5	14.6	19.9	21.9
Female				
+	3.4	26.9	16.0	21.7
0	72.4	53.7	49.3	42.0
−	24.3	18.7	30.9	35.9

+ = positive messages; 0 = neutral messages; − = negative messages.

The interaction of marital adjustment level and channel showed a tendency for low marital adjustment subjects to use more negatives over all channels, with the exception of the visual channel (see figure 11.3).

To summarize, positive messages were used more by high and moderate marital adjustment subjects and negative messages were used more by low marital adjustment subjects. Neutral messages were used more by males than females, and the difference in neutral message use between males and females was larger for the low marital adjustment subjects than for other subjects. Over all levels of marital adjustment, neutral messages were used more in the verbal

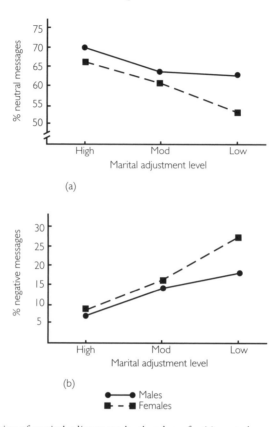

Figure 11.2   Interaction of marital adjustment level and sex for (a) neutral messages and (b) negative messages

Table 11.7   Results for analyses of variance on discrepancies between the visual and verbal and visual and vocal channels

Effect	Results			
	df	F	p<	*Magnitude* (d)
Marital adjustment	2, 39	5.5	.009	.469[a]
Sex	1, 39	6.8	.02	.833
Type of discrepancy	1, 39	60.65	.001	2.49
Direction	1, 39	56.9	.001	2.416
Marital adjustment × Direction	2, 39	7.3	.003	.522[a]
Sex × Direction	1, 39	4.6	.05	.687
Marital adjustment × Sex × Direction	2, 39	3.13	.054	.372

[a] Effect magnitude given is η, rather than *d*.

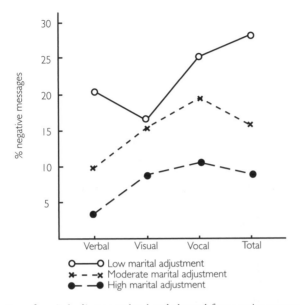

Figure 11.3 Interaction of marital adjustment level and channel for negative messages

Table 11.8 Mean percentage of discrepant communications for each sex and marital adjustment level

Marital adjustment	Channel			
	Visual/vocal		Visual/verbal	
	+ −	− +	+ −	− +
High				
Males	4.5	2.3	1.2	.19
Females	4.23	3.15	1.54	.7
Moderate				
Males	6.14	2.64	2.53	.0
Females	8.0	2.36	3.88	.49
Low				
Males	6.68	2.41	3.84	.31
Females	9.52	1.83	7.31	.00

+ = positive messages; − = negative messages.

channel than in any other, positive messages were used less in the verbal channel than in any other, and negative messages were used less in the verbal and visual channels.

Results of the *F* tests are presented in table 11.7 and cell means are presented in table 11.8. Marital adjustment level was again treated as a between-subjects variable, whereas sex, type of discrepancy, and direction of discrepancy were treated as within-subjects variables.

Analysis of discrepancies

A four-way analysis of variance was carried out using the discrepancy scores – that is, the percentage of thought units on which there was a discrepancy between the visual and verbal channels and the visual and vocal channels. The independent variables for the analysis were marital adjustment level, sex, type of discrepancy (visual/verbal or visual/vocal) and direction of discrepancy (+ − or − +).

Low marital adjustment subjects sent a greater number of discrepant communications than did moderate- or high-adjustment subjects, and females sent more discrepant communications than males. There were more communications with discrepancies between the visual and vocal channels than between the visual and verbal channels, and there were more discrepancies with positive in the visual channel and negative in the verbal or vocal channels than there were discrepancies in the other direction. These latter two results taken together indicate that discrepancies are more likely to involve positivity in the visual channel and that the negativity is more likely to be in the tone of voice or in the words plus tone of voice than in the words alone.

As can be seen from figure 11.4, the interaction of marital adjustment level and direction indicates that the differences between the marital adjustment levels were greater for those discrepancies with positive visual messages and negative messages in the verbal or vocal

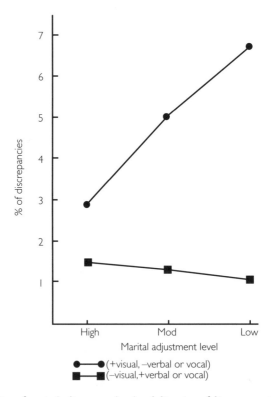

Figure 11.4   Interaction of marital adjustment level and direction of discrepancy. (+ = positive messages; − = negative messages.)

channels. This effect was due to the increase in discrepancies involving positive messages in the visual channel in subjects moving from high to low in marital adjustment.

There was also an interaction of sex and direction, with the differences between males and females being greater for discrepancies with positive visual messages and negative messages in the verbal or vocal channels (see table 11.8).

There was also a three-way interaction of marital adjustment level, sex, and direction. For both males and females, the percentage of communications involving positivity in the visual channel increased in a linear fashion from high to low adjustment, with female scores generally being higher than male scores. There was no such relationship for discrepancies with negativity in the visual channel; as mentioned before, there were few of these.

Analysis of how items with discrepancies between visual and vocal channels were coded in the total channel

A further four-way analysis of variance was carried out to check how the most common discrepant messages, those with discrepancies between the visual and vocal channels, were coded in the total channel. The dependent variable for this analysis was the percentage of thought units with discrepancies that were coded positive, neutral, or negative in the total channel. The independent variables for the analysis were marital adjustment level, sex, direction, and type of coding. Since subjects who had no discrepancies of this type were not included in this analysis, the number of subjects in each cell was reduced to 12.

Results for this analysis indicated that messages with discrepancies between the visual channel and the vocal channel were more likely to be coded positive, $F(2, 132) = 5.3, p < .001$, $\eta = .27$. Newman-Keuls tests showed that such messages were more likely to be coded positive than neutral ($p < .05$), but the percentage coded negative was not significantly different from the percentage coded positive. There was also an interaction of sex and type of coding, $F(2, 132) = 3.7, p < .03, \eta = .23$, with more units being coded positive in the total channel for males (but not for females).

Since the main interest of the study was messages with positive visual and negative vocal components, these were analyzed separately. There was a main effect for type of coding, $F(2, 132) = 4.43, p < .02$. Fewer of these messages were coded neutral than either positive or negative, with more coded negative than positive. The interaction of sex and type of coding, $F(2, 132) = 4.88, p < .01$, indicated that although females had fewer of their discrepant messages coded positive or neutral than did the males, they had many more coded negative.

To summarize, messages with discrepancies between the visual channel and the vocal channel were more likely to be coded positive, particularly for males. Discrepancies with positive meassages in the visual channel and negative messages in the vocal channel were more likely to be coded positive for males and negative for females.

Analysis to test for chance effects

Because of the possibility that these discrepancy results were affected by chance and because the co-occurrence of positive visual and negative verbal messages observed in the wives with low marital adjustment could have been the result of the frequency of these two behaviors in that group, another analysis was carried out to examine the data further.

For each subject, the expected probability of the co-occurrence of positive visual and negative verbal messages was calculated as a product of that subject's probability of using positive visual behavior and their probability of making a negative statement. The subject was then given a score that was the ratio of the observed probability of the target behavior (positive visual behavior while making a negative statement) to the expected probability of that behavior; the scores were then transformed to logarithms. When the score was 0, −1 was used as the appropriate logarithm, since this was considered a conservative estimate of log 0 (minus infinity).

An analysis of variance was carried out using these log transformations as the dependent variables and marital adjustment level and sex as the independent variables. There was a main effect for marital adjustment level, $F(2, 78) = 3.983, p < .03$ $\eta = .30$, showing that when chance was controlled for, high and moderate marital adjustments subjects used fewer positive visual behaviors with negative verbal messages than the low marital adjustment subjects. There was no significant effect for sex and no interaction, but the effects were in the expected direction. The wives in the low marital adjustment group particularly showed more of the target behavior than the husbands. However, this analysis does show that when amount of positive visual behavior is controlled for, husbands in this group are as likely as their wives to use a positive facial impression when making a negative statement.

Discussion

The finding of greater positivity in the high marital adjustment group and greater negativity in the low marital adjustment group is not surprising and fits with previous findings (e.g., Birchler, Weiss, and Vincent, 1975). It should be realized that this finding is at least in part a function of the task in which the couples were engaged.

The finding that neutral messages were used more in the verbal channel than in other channels indicates that a fairly large proportion of communications (about 30% in these couples) involve neutral or ambiguous words, with the message then being modified by one or both of the nonverbal channels (visual or vocal) to become other than a neutral message. The finding that positives were used less in the verbal channel than in other channels indicates that it is particularly positive messages that are likely to be sent in this way.

Also relevant is the finding in an earlier study in the present series (Noller, 1980b) that positive messages in particular come across more negatively than intended, with males especially having difficulty sending positive messages. Since such positive messages are often sent with neutral words, one would expect the males in the interaction setting (particularly the low marital adjustment males) to experience the same kinds of difficulties with sending positive messages that they experienced in the experiment using the ambiguous messages.

The finding that females were more often coded positive or negative, whereas males were more often coded neutral, could be related to the lack of expressivity in males often discussed in the literature (e.g., Balswick and Peek, 1971).

The findings with regard to discrepancies fit with previous data, particularly with the work of Bugental and her associates (Bugental, 1974; Bugental, Kaswan, and Love, 1970; Bugental, Kaswan, Love, and Fox, 1970; Bugental, Love, and Gianetto, 1971; Bugental, Love, Kaswan, and April, 1971). These researchers also found greater use of inconsistent messages by females: Positive facial expressions, particularly smiles, bore little relationship to the verbal content of the message. The fact that previous investigators found this behavior in families with disturbed children and that here it was linked to low marital adjustment implies that this behavior is related to disturbed relationships, though whether as a cause or an effect is not clear. The finding that the behavior increased directly from the high marital adjustment group through the moderate to the low adjustment group (and was almost nonexistent in the high adjustment group) may indicate that it is an effect. However, another possible explanation is that the behavior limits problem solving and hence may be a cause of poor adjustment. Certainly couples in the high marital adjustment group talked of having had problems in earlier times, but said they had worked through the problems to a place of greater intimacy and closeness.

Gottman's finding (Gottman, Notarius, Markman, Banks, Yoppi, and Rubin, 1976) that messages between the members of an unhappy couple were received more negatively than the sender intended is relevant to the present findings, with encoding seeming the most likely explanation. It would seem though, that there could be different reasons for the effect, depending on the sex of the sender. Males could be having a more negative effect than they intend because of lack of expressivity, whereas females may believe that their positive facial expressions are making their messages less negative when, in fact, it seems they are not.

An important question for this research was whether the high co-occurrence of positive visual behavior with negative verbal and/or vocal behavior in the low marital adjustment females was a chance effect due only to the higher occurrence of negative verbal behavior in this group and the greater amount of smiling in the females. The analysis looking at the probability of co-occurrence of these two behaviors showed that this behavior occurred more in low marital adjustment couples than others and that males in this group were also likely to produce discrepant messages.

Another important point is that although males and females in the low marital adjustment group were both likely to produce a discrepant message when they smiled, the women smiled much more and hence their behavior would tend to be more prominent and perhaps have more effect on the relationship.

There has been some discussion in the literature about why these women might smile when they make negative statements. One reason that has been suggested is that women see the smile as part of their culturally prescribed role (Bugental, Love, and Gianetto, 1971) and may particularly use the smile to mask negativity and criticism that does not fit with the warm compliance that is expected. Others have suggested that women smile to appease the person they are criticizing (Eibl-Eibesfeldt, 1970; Frieze, Parsons, Johnson, Ruble, and Zellman, 1978; Mehrabian, 1972), and others have found a strong relationship between approval seeking and smiling (Andrew, 1965; Rosenfeld, 1996).

Other reasons that have been suggested for smiling when being negative that could be relevant for either sex include uneasiness in the situation (Landis, 1924; Mehrabian, 1971), pleasure at the unpleasant action he or she is taking (Mehrabian and Wiener, 1967), and servicing the relationship in the nonverbal channel while disagreeing in the verbal channel (Danziger, 1976; Fraser, 1976).

Although there is evidence that a verbal insult accompanied by smiling generally conveys an affectionate attitude, it would seem to be more true for men than for women (Bugental, Kaswan, and Love, 1970). In the present study, there was also evidence that discrepancies involving negative verbal messages and positive visual messages are interpreted more negatively when sent by females. Relevant here also is the finding of Gottman and his associates (Gottman et al., 1976) with regard to messages from dissatisfied spouses coming across more negatively than intended. These subjects may intend to convey some affection, but the evidence suggests, particularly in the case of the wives, that they are not successful at conveying this affection because their smiles are ignored.

Another group of researchers has suggested that the use of discrepancies may be a deliberate attempt to confuse so that the person using such communication is less accountable for the message and for reactions to it (Ekman and Friesen, 1969). On the other hand, the discrepancy may be merely an expression of the ambivalence that the person feels about the relationship (Morris, 1977).

It is unlikely that a single explanation for these channel discrepancies covers all cases or that any one explanation entirely covers any one case; rather, several processes are occurring together. Marital communication is clearly a complex process and this research is only one step in the equally complex process of gaining some understanding into communication styles that help or hinder marital relationships.

NOTES

Thanks to Glen McBride, Janet Khan, Peter Pamment, Fred Foenander, and Vikki Uhlmann for help with this project, to Ray Pike for help with the analyses, and to the couples, without whom the study would not have been possible. Thanks also to John Gottman of the University of Illinois for making his coding system available, as well as to Robert Weiss of the Marital Studies Program, University of Oregon, for the Areas of Change Questionnaire.
[1] Readers interested in more data about these couples should consult Noller (1980b).

REFERENCE NOTE

1 Gottman, J., Notarius, C., and Markman, H. Couples' Interaction Scoring System (C.I.S.S.). Unpublished manuscript, University of Illinois at Urbana-Champaign, 1976.

REFERENCES

Alger, I., and Hogan, P. The use of videotape recordings in conjoint marital therapy. *American Journal of Psychiatry*, 1967, *123*, 1425–30.

Andrew, R.J. The origins of facial expressions. *Scientific American*, 1965, *213*, 88–94.

Argyle, M., Alkema, F., and Gilmour, R. The communication of friendly and hostile attitudes by verbal and nonverbal signals. *European Journal of Social Psychology*, 1972, *1*, 385–402.

Argyle, M., Salter, V., Nicholson, H., Williams, M., and Burgess, P. The communication of inferior and superior attitudes by verbal and nonverbal signals. *British Journal of Social and Clinical Psychology*, 1970, *9*, 222–31.

Balswick, J., and Peek, C. The inexpressive male: A tragedy of American society. *Family Coordinator*, 1971, *20*, 363–8.

Bateson, G., Jackson, D.D., Haley, J., and Weakland, J. Toward a theory of schizophrenia. *Behavioral Science*, 1956, *1*, 251–64.

Birchler, G.R., Weiss, R.L., and Vincent, J.P. Multimethod analysis of social reinforcement exchange between maritally distressed and nondistressed spouse and stranger dyads. *Journal of Personality and Social Psychology*, 1975, *31*, 349–60.

Bugental, D.E. Interpretations of naturally occurring discrepancies betwwen words and intonation: Modes of inconsistency resolution. *Journal of Personality and Social Psychology*, 1974, *30*, 125–33.

Bugental, D.E., Kaswan, J.W., and Love, L.R. Perception of contradictory meanings conveyed by verbal and nonverbal channels. *Journal of Personality and Social Psychology*, 1970, *16*, 647–55.

Bugental, D.E., Love, L.R., and Gianetto, R.M. Perfidious feminine faces. *Journal of Personality and Social Psychology*, 1971, *17*, 314–18.

Bugental, D.E., Kaswan, J.W., Love, L.R., and Fox, M.N. Child versus adult perception of evaluative messages in verbal, vocal, and visual channels. *Developmental Psychology*, 1970, *2*, 367–75.

Bugental, D.E., Love, L.R., Kaswan, J.W., and April, C. Verbal–nonverbal conflict in parental messages to normal and disturbed children. *Journal of Abnormal Psychology*, 1971, *77*, 6–10.

Cohen, J. *Statistical power analysis for the behavioral sciences.* New York: Academic Press, 1969.

Danziger, K. *Interpersonal communication.* London: Pergamon Press, 1976.

DePaulo, B., and Rosenthal, R. Telling lies. *Journal of Personality and Social Psychology*, 1979, *37*, 1713–22.

Eibl-Eibesfeldt, I. *Ethology: The biology of behavior.* New York: Holt, Rinehart and Winston, 1970.

Ekman, P., and Friesen, W.V. Nonverbal leakage and clues to deception. *Psychiatry*, 1969, *32*, 88–106.

Ekman, P., and Friesen, W.V. Detecting deception from the body or face. *Journal of Personality and Social Psychology*, 1974, *29*, 288–98.

Fleiss, J.L. Measuring agreement between two judges on the presence or absence of a trait. *Biometrica*, 1975, *31*, 651–9.

Fraser, C. An analysis of face to face communication. In A.E. Bennett (ed.), *Communication between doctors and patients.* Oxford: Oxford University Press, 1976.

Friedman, H. Magnitude of experimental effect and a table for its rapid estimation. *Psychological Bulletin*, 1968, *70*, 245–51.

Frieze, I.H., Parsons, J.E., Johnson, P.B., Ruble, D.N., and Zellman, G.L. *Women and sex roles: A social psychological perspective.* New York: Norton, 1978.

Gottman, J., Notarius, C., Markman, H., Banks, S., Yoppi, B., and Rubin, M.E. Behavior exchange theory and marital decision making. *Journal of Personality and Social Psychology*, 1976, *34*, 14–23.

Landis, C. Studies of emotional reactions: II. General behavior and facial expression. *Journal of Comparative Psychology*, 1924, *4*, 447–509.

Locke, H.J., and Wallace, K.M. Short marital adjustment and prediction tests: Their reliability and validity. *Marriage and Family Living*, 1959, *21*, 251–5.

Mehrabian, A. Nonverbal betrayal of feeling. *Journal of Experimental Research in Personality*, 1971, *5*, 64–73.

Mehrabian, A. *Nonverbal communication.* Chicago: Aldine-Atherton, 1972.

Mehrabian, A., and Ferris, S.R. Inference of attitudes from nonverbal communication in two channels. *Journal of Consulting Psychology*, 1967, *31*, 248–52.

Mehrabian, A., and Wiener, M. Decoding of inconsistent communications. *Journal of Personality and Social Psychology*, 1967, *6*, 109–14.

Morris, D. Nonverbal leakage: How you can tell if someone's lying. *New York Magazine*, October 17, 1977, pp. 43–6.

Noller, P. Gaze in married couples. *Journal of Nonverbal Behavior*, 1980, *5*, 115–29. (a)

Noller, P. Marital misunderstanding: A study of couples' nonverbal communication. *Journal of Personality and Social Psychology*, 1980, *39*, 1135–48. (b)

Noller, P. Gender and marital adjustment level differences in decoding messages from spouses and strangers. *Journal of Personality and Social Psychology*, 1981, *41*, 272–8.

Raush, H.L., Barry, W.A., Hertel, R.K., and Swain, M.E. *Communication, conflict and marriage.* San Francisco: Jossey-Bass, 1974.

Rogers, C.R. The necessary and sufficient conditions of therapeutic personality change. *Journal of Consulting Psychology*, 1957, *21*, 95–103.

Rosenfeld, H.M. Approval-seeking and approval-inducing functions of verbal and nonverbal responses in the dyad. *Journal of Personality and Social Psychology*, 1966, *4*, 597–605.

Truax, C.B., and Carkhuff, R.B. *Towards effective counseling and psychotherapy: Training and practice.* Chicago: Aldine, 1967.

Weiss, R.L., Hops, W., and Patterson, G.R. A framework for conceptualizing marital conflict, a technology for altering it, some data for evaluating it. In F.W. Clark and L.A. Hamerlynck (eds), *Critical issues in research and practice: Proceedings of the Fourth Banff International Conference on Behavior Modification.* Champaign, Illinois: Research Press, 1973.

Zaidel, S., and Mehrabian, A. The ability to communicate and infer positive and negative attitudes facially and vocally. *Journal of Experimental Research in Personality*, 1969, *3*, 233–41.

12 Affiliation, Attraction and Close Relationships

Romantic love conceptualized as an attachment process

C. Hazan and P. Shaver

Editors'
Introduction

Theoretical Background

For the last few decades, research on interpersonal attraction and relationships has been dominated by utilitarian approaches such as exchange or interdependence theory. These rely on economic metaphors and assume that attraction or love is determined by the outcomes people anticipate or experience in relationships. Social psychologists were therefore very slow in adopting attachment theory, which is strongly influenced by evolutionary or sociobiological thinking and has its main focus on the development of attachment relationships in children. Stimulated by Weiss's (1982) application of attachment theory to loneliness, Hazan and Shaver were the first mainstream social psychologists to use attachment theory as a theoretical framework in the study of relationship formation.

Bowlby's (1971, 1975, 1981) attachment theory grew out of observations that both human and primate infants proceed through a predictable series of emotional reactions when separated from their mothers, beginning with protest, followed by despair and ending with detachment. Because of the remarkable similarities across species, Bowlby was led to consider the evolutionary significance of infant–caregiver attachment and its maintenance in the face of separation. The attachment system, as Bowlby called the complex constellation of feelings and behaviours, seems to have evolved to protect infants from danger by keeping them close to their mother.

According to Bowlby, one of the major functions served by an attachment figure, particularly a mother, is that of providing a base of security from which the infant can explore the environment. Whenever an infant is confronted with a frightening stimulus, it not only withdraws but also retreats towards the attachment figure. When the attachment figure is gone, there is no longer a secure base to which to retreat, which is a terrifying experience and results in distress. Bowlby suggested that confidence in the availability of attachment figures builds up slowly during the years of immaturity, and that the expectations developed during

Journal of Personality and Social Psychology (1987), 52:511–24.

those years tend to persist relatively unchanged throughout the rest of life (continuity hypothesis). This is why the quality of the attachment relationships developed during childhood is assumed to have a lasting influence on the way the individual views relationships in later life.

In their classic study of attachment styles based on observations of the interaction of young children with their mothers, Ainsworth et al. (1978) distinguished three attachment styles. These refer to infants' expectations concerning their mother's accessibility and responsiveness: secure attachment, anxious/ambivalent attachment and avoidant attachment. Ainsworth and colleagues suggested that these expectations are incorporated into the mental model which infants construct of themselves and their major social-interaction partners. The expectations incorporated into these models are important sources of *continuity* between early and later attachment feelings and behaviour. The study by Hazan and Shaver is the first empirical test of the hypothesis that this continuity can be demonstrated in adulthood.

Hypotheses

The following five hypotheses were tested in the two studies reported in this paper:

1   The distribution of attachment styles in adulthood will be similar to that observed in research on children.
2   The love experiences of the three attachment types are characterized by different feelings.
3   The mental models of self and relationships differ according to attachment style.
4   Attachment histories should differ between the three styles.
5   Different attachment types are differentially vulnerable to experiencing loneliness, with anxious/ambivalent respondents being most vulnerable and securely attached respondents least vulnerable.

STUDY I

Design

There is no experimental design. No factors were manipulated. The study is cross-sectional (i.e. all variables are assessed at the same time).

Method

This is a questionnaire study conducted on a sample of convenience (i.e. readers who filled in a questionnaire published in an American newspaper). The questionnaire consisted of three sections: part 1 contained fifty-six statements on which respondents had to rate their most important relationships. These statements had been adapted from already existing love questionnaires or suggested from the infant caretaker literature, and were assumed to form fourteen subscales measuring dimensions thought by the authors to be theoretically important. Part 2 asked details about the characteristics of this relationship (e.g. current or past, duration). Part

3 assessed attachment style, attachment history and mental models of attachment relationships. Attachment style was measured in a surprisingly simple manner: respondents had to choose from three descriptions of attachment types the one which most closely fitted the way they typically felt in relationships. Attachment history was assessed by questions about parental divorce and evaluations of the relationship that existed between parents and between the respondents and their parents. Mental models of attachment relationships were assessed by means of presenting respondents with descriptions of the typical course of romantic love, and asking them to indicate their agreement with these descriptions.

Results

The responses of the first 620 of the more than 1,200 readers who replied were used in the analysis. (Since we do not know how many readers read the relevant section of the paper, we have no possibility of determining the response rate, that is, the percentage of readers who actually replied.) Before testing the main hypotheses, investigators had to verify whether the questions in part 1 really reflected the dimensions they were intended to measure. In order to do this, responses to the fifty-six items or questions of part 1 were factor analysed. Factor analysis is a statistical procedure which allows one to identify from a pool of items subscales of items which measure the same dimension. This factor analysis reproduced twelve of the fourteen original scales (see table 12.1).

Hypothesis 1 postulated that the distribution of attachment styles in adulthood would be similar to that observed in children. It was supported by the distribution of the respondents' self-classifications into different attachment styles (table 12.2). Hypothesis 2 postulated systematic differences between the three attachment styles in the way they characterized their most important love experience. This hypothesis was tested (and supported) by the differences between the three attachment types in their mean scores on the love subscales (table 12.3). Hypothesis 3 postulated differences in the mental models of relationships between the three attachment styles. This hypothesis was tested by looking at differences between the three attachment types in the proportion of respondents who agreed with each of the mental model statements. Again, the differences observed between the three attachment types were consistent with hypotheses (table 12.4). Hypothesis 4 postulated differences between attachment styles in attachment history. Although there were no systematic differences between the different types in frequency of parental divorce or parental separation, ratings of parental behaviour and of relationship between the parents and between the respondent and his or her parents were systematically related to attachment type (table 12.5, figure 12.1).

STUDY 2

Study 2 was conducted in order to replicate findings of study 1 with a sample that was less self-selected, and with a better measure of mental models. In addition, a measure of loneliness was included to allow for a test of hypothesis 5. Respondents in study 2 were undergraduate students. In general, the findings of study 1 were replicated. In addition, the test of hypothesis 5 indicated that consistent with predictions, anxious/ambivalent subjects had the highest loneliness scores and securely attached subjects the lowest.

Discussion

With their measure of attachment styles, Hazan and Shaver offered a simple solution to a baffling problem, namely how to assess in adulthood attachment styles that presumably developed during childhood, and moreover to do this without using time-intensive, in-depth interviews. The findings of the study provide encouraging support for the attachment theoretical perspective on romantic love, and thus inspire trust in the validity of their attachment measure. However, the plausiblity of the continuity hypothesis – that is, the assumption that the attachment styles assessed by Hazan and Shaver had indeed been developed in childhood – rests mainly on the similarity in the distribution of the different styles. This is weak evidence, for a number of reasons. First, the samples investigated by the authors were not representative of the population, and the same is probably true for the children assessed by Ainsworth. Second, it is quite possible that attachment styles can be distributed in the same way in adulthood and childhood without there being any continuity in style across the lifespan. For a definite proof of such continuity of attachment styles, a longitudinal study would be needed, assessing attachment styles of the same individuals in both childhood and adulthood. However, the fact that a number of important differences in respondents' experience with, and perspective on, relationships were systematically related to the measure of attachment style, in a theoretically meaningful way, increases one's confidence in the validity of the interpretations offered by Hazan and Shaver.

FURTHER READING

Bowlby, J. (1977). The making and breaking of affectional bonds. *British Journal of Psychiatry*, 130, 201–10. Brief summary of Bowlby's theory of attachment.
Weiss, R. (1982). Issues in the study of loneliness. In L.A. Peplau and D. Perlman (eds), *Loneliness: A Sourcebook of Current Theory, Research and Therapy* (pp. 71–80). New York: Wiley. Brief presentation of Weiss's theory of loneliness and his distinction of the two types of loneliness.

REFERENCES

Ainsworth, M.D.S., Blehar, M.C., Waters, E. and Wall, S. (1978). *Patterns of Attachment: A Psychological Study of the Strange Situation*. Hillsdale, NJ: Erlbaum.
Bowlby, J. (1971). *Attachment and Loss (vol. 1): Attachment*. Harmondsworth: Pelican.
Bowlby, J. (1975). *Attachment and Loss (vol 2): Loss*. Harmondsworth: Pelican.
Bowlby, J. (1981). *Attachment and Loss (vol 3): Loss: Sadness and Depression*. Harmondsworth: Pelican.

- - - - -
Primary
Reading
- - - - - - - -

One of the landmarks of contemporary psychology is Bowlby's (1969, 1973, 1980) three-volume exploration of attachment, separation, and loss, the processes by which affectional bonds are forged and broken. Bowlby's major purpose was to describe and explain how infants become emotionally attached to their primary caregivers and emotionally distressed when separated from them, although he also contended that "attachment behavior [characterizes] human beings from the cradle to the grave" (1979, p. 129). In recent years, laboratory and naturalistic studies of infants and children (summarized by Bretherton, 1985, and Maccoby, 1980) have provided considerable support for attachment theory, which was proposed by Bowlby and elaborated by several other investigators. The purpose of this article is to explore the possibility that this theory, designed primarily with infants in mind, offers a valuable perspective on adult romantic love. We will suggest that romantic love is an attachment process (a process of becoming attached), experienced somewhat differently by different people because of variations in their attachment histories.

For our purpose, which is to create a coherent framework for understanding love, loneliness, and grief at different points in the life cycle, attachment theory has several advantages over existing approaches to love (Shaver, Hazan, and Bradshaw, in press). First, although many researchers (e.g., Rubin, 1973; Hatfield and Sprecher, 1985) have attempted to assess love with unidimensional scales, love appears to take multiple forms (e.g., Dion and Dion, 1985; Hendrick and Hendrick, 1986; Lee, 1973; Steck, Levitan, McLane, and Kelley, 1982; Sternberg, 1986; Tennov, 1979). Attachment theory explains how at least some of these forms develop and how the same underlying dynamics, common to all people, can be shaped by social experience to produce different relationship styles. Second, although various authors have portrayed certain forms of love as healthy and others as unhealthy, or at least problematic (e.g., Hindy and Schwarz, 1984; Tennov, 1979), they have not said how the healthy and unhealthy forms fit together in a single conceptual framework. Attachment theory not only provides such a framework, but also explains how both healthy and unhealthy forms of love originate as reasonable adaptations to specific social circumstances. The portrait of love offered by attachment theory includes negative as well as positive emotions: for example, fear of intimacy (discussed by Hatfield, 1984), jealousy (e.g., Hindy and Schwarz, 1985), and emotional ups and downs (Tennov, 1979) as well as caring (Rubin, 1973), intimacy (Sternberg, 1986), and trust (Dion and Dion, 1985). Third, attachment theory deals with separation and loss and helps explain how loneliness and love are related (Shaver and Rubenstein, 1980; Parkes and Weiss, 1983; Weiss, 1973). Finally, attachment theory links adult love with socioemotional processes evident in children and nonhuman primates; it places love within an evolutionary context (Wilson, 1981). (See Sternberg and Barnes, in press, for an anthology of recent approaches to the study of adult love.)

Attachment Theory and Research

Bowlby's attachment theory grew out of observations of the behavior of infants and young children who were separated from their primary caregiver (usually the mother) for various lengths of time. Bowlby noticed what primate researchers had also observed in the laboratory and the field: When a human or primate infant is separated from its mother, the infant goes through a predictable series of emotional reactions. The first is *protest*, which involves crying, active searching, and resistance to others' soothing efforts. The second is *despair*, which is a state of passivity and obvious sadness. And the third, discussed only with reference to humans, is *detachment*, an active, seemingly defensive disregard for and avoidance of the mother if she returns. Because of the remarkable similarities between human infants and other primate infants, Bowlby was led to consider the evolutionary significance of infant–caregiver attachment and its maintenance in the face of separation.

The attachment system, as Bowlby called the complex constellation of attachment feelings and behaviors, seems to have evolved to protect infants from danger by keeping them close to the mother. When very young, a human infant can do little more than cry, make eye contact, smile, and snuggle in to encourage its mother to keep it near. Once mobile, however, it can actively pursue its mother and vocalize to her. Bowlby and other observers of both human and primate behavior have noticed that when an infant is healthy, alert, unafraid, and in the presence of its mother, it seems interested in exploring and mastering the environment and in establishing affiliative contact with other family and community members. Researchers call this using the mother as a secure base.

Attachment theory can be summarized in three propositions, phrased clearly in the second volume of Bowlby's trilogy:

> The first [proposition] is that when an individual is confident that an attachment figure will be available to him whenever he desires it, that person will be much less prone to either intense or chronic fear than will an individual who for any reason has no such confidence. The second proposition concerns the sensitive period during which such confidence develops. It postulates that confidence in the availability of attachment figures, or lack of it, is built up slowly during the years of immaturity – infancy, childhood, and adolescence – and that whatever expectations are developed during those years tend to persist relatively unchanged throughout the rest of life. The third proposition concerns the role of actual experience. It postulates that the varied expectations of the accessibility and responsiveness of attachment figures that individuals develop during the years of immaturity are tolerably accurate reflections of the experiences those individuals have actually had. (Bowlby, 1973, p. 235)

The formation during early childhood of a smoothly functioning (i.e., secure) attachment relationship with a primary caregiver, although the norm in our society, is by no means guaranteed. Research by Ainsworth and others suggests that a mother's sensitivity and responsiveness to her infant's signals and needs during the first year of life are important prerequisites. Mothers who are slow or inconsistent in responding to their infant's cries or who regularly intrude on or interfere with their infant's desired activities (sometimes to force affection on the infant at a particular moment) produce infants who cry more than usual, explore less than usual (even in the mother's presence), mingle attachment behaviors with overt expressions of anger, and seem generally anxious. If, instead, the mother consistently rebuffs or rejects the infant's attempts to establish physical contact, the infant may learn to avoid her. On the basis of their observations, Ainsworth, Blehar, Waters, and Wall (1978) delineated three styles or types of attachment, often called *secure*, *anxious/ambivalent*, and *avoidant*. Infants in the anxious/ambivalent category frequently exhibit the behaviors Bowlby called *protest*, and the avoidant infants frequently exhibit the behaviors he called *detachment*. A major goal of this article is to apply this three-category system to the study of romantic love.

In their description of the three attachment styles, Ainsworth et al. (1978) referred to infants' expectations concerning their mothers' accessibility and responsiveness. This fits with Bowlby's claim that infants and children construct inner working models of themselves and their major social-interaction partners. Because the expectations incorporated in these models are some of the most important sources of continuity between early and later feelings and behaviors, they deserve special attention. According to Bowlby, working models (which we will also call *mental models*) and the behavior patterns influenced by them are central components of personality. The claim of cross-situational and cross-age continuity is still controversial but is supported by a growing list of longitudinal studies from infancy through the early elementary school years (Dontas, Maratos, Fafoutis, and Karangelis, 1985; Erickson, Sroufe, and Egeland, 1985; Main, Kaplan, and Cassidy, 1985; Sroufe, 1983; Waters, Wippman, and Sroufe, 1979). This evidence for continuity adds plausibility to the notion that a person's adult style of romantic attachment is also affected by attachment history.

Continuity, according to Bowlby (1973), is due primarily to the persistence of interrelated mental models of self and social life in the context of a fairly stable family setting:

> Confidence that an attachment figure is, apart from being accessible, likely to be responsive can be seen to turn on at least two variables: (a) whether or not the attachment figure is judged to be the sort of person who in general responds to calls for support and protection; [and] (b) whether or not the self is judged to be the sort of person towards whom anyone, and the attachment figure in particular, is likely to respond in a helpful way. Logically these variables are independent. In practice they are apt to be confounded. As a result, the model of the attachment figure and the model of the self are likely to develop so as to be complementary and mutually confirming. (Bowlby, 1973, p. 238)

Love as Attachment

So far, no one has attempted to conceptualize the entire range of romantic love experiences in a way that parallels the typology developed by Ainsworth and her colleagues. Nor has anyone with an interest in romantic relationships pursued Bowlby's idea that continuity in relationship style is a matter of mental models of self and social life. Finally, no one has explored the possibility that the specific characteristics of parent–child relationships identified by Ainsworth et al. as the probable causes of differences in infant attachment styles are also among the determinants of adults' romantic attachment styles. These are the major aims of this article.

We derived the following hypotheses by applying Bowlby's and Ainsworth's ideas and findings as literally as possible to the domain of adult love.

Hypothesis 1

Given the descriptions of the secure, avoidant, and anxious/ambivalent styles, we expected roughly 60% of adults to classify themselves as secure and the remainder to split fairly evenly between the two insecure types, with perhaps a few more in the avoidant than in the anxious/ambivalent category. In a summary of American studies of the three types of infants, Campos, Barrett, Lamb, Goldsmith, and Stenberg (1983) concluded that 62% are secure, 23% are avoidant, and 15% are anxious/ambivalent. Given a diverse sample of American adults, we thought it reasonable to expect approximately the same proportions.

Hypothesis 2

Just as the feelings an infant presumably experiences in the relationship with his or her mother are thought to reflect the quality of attachment to her, we expected that different types of respondents – secure, avoidant, and anxious/ambivalent – would experience their most important love relationships differently. We predicted that the most important love experience of a secure adult would be characterized by trust, friendship, and positive emotions. For avoidant adults, love was expected to be marked by fear of closeness and lack of trust. Anxious/

ambivalent adults were expected to experience love as a preoccupying, almost painfully exciting struggle to merge with another person. This last style is similar to what Hindy and Schwarz (1984) called anxious romantic attachment and Tennov (1979) called limerence.

Hypothesis 3

Respondents' working models of self and relationships were also expected to differ according to attachment style. Secure types should believe in enduring love, generally find others trustworthy, and have confidence that the self is likable. Avoidant types should be more doubtful of the existence or durability of romantic love and believe that they do not need a love partner in order to be happy. Anxious/ambivalent types should fall in love frequently and easily but have difficulty finding true love. They should also have more self-doubts than the other two types because, unlike avoidant respondents, they do not repress or attempt to hide feelings of insecurity.

Hypothesis 4

Because attachment style is thought to develop in infancy and childhood, we expected respondents of the three types to report different attachment histories. According to the theory, secure respondents should remember their mothers as dependably responsive and caring; avoidant respondents should report that their mothers were generally cold and rejecting; and anxious/ambivalent respondents should remember a mixture of positive and negative experiences with their mothers. As less research has been conducted with fathers, we tentatively expected the findings related to them to be roughly similar to the findings for mothers.

Hypothesis 5

Finally, because the attachment needs of insecure respondents are unlikely to be fully met, avoidant and anxious/ambivalent respondents should be especially vulnerable to loneliness. The avoidant types, however, may defend against or attempt to hide this vulnerable feeling and so report less loneliness than anxious/ambivalent respondents do.

Study 1

In an initial effort to test the attachment-theory approach to romantic love, we designed a "love quiz" to be printed in a local newspaper. As explained by Shaver and Rubenstein (1983), the newspaper questionnaire method has been used in a wide variety of studies, always with results that approximate those from more expensive, more strictly representative surveys. The main difference between newspaper survey respondents and participants in representative sample surveys is that the former have slightly higher education levels. Also, depending on the topic, newspaper surveys tend to draw more female than male respondents. Neither of these biases seemed to preclude a valuable initial test of our ideas, and the gains in sample size and heterogeneity appeared to outweigh the cost of mild unrepresentativeness.

A single-item measure of the three attachment styles was designed by translating

Ainsworth et al.'s (1978) descriptions of infants into terms appropriate to adult love. The love-experience questionnaire, which we will describe in detail, was based on previous adult-love measures and extrapolations from the literature on infant–caregiver attachment. The measure of working models was based on the assumption that conscious beliefs about romantic love – concerning, for example, whether it lasts forever and whether it is easy or difficult to find – are colored by underlying, and perhaps not fully conscious, mental models. The measure of attachment history was a simple adjective checklist used to describe childhood relationships with parents and the parents' relationship with each other.

Method

Subjects
Analyses reported here are based on the first 620 of over 1,200 replies received within a week following publication of the questionnaire. (The major findings were stable after the first few hundred, so additional replies were not keypunched.) Of these 620 replies, 205 were from men and 415 were from women. The subjects ranged in age from 14 to 82, with a median age of 34 and a mean of 36. Average household income was $20,000 to $30,000; average education level was "some college." Just over half (51%) were Protestant, 22% were Catholic, 3% were Jewish, 10% were atheist or agnostic, and 13% were "other." Ninety-one percent were "primarily heterosexual," 4% were "primarily homosexual," and 2% were "primarily bisexual" (3% chose not to answer). Forty-two percent were married at the time of the survey; 28% were divorced or widowed, 9% were "living with a lover," and 31% were dating. (Some checked more than one category.)

Measures and procedure
The questionnaire appeared in the July 26, 1985, issue of the *Rocky Mountain News* on the first and second pages of the Lifestyles section. Besides being highly visible there, it was referred to in a banner headline at the top of the paper's front page: "Tell us about the love of your life; experts ask 95 questions about your most important romance." The instructions included the following sentences: "The questionnaire is designed to look at the most important love relationship you have ever had, why you got involved in it, and why it turned out the way it did. . . . It may be a past or a current relationship, but choose only the most important one." Given that there was only enough room to ask about one relationship, we decided to have subjects focus on the one they considered most important.

The questionnaire was divided into three parts. The first contained 56 statements concerning the subject's most important relationship, for example, "I (considered/consider) —— one of my best friends" and "I (loved/love) —— so much that I often (felt/feel) jealous." (The blank referred to the most important lover's name.) Responses were recorded by circling *SD*, *D*, *A*, or *SA* to indicate points along a *strongly disagree* to *strongly agree* continuum. The 56 statements, 4 each for 14 a priori subscales, were adapted from previous love questionnaires (Dion and Dion, 1985; Hatfield and Sprecher, 1985; Hindy and Schwarz, 1984; Lasswell and Lobsenz, 1980; Rubin, 1973; Steffen, McLaney, and Hustedt, 1984) or suggested by the literature on infant–caretaker attachment (e.g., Ainsworth et al., 1978).

A principal-components analysis followed by equimax rotation was performed on the 56-item measure. Thirteen factors had eigenvalues greater than 1.0, and 12 corresponded to a

Table 12.1   Information on love-experience scales

Scale name	Sample item	No. of items	α
Happiness	My relationship with _____ (made/makes) me very happy.	4	.84
Friendship	I (considered/consider) _____ one of my best friends.	4	.78
Trust	I (felt/feel) complete trust in _____.	4	.83
Fear of closeness	I sometimes (felt/feel) that getting too close to _____ could mean trouble.	3	.64
Acceptance	I (was/am) well aware of _____'s imperfections but it (did/does) not lessen my love.	2	.67
Emotional extremes	I (felt/feel) almost as much pain as joy in my relationship with _____.	3	.81
Jealousy	I (loved/love) _____ so much that I often (felt/feel) jealous.	4	.82
Obsessive preoccupation	Sometimes my thoughts (were/are) uncontrollably on _____.	3	.70
Sexual attraction	I (was/am) very physically attracted to _____.	4	.80
Desire for union	Sometimes I (wished/wish) that _____ and I were a single unit, a "we" without clear boundaries.	3	.79
Desire for reciprocation	More than anything, I (wanted/want) _____ to return my feelings.	3	.70
Love at first sight	Once I noticed _____, I was hooked.	4	.70

priori scales. Items loading above .40 on 1 of the 12 predicted factors were analyzed for reliability, and items that reduced coefficient alpha were deleted. Table 12.1 provides the names of the 12 scales and a sample item, the number of items retained, and coefficient alpha for each. Alpha ranged from .64 to .84 with a mean of .76, which seemed adequate for preliminary tests of the hypotheses.

Part 2 of the questionnaire asked whether the described relationship was current or past (61% were current, 39% were past), what the subject's relationship to that person was at the time of the survey, how long the relationship had lasted, how many times the subject had been in love, and whether he or she had experienced crushes before age 10. This part of the questionnaire also contained demographic questions.

Part 3 dealt with attachment style and attachment history. It included sections dealing with the subject's childhood relationships with his or her mother and father and the parents' relationship with each other (the specific items will be discussed more fully in the *Results and Discussion* section). Also included were questions concerning how the subject typically felt in relationships (the exact wording appears in table 12.2) and what he or she believed concerning the typical course of romantic love. The questionnaire concluded with the open-ended question "Can you add anything that might help us understand romantic love?" and a request for the subject's name and phone number if he or she was willing to be interviewed. (Over 60% of the subjects provided this information.)

Subjects were asked to mail their reply forms to the *Rocky Mountain News* within a week.

Results and discussion

Frequencies of the three attachment styles

Hypothesis 1 concerned whether newspaper readers could meaningfully classify themselves as avoidant, anxious/ambivalent, or secure in their most important romantic relationship, given fairly simple descriptions of the three attachment styles, and in particular whether the frequencies of the types would be similar to those found in studies of infants and young children. Table 12.2 shows how the alternatives were worded and provides the percentage of subjects endorsing each description.

Just over half (56%) classified themselves as secure, whereas the other half split fairly evenly between the avoidant and anxious/ambivalent categories (25% and 19%, respectively). These figures are similar to proportions reported in American studies of infant–mother attachment (Campos et al., 1983, summarized the proportions obtained in these studies as 62% secure, 23% avoidant, and 15% anxious/ambivalent). Our results suggest, but of course do not prove, that subjects' choices among the alternatives were nonrandom and may have been determined by some of the same kinds of forces that affect the attachment styles of infants and children. The remainder of the results argue for the validity of subjects' self-classifications.

Differences in love experiences

The second hypothesis predicted that subjects with different self-designated attachment styles would differ in the way they characterized their most important love relationship. Table 12.3 presents the mean subscale scores (each with a possible range of 1 to 4) for each attachment type, along with the F ratio from a one-way analysis of variance (ANOVA) on scores for each subscale.

In line with the hypothesis, secure lovers described their most important love experience as especially happy, friendly, and trusting. They emphasized being able to accept and support their partner despite the partner's faults. Moreover, their relationships tended to endure longer: 10.02 years, on the average, compared with 4.86 years for the anxious/ambivalent subjects and 5.97 years for the avoidant subjects, $F(2, 568) = 15.89, p < .001$. This was the case even though

Table 12.2 Adult attachment types and their frequencies (newspaper sample)

Question: Which of the following best describes your feelings?

Answers and percentages:

    Secure (N = 319, 56%): I find it relatively easy to get close to others and am comfortable depending on them and having them depend on me. I don't often worry about being abandoned or about someone getting too close to me.

    Avoidant (N = 145, 25%): I am somewhat uncomfortable being close to others; I find it difficult to trust them completely, difficult to allow myself to depend on them. I am nervous when anyone gets too close, and often, love partners want me to be more intimate than I feel comfortable being.

    Anxious/Ambivalent (N = 110, 19%): I find that others are reluctant to get as close as I would like. I often worry that my partner doesn't really love me or won't want to stay with me. I want to merge completely with another person, and this desire sometimes scares people away.

Twenty-one subjects failed to answer this question, and 25 checked more than one answer alternative.

Table 12.3   Love-subscale means for the three attachment types (newspaper sample)

Scale name	Avoidant	Anxious/ambivalent	Secure	F(2, 571)
Happiness	3.19$_a$	3.31$_a$	3.51$_b$	14.21***
Friendship	3.18$_a$	3.19$_a$	3.50$_b$	22.96***
Trust	3.11$_a$	3.13$_a$	3.43$_b$	16.21***
Fear of closeness	2.30$_a$	2.15$_a$	1.88$_b$	22.65***
Acceptance	2.86$_a$	3.03$_b$	3.01$_b$	4.66**
Emotional extremes	2.75$_a$	3.05$_b$	2.36$_c$	27.54***
Jealousy	2.57$_a$	2.88$_b$	2.17$_c$	43.91***
Obsessive preoccupation	3.01$_a$	3.29$_b$	3.01$_a$	9.47***
Sexual attraction	3.27$_a$	3.43$_b$	3.27$_a$	4.08*
Desire for union	2.81$_a$	3.25$_b$	2.69$_a$	22.67***
Desire for reciprocation	3.24$_a$	3.55$_b$	3.22$_a$	14.90***
Love at first sight	2.91$_a$	3.17$_b$	2.97$_a$	6.00**

Within each row, means with different subscripts differ at the .05 level of significance according to a Scheffé test.
*$p < .05$.
**$p < .01$.
***$p < .001$.

members of all three groups were 36 years old on the average. Only 6% of the secure group had been divorced, compared with 10% of the anxious/ambivalent group and 12% of the avoidant group, $F(2, 573) = 3.36$, $p < .05$.

The avoidant lovers were characterized by fear of intimacy, emotional highs and lows, and jealousy. They never produced the highest mean on a positive love-experience dimension. The anxious/ambivalent subjects experienced love as involving obsession, desire for reciprocation and union, emotional highs and lows, and extreme sexual attraction and jealousy. They provided a close fit to Tennov's (1979) description of limerence and Hindy and Schwarz's (1984) conception of anxious romantic attachment, suggesting that the different between what Tennov called love and limerence is the difference between secure and anxious/ambivalent attachment.

Although the average love experiences of people in the three different attachment categories differed significantly, for most of the subscales all three types scored on the same side of the midpoint (2.50), emotional extremes and jealousy being the only exceptions. Thus, there appears to be a core experience of romantic love shared by all three types, with differences in emphasis and patterning between the types. The results also support the ideas that love is a multidimensional phenomenon and that individuals differ in more ways than the intensity of their love experiences. Especially noteworthy was the fact that the ordering of means for the different attachment styles differed for different dimensions. For the dimensions of happiness, friendship, trust, and fear of closeness, secure subjects differed significantly from avoidant and anxious/ambivalent subjects but these two insecure groups did not differ from each other. On the dimensions of obsessive preoccupation, sexual attraction, desire for union, desire for reciprocation, and love at first sight, anxious/ambivalent subjects differed significantly from avoidant and secure subjects, who did not differ from each other. On the acceptance dimension, avoidant subjects (the least accepting) differed from anxious/ambivalent and secure subjects, and on emotional extremes and jealousy, all three groups were statistically distinct. This variety of patterns supports the claim that there are three different love styles, not simply three points along a love continuum.

Differences in mental models

We attempted to assess what Bowlby (1969) called working models of relationships by using the items shown in table 12.4. Each was either checked or not checked as describing how the subject generally "view[s] the course of romantic love over time." These dichotomous answers were analyzed by attachment style, using a one-way ANOVA. (Because the answers were scored as either 0 or 1, the means can be read as proportions.)

In line with the third hypothesis, secure lovers said that romantic feelings wax and wane but at times reach the intensity experienced at the start of the relationship and that in some relationships romantic love never fades. The avoidant lovers said the kind of head-over-heels romantic love depicted in novels and movies does not exist in real life, romantic love seldom lasts, and it is rare to find a person one can really fall in love with. The anxious/ambivalent subjects claimed that it is easy to fall in love and that they frequently feel themselves beginning to fall, although (like the avoidant subjects) they rarely find what they would call real love. Like the secure subjects, the anxious/ambivalent subjects said they believe that romantic feelings wax and wane over the course of a relationship.

Table 12.4 Proportion of respondents who endorsed each mental-model statement about love (newspaper sample)

Statement	Avoidant	Anxious/ambivalent	Secure	F(2, 571)
1 The kind of head-over-heels romantic love depicted in novels and movies doesn't exist in real life.	.25$_a$	.28$_a$	.13$_b$	8.81***
2 Intense romantic love is common at the beginning of a relationship, but it rarely lasts forever.	.41$_a$	.34$_b$	.28$_b$	3.83*
3 Romantic feelings wax and wane over the course of a relationship, but at times they can be as intense as they were at the start.	.60$_a$	.75$_b$	.79$_b$	9.86***
4 In some relationships, romantic love really lasts; it doesn't fade with time.	.41$_a$	.46$_a$	.59$_b$	7.48***
5 Most of us could love many different people equally well; there is no "one true love" which is "meant to be."	.39	.36	.40	*ns*
6 It's easy to fall in love. I feel myself beginning to fall in love often.	.04$_a$	.20$_b$	.09$_a$	9.33***
7 It's rare to find someone you can really fall in love with.	.66$_a$	.56$_a$	.43$_b$	11.61***

Within each row, means with different subscripts differ at the .05 level of significance according to a Scheffé test.
*p < .05.
**p < .01.
***p < .001.

Differences in attachment history

Attachment history with parents was assessed in two ways. Subjects were asked whether they had ever been separated from either parent for "what seemed like a long time" and whether the parents ever separated or divorced. They were also asked to describe how each parent had generally behaved toward them during childhood (using 37 adjectives, such as *responsive, caring, critical*, and *intrusive*, derived from a pilot study in which subjects answered open-ended questions about their childhood relationships with parents) and the parents' relationship with each other (using 12 similarly derived adjectives such as *affectionate, unhappy*, and *argumentative*).

There were no significant differences among the three attachment types in likelihood or duration of separation from parents during childhood, even when analyzed by reason for separation. In addition, parental divorce seemed unrelated to attachment type, even though quality of relationships with parents was associated with type. The best predictors of adult attachment type were respondents' perceptions of the quality of their relationship with each parent and the parents' relationship with each other.

A one-way ANOVA, with attachment style as the independent variable, on each of the 86 child–parent and parent–parent relationship variables yielded 51 Fs that were significant at the .05 level, clearly more than expected by chance. (Thirty-seven of these were significant at the .01 level; 15 were significant at the .001 level.) Because many of the variables were correlated, which meant that many of the ANOVA results were redundant, a hierarchical discriminant-function analysis was performed to assess predictability of membership in the three attachment categories from a combination of attachment-history variables. Subjects with no missing data on the variables involved ($N = 506$) were included in the analysis. The 22 attachment-history variables shown in table 12.5 (plus one with a correlation below .20) were retained as significant predictors of attachment type. Both discriminant functions (two being the maximum possible number given three target groups) were statistically significant, with a combined $\chi^2(46, N = 506) = 131.16, p < .001$. After removal of the first function, $\chi^2(22, N = 506)$ was 40.94 ($p < .01$). The two functions accounted for 69.87% and 30.13%, respectively, of the between-groups variability.

As shown in figure 12.1, the first discriminant function separated secure subjects from the two kinds of insecure subjects. The second function separated avoidant from anxious/ambivalent subjects. Together, the two functions correctly classified 56% of the avoidant subjects, 51% of the anxious/ambivalent subjects, and 58% of the secure subjects. (The incorrectly classified subjects were distributed fairly evenly across the remaining categories.)

Correlations of the 22 predictor variables with the two discriminant functions are shown in table 12.5. The best discriminators between secure and insecure subjects included (a) a relationship between parents that was affectionate ($r = .44$), caring (.32), and not unhappy (−.34); (b) a mother who was respectful of the subject (.43), confident (.35), accepting (.33), responsible (.31), not intrusive (−.42), and not demanding (−.40), among other qualities; and (c) a father who was, among other things, caring (.41), loving (.40), humorous (.40), and affectionate (.30). The top discriminators between avoidant and anxious/ambivalent groups, with positively correlated variables being those named more frequently by anxious/ambivalent subjects, included (a) no parental relationship variables; (b) a mother who was relatively humorous (.43), likable (.38), respected (.37), and not rejecting (−.30); and (c) a father who was relatively unfair (.47).

These results can be summarized by saying that secure subjects, in comparison with insecure subjects, reported warmer relationships with both parents and between their two parents.

Table 12.5 Significant correlations between attachment-history variables and discriminant functions (newspaper sample)

Variable	Function 1	Function 2
Affectionate parental relationship	.44*	
Respectful mother	.43*	.22
Intrusive mother	−.42*	
Caring father	.41*	
Demanding mother	−.40*	
Loving father	.40*	.25
Humorous father	.40*	
Confident mother	.35*	
Unhappy parental relationship	−.34*	.24
Accepting mother	.33*	
Caring parental relationship	.32*	
Responsible mother	.31*	
Affectionate father	.30*	.26
Sympathetic father	.28*	
Strong mother	.28*	
Disinterested mother	−.28*	
Unresponsive father	−.24*	
Unfair father	−.20	.47*
Humorous mother		.43*
Likable mother		.38*
Respected mother	.30	.37*
Rejecting mother	−.27	−.30*

Correlations marked with an asterisk in the first column correlated more highly with Function 1 than with Function 2; the reverse is true in the second column.

Avoidant subjects, in comparison with anxious/ambivalent subjects, described their mothers as cold and rejecting. Anxious/ambivalent subjects saw their fathers as unfair. Both sets of correlations are compatible with expectations based on Ainsworth et al.'s (1978) studies of infant–caregiver attachment.

Sex differences and similarities

There were a few significant sex differences on individual items. Most notably, respondents tended to describe their opposite-sex parent more favorably than their same-sex parent. For example, 62% of the women (vs. 44% of the men) described their fathers as loving, $t(563) = 4.16, p < .001$, and 78% of the men (vs. 69% of the women) described their mothers as loving, $t(614) = 2.36, p < .05$. This same pattern was found for the adjectives *affectionate* and *understanding*. Moreover, on negative trait dimensions, respondents tended to judge their same-sex parent more harshly. For instance, 39% of the women, but only 27% of the men, described their mothers as critical, $t(614) = 2.91, p < .01$. When reporting about their fathers, on the other hand, 53% of the men chose *critical*, compared with 39% of the women, $t(563) = 3.06$, $p < .01$. The same was true for *demanding*. There were no significant sex differences in prevalence

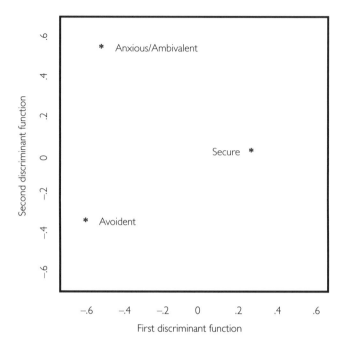

Figure 12.1   Plot of three group centroids on two discriminant functions derived from attachment-history variables (newspaper sample)

of the three attachment styles and only small differences on two of the love dimensions: Men agreed slightly more than women did with the sexual-attraction items (3.35 vs. 3.26), $t(618)$ = 1.99, $p < .05$, and also reported greater desire for union (2.94 vs. 2.78), $t(616) = 2.45$, $p <$ .05. Overall, what stood out was the marked similarity of the results for men and women.

Study 2

Method

Study 1 suffered from several limitations that made it desirable to conduct a conceptual replication. First, the newspaper sample might have been biased because of self-selection. This could have affected our estimate of the prevalence of each of the three attachment types and distorted other results in unanticipated and undetectable ways. It seemed wise, therefore, to test a non-self-selected college-student group in our second study, students being the usual subjects in social psychological research. Second, Study 1 examined only limited aspects of subjects' mental models. An interesting part of Bowlby's (1969) analysis was the claim that these models involve complementary portrayals of self and relationships. In Study 1, because of space limitations imposed by newspaper editors, we neglected the self side of subjects' mental models; in Study 2 we focused on them. Third, because previous research on loneliness (e.g., Rubenstein and Shaver, 1982) has linked loneliness to attachment history without using the attachment-classification item designed for our research on romantic love, we decided to include in Study 2 brief measures of state and trait loneliness (Shaver, Furman, and Buhrmester, 1985). The hypotheses were the same as in Study 1, but Hypotheses 4 and 5 were especially important in Study 2 because new self-model items and measures of loneliness were included.

Subjects

One hundred eight undergraduates (38 men and 70 women) who were enrolled in a course entitled Understanding Human Conflict completed the questionnaire as a class exercise. Approximately three fourths of the students were first-quarter freshmen; the mean age was 18 years.

Measures and procedure

As in Study 1, subjects were asked to describe their most important love relationship in terms of 56 agree–disagree items. They also classified themselves by using the same attachment-style item. To measure additional aspects of subjects' mental models, we included several self-descriptive items and some new items concerning relationships with other people (see table 12.8). State and trait loneliness were measured (in a separate questionnaire to be described) with two parallel 11-item scales similar to those described by Shaver et al. (1985). These were based in part on the revised UCLA Loneliness Scale (Russell, Peplau, and Cutrona, 1980). Each item was answered on a 5-point response scale; trait items referred to feelings experienced "during the past few years" and state items referred to "the past few weeks." Sample trait items included "During the past few years, I have lacked companionship" and "During the past few years, about how often have you felt lonely?"

Subjects received their questionnaires as part of a series of class exercises due at different points during the quarter. Each exercise was due a week before related issues were discussed in class. Confidentiality was assured by checking off the names of students who handed in the exercise on time and then analyzing all data by number rather than by name. To decrease possible halo effects, the loneliness questionnaire was administered 4 weeks after the love-quiz exercise was completed.

Results and discussion

Frequencies of the three attachment styles

The proportions of each of the three attachment styles were highly similar in Study 2 to what they were in Study 1: secure, 56% (vs. 56% of newspaper respondents); avoidant, 23% (vs. 25%); and anxious/ambivalent, 20% (vs. 19%). It seems unlikely, therefore, that the newspaper sample was biased in this respect.

Differences in love experiences

The effects of attachment style on love experiences were also similar across the two studies, as seen by comparing tables 12.3 and 12.6. Even though only 8 of the 12 subscales yielded significant mean differences with the smaller sample, nearly all exhibited the same pattern of means found in Study 1. Secure respondents characterized their love experiences as friendly, happy, and trusting, whereas avoidant subjects reported fear of closeness, and anxious/ambivalent subjects described relationships marked by jealousy, emotional highs and lows, and desire for reciprocation.

Table 12.6 Love-subscale means for the three attachment types (undergraduate sample)

Scale name	Avoidant	Anxious/ambivalent	Secure	F(2, 104)
Happiness	3.06	3.26	3.30	ns
Friendship	3.34$_a$	3.39$_a$	3.61$_b$	3.30*
Trust	3.25$_a$	3.35$_b$	3.57$_b$	3.03*
Fear of closeness	2.63$_a$	2.45$_a$	2.13$_b$	4.48**
Acceptance	2.96	3.11	2.91	ns
Emotional extremes	2.79$_a$	2.86$_a$	2.33$_b$	4.67**
Jealousy	2.52$_a$	3.26$_b$	2.40$_a$	13.24***
Obsessive preoccupation	3.03	3.09	3.09	ns
Sexual attraction	3.05	3.31	3.23	ns
Desire for union	2.83$_a$	3.29$_b$	2.92$_a$	3.41*
Desire for reciprocation	3.21$_a$	3.64$_b$	3.18$_a$	7.50***
Love at first sight	2.67$_a$	3.10$_b$	2.83$_a$	3.76*

Within each row, means with different subscripts differ at the .05 level of significance according to a Scheffé test.
*$p < .05$.
**$p < .01$.
***$p < .001$.

Differences in mental models (old items)

As seen by comparing tables 12.4 and 12.7, the results for six of the seven mental-model items used in Study 1 were replicated in Study 2, the exception being Item 3. (In Study 1, avoidant subjects were distinguishable by their denial that love can be rekindled after it wanes, but in Study 2 they were not.) However, only two of the items produced significant differences: Item 6 ("It's easy to fall in love . . ."; endorsed by 32% of the anxious/ambivalent, 15% of the secure, and none of the avoidant subjects) and Item 7 ("It's rare to find someone . . ."; endorsed by 80% of the avoidant, 55% of the secure, and 41% of the anxious/ambivalent subjects). One possible reason for differences between the two sets of results is that the college student subjects had less relationship experience; their average relationship had lasted about 1 year, compared with 8 years for the newspaper sample. Fewer of them were willing to say that Hollywood romance doesn't exist in real life (Item 1), more said that love doesn't fade over time (Item 4), and so on.

Differences in mental models (new items)

Table 12.8 shows the proportion of each attachment group endorsing the new mental-model statements designed for Study 2. Attachment style had a significant effect on six of the eight, including all but one of the items concerning self. The secure subjects described themselves as easy to get to know and as liked by most people and endorsed the claim that other people are generally well-intentioned and good-hearted. The anxious/ambivalent subjects reported having more self-doubts, being misunderstood and underappreciated, and finding others less willing and able than they are to commit themselves to a relationship. The avoidant subjects generally fell between the extremes set by the secure and anxious/ambivalent subjects, and in most cases were closer to the anxious/ambivalent than to the secure. Although the differences on the last two items did not reach significance, the means were ordered in theoretically meaningful ways. The two insecure groups more often said that one has to "watch out in

Table 12.7 Proportion of respondents who endorsed each statement about love (undergraduate sample)

Statement	Avoidant	Anxious/ ambivalent	Secure	F Ratio (2, 104)
1 The kind of head-over-heels romantic love depicted in novels and movies doesn't exist in real life.	.16	.18	.12	ns
2 Intense romantic love is common at the beginning of a relationship, but it rarely lasts forever.	.40	.27	.17	ns
3 Romantic feelings wax and wane over the course of a relationship, but at times they can be as intense as they were at the start.	.64	.68	.50	ns
4 In some relationships, romantic love really lasts; it doesn't fade with time.	.56	.59	.77	ns
5 Most of us could love many different people equally well; there is no "one true love" which is "meant to be."	.28	.36	.28	ns
6 It's easy to fall in love. I feel myself beginning to fall in love often.	$.00_a$	$.32_b$	$.15_{ab}$	4.96**
7 It's rare to find someone you can really fall in love with.	$.80_a$	$.41_b$	$.55_b$	4.10*

Within each row, means with different subscripts differ at the .05 level of significance according to a Scheffé test.
*$p < .05$.
**$p < .01$.

Table 12.8 Proportion of respondents who endorsed each new mental-model item (undergraduate sample)

Item	Avoidant	Anxious/ ambivalent	Secure	F(2, 104)
1 I am easier to get to know than most people.	$.32_a$	$.32_a$	$.60_b$	4.39*
2 I have more self-doubts than most people.	$.48_a$	$.64_a$	$.18_b$	9.96***
3 People almost always like me.	$.36_a$	$.41_a$	$.68_b$	5.19**
4 People often misunderstand me or fail to appreciate me.	$.36_a$	$.50_a$	$.18_b$	4.56*
5 Few people are as willing and able as I am to commit themselves to a long-term relationship.	$.24_a$	$.59_b$	$.23_a$	5.57**
6 People are generally well-intentioned and good-hearted.	$.44_a$	$.32_a$	$.72_b$	6.99***
7 You have to watch out in dealing with most people; they will hurt, ignore, or reject you if it suits their purposes.	.32	.32	.15	ns
8 I am more independent and self-sufficient than most people; I can get along quite well by myself.	.80	.59	.68	ns

Within each row, means with different subscripts differ at the .05 level of significance according to a Scheffé test.
*$p < .05$.
**$p < .01$.
***$p < .001$.

dealing with most people," and more of the avoidant subjects (80%) than of the secure (68%) or anxious/ambivalent (59%) subjects agreed that "I can get along quite well by myself."

Differences in attachment history

In an attempt to replicate the attachment-history findings of Study 1 using data from Study 2, we again performed a hierarchical discriminant-function analysis. Subjects with no missing data on the variables involved ($N = 101$) were included in the analysis. Once again, both functions proved to be statistically significant, with a combined $\chi^2(50, N = 101) = 128.30$, $p < .001$. After removal of the first function, $\chi^2(24, N = 101)$ was 39.84 ($p < .05$). The two functions accounted for 75.31% and 24.69%, respectively, of the between-groups variability. As shown in the upper panel of figure 12.2, the first discriminant function separated anxious/ambivalent subjects from the other two attachment groups, a pattern different from that obtained in Study 1. The second function separated avoidant from secure subjects. Together, the two functions correctly classified 75.0% of the avoidant subjects, 90.5% of the anxious/ambivalent subjects, and 85.7% of the secure subjects.

The new pattern was due primarily to the fact that avoidant subjects in Study 2 described their attachment histories as more similar to those of secure subjects on positive trait dimensions than did avoidant subjects in Study 1. In Study 1, for example, only 12% of avoidant subjects said their mother had been accepting; in Study 2 this figure jumped to 50%. For *sympathetic*, the figure jumped from 32% to 79%. The same kinds of differences were evident in descriptions of the relationship with father and the parental relationship. For example, 29% of avoidant subjects in Study 1 described their parents' relationship as happy; the corresponding figure in Study 2 was 63%. For *good-humored*, the percentage increased from 19 to 54. This tendency toward more favorable descriptions on the part of Study 2's avoidant subjects resulted in greater apparent similarity to the secure subjects; on several items, in fact, slightly more avoidant than secure subjects gave their parents favorable reports. This did not keep them, however, from also mentioning more negative descriptors, such as *critical*, *rejecting*, and *disinterested*. These negative descriptors allowed the second discriminant function to distinguish between secure and avoidant groups.

Correlations between the 17 significant predictor variables with coefficients above .15 and the two discriminant functions are shown in table 12.9. The best discriminators between anxious/ambivalent subjects and secure subjects were (a) a relationship between parents that was perceived not to be good-humored (−.16), (b) a mother who was not understanding (−.22), and (c) a father who was cold (.25), not caring (−.24), and not confident (−.23). In contrast to avoidant subjects, secure subjects described their mothers as respectful (.21), accepting (.17), not rejecting (−.42), and not critical (−.19), and their fathers as fair (.19).

Why should avoidant subjects' attachment histories appear more similar to secure subjects' attachment histories in the younger (college student) sample? Central to avoidant attachment is defensiveness. Main et al. (1985) and Kobak and Sceery (in press) have shown that avoidant adults and college students tend to idealize their relationships with parents to avoid the negative feelings associated with those relationships. Evidently, it is only with maturity and distance from parents that an avoidant person can begin to acknowledge severely negative aspects of his or her early relationships. To test the hypothesis that youth is an important factor, we performed a third discriminant-function analysis, using data from the 100 youngest newspaper respondents (all under 26 years of age). The pattern of results proved to be highly similar to the results from Study 2, as seen by comparing the upper and lower panels of figure

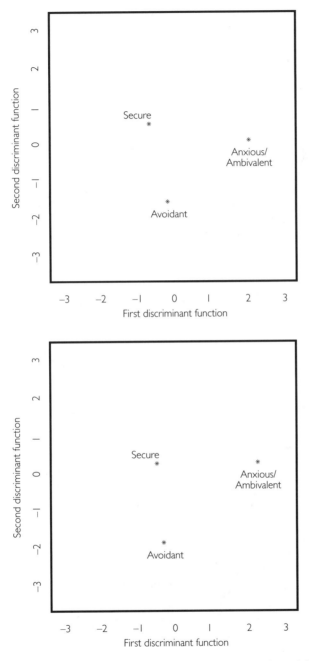

Figure 12.2 Plots of three group centroids on two discriminant functions derived from attachment-history variables. (The upper portion of the figure displays results for Study 2; the lower portion, results from newspaper respondents below 26 years of age.)

Table 12.9 Significant correlations between attachment-history variables and discriminant functions (undergraduate sample)

Variable	Function 1	Function 2
Cold father	.25*	
Caring father	−.24*	
Confident father	−.23*	
Understanding mother	−.22*	
Humorous father	−.21*	
Warm father	−.18*	
Respectful father	−.17*	
Good-humored parental relationship	−.16*	
Rejecting mother		−.42*
Confident mother		.31*
Respectful mother		.21*
Fair father		.19*
Critical mother		−.19*
Disinterested mother		−.18*
Accepting mother		.17*
Insecure mother		−.17*
Cold mother		−.16*

Correlations marked with asterisks in the first column correlated more highly with Function 1 than with Function 2; the reverse is true in the second column.

12.2. There were two statistically significant discriminant functions, and, as in Study 2, the first distinguished primarily between anxious/ambivalent subjects and the other two groups. The second function distinguished primarily between avoidant and secure subjects.

As a further test of whether differences were due to younger avoidant subjects describing their attachment histories more favorably than did older avoidant subjects, we compared the means on attachment variables for young (again, under 26 years of age) with those of older newspaper subjects who had classified themselves as avoidant. We found that more younger than older avoidant subjects described relationships with and between their parents in favorable terms. For example, more described their mothers as loving (.77 vs. .57), $t(51) = 2.15$, $p < .05$. They were also significantly ($p < .05$) more likely to say their mothers were responsive, not intrusive, and not rejecting. The same pattern was found in their descriptions of their fathers. For example, 65% of the young avoidants but only 54% of the older group called their fathers loving, $t(157) = 2.13$, $p < .05$, and they described their fathers as significantly more good-humored. Thus, differences between discriminant-function analyses from the two studies seem to be due to age differences between the two samples and the tendency for young avoidant subjects to idealize their attachment histories.

Differences in state and trait loneliness
Finally, table 12.10 reports mean trait- and state-loneliness scores (on 5-point scales) for each of the three attachment groups in Study 2. In line with Hypothesis 5, the highest scores were obtained by the anxious/ambivalent subjects and the lowest scores by the secure subjects. These

Table 12.10 Trait and state loneliness as a function of adult attachment style (undergraduate sample)

Loneliness type	Avoidant	Anxious/ ambivalent	Secure	F(2, 104)	p
Trait	2.30$_{ab}$	2.59$_a$	2.01$_b$	7.12	.001
State	2.57$_{ab}$	3.02$_a$	2.21$_b$	6.43	.003

Within each row, means with different subscripts differ at the .05 level of significance according to a Scheffé test.

findings fit with other indications throughout the two studies that anxious/ambivalent adults yearn for a love relationship involving merger, reciprocation, and intense passion – a relationship for which they find too few willing partners.

In an attempt to understand why avoidant subjects did not receive trait-loneliness scores equal to those of anxious/ambivalent subjects, we looked at individual items, including some extreme ones not included in the two scales. (The extra items were taken from the NYU Loneliness Scale; Rubenstein and Shaver, 1982.) Two kinds of items were of special interest: one that blatantly emphasized being a lonely person (e.g., "I am a lonely person," "I always was a lonely person") and another that referred to distance from others but without indicating that a lonely self was to blame (e.g., "During the past few years, no one has really known me well," "During the past few years, I have felt left out").

In an exploratory analysis, two items of each type were averaged and contrasted by means of planned comparisons. The comparison of anxious/ambivalent subjects and the other two groups on items that implicated a trait-lonely self produced $F(1, 80) = 17.88$, $p < .001$; the comparison of secure and insecure groups on the more ambiguous items produced $F(1, 80) = 7.05$, $p < .01$. No other comparisons were significant.

These exploratory analyses are compatible with findings reported by Kobak (1985). In his study, both avoidant and anxious/ambivalent subjects were rated by peers as less socially competent than secure subjects, but when asked to describe themselves, only the anxious/ ambivalent subjects reported less social competence.

Sex differences and similarities
In Study 2 there were no significant sex differences in any of the variables or patterns for which we had sufficient numbers of men to make comparisons.

General Discussion

Five hypotheses concerning adult love and loneliness were derived from attachment theory and research. The first was the simplest prediction we could make regarding the relative frequencies of the three attachment styles: that they would be about as common in adulthood as they are in infancy. The results supported this hypothesis. Across both studies, approximately 56% of the subjects classified themselves as secure, approximately 24% as avoidant, and approximately 20% as anxious/ambivalent. Campos et al. (1983) estimated the figures for infancy as 62%

secure, 23% avoidant, and 15% anxious/ambivalent. Of course, it is unlikely that our single-item measure of attachment style measures exactly the same thing that Ainsworth et al. (1978) coded from behavioral observations of infant–mother dyads, and it would be naive to think that a style adopted in infancy remains unchanged or unelaborated all through life. Still, the search for connections between attachment in childhood and attachment in adulthood must begin somewhere, and our simple measure and straightforward hypothesis fared surprisingly well in their initial tests.

The second hypothesis predicted different kinds of love experiences for people in the three attachment-style categories. The data supported this hypothesis, indicating a unique constellation of emotions for each of the three attachment categories despite the existence of a general core experience of romantic love. The results were weaker in Study 2 than in Study 1, partly because of sample size but also, perhaps, because of younger subjects' lack of relationship experience.

The third hypothesis predicted that subjects' working models of self and relationships would be related to attachment style. The results supported this prediction, indicating that people with different attachment orientations entertain different beliefs about the course of romantic love, the availability and trustworthiness of love partners, and their own love-worthiness. These beliefs may be part of a cycle (a vicious cycle in the case of insecure people) in which experience affects beliefs about self and others and these beliefs in turn affect behavior and relationship outcomes (Wachtel, 1977).

The fourth hypothesis, like the first, predicted straightforward parallels between infant–mother interactions and adults' reports about their childhood relationships with parents. Simple adjective checklists were used to assess remembered relationships with parents and the parents' relationship with each other. Study 1 indicated that two discriminant functions based on attachment-history items could distinguish significantly between members of the three attachment categories. The most powerful function discriminated between secure and insecure subjects; the second function discriminated mainly between the two insecure groups. These results fit well with Ainsworth et al.'s (1978) findings.

The results were not so straightforward for Study 2, which involved a younger group of subjects. For them, the easiest attachment styles to distinguish, based on reports about childhood experiences with parents, were anxious/ambivalent on the one hand and avoidant and secure on the other. A second function discriminated mainly between the latter two groups. The differences between Study 1 and Study 2 were interpreted in terms of the defensiveness of young avoidant subjects. An analysis distinguishing younger from older subjects in Study 1 supported this interpretation.

The fifth hypothesis predicted greater reported trait loneliness among insecure than secure subjects, especially among the anxious/ambivalents. This prediction was tested in Study 2 and was supported by measures of both trait and state loneliness. Additional analyses revealed that avoidant subjects admitted being distant from other people but did not report feeling lonely. It was impossible to evaluate their claims more deeply to see whether they are accurate or should be interpreted as additional examples of defensive avoidance.

Overall, the results provide encouraging support for an attachment-theoretical perspective on romantic love, although a number of caveats are in order.

Because the Study 1 and Study 2 questionnaires had to be brief (one due to the constraints of newspaper space, the other to limitations of a class-exercise format), we were able to inquire about only a single romantic relationship – the one that each subject considered most important. To increase the chances of detecting features of relationship experience due to subjects' attachment styles, it would be better to ask about more than one relationship. Hindy and Schwarz (1984) questioned their subjects (all recent college graduates) about four relationships and treated these as items on an anxious-attachment measure. They found correlations in the neighborhood of .40 between each pair of relationships in terms of anxious attachment, suggesting both considerable continuity (due, we suspect, to subjects' attachment style) and considerable variation across relationships. Degree of security or anxiety in a relationship is, as one would expect, a joint function of attachment style and factors unique to particular partners and circumstances. This matter obviously deserves further study.

It may be useful to assess both partners in a relationship; so far, we and Hindy and Schwarz have relied on reports from only one. It should be possible, using methods like those of Gottman (1979) and Gottman, Markman, and Notarius (1977), to examine not only reports about relationship qualities but also observable features of couple interaction in the laboratory. This is one way to extend measurement beyond the realm of self-report.

In general, we have probably overemphasized the degree to which attachment style and attachment-related feelings are traits rather than products of unique person–situation interactions. Attachment researchers often vacillate between using the terms *secure, avoidant,* and *anxious/ambivalent* to describe relationships and using them to categorize people. We have focused here on personal continuity, but we do not wish to deny that relationships are complex, powerful phenomena with causal effects beyond those predictable from personality variables alone. A secure person trying to build a relationship with an anxious/ambivalent person might be pushed to feel and act avoidant. An avoidant person might cause a secure partner to feel and act anxious, and so on. These kinds of interactions deserve study in their own right.

Our measures were limited in terms of number of items and simplicity of answer alternatives, and this should be corrected in future work. However, there are reasons to suspect that no amount of psychometric improvement will solve all the problems associated with self-report assessment of attachment-related variables. First of all, subjects may be unable to articulate exactly how they feel in love relationships. Second, subjects are unlikely to have anything like perfect memory for their love experiences or for the nature of their relationships with parents, especially those during the preschool years. Third, subjects are likely to be defensive and self-serving in their recall and description of some of the events we wish to inquire about.

One way around some of the problems with self-report measures is to ask outsiders to describe subjects' relationship-relevant characteristics. Kobak and Sceery (in press) did so in a recent study of attachment styles of college freshmen. They had two acquaintances of each subject describe him or her by using a Q-sort procedure, and the two sets of results were averaged. Subjects' attachment styles were assessed by a long clinical interview designed by George, Kaplan, and Main (1984). The results indicated that secure subjects were described by acquaintances as more socially competent, charming, cheerful, and likable than their avoidant and anxious/ambivalent classmates. The two insecure groups differed in theoretically expected ways, the avoidant group being described as more hostile and defensive, for example, and the anxious/ambivalent group as more self-conscious and preoccupied with relationship issues.

The attachment interview designed by George et al. (1984) is itself an important alternative to the kinds of self-report measures we used because it includes assessments of defensiveness, apparently blocked memories of important relational episodes with parents, and preoccupation with attachment issues (on the part of anxious/ambivalent subjects). In fact, focusing on defensiveness and information-processing style led Main et al. (1985) to conceptualize mental models somewhat differently than we did. Whereas we attempted to assess consciously held beliefs about self and relationships, Main et al. attempted to assess how information is processed and distorted.

Even within the self-report domain, it should be possible to improve on our single-item measure of attachment style. Each of our answer alternatives included more than one issue or dimension, for example, ease of getting close to others, feeling comfortable with caregiving and care receiving, fear of abandonment. In principle, each such issue could be assessed separately, with a multi-item scale, and then attachment types could be derived by profile analysis. Besides being potentially more reliable, such a method would allow subjects to endorse parts of what is currently forced on them as a single alternative.

Aside from measurement problems, the attachment approach to romantic love must overcome important conceptual dilemmas. In our preliminary studies, we have chosen to overlook the fact that child–parent relationships differ in important ways from adult romantic relationships. One of the most important differences is that romantic love is usually a two-way street; both partners are sometimes anxious and security-seeking and at other times able providers of security and care. A second important difference is that romantic love almost always involves sexual attraction (Tennov, 1979), whereas only the most speculative psychoanalysts have claimed that infants' attachments to the mother are sexual in nature. Bowlby (1979) and Ainsworth et al. (1978), taking their cue from ethology, have dealt with problems such as these by postulating distinct behavioral systems. These include, among others, the attachment system, the caregiving system, and the mating or reproductive system. Adult romantic love seems to involve the integration of these three systems, with the form of the integration being influenced by attachment history (Shaver et al., in press).

Another important issue has to do with continuity and change in attachment style. For theoretical reasons, we were interested in examining evidence for continuity of attachment style between childhood and adulthood, and we consider it important that there is good evidence for continuity between ages 1 and 6 and preliminary retrospective evidence for continuity in our own adult data. Nevertheless, it would be overly pessimistic – from the perspective of insecurely attached people – to conclude that continuity is the rule rather than the exception between early childhood and adulthood. The correlations we obtained between parent variables and current attachment type were statistically significant but not strong. They were higher in Study 2, where the average subject was 15 to 20 years younger than in Study 1. (Also, when we divided the newspaper sample into younger and older age groups in an analysis not reported here, correlations with parent variables were higher for the younger group.) It seems likely that continuity between childhood and adult experiences decreases as one gets further into adulthood. (See Skolnick, in press, for relevant longitudinal evidence.) The average person participates in several important friendships and love relationships, each of which provides an opportunity to revise mental models of self and others.

Main et al. (1985) reported that, despite an impressive association between adults' attachment history and the attachment styles of their own young children, some parents had freed themselves from the chain of cross-generational continuity. That is, some adults who reported being insecure in their relationships with parents managed to produce children who were securely attached at ages 1 and 6. Careful study of these cases suggested to Main et al. that the adults had mentally worked through their unpleasant experiences with parents and now had mental models of relationships more typical of secure subjects. The process by which an insecure person becomes increasingly secure, probably by participating in relationships that disconfirm negative features of experience-based mental models, offers an important avenue for future research. Our results suggest that younger avoidant adults are especially prone to defensive distortion of memories of relationships with and between parents. Older avoidant subjects presented a much less favorable portrait of their parents.

Because many social psychologists are likely to misread our approach as Freudian, it may be worthwhile to contrast Freudian conceptions of infant-to-adult continuity on the one hand with attachment theory's conception on the other. Unlike the Freudian conception, according to which the supposed irrationalities of adult love indicate regression to infancy or fixation at some earlier stage of psychosexual development, attachment theory includes the idea that social development involves the continual construction, revision, integration, and abstraction of mental models. This idea, which is similar to the notion of scripts and schemas in cognitive social psychology (e.g., Fiske and Taylor, 1984), is compatible with the possibility of change based on new information and experiences, although change may become more difficult with repeated, uncorrected use of habitual models or schemas.

Freud argued his case beautifully, if not persuasively, by likening the unconscious to the city of Rome, which has been ravaged, revised, and rebuilt many times over the centuries. In the case of the unconscious, according to Freud, it is as if all the previous cities still exist, in their original form and on the same site. Bowlby's conception is more in line with actual archeology. The foundations and present shapes of mental models of self and social life still bear similarities and connections to their predecessors – some of the important historical landmarks, bridges, and crooked streets are still there. But few of the ancient structures exist unaltered or in mental isolation, so simple regression and fixation are unlikely.

The attachment-theory approach to romantic love suggests that love is a biological as well as a social process, based in the nervous system and serving one or more important functions. This view runs counter to the increasingly popular idea that romantic love is a historical–cultural invention, perhaps a creation of courtly lovers in 13th-century Europe (e.g., Averill, 1985; de Rougement, 1940). This is obviously a matter for serious cross-cultural and historical research, but in the absence of strong evidence to the contrary, we hypothesize that romantic love has always and everywhere existed as a biological potential, although it has often been precluded as a basis for marriage. There are explicit records of romantic love in all of the great literate civilizations of early historic times, from Egypt and China to Greece and Rome (Mellen, 1981).

Finally, we should make clear that by calling romantic love an attachment process we do not mean to imply that the early phase of romance is equivalent to being attached. Our idea, which requires further development, is that romantic love is a biological process designed by evolution to facilitate attachment between adult sexual partners who, at the time love evolved, were likely to become parents of an infant who would need their reliable care.

The noticeable decrease in fascination and preoccupation as lovers move from the romantic (attaching) phase to what can become a decades-long period of secure attachment is evident not only in the case of romantic love but also in early childhood, when most secure children begin to take parental support for granted (barring unexpected separations). As Berscheid (1983) has shown in her analysis of the apparent unemotionality of many marriages, disruptions such as divorce and widowhood often "activate the attachment system," to use Bowlby's phrase, and reveal the strength of attachment bonds that were previously invisible. Loneliness and grieving are often signs of the depth of broken attachments.

In sum, love and loneliness are emotional processes that serve biological functions.

Attachment theory portrays them in that light and urges us to go beyond simpler and less theoretically integrative models involving concepts such as attitude (e.g., Rubin, 1973) and physiological arousal (Berscheid and Walster, 1974). For that reason, the attachment approach seems worth pursuing even if future study reveals (as it almost certainly will) that adult romantic love requires additions to or alterations in attachment theory. It would not be surprising to find that adult love is more complex than infant–caretaker attachment, despite fundamental similarities.

NOTE

We are grateful to Donna Bradshaw for sharing her expertise in the areas of attachment theory and research, to Marty Meitus for allowing us to conduct Study 1 in the *Rocky Mountain News*, to Kathy Purcell for keypunching, to Rick Canfield for assistance in all phases of the project, and to Mary Ainsworth, John Bowlby, Harry Gollob, Lee Kirkpatrick, Roger Kobak, Anne Peplau, Harry Reis, Judith Schwartz, Arlene Skolnick, and Robert Sternberg for helpful comments on convention presentations and earlier drafts of this article.

REFERENCES

Ainsworth, M.D.S., Blehar, M.C., Waters, E., and Wall, S. (1978). *Patterns of attachment: A psychological study of the strange situation.* Hillsdale, NJ: Erlbaum.

Averill, J.R. (1985). The social construction of emotion: With special reference to love. In K.J. Gergen and K.E. Davis (eds), *The social construction of the person* (pp. 89–109). New York: Springer-Verlag.

Berscheid, E. (1983). Compatibility and emotion. In W. Ickes (ed.), *Compatible and incompatible relationships* (pp. 143–61). New York: Springer-Verlag.

Berscheid, E., and Walster, E. (1974). A little bit about love. In T.L. Huston (ed.), *Foundations of interpersonal attraction* (pp. 355–81). New York: Academic Press.

Bowlby, J. (1969). *Attachment and loss: Vol. 1. Attachment.* New York: Basic Books.

Bowlby, J. (1973). *Attachment and loss: Vol. 2. Separation: Anxiety and anger.* New York: Basic Books.

Bowlby, J. (1979). *The making and breaking of affectional bonds.* London: Tavistock.

Bowlby, J. (1980). *Attachment and loss: Vol. 3. Loss.* New York: Basic Books.

Bretherton, I. (1985). Attachment theory: Retrospect and prospect. *Monographs of the Society for Research in Child Development,* 50(1 and 2), 3–35.

Campos, J.J., Barrett, K.C., Lamb, M.E., Goldsmith, H.H., and Stenberg, C. (1983). Socioemotional development. In M.M. Haith and J.J. Campos (eds), *Handbook of child psychology: Vol. 2. Infancy and psychobiology* (pp. 783–915). New York: Wiley.

de Rougement, D. (1940). *Love in the Western world.* New York: Harcourt.

Dion, K.K., and Dion, K.L. (1985). Personality, gender, and the phenomenology of romantic love. In P. Shaver (ed.), *Review of personality and social psychology* (vol. 6, pp. 209–39). Beverly Hills, CA: Sage.

Dontas, C., Maratos, O., Fafoutis, M., and Karangelis, A. (1985). Early social development in institutionally reared Greek infants: Attachment and peer interaction. *Monographs of the Society for Research in Child Development,* 50(1 and 2), 136–46.

Erickson, M.F., Sroufe, L.A., and Egeland, B. (1985). The relationship between quality of attachment and behavior problems in preschool in a high-risk sample. *Monographs of the Society for Research in Child Development,* 50(1 and 2), 147–66.

Fiske, S.T., and Taylor, S.E. (1984). *Social cognition.* Reading, MA: Addison-Wesley.

George, C., Kaplan, N., and Main, M. (1984). Attachment interview for adults. Unpublished manuscript, University of California, Berkeley.

Gottman, J.M. (1979). *Marital interaction: Experimental investigations*. New York: Academic Press.

Gottman, J.M., Markman, H., and Notarius, C. (1977). The topography of marital conflict: A sequential analysis of verbal and nonverbal behavior. *Journal of Marriage and the Family*, 39, 461–77.

Hatfield, E. (1984). The dangers of intimacy. In V.J. Derlega (ed.), *Communication, intimacy, and close relationships* (pp. 207–20). New York: Academic Press.

Hatfield, E., and Sprecher, S. (1985). Measuring passionate love in intimate relations. Unpublished manuscript, University of Hawaii at Manoa.

Hendrick, C., and Hendrick, S. (1986). A theory and method of love. *Journal of Personality and Social Psychology*, 50, 392–402.

Hindy, C.G., and Schwarz, J.C. (1984). Individual differences in the tendency toward anxious romantic attachments. Paper presented at the Second International Conference on Personal Relationships, Madison, WI.

Hindy, C.G., and Schwarz, J.C. (1985). "Lovesickness" in dating relationships: An attachment perspective. Paper presented at the annual convention of the American Psychological Association, Los Angeles.

Kobak, R.R. (1985). The transition to college: Attitudes toward attachment and social competence. Unpublished doctoral dissertation, University of Virginia, Charlottesville.

Kobak, R.R., and Sceery, A. (in press). Attachment in late adolescence: Working models, affect regulation, and perception of self and others. *Child Development*.

Lasswell, M., and Lobsenz, N.M. (1980). *Styles of loving: Why you love the way you do*. New York: Doubleday.

Lee, J.A. (1973). *The colors of love: An exploration of the ways of loving*. Don Mills, Ontario, Canada: New Press.

Maccoby, E.E. (1980). *Social development: Psychological growth and the parent–child relationship*. New York: Harcourt Brace Jovanovich.

Main, M., Kaplan, N., and Cassidy, J. (1985). Security in infancy, childhood, and adulthood: A move to the level of representation. *Monographs of the Society for Research in Child Development*, 50(1 and 2), 66–104.

Mellen, S.L.W. (1981). *The evolution of love*. San Francisco: Freeman.

Parkes, C.M., and Weiss, R.S. (1983). *Recovery from bereavement*. New York: Basic Books.

Rubenstein, C., and Shaver, P. (1982). *In search of intimacy*. New York: Delacorte.

Rubin, Z. (1973). *Liking and loving: An invitation to social psychology*. New York: Holt, Rinehart and Winston.

Russell, D., Peplau, L.A., and Cutrona, C. (1980). The revised UCLA Loneliness Scale: Concurrent and discriminant validity evidence. *Journal of Personality and Social Psychology*, 39, 472–80.

Shaver, P., and Rubenstein, C. (1980). Childhood attachment experience and adult loneliness. In L. Wheeler (ed.), *Review of personality and social psychology* (vol. 1, pp. 42–73). Beverly Hills, CA: Sage.

Shaver, P., and Rubenstein, C. (1983). Research potential of newspaper and magazine surveys. In H.T. Reis (ed.), *Naturalistic approaches to studying social interaction* (pp. 75–91). San Francisco: Jossey-Bass.

Shaver, P., Furman, W., and Buhrmester, D. (1985). Transition to college: Network changes, social skills, and loneliness. In S. Duck and D. Perlman (eds), *Understanding personal relationships: An interdisciplinary approach* (pp. 193–219). London: Sage.

Shaver, P., Hazan, C., and Bradshaw, D. (in press). Love as attachment: The integration of three behavioral systems. In R. Sternberg and M. Barnes (eds), *The anatomy of love*. New Haven, CT: Yale University Press.

Skolnick, A. (in press). Early attachment and personal relationships across the life course. In R. Lerner and D. Featherman (eds), *Life span development and behavior* (vol. 7). Hillsdale, NJ: Erlbaum.

Sroufe, L.A. (1983). Infant–caregiver attachment and patterns of adaptation in preschool: The roots of maladaptation and competence. In M. Perlmutter (ed.), *Minnesota Symposium on Child Psychology* (vol. 16, pp. 41–83). Hillsdale, NJ: Erlbaum.

Steffen, J.J., McLaney, M.A., and Hustedt, T.K. (1984). The development of a measure of limerence. Unpublished manuscript, University of Cincinnati, Ohio.

Steck, L., Levitan, D., McLane, D., and Kelley, H.H. (1982). Care, need, and conceptions of love. *Journal of Personality and Social Psychology*, *43*, 481–91.

Sternberg, R.J. (1986). A triangular theory of love. *Psychological Review*, *93*, 119–35.

Sternberg, R.J., and Barnes, M. (in press). *The anatomy of love*. New Haven, CT: Yale University Press.

Tennov, D. (1979). *Love and limerence: The experience of being in love*. New York: Stein and Day.

Wachtel, P.L. (1977). *Psychoanalysis and behavior therapy: Toward an integration*. New York: Basic Books.

Waters, E., Wippman, J., and Sroufe, L.A. (1979). Attachment, positive affect, and competence in the peer group: Two studies in construct validation. *Child Development*, *50*, 821–9.

Weiss, R.S. (1973). *Loneliness: The experience of emotional and social isolation*. Cambridge, MA: MIT Press.

Wilson, G. (1981). *The Coolidge effect: An evolutionary account of human sexuality*. New York: Morrow.

Commitment and satisfaction in romantic associations: A test of the investment model

C.E. Rusbult

- - - - -
Editors'
Introduction
- - - - - - - -

Theoretical Background

The investment model presented in this article is an elaboration of the exchange theory of Thibaut and Kelley (1959; Kelley and Thibaut, 1978). Fundamental to both theories is the assumption that individuals are generally attracted to and form relationships with those with whom interaction promises the best outcomes (i.e. relatively high rewards at low costs). Furthermore both theories postulate that satisfaction with, and attraction to, a relationship depend on the relation of the outcomes experienced in a given relationship to a comparison level. Outcomes above the comparison level are experienced as satisfying, those below as dissatisfying. The comparison level reflects the modal valence of outcomes the individual has experienced in previous relationships and/or his or her perceptions of the valence of outcomes experienced by similar others.

The novel contribution of the investment model is the focus on determinants of 'relationship commitment'. It seems plausible to suggest that individuals stay in relationships which provide them with satisfying outcomes and leave those which do not. But as Thibaut and Kelley (1959) had already pointed out, relationship satisfaction is not the only determinant of commitment. People may walk out of relationships with which they are satisfied, if there are even better alternative relationships available, or they may stay in relationships which are unsatisfactory, if there are no more satisfying alternatives open to them. Thus, the degree to which partners are committed to a relationship is strongly determined by the quality of the outcomes available to them from alternative relationships (i.e. their comparison level for alternatives). The investment model emphasized in addition that commitment is also affected by investment size. The more people have to lose by leaving the relationship, the more they should be committed to it. Thus, joint property ownership will do wonders for relationship stability.

Journal of Experimental Social Psychology (1980), 16:172–86.

Hypotheses

1 Commitment to a relationship is determined by relationship outcomes, outcomes expected from alternative relationships, and size of investment.
2 Satisfaction depends only on relationship outcomes. It is not affected by the outcomes expected from alternative relationships or by investment size.

STUDY I

Design

The study is an experiment with a 3 (investment size: low/medium/high) × 2 (relationship costs: low/high) × 2 (alternative outcome: poor/good) × 2 (sex of participant: female/male) between-subjects design.

Method

Subjects were female and male undergraduate students who were asked to role-play the position of the major character in a story about a relationship described in an essay. The essays given to male and female subjects were identical, except for changes in the sex of the major character.

The independent variables were operationalized as follows: *investment size* was manipulated by varying the duration of the relationship (intrinsic investment) and the fact that the major character was employed by the father of the partner and would have to quit that job, if she or he left the relationship (extrinsic investment). *Relationship costs* were manipulated by the fact that the partner had had to move to another town which was either 60 miles (low costs) or 1,000 miles (high costs) away. *Alternative outcomes* were manipulated by information about an alternative relationship which the major character could form with a person who was described as either high or moderate on valued dimensions such as intelligence, humour and physical attractiveness.

The dependent measures were assessed as follows: *commitment* was measured with three items ('How likely is it that you will begin dating the alternative? How attached are you to your current relationship? How committed are you to your current relationship?'). *Satisfaction* was assessed with two items ('How satisfied are you with your current relationship? How attracted are you to your current relationship?'). In addition a number of questions were asked as *checks* of the effectiveness of the manipulation of the different independent variables. By using several items to assess each dependent variable and for each manipulation check, Rusbult made certain that these measures were reasonably reliable.

Results

Data were analysed using three-factor between-subjects multivariate analyses of variance (MANOVA) involving relationship costs, alternative outcomes, and investment size. (Initially four-factor MANOVAs were conducted, including sex as the fourth factor. There were no significant sex differences.) The use of a multivariate analysis of variance allowed the joint assessment of the significance of the impact of a given factor on several dependent measures by means of multivariate *F*s. This procedure reduces the number of independent statistical tests which have to be conducted and thus the likelihood of reporting as significant differences that in fact may have been due to chance.

Manipulation checks

The first set of analyses conducted on the manipulation checks associated with each of the independent variables suggested that all manipulations had been successful.

Commitment

Whereas investment size and alternative outcome had the predicted significant effect on the three items which served as measures of commitment, the effect of relationship cost, though in line with predictions, did not reach an acceptable level of significance.

Satisfaction

In line with predictions, satisfaction was significantly affected by the manipulation of relationship costs, and not by investment size or alternative outcome.

STUDY 2

The second study, which is not an experiment (i.e. no independent variables were manipulated) but a field study, was conducted to test whether the main parameters of the investment model could predict commitment and satisfaction in real, ongoing relationships. Values of each parameter of the investment model were measured in a questionnaire administered to a small sample of female and male undergraduate students. Respondents had to answer questions concerning a romantic relationship. This could be either an ongoing or a past relationship. Each parameter of the model (i.e. relationship outcome, alternative outcome and investment size) was briefly described in everyday terms and then assessed by means of a number of questions. Similarly, relationship satisfaction and commitment (i.e. the criterion variables) were assessed with four and six questions, respectively.

Thus, instead of manipulating the independent variables experimentally, relationship outcome, alternative outcome and investment size were assessed as they occur naturally in romantic relationships. Commitment to, and satisfaction with, the relationship were also measured. Using multiple regression procedures, which allow one to test both the independent and the joint impact of the various predictor variables, the researchers then tested whether the independent variables (now called predictor variables) were related to the dependent variables (now called criterion variables) in the manner predicted by the theory. In line with predictions, commitment was significantly influenced by relationship outcome, alternative outcome and investment size. Deletion of any of these variables resulted in a significant reduction in predictive power. Also consistent with predictions, satisfaction was significantly influenced by relationship outcome, but not influenced by alternative outcome or investment size.

Discussion

The two studies reported in this paper provide consistent support for the predictions derived from investment theory about the joint influence of relationship outcome, alternative outcome and investment size on commitment and on satisfaction. The pattern of findings reported in this article is even more persuasive because the methodologies chosen for the two studies, while not unproblematic taken individually, are nicely complementary. Thus, by having subjects role-play romantic relationships rather than manipulating real relationships (which would not have been possible), Rusbult may have measured subjects' theories about how they would behave in such situations rather than their 'real' behaviour. However, this criticism applies much less to the second study, where subjects had to rate their own real-life romantic relationships. The weakness of the second study is that due to its cross-sectional nature (i.e. all variables measured at the same time), it does not really allow one to test causal hypotheses. The issue of causality can be more readily addressed in longitudinal studies, which allow one to study the impact of the assumed causes on the assumed consequences over time. In the meantime, such studies have been conducted and tend to support the investment model (e.g. Rusbult, 1983).

Finally, it is worth noting that the strong support which the investment model received from these studies is somewhat inconsistent with findings reported by Clark and Mills (1979), showing that the economic principles underlying the investment model should be more applicable to 'exchange relationships' as they exist between acquaintances and business partners than to 'communal relationships' as they exist between lovers.

FURTHER READING

Clark, M.S. and Mills, J. (1979). Interpersonal attraction in exchange and communal relationships. *Journal of Personality and Social Psychology*, 37, 12–24. Distinguishes communal relationships, in which the giving of a benefit in response to a need for the benefit is appropriate, from exchange relationships, in which the giving of a benefit in response to the receipt of a benefit is appropriate. Empirical findings are presented which support this distinction.
Rusbult, C.E. (1983). A longitudinal test of the investment model: The development (and deterioration) of satisfaction and commitment in heterosexual involvements. *Journal of Personality and Social Psychology*. 45, 101–17. A longitudinal study testing the investment model.

REFERENCES

Kelley, H.H. and Thibaut, J.W. (1978). *Interpersonal Relations: A Theory of Interdependence.* New York: Wiley.
Thibaut, J.W. and Kelley, H.H. (1959). *The Social Psychology of Groups.* New York: Wiley.

Psychologists concerned with interpersonal relationships have typically concentrated on the study of attraction and its antecedents (Aronson and Linder, 1965; Byrne and Nelson, 1965; Gerard and Mathewson, 1966; Insko and Wilson, 1977). Variations in factors such as attitudinal similarity (Byrne and Nelson, 1965), physical attributes of the target person (Walster, Aronson, Abrahams, and Rottman, 1966), positivity of target evaluation of the subject (Aronson and Linder, 1965), and social interaction (Insko and Wilson, 1977) have been shown to affect initial liking for another. Reinforcement–affect theory (Clore and Byrne, 1974) and consistency theories (Festinger, 1957; Heider, 1958; Newcomb, 1968) are thus helpful in understanding initial attraction toward strangers. However, they do not adequately account for temporal changes in relationships, nor do they deal with the development or deterioration of commitment to ongoing associations.

Several psychologists have recently proposed models of interpersonal attraction in ongoing associations (Altman and Taylor, 1973; Levinger and Snoek, 1972). Each theory attempts to identify variables that account for the growth and deterioration of attraction, and to describe the course of development and dissolution of associations. The model to be described in this paper is in this general tradition. The primary goal of the investment model is to predict degree of commitment to and satisfaction with a variety of forms of ongoing association (e.g., romantic, friendship, business) with wide ranges of duration and involvement.

The investment model is based on several principles of interdependence theory (Kelley and Thibaut, 1978), and assumes that individuals are in general motivated to maximize rewards while minimizing costs. As interdependence theory states, satisfaction with and attraction to an association is a function of the discrepancy between the outcome value of the relationship and the individual's expectations concerning the quality of relationships in general, or his comparison level (*CL*) (Thibaut and Kelley, 1959). The outcome value of a relationship (O_X is defined as:

$$O_X = \Sigma w_i a_i \qquad [1]$$

where a_i represents the individual's subjective estimate of the value of attribute i available in relationship X, and w_i represents its subjective importance. Attribute values may be positive or negative (i.e., rewards or costs), material or psychological, and may either exist objectively or merely in the subjective perception of the individual. Some examples of potentially important attributes are intelligence, physical appearance, complementary needs, sense of humor, sexual satisfaction, and attitudinal similarity.

The individual's comparison level is the standard against which the attractiveness of a relationship is evaluated. It represents the average relationship outcome value that the individual has come to expect, and is determined by the quality of past experiences with relationships and comparison to associations of similar others. Individuals evaluate their present relationships in relation to their comparison levels in order to assess degree of satisfaction and with attraction to the association. Satisfaction with relationship X (SAT_X) is represented as:

$$SAT_X = O_X - CL \qquad [2]$$

The individual should be more satisfied with and attracted to a relationship as the rewards associated with the relationship increase, costs decrease, and expectations become lower.

Satisfaction and attraction refer to the degree of positive affect associated with a relationship. The individual's commitment to an association, however, is related to the probability that he/she will leave the relationship, and involves feelings of psychological attachment. Commitment is *in part* a function of the relationship outcome value and the outcome value of the individual's best available alternative (or CL_{alt}). Alternative outcome value (O_Y) represents the quality of the best available alternative to a relationship X, whether solitude or an alternative association. It is mathematically defined in the same manner as is satisfaction with the current relationship:

$$A_Y = O_Y - CL \qquad [3]$$

The individual should evaluate alternatives more positively as the rewards associated with the best alternative increase, as its costs decrease, and as comparison level decreases. However, although evaluations of the quality of the current relationship and the alternative both depend on comparison level, comparisons of the relative merits of the two (i.e., $SAT_X - A_Y$) depend solely on the difference between the rewards and costs of one's current association and those of the alternative.

The investment model states that commitment is affected not just by the outcome values of the current relationship and alternative, but also by investment size. Commitment increases with the passage of time in part because the resources "put into" a relationship increase the costs of withdrawing from it. Investments may be of two sorts. *Extrinsic* investments occur when previously extraneous interests are linked to current behavior. For example, an individual's home and his current relationship may not have been initially associated. However, if he believes that dissolution of the relationship with his current partner would cause him to lose his home, commitment should be increased and the individual should be less likely to leave the relationship. The *intrinsic* investment of resources such as time, emotional involvement, self-disclosures, money, and so on, should also increase commitment. Since investments of both types are nonportable and would be lost on dissolution of the relationship, the individual who has made investments should be less likely to leave his ongoing association. Investment size (I_X) is defined as:

$$I_X = \Sigma w_j r_j \qquad [4]$$

where r_j refers to the size of the investment of resource j in relationship X, and w_j refers to the importance of this resource.

Commitment is generally increased over time by the investment of resources in a relationship, but it is also a function of the relationship and alternative outcome values. Commitment to the current association (COM_X) is therefore defined as follows:

$$COM_X = O_X + I_X - O_Y \qquad [5]$$

Thus, commitment should increase as the relationship becomes more "valuable" (or rewarding, with fewer costs), as alternatives decrease in quality, and as the magnitude of the individual's investment in the association becomes larger. It should be noted that satisfaction/attraction and commitment are not isomorphically related. High investments and/or poor alternatives may sometimes serve to "trap" the individual in an unhappy, unsatisfying relationship – commitment may be high while satisfaction and attraction are low.

Although the investment model is a new means of formally distinguishing between the concepts of satisfaction/attraction and commitment, similar concepts have been introduced in the past by other social scientists. The reward/cost (outcome value), comparison level, and alternative value parameters are borrowed directly from interdependence theory (Thibaut and Kelley, 1959; Kelley and Thibaut, 1978), although the explication of their effect on commitment is new to the investment model. Becker (1960) discussed a notion similar to the concept of extrinsic investments when he argued that one of the primary aspects of commitment was "prior actions of the person staking some originally extraneous interest on his following a consistent line of activity" (Becker, 1960, p. 36). An identical factor was identified by Schelling (1956), who referred to extrinsic investments as a "side bet." Rubin (reference note 1) introduced the notion of "entrapment," which is closely related to the concept of commitment. Entrapment refers to the investment of greater resources (e.g., time, energy, money) than an exchange objectively warrants. The process of entrapment directly parallels that of increasing commitment through intrinsic investments, as discussed in the investment model. Finally, Blau (1967) captured much of the content of the investment model when he argued that: "Alternative opportunities foregone strengthen commitments, and together with the investments made sometimes produce firm attachments" (Blau, 1967, p. 160). Thus, although the investment model is a new approach to the study of interpersonal relationships, its basic concepts are firmly rooted in existing psychological and sociological literature.

An experiment and a cross-sectional survey questionnaire were designed to examine the effects of variations in relationship outcome value, alternative outcome value, and investment size on commitment and satisfaction in romantic associations.[1] In the first experiment, subjects were asked to place themselves in the position of the major character in a written scenario, and to answer a number of questions concerning their probable behavior, the value of the relationship with their partner, their attraction to and satisfaction with both the current relationship and the alternative, and their commitment to the current relationship. The second experiment was a survey of individuals who were involved in ongoing romantic associations. These subjects answered questions related to a number of parameters of the investment mode. Multiple regression procedures were employed to determine the extent to which the model parameters accurately predicted their degree of commitment to and satisfaction with the relationships in which they were involved. Together, the two experiments provide a good test of the predictive ability of the investment model, since the strengths of one method correspond to the weaknesses of the other. The experiment is highly controlled and clearly demonstrates causal relations, while the survey possesses greater real-world validity.

Experiment I

Experiment 1 examined the effects of relationship outcome value, intrinsic and extrinsic investment size and alternative outcome value on satisfaction/attraction and commitment in romantic associations. Since it is both unethical and nearly impossible to manipulate these factors systematically in real, developing relationships, these variables were manipulated in a role-playing paradigm. The use of role-playing as an experimental method is not completely satisfactory (Cooper, 1976; Darroch and Steiner, 1970; Freedman, 1972), but is generally seen as enlightening when used in combination with other forms of experimentation (Freedman, 1972) or when appropriate as a complement to standard experimental methods (Cooper, 1976).

Each participant read a role-playing essay that described the major character's dilemma – should he/she remain in the current romantic association or begin to date an alternative person? It was predicted that decreases in the costs associated with the current relationship, increases in intrinsic and extrinsic investment size, and decreases in the quality of the alternative would lead to decreases in the probability that the participant would choose to date the alternative and increases in reported commitment to the current relationship (see Eq. [5]). Satisfaction with and attraction to the current relationship were expected to be significantly affected by variations in the outcome value of the current association, but not by investment size or alternative outcome value (Eq. [2]).

Method

Participants
Eighty-two males and 89 females participated in the experiment in partial fulfillment of the requirements for an introductory psychology course at the University of North Carolina at Chapel Hill. Fourteen to twenty-two participants were present in each experimental session, and the ratio of males to females was approximately equal across experimental conditions.

Procedure
Upon arrival at the experimental session, participants were seated at tables and were given essay booklets and questionnaire materials. The experimenter administered verbal instructions outlining the experimental task. Each participant was asked to place him/herself in the position of the major character of the four-page essay (Robert for male participants, Sarah for females), imagining that person's feelings, attitudes, beliefs, and behavior. Participants were to try to imagine they were experiencing the situations the fictional character experienced and behaving as the essay character behaved, forgetting their own attitudes and characteristic manners of behaving.

Each essay began with a brief description of the character to be role-played by the participant. Male and female essays were identical except for changes in the sex of the major character, current partner, and alternative person. In females' essays, the protagonist (Sarah) was described as a typical 21-year-old junior at the University of North Carolina. Sarah had met Robert, her current romantic partner, at work through her employer (Robert's father), and had dated him for a specified period of time. Robert had recently moved some distance away from Sarah for academic reasons, and the two were now able to see one another less often than they had previously. John, an alternative who was interested in dating Sarah, then entered the scene. Sarah had to decide whether to remain in the current relationship or begin dating the alternative.

The experiment effected four independent variable manipulations: relationship cost (high or low), alternative outcome value (high or low), investment size (high, medium, or low), and sex of participant. *Relationship cost* was manipulated through changes in the difficulty of maintaining the relationship. In the high cost condition, Robert had moved 1,000 miles away and he and Sarah were able to see one another only once a month, and in the low cost condition, he had moved 60 miles away, enabling one or two visits per week. *Alternative outcome value* was manipulated through variations in John's intelligence, personality, physical attributes, and wit, producing a moderately attractive or a moderately unattractive alternative. The third independent variable manipulation effected variations in both intrinsic and extrinsic investment size, and therefore had three levels. In the small investment condition, Sarah had dated Robert for 1 month prior to his move, and in the medium investment condition they had been dating one another for 1 year. A comparison of these two conditions, therefore, tests the effects of the intrinsic investment in the relationship of time. The large investment condition was similar to the medium in that the two had dated for 1 year, but an extrinsic investment was added – if Sarah were to begin dating the alternative, her employer, Robert's father, would know and she would feel compelled to quit her job. A comparison of the medium and large investment conditions, therefore, tests the effects of the extrinsic investment in the current association of the essay character's job.

After reading the essay as many times as was necessary to achieve complete familiarity (this required approximately 15 min), participants placed their essays face down and proceeded to complete their experimental questionnaires. Nineteen nine-point semantic-differential items were designed to measure participants' judged satisfaction with and commitment to the current association, and to assess the effectiveness of the experimental manipulations. Manipulation checks and dependent variables were assessed in a single random order that was constant over questionnaires. Two items served as checks on the intrinsic investment size manipulation (current relationship is very long/short in duration, time investment is very small/large), three served as checks on the extrinsic investment size manipulation (job is extremely/not at all important and connected to current relationship, investment of job in relationship is very small/large), four items assessed the effects of the partner costs manipulation (partner's move is extremely/not at all distant, frequency of visits is likely to be very large/small, current association is extremely/not at all difficult and costly), and five items were designed to evaluate the success of the manipulation of alternative outcome value (the alternative is extremely/not at all intelligent, witty, and physically attractive, his/her personality is extremely/not at all pleasant, dating him/her would be extremely/not at all pleasant). Partipants also answered two questions concerning satisfaction with the current association (I am not at all/extremely satisfied, attracted to relationship), and three related to commitment (it is extremely/not at all likely that I will begin dating the alternative, I am not at all/extremely attached and committed to the current relationship). After completing the questionnaire, participants were thoroughly debriefed, thanked, and excused.

Results

Manipulation checks
The set of manipulation checks associated with each independent variable was subjected to a three-factor nonorthogonal multivariate analysis of variance involving relationship costs, alternative value, and investment size (Appelbaum and Cramer, 1974). Compared to participants in the low cost condition, participants in the high cost condition reported that the relationship was more "costly," that the partner had moved a greater distance, that they could see one another less frequently, and that the relationship had become more difficult (Mult. $F(4, 156) = 745.23, p < .001$). Participants in the high alternative value condition judged their alternative to be more intelligent, physically attractive, and funny, to have a more pleasant personality, and guessed that dating him/her would be more enjoyable, than did participants in the low alternative outcome value condition (Mult. $F(5, 155) = 76.43, p < .001$). Two contrasts assessed the effectiveness of the investment size manipulations. A contrast of the low and medium investment conditions tested the effectiveness of the intrinsic investment manipulation on

measures of subjective duration and size of time investment in the relationship. The two conditions differed as expected (Mult. $F(2, 158) = 173.91$, $p < .001$). The contrast of the medium and high investment conditions on measures of the importance and connectedness of the job to the current partner and the investment of the job in the current relationship also revealed a significant effect (Mult. $F(3, 157) = 82.33$, $p < .001$). Sex of essay character/participant did not significantly affect any set of manipulation checks. Thus, the experimental manipulations appear to have been successful.

Commitment

Three questionnaire items served as measures of commitment: how likely is it that you will begin to date John/Lisa, how attached are you to your relationship with Robert/Sarah, and how committed are you to your current relationship? These data, for the three measures combined, are summarized in table 12.11. A three-factor multivariate analysis of variance was performed on the commitment dependent variables. It was expected that variations in costs, alternative value, and intrinsic and extrinsic investments would significantly affect commitment (see Eq. [5]). Participants in the low cost condition reported that they were less likely to date the alternative and were more attached and committed to their relationship than were those in the high cost condition, but this effect was not significant (Mult. $F(3, 154) = 1.96$, $p < .12$). Low alternative outcome value led to greater reported attachment and commitment and less probability of dating the alternative than did high alternative outcome value (Mult. $F(3, 154) = 13.74$, $p < .001$). The main effect of investment size on the commitment measures was significant (Mult. $F(6, 308) = 2.79$, $p < .01$), so specific contrasts were performed in order to explore the independent effects of intrinsic and extrinsic investments. The contrast of the low and medium investment size conditions revealed that larger intrinsic investments produced greater commitment and attachment and less likelihood of dating the alternative (Mult. $F(3, 154) = 3.50$, $p < .02$). A similar effect was obtained for extrinsic investments, tested by the contrast of the medium and large investment conditions (Mult. $F(3, 154) = 4.51$, $p < .005$). Sex of participant had no significant effect on the commitment measures, and there were no significant interactions. These multivariate analyses indicate that both alternative value and investment size significantly affect commitment. The three measures of commitment were similarly affected by the independent variable manipulations, greater commitment resulting from poorer alternatives, larger intrinsic investments, and larger extrinsic investments. Increases in costs resulted in decreased commitment, but this effect was not statistically significant.

Table 12.11   Mean commitment for each experimental condition

	High cost		Low cost	
	Poor alternative	Good alternative	Poor alternative	Good alternative
Low investment size	17.13	15.14	18.29	15.87
Medium investment size	18.15	16.36	19.69	15.79
Large investment size	18.93	17.43	19.80	18.15

Values shown are the sum of the means of the individual dependent measures. Higher numbers indicate less likelihood of leaving the relationship, greater commitment, and greater attachment.

Further analyses were performed in order to determine why the manipulation of relationship cost failed to affect commitment significantly. Composite values for relationship cost value, alternative value, investment size, and commitment were formed by summing reported values on the individual measures of each concept. The multiple regression of relationship cost, alternative value, and investment size onto commitment was significant ($R = .52$, $p < .001$), and reduced models (eliminating one or more predictor variables) were less powerful. The cost variable, however, was only weakly related to commitment. The fact that the regression of cost value onto commitment revealed a significant relationship, while the analysis of variance reported above did not, suggests that the manipulation of costs was either weak or produced inconsistent effects across participants. However, even in the regression analyses, relationship cost was at best only weakly related to commitment. Thus, except for the weak effects of cost on commitment, these data are in agreement with the hypotheses.

Satisfaction

The investment model predicts that increases in the costs of a relationship should result in decreased attraction to and satisfaction with that relationship (refer to Eq. [2]). A three-factor nonorthogonal analysis of variance performed on the measures of satisfaction with and attraction to the current relationship revealed a significant main effect of relationship cost (Mult. $F(2, 158) = 3.82$, $p < .02$). Participants in the low cost condition were more satisfied with their relationships than were those in the high cost condition (the means were 4.44 and 3.99, $F(1, 157) = 4.25$, $p < .04$), and were more attracted to their current associations (the means were 4.58 and 4.30, $F(1, 157) = 7.04$, $p < .009$). As expected, the correlation between satisfaction/attraction and commitment was weak ($R = .24$, $p < .001$). The sex of participant, investment size, and alternative outcome value variables did not significantly affect satisfaction and attraction. These results provide good support for the prediction concerning the determinants of satisfaction (see Eq. [2]).

Experiment 2

The second experiment explored the ability of several parameters of the investment model to predict commitment and satisfaction in real, ongoing associations. Values of each parameter of the investment model were measured in a survey questionnaire. The reward and cost components of relationship outcome value were measured separately in this experiment because of the weak effects of the cost manipulation in Experiment 1. In light of that problem it seemed useful to obtain measures of both components in this experiment. The adequacy of the investment model in predicting commitment to and satisfaction with current relationships was examined through the use of multiple regression procedures. The best predictions of satisfaction/attraction and commitment should follow the equations presented in the introduction of the paper (Eq. [2] for satisfaction and Eq. [5] for commitment).

Method

Respondents

Fifty-eight male and 53 female students from the University of North Carolina at Chapel Hill participated in the study in partial fulfillment of the requirements for an introductory psychology course. The participant recruitment sheet provided a brief explanation of the study and a description of the type of relationship to be explored (of any duration and degree of "seriousness," ongoing or past) in order to make certain that all respondents would be capable of completing the questionnaire. Approximately 12 participants attended each session.

Procedure

Upon arrival at the session, respondents received verbal instructions outlining the purpose and nature of the questionnaire and were assured that their responses would be completely anonymous. The experimenter stated that she was interested in examining the course of development of romantic relationships, and announced that respondents would be asked to answer a number of questions concerning a romantic association in which they had at some time been involved. She asked that respondents describing past relationships discuss one in which the dissolution of the relationship occurred as a result of their own actions or was agreeable to them. Respondents describing ongoing relationships were asked to respond with respect to how they felt at present about their relationships, while those describing past relationships were to respond with respect to how they felt about their relationships at the time they ended. The partner was to be referred to as "X," and respondents were asked to make an active effort to be honest in completing the questionnaire items. Materials were then distributed and respondents proceeded to complete the experimental questionnaires. The questionnaire required approximately 30 min to complete.

Questionnaire

The questionnaire contained items designed to measure relationship outcome value (both rewards and costs), alternative outcome value, investment size, satisfaction, and commitment. Since it was anticipated that respondents would not easily be able to answer questions such as "what is the outcome value of your best available alternative," the parameters of the investment model were "translated" into the language of everyday relationships, specifically, (1) each parameter was briefly defined, (2) a series of questions representing concrete operationalizations of each parameter was answered, and (3) several estimates of each model parameter were then obtained. Values of the single estimates for each predictor variable and criterion measure were summed to form a single index of each investment model parameter. Unless otherwise indicated, questionnaire items were nine-point semantic differentials, and end anchors were "extremely/not at all," "none/many," or "very small/large."

The *reward value* of the relationship (reward component of O_X) was defined for respondents as the extent to which they believed their relationships possessed good attributes and their partners had positive qualities and traits. Eight concrete measures were designed to assess physical attractiveness, complementary needs, similarity of attitudes and background, personality pleasantness, intelligence, sense of humor, ability to coordinate activities, and sexual satisfaction. In addition, two parameter estimates concerned the extent to which their relationships were rewarding and compared favorably to their ideal relationships.

The *cost value* of the relationship (cost component of O_X) was defined as the extent to which respondents believed their relationships had bad attributes and their partners had negative qualities and traits. Nine concrete measures assessed giving up enjoyable activities, monetary costs, time constraints, embarrassing behaviors, unattractive and persistent personal qualities, unattractive and persistent attitudes, failure to live up to agreements, conflict, and lack of faithfulness. Two parameter estimates evaluated the extent to which it was costly to maintain a relationship with X and compared the costs of that relationship to those they felt were normally associated with relationships.

Alternative outcome value (A_Y) was defined as the quality of the best available alternative to the current relationship – beginning a relationship with another person, dating several other people, or spending time alone. Five concrete measures assessed the attractiveness of alternative persons, difficulty of replacing X, how appealing dating many persons would be, importance of any sort of exclusive romantic involvement, and their happiness when not involved in a romantic association. The parameter estimates concerned degree of expected satisfaction of the alternative, a comparison of the alternative to the respondent's ideal, and a comparison of the alternative to the current relationship. Respondents made these parameter estimates in an abstract sense, without being required to state whether their best alternative was solitude or an alternative association.

Investment size (I_X) was defined for respondents as the extent to which: (1) they had "put things into" their relationships; and (2) there were objects/events/persons/activities uniquely associated with their relationships. Three fill-in concrete items concerned the duration of the relationship, the number of hours per week on the average spent with the partner, and the number of children born of the relationship. Eight concrete measures concerned degree of exclusiveness of the relationship, mutual friends, shared memories, monetary investments, shared material possessions, activities uniquely associated with X, emotional investments, and self-disclosures. Three parameter estimates assessed the extent to which there were important objects/persons/events/activities connected to the relationship, measured the size of the respondent's investment in the relationship, and evaluated the importance of the relationship with X, considering investment size.

Only parameter estimates of the criterion variables of *satisfaction* (SAT_X) and *commitment* (COM_X) were obtained. Four satisfaction measures were designed to assess respondents' attraction to their relationships, positivity of feelings for their partners, satisfaction with their relationships, and closeness of their relationships to their ideals. Six commitment criterion measures assessed the likelihood that respondents would end their relationships in the near future, probable duration of their relationships (very long/short), desired duration of their relationships (very long/short), commitment to their relationships, required attractiveness of alternatives before they would leave their relationships, and degree of attachment to their relationships.

Results

Parameter estimate reliability

In order to obtain estimates of the reliability of the parameter estimates, the set of concrete measures associated with each parameter was regressed onto the parameter estimate. These multiple regressions were significant for reward value ($R = .70, p < .001$), cost value ($R = .42, p < .001$), alternative value ($R = .61, p < .001$), and investment size ($R = .56, p < .001$), so the parameter estimates were judged to be reliable. It should be noted, however, that the multiple correlation onto relationship cost value was low ($.42$). The estimate of cost value may, therefore, have been somewhat unreliable.

Satisfaction

The model testing methods employed to assess the predictive ability of the investment model follow the step-down regression procedures outlined by Cramer (1972). Recall that according to Eq. [2], satisfaction with a relationship should be best predicted by relationship outcome value, a combination of rewards and costs, and that alternative value and investment size should not contribute to this prediction significantly. Judged satisfaction with relationships was significantly correlated with both relationship reward value ($R = .66, p < .001$) and cost value ($R = .17, p < .001$). Multiple regression analyses indicated that both of these factors contributed significantly to the prediction of satisfaction ($R = .68, p < .001$). The deletion of either variable from the regression formula resulted in a significant reduction in predictive ability, and the addition of other variables (alternative outcome value or investment size) did not significantly improve its prediction.

Commitment

According to Eq. [5], commitment to relationships ought to be best predicted by a combination of relationship outcome value, alternative value, and investment size. This experiment provides direct measures of alternative value and investment size, and relationship outcome value is best approximated by either the satisfaction measure or the relationship reward and cost measures. Regression of satisfaction/attraction to current relationships, alternative value, and investment size onto the commitment measure yielded a significant multiple correlation ($R = .78, p < .001$). Deletion of any variable (or pair) from the full investment model produced a significant reduction in predictive power. Predictions of commitment from satisfaction/ attraction alone were significantly less accurate ($R = .65$) than were predictions based on the full model described by Eq. [5] ($F(2, 107) = 24.52, p < .01$).

The contributions of relationship reward and cost values to the prediction of commitment were also explored. Commitment was significantly predicted by the four parameter model consisting of relationships reward and cost values, alternative outcome value, and investment size ($R = .61, p < .001$). Comparisons of this full model to reduced models resulted in significant reductions in predictive power, although the reduction resulting from elimination of the cost variable was minimal (.03 of the variance). Thus, the simplest and most parsimonious prediction of commitment follows from the full investment model – relationship value (rewards *and* costs), alternative value, and investment size, with the qualification that the contributions of relationship cost, although statistically significant, were weak.

Discussion

The primary goal of the present experiments was to assess the adequacy of the investment model in predicting commitment and satisfaction/attraction in ongoing associations. In Experiment 1, decreases in relationship cost value increased perceived satisfaction with an ongoing association, and in Experiment 2, relationship reward value and relationship cost value were both related to satisfaction. These findings are consistent with the investment model. With respect to the prediction of commitment, Experiment 1 demonstrated that an attractive alternative decreased perceived commitment, and increases in both intrinsic and extrinsic investments increased perceived commitment. However, decreases in relationship costs had at best a weak effect on commitment. A similar pattern of results was observed in Experiment 2, where commitment was best predicted by a model including relationship reward and cost values, alternative outcome value, and investment size, but where cost contributed only weakly to these predictions.

The results of the two experiments are thus consistent. Moreover, except for the weak effect of relationship cost on commitment, the results are in complete agreement with the proposed investment model. The romantic ideal that one accepts a mate "for better or worse" may prevent individuals from admitting that they become less committed to another as the costs of doing so increase. However, in recent research (Rusbult, reference note 2; Farrell and Rusbult, reference note 3) it was found that relationship cost value (along with the other investment model parameters) *did* predict commitment in friendships and business associations, where the romantic ideal does not apply. Although this line of reasoning provides a reasonable post hoc explanation for these findings, it may alternatively be that the weak effect of costs is accounted for by poor measurement in Experiment 2, a weak manipulation in Experiment 1, or more general problems with the investment model. These issues must be resolved in future research.

These experiments provide relatively strong support for the investment model. Satisfaction with and attraction to a relationship are a simple function of the rewards and costs (or outcome value) associated with the relationship. An individual's commitment to another, however, cannot be viewed as a simple function of degree of satisfaction with the relationship, nor does it result from a straightforward evaluation of the relative merits of partner and alternative. The magnitude of an individual's investment in a relationship, along with relationship outcome value and alternative outcome value, is a powerful determinant of the stability of that relationship.

The present experiments have demonstrated the utility of the investment model in predicting commitment and satisfaction/attraction in ongoing associations. The model extends our knowledge of interpersonal relationships by focusing on the determinants of both satisfaction and commitment intrelationships that are of a greater duration and degree of involvement than are those explored in most interpersonal attraction research. It goes beyond traditional theories of attraction (Clore and Byrne, 1974; Newcomb, 1968) by exploring the determinants of commitment, an aspect of relationship stability, along with the more traditional issue of positivity of affect (satisfaction/attraction). Whereas Altman and Taylor's (1973) social penetration theory focuses largely on self-disclosures (with some reference to anticipated rewards and costs) as the cause of increasing intimacy, this model deals with a broad range of specific variables that may be subsumed under the more general investment model parameters. While the Levinger and Snoek (1972) model of relationship growth is mainly descriptive, the investment model is highly formalized and predictive in nature. In addition, the investment model extends and formalizes some basic variables of interdependence theory, one of the few general theories of social behavior, and adds to that theory the concepts of investments and commitment. The model is logically consistent, agrees with existing data, is simple, and has a broad range of applicability (it has also been shown to predict satisfaction, commitment, and "turnover" in business associations and in friendships) (Rusbult, reference note 2; Farrell and Rusbult, reference note 3). There exists a clear potential for applying the model to other issues in the study of interpersonal relationships.

NOTES

These experiments are based on a dissertation submitted by the author in partial fulfillment of the requirements for the degree of Doctor of Philosophy at the University of North Carolina at Chapel Hill. The author is grateful to John Thibaut, her committee chairman, and also to Mark Appelbaum, Chester

Insko, John Schopler, and Vaida Thompson, the other committee members. The study was supported by a grant to the author from the National Institute of Child and Human Development.

[1] No attempt was made to measure *CL* in these experiments because of the intimate connection of respondents' reports of reward and cost values with their general expectations (most people cannot separate what exists objectively from what they expect in general). However, when *CL* is experimentally varied, it does significantly affect satisfaction with outcomes.

REFERENCE NOTES

1　Rubin, J.Z. Conflict escalation and entrapment in international relations: A proposal. Research proposal, 1975

2　Rusbult, C.E. The effects of relationship outcome value, alternative outcome value, and investment size upon satisfaction and commitment in friendships. Unpublished manuscript, University of Kentucky, 1979.

3　Farrell, D., and Rusbult, C.E. Job satisfaction, commitment, and turnover. Unpublished manuscript, University of Kentucky, 1979.

REFERENCES

Altman, I., and Taylor, D.A. *Social penetration: The development of interpersonal relationships.* New York: Holt, Rinehart, and Winston, 1973.

Appelbaum, M.I., and Cramer, E.M. Some problems in the nonorthogonal analysis of variance, *Psychological Bulletin*, 1974, *81*, 335–43.

Aronson, E., and Linder, D. Gain and loss of esteem as determinants of interpersonal attractiveness. *Journal of Experimental Social Psychology*, 1965, *1*, 156–71.

Becker, H.S. Notes on the concept of commitment. *American Sociological Review*, 1960, *66*, 32–40.

Blau, P.M. *Exchange and power in social life.* New York, Wiley, 1967.

Byrne, D., and Nelson, D. Attraction as a linear function of proportion of positive reinforcements. *Journal of Personality and Social Psychology*, 1965, *1*, 695–63.

Clore, G.L., and Byrne, D. A reinforcement–affect model of attraction. In T.L. Huston (ed.), *Foundations of interpersonal attraction.* New York: Academic Press, 1974.

Cooper, J. Deception and role playing: On telling the good guys from the bad guys. *American Psychologist*, 1976, *31*, 605–10.

Cramer, E.M. Significance tests and tests of models in multiple regression. *American Statistician*, 1972, *26*, 26–30.

Darroch, R.K., and Steiner, I.D. Role playing: An alternative to laboratory research? *Journal of Personality*, 1970, *38*, 302–11.

Festinger, L. *A theory of cognitive dissonance.* Evanston, II: Row, Peterson, 1957.

Freedman, J.L. Role playing: Psychology by consensus. In A.G. Miller (ed.), *The social psychology of psychological research.* New York: Free Press, 1972.

Gerard, H.B., and Mathewson, G.C. The effects of severity of initiation on liking for a group: A replication. *Journal of Experimental Social Psychology*, 1966, *2*, 278–87.

Heider, F. *The psychology of interpersonal relationships.* New York: Wiley, 1958.

Insko, C.A., and Wilson, M. Interpersonal attraction as a function of social interaction. *Journal of Personality and Social Psychology*, 1977, *35*, 903–11.

Kelley, H.H., and Thibaut, J.E. *Interpersonal relations: A theory of interdependence.* New York: Wiley, 1978.

Levinger, G., and Snoek, J.D. *Attraction in relationships: A new look at interpersonal attraction.* Morristown, NJ: General Learning Press, 1972.

Newcomb, T.M. Interpersonal balance. In R. Abelson, E. Aronson, W.J. McGuire, T.M. Newcomb, M.J. Rosenberg, and P.H. Tannenbaum (eds), *Theories of cognitive consistency: A sourcebook.* Chicago: Rand McNally, 1968.

Schelling, J.C. An essay on bargaining. *American Economic Review*, 1956, 46, 281–306.

Thibaut, J.W., and Kelley, H.H. *The social psychology of groups.* New York: Wiley, 1959.

Walster, E., Aronson, V., Abrahams, D., and Rottman, L. Importance of physical attractiveness in dating behavior. *Journal of Personality and Social Psychology*, 1966, 4, 508–16.

13 Prosocial Behaviour

'From Jerusalem to Jericho': A study of situational and dispositional variables in helping behavior

J.M. Darley and C.D. Batson

Editors'
Introduction

Theoretical Background

Research on helping behaviour, that is on 'voluntary acts performed with the intent of providing benefits to another person' (Dovidio, 1995, p. 290), has developed in several stages. Early research was concerned with the influence of norms, such as reciprocity or social responsibility, on help giving. Subsequently, researchers became fascinated with the problem of bystander apathy and focused mainly on the study of the conditions under which people help (for a review see, Latané and Darley, 1970). In the early 1980s, researchers' questions moved from *when* people help to *why* people help (Dovidio, 1995). They tried to understand the motivational processes underlying helping behaviour, frequently distinguishing egoistic helping, which primarily serves the goal of benefiting oneself, from altruistic helping, aimed at improving the welfare of others (Dovidio, 1995).

Although the focus of the present article is still very much on the situational factors that inhibit helping (e.g. time pressure), it also begins to address the question of why people help and what motivates them to intervene on behalf of others. The study was inspired by the parable of the Good Samaritan and investigates the effects of both personality and situational variables, which according to this parable are relevant to helping. The parable describes how both a priest and a Levite (type of religious functionary) passed a robbery victim on the road to Jericho without helping, whereas a Samaritan helped. The authors reasoned that the main differences between the religious men and the Samaritan were in terms of the content of their thoughts (religious/mundane), the extent to which they travelled under time pressure, and the type of their religiousness.

Journal of Personality and Social Psychology (1973), 27:100–8.

Hypotheses

Three hypotheses were formulated, ostensibly derived from the parable:

1 People who encounter a potential helping situation while thinking religious and ethical thoughts will be no more likely to offer help than people thinking about something else. This first prediction is counter-intuitive, non-obvious and in favour of the null-hypothesis, and thus difficult to test. It also does not really follow from the parable.
2 People encountering a helping situation are less likely to help when they are in a hurry than when they are not.
3 Type of religiosity will make a difference.

Design

The main design of the study was a 2 (message: task relevant/helping relevant) × 3 (hurry: high, medium, low) between-subjects design. In addition, a religiousness scale allowed the analysis of the impact of individual differences in religiousness on helping.

Method

Subjects in this experiment were students at a theological seminary who thought they were participating in a study on religious education and vocation. For the independent variables, subjects were induced to think either about the parable of the Good Samaritan (helping-relevant message) or about professional problems (task-relevant message); they were then sent to another building ostensibly for the second part of the experiment with instructions that imposed different degrees of time pressure. For example, in the high-hurry condition they were told that they were late and had been expected in the other building minutes earlier; in the low-hurry condition they were told that it would be a few minutes before the assistant in the other building would be ready for them. In addition, type of religiosity was measured with three scales. The helping incident happened after the independent variables had been manipulated or measured. While in transit to the other building, the subjects passed a slumped victim 'planted' in an alleyway, who had his head down and his eyes closed. The dependent measure assessed the extent to which the subject helped. It could be used either as a dichotomous variable (helping/not helping) or as a continuous variable expressing degrees of helpfulness.

Results

Helping scores were analysed with a 3 (hurry) × 2 (message) unequal-N analysis of variance, which resulted in a significant main effect for hurry. (The results of this analysis were replicated with a multiple regression.) The more people were put under time pressure, the less likely they were to help. Also in line with the authors' predictions, helping was not significantly affected by whether or not subjects were put in a helping frame of mind through thinking about the story of the Good Samaritan. Finally, the relationship between religious personality variables and type of helping behaviour was analysed by means of correlations. Religious personality did not predict whether an individual would help the victim or not. However, if a subject did stop to offer help, the character of the helping response was related to type of religiosity.

Discussion

This study is a prime example of the creative and daring field experiments which began to grasp the imagination of social psychologists in the 1970s. It supported both main hypotheses, namely that time pressure decreased helping behaviour and that thinking religious and ethical thoughts had no impact on helping. The latter finding becomes even more suprising when translated into modern terminology: priming subjects with helping thoughts by getting them to read the parable of the Good Samaritan did not increase helping behaviour. However, the fact that the pattern of means (table 13.1) as well as figure 13.1 in the textbook (chapter 13) suggest a consistent and stable difference between the two message conditions makes one wonder whether this effect might not have become significant if more than forty-six subjects had been included in the present study. These doubts are further strengthened by the results of a reanalysis of the data of this study in terms of Bayesian statistics, which showed that there was substantial evidence for the alternative hypothesis that reading the parable did, in fact, increase the odds in favour of helping (Greenwald, 1975).

FURTHER READING

Batson, C.D., Batson, J.G., Griffitt, C.A. et al. (1989). Negative-state relief and the empathy–altruism hypothesis. *Journal of Personality and Social Psychology*, 56, 922–33. Reviews a series of studies which pit two motivational explanations of altrusim against each other.
Greenwald, A.G. (1975). Does the Good Samaritan parable increase helping? A comment on Darley and Batson's no-effect conclusion. *Journal of Personality and Social Psychology*, 32, 578–83. Presents a reanalysis of the Darley and Batson findings in terms of a different statistical model (Bayes) and arrives at the conclusion that there was a great deal of evidence that reading the parable of the Good Samaritan increased helping behaviour.

REFERENCES

Dovidio, J.F. (1995). Helping behaviour. In A.S.R. Manstead and M. Hewstone (eds), *The Blackwell Encyclopedia of Social Psychology* (pp. 290–5). Oxford: Blackwell.
Latané, B. and Darley, J.M. (1970). *The Unresponsive Bystander: Why Doesn't He Help?*. New York: Appleton-Century-Crofts.

Helping other people in distress is, among other things, an ethical act. That is, it is an act governed by ethical norms and precepts taught to children at home, in school, and in church. From Freudian and other personality theories, one would expect individual differences in internalization of these standards that would lead to differences between individuals in the likelihood with which they would help others. But recent research on bystander intervention in emergency situations (Bickman, 1969; Darley and Latané, 1968; Korte, 1969; but see also Schwartz and Clausen, 1970) has had bad luck in finding personality determinants of helping behavior. Although personality variables that one might expect to correlate with helping behavior have been measured (Machiavellianism, authoritarianism, social desirability, alienation, and social responsibility), these were not predictive of helping. Nor was this due to a generalized lack of predictability in the helping situation examined, since variations in the experimental situation, such as the availability of other people who might also help, produced marked changes in rates of helping behavior. These findings are reminiscent of Hartshorne and May's (1928) discovery that resistance to temptation, another ethically relevant act, did not seem to be a fixed characteristic of an individual. That is, a person who was likely to be honest in one situation was not particularly likely to be honest in the next (but see also Burton, 1963).

The rather disappointing correlation between the social psychologist's traditional set of personality variables and helping behavior in emergency situations suggests the need for a fresh perspective on possible predictors of helping and possible situations in which to test them. Therefore, for inspiration we turned to the Bible, to what is perhaps the classical helping story in the Judeo-Christian tradition, the parable of the Good Samaritan. The parable proved of value in suggesting both personality and situational variables relevant to helping.

> "And who is my neighbor?" Jesus replied, "A man was going down from Jerusalem to Jericho, and he fell among robbers, who stripped him and beat him, and departed, leaving him half dead. Now by chance a priest was going down the road; and when he saw him he passed by on the other side. So likewise a Levite, when he came to the place and saw him, passed by on the other side. But a Samaritan, as he journeyed, came to where he was; and when he saw him, he had compassion, and went to him and bound his wounds, pouring on oil and wine; then he set him on his own beast and brought him to an inn, and took care of him. And the next day he took out two denarii and gave them to the innkeeper, saying, "Take care of him; and whatever more you spend, I will repay you when I come back." Which of these three, do you think, proved neighbor to him who fell among the robbers? He said, "The one who showed mercy on him." And Jesus said to him, "Go and do likewise." (Luke 10: 29–37 RSV)

To psychologists who reflect on the parable, it seems to suggest situational and personality differences between the nonhelpful priest and Levite and the helpful Samaritan. What might each have been thinking and doing when he came upon the robbery victim on that desolate road? What sort of persons were they?

One can speculate on differences in thought. Both the priest and the Levite were religious functionaries who could be expected to have their minds occupied with religious matters. The priest's role in religious activities is obvious. The Levite's role, although less obvious, is equally important: The Levites were necessary participants in temple ceremonies. Much less can be said with any confidence about what the Samaritan might have been thinking, but, in contrast to the others, it was most likely not of a religious nature, for Samaritans were religious outcasts.

Not only was the Samaritan most likely thinking about more mundane matters than the priest and Levite, but, because he was socially less important, it seems likely that he was operating on a quite different time schedule. One can imagine the priest and Levite, public figures, hurrying along with little black books full of meetings and ap glancing furtively at their sundials. In contrast, the Samaritan would likely have .. less important people counting on him to be at a particular place at a particular time, .. therefore might be expected to be in less of a hurry than the prominent priest or Levite.

In addition to these situational variables, one finds personality factors suggested as well. Central among these, and apparently basic to the point that Jesus was trying to make, is a distinction between types of religiosity. Both the priest and Levite are extremely "religious." But it seems to be precisely their type of religiosity that the parable challenges. At issue is the motivation for one's religion and ethical behavior. Jesus seems to feel that the religious leaders of his time, though certainly respected and upstanding citizens, may be "virtuous" for what it will get them, both in terms of the admiration of their fellowmen and in the eyes of God. New Testament scholar R.W. Funk (1966) noted that the Samaritan is at the other end of the spectrum: "The Samaritan does not love with side glances at God. The need of neighbor alone is made self-evident, and the Samaritan responds without other motivation" (pp. 218–19). That is, the Samaritan is interpreted as responding spontaneously to the situation, not as being preoccupied with the abstract ethical or organizational dos and don'ts of religion as the priest and Levite would seem to be. This is not to say that the Samaritan is portrayed as irreligious. A major intent of the parable would seem to be to present the Samaritan as a religious and ethical example, but at the same time to contrast his type of religiosity with the more common conception of religiosity that the priest and Levite represent.

To summarize the variables suggested as affecting helping behavior by the parable, the situational variables include the content of one's thinking and the amount of hurry in one's journey. The major dispositional variable seems to be differing types of religiosity. Certainly these variables do not exhaust the list that could be elicited from the parable, but they do suggest several research hypotheses.

Hypothesis 1   The parable implies that people who encounter a situation possibly calling for a helping response while thinking religious and ethical thoughts will be no more likely to offer aid than persons thinking about something else. Such a hypothesis seems to run counter to a theory that focuses on norms as determining helping behavior because a normative account would predict that the increased salience of helping norms produced by thinking about religious and ethical examples would increase helping behavior.

Hypothesis 2   Persons encountering a possible helping situation when they are in a hurry will be less likely to offer aid than persons not in a hurry.

Hypothesis 3   Concerning types of religiosity, persons who are religious in a Samaritanlike fashion will help more frequently than those religious in a priest or Levite fashion.

Obviously, this last hypothesis is hardly operationalized as stated. Prior research by one of the investigators on types of religiosity (Batson, 1971), however, led us to differentiate three distinct ways of being religious: (a) for what it will gain one (cf. Freud, 1953, and perhaps the priest and Levite), (b) for its own intrinsic value (cf. Allport and Ross, 1967), and (c) as a response to and quest for meaning in one's everyday life (cf. Batson, 1971). Both of the latter conceptions would be proposed by their exponents as related to the more Samaritanlike "true" religiosity. Therefore, depending on the theorist one follows, the third hypothesis may be stated like this: People (a) who are religious for intrinsic reasons (Allport and Ross, 1967) or

(b) whose religion emerges out of questioning the meaning of their everyday lives (Batson, 1971) will be more likely to stop to offer help to the victim.

The parable of the Good Samaritan also suggested how we would measure people's helping behavior – their response to a stranger slumped by the side of one's path. The victim should appear somewhat ambiguous – ill-dressed, possibly in need of help, but also possibly drunk or even potentially dangerous.

Further, the parable suggests a means by which the incident could be perceived as a real one rather than part of a psychological experiment in which one's behavior was under surveillance and might be shaped by demand characteristics (Orne, 1962), evaluation apprehension (Rosenberg, 1965), or other potentially artifactual determinants of helping behavior. The victim should be encountered not in the experimental context but on the road between various tasks.

Method

In order to examine the influence of these variables on helping behavior, seminary students were asked to participate in a study on religious education and vocations. In the first testing session, personality questionnaires concerning types of religiosity were administered. In a second individual session, the subject began experimental procedures in one building and was asked to report to another building for later procedures. While in transit, the subject passed a slumped "victim" planted in an alleyway. The dependent variable was whether and how the subject helped the victim. The independent variables were the degree to which the subject was told to hurry in reaching the other building and the talk he was to give when he arrived there. Some subjects were to give a talk on the jobs in which seminary students would be most effective, others, on the parable of the Good Samaritan.

Subjects

The subjects for the questionnaire administration were 67 students at Princeton Theological Seminary. Forty-seven of them, those who could be reached by telephone, were scheduled for the experiment. Of the 47, 7 subjects' data were not included in the analyses – 3 because of contamination of the experimental procedures during their testing and 4 due to suspicion of the experimental situation. Each subject was paid $1 for the questionnaire session and $1.50 for the experimental session.

Personality measures

Detailed discussion of the personality scales used may be found elsewhere (Batson, 1971), so the present discussion will be brief. The general personality construct under examination was religiosity. Various conceptions of religiosity have been offered in recent years based on different psychometric scales. The conception seeming to generate the most interest is the Allport and Ross (1967) distinction between "intrinsic" versus "extrinsic" religiosity (cf. also Allen and Spilka, 1967, on "committed" versus "consensual" religion). This bipolar conception of religiosity has been questioned by Brown (1964) and Batson (1971), who suggested three-dimensional analyses instead. Therefore, in the present research, types of religiosity were measured with three instruments which together provided six separate scales: (a) a *doctrinal orthodoxy* (D-O) scale patterned after that used by Glock and Stark (1966), scaling agreement with classic doctrines of Protestant theology; (b) the Allport–Ross *extrinsic* (AR-E) scale, measuring the use of religion as a means to an end rather than as an end in itself; (c) the Allport–Ross *intrinsic* (AR-I) scale, measuring the use of religion as an end in itself; (d) the *extrinsic external* scale of Batson's Religious Life Inventory (RELI-EE), designed to measure the influence of significant others and situations in generating one's religiosity; (e) the *extrinsic internal* scale of the Religious Life Inventory (RELI-EI), designed to measure the degree of "drivenness" in one's religiosity; and (f) the *intrinsic* scale of the Religious Life Inventory (RELI-I), designed to measure the degree to which one's religiosity involves a questioning of the meaning of life arising out of one's interactions with his social environment. The order of presentation of the scales in the questionnaire was RELI, AR, D-O.

Consistent with prior research (Batson, 1971), a principal-component analysis of the total scale scores and individual items for the 67 seminarians produced a theoretically meaningful, orthogonally rotated three-component structure with the following loadings:

Religion as means received a single very high loading from AR-E (.903) and therefore was defined by Allport and Ross's (1967) conception of this scale as measuring religiosity as a means to other ends. This component also received moderate negative loadings from D-O (−.400) and AR-I (−.372) and a moderate positive loading from RELI-EE (.301).

Religion as end received high loadings from RELI-EI (.874), RELI-EE (.725), AR-I (.768), and D-O (.704). Given this configuration, and again following Allport and Ross's conceptualization, this component seemed to involve religiosity as an end in itself with some intrinsic value.

Religion as quest received a single very high loading from RELI-I (.945) and a moderate loading from RELI-EE (.75). Following Batson, this component was conceived to involve religiosity emerging out of an individual's search for meaning in his personal and social world.

The three religious personality scales examined in the experimental research were constructed through the use of complete-estimation factor score coefficients from these three components.

Scheduling of experimental study

Since the incident requiring a helping response was staged outdoors, the entire experimental study was run in 3 days, December 14–16, 1970, between 10 a.m. and 4 p.m. A tight schedule was used in an attempt to maintain reasonably consistent weather and light conditions. Temperature fluctuation according to the *New York Times* for the 3 days during these hours was not more than 5 degrees Fahrenheit. No rain or snow fell, although the third day was cloudy, whereas the first two were sunny. Within days the subjects were randomly assigned to experimental conditions.[1]

Procedure

When a subject appeared for the experiment, an assistant (who was blind with respect to the personality scores) asked him to read a brief statement which explained that he was participating in a study of the vocational careers of seminary students. After developing the rationale for the study, the statement read:

What we have called you in for today is to provide us with some additional material which will give us a clearer picture of how you think than does the questionnaire material we have gathered thus far. Questionnaires are helpful, but tend to be somewhat oversimplified. Therefore, we would like to record a 3–5-minute talk you give based on the following passage. . . .

Variable 1: Message

In the task-relevant condition the passage read,

With increasing frequency the question is being asked: What jobs or professions do seminary students subsequently enjoy most, and in what jobs are they most effective? The answer to this question used to be so obvious that the question was not even asked. Seminary students were being trained for the ministry, and since both society at large and the seminary student himself had a relatively clear understanding of what make a "good" minister, there was no need even to raise the question of for what other jobs seminary experience seems to be an asset. Today, however, neither society nor many seminaries have a very clearly defined conception of what a "good" minister is or of what sorts of jobs and professions are the best context in which to minister. Many seminary students, apparently genuinely concerned with "ministering," seem to feel that it is impossible to minister in the professional clergy. Other students, no less concerned, find the clergy the most viable profession for ministry. But are there other jobs and/or professions for which seminary experience is an asset? And, indeed, how much of an asset is it for the professional ministry? Or, even more broadly, can one minister through an "establishment" job at all?

In the helping-relevant condition, the subject was given the parable of the Good Samaritan exactly as printed earlier in this article. Next, regardless of condition, all subjects were told.

You can say whatever you wish based on the passage. Because we are interested in how you think on your feet, you will not be allowed to use notes in giving the talk. Do you understand what you are to do? If not, the assistant will be glad to answer questions.

After a few minutes the assistant returned, asked if there were any questions, and then said:

Since they're rather tight on space in this building, we're using a free office in the building next door for recording the talks. Let me show you how to get there [draws and explains map on 3 × 5 card]. This is where Professor Steiner's laboratory is. If you go in this door [points at map], there's a secretary right here, and she'll direct you to the office we're using for recording. Another of Professor Steiner's assistants will set you up for recording your talk. Is the map clear?

Variable 2: Hurry

In the high-hurry condition the assistant then looked at his watch and said, "Oh, you're late. They were expecting you a few minutes ago. We'd better get moving. The assistant should be waiting for you so you'd better hurry. It shouldn't take but just a minute." In the intermediate-hurry condition he said, "The assistant is ready for you, so please go right over." In the low-hurry condition he said, "It'll be a few minutes before they're ready for you, but you might as well head on over. If you have to wait over there, it shouldn't be long."

The incident

When the subject passed through the alley, the victim was sitting slumped in a doorway, head down, eyes closed, not moving. As the subject went by, the victim coughed twice and groaned, keeping his head down. If the subject stopped and asked if something was wrong or offered to help, the victim, startled and somewhat groggy, said, "Oh, thank you [cough]. . . . No, it's all right. [Pause] I've got this respiratory condition [cough]. . . . The doctor's given me these pills to take, and I just took one. . . . If I just sit and rest for a few minutes I'll be O.K. . . . Thanks very much for stopping though [smiles weakly]." If the subject persisted, insisting on taking the victim inside the building, the victim allowed him to do so and thanked him.

Helping ratings

The victim rated each subject on a scale of helping behavior as follows: 0 = failed to notice the victim as possibly in need at all; 1 = perceived the victim as possibly in need but did not offer aid; 2 = did not stop but helped indirectly (e.g., by telling Steiner's assistant about the victim); 3 = stopped and asked if victim needed help; 4 = after stopping, insisted on taking the victim inside and then left him.

The victim was blind to the personality scale scores and experimental conditions of all subjects. At the suggestion of the victim, another category was added to the rating scales, based on his observations of pilot subjects' behavior: 5 = after stopping, refused to leave the victim (after 3–5 minutes) and/or insisted on taking him somewhere outside experimental context (e.g., for coffee or to the infirmary). (In some cases it was necessary to distinguish Category 0 from Category 1 by the postexperimental questionnaire and Category 2 from Category 1 on the report of the experimental assistant.)

This 6-point scale of helping behavior and a description of the victim were given to a panel of 10 judges (unacquainted with the research) who were asked to rank order the (unnumbered) categories in terms of "the amount of helping behavior displayed toward the person in the doorway." Of the 10, 1 judge reversed the order of Categories 0 and 1. Otherwise there was complete agreement with the ranking implied in the presentation of the scale above.

The speech

After passing through the alley and entering the door marked on the map, the subject entered a secretary's office. She introduced him to the assistant who gave the subject time to prepare and privately record his talk.

Helping behavior questionnaire

After recording the talk, the subject was sent to another experimenter, who administered "an exploratory questionnaire on personal and social ethics." The questionnaire contained several initial questions about the interrelationship between social and personal ethics, and then asked three key questions: (a) "When was the last time you saw a person who seemed to be in need of help?" (b) "When was the last time you stopped to help someone in need?" (c) "Have you had experience helping persons in need? If so, outline briefly." These data were collected as a check on the victim's ratings of whether subjects who did not stop perceived the situation in the alley as one possibly involving need or not.

When he returned, the experimenter reviewed the subject's questionnaire, and, if no mention was mede of the situation in the alley, probed for reactions to it and then phased into an elaborate debriefing and discussion session.

Debriefing

In the debriefing, the subject was told the exact nature of the study, including the deception involved, and the reasons for the deception were explained. The subject's reactions to the victim and to the study in general were discussed. The role of situational determinants of helping behavior was explained in relation to this particular incident and to other experiences of the subject. All subjects seemed readily to understand the necessity for the deception, and none indicated any resentment of it. After debriefing, the subject was thanked for his time and paid, then he left.

Results and Discussion

Overall helping behavior

The average amount of help that a subject offered the victim, by condition, is shown in table 13.1. The unequal-N analysis of variance indicates that while the hurry variable was significantly ($F = 3.56$, $df = 2/34$, $p < .05$) related to helping behavior, the message variable was not. Subjects in a hurry were likely to offer less help than were subjects not in a hurry. Whether the subject was going to give a speech on the parable of the Good Samaritan or not did not significantly affect his helping behavior on this analysis.

Other sudies have focused on the question of whether a person initiates helping action or not, rather than on scaled kinds of helping. The data from the present study can also be analyzed on the following terms: Of the 40 subjects, 16 (40%) offered some form of direct or indirect aid to the victim (Coding Categories 2–5), 24 (60%) did not (Coding Categories 0 and 1). The percentages of subjects who offered aid by situational variable were, for low hurry, 63% offered help, intermediate hurry 45%, and high hurry 10%; for helping-relevant message 53%,

Table 13.1   Means and analysis of variance of graded helping responses

	M			
	Hurry			
Message	*Low*	*Medium*	*High*	*Summary*
Helping relevant	3.800	2.000	1.000	2.263
Task relevant	1.667	1.667	.500	1.333
Summary	3.000	1.818	.700	

Analysis of variance				
Source	SS	df	MS	F
Message (A)	7.766	1	7.766	2.65
Hurry (B)	20.884	2	10.442	3.56*
A × B	5.237	2	2.619	.89
Error	99.633	34	2.930	

$N = 40$.
*$p < .05$.

task-relevant message 29%. With regard to this more general question of whether help was offered or not, an unequal-N analysis of variance (arc sine transformation of percentages of helpers, with low- and intermediate-hurry conditions pooled) indicated that again only the hurry main effect was significantly ($F = 5.22, p < .05$) related to helping behavior; the subjects in a hurry were more likely to pass by the victim than were those in less of a hurry.

Reviewing the predictions in the light of these results, the second hypothesis, that the degree of hurry a person is in determines his helping behavior, was supported. The prediction involved in the first hypothesis concerning the message content was based on the parable. The parable itself seemed to suggest that thinking pious thoughts would not increase helping. Another and conflicting prediction might be produced by a norm salience theory. Thinking about the parable should make norms for helping salient and therefore produce more helping. The data, as hypothesized, are more congruent with the prediction drawn from the parable. A person going to speak on the parable of the Good Samaritan is not significantly more likely to stop to help a person by the side of the road than is a person going to talk about possible occupations for seminary graduates.

Since both situational hypotheses are confirmed, it is tempting to stop the analysis of these variables at this point. However, multiple regression analysis procedures were also used to analyze the relationship of all of the independent variables of the study and the helping behavior. In addition to often being more statistically powerful due to the use of more data information, multiple regression analysis has an advantage over analysis of variance in that it allows for a comparison of the relative effect of the various independent variables in accounting for variance in the dependent variable. Also, multiple regression analysis can compare the effects of continuous as well as nominal independent variables on both continuous and nominal dependent variables (through the use of point biserial correlations. r_{pb}) and shows considerable robustness to violation of normality assumptions (Cohen, 1965, 1968). Table 13.2 reports the results of the multiple regression analysis using both help versus no help and the graded

Table 13.2 Stepwise multiple regression analysis

Help vs. no help					Graded helping				
	Individual variable		Overall equation			Individual variable		Variable equation	
Step	r^a	F	R	F	Step	r	F	R	F
1 Hurry[b]	−.37	4.537*	.37	5.884*	1 Hurry	−.42	6.665*	.42	8.196**
2 Message[c]	.25	1.495	.41	3.834*	2 Message	.25	1.719	.46	5.083*
3 Religion as quest	−.03	.081	.42	2.521	3 Religion as quest	−.16	1.297	.50	3.897*
4 Religion as means	−.03	.003	.42	1.838*	4 Religion as means	−.08	.018	.50	2.848*
5 Religion as end	.06	.000	.42	1.430	5 Religion as end	−.07	.001	.50	2.213

$N = 40$. Helping is the dependent variable. $df = 1/34$.
[a] Individual variable correlation coefficient is a point biserial where appropriate.
[b] Variables are listed in order of entry into stepwise regression equations.
[c] Helping-relevant message is positive.
*$p < .05$.
**$p < .01$.

helping scale as dependent measures. In this table the overall equation Fs show the F value of the entire regression equation as a particular row variable enters the equation. Individual variable Fs were computed with all five independent variables in the equation. Although the two situational variables, hurry and message condition, correlated more highly with the dependent measure than any of the religious dispositional variables, only hurry was a significant predictor of whether one will help or not (column 1) or of the overall amount of help given (column 2). These results corroborate the findings of the analysis of variance.[2]

Notice also that neither form of the third hypothesis, that types of religiosity will predict helping, received support from these data. No correlation between the various measures of religiosity and any form of the dependent measure ever came near statistical significance, even though the multiple regression analysis procedure is a powerful and not particularly conservative statistical test.

Personality difference among subjects who helped

To further investigate the possible influence of personality variables, analyses were carried out using only the data from subjects who offered some kind of help to the victim. Surprisingly (since the number of these subjects was small, only 16) when this was done, one religiosity variable seemed to be significantly related to the kind of helping behavior offered. (The situational variables had no significant effect.) Subjects high on the religion as quest dimension appear likely, when they stop for the victim, to offer help of a more tentative or incomplete nature than are subjects scoring low on this dimension ($r = -.53, p < .05$).

This result seemed unsettling for the thinking behind either form of Hypothesis 3. Not only do the data suggest that the Allport–Ross-based conception of religion as *end* does not predict the degree of helping, but the religion as quest component is a significant predictor of offering less help. This latter result seems counterintuitive and out of keeping with previous research (Batson, 1971), which found that this type of religiosity correlated positively with other socially valued characteristics. Further data analysis, however, seemed to suggest a different interpretation of this result.

It will be remembered that one helping coding category was added at the suggestion of the victim after his observation of pilot subjects. The correlation of religious personality variables with helping behavior dichotomized between the added category (1) and all of the others (0) was examined. The correlation between religion as quest and this dichotomous helping scale was essentially unchanged ($r_{pb} = -.54, p < .05$). Thus, the previously found correlation between the helping scale and religion as quest seems to reflect the tendency of those who score low on the quest dimension to offer help in the added helping category.

What does help in this added category represent? Within the context of the experiment, it represented an embarrassment. The victim's response to persistent offers of help was to assure the helper he was all right, had taken his medicine, just needed to rest for a minute or so, and, if ultimately necessary, to request the helper to leave. But the *super* helpers in this added category often would not leave until the final appeal was repeated several times by the victim (who was growing increasingly panicky at the possibility of the arrival of the next subject). Since it usually involved the subject's attempting to carry through a preset plan (e.g., taking the subject for a cup of coffee or revealing to him the strength to be found in Christ), and did not allow information from the victim to change that plan, we originally labeled this kind of helping as rigid – an interpretation supported by its increased likelihood among highly doctrinal orthodox subjects ($r = .63, p < .01$). It also seemed to have an inappropriate character. If this more extreme form of helping behavior is indeed effectively less helpful, then the second form of Hypothesis 3 does seem to gain support.

But perhaps it is the experimenters rather than the super helpers who are doing the inappropriate thing; perhaps the best characterization of this kind of helping is as different rather than as inappropriate. This kind of helper seems quickly to place a particular interpretation on the situation, and the helping response seems to follow naturally from this interpretation. All that can safely be said is that one style of helping that emerged in this experiment was directed toward the presumed underlying needs of the victim and was little modified by the victim's comments about his own needs. In contrast, another style was more tentative and seemed more responsive to the victim's statements of his need.

The former kind of helping was likely to be displayed by subjects who expressed strong doctrinal orthodoxy. Conversely, this fixed kind of helping was unlikely among subjects high on the religion as quest dimension. These latter subjects, who conceived their religion as involving an ongoing search for meaning in their personal and social world, seemed more responsive to the victim's immediate needs and more open to the victim's definitions of his own needs.

Conclusion and Implications

A person not in a hurry may stop and offer help to a person in distress. A person in a hurry is likely to keep going. Ironically, he is likely to keep going even if he is hurrying to speak on the parable of the Good Samaritan, thus inadvertently confirming the point of the parable. (Indeed, on several occasions, a seminary student going to give his talk on the parable of the Good Samaritan literally stepped over the victim as he hurried on his way!)

Although the degree to which a person was in a hurry had a clearly significant effect on his likelihood of offering the victim help, whether he was going to give a sermon on the parable or on possible vocational roles of ministers did not. This lack of effect of sermon topic raises certain difficulties for an explanation of helping behavior involving helping norms and their salience. It is hard to think of a context in which norms concerning helping those in distress are more salient than for a person thinking about the Good Samaritan, and yet it did not significantly increase helping behavior. The results were in the direction suggested by the norm salience hypothesis, but they were not significant. The most accurate conclusion seems to be that salience of helping norms is a less strong determinant of helping behavior in the present situation than many, including the present authors, would expect.

Thinking about the Good Samaritan did not increase helping behavior, but being in a hurry decreased it. It is difficult not to conclude from this that the frequently cited explanation that ethics becomes a luxury as the speed of our daily lives increases is at least an accurate description. The picture that this explanation conveys is of a person seeing another, consciously noting his distress, and consciously choosing to leave him in distress. But perhaps this is not entirely accurate, for, when a person is in a hurry, something seems to happen that is akin to Tolman's (1948) concept of the "narrowing of the cognitive man." Our seminarians in a hurry noticed the victim in that in the postexperiment interview almost all mentioned him as, on reflection, possibly in need of help. But it seems that they often had not worked this out when they were near the victim. Either the interpretation of their visual picture as a person in distress or the empathic reactions usually associated with that interpretation had been deferred because they were hurrying. According to the reflections of some of the subjects, it would be inaccurate to say that they realized the victim's possible distress, then chose to ignore it; instead, because of the time pressures, they did not perceive the scene in the alley as an occasion for an ethical decision.

For other subjects it seems more accurate to conclude that they decided not to stop. They appeared aroused and anxious after the encounter in the alley. For these subjects, what were the elements of the choice that they were making? Why were the seminarians hurrying? Because the experimenter, *whom the subject was helping*, was depending on him to get to a particular place quickly. In other words, he was in conflict between stopping to help the victim and continuing on his way to help the experimenter. And this is often true of people in a hurry; they hurry because somebody depends on their being somewhere. Conflict, rather than callousness, can explain their failure to stop.

Finally, as in other studies, personality variables were not useful in predicting whether a person helped or not. But in this study, unlike many previous ones, considerable variations were possible in the kinds of help given, and these variations did relate to personality measures – specifically to religiosity of the quest sort. The clear light of hindsight suggests that the dimension of kinds of helping would have been the appropriate place to look for personality differences all along; *whether* a person helps or not is an instant decision likely to be situationally controlled. How a person helps involves a more complex and considered number of decisions, including the time and scope to permit personality characteristics to shape them.

NOTES

For assistance in conducting this research thanks are due Robert Wells, Beverly Fisher, Mike Shafto, Peter Sheras, Richard Detweiler, and Karen Glasser. The research was funded by National Science Foundation Grant GS-2293.

[1] An error was made in randomizing that increased the number of subjects in the intermediate-hurry conditions. This worked against the prediction that was most highly confirmed (the hurry prediction) and made no difference to the message variable tests.

[2] To check the legimacy of the use of both analysis of variance and multiple regression analysis, parametric analyses, on this ordinal data, Kendall rank correlation coefficients were calculated between the helping scale and the five independent variables. As expected τ approximated the correlation quite closely in each case and was significant for hurry only (hurry, $\tau = -.38$, $p < .001$).

REFERENCES

Allex, R.O., and Spilka, B. Committed and consensual religion. A specification of religion–prejudice relationships. *Journal for the Scientific Study of Religion*, 1967, 6, 191–206.

Allport, G.W., and Ross, J.M. Personal religious orientation and prejudice. *Journal of Personality and Social Psychology*, 1967, 5, 432–43.

Batson, C.D. Creativity and religious development: Toward a structural-functional psychology of religion. Unpublished doctoral dissertation, Princeton Theological Seminary, 1971.

Bickman, L.B. The effect of the presence of others on bystander intervention in an emergency. Unpublished doctoral dissertation, City College of the City University of New York, 1969.

Brown, L.B. Classifications of religious orientation. *Journal for the Scientific Study of Religion*, 1964, *4*, 91–9.

Burton, R.V. The generality of honesty reconsidered. *Psychological Review*, 1963, *70*, 481–99.

Cohen, J. Some statistical issues in psychological research. In B.B. Wolman (ed.), *Handbood of clinical psychology*. New York: McGraw-Hill, 1965.

Cohen, J. Multiple regression as a general data-analytic system. *Psychological Bulletin*, 1968, *70*, 426–43.

Darley, J.M., and Latané, B. Bystander intervention in emergencies: Diffusion of responsibility. *Journal of Personality and Social Psychology*, 1968, *8*, 377–83.

Freud, S. *The future of an illusion*. New York: Liveright, 1953.

Funk, R.W. *Language, hermeneutic, and word of God*. New York: Harper and Row, 1966.

Glock, C.Y., and Stark, R. *Christian beliefs and anti-Semitism*. New York: Harper and Row, 1966.

Hartshorne, H., and May, M.A. *Studies in the nature of character*. Vol. 1. *Studies in deceit*. New York: Macmillan, 1928.

Korte, C. Group effects on help-giving in an emergency. *Proceedings of the 77th Annual Convention of the American Psychological Association*, 1969, *4*, 383–4. (Summary)

Orne, M.T. On the social psychology of the psychological experiment: With particular reference to demand characteristics and their implications. *American Psychologist*, 1962, *17*, 776–83.

Rosenberg, M.J. When dissonance fails: On eliminating evaluation apprehension from attitude measurement. *Journal of Personality and Social Psychology*, 1965, *1*, 28–42.

Schwartz, S.H., and Clausen, G.T. Responsibility, norms, and helping in an emergency. *Journal of Personality and Social Psychology*, 1970, *16*, 299–310.

Tolman, E.C. Cognitive maps in rats and men. *Psychological Review*, 1948, *55*, 189–208.

A lady in distress: Inhibiting effects of friends and strangers on bystander intervention

B. Latané and J. Rodin

Editors'
Introduction

Theoretical Background

Research on bystander intervention was stimulated in the 1960s by a shocking example of bystander apathy, the story of the murder of Kitty Genovese, a young women who was stabbed to death in the middle of a street in a residential section of New York City. Although at least thirty-eight witnesses had observed the attack, and although the attacker took more than half an hour to kill his victim, none of the observers who watched from the safety of their apartments did anything to help. They even failed to phone the police. The present study is a follow-up to a similar study by Latané and Darley (1968) and forms part of an innovative research programme aimed at unravelling the motivational underpinnings of bystander apathy. In particular, it addresses the question why bystanders are so much less likely to help when they are in a group rather than being on their own.

The authors suggested two explanations for this phenomenon, namely diffusion of responsibility and social influence. Basic to the first interpretation is the assumption that a single bystander may feel that he or she is totally responsible for intervening. With other bystanders present, the responsibility is shared or diffused. (This intepretation is similar to perceived dispensability, one of the mechanisms suggested in explanation of the Ringelmann Effect: see reading by Latané, Williams and Harkings, chapter 15). The second interpretation is based on the assumption that most situations in which people require help are ambiguous with regard both to whether people are really in need of help and to what type of help is needed. Therefore potential helpers are uncertain and use each other as models or sources of information to interpret the situation. Especially if people try to project an image of coolness and control, their apparent inaction can lead to misinterpretations regarding their true feelings.

Hypotheses

It was implicitly assumed that bystanders would be most likely to help in an emergency when they were alone, and least likely when they are with another bystander who did not help (confederate of the experimenter).

Design

Four experimental groups were used. The design was not factorial.

Method

Male student subjects were led to believe that they were participating in a study on consumer attitudes. While completing a questionnaire, they overheard a woman in an adjoining room fall and cry out in pain. The independent variables were whether subjects were alone or with a second person and whether the second person was a friend or a stranger. For half of the subjects in the stranger condition, the other subject was a confederate of the experimenter who had been instructed not to help; for the other half, it was another participant who was unacquainted to the subject. Thus, there were four conditions: alone, with a friend, with a stranger subject, and with a stranger confederate. The dependent variable was whether subjects tried to help and how long they took to do so.

Results

Seventy per cent of subjects helped in the alone condition and when they were with a friend, 40 per cent helped when they were with a stranger who was a subject, and 7 per cent helped when they were with the unresponsive (confederate) stranger. However, as the authors pointed out, these raw results can be misleading. Interpretations are complicated by the fact that because only one member of the group is needed to help, everything else remaining equal, the probability that there will be at least one person to help should increase with group size. In fact this situation is equivalent to the disjunctive model of group productivity suggested by Steiner (1972; see also textbook, chapter 15).

Obviously, the authors do not suggest that everything else remains equal. In fact, they assume that due to social inhibition and diffusion of responsibility, bystanders should be less helpful in groups than alone. But in order to assess the influence of social inhibition and responsibility diffusion on helping, we need to control for other factors associated with group size which influence the likelihood of helping behaviour in groups. The probability that at least one member of a two-person group will help can be predicted with a formula suggested by Lorge and Solomon (1955). If in a given population the proportion of people who are helpful is P (e.g. .7 in the present study), and the probability of people not being helpful is Q ($1 - P$; or .3), the probability of drawing at random from the population a single unhelpful person is Q. The probability that nobody in a randomly assembled group of n individuals will be helpful is Q^n. Finally, the probability that at least one member of the group will be helpful is $1 - Q^n$. Thus, the proportion of two-person groups where at least one member will help should be $1 - .3^2 = .91$. To predict the response time, the authors mathematically combined all possible 'groups' of two response-time-scores obtained from subjects in the alone condition, and took the distribution of the fastest scores in each 'group' as a hypothetical baseline (figure 13.2). The authors then used significance tests to test whether the differences between the actual and the hypothetical scores were significant.

Thus, in contrast to the (erroneous) conclusions one would have drawn from the raw data, a comparison with the baseline indicates that the presence of a friend in fact substantially reduced the probability that a person would help (i.e. from 91 per cent to 70 per cent). Because the same control should also be applied to the (real-subject) stranger condition, we now can see that the impact of the presence of the stranger on helpfulness is much larger than suggested by the raw data, namely 51 per cent instead of 30 per cent.

Discussion

This innovative study marked the start of a new research area, namely the social psychological study of prosocial or helping behaviour. Although the study was designed to be more illustrative than theory testing, the findings throw some light on the theoretical mechanisms assumed to underlie the bystander apathy effect. For example, the fact that helping was reduced to near-zero with the unresponsive bystander is consistent with an interpretation in terms of social influence, as is the finding that more helping occurred in pairs of friends than in pairs of strangers. If one assumes that fear of embarrassment due to a misinterpretation of a situation as an emergency was a powerful motive resulting in inaction, then this should have been highest with the non-responsive stranger and lowest with a friend.

FURTHER READING

Latané, B. and Darley, J.M. (1968). Group inhibition of bystander in emergencies. *Journal of Personality and Social Psychology*, 10, 215–21. Probably the first bystander study. Demonstrates that subjects who found themselves in a smoke-filling room were less likely to report the smoke when in the presence of passive others or in groups of three than when alone.

Latané, B. and Darley, J.M. (1970). *The Unresponsive Bystander: Why Doesn't He Help?*. New York: Appleton-Century-Crofts. Classic monograph summarizing the authors' research programme on bystander intervention.

REFERENCES

Lorge, I. and Solomon, H. (1955) Two models of group behavior in the solution of eureka-type problems. *Psychometrika*, 20, 139–48.

Steiner, I. (1972). *Group Processes and Productivity*. New York: Academic Press.

Primary
Reading

"There's safety in numbers," according to an old adage, and modern city dwellers seem to believe it. They shun deserted streets, empty subway cars, and lonely walks in dark parks, preferring instead to go where others are or to stay at home. When faced with stress, most individuals seem less afraid when they are in the presence of others than when they are alone (Wrightsman, 1959). Dogs are less likely to yelp when they face a strange situation with other dogs (Scott and Fuller, 1965); even rats are less likely to defecate and freeze when they are placed in a frightening open field with other rats (Latané, 1969, Latané and Glass, 1968).

A feeling so widely shared must have some basis in reality. Is there safety in numbers? If so, why? Two reasons are often suggested: Individuals are less likely to find themselves in trouble if there are others about, and even if they do find themselves in trouble, others are likely to help them deal with it.

Ecologists have long puzzled over the adaptive functions of such phenomena as schooling in fish and flocking in birds. Such congregations seem ideally designed to make life easy for predators; yet they are widespread in nature. Why? Predators may be inhibited by fear from attacking large troops of animals (Lorenz, 1966), and they may be "confused" by the presence of many individuals, unable to focus on any one (Allee, 1951; Shaw, 1962). Similar processes may operate in humans. Roving psychopaths are probably more likely to hit isolated farm dwellings than urban apartment houses. Rapists do not usually work in Times Square.

Even if trouble comes, individuals may feel more certain of getting help if others are present. In 1871, Charles Darwin, In *The Descent of Man*, wrote "As man is a social animal it is almost certain that . . . he would from an inherited tendency be willing to defend, in concert with others, his fellow men; and be ready to aid them in any way, which did not too greatly interfere with his own welfare or his own strong desires." We may quarrel with Darwin's assertion of an *inherited* tendency, but most of us seem ready to assume that others are willing to help us in our distress.

While it is certainly true that a victim is unlikely to receive help if nobody knows of his plight, recent research casts doubt on the suggestion that he will be more likely to receive help if more people are present. In fact, experiments by Darley and Latané (1968) and by Latané and Darley (1968) show the opposite to be true. In the former study, students overhearing someone in the midst of a serious nervous seizure were more likely to attempt help, and did so sooner, if they thought they were the only person present and aware of the emergency than if they thought other people were also listening to it. In the latter study, subjects alone in a waiting room were more likely to report a possible fire than were subjects waiting in groups. In both these experiments, an emergency was less likely to be reported the more people who witnessed it.

The results of these studies may provide some insight into such widely publicized and distressing incidents as the murder of Kitty Genovese, a murder which 38 people witnessed from the safety of their apartments but did nothing to prevent. As in our laboratory studies, the presence of others served in a variety of ways to inhibit taking positive action.

These incidents have been widely cited as examples of "apathy" and "dehumanization" stemming from the urbanization of our society. These glib phrases may contain some truth since startling cases like the Genovese murder often occur in large cities, but such terms may also be misleading. The studies above suggest that situational factors, specifically factors involving the immediate social environment, may be of greater importance in determining an individual's reaction to an emergency than such vague cultural or personality concepts as "apathy" or "alienation due to urbanization."

If the social inhibition effects demonstrated by Latané and Darley and by Darley and Latané are general, they may explain why the failure to intervene seems to be more characteristic of large cities than rural areas. Bystanders to urban emergencies are more likely to be, or at least think they are, in the presence of other bystanders than witnesses of non-urban emergencies.

A second way in which urban emergencies differ from emergencies in other settings is that, in the former, bystanders are not likely to know each other. It is possible that the kinds of social inhibition and diffusion of responsibility generated by the presence of strangers may not arise from the presence of friends. Groups of friends may be even more able and willing to intervene in an emergency than single individuals. It is the purpose of the present experiment to test these possibilities, and to do so in a new emergency setting. In addition to demonstrating possible differences between friends and strangers, this will further test the generalities of social inhibition effects.

Method

Subjects waited either alone, with a friend, or with a stranger to participate in a market research study. As they waited, they heard someone fall and apparently injure herself in the room next door. Whether they tried to help and how long they took to do so were the main dependent variables of the study.

Subjects

One hundred fifty-six male Columbia undergraduates between the ages of 18 and 21 were selected at random from the college dormitory list. They were telephoned and offered $2.00 to participate in a survey of game and puzzle preferences conducted at Columbia by the Consumer Testing Bureau (CTB), a market research organization. Each person contacted was asked to find a friend who would also be interested in participating. Only those students who recommended friends, and the friends they suggested, were used as subjects. Fourteen per cent of the students called were unwilling to participate and 9% with appointments did not come, leaving 120 who served in the study.

Procedure

Subjects were met at the door by the market research representative and taken to the testing room. On the way they passed the CTB office and through its open door they were able to see a desk and bookcases piled high with papers and filing cabinets. They entered the adjacent testing room which contained a table and chairs and a variety of games, and they were given a preliminary background information and game preference questionnaire to fill out.

The representative told subjects that she would be working next door in her office for about ten minutes while they completed the questionnaires, and left by opening the collapsible curtain which divided the two rooms. She made sure that subjects were aware that the curtain was unlocked and easily opened and that it provided means of entry to her office. The representative stayed in her office, shuffling papers, opening drawers, and making enough noise to remind the subjects of her presence. Four minutes after leaving the testing area, she turned on a high fidelity stereophonic tape recorder.

The emergency

If the subject listened carefully, he heard the representative climb on a chair to reach for a stack of papers on the bookcase. Even if he were not listening carefully, he heard a loud crash and a scream as the chair collapsed and she fell to the floor. "Oh, my God, my foot . . . I . . . I . . . can't move it. Oh . . . my ankle," the representative moaned. "I . . . can't get this . . . thing . . . off me." She cried and moaned for about a minute longer, but the cries gradually got more subdued and controlled. Finally she muttered something about getting outside, knocked around the chair as she pulled herself up, and thumped to the door, closing it behind her as she left. The entire incident took 130 seconds.

If a subject intervened, the post-experimental interview was begun immediately. If he did not intervene, the representative waited one minute after the end of the tape and then entered the testing room through the door, visibly limping. The representative asked all subjects about the noises next door, their reactions to them, and the reasons for the course of action they had taken, and then explained in detail the true purposes of the experiment. At the end of the interview, subjects were paid and asked to fill out an anonymous questionnaire concerning their feelings about the experiment. Reasons for secrecy were discussed and all subjects readily agreed.

Measures

The main dependent variables of the study were whether the subject took action to help the victim and how long it took him to do so. There were actually several modes of interaction available. A subject could open the screen dividing the two rooms, leave the testing room and enter the CTB office by the door, find someone else, or, most simply, call out to see if the representative needed help.

Design of the experiment

Four experimental groups were used. In one condition (Alone, $N = 26$), each subject was by himself in the testing room while he filled out the questionnaire and heard the fall. In a second condition (Stooge, $N = 14$), a stranger, actually a confederate of the experimenter, was also present. The confederate had instructions to be as passive as possible and to answer questions put to him by the subject with a brief gesture or remark. During the emergency, he looked up, shrugged his shoulders, and continued working on his questionnaire. Subjects in the third condition (Strangers, $N = 20$ pairs) were placed in the testing room in pairs. Each subject in the pair was unacquainted with the other before entering the room and they were not introduced. Only one subject in this condition spontaneously introduced himself to the other. In a final condition (Friends, $N = 20$ pairs), each subject had been scheduled with a friend and remained with him throughout the experiment.

Results

Check on manipulation

In the post-experimental interview, subjects were asked to describe what they thought had taken place next door. All thought the market research representative had fallen and hurt her foot. Less than 5% reported any suspicion that they had been listening to a tape recording. All subjects in the Two Strangers condition reported that they were unacquainted before the experiment.

Mode of intervention

Across all experimental groups, the majority of subjects who intervened did so by pulling back the room divider and coming into the CTB office (61%). Few subjects came the round-about way through the door to offer their assistance (14%), and a surprisingly small number (24%) chose the easy solution of calling out to offer help. No one tried to find someone else to whom to report the accident. Thus all interveners offered some kind of direct assistance to the injured woman. Since experimental conditions did not differ in the proportions choosing various modes of intervention, the comparisons below will deal only with the total proportions of subjects offering help.

Alone vs. Stooge conditions

Seventy percent of all subjects who heard the fall while alone in the waiting room offered to help the victim before she left the room. By contrast, the presence of a nonresponsive bystander markedly inhibited helping. Only 7% of subjects in the Stooge condition intervened. These subjects seemed upset and confused during the emergency and frequently glanced at the passive confederate who continued working on his questionnaire. The difference between the Alone and Stooge conditions is, of course, highly significant ($\chi^2 = 13.92$, $p < .001$).[1]

Figure 13.1 presents the cumulative proportion of subjects who had intervened by any point in time following the accident. For example, figure 13.1 shows that by the end of 60 seconds, 64% of Alone subjects and only 7% of subjects tested with a stooge had intervened. The shapes of these curves indicate that even had the emergency lasted longer than 130 seconds, little further intervention would have taken place. In fact, over the experiment as a whole, 90% of all subjects who ever intervened did so in the first half of the time available to them.

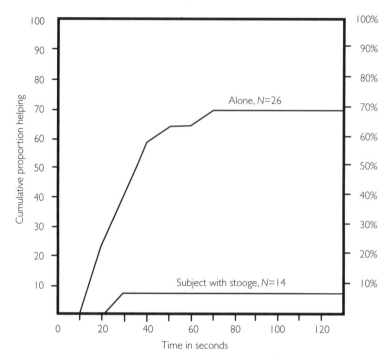

Figure 13.1   Cumulative proportion helping in the Alone and Stooge conditions

It is clear that the presence of an unresponsive bystander strongly inhibited subjects from offering to help the injured woman. Let us look now at whether this effect depends upon some specific characteristic or unnatural behavior of the passive confederate. Will the same social inhibition occur when two naive subjects are tested together?

Alone vs. Two Strangers

Once one person in a group of two bystanders has intervened, the situation confronting the other bystander changes. It is no longer necessary for him to act (and indeed, nobody did so). For this reason, we took the latency of the *first* person's response as our basic measure. This procedure, however, complicates a simple comparison between the Alone and Two Strangers conditions. Since there are twice as many people available to respond in the latter condition, we should expect an increased probability that at least one person would intervene by chance alone.

To compare the two groups, we computed a hypothetical baseline from the Alone distribution. This was achieved by mathematically combining all possible "groups" of two scores obtained from subjects in the Alone condition, and taking the distribution of the fastest scores in each "group" for the hypothetical baseline. This baseline is graphed in figure 13.2, and represents the *expected* cumulative proportion of pairs in which at least one person helps if the members of the pairs are entirely independent (i.e., behave exactly like Alone subjects). Since 70% of Alone subjects intervened, we should expect that at least one person in 91% of all two-person groups would offer help, even if members of a pair had no influence upon each other.[2]

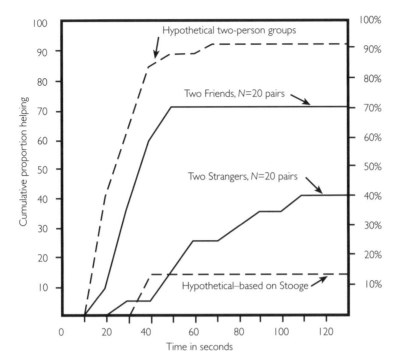

Figure 13.2 Cumulative proportion helping in the Friends and Strangers conditions and hypothetical baselines

In fact, the results show that members of a pair had a strong influence on each other. In only 40% of the groups of subjects in the Two Strangers condition did even one person offer help to the injured woman. Only 8 subjects of the 40 who were run in this condition intervened. This response rate is significantly below the hypothetical base rate ($\chi^2 = 11.34$, $p < .001$). Figure 13.2 shows that at every point in time, fewer subjects in the Two Strangers condition had intervened than would be expected on the basis of the Alone response rate ($p < .01$ by Kolmogorov-Smirnov). This result demonstrates that the presence of another person strongly inhibits individuals from responding, and that this inhibition is not a function of some artificiality of a stooge's behavior.

Strangers vs. Stooge

The response rate of 40% in the Two Strangers condition appears to be somewhat higher than the 7% rate in the Stooge condition. Making a correction similar to that used for the Alone scores, the expected response rate based on the Stooge condition is 13%. This is significantly lower than the response rate in the Strangers condition ($p < .05$ by binomial test).

The results above strongly replicate the finding by Latané and Darley (1968) in a different experimental setting: Smoke trickling into a waiting room. In both experiments, subjects were less likely to take action if they were in the presence of passive confederates than if they were alone, and in both studies, this effect showed up even when groups of naive subjects were tested together. This congruence of findings from different experimental settings supports their validity and generality: It also helps rule out a variety of explanations suitable to either situation alone. For example, the smoke may have represented a threat to the subject's own personal safety. It is possible that subjects in groups were less likely to respond than single subjects because of a greater concern to appear "brave" in the face of a possible fire. This explanation, however, does not fit the present experiment in which the same pattern of results appeared. In the present experiment, non-intervention cannot signify bravery.

Comparison of the two experiments also suggests that the absolute number of nonresponsive bystanders may not be a critical factor in producing social inhibition of intervention. One passive confederate in the present experiment was as effective as two in the smoke study; pairs of strangers in the present study inhibited each other as much as did trios in the former study.

Let us look now at our final experimental condition in which pairs of friends were tested together.

Alone vs. Two Friends

Pairs of friends often talked about the questionnaire before the accident, and sometimes discussed a course of action after the fall. Even so, in only 70% of the pairs did even one person intervene. While, superficially, this appears as high as the Alone condition, again there must be a correction for the fact that two people are free to act. When compared to the 91% base rate of hypothetical two-person groups, friends do inhibit each other from intervening ($\chi^2 = 2.84$, $p < .10$). Friends were less likely, and they were also slower, to intervene than would be expected on the basis of the Alone rate ($p < .05$ by Kolmogorov-Smirnov).

Friends vs. Strangers

Although pairs of friends were inhibited from helping when compared to the Alone condition, they were significantly faster to intervene than were pairs of strangers ($U = 96$, $p < .01$). The median latency of the first response from pairs of friends was 36 seconds; the median pair of strangers did not respond at all within the arbitrary 130-second duration of the emergency.

One sort of alternative explanation which plagues comparisons of friends and strangers in many experiments was ruled out by the present procedure. If some subjects are asked to recruit friends, and others are not, different degrees of commitment may be aroused. In this experiment, all subjects either recruited friends or were recruited by them, equalizing commitment across conditions.

From the victim's viewpoint

In order to determine whether an individual's likelihood of responding is affected by the presence of other people, we have compared scores in the Friends and Strangers conditions with a hypothetical base rate computed from the distribution of responses in the Alone condition. By this procedure, we have shown that an individual is less likely to respond when he is with either a friend or a stranger. But what of the victim? Under what conditions is she most likely to get help? For this question, the use of hypothetical baselines is unjustified. The results show that the victim is no better off if two friends hear her cry for help than if only one person does. When the bystanders are strangers, social inhibition was so strong that the victim actually got help significantly faster the fewer people who heard her distress (Alone vs. Strangers, $U = 112$, $p < .01$). In this instance, she would be foolish indeed to count on safety in numbers.

Post-experimental interview

Although the interview began differently for the interveners and noninterveners, all subjects were encouraged to discuss the accident and their reactions to it in some detail before they were told about the tape and the purpose of the experiment.

Subjects who intervened usually claimed that they did so either because the fall sounded very serious or because they were uncertain what had occurred and felt they should investigate. Many talked about intervention as the "right thing to do" and asserted they would help again in any situation.

Many of the noninterveners also claimed that they were unsure what had happened (59%), but had decided it was not too serious (46%). A number of subjects reported that they thought other people would or could help (25%), and three said they refrained out of concern for the victim – they did not want to embarrass her.[3] Whether to accept these explanations as reasons or rationalizations is moot – they certainly do not explain the differences among conditions. The important thing to note is that noninterveners did not seem to feel that they had behaved callously or immorally. Their behavior was generally consistent with their interpretation of the situation. Subjects almost uniformly claimed that in a "real" emergency, they would be among the first to help the victim.

Interestingly, when subjects were asked whether they had been influenced by the presence or action of their co-worker, they were either unwilling or unable to believe that they had. Subjects in the passive confederate condition reported, on the average, that they were "very little" influenced by the stooge. Subjects in the Two Strangers condition claimed to having been only "a little bit" influenced by each other, and friends admitted to "moderate" influence. Put another way, only 14, 30, and 70% of the subjects in these three conditions admitted to at least a "moderate" degree of influence ($\chi^2 = 12.2$, 2 *df*, $p < .01$). These claims, of course, run directly counter to the experimental results, in which friends were the least inhibited and subjects in the Stooge condition most inhibited by the other's actions.

Reactions to the experiment

After the post-experimental interview, debriefing, and payment of the promised $2.00, subjects were asked to fill out a final questionnaire concerning their mood and their reactions to the experiment. Subjects were convincingly assured that their answers would be entirely anonymous and the experimenter departed. On an adjective check list, 85% of the subjects said they were "interested," 77% "glad to have taken part," 59% "concerned about the problem," 33% "surprised," 24% "satisfied," 18/% "relieved," 12% "happy," 2% "confused," 2% "annoyed," 1% "angry at myself," and 0% "angry at the experimenter," "afraid," or "ashamed."[4] One hundred per cent said they would be willing to take part in similar experiments in the future, 99% that they understood what the experiment was really about, 99% that the deceptions were necessary, and 100% that they were justified. On a 5-point scale, 96% found the experiment either "very interesting" or "interesting," the two extreme points. The only sign of a difference in reaction between interveners and noninterveners was that 47% of the former and only 24% of the latter checked the most extreme interest ($\chi^2 = 4.64$, $p < .05$). In general, then, reactions to the experiment were highly positive.

Discussion

The idea of "safety in numbers" receives no support from the results of this experiment. When it was first designed, our major worry was that everyone would act, or at least call out to offer help to the injured woman. Yet on almost 40 occasions, she limped away from her accident without even the offer of help. In general she fared fairly well when only one person heard her distress. Her luck was much worse when several did. Although in the combined group conditions, 23 people offered help, 49 did not. What is there about a group setting which caused such ungentlemanly behavior? Two lines of explanation seem plausible. The first involves the workings of social influence processes (Latané and Darley, 1968), and the second the concept of "diffusion of responsibility" (Darley and Latané, 1968). Let us consider each of these lines of explanation and see how they fit the present case.

A bystander to an emergency must first come to some general interpretation of the situation, and then, on the basis of this interpretation, he may choose what to do. Many emergencies are rather ambiguous: It is unclear whether anything is really wrong or whether anything can be done about it. In a previous experiment, smoke might have represented fire, but it might have been nothing more than steam from a radiator. In the present experiment, a crash and the sounds of sobbing might have indicated a girl with a badly injured leg, but it might have meant nothing more than a slight sprain and a good deal of chagrin.

In deciding what interpretation to put on a particular configuration of emergency symptoms, a bystander will be influenced by his experience and his desires as well as by what he sees. In addition, if other people are present, he will be guided by their apparent reactions in formulating his own impressions. Unfortunately, their apparent reactions may not be a good indication of their true feelings. Apparent passivity and lack of concern on the part of other bystanders may indicate that they feel the emergency is not serious, but it may simply mean that they have not yet had time to work out their own interpretation or even that they are assuming a bland exterior to hide their inner uncertainty and concern. The presence of other bystanders provides models for each individual to observe, but it also provides an audience to any action he may undertake. In public, Americans generally wish to appear poised and in control of themselves. Thus it is possible for a state of "pluralistic ignorance" to develop, in which each bystander is led by the *apparent* lack of concern of the others to interpret the situation as being less serious than he would if he were alone. To the extent that he does not feel the situation is an emergency, of course, he will be unlikely to take any helpful action.

Even if an individual does decide that an emergency is actually in process and that something ought to be done, he still is faced with the choice of whether he himself will intervene. His decision will presumably be made in terms of the rewards and costs associated with the various alternative courses of action open to him. The presence of other people can alter these rewards and costs – perhaps most importantly, they can alter the cost of not acting. If only one bystander is present at an emergency, he bears 100% of the responsibility for dealing with it; he will feel 100% of the guilt for not acting; he will bear 100% of any blame others may level for nonintervention. If others are present, the onus of responsibility is diffused, and the individual may be more likely to resolve his conflict between intervening and not intervening in favor of the latter alternative.

Both the "social influence" and "diffusion of responsibility" explanations seem valid, and there is no reason why both should not be jointly operative. Neither alone can account for all the data. For example, the "diffusion" explanation cannot account for the significant difference in response rate between the Strangers and Stooge conditions – there should be equal diffusion in either case. The difference can more plausibly be attributed to the fact that strangers typically did not show such complete indifference to the accident as did the stooge. The diffusion process also does not seem applicable to results from the Smoke situation (Latané and Darley, 1968). Responsibility for protecting oneself should not diffuse. On the other hand, social influence processes cannot account for results in the Seizure situation (Darley and Latané, 1968). Subjects in that experiment could not communicate with one another and thus could not be influenced by each other's reactions.

Although both processes probably operate, they may not do so at the same time. To the extent that social influence leads an individual to define the situation as nonserious and not requiring action, his responsibility is eliminated, making diffusion unnecessary. Only if social influence is unsuccessful in leading subjects to misinterpret the situation should diffusion play a role. Indirect evidence supporting this analysis comes from observation of nonintervening subjects in the various emergency settings. In settings involving face-to-face contact among bystanders, as in the present study and in the Smoke situation, noninterveners typically redefined the situation and did not see it as a serious emergency. Consequently they avoided the moral choice of whether or not to take action. During the post-experimental interviews, subjects in these experiments seemed relaxed and self-assured. In the Seizure situation, on the other hand, face-to-face contact was prevented, social influence could not help subjects define the situation as nonserious, and they were faced with the moral dilemma of whether to intervene. Although the imagined presence of other people led many subjects to delay intervention, their conflict was exhibited in the post-experimental interviews. If anything, subjects who did not intervene seemed more emotionally aroused than did subjects who reported the emergency.

How can we fit friend–stranger differences into this framework? There are several possibilities. It may be that people are less likely to fear possible embarrassment in front of friends than before strangers, and that friends are less likely to misinterpret each other's inaction than are strangers. If so, social influence may be less likely to lead friends to decide there is no emergency. It also may be that individuals are less likely to lay off responsibility on their friends than on strangers, reducing the effectiveness of responsibility diffusion. There is some evidence consistent with both these possibilities.

When strangers overheard the emergency, they seemed noticeably confused and concerned, attempting to interpret what they heard and to decide on a course of action. They often glanced furtively at one another, apparently anxious to discover the other's reaction yet unwilling to meet eyes and betray their own concern. Friends, on the other hand, seemed better able to convey their concern nonverbally, and often discussed the incident and arrived at a mutual plan of action. Although these observations are admittedly impressionistic, they are consistent with a further piece of data. During the emergency, a record was kept of whether the bystanders engaged in verbal conversation. Unfortunately, no attempt was made to code the amount or content of what was said, but it is possible to break down whether there was any talking at all. Only 29% of subjects attempted any conversation with the stooge; while 60% of the pairs of strangers engaged in some conversation, mostly desultory and often unrelated to the accident. Although the latter rate seems higher than the former, it really is not, since there are two people free to initiate a conversation rather than just one. Friends, on the other hand, were somewhat more likely to talk than strangers. Eighty-five per cent of the pairs did so ($p < .15$

by Fisher's Exact test). Friends, then, may show less mutual inhibition than strangers because they are less likely to develop a state of "pluralistic ignorance."

Friends may also be less likely to diffuse responsibility than strangers. In a variation on the Seizure situation, Darley and Darley[5] recruited pairs of friends to serve as subjects at the same time. During the course of the emergency, friends could have no contact with each other and thus could have no direct influence on each other. Even so, subjects tested with friends were quicker to intervene than subjects tested with strangers.

Conclusions

The results of this experiment, in conjunction with those of previous studies in this series, suggest that social inhibition effects may be rather general over a variety of emergency situations. In three different experiments, bystanders have been less likely to intervene if other bystanders are present. The nature of the other bystander seems to be important: A nonreactive confederate provides the most inhibition, a stranger provides a moderate amount, and a friend the least. Overall, the results are consistent with a multiprocess model of intervention: The effect of other people seems to be mediated both through the interpretations that bystanders place on the situation, and through the decisions they make once they have come up with an interpretation. The results suggest situational reasons why our large cities may be less safe than smaller towns: Even if there be an equal likelihood of getting involved in an emergency, the presence of many strangers may prevent you from getting help. There may be safety in numbers, but these experiments suggest that if you are involved in an emergency, the best number of bystanders is one.

In a less sophisticated era, Rudyard Kipling prayed "That we, with Thee, may walk uncowed by fear or favor of the crowd; that, under Thee, we may possess man's strength to comfort man's distress." It appears that the latter hope may depend to a surprising extent upon the former.

NOTES

This research was supported by National Science Foundation Grant GS1239 to Bibb Latané and was conducted while Judith Rodin held an NDEA Title IV Fellowship.

[1]   All statistical tests in this paper are two-tailed.

[2]   The probability that at least one number of a group will help by a given time is $1 - (1 - p)^n$, where n is the number of people in the group and p is the probability of a single individual helping by that time.

[3]   Noninterveners reported an average of 1.9 different reasons.

[4]   Subjects checked an average of 3.1 adjectives.

[5]   Personal communication.

REFERENCES

Allee, W.C. *The Social life of animals.* Boston: Beacon Press, 1951.

Darley, J.M., and Latané, B. Bystander intervention in emergencies: Diffusion of responsibility. *Journal of Personality and Social Psychology*, 1968, 8, 377–83.

Latané, B. Gregariousness and fear in the laboratory rat. *Journal of Experimental Social Psychology*, 1969, 5, 61–9.

Latané, B., and Darley, J.M. Group inhibition of bystander intervention in emergencies. *Journal of Personality and Social Psychology*, 1968, *10*, 215–21.

Latané, B., and Glass, D.C. Social and nonsocial attraction in rats. *Journal of Personality and Social Psychology*, 1968, 9, 142–6.

Lorenz, Konrad. *On aggression*. New York: Harcourt, Brace and World, 1966.

Scott, J.P., and Fuller, J.L., *Genetics and the social behavior of the dog*. Chicago: University of Chicago Press, 1965.

Shaw, E. The schooling of fishes. *Scientific American*, 1962, *206*, No. 6, 128–38.

Wrightsman, Lawrence, S., Jr. The effects of small group membership on level of concern. Unpublished doctoral dissertation, University of Minnesota, 1959.

Weapons as aggression-eliciting stimuli
L. Berkowitz and A. LePage

Theoretical Background

To what extent can aggressive actions be 'automatically' elicited by situational stimuli? This is the theoretical issue that lies behind this well-known experiment. Instead of regarding human action as essentially purposive and goal-directed, the authors contend that there are some situations in which people respond more automatically and habitually to the available stimuli. In relation to aggressive behaviour, it is suggested that there may be certain kinds of stimulus that automatically and without conscious cognitive mediation elicit such behaviour. The authors cite a previous experiment by Loew (1965) as supporting their theoretical argument. Subjects who had learned a list of twenty aggressive words later gave stronger electric shocks to another person as punishment for mistakes on a learning task than did subjects who had learned a list of twenty neutral words. The aggressive words had presumably 'automatically' elicited aggressive responses, which then resulted in more aggressive behaviour. In more modern terms, we might speak of the aggressive words as having 'primed' the aggressive behaviour. The authors' own experiment was designed to see whether a similar effect could be induced by the presence of weapons. The rationale is simple: weapons are symbols of aggression. If we think of weapons as devices for harming other people, the simple presence of a weapon might encourage us to aggress against others to a greater extent than we would in the absence of such weapons.

Hypotheses

The main hypothesis tested in this experiment is stated at the end of the penultimate paragraph of the Introduction: the presence of aggressive objects (i.e. weapons) should lead to more

Journal of Personality and Social Psychology (1967), 7:202–7.

intense attacks upon an available target than would occur in the presence of a neutral object. An additional hypothesis is mentioned in the first paragraph of the Procedure section. Here it is suggested that aggression might be even greater if the 'available target' was the owner of the weapons.

Design

The experiment involved seven conditions. Six of these resulted from the factorial combination of two independent variables, and the seventh was a control condition. One of the independent variables was the number of shocks (one or seven) administered to the subject by a confederate of the experimenters who was posing as a fellow subject. Subjects who received only one shock were supposedly not angry with the confederate, whereas those who received seven shocks were supposedly angry with the confederate. The other independent variable was the presence of weapons, and here there were three conditions. Two of these conditions were 'aggressive-weapons' conditions, in which a shotgun and a revolver were lying on a table in full view. In one of these conditions it was said that the weapons belonged to the confederate ('associated weapons'); in the other it was said that the weapons belonged to a previous experimenter ('unassociated weapons'). In the third condition ('no object'), there was nothing on the table. In the control condition ('badminton racquets') subjects who had been angered by receiving seven shocks were exposed to neutral stimuli, in the form of two racquets that were said to belong to a previous experimenter.

Method

The experiment was presented as a study of physiological reactions to stress. The stress was to be created by the administration of mild electric shocks. Subjects, who were all men, were run in pairs, one being the real subject, the other being a confederate. Each member of a pair had five minutes in which to solve a task that would later be evaluated by the other member. The evaluations took the form of electric shocks, with one shock representing a very positive evaluation, and ten shocks a very negative evaluation. After completing the tasks, the subjects were placed in separate rooms. The real subject was attached to one set of electrodes supposedly measuring electrodermal activity (GSR) and another for the electric shock administration. It was explained that he would be the first to receive his 'evaluation'. Then, according to condition, he received either one or seven shocks, after which he completed a brief self-report of mood. Then it was the subject's turn to deliver his 'evaluation' to the confederate, which required going to another room. Next to the apparatus for delivering the shock to the confederate (referred to in the paper as a 'shock key') were the weapons, badminton racquets or nothing, as appropriate. In the weapons conditions it was explained that the weapons had been left there either by someone else who must have been running an experiment in the same room, or by the confederate; in both cases, subjects were told to disregard the guns. In the racquets condition, it was said that the racquets belonged to someone else. Subjects were then given the confederate's solution to the task, and asked to evaluate it by giving an appropriate number of shocks. The number of shocks given by the subjects was the primary dependent variable in this study. Finally, the subject completed a second self-report of mood, was then interviewed about his reactions to the experiment, and was debriefed.

Results

The data were analysed using 2 (level of shock) × 3 (weapons condition) analyses of variance. Subjects who received seven shocks did report themselves as feeling significantly angrier than did subjects who received one shock. So the manipulation of anger was effective. Furthermore, there were no differences in self-reported anger as a function of the weapons manipulation. The main results of this experiment are shown in Table 14.2. There it can be seen that the mean number of shocks administered by the subject was consistently higher in the seven-shock condition than in the one-shock condition, suggesting that angrier subjects delivered more shocks to the confederate. More important are the differences *within* the seven-shock condition. There it can be seen that subjects in the two 'weapons' conditions delivered significantly more shocks than did subjects in the 'badminton racquets' condition; furthermore, subjects in the 'associated weapons' condition delivered significantly more shocks than did subjects in the 'no object' condition. The difference between the 'unassociated weapons' and 'no object' conditions is in the predicted direction but is not statistically significant. Supplementary findings are shown in Table 14.3, which shows the mean duration of the shocks administered by subjects. Those in the seven-shock condition delivered longer shocks than did those in the one-shock condition; however, within the seven-shock condition there were no significant differences as a function of the presence of weapons, although the means are in the direction predicted by the hypothesis.

Discussion

The authors argue that a common-sense interpretation of firing a gun is that the person either pulls the trigger deliberately, or does so accidentally. They suggest that their findings point to another possibility: sometimes the gun might act as an 'aggressive cue'. Instead of the finger pulling the trigger, in other words, there may be a sense in which the trigger pulls the finger. This conclusion carries clear implications for laws governing the availability of weapons such as guns and knives to members of the general public. Perhaps the first question to address here is whether or not this 'weapons effect' is replicable. Later research shows that it is, although there have also been some failures to replicate (see Turner et al., 1977, for a review).

A second issue to consider is whether the effect is limited to those who have been angered, which is what Berkowitz and LePage found in their study. Some of the later studies found that even non-angered persons were more aggressive in the presence of weapons. So what is the role of anger in the weapons effect? Berkowitz (1993) argues that when people are angry two different effects can arise: (1) inhibitions against aggression are reduced; and (2) aggression-related motor reactions occur which can intensify the aggressive response to aggression-related cues (such as weapons).

A third issue is the role played in this and other weapons effect studies by 'demand characteristics'. The argument made by critics of Berkowitz and Page's experiment, and others like it, is that subjects were at some level aware of the hypothesis under investigation, and that they acted to confirm this hypothesis by responding to the 'demands' of the experimental situation. Turner and Simons's (1974) study addressed this criticism by deliberately manipulating how much subjects knew about the researchers' interest in the effects of weapons on their behaviour. Contrary to the demand characteristic interpretation of the weapons effect, those subjects who were more aware of the experimenters' interest in aggression administered fewer shocks than did those who were less aware of this interest in aggression.

In conclusion, then, it seems that the presence of weapons automatically intensifies aggressive behaviour, and that under conditions where inhibitions against behaving aggressively are weak, their presence may even automatically elicit aggression. Recent research by Anderson et al. (1996) suggests that this intensification of aggressive behaviour is mediated by cognitions: they found that exposure to photos of weapons automatically increased the accessibility of hostility-related thoughts, but did not increase hostile attitudes or feelings.

FURTHER READING

Anderson, C.A., Anderson, K.B. and Deuser, W.E. (1996). Examining an affective aggression framework: Weapon and temperature effects on aggressive thoughts, affect, and attitudes. *Personality and Social Psychology Bulletin*, 22, 366–76. A study that locates the 'weapons effect' within a more general theoretical framework.

Turner, C.W. and Simons, L.S. (1974). Effect of subject sophistication and evaluation apprehension on aggressive responses to weapons. *Journal of Personality and Social Psychology*, 30, 341–8. As noted above, this study attempts to rule out a demand characteristic interpretation of the weapons effect.

REFERENCES

Berkowitz, L. (1993). *Aggression: Its Causes, Consequences, and Control*. New York: McGraw-Hill.

Loew, C.A. (1965). Acquisition of a hostile attitude and its relationship to aggressive behavior. Unpublished doctoral dissertation, State University of Iowa.

Turner, C.W., Simons, L.S., Berkowitz, L. and Frodi, A. (1977). The stimulating and inhibiting effects of weapons on aggressive behavior. *Aggressive Behavior*, 3, 355–78.

Human behavior is often goal directed, guided by strategies and influenced by ego defenses and strivings for cognitive consistency. There clearly are situations, however, in which these purposive considerations are relatively unimportant regulators of action. Habitual behavior patterns become dominant on these occasions, and the person responds relatively automatically to the stimuli impinging upon him. Any really complete psychological system must deal with these stimulus-elicited, impulsive reactions as well as with more complex behavior patterns. More than this, we should also be able to specify the conditions under which the various behavior determinants increase or decrease in importance.

Primary
Reading

The senior author has long contended that many aggressive actions are controlled by the stimulus properties of the available targets rather than by anticipations of ends that might be served (Berkowitz, 1962, 1964, 1965). Perhaps because strong emotion results in an increased utilization of only the central cues in the immediate situation (Easterbrook, 1959; Walters and Parke, 1964), anger arousal can lead to impulsive aggressive responses which, for a short time at least, may be relatively free of cognitively mediated inhibitions against aggression or, for that matter, purposes and strategic considerations.[1] This impulsive action is not necessarily pushed out by the anger, however. Berkowitz has suggested that appropriate cues must be present in the situation if aggressive responses are actually to occur. While there is still considerable uncertainty as to just what characteristics define aggressive cue properties, the association of a stimulus with aggression evidently can enhance the aggressive cue value of this stimulus. But whatever its exact genesis, the cue (which may be either in the external environment or represented internally) presumably elicits the aggressive response. Anger (or any other conjectured aggressive "drive") increases the person's reactivity to the cue, possibly energizes the response, and may lower the likelihood of competing reactions, but is not necessary for the production of aggressive behavior.[2]

A variety of observations can be cited in support of this reasoning (cf. Berkowitz, 1965). Thus, the senior author has proposed that some of the effects of observed violence can readily be understood in terms of stimulus-elicited aggression. According to several Wisconsin experiments, observed aggression is particularly likely to produce strong attacks against anger instigators who are associated with the victim of the witnessed violence (Berkowitz and Geen, 1966, 1967; Geen and Berkowitz, 1966). The frustrater's association with the observed victim presumably enhances his cue value for aggression, causing him to evoke stronger attacks from the person who is ready to act aggressively.

More direct evidence for the present formulation can be found in a study conducted by Loew (1965). His subjects, in being required to learn a concept, either aggressive or nature words, spoke either 20 aggressive or 20 neutral words aloud. Following this "learning task," each subject was to give a peer in an adjacent room an electric shock whenever this person made a mistake in his learning problem. Allowed to vary the intensity of the shocks they administered over a 10-point continuum, the subjects who had uttered the aggressive words gave shocks of significantly greater intensity than did the subjects who had spoken the neutral words. The aggressive words had evidently evoked implicit aggressive responses from the subjects, even though they had not been angered beforehand, which then led to the stronger attacks upon the target person in the next room when he supposedly made errors.

Cultural learning shared by many members of a society can also associate external objects with aggression and thus affect the objects' aggressive cue value. Weapons are a prime example. For many men (and probably women as well) in our society, these objects are closely associated with aggression. Assuming that the weapons do not produce inhibitions that are stronger than the evoked aggressive reactions (as would be the case, e.g., if the weapons were labeled as morally "bad"), the presence of the aggressive objects should generally lead to more intense attacks upon an available target than would occur in the presence of a neutral object.

The present experiment was designed to test this latter hypothesis. At one level, of course, the findings contribute to the current debate as to the desirability of restricting sales of firearms. Many arguments have been raised for such a restriction. Thus, according to recent statistics, Texas communities having virtually no prohibitions against firearms have a much higher homicide rate than other American cities possessing stringent firearm regulations, and J. Edgar Hoover has maintained in *Time* magazine that the availability of firearms is an important factor in murders (Anonymous, 1966). The experiment reported here seeks to determine how this influence may come about. The availability of weapons obviously makes it easier for a person who wants to commit murder to do so. But, in addition, we ask whether weapons can serve as aggression-eliciting stimuli, causing an angered individual to display stronger violence than he would have shown in the absence of such weapons. Social significance aside, and at a more general theoretical level, this research also attempts to demonstrate that situational stimuli can exert "automatic" control over socially relevant human actions.

Method

Subjects

The subjects were 100 male undergraduates enrolled in the introductory psychology course at the University of Wisconsin who volunteered for the experiment (without knowing its nature) in order to earn points counting toward their final grade. Thirty-nine other subjects had also been run, but were discarded because they suspected the experimenter's confederate (21), reported receiving fewer electric shocks than were actually given them (7), had not attended to information given them about the procedure (9), or were run while there was equipment malfunctioning (2).

Procedure

General design
Seven experimental conditions were established, six organized in a 2 × 3 factorial design, with the seventh group serving essentially as a control. Of the men in the factorial design, half were made to be angry with the confederate, while the other subjects received a friendlier treatment from him. All of the subjects were then given an opportunity to administer electric shocks to the confederate, but for two-thirds of the men there were weapons lying on the table near the shock apparatus. Half of these people were informed the weapons belonged to the confederate in order to test the hypothesis that aggressive stimuli which also were associated with the anger instigator would evoke the strongest aggressive reaction from the subjects. The other people seeing the weapons were told the weapons had been left there by a previous experimenter. There was nothing on the table except the shock key when the last third of the subjects in both the angered and nonangered conditions gave the shocks. Finally, the seventh group consisted of angered men who gave shocks with two badminton racquets and shuttlecocks lying near the shock key. This condition sought to determine whether the presence of *any* object near the shock apparatus would reduce inhibitions against aggression, even if the object were not connected with aggressive behavior.

Experimental manipulations
When each subject arrived in the laboratory, he was informed that two men were required for the experiment and that they would have to wait for the second subject to appear. After a 5-minute wait, the experimenter, acting annoyed, indicated that they had to begin because of his other commitments. He said he would have to look around outside to see if he could find another person who might serve as a substitute for the missing subject. In a few minutes the experimenter returned with the confederate. Depending upon the condition, this person was

introduced as either a psychology student who had been about to sign up for another experiment or as a student who had been running another study.

The subject and confederate were told the experiment was a study of physiological reactions to stress. The stress would be created by mild electric shocks, and the subjects could withdraw, the experimenter said, if they objected to these shocks. (No subjects left.) Each person would have to solve a problem knowing that his performance would be evaluated by his partner. The "evaluations" would be in the form of electric shocks, with one shock signifying a very good rating and 10 shocks meaning the performance was judged as very bad. The men were then told what their problems were. The subject's task was to list ideas a publicity agent might employ in order to better a popular singer's record sales and public image. The other person (the confederate) had to think of things a used-car dealer might do in order to increase sales. The two were given 5 minutes to write their answers, and the papers were then collected by the experimenter who supposedly would exchange them.

Following this, the two were placed in separate rooms, supposedly so that they would not influence each other's galvanic skin response (GSR) reactions. The shock electrodes were placed on the subject's right forearm, and GSR electrodes were attached to fingers on his left hand, with wires trailing from the electrodes to the next room. The subject was told he would be the first to receive electric shocks as the evaluation of his problem solution. The experimenter left the subject's room saying he was going to turn on the GSR apparatus, went to the room containing the shock machine and the waiting confederate, and only then looked at the schedule indicating whether the subject was to be angered or not. He informed the confederate how many shocks the subject was to receive, and 30 seconds later the subject was given seven shocks (angered condition) or one shock (nonangered group). The experimenter then went back to the subject, while the confederate quickly arranged the table holding the shock key in the manner appropriate for the subject's condition. Upon entering the subject's room, the experimenter asked him how many shocks he had received and provided the subject with a brief questionnaire on which he was to rate his mood. As soon as this was completed, the subject was taken to the room holding the shock machine. Here the experimenter told the subject it was his turn to evaluate his partner's work. For one group in both the angered and nonangered conditions the shock key was alone on the table (no-object groups). For two other groups in each of these angered and nonangered conditions, however, a 12-gauge shotgun and a .38-caliber revolver were lying on the table near the key (aggressive-weapon conditions). One group in both the angered and nonangered conditions was informed the weapons belonged to the subject's partner. The subjects given this treatment had been told earlier that their partner was a student who had been conducting an experiment.[3] They now were reminded of this, and the experimenter said the weapons were being used in some way by this person in his research (associated-weapons condition); the guns were to be disregarded. The other men were told simply the weapons "belong to someone else" who "must have been doing an experiment in here" (unassociated-weapons group), and they too were asked to disregard the guns. For the last treatment, one group of angered men found two badminton racquets and shuttlecocks lying on the table near the shock key, and these people were also told the equipment belonged to someone else (badminton-racquets group).

Immediately after this information was provided, the experimenter showed the subject what was supposedly his partner's answer to his assigned problem. The subject was reminded that he was to give the partner shocks as his evaluation and was informed that this was the last time shocks would be administered in the study. A second copy of the mood questionnaire was then completed by the subject after he had delivered the shocks. Following this, the subject was asked a number of oral questions about the experiment, including what, if any, suspicions he had. (No doubts were voiced about the presence of the weapons.) At the conclusion of this interview the experiment was explained, and the subject was asked not to talk about the study.

Dependent variables

As in nearly all the experiments conducted in the senior author's program, the number of shocks given by the subjects serves as the primary aggression measure. However, we also report here findings obtained with the total duration of each subject's shocks, recorded in thousandths of a minute. Attention is also given to each subject's rating of his mood, first immediately after receiving the partner's evaluation, and again immediately after administering shocks to the partner. These ratings were made on a series of 10 13-point bipolar scales with an adjective at each end, such as "calm–tense" and "angry–not angry."

Results

Effectiveness of arousal treatment

Analyses of variance of the responses to each of the mood scales following the receipt of the partner's evaluation indicate the prior-shock treatment succeeded in creating differences in anger arousal. The subjects getting seven shocks rated themselves as being significantly angrier than the subjects receiving only one shock ($F = 20.65$, $p < .01$). There were no reliable differences among the groups within any one arousal level. Interestingly enough, the only other mood scale to yield a significant effect was the scale "sad–happy." The aroused–seven-shocks men reported a significantly stronger felt sadness than the men getting one shock ($F = 4.63$, $p > .05$).

Aggression toward partner

A preliminary analysis of variance of the shock data for the six groups in the 3×2 factorial design yielded the findings shown in table 14.1. As is indicated by the significant interaction, the presence of the weapons significantly affected the number of shocks given by the subject when the subject had received seven shocks. A Duncan multiple-range test was then made of the differences among the seven conditions means, using the error variance from a seven-group one-way analysis of variance in the error term. The mean number of shocks administered in each experimental condition and the Duncan test results are given in table 14.2. The hypothesis guiding the present study receives good support. The strongly provoked men delivered more frequent electrical attacks upon their tormentor in the presence of a weapon than when nonaggressive objects (the badminton racquets and shuttlecocks) were present or when only the shock key was on the table. The angered subjects gave the greatest number of shocks in the presence of the weapons associated with the anger instigator, as predicted, but this group was not reliably different from the angered–unassociated-weapons conditions. Both of these groups expressing aggression in the presence of weapons were significantly more aggressive than the

Table 14.1   Analysis of variance results for number of shocks given by subjects in factorial design

Source	df	MS	F
No. shocks received (A)	1	182.04	104.62*
Weapons association (B)	2	1.90	1.09
A × B	2	8.73	5.02*
Error	84	1.74	

*$p < .01$.

Table 14.2   Mean number of shocks given in each condition

	Shocks received	
Condition	1	7
Associated weapons	2.60$_a$	6.07$_a$
Unassociated weapons	2.20$_a$	5.67$_{cd}$
No object	3.07$_a$	4.67$_{bc}$
Badminton racquets	–	4.60$_b$

Cells having a common subscript are not significantly different at the .05 level by Duncan multiple-range test. There were 10 subjects in the seven-shocks-received–badminton-racquets group and 15 subjects in each of the other conditions.

angered–neutral-object condition, but only the associated-weapons condition differed significantly from the angered–no-object group.

Some support for the present reasoning is also provided by the shock-duration data summarized in table 14.3. (We might note here, before beginning, that the results with duration scores – and this has been a consistent finding in the present research program – are less clearcut than the findings with number of shocks given.) The results indicate that the presence of weapons resulted in a decreased number of attacks upon the partner, although not significantly so, when the subjects had received only one shock beforehand. The condition differences are in the opposite direction, however, for the men given the stronger provocation. Consequently, even though there are no reliable differences among the groups in this angered condition, the angered men administering shocks in the presence of weapons gave significantly longer shocks than the nonangered men also giving shocks with guns lying on the table. The angered–neutral-object and angered–no-object groups, on the other hand, did not differ from the nonangered–no-object condition.

Mood changes

Analyses of covariance were conducted on each of the mood scales, with the mood ratings made immediately after the subjects received their partners' evaluation held constant in order to

Table 14.3   Mean total duration of shock given in each condition

Condition	Shocks received	
	1	7
Associated weapons	17.93$_c$	46.93$_a$
Unassociated weapons	17.33$_c$	39.47$_{ab}$
No object	24.47$_{bc}$	34.80$_{ab}$
Badminton racquets	–	34.90$_{ab}$

The duration scores are in thousandths of a minute. Cells having a common subscript are not significantly different at the .05 level by Duncan multiple-range test. There were 10 subjects in the seven-shocks-received–badminton-racquet group and 15 subjects in each of the other conditions.

determine if there were condition differences in mood changes following the giving of shocks to the partner. Duncan range tests of the adjusted condition means yielded negative results, suggesting that the attacks on the partner did not produce any systematic condition differences. In the case of the felt anger ratings, there were very high correlations between the ratings given before and after the shock administration, with the Pearson *rs* ranging from .89 in the angered–unassociated-weapons group to .99 in each of the three unangered conditions. The subjects could have felt constrained to repeat their initial responses.

Discussion

Common sense, as well as a good deal of personality theorizing, both influenced to some extent by an egocentric view of human behavior as being caused almost exclusively by motives within the individual, generally neglect the type of weapons effect demonstrated in the present study. If a person holding a gun fires it, we are told either that he wanted to do so (consciously or unconsciously) or that he pulled the trigger "accidentally." The findings summarized here suggest yet another possibility: The presence of the weapon might have elicited an intense aggressive reaction from the person with the gun, assuming his inhibitions against aggression were relatively weak at the moment. Indeed, it is altogether conceivable that many hostile acts which supposedly stem from unconscious motivation really arise because of the operation of aggressive cues. Not realizing how these situational stimuli might elicit aggressive behavior, and not detecting the presence of these cues, the observer tends to locate the source of the action in some conjectured underlying, perhaps repressed, motive. Similarly, if he is a Skinnerian rather than a dynamically oriented clinician, he might also neglect the operation of aggression-eliciting stimuli by invoking the concept of operant behavior, and thus sidestep the issue altogether. The sources of the hostile action, for him, too, rest within the individual, with the behavior only steered or permitted by discriminative stimuli.

Alternative explanations must be ruled out, however, before the present thesis can be regarded as confirmed. One obvious possibility is that the subjects in the weapons condition reacted to the demand characteristics of the situation as they saw them and exhibited the kind of behavior they thought was required of them. ("These guns on the table mean I'm supposed to be aggressive, so I'll give many shocks.") Several considerations appear to negate this explanation. First, there are the subjects' own verbal reports. None of the subjects voiced any suspicions of the weapons and, furthermore, when they were queried generally denied that the weapons had any effect on them. But even those subjects who did express any doubts about the experiment typically acted like the other subjects. Thus, the eight nonangered-weapons subjects who had been rejected gave only 2.50 shocks on the average, while the 18 angered–no-object or neutral-object men who had been discarded had a mean of 4.50 shocks. The 12 angered–weapons subjects who had been rejected, by contrast, delivered an average of 5.83 shocks to their partner. These latter people were evidently also influenced by the presence of weapons.

Setting all this aside, moreover, it is not altogether certain from the notion of demand characteristics that only the angered subjects would be inclined to act in conformity with the experimenter's supposed demands. The nonangered men in the weapons group did not display a heightened number of attacks on their partner. Would this have been predicted beforehand by researchers interested in demand characteristics? The last finding raises one final observation. Recent unpublished research by Allen and Bragg indicates that awareness of the experimenter's purpose does not necessarily result in an increased display of the behavior the experimenter supposedly desires. Dealing with one kind of socially disapproved action (conformity), Allen and Bragg demonstrated that high levels of experimentally induced awareness of the experimenter's interests generally produced a decreased level of the relevant behavior. Thus, if the subjects in our study had known the experimenter was interested in observing their *aggressive* behavior, they might well have given less, rather than more, shocks, since giving shocks is also socially disapproved. This type of phenomenon was also not observed in the weapons conditions.

Nevertheless, any one experiment cannot possibly definitely exclude all of the alternative explanations. Scientific hypotheses are only probability statements, and further research is needed to heighten the likelihood that the present reasoning is correct.

NOTES

The present experiment was conducted by Anthony LePage under Leonard Berkowitz' supervision as part of a research program sponsored by Grant G-23988 from the National Science Foundation to the senior author.

[1] Cognitive processes can play a part even in impulsive behavior, most notably by influencing the stimulus qualities (or meaning) of the objects in the situation. As only one illustration, in several experiments by the senior author (cf. Berkowitz, 1965) the name applied to the available target person affected the magnitude of the attacks directed against this individual by angered subjects.

[2] Buss (1961) has advanced a somewhat similar conception of the functioning of anger.

[3] This information evidently was the major source of suspicion; some of the subjects doubted that a student running an experiment would be used as a subject in another study, even if he were only an undergraduate. This information was provided only in the associated-weapons conditions, in order to connect the guns with the partner, and, consequently, this ground for suspicion was not present in the unassociated-weapons groups.

REFERENCES

Anonymous. A gun-toting nation. *Time*, August 12, 1966.

Berkowitz, L. *Aggression: A social psychological analysis*. New York: McGraw-Hill, 1962.

Berkowitz, L. Aggressive cues in aggressive behavior and hostility catharsis. *Psychological Review*, 1964, 71, 104–22.

Berkowitz, L. The concept of aggressive drive: Some additional considerations. In L. Berkowitz (ed.), *Advances in experimental social psychology*. Vol. 2. New York: Academic Press, 1965. Pp. 301–29.

Berkowitz, L., and Geen, R.G. Film violence and the cue properties of available targets. *Journal of Personality and Social Psychology*, 1966, 3, 525–30.

Berkowitz, L., and Geen, R.G. Stimulus qualities of the target of aggression: A further study. *Journal of Personality and Social Psychology*, 1967, 5, 365–8.

Buss, A. *The psychology of aggression*. New York: Wiley, 1961.

Easterbrook, J.A. The effect of emotion on cue utilization and the organization of behavior. *Psychological Review*, 1959, 66, 183–201.

Geen, R.G., and Berkowitz, L. Name-mediated aggressive cue properties. *Journal of Personality*, 1966, 34, 456–65.

Loew, C.A. Acquisition of a hostile attitude and its relationship to aggressive behavior. Unpublished doctoral dissertation, State University of Iowa, 1965.

Walters, R.H., and Parke, R.D. Social motivation, dependency, and susceptibility to social influence. In L. Berkowitz (ed.), *Advances in experimental social psychology*. Vol. 1. New York: Academic Press, 1964. Pp. 231–76.

Attribution of apparent arousal and proficiency of recovery from sympathetic activation affecting excitation transfer to aggressive behavior

D. Zillmann, R.C. Johnson and K.D. Day

- - - - -
Editors'
Introduction
- - - - - - - -

Theoretical Background

The experiment reported in this paper is one of a series of studies of 'excitation transfer' conducted by Zillmann and his colleagues. 'Excitation transfer' is the term they use to refer to a process whereby physiological arousal generated by one source combines with the arousal generated by a second, emotional source, thereby intensifying the emotional response to the second source. This process of excitation transfer depends on *misattribution of arousal*. That is, the cause of the arousal is perceived as being the second source exclusively; the part of the arousal that is actually due to the first source is integrated with arousal from the second source.

This line of reasoning is a clever extension of Schachter's (1964) 'two-factor' theory of emotion (see the reading by Schacter and Singer, chapter 10). As in two-factor theory, it is

Journal of Experimental Social Psychology (1974), 10:503–15.

assumed that arousal can be non-specific enough to be the basis of any kind of emotional response, given the right cognitive labelling. This means that arousal from different sources can in principle be 'pooled' and thereby enhance the strength of reaction to an emotional stimulus. The different sources of arousal can both be emotional (e.g. sexual arousal could combine with angry arousal to increase the strength of reaction to provocation); or one source can be non-emotional (e.g. physical exercise) and the other emotional (e.g. erotic films, the result being a strengthening of the subjective response to the films).

The present experiment involves one non-emotional source of arousal (exercise) and one emotional source (provocation). A key feature of this study is that it establishes some of the limits on the excitation transfer process. Zillmann and his colleagues argue that if the situation contains any factor that leads subjects to attribute arousal correctly to the first source, it cannot be transferred to the second source. One such factor is time: if we pedal hard on an exercise cycle and immediately afterwards we are shown erotic films, there is less chance that we will attribute the exercise-induced arousal to the films than if the films are shown to us after a delay, because in the delay condition the remaining ('residual') arousal will be less salient, and will be less likely to be attributed to the exercise.

However, individual differences in physical fitness will complicate this process, in the sense that those who are very fit will recover their baseline arousal faster than those who are less fit. Thus the optimal set of circumstances for excitation transfer should be when less fit people first exercise, then have a delay long enough for obvious signs of arousal to disappear, and then be exposed to an emotional stimulus. This is the logic tested in the present experiment, which is concerned with the potential for exercise-induced arousal to enhance aggressive behaviour.

Hypothesis

The hypothesis tested in this experiment is that aggressive behaviour should be enhanced by exercise-induced arousal under conditions in which cues linking the arousal to its real source are absent (i.e. with delay between exercise and aggression), and that this enhancement of aggression will be especially apparent among less fit persons (because they will have more residual arousal available for transfer).

Design

The design is a 2 (delay vs. no delay) × 2 ('recovery proficiency': high, intermediate, or low) factorial, which means that all possible combinations of the two factors were tested. 'Delay' refers to the delay between exercising and having the opportunity to engage in aggressive behaviour, and this manipulation was intended to vary the decay of the exercise-induced arousal (no delay = undecayed; delay = partially decayed). 'Recovery proficiency' refers to the physical fitness of the subjects, who were divided into three groups on the basis of a pretest: high, intermediate or low proficiency. Note that the fact that subjects were allocated to the different levels of proficiency on the basis of a pretest means that they were not randomly allocated to fitness conditons, which raises the possibility that fitness might be associated with aggressiveness, such that less fit people are more aggressive. However implausible this possibility may seem, it is important to rule it out as an alternative possible explanation for any differences in aggressiveness found between the different fitness levels. This is why Zillmann and his colleagues also assessed unprovoked aggressiveness in the six experimental conditions.

Method

The pretest was presented as being concerned with ability to recall material while being physically distracted. Under this pretext subjects were shown a series of slides while pedalling an exercise cycle. Heart rate and blood pressure were monitored during 8 minutes after this exercise. This enabled the subjects to be divided into three fitness groups.

The main experiment was conducted 1–2 weeks later, and was presented as concerned with the relationship between ability to recall information and ability to teach using positive and negative feedback. The subject was always given the role of 'teacher' in a teacher–learner pair, the learner role being filled by a confederate. The 'negative feedback' took the form of electric shock, and subjects were told to choose the shock level they thought appropriate whenever the learner made an error. The learner made five prescheduled errors. The subject's choice of shock level for these five errors forms the measure of 'unprovoked' aggression. There then followed a procedure supposed to measure 'rapport' between teacher and learner: the subject expressed his attitudes on twelve issues, and the learner indicated his disagreement with the subject on nine of these issues by administering a painful shock to the subject. This constitutes the provocation. Next, the subject was asked either first to view some slides and then to pedal on the exercise cycle (no decay of arousal) or first to pedal on the cycle and then to view some slides (partial decay of arousal). Finally, there followed a further session of the 'teaching' task. Of the twenty-eight answers given by the learner, eighteen were prescheduled errors. The level of shock chosen by the subject for these errors is the measure of 'provoked aggressiveness', and is the main dependent variable in this study.

Results

The data are analysed by means of 2×3 analyses of variance. The findings are summarized in Table 14.4. The first row shows mean levels of systolic blood pressure (expressed as changes from baseline) at the beginning of the 'provoked aggressiveness' task. (Note that these means are derived from the pretest, since physiological measures were not taken in the main experiment.) These means show that blood pressure was higher in the 'undecayed' condition than in the 'partially decayed' condition, as would be expected; blood pressure also varies with recovery proficiency, as would be expected. The remaining data in the table all refer to shock intensity (i.e. the mean shock level chosen by the subject). The second row of the table shows that there were no differences between the conditions with regard to unprovoked aggression. The third row shows that there were significant differences in provoked aggression, but that these differences are confined to the partially decayed condition, and moreover that aggressiveness was only higher in the intermediate- and low-proficiency groups. The last row of the table simply shows the difference between mean unprovoked and mean provoked aggressiveness, with a pattern exactly the same as that for provoked aggressiveness. Only subjects in the intermediate- and low-proficiency groups chose significantly more intense shocks after provocation, and their difference scores were significantly larger than those in the other four conditions.

Discussion

The findings support the authors' hypothesis. When there was a delay between exercise and the opportunity to aggress against someone who had behaved provocatively, aggression was greater than when there was no delay. This finding is consistent with the idea that arousal only 'transfers' under conditions where that arousal is unlikely to be attributed to its real source. However, this finding was only obtained for those who were intermediate or low in physical fitness. Again, this is consistent with the authors' hypothesis, because the pretest data showed that subjects high in fitness would have recovered from their exercise fully by the time they had the opportunity to aggress against the provoker. For them, therefore, there was no residual arousal available for transfer. By contrast, the subjects in the intermediate and low fitness groups still had residual arousal (see row 1 of Table 14.4).

One important implication of this experiment and others in Zillmann's research programme is that arousal does not facilitate all types of behaviour. Rather, its impact on subsequent behaviour depends on the cognitive process of attribution. The original source of the arousal has to be 'out of mind' in order for the arousal to be 'free' to be transferred to another plausible source (such as an emotional stimulus). In the present experiment the plausible source of the arousal is the provoker. Note that we have to make some assumptions about what is happening in this situation. Being confronted with the provoker supposedly generates some level of arousal, and when there is residual arousal present, this pools with the arousal elicited by the provoker to result in enhanced aggressiveness against the provoker. Although the findings are supportive of the authors' reasoning, there is no direct evidence to support some steps of their argument. However, this is just one experiment from a large programme of work (see Zillmann, 1983, 1996). If we consider the programme as a whole, there is an impressive degree of support for the notion of excitation transfer.

FURTHER READING

Cantor, J.R., Zillmann, D. and Bryant, J. (1975). Enhancement of experienced sexual arousal in reponse to erotic stimuli through misattribution of unrelated residual activation. *Journal of Personality and Social Psychology*, 32, 69–75. A study showing that exercise-induced arousal can influence later judgments of sexual arousal.

Zillmann, D. (1983). Transfer of excitation in emotional behavior. In J.T. Cacioppo and R.E. Petty (eds), *Handbook of Social Psychophysiology* (pp. 215–30). New York: Guilford Press. An updated statement of excitation transfer theory and a review of the empirical evidence.

REFERENCES

Schachter, S. (1964). The interaction of cognitive and physiological determinants of emotional state. In L. Berkowitz (ed.), *Advances in Experimental Social Psychology* (vol. 1, pp. 49–80). New York: Academic Press.

Zillmann D. (1996). Sequential dependencies in emotional experience and behavior. In R.D. Kavanaugh, B. Zimmerberg and S. Fein (eds), *Emotion: Interdisciplinary Perspectives*. Mahwah, NJ: Erlbaum.

It has been demonstrated that under conditions of prior provocation, residual portions of an excitatory response induced by strenuous exercise can markedly facilitate aggression (Zillmann, Katcher, and Milavsky, 1972). Similarly, it has been observed that such residues can intensify the experience of anger and thereby facilitate retaliatory aggression after arousal has subsided (Zillmann and Bryant, in press). These findings were interpreted as consistent with expectations derived from excitation-transfer theory (cf. Zillmann, 1972). It was assumed that essential elements of exertion-induced excitation, known to decay rather slowly, combine inseparably with the excitatory response to stimuli to which the organism is subsequently exposed. Involving the two-factor theory of emotion (cf. Schachter, 1964, 1970), it was proposed that, to the extent that residual excitation from prior activities is transferred into subsequent behavior, the individual experiences any emotional state more intensely because he causally attributes his acute excitation to the stimuli in his immediate environment. Clearly then, the intensification of emotional states and dependent behaviors is seen as resulting from the causal misattribution of potentially unrelated excitatory residues.

The misattribution of residual excitation should not be seen as occurring by necessity, however. Transfer effects, it would appear, can be impaired and possibly prevented by the presence of extero- and interoceptive feedback of the excitation associated with the initial emotional experience. It may be assumed that the individual who has attributed his excitatory response to a particular inducer is provided, for some time, with apparent cues indicative of his dependent state of arousal. This is not to say that he receives highly specific, reliable feedback, but rather that he may notice, e.g., a shiver or tremble in a state of acute anxiety, erection in a state of sexual arousal, flushing in a state of euphoria or rage, or heart pounding after exertion. Based on this assumption of the involvement of feedback, it is proposed that the individual is unlikely to reattribute or misattribute residual excitation to alternative, subsequently provided potential inducers of emotional responses as long as he has apparent cues of the state of arousal which he linked to particular prior inducers. Thus, during this feedback period, transfer should not be expected.

This proposition has been tested recently (Cantor, Zillmann, and Bryant, in press). The time periods of actual and perceived recovery from elevated exertion-induced excitation were determined in a pretest to ascertain three distinct phases: a first one, in which excitation was measured to be elevated and in which, through the perception of apparent cues, it was recognized by the subject as still being elevated; a second one, in which measured excitation was still elevated, but was no longer recognized as elevated; and a final one, in which recovery was measured to be achieved and recognized as completed. In the main experiment, subjects were exposed to moderately explicit, erotic film segments during the first, second, or third recovery phase. They were instructed to report the degree to which they perceived themselves

- - - - -
Primary
Reading
- - - - - - - -

to be sexually aroused by these segments. With the data deriving from the final-phase condition serving as a control (no residual excitation), it was expected that sexual arousal, combing with residues from exertion, would be overexperienced only in the second-phase condition and that in the first-phase condition, although residues were more substantial, the attribution of prevailing excitation to exertion could only hamper feelings of sexual arousal. The findings were entirely consistent with these expectations.

Applied to the facilitation of aggression via transferred excitation, these findings have implications of interest. Counter to the popular notion that excitation, conceived of as generalized drive or energy, will enhance any and every response the individual is called upon to perform, it must be expected that, since residual excitation presumably becomes less pronounced as apparent cues vanish, predisposed aggression will be intensified to a greater extent by smaller, but more readily misattributable excitatory residues.

The present investigation sought to establish that the intensification of aggressive behavior by excitation transfer can be impaired and prevented by the presence of apparent cues associated with prior arousal. In earlier transfer studies (e.g., Zillmann, 1971; Zillmann et al., 1972), the problem of apparent cues was circumvented by delaying the performance of aggressive activities with instructions lasting at least one minute. In the present study, a delay condition was maintained, and a no-delay condition was added to accomplish an absence vs. presence variation of apparent cues.

A second goal of this investigation was to establish a relationship between a basic physical capability of a person, the proficiency to recover physiologically from exertion, and the degree to which he is susceptible to aggression-intensifying transfer effects. The reasoning on recovery proficiency simply takes transfer theory, modified to accommodate the problem of apparent cues, and applies it to individual differences.

1   Given a situation in which (a) an individual appraises, assimilates, and responds to emotion-inducing stimuli, (b) he experiences a level of sympathetic arousal that is still elevated from prior stimulation, and (c) he is not provided with apparent extero- and/or interoceptive cues which would indicate that his arousal results from this prior stimulation, excitatory residues from prior arousal will combine inseparably with the excitatory response to present stimuli and intensify emotional behavior.

2   Emotional behavior will be enhanced in proportion to the magnitude of residual excitation prevailing.

3   Both the period of time in which transfer can manifest itself and the magnitude of transferable residues are a function of (a) the magnitude of the preceding excitatory response and/or (b) the rate of recovery from the excitatory state.

Assuming appreciable individual differences in excitatory responsiveness and recovery proficiency, proposition 3 yields the following corollaries.

(a)   The individual's potential for transfer varies proportionally with his excitatory responsiveness.

(b)   The individual's potential for transfer is inversely proportional to his proficiency to recover from states of excitatory elevation.

Clearly, the magnitude of excitatory residues depends directly upon the magnitude of the excitatory response these residues derive from. The more responsive the individual is, the larger are the residues provided for transfer. Also, the less efficiently the individual recovers, i.e., controls his own responsiveness, the more likely it is that the conditions for excitation transfer will be met. Other things equal, the highly proficient recoverer retains transferable excitatory residues for a shorter period of time than the less proficient recoverer.

For the purpose of the present investigation it is posited that there are appreciable and consistent differences in (a) individuals' excitatory responses to strenuous exercise, and/or (b) their proficiency to recover from the excitatory responses thus induced (cf. Schneider and Truesdell, 1922; LeBlanc, 1957; Monod, 1967; Campbell, 1969). It is proposed that with exertion held constant, individuals who display pronounced excitatory elevation and/or fail to recover efficiently are more likely to transfer residual excitation into subsequent behavior than those who are less responsive and/or recover more efficiently. Since low responsiveness and high recovery proficiency are generally considered salient criteria of physical fitness, this proposition may be alternatively expressed by stating that the potential for excitation transfer is negatively related to physical fitness.

In order to explore the validity of the postulated relationship, the present study involved the division of a population into subpopulations representing various levels of responsiveness and/or recovery proficiency (high, intermediate, low). This division was accomplished by assessing each individual's excitatory recovery from strenuous exercise. In a factorial design, levels of recovery proficiency were varied with the absence (delay) vs. presence (no delay) of apparent cues of prior arousal.

Involving the entire design, it is expected, then, that under conditions in which apparent cues linking arousal to its prior induction are absent, aggressive behavior should augment as a function of the incompleteness of recovery, that is, the least fit individuals should display the greatest aggression-intensifying transfer effects. In contrast, it is expected that under conditions in which apparent cues link arousal to prior exertion, aggressive behavior should be at similar, low levels in all conditions of recovery proficiency.

It may, of course, be argued that the grouping of recovery proficiency inadvertently effects a grouping of personality traits with relevant implications for aggression. Conceivably, in comparison to the person in bad shape, the physically fit person is more skillful as an aggressor, has developed a greater habit strength for aggressiveness, is less inhibited to aggress against a tormentor, and so on. The excellent recoverer may thus be expected to display altogether more rather than less aggressiveness. To cope with such an alternative explanation, the present investigation involved an assessment of unprovoked aggressiveness in the various conditions.

Method

Pretest[1]

Subjects

Sixty male undergraduates from a large-enrollment introductory communications course at Indiana University were recruited to participate in two experimental sessions. The students met a course requirement by serving as subjects.

Procedure

All instructions were tape-recorded. The subject was informed that the purpose of the first experimental session was to determine his ability to recall complex communication content under conditions of physical distraction. Specifically, he was told that he would be exposed to visual stimuli while riding a bicycle and that physiological measures would be taken to assess the degree of his physical involvement. Each subject was seated on an exercise bicycle and was hooked up to physiological measuring devices. Electrodes were placed on both arms to obtain the cardiogram, and a brachial artery cuff was placed on the left arm to record blood pressures intermittently. After base level measures were taken, the subject was exposed to slides, projected in front of him. While being exposed to these slides, he pedaled the bicycle ergometer for 1 min and 30 sec with a work-load setting of 1500 kilopond m per min, or 245.3 W. After completing this strenuous task, he continued to be exposed to slides for another 8 min, remaining seated on the bicycle. During this period, physiological measures were obtained immediately after termination of the riding task and in 2-min intervals, that is 2, 4, 6, and 8 min after termination. At these times, heart rate was measured during a 20-sec interval, and blood pressures were recorded immediately thereafter. Finally, in order to disguise the true purpose of the pretest, the subject was given a series of highly specific questions about the content of the slides. After completing this task, he was informed that he would be assigned a particular role in the second experimental session according to his score in the first part.

Materials

The visual stimuli involved were not related to aggression or to anything that potentially could produce nontrivial degrees of arousal. The slides displayed campus scenery, wildlife, complex woven designs, and the like. Each slide was shown for 15 sec.

Apparatus

A Schwinn bicycle ergometer was used for the exertion task. Blood pressures were recorded on a Sears sphygmomanometergraph, and heart rate on a Sanborn cardiograph.

Determination of levels of recovery proficiency

Systolic blood pressure taken 6 min after exertion was used as the blocking criterion (a) because earlier research showed systolic pressure to be the most reliable single index of sympathetic activation induced by exertion (cf. Zillmann et al., 1972), (b) because at this time of measurement maximal between-subjects variability was observed, and (c) because at this time apparent cues of prior arousal should have vanished (cf. Cantor et al., in press). Subjects were rank ordered on this criterion, and the ranked sequence was broken down into pairs of adjacently placed subjects. Three levels of recovery proficiency, high, intermediate, and low, were formed by dividing the sequence of ranked pairs into thirds. One subject in each pair was then randomly assigned to the no-delay condition, and the other was placed in the delay condition.

An analysis of means scores revealed that recovery to base level was achieved after 4 min in the high-proficiency condition and after 8 min in the intermediate-proficiency condition. In the low-proficiency condition, recovery was not achieved during the period in which measures were taken: after 8 min, systolic blood pressure was still 10 mm of mercury above base level. Thus, recovery proficiency differed markedly within the population sampled, justifying the blocking of that variable as planned for the main experiment.

Main Experiment[2]

Subjects

Forty-eight of the 60 subjects who participated in the pretest served as subjects in the main experiment. Of the remaining 12 pretested subjects, 10 did not return for the main experiment: one who proved to be physically incapacitated, eight who were not available during the time allotted for completion of the experiment, and one who was excluded in the interest of equal cell size. In addition, one subject was dismissed because he spontaneously reported having participated in a "similar aggression study," and another refused to participate because he objected to the use of shock.

To prevent any discussion of the experiment or its purpose during class sessions which would bring former and potential subjects together, the entire main experiment was conducted in the period between two successive meetings of the class from which the subjects were recruited. All subjects served in the main experiment between 7 and 14 days after the pretest.

Procedure

All instructions were tape-recorded. The subject was informed that the purpose of this second part of the experiment was to investigate the relationship between the ability to recall complex visual materials and the ability to teach by providing coded information to a learner together with positive and negative feedback about his progress. The subject was told that he had received a rather high score on the retention pretest, and that he was assigned to an experimental condition in which a high-scorer taught a low-scorer. It was explained that he was to play the part of the teacher and that another subject would be the learner. The subject was told that the other subject (actually a confederate of the experimenter) had been scheduled to come earlier and was already well under way on his learning task in the adjoining room. He was told that both subjects would interact over an intercom, but that to maintain strict experimental control they would never meet each other in person. The subject was then informed that, in the experiment, negative feedback would be operationalized in the delivery of electric shock, and he was given an opportunity to withdraw from the experiment if the use of shock was unacceptable to him.

The subject was then given instructions on how to provide the learner with coded information and how to give him negative feedback whenever he made erroneous responses (cf. Zillmann et al., 1972, for further details). The subject was told that he had to deliver shock every time his apparatus signalled that the learner had made an error, but that he could vary the intensity of the shocks from "quite mild" (button #1) through "rather painful" (#10). It was suggested that he choose *the intensity he felt was most appropriate in this particular learning situation.* The subject was left alone during this teaching task, in which the learner made five prescheduled errors in 12 responses.

After this task, the subject was informed that, since the rapport between teacher and learner critically influences the learning process, it would be necessary to take a measure of how the two were "in tune with one another." Following procedures reported in earlier studies (e.g., Zillmann et al., 1972), the subject was given a list of 12 controversial issues on which he stated his opinion over the intercom. For each attitude expressed by the subject, the learner signalled his agreement by illuminating a light signal or his disagreement by administering shock to the subject. No matter what opinions the subject expressed, he received painful shocks in response to nine out of his 12 expressed opinions. This procedure was employed to induce anger in the subject and to give him the impression that the learner was disagreeable and obnoxious.

The subject was then informed that a measure of his ability to retrieve complex verbal communication content was needed (the pretest involved nonverbal stimuli only). The subject was exposed to slides and, depending on the condition to which he had been randomly assigned, he viewed the slides either while first sitting in a chair for 6 min and then engaging in strenuous exercise for 1.5 min (no decay) or while first engaging in strenuous exercise for 1.5 min and then sitting in a chair for 6 min (partial decay). Subjects in the no-decay condition were not informed about the forthcoming exercise until it was time for them to perform it. The strenuous exercise consisted of bicycle riding under conditions identical to those of the pretest.

After completion of the exercise session, the subject was told that the learner would now be ready for a final exchange similar to the first teaching task. Prior to this, no mention was made of this final teacher–learner encounter. The subject was given a list of coded items and was told to use the procedure he had used before, giving shocks in response to the learner's errors. The subject started the teaching task about 30 sec after having completed the exercise portion of the session. The task involved 28 responses to coded information, 18 of which were prescheduled as erroneous.

Finally, the subject was taken to another room and was asked to fill out a questionnaire concerning the content of the slides he had seen. As in the pretest, this was for the purpose of effective disguise only. Two questions concerning the subject's response to the strenuous exercise were added: he rated (a) the degree to which he had experienced the task as physically demanding, and (b) the degree to which he had liked or disliked the task. The subject was then dismissed. All subjects were given a delayed debriefing by their instructors after the experiment had been completed.

Materials

The slides used were copies of recent magazine advertisements. Each slide was shown for 15 sec.

Apparatus

Electric shock was generated by a Harvard shock inducer. Eight volts were delivered for about .5 sec to the distal pads of the index and ring fingers of one hand.

Shock was ostensibly delivered via a so-called aggression machine and was recorded on a Gerbrands multichannel event recorder.

Dependent measures

Both intensity and duration of shock ostensibly delivered to the learner were employed as indices of aggressiveness. The mean of the five pre-provocation scores served as a measure of unprovoked aggressiveness. It also served as a base level of aggressiveness in the determination of differences scores, the measure of aggressiveness after provocation. For analysis, the 18 difference scores obtained ($\Delta_{ij} = X_{ij} - B_i$, where X_{ij} is the jth retaliation score of the ith subject, and B_i is the arithmetic mean of all preprovocation scores of that subject) were reduced to six blocks of three responses each.

The difficulty of the strenuous task was assessed on a scale ranging from "extremely easy" (−100) to "extremely strenuous" (100). The attitude toward this task was assessed on a scale ranging from "I really hated it" (−100) to "I really loved it" (100). Both scales were marked at intervals of 10.

Results

Recovery proficiency

The difference scores (deviations from basal measures) of the physiological measures taken in the pretest on the 48 subjects who participated in the main experiment were subjected to analyses of variance (a) to validate the proficiency blocking and (b) to guard aginst possible sampling bias in the no-delay vs. delay conditions. No sampling bias was detected. Randomization in the decay conditions proved fully satisfactory, since all effects of the resulting grouping were trivial and insignificant.

Systolic blood pressure

The main effect of recovery proficiency on systolic blood pressure was highly significant ($F(2,42) = 37.86$; $p < .001$). The means were differentiated as required: 1.262 mm of mercury for high recovery proficiency, 18.80 for intermediate proficiency, and 36.40 for low proficiency, all contrasting significantly ($p < .001$) from one another. The main effect of repeated measures was also highly significant ($F(4,168) = 103.12$; conservatively corrected by the Geisser–Greenhouse method, $p < .001$). All the means in the sequence, 49.75, 32.21, 14.08, 3.12, −5.06, differed significantly ($p < .05$) from each other. There was, however, no appreciable interaction between recovery proficiency and repeated measures ($F < 1$). Given the highly significant differentiation of recovery proficiency and the lack of an interaction, differences in *de facto* recovery, measured in time, clearly resulted from a well-differentiated initial excitatory response to exertion rather than from differential decay gradients.

Alternative indices of excitation

On heart rate, the differentiation of proficiency conditions paralleled that of systolic blood pressure, but it failed to be statistically reliable. There was only a negligible interaction between proficiency and decay, and deceleration over time was highly significant and nonlinear (cf. Monod, 1967). The analysis of mean blood pressure (estimated as the systolic pressure minus one third of the systolic–diastolic difference) and that of sympathetic activation (estimated as the product of mean blood pressure and heart rate) both yielded results which were redundant with those reported for systolic blood pressure.

Excitation prior to provoked aggression

Table 14.4 shows the mean changes in systolic blood pressure, the primary index of excitation, which were obtained in the pretest and which have been treated as estimates of the excitation prevailing at the outset of the retaliatory encounter in the main experiment. As can be seen, the means are differentiated as required. Comparisons on sympathetic activation closely paralleled those on systolic blood pressure.

Evaluation of strenuous exercise

The postexperimental ratings concerning the strenuous exercise indicated that subjects tended to perceive the difficulty of the task as a function of their proficiency to recover from it. Subjects in all conditions found it strenuous, but those in the high-proficiency conditions found it less so than those in the intermediate and low conditions. Mean ratings were 16.06, as compared to 32.00 and 32.50, respectively. The differences were not statistically reliable, however.

Table 14.4   Indices of excitation prior to retaliation and measures of unprovoked and provoked aggressiveness

| | Exertion-induced excitation | | | | | |
| | Undecayed: recovery proficiency | | | Partially decayed: recovery proficiency | | |
Dependent measure	High	Intermediate	Low	High	Intermediate	Low
Excitation:						
Δ Systolic blood pressure	37.62^{cd}	45.00^d	70.12^e	−16.50^a	3.25^b	23.50^c
Aggression:						
Shock intensity						
before provocation	2.40^A	3.99^A	3.90^A	3.35^A	3.35^A	3.30^A
after provocation	3.09^A	4.52^A	4.33^A	3.36^A	5.05^B	5.28^B
Δ Shock intensity	.69^{ab}	.62^{ab}	.43^a	.01^a	1.70^b	1.98^b

Comparisons across conditions (horizontal) are denoted by lower-case superscripts, those on repeated measures within conditions (vertical), by upper-case superscripts. Means having no letter in their superscripts in common differ significantly at $p < .05$.

Subjects in all conditions found the task unenjoyable, but their ratings bore no consistent relationship to recovery proficiency. The mean ratings were −8.81, −4.81, and −11.06 from high through low proficiency. Again, the differentiation was statistically unreliable.

For both rated difficulty and disliking of the task, there were no significant effects of the decay manipulation or of the interaction of decay with recovery proficiency.

Aggressive behavior

As in earlier studies (e.g., Zillmann, 1971; Zillmann et al., 1972), no statistically reliable effects were obtained in the duration of shock. Given the repeatedly observed within-subject consistency of duration over trials, it would appear that this measure assesses mainly the subject's habit of pressing buttons. Shock duration as a measure of aggressiveness will thus be omitted from further discussion.

Unprovoked aggressiveness
The analysis of variance performed on the mean shock intensity of the five punitive responses made prior to provocation disclosed entirely negligible effects for all sources of variation (all $Fs \approx 1$).

Provoked aggressiveness
As the most pertinent finding, the analysis of variance on the difference scores of shock intensity revealed the expected interaction between decay and recovery proficiency ($F(2,42) = 3.36$, $p < .05$). The associated differentiation of means is displayed in table 14.4. Whereas under conditions of undecayed excitation all differences between means were negligible, under conditions of partially decayed excitation measured aggressiveness decreased with recovery

proficiency. Shock intensity in the high-proficiency condition was significantly lower than in the intermediate-proficiency condition; in the intermediate-proficiency condition it was lower than in the low-proficiency condition, the latter difference not being statistically reliable, however.

The main effect of the decay variation fell short of significance ($F(1,42) = 3.08$, $p < .10$). Similarly, the main effect of recovery proficiency was insignificant ($F(2,42) = 2.26$, $p > .10$). In contrast, the main effect of the six shock blocks was significant ($F(5,210) = 7.95$; conservatively corrected, $p < .01$). The associated differentiation of means (-0.096, 0.647, 1.140, 1.231, 1.306, 1.198) exhibits the repeatedly observed (cf. Baron and Kepner, 1970; Zillmann et al., 1972) successive increment of shock intensity. All interactions involving shock blocks were negligible (all $ps > .10$).

The analysis of the raw shock-intensity scores paralleled the analysis of the difference scores, but failed to yield a reliable interaction between proficiency and decay conditions. However, when a repeated-measures analysis was performed on the means of the shock intensities employed prior to and following the provocation treatment, the significant interaction reported for the difference scores was corroborated. As can be seen from table 14.4, the increase in shock intensity due to provocation was significant only for low and intermediate recovery proficiency under conditions of delay (both comparisons are associated with $p < .001$). This increase was negligible in all remaining conditions (for all comparisons, $p > .10$).

Discussion

The findings are consistent with the proposition that the facilitatory effect which residual excitation can exert on aggressive behavior presupposes the absence of a decisive attribution of experienced arousal, or portions thereof, to prior stimulation. Under conditions in which apparent extero- and/or interoceptive cues of prior arousal were present, provocation failed to increase aggressiveness significantly, and the magnitude of residual arousal failed to affect aggressiveness. In contrast, significant increments of aggressiveness were observed under conditions in which cues of prior arousal were no longer present but excitatory residues still prevailed. Considering all conditions, provoked aggressiveness was not found to be proportional to the magnitude of arousal active at the time retaliatory opportunities were provided. Together with earlier findings (Zillmann et al., 1972), the present results constitute evidence against the proposal that residual excitation will energize and facilitate, as a simple function of its magnitude, any and every behavior the individual engages in.

It may be speculated, of course, that the low levels of aggressiveness observed immediately after exertion were not so much the result of an attribution process in which anger and aggression were deprived of their excitatory component, as they were a direct consequence of the subjects' exhaustion. In this state, the subjects may have been preoccupied with "catching their breath." Or, it may be argued that the intense arousal they experienced distracted them sufficiently to impair anger and aggression. Both explanations seem unlikely, however, because the state of arousal induced was certainly not extreme enough to reduce the individual's mental or physical functioning as far as anger and aggression are concerned. Moreover, if either the physical impairment or the distraction argument were valid, provoked aggressiveness should have declined with decreasing fitness.

Concerning fitness, the findings are consistent with the proposition that proficiency of recovery from exertion reduces the likelihood of aggression facilitation by residual excitation. Assuming that cardiovascular recovery proficiency is representative of physical fitness in a more general sense, the physically most fit persons proved to be the least susceptible to behavior-modifying transfer effects, apparently because they had best recovered from the induced state of sympathetic arousal.

It could alternatively be argued that the strenuous task had a frustrating effect on the less fit persons, and that they displaced their anger about the task onto their opponents. The data on the task evaluation do not support this suggestion, however. Furthermore, the argument fails to account for the lack of increased aggressiveness in low and intermediate recoverers immediately after exertion, when any frustration should have been at a maximum.

Considering the findings on both unprovoked and provoked aggressiveness, the possibility that the grouping of recovery proficiency effected a contaminating grouping in aggressive traits seems remote. The results give no support whatsoever to the notion that physical fitness promotes aggressiveness. Contrary to such a notion, provoked subjects enjoying excellent fitness displayed the least aggressive behavior, and those showing the poorest fitness displayed the most. This outcome is more in line with the argument that the "cowardly" person in poor shape, when provided with an opportunity to attack an opponent without being counterattacked, gives in to the temptation "to let him have it" more than others, because under normal circumstances he would be afraid of the repercussions of such behavior. The argument does not hold up, however, since in the unprovoked exchange, where counteraggression seemed least likely, the aggressiveness of unfit subjects was comparable to that of subjects in a superior state of fitness. However, in accord with the results it may be speculated that persons of superior fitness are emotionally more secure (cf. Layman, 1972) and therefore less readily provoked and less eager to retaliate. This account seems to provide an adequate explanation for the significant differences obtained, and it cannot be ruled out at present.

NOTES

This research was supported by Grant GS-35165 from the National Science Foundation to Dolf Zillmann.
[1]   Jennings Bryant conducted the pretest.
[2]   KDD conducted the main experiment.

REFERENCES

Baron, R.A., and Kepner, R. Model's behavior and attraction toward the model as determinants of adult aggressive behavior. *Journal of Personality and Social Psychology*, 1970, *14*, 335–44.

Campbell, D.E. Trend analysis of heart rate deceleration following graded intensities of exercise of two groups of pubescent boys. *Journal of Sports Medicine and Physical Fitness*, 1969, *9*, 110–18.

Cantor, J.R., Zillman, D., and Bryant, J. Enhancement of experienced sexual arousal in response to erotic stimuli through misattribution of unrelated residual excitation. *Journal of Personality and Social Psychology*, in press.

Layman, E.M. The contribution of play and sports to emotional health. In J.E. Kane (ed.), *Psychological aspects of physical education and sport*. London: Routledge and Kegan Paul, 1972.

Le Blanc, J.A. Use of heart rate as an index of work output. *Journal of Applied Physiology*, 1957, *10*, 275–80.

Monod, H. La validité des mesures de fréquence cardiaque en ergonomie. *Ergonomics*, 1967, *10*, 485–537.

Schachter, S. The interaction of cognitive and physiological determinants of emotional state. In P.H. Leiderman and D. Shapiro (eds), *Psychobiological approaches to social behavior*. Stanford: University Press, 1964.

Schachter, S. The assumption of identity and peripheralist–centralist controversies in motivation and emotion. In M.B. Arnold (ed.), *Feelings and emotions*. New York: Academic Press, 1970.

Schneider, E.C. and Truesdell, D. A statistical study of the pulse rate and the arterial blood pressures in recumbency, standing, and after a standard exercise. *American Journal of Physiology*, 1922, *61*, 429–74.

Zillmann, D. Excitation transfer in communication-mediated aggressive behavior. *Journal of Experimental Social Psychology*, 1971, *7*, 419–34.

Zillmann, D. The role of excitation in aggressive behavior. In *Proceedings of the Seventeenth International Congress of Applied Psychology, 1971*. Brussels: Editest, 1972.

Zillmann, D., and Bryant, J. The effect of residual excitation on the emotional response to provocation and delayed aggressive behavior. *Journal of Personality and Social Psychology*, in press.

Zillmann, D., Katcher, A.H. and Milavsky, B. Excitation transfer from physical exercise to subsequent aggressive behavior. *Journal of Experimental Social Psychology*, 1972, *8*, 247–59.

Part IV
Social Groups

15 Group Performance

Many hands make light the work: The causes and consequences of social loafing

B. Latané, K. Williams and S. Harkins

- - - - -
Editors'
Introduction
- - - - - - - -

Theoretical Background

In contrast to early group researchers who believed that individuals perform better in groups than individually, more recent group research has taken the position that individuals typically perform suboptimally in groups. This position was expressed most succinctly by Steiner (1972), who stated that group productivity was equal to the potential productivity of a group minus the productivity loss. The present study examines potential causes of one of the best known examples of productivity loss in groups, namely the 'Ringelmann effect' (Ringelmann, 1913). Because the Ringelmann effect became known to American social psychology through Dashiell (1935), who, like many early American psychologists, was able to read German, and had read about Ringelmann's studies in books and articles published by the German industrial psychologist Moede (1927), everybody assumed that Ringelmann was German and a student of Moede. As Kravitz and Martin (1986) later pointed out, Ringelmann was in fact French and a professor of agricultural engineering. His studies, which were carried out between 1882 and 1887, probably constitute the first experiments in social psychology, although they were published well after the experiment by Tripplett (1898) which is usually accorded this honour (at least in American textbooks of social psychology).

Ringelmann got subjects to pull a rope either individually or in groups which varied in size from two to eight members. He found that groups of two pulled only at 93 per cent of the sum of their individual efforts, trios at 85 per cent, and groups of eight at only 49 per cent. Thus, for eight-person groups there was a productivity loss of just over 50 per cent. As Steiner (1972) pointed out, this 'productivity loss' could have been due either to losses in the coordination of their individual efforts or in the motivation of group members. Thus, group members may not have pulled at exactly the same time or in the same direction (coordination loss) or they may have pulled less hard in groups than individually (motivation loss). This type of motivation loss in groups was later termed 'social loafing' by Latané and colleagues (in this reading).

Journal of Personality and Social Psychology (1979), 37:822–32.

With their concept of 'pseudogroups', Ingham et al. (1974) had some years earlier developed a procedure which allows one to distinguish between the two types of loss. Pseudogroups consist of individuals who are led to believe that they are working in a group of a given size when they are in fact performing on their own. With a rope-pulling task this can be achieved by getting only the first subject in the row to pull, with the subjects behind the first being confederates of the experimenter and instructed merely to pretend to pull. Because there can be no coordination loss in pseudogroups, any productivity loss must reflect a loss of motivation. Ingham and colleagues (1974) demonstrated that both types of loss were responsible for the discrepancy observed between potential and actual productivity in the Ringelmann study. The goal of the present experiment was to replicate the findings of Ringelmann and of Ingham and colleagues (1974) using a completely different task.

EXPERIMENT I

Hypotheses

Individuals will perform less well when clapping or cheering in groups rather than individually.

Design

The experimental design was a 4 (group size: 1, 2, 4, 6) × 2 (response mode: clapping vs. shouting) × 2 (replications: 1, 2) within-subjects design.

Method

Forty-eight male undergraduate students participated in groups of six as subjects in this experiment. They sat in a semi-circle in the laboratory and on each trial either all of them or only some of them were asked to either cheer or clap for 5 seconds as loud as they could. There were thirty-six trials of yelling and thirty-six trials of clapping. Within each modality, each person performed twice alone, four times in pairs, four times in groups of four, and six times in groups of six. Apparently, the whole seventy-two-trial sequence of shouting and clapping was repeated, constituting the replication factor (Harkins, personal communication). Since each person's performance could affect and be affected by the others, the group rather than the individual was the unit in the analysis of variance, and each score was based on the average output per person. Performance was measured with a sound-level meter which was placed exactly 4 m away from each performer. The dependent measure was the average sound pressure generated per person (dynes/cm^2).

This is a somewhat unusual and very complex procedure. The design would have been more transparent if group size had been manipulated as a between-subjects factor, using only clapping versus cheering as a within-subjects factor. The order of this factor could then have been counterbalanced by getting subjects either to clap first and then cheer, or to cheer first and then clap. Another unusual feature is that the average score of subjects to be entered into the group score was based on different numbers of trials varying with group size.

Results

Results were analysed using 4 (group size) × 2 (response mode) × 2 (replications) analysis of variance. In line with patterns of productivity observed in previous studies, the average sound pressure per person decreased with increasing group size. People averaged approximately 3.7 dynes/cm^2 alone, 2.6 in pairs, 1.8 in foursomes, and 1.5 in groups of six (see figure 15.1). Thus, two-person groups performed at 71 per cent of the sum of their individual capacity, four-person groups at 51 per cent and six-person groups at 40 per cent.

EXPERIMENT 2

The results of experiment 1 replicated the findings reported by Ringelmann. However, like the study conducted by Ringelmann, experiment 1 does not allow one to differentiate between deficits in motivation or coordination as causes of the productivity loss observed in groups. The authors discuss a number of ways in which coordination losses could have occurred in the present task, for example because of sound cancellation, because individuals are not all directed towards the microphone while making noise, or because they do not all produce their maximum at the same point in time. Experiment 2 used pseudogroups to examine whether productivity losses would still occur under conditions which eliminate performance losses due to faulty coordination.

Hypotheses

Productivity loss was predicted to increase in actual groups and pseudogroups with increasing group size. The increase in productivity loss ought to be greater in actual than in pseudogroups.

Design

Two factors were manipulated, namely group size (1, 2, 6 persons) and type of group (actual groups/pseudogroups). Since the whole series of trials was repeated three times, there was a third factor, namely trial blocks (1–3). Thus, the experiment constituted a 3 × 2 × 3 within-subjects design.

Method

Subjects shouted either alone, in actual groups of two and six persons, or in pseudogroups of two and six persons. When shouting in a pseudogroup a subject in fact shouted alone, but believed that he was shouting together with either another subject (two-person pseudogroup) or five other subjects (six-person pseudogroup). This was achieved by blindfolding subjects and getting them to wear earphones that exposed them to constant noise during each trial, thus making it impossible for subjects to detect whether or not others shouted. The dependent measure was the average sound pressure generated per person (dynes/cm^2).

Results

The data were analysed with two separate 3 (group size) $\times$ 3 (trial blocks) analyses of variance. Thus, separate analyses were run on actual and pseudogroups, probably because the same individual condition had to be included in both analyses. Findings supported the hypotheses (see figure 15.2). Productivity loss increased with group size and this effect, at least descriptively, was more marked in actual rather than pseudogroups.

Discussion

The findings of the two studies closely replicate the results reported by Ringelmann (1913) and Ingham et al. (1974). Productivity of individual members decreased with increasing group size. The fact that productivity decreased even in pseudogroups, where coordination losses can be ruled out, indicates that the mere thought of working as part of a group is sufficient to reduce performance. However, because the productivity loss was greater in actual than in pseudogroups, coordination losses must also play a role. Further research has identified perceived identifiability, self-evaluation and perceived dispensability as major reasons for these motivation losses. It has been demonstrated that these productivity losses can be reduced or eliminated when subjects believe that their individual contributions can be evaluated through comparison with the contributions of others (perceived identifiability, self-evaluation; e.g. Szymanski and Harkins, 1987) and/or when they believe that their contributions are essential for the group to succeed (perceived dispensability; e.g. Kerr and Bruun, 1983). The economic theory of group productivity developed by Stroebe and Frey (1982) offers a theoretical framework to explain some of these findings.

FURTHER READING

Karau, S.J. and Williams, K.D. (1993). Social loafing: A meta-analytic review and theoretical integration. *Journal of Personality and Social Psychology*, 65, 681–706. Presents a theoretical and a statistical integration of the body of findings on social loafing.

Kerr, N.L. and Bruun, S. (1983). The dispensability of member effort and group motivation losses: Free rider effects. *Personality and Social Psychology Bulletin*, 44, 78–94. Demonstrates empirically that group members' perceptions that their contributions are not really needed to produce a group product (i.e. dispensability) encourages social loafing.

Szymanski, K. and Harkins, S. (1987). Social loafing and self-evaluation with a social standard. *Journal of Personality and Social Psychology*, 53, 891–7. Demonstrates empirically that social loafing is reduced if group members are given the opportunity to evaluate their own outputs.

REFERENCES

Dashiell, J.F. (1935). Experimental studies of the influence of social situations on the behavior of individual human adults. In C. Murchison (ed.), *Handbook of Social Psychology* (pp. 1097–158). Worcester, MA: Clark University Press.

Ingham, A.G., Levinger, G., Graves, J. and Peckham, V. (1974). The Ringelmann effect: Studies of group size and group performance. *Journal of Experimental Social Psychology*, 10, 371–84.

Kravitz, D.A. and Martin, B. (1986). Ringelmann rediscovered: The original article. *Journal of Personality and Social Psychology*, 50, 936–41.

Moede, W. (1927). Die Richtlinien der Leistungspsychologie. [Guidelines for a psychology of performance]. *Industrielle Psychotechnik*, 4, 193–207.

Ringelmann, M. (1913). Recherches sur les moteurs animés: Traveil de l'homme. [Research on animate sources of power: The work of man]. *Annales de l'Institut National Agronomique* (2nd series), XII, 1–40.

Steiner, I. (1972). *Group Process and Productivity*. New York: Academic Press.

Stroebe, W. and Frey, B.S. (1982). Self-interest and collective action: The economics and psychology of public goods. *British Journal of Social Psychology*, 21, 121–37.

Triplett, N.D. (1898). The dynamogenic factor in pacemaking and competition. *American Journal of Psychology*, 9, 507–33.

There is an old saying that "many hands make light the work." This saying is interesting for two reasons. First, it captures one of the promises of social life – that with social organization people can fulfill their individual goals more easily through collective action. When many hands are available, people often do not have to work as hard as when only a few are present. The saying is interesting in a second, less hopeful way – it seems that when many hands are available, people actually work less hard than they ought to.

Over 50 years ago a German psychologist named Ringelmann did a study that he never managed to get published. In rare proof that unpublished work does not necessarily perish, the results of that study, reported only in summary form in German by Moede (1927), have been cited by Dashiell (1935), Davis (1969), Köhler (1927), and Zajonc (1966) and extensively analyzed by Steiner (1966, 1972) and Ingham, Levinger, Graves, and Peckham (1974). Apparently Ringelmann simply asked German workers to pull as hard as they could on a rope, alone or with one, two, or seven other people, and then he used a strain gauge to measure how hard they pulled in kilograms of pressure.

Rope pulling is, in Steiner's (1972) useful classification of tasks, maximizing, unitary, and additive. In a maximizing task, success depends on how much or how rapidly something is accomplished and presumably on how much effort is expended, as opposed to an optimizing task, in which precision, accuracy, or correctness are paramount. A unitary task cannot be

- - - - -
Primary
Reading
- - - - - - - -

divided into separate subtasks – all members work together doing the same thing and no division of labor is possible. In an additive task, group success depends on the *sum* of the individual efforts, rather than on the performance of any subset of members. From these characteristics, we should expect three people pulling together on a rope with perfect efficiency to be able to exert three times as much force as one person can, and eight people to exert eight times as much force.

Ringelmann's results, however, were strikingly different. When pulling one at a time, individuals averaged a very respectable 63 kg of pressure. Groups of three people were able to exert a force of 160 kg, only two and a half times the average individual performance, and groups of eight pulled at 248 kg, less than four times the solo rate. Thus the collective group performance, while increasing somewhat with group size, was substantially less than the sum of the individual efforts, with dyads pulling at 93% of the sum of their individual efforts, trios at 85%, and groups of eight at only 49%. In a way somewhat different from how the old saw would have it, many hands apparently made light the work.

The Ringelmann effect is interesting because it seems to violate both common stereotype and social psychological theory. Common stereotype tells us that the sense of team participation leads to increased effort, that group morale and cohesiveness spur individual enthusiasm, that by pulling together groups can achieve any goal, that in unity there is strength. Social psychological theory holds that, at least for simple, well-learned tasks involving dominant responses, the presence of other people, whether as co-workers or spectators, should facilitate performance. It is thus important to find out whether Ringelmann's effect is replicable and whether it can be obtained with other tasks.

The Ringelmann effect is also interesting because it provides a different arena for testing a new theory of social impact (Latané, 1973). Social impact theory holds that when a person stands as a target of social forces coming from other persons, the amount of social pressure on the target person should increase as a multiplicative function of the strength, immediacy, and number of these other persons. However, if a person is a member of a group that is the target of social forces from outside the group, the impact of these forces on any given member should diminish in inverse proportion to the strength, immediacy, and number of group members. Impact is divided up among the group members, in much the same way that responsibility for helping seems to be divided among witnesses to an emergency (Latané and Darley, 1970). Latané further suggests that just as psychophysical reactions to external stimuli can be described in terms of a power law (Stevens, 1957), so also should reactions to social stimuli, but with an exponent having an absolute value less than 1, so that the nth person should have less effect than the $(n - 1)$th. Ringelmann's asking his workers to pull on a rope can be considered social pressure. The more people who are the target of this pressure, the less pressure should be felt by any one person. Since people are likely to work hard in proportion to the pressure they feel to do so, we should expect increased group size to result in reduced efforts on the part of individual group members. These reduced efforts can be called "social loafing" – a decrease in individual effort due to the social presence of other persons. With respect to the Ringelmann phenomenon, social impact theory suggests that at least some of the effect should be due to reduced efforts on the part of group participants, and that this reduced effort should follow the form of an inverse power function having an exponent with an absolute value less than one.

The Ringelmann effect is interesting for a third reason: If it represents a general phenomenon and is not restricted to pulling on a rope, it poses the important practical question of when and why collective efforts are less efficient that individual ones. Since many components of our standard of life are produced through one form or another of collective action, research identifying the causes and conditions of inefficient group output and suggesting strategies to overcome these inefficiencies is clearly desirable.

For these three and other reasons, we decided to initiate a program of research into the collective performance of individuals in groups.

Experiment I

Clap your hands and shout out loud

One of the disadvantages of Ringelmann's rope-pulling task is that the equipment and procedures are relatively cumbersome and inefficient. Therefore, we decided to keep our ears open for other tasks that would allow us to replicate the Ringelmann finding conceptually and would provide the basis for extended empirical and theoretical analysis. We chose cheering and clapping, two activities that people commonly do together in social settings and that are maximizing, unitary, and additive. As with rope pulling, output can be measured in simple physical units that make up a ratio scale.

Method

On eight separate occasions, groups of six undergraduate males were recruited from introductory psychology classes at Ohio State University; they were seated in a semicircle, 1 m apart, in a large soundproofed laboratory and told, "We are interested in judgments of how much noise people make in social settings, namely cheering and applause, and how loud they seem to those who hear them. Thus, we want each of you to do two things: (1) Make noises, and (2) judge noises." They were told that on each trial "the experimenter will tell you the trial number, who is to perform and whether you are to cheer (Rah!) or clap. When you are to begin, the experimenter will count backwards from three and raise his hand. Continue until he lowers it. We would like you to clap or cheer for 5 seconds as loud as you can." On each trial, both the performers and the observers were also asked to make magnitude estimates of how much noise had been produced (Stevens, 1966). Since these data are not relevant to our concerns, we will not mention them further.

After some practice at both producing and judging noise, there were 36 trials of yelling and 36 trials of clapping. Within each modality, each person performed twice alone, four times in pairs, four times in groups of four, and six times in groups of six. These frequencies were chosen as a compromise between equating the number of occasions on which we measured people making noise alone or in groups (which would have required more noisemaking in fours and sixes) and equating the number of individual performances contributing to our measurements in the various group sizes (which would have required more noisemaking by individuals and pairs). We also arranged the sequence of performances to space and counterbalance the order of conditions over each block of 36 trials, while making sure that no one had to perform more than twice in a row.

Performances were measured with a General Radio sound-level meter, Model 1565A, using the C scale and the slow time constant, which was placed exactly 4 m away from each performer. The C scale was used so that sounds varying only in frequency or pitch would be recorded as equally loud. Sound-level meters are read in decibel (dB) units, which are intended to approximate the human reaction to sound. For our purposes, however, the appropriate measure is the effort used in generating noise, not how loud it sounds. Therefore, our results are presented in terms of dynes/cm^2, the physical unit of work involved in producing sound pressure.

Because people shouted and clapped in full view and earshot of each other, each person's performance could affect and be affected by the others. For this reason, the group, rather than the individual, was the unit of analysis, and each score was based on the average output per person. Results were analyzed in a $4 \times 2 \times 2$ analysis of variance, with Group Size (1, 2, 4, 6), Response Mode (clapping vs. shouting), and Replications (1, 2) as factors.

Results

Participants seemed to adapt to the task with good humor if not great enthusiasm. Nobody refused to clap or shout, even though a number seemed somewhat embarrassed or shy about making these noises in public. Despite this, they did manage to produce a good deal of noise. Individuals averaged 84 dB (C) clapping and 87 dB cheering, while groups of six clapped at 91 dB and shouted at 95 dB (an increment of 6 dB represents a doubling of sound pressure).

As might be expected, the more people clapping or cheering together, the more intense the noise and the more the sound pressure produced. However, it did not grow in proportion to the number of people: The average sound pressure generated *per person* decreased with increasing group size, $F(3, 21) = 41.5, p < .001$. People averaged about 3.7 dynes/cm^2 alone, 2.6 in pairs, 1.8 in foursomes, and about 1.5 in groups of six (figure 15.1). Put another way, two-person groups performed at only 71% of the sum of their individual capacity, four-person groups at 51%, and six-person groups at 40%. As in pulling ropes, it appears that when it comes to clapping and shouting out loud, many hands do, in fact, make light the work.

People also produced about 60% more sound power when they shouted than when they clapped, $F(1, 7) = 8.79, p < .01$, presumably reflecting physical capacity rather than any psychological process. There was no effect due to blocks of trials, indicating that the subjects needed little or no practice and that their performance was not deleteriously affected by fatigue. In addition, there were no interactions among the variables.

Discussion

The results provide a strong replication of Ringelmann's original findings, using a completely different task and in a different historical epoch and culture. At least when people are making noise as part of a task imposed by someone else, voices raised together do not seem to be raised as much as voices raised alone, and the sound of 12 hands clapping is not even three times as intense as the sound of 2.

Zajonc's (1965) elegant theory of social facilitation suggests that people are aroused by the mere presence of others and are thus likely to work harder (though not necessarily to achieve more) when together. Although social facilitation theory might seem to predict enhanced group performance on a simple task like clapping or shouting, in the present case it would not predict any effect due to group size, since the number of people present was always eight, six participants and two experimenters. Evaluation apprehension theory (Cottrell, 1972) would also not predict any effect as long as it is assumed that coactors and audience members are

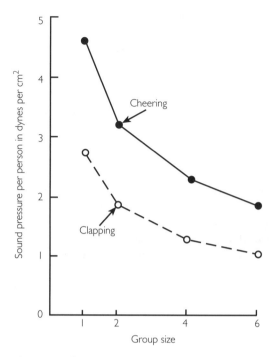

Figure 15.1   Intensity of noise as a function of group size and response mode, Experiment 1

equally effective in arousing performance anxiety. Therefore, these theories are not inconsistent with our position that an unrelated social process is involved. The results of Experiment 1 also can be taken as support for Latané's (1973) theory of social impact: The impact that the experimenters have on an individual seems to decrease as the number of coperformers increases, leading to an apparent drop in individual performance, a phenomenon we call social loafing.

However, there is an alternative explanation to these results. It may be, not that people exert less effort in groups, but that the group product suffers as a result of group inefficiency. In his invaluable theoretical analysis of group productivity, Steiner (1972) suggests that the discrepancy between a group's potential productivity (in this case *n* times the average individual output) and its actual productivity may be attributed to faulty social process. In the case of Ringelmann's rope pull, Steiner identifies one source of process loss as inadequate social coordination. As group size increases, the number of "coordination links," and thus the possibility of faulty coordination (pulling in different directions at different times), also increases. Steiner shows that for Ringelmann's original data the decrement in obtained productivity is exactly proportional to the number of coordination links.

Ingham et al. (1974) designed an ingenious experiment to determine whether the process losses found in rope pulling were mainly due to problems of coordinating individual efforts and the physics of the task, or whether they resulted from reductions in personal exertion (what we have called social loafing). First, they conducted a careful replication of Ringelmann's original rope-pulling study and found similar results – dyads pulled at 91% of the sum of their individual capacities, trios at 82%, and groups of six at only 78%.

In a second experiment, Ingham et al. cleverly arranged things so that only the individual's perception of group size was varied. Individuals were blindfolded and led to believe that others were pulling with them, but in fact, they always pulled alone. Under these conditions, of course, there is no possibility of loss due to faulty synchronization. Still there was a substantial drop in output with increases in perceived group size: Individuals pulled at 90% of their alone rate when they believed one other person was also pulling, and at only 85% with two to six others believed pulling. It appears that virtually all of the performance decrement in rope pulling observed by Ingham et al. can be accounted for in terms of reduced effort or social loafing.

With respect to clapping and especially shouting, however, there are several possible sources of coordination loss that might have operated in addition to social loafing: (a) Sound cancellation will occur to the extent that sound pressure waves interfere with each other, (b) directional coordination losses will occur to the extent that voices are projected toward different locations, and (c) temporal coordination losses will occur to the extent that moment-to-moment individual variations in intensity are not in synchrony. Our second experiment was designed to assess the relative effects of coordination loss and social loafing in explaining the failure of group cheering to be as intense as the sum of individual noise outputs.

Experiment 2

Coordination loss or reduced effort?

For Experiment 2 we arranged things so that people could not hear each other shout; participants were asked to wear headphones, and during each trial a constant 90-dB recording of six people shouting was played over the earphones, ostensibly to reduce auditory feedback and to signal each trial. As a consequence, individuals could be led to believe they were shouting in groups while actually shouting alone. Ingham et al. (1974) accomplished this through the use of "pseudosubjects," confederates who pretended to be pulling with the participants but who in fact did not pull any weight at all. That is an expensive procedure – each of the 36 participants tested by Ingham et al. required the services of 5 pseudosubjects as well as the experimenter. We were able to devise a procedure whereby, on any given trial, one person could be led to believe that he was performing in a group, while the rest thought he was performing alone. Thus, we were able to test six real participants at one time.

Additionally, although we find the interpretation offered by Ingham et al. plausible and convincing, the results of their second experiment are susceptible to an alternative explanation. When participants were not pulling the rope, they stood and watched the pseudosubjects pull. This would lead people accurately to believe that while they were pulling the rope, idle participants would be watching (Levinger, reference note 1). Thus, as the number of performers decreased, the size of the audience increased. According to Cottrell's evaluation apprehension hypothesis (1972), the presence of an evaluative audience should enhance performance for a simple, well-learned task such as rope pulling, and, although there is little supportive evidence, it seems reasonable that the larger the audience, the greater the enhancement (Martens and Landers, 1969; Seta, Paulus, and Schkade, 1976). Thus, it is not clear whether there was a reduced effort put forth by group members because they believed other people were pulling with them, or an increase in the effort exerted by individuals because they believed other people were watching them. In Experiment 2, therefore, we arranged to hold the size of the audience constant, even while varying the number of people working together.

Method

Six groups of six male undergraduate volunteers heard the following instructions:

> In our experiment today we are interested in the effects of sensory feedback on the production of sound in social groups. We will ask you to produce sounds in groups of one, two, or six, and we will record the sound output on the sound-level meter that you can see up here in front. Although this is not a competition and you will not learn your scores until the end of the experiment, we would like you to make your sounds as loud as possible. Since we are interested in sensory feedback, we will ask you to wear blindfolds and earphones and, as you will see, will arrange it so that you will not be able to hear yourself as you shout.
>
> We realize it may seem strange to you to shout as loud as you can, especially since other people are around. Remember that the room is soundproofed and that people outside the room will not be able to hear you. In addition, because you will be wearing blindfolds and headsets, the other participants will not be able to hear you or to see you. Please, therefore, feel free to let loose and really shout. As I said, we are interested in how loud you can shout, and there is no reason not to do your best. Here's your chance to really give it a try. Do you have any questions?

Once participants had donned their headsets and blindfolds, they went through a series of 13 trials, in which each person shouted four times in a group of six, once in a group of two, and once by himself. Before each trial they heard the identification letters of those people who were to shout.

Interspersed with these trials were 12 trials, two for each participant, in which the individual's headset was switched to a separate track on the stereophonic instruction tape. On these trials, everybody else was told that only the focal person should shout, but that individual was led to believe either that one other person would shout with him or that all six would shout.

Thus, each person shouted by himself, in actual groups of two and six, and in pseudogroups of two and six, with trials arranged so that each person would have approximately equal rest periods between the trials on which he performed. Each trial was preceded by the specification of who was to perform. The yells were coordinated by a tape-recorded voice counting backwards from three, followed by a constant 90-dB 5-sec recording of the sound of six people shouting. This background noise made it impossible for performers to determine whether or how loudly other people were shouting, or, for that matter, to hear themselves shout. Each trial was terminated by the sound of a bell. This sequence of 25 trials was repeated three times, for a total of 75 trials, in the course of which each subject shouted 24 times.

As in Experiment 1, the data were transformed into dynes/cm^2 and subjected to analyses of variance, with the group as the unit of analysis and each score based on the average output per person. Two separate 3×3 analyses of variance with group size (1, 2, 6) and trial block (1–3) were run, one on the output of trials in which groups actually shouted together, and one on the pseudogroup trials in which only one person actually shouted.

Results

Overall, participants shouted with considerably more intensity in Experiment 2 than in Experiment 1, averaging 9.22 dynes/cm^2 when shouting alone, as compared to 4.73 dynes/cm^2, $t(12) = 4.05$, $p < .01$. There are several plausible reasons for this difference. The new rationale involving the effects of reduced sensory feedback may have interested or challenged individuals to perform well. The constant 90-dB background noise may have led people to shout with more intensity, just as someone listening to music through headphones will often speak inappropriately loudly (the Lombard reflex). The performers may have felt less embarrassed because the room was soundproof and the others were unable to see or hear them. Finally, through eliminating the possibility of hearing each other, individuals could no longer be influenced by the output of the others, thereby lifting the pressure of social conformity.

As in Experiment 1, as the number of actual performers increase, the total sound output also increased, but at a slower rate than would be expected from the sum of the individual outputs. Actual groups of two shouted at only 66% of capacity, and groups of six at 36%, $F (2, 10) = 226, p < .001$. The comparable figures for Experiment 1 are 71% and 40%. These similarities between experiments suggest that our procedural changes, even though they made people unable to hear or see each other, did not eliminate their feeling of being in a group or reduce the amount of incoordination or social loafing.

The line connecting the solid circles in figure 15.2 shows the decreased output per person when actually performing in groups. The dashed line along the top represents potential productivity – the output to be expected if there were no losses due to faulty coordination or to social loafing. The striped area at the bottom represents the obtained output per person in actual groups. Output is obviously lower than potential productivity, and this decrease can be considered as representing the sum of the losses due to incoordination and to reduced individual effort.

In addition to shouting in actual groups, individuals also performed in pseudogroups in which they believed that others shouted with them but in which they actually shouted alone, thus preventing coordination loss from affecting output. As shown in figure 15.2, people

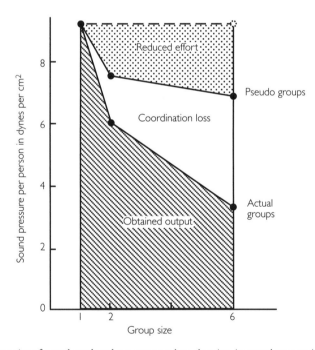

Figure 15.2   Intensity of sound produced per person when cheering in actual or perceived groups of one, two, and six, as a result of reduced effort and faulty coordination of group efforts, Experiment 2

shouted with less intensity in pseudogroups than when alone, $F(2, 10) = 37.0, p < .0001$. Thus, group size made a significant difference even in pseudogroups in which coordination loss is not a factor and only social loafing can operate.

When performers believed one other person was yelling, they shouted 82% as intensely as when alone, and when they believed five others to be yelling, they shouted 74% as intensely. The stippled area defined at the top of figure 15.2 by the data from the pseudogroups represents the amount of loss due to social loafing. By subtraction, we can infer that the white area of figure 15.2 represents the amount of loss due to faulty coordination. Since the latter comprises about the same area as the former, we can conclude that, for shouting, half the performance loss decrement is due to incoordination and half is due to social loafing.

Discussion

Despite the methodological differences between Experiments 1 and 2, both experiments showed that there is a reduction in sound pressure produced per person when people make noise in groups compared to when alone. People in Experiment 1 applauded and cheered in full view of each other, with all the excitement, embarrassment, and conformity that goes along with such a situation. In Experiment 2, no one could see or hear any other person. Only the experimenters could see the people perform. And finally, the rationale changed drastically, from the experimenters' interest in "judgments of how much noise people make in social settings" to their interest in "the effects of sensory feedback on the production of sound in social groups." Yet, despite differences in the task characteristics and supposed purpose, the two studies produced similar results. This points to the robust nature of both the phenomenon and the paradigm.

General Discussion

Noise production as group performance

Although we do not usually think about it that way, making noise can be hard work, in both the physical and the psychological sense. In the present case, the participants were asked to produce sound pressure waves, either by rapidly vibrating their laryngeal membranes or by vigorously striking their hands together. Although superficially similar in consequence, this task should not be confused with more normal outbreaks of shouting and clapping that occur as spontaneous outbursts of exuberant expressiveness. Our participants shouted and clapped because we asked them to, not because they wanted to.

This effortful and fatiguing task resulted in sound pressure waves, which, although invisible, can be easily and accurately measured in physical units that are proportional to the amount of work performed. The making of noise is a useful task for the study of group processes from the standpoint both of production and of measurement – people are practiced and skilled at making noise and can do so without the help of expensive or cumbersome apparatus, and acoustics and audio engineering are sufficiently advanced to permit sophisticated data collection. We seem to have found a paradigm wherein people get involved enough to try hard and become somewhat enthusiastic, yet the task is still effortful enough so that they loaf when given the opportunity.

The causes of social loafing

The present research shows that groups can inhibit the productivity of individuals so that people reduce their exertions when it comes to shouting and clapping with others. Why does this occur? We suggest three lines of explanation, the first having to do with attribution and equity, the second with submaximal goal setting, and the third with the lessening of the contingency between individual inputs and outcomes.

1 *Attribution and equity*   It may be that participants engaged in a faulty attribution process, leading to an attempt to maintain an equitable division of labor. There are at least three aspects of the physics and psychophysics of producing sound that could have led people to believe that the other persons in their group were not working as hard or effectively as themselves. First, individuals judged their own outputs to be louder than those of the others, simply because they were closer to the sound source. Second, even if everyone worked to capacity, sound cancellation would cause group outputs to seem much less than the sum of their individual performances. Finally, the perception of the amount of sound produced in a group should be much less than the actual amount − growing only as the .67 power of the actual amount of sound, according to Stevens's psychophysical power law (1975).

These factors may have led individuals to believe that the other participants were less motivated or less skillful than themselves − in short, were shirkers or incompetents. Thus, differences in the perception of sound production that were essentially the result of physical and psychophysical processes may have been mistakenly attributed to a lack of either skill or motivation on the part of the others, leading individuals to produce less sound in groups because there is no reason to work hard in aid of shirkers or those who are less competent.

This process cannot explain the results of Experiment 2, since the capacity to judge the loudness of one's own output, much less that of others, was severely impaired by the 90-dB background masking noise used to signal the trials. However, rather than "discovering" social loafing while participating in the experiment, the participants may have arrived with the preexisting notion that people often do not pull their own weight in groups. Thus, despite being unable to hear or see one another, lack of trust and the propensity to attribute laziness or ineptitude to others could have led people to work less hard themselves.

2 *Submaximal goal setting*   It may be that despite our instructions, participants redefined the task and adopted a goal, not of making as much noise as possible, but merely of making enough noise or of matching some more or less well-defined standard. Individuals would clearly expect it to be easier to achieve this goal when others are helping, and might work less hard as a consequence. This, of course, would change the nature of noise production from what Steiner (1972) would term a *maximizing* task to an *optimizing* task. A maximizing task makes success a function of how much or how rapidly something is accomplished. For an optimizing task, however, success is a function of how closely the individual or group approximates a predetermined "best" or correct outcome. If participants in our experiments perceived sound production as an optimizing rather than a maximizing task, they might feel the optimal level of sound output could be reached more easily in groups than alone, thereby allowing them to exert less effort.

The participants in Experiment 2 could hear neither themselves nor others and would not be able to determine whether their output was obnoxious or to develop a group standard for an optimal level. Furthermore, in both experiments, the experimenters reiterated their request to yell "as loud as you can, every time," over and over again. Before the first trial they would ask the group how loud they were supposed to yell. In unison, the group would reply, "As loud as we can!" We think it unlikely that participants perceived the task to be anything other than maximizing.

3 *Lessened contingency between input and outcome*   It may be that participants felt that the contingency between their input and the outcome was lessened when performing in groups. Individuals could "hide in the crowd" (Davis, 1969) and avoid the negative consequences of slacking off, or they may have felt "lost in the crowd" and unable to obtain their fair share of the positive consequences for working hard. Since individual scores are unidentifiable when groups perform together, people can receive neither precise credit nor appropriate blame for their performance. Only when performing alone can individual outputs be exactly evaluated and rewarded.

Let us assume that group members expect approval or other reward proportional to the total output of a group of n performers, but that since individual efforts are indistinguishable, the reward is psychologically divided equally among the participants, each getting $1/n$ units of reward. Under these assumptions, the average group, if it performed up to capacity and suffered no process loss, could expect to divide up n times the reward of the average individual, resulting in each member's getting $n \times 1/n$, or n/n, units of reward, the same amount as an individual.

Although the total amount of reward may be the same, the contingency on individual output is not. Any given individual under these assumptions will get back only one nth of his own contribution to the group; the rest will be shared by the others. Even though he may also receive unearned one nth of each other person's contribution, he will be tempted, to the extent that his own performance is costly or effortful, to become a "free rider" (Olson, 1965). Thus, under these assumptions, if his own performance cannot be individually monitored, an individual's incentive to perform should be proportional to $1/n$.

Seligman (1975) has shown that animals and people become lethargic and depressed when confronted with tasks in which they have little or no control over the outcomes. Likewise, in our experiments, people may have felt a loss of control over their fair share of the rewards when they performed in groups, leading them also to become, if not lethargic and depressed, at least less enthusiastic about making lots of noise.

Since people were asked to shout both alone and in groups, they may have felt it smart to save their strength in groups and to shout as lustily as possible when scores were individually identifiable, marshalling their energy for the occasions when they could earn rewards. This line of reasoning suggests that if inputs were made identifiable and rewards contingent on them, even when in groups, it would be impossible for performers to get a free ride and they would have an incentive to work equally hard in groups of different sizes.

Social loafing and social impact theory

Each of these three lines of explanation may be described in terms of Latané's (1973) theory of social impact. If a person is the target of social forces, increasing the number of other persons also in the target group should diminish the pressures on each individual because the impact is divided among the group members. In a group performance situation in which pressures to work come from outside the group and individual outputs are not identifiable, this division of impact should lead each individual to work less hard. Thus, whether the subject is dividing up the amount of work he thinks should be performed or whether he is dividing up the amount of reward he expects to earn with his work, he should work less hard in groups.

The theory of social impact further stipulates the form that the decrease in output should follow. Just as perceptual judgments of physical stimuli follow power functions (Stevens, 1957), so also should judgments of social stimuli, and the exponent of the psychosocial power function should have an exponent of less than one, resulting in a marginally decreasing impact of additional people. Thus, social impact theory suggests that the amount of effort expended on group tasks should decrease as an inverse power function of the number of people in the group. This implication cannot be tested in Experiment 1 or with the actual groups of Experiment 2, inasmuch as coordination loss is confounded with social loafing. However, a power function with an exponent of $-.14$ accounted for 93% of the variance for the pseudogroups of Experiment 2. It appears that social impact theory provides a good account of both the existence and the magnitude of social loafing.

The transsituational and transcultural generality of social loafing

The present research demonstrates that performance losses in groups occur with tasks other than rope pulling and with people other than prewar German workers. There are, in addition, other instances of experimental research that demonstrate similar cases of social loafing. For example, Marriott (1949) and Campbell (1952) have shown that factory workers produce less per person in larger groups than in smaller ones. Latané and Darley (1970) have found that the likelihood that a bystander will intervene in a situation in which someone requires assistance is substantially reduced by the addition of other bystanders who share in the responsibility for help. Wicker (1969) has found that the proportion of members taking part in church activities is lower in large than in small churches, presumably because the responsibility for taking part is more diffuse. Similarly, Petty, Harkins, Williams, and Latané (1977) found that people perceived themselves as exerting less cognitive effort on evaluating poems and editorials when they were among groups of other unidentifiable evaluators than when they alone were responsible for the task.

These experimental findings have demonstrated that a clear potential exists in human nature for social loafing. We suspect that the effects of social loafing have far-reaching and profound consequences both in our culture and in other cultures. For example, on collective farms (kolkhoz) in Russia, the peasants "move all over huge areas, working one field and one task one day, another field the next, having no sense of responsibility and no direct dependence on the results of their labor" (Smith, 1976, p. 281). Each peasant family is also allowed a private plot of up to an acre in size that may be worked after the responsibility to the collective is discharged. The produce of these plots, for which the peasants are individually responsible, may be used as they see fit. Although these plots occupy less than 1% of the nation's agricultural lands (about 26 million acres), they produce 27% of the total value of Soviet farm output (about $32.5 billion worth) (Yemelyanov, 1975, cited in Smith, 1976, p. 266). It is not, however, that the private sector is so highly efficient; rather, it is that the efficiency of the public sector is so low (Wädekin, 1973, p. 67).

However, before we become overly pessimistic about the potential of collective effort, we should consider the Israeli kibbutz, an example that suggests that the effects of social loafing can be circumvented. Despite the fact that kibbutzim are often located in remote and undeveloped areas on the periphery of Israel to protect the borders and develop these regions, these communes have been very successful. For example, in dairying, 1963 yields per cow on the kibbutz were 27% higher than for the rest of Israel's herds, and in 1960 yields were 75% higher than in England. In 1959, kibbutz chickens were producing 22% of the eggs with only 16% of the chickens (Leon, 1969). The kibbutz and the kolkhoz represent the range of possibilities for collective effort, and comparisons of these two types of collective enterprise may suggest conditions under which per person output would be greater in groups than individually.

Social loafing as a social disease

Although some people still think science should be value free, we must confess that we think social loafing can be regarded as a kind of social disease. It is a "disease" in that it has negative consequences for individuals, social institutions, and societies. Social loafing results in a reduction in human efficiency, which leads to lowered profits and lowered benefits for all. It is "social" in that it results from the presence or actions of other people.

The "cure," however, is not to do away with groups, because despite their inefficiency, groups make possible the achievement of many goals that individuals alone could not possibly accomplish. Collective action is a vital aspect of our lives: From time immemorial it has made possible the construction of monuments, but today it is necessary to the provision of even our food and shelter. We think the cure will come from finding ways of channeling social forces so that the group can serve as a means of intensifying individual responsibility rather than diffusing it.

NOTES

This research was supported by National Science Foundation Grant GS40194.

The authors would like to thank Levis Hinkle for technical assistance and Edward Diener, John Harvey, Norbert Kerr, Robert Kidd, George Levinger, Thomas Ostrom, Richard Petty, and Ladd Wheeler for their valuable comments.

REFERENCE NOTE

1 Levinger, G. Personal communication, June 1976.

REFERENCES

Campbell, M. Group incentive payment schemes: The effects of lack of understanding and group size. *Occupational Psychology*, 1952, *26*, 15–21.
Cottrell, N. Social facilitation. In C. McClintock (ed.), *Experimental social psychology*. New York: Holt, Rinehart and Winston, 1972.
Dashiell, J.F. Experimental studies of the influence of social situations on the behavior of individual

human adults. In C. Murchison (ed.), *A handbook of social psychology*. Worcester, MA: Clark University Press, 1935.

Davis, J.H. *Group performance*. Reading, MA: Addison-Wesley, 1969.

Ingham, A.G., Levinger, G., Graves, J., and Peckham, V. The Ringelmann effect: Studies of group size and group performance. *Journal of Experimental Social Psychology*, 1974, *10*, 371–84.

Köhler, O. Ueber den Gruppenwirkungsgrad der menschlichen Körperarbeit und die Bedingung optimaler Kollektivkraftreaktion. *Industrielle Psychotechnik*, 1927, *4*, 209–26.

Latané, B. *A theory of social impact*. St Louis, MO: Psychonomic Society, 1973.

Latané, B., and Darley, J.M. *The unresponsive bystander: Why doesn't he help?*. New York: Appleton-Century-Crofts, 1970.

Leon, D. *The kibbutz: A new way of life*. London: Pergamon Press, 1969.

Marriott, R. Size of working group and output. *Occupational Psychology*, 1949, *23*, 47–57.

Martens, R., and Landers, D.M. Coaction effects on a muscular endurance task. *Research Quarterly*, 1969, *40*, 733–7.

Moede, W. Die Richtlinien der Leistungs-Psychologie. *Industrielle Psychotechnik*, 1927, *4*, 193–207.

Olson, M. *The logic of collective action: Public goods and the theory of groups*. Cambridge, MA: Harvard University Press, 1965.

Petty, R., Harkins, S., Williams, K., and Latané, B. The effects of group size on cognitive effort and evaluation. *Personality and Social Psychology Bulletin*, 1977, *3*, 579–82.

Seligman, M. *Helplessness*. San Francisco: Freeman, 1975.

Seta, J.J., Paulus, P.B., and Schkade, J.K. Effects of group size and proximity under cooperative and competitive conditions. *Journal of Personality and Social Psychology*, 1976, *34*, 47–53.

Smith, H. *The Russians*, New York: Ballantine Books, 1976.

Steiner, I.D. Models for inferring relationships between group size and potential group productivity. *Behavioral Science*, 1966, *11*, 273–83.

Steiner, I.D. *Group process and productivity*. New York: Academic Press, 1972.

Stevens, S.S. On the psychological law. *Psychological Review*, 1957, *64*, 153–81.

Stevens, S.S. A metric for the social consensus. *Science*, 1966, *155*, 530–41.

Stevens, S.S. *Psychophysics: Introduction to its perceptual, neural and social prospects*. New York: Wiley, 1975.

Wädekin, K. *The private sector in Soviet agriculture*. Los Angeles: University of California Press, 1973.

Wicker, A.N. Size of church membership and members' support of church behavior settings. *Journal of Personality and Social Psychology*, 1969, *13*, 278–88.

Zajonc, R.B. Social facilitation. *Science*, 1965, *149*, 269–74.

Zajonc, R.B. *Social psychology: An experimental approach*. Belmont, CA: Brooks/Cole, 1966.

Productivity loss in brainstorming groups: Toward the solution of a riddle

M. Diehl and W. Stroebe

- - - - -
Editors'
Introduction
- - - - - - - -

Theoretical Background

There are two paradoxical aspects to the history of brainstorming as a method of increasing creativity in groups. One is that brainstroming remained extremely popular among practitioners despite early and overwhelming evidence that it did not work. The other is that even after

Journal of Personality and Social Psychology (1987), 53:497– 509.

evidence accumulated that demonstrated the superior productivity of individual over group brainstormers, there was relatively little research effort on the part of social psychologists to find theoretical explanations for this effect.

The first empirical study demonstrating the superiority of individual over group brainstorming was published in 1958 by Taylor et al., just five years after the appearance of the book that popularized the notion that group brainstorming is effective (Osborn, 1953). Taylor and colleagues used an important methodological device to compare individual and group brainstorming: the *nominal group*. Nominal groups consist of the same number of individuals as the real groups to which they are compared, but are comprised of individuals who brainstorm alone. Only afterwards are their ideas pooled to make a group product. Since the same idea may be suggested several times by four persons working alone, whereas such repetition would not be allowed in an interacting group, these redundant ideas are eliminated from the pooled set of ideas that constitutes the 'group product' of the nominal group. The performance of nominal groups formed a baseline which indicated the productivity of a set of individuals who are neither helped nor hindered by interaction. Taylor and colleagues found that nominal groups produced substantially more ideas than real groups. This finding has since been replicated in numerous studies (for a meta-analytic review see Mullen et al., 1991). And yet, brainstorming is still widely used by advertising agencies and business organizations as a procedure for increasing group productivity.

Diehl and Stroebe became interested in brainstorming when they were looking for a cognitive task which was additive and would allow the testing of predictions from the economic theory of group productivity developed by Stroebe and Frey (1982). According to this theory there should be a temptation to free-ride on the efforts of others in brainstorming groups, because, due to the pooling of their ideas, group members should perceive their individual contributions as more dispensable and less identifiable than would individual brainstormers. As Stroebe and Diehl (1983) pointed out, this explanation could resolve a number of discrepancies in the brainstorming literature (such as between the findings of Maginn and Harris, 1980, and Collaros and Anderson, 1969). Study 1 was conducted to test this hypothesis.

STUDY 1

Hypothesis

If the difference in productivity between real and nominal groups is due to the fact that members of real groups are tempted to free-ride because they expect that their ideas will be pooled, then a manipulation of this expectation should eliminate the productivity difference between real and nominal groups.

Design

The study used a 2 (type of session: individual/group) $\times$ 2 (assessment expectation: personal/collective) between-subjects design.

Method

For the independent variables, subjects (male high school students) brainstormed either individually or in four-person groups. Subjects in both types of session were told that their ideas would be either pooled into a group product or examined individually. The dependent variables consisted of the numbers of non-redundant ideas and of non-redundant good ideas produced by real and nominal groups. Redundant ideas were eliminated by raters from sets of ideas which constituted the product of either real or nominal groups. The raters were blind as to the conditions under which a given set was produced. In a second step, ideas were rated according to their originality and feasibility. An idea was defined as 'good' if it was rated high on both dimensions.

Results

Two 2 (type of session) × 2 (type of assessment) analyses of variance (ANOVAs) conducted on quantity and quality scores resulted in two main effects. Subjects produced more ideas and more good ideas when brainstorming individually rather than in groups, and when expecting to be assessed personally rather than having their ideas pooled. The ANOVA also allows one to partition the total variability or variance in idea production into the variability produced by the different factors or independent variables as a measure of the impact these manipulations had on idea production. Since, according to the variance accounted for by each factor, the impact of the type of session was much larger than that of type of assessment, the authors concluded that free-riding was not a major cause of productivity loss in brainstorming groups.

A second conclusion from this study was that the correlation between the number of ideas and the number of good ideas was so high ($r = .82$) that the additional information gained by looking at these quality ratings did not seem to justify the costly effort involved in conducting them. Therefore they used only quantity as an indicator of brainstorming productivity in their later studies.

STUDIES 2 AND 3

Studies 2 and 3 checked whether the productivity loss could be due to evaluation apprehension. This explanation assumes that despite instructions, group members still fear the criticism of their fellow brainstormers and thus produce fewer ideas than individual brainstormers who have no such fears. In contrast to Maginn and Harris (1980), in experiment 2 Diehl and Stroebe found that increasing evaluation apprehension in individual sessions reduced brainstorming productivity. However, the pattern of findings of experiment 3, in which evaluation apprehension and type of session were manipulated independently, eliminated evaluation apprehension as a major explanation of productivity loss in brainstorming groups. If the difference in evaluation apprehension between individual and group sessions was responsible for the lower productivity in groups, it would be difficult to explain why type of session still accounted for most of the variance in idea production, although evaluation apprehension had been manipulated independently of type of session in this experiment.

STUDY 4

Having established that neither free-riding nor evaluation apprehension could account for the powerful effect of type of session, Diehl and Stroebe tested whether 'production blocking' could be responsible. This explanation attributes the lower productivity of brainstorming groups to production blocking due to the fact that in groups only one member can speak at any given time. Because production blocking cannot be eliminated in real groups, they examined its role by introducing blocking into individual sessions. They had groups of four subjects who worked in separate rooms connected via a communication apparatus that functioned like a set of traffic lights. These lights were voice controlled, giving the red light to three of the subjects when the fourth one was talking. As soon as that subject stopped talking, green lights went on, indicating that somebody else could take the word. When somebody did, the red lights went on for the other 'group members'. Thus, these lights imposed turn-taking. Diehl and Stroebe found that whenever this was the case, productivity was lower than that of real groups, regardless of whether subjects could or could not listen to the ideas presented by others. This effect was so powerful that it accounted for 96 per cent of the variance due to experimental conditions.

Discussion

This series of studies set out to test three theoretical explanations for the lower productivity of brainstorming groups as compared to individual brainstormers. The major strategy followed was to introduce a factor suspected to be a cause of the productivity loss in brainstorming groups into individual sessions, to test whether its impact on individual brainstorming was powerful enough to account for the substantial difference observed between individuals and groups. Whereas the expectation that ideas will be pooled (free-riding) or that one's ideas will be evaluated (evaluation apprehension) failed this test, blocking was powerful enough to make it a likely cause of the productivity loss in groups. In their more recent research the authors have searched for strategies to reduce or eliminate the blocking effect (for a review, see Stroebe and Diehl, 1994).

FURTHER READING

Paulus, P.B. and Dzindolet, M.T. (1993). Social influence processes in group brainstorming. *Journal of Personality and Social Psychology*, 64, 575–86. Presents and tests a social influence theory of brainstorming productivity. The authors argue that social matching of low performance levels of interactive group members may be an important factor in the productivity loss observed in brainstorming groups.

Stroebe, W. and Diehl, M. (1994). Why groups are less effective than their members. In W. Stroebe and M. Hewstone (eds), *European Review of Social Psychology* (vol. 5, pp. 272–303). Evaluates all theoretical explanations of the productivity loss in brainstorming in the light of empirical evidence.

REFERENCES

Collaros, P.A. and Anderson, L.R. (1969). Effects of perceived expertness upon creativity of members of brainstorming groups. *Journal of Applied Psychology*, 53, 159–63.

Maginn, B.K. and Harris, R.J. (1980). Effect of anticipated evaluation on individual brainstorming performance. *Journal of Applied Psychology*, 12, 3–24.

Mullen, B., Johnson, C. and Salas, E. (1991). Productivity loss in brainstorming groups: A meta-analytic integration. *Basic and Applied Social Psychology*, 12, 3–24.

Osborn, A.F. (1953). *Applied Imagination*. New York: Scribner (rev. edns 1957, 1963).

Stroebe, W. and Diehl, M. (1983). The effect of free-riding and social inhibition on brainstorming productivity. Paper given at the European–Israeli conference on group processes and intergroup conflict. Tel Aviv, Israel.

Stroebe, W. and Frey, B. (1982). Self-interest and collective action: The economics and psychology of public goods. *British journal of Social Psychology*, 21, 121–37.

Taylor, D.W., Berry, P.C. and Block, C.H. (1958). Does group participation when using brainstorming facilitate or inhibit creative thinking? *Administrative Science Quarterly*, 3, 23–47.

- - - - -
Primary
Reading
- - - - - - - -

In his influential book, Osborn (1957) suggested brainstorming as a method of group problem solving that considerably increases the quality and quantity of ideas produced by group members. Brainstorming groups are traditionally given instructions designed to free the individual members from the inhibiting effects of self-criticism and the criticism by others during the problem-solving session. The rules behind brainstorming are as follows: keep in mind that the more ideas the better and the wilder the ideas the better; improve or combine ideas already suggested; and do not be critical. Osborn (1957) claimed that if these rules are followed "the average person can think up twice as many ideas when working with a group than when working alone" (p. 229).

Taylor, Berry, and Block (1958) were the first to test Osborn's claim in a study in which subjects were asked to brainstorm for a period of 12 min either individually or in 4-person groups. To allow for a statistical comparison between results from individual and group sessions, nominal groups were formed from subjects who had brainstormed individually. For each nominal group the ideas of 4 subjects were combined, eliminating redundant ideas by counting only once any idea that had been suggested several times. Thus, the scores of nominal groups represent the level of productivity one would expect if group interaction neither facilitated nor inhibited group productivity. Contrary to Osborn's claim, Taylor et al. found that nominal groups produced nearly twice as many different ideas as the real groups. This finding has since been frequently replicated. Of the 22 experiments listed in table 15.1, 18 reported the performance of nominal groups to be superior to that or real groups, and only 4, all involving 2-person groups (Cohen, Whitmyre, and Funk, 1960; Pape and Bölle, 1984; Torrance, 1970, Experiments 1 and 2), reported no difference.

Results have been more equivocal with regard to quality of ideas. Of the few studies that assessed quality, most have reported a measure of *total quality* (i.e., the sum of the quality ratings of the ideas produced by a given subject or group). Because the total quality is highly related to the number of ideas, some authors have preferred to use *average quality*. However, as brainstorming is assumed to increase the production of good ideas, the number of good ideas appears to be a more appropriate measure of quality. Consequently, in these studies that

Table 15.1   Results of studies that compare brainstorming productivity of real groups (R) with productivity of nominal groups (N)

Study	Group size	Productivity Quantity	Quality
Taylor, Berry, and Block (1958)	4	$R < N$	TQ:$R < N$
			AQ:equivocal[a]
			NO:$R < N$
Cohen, Whitmyre, and Funk (1960)	2	$R = N$	NO:equivocal
Dunette, Campbell, and Jaastad (1963)	4	$R < N$	TQ:$R < N$
			AQ:equivocal
Milton (1965)	4	$R < N$	TQ:$R < N$
Gurman (1968)	3	$R < N$	TQ:$R < N$
Bouchard (1969)	4	$R < N$	TQ:$R < N$
Experiment 2			AQ:equivocal
			NG:$R < N$
Rotter and Portugal (1969)	4	$R < N$	–
Vroom, Grant, and Cotton (1969)	4	$R < N$	TQ:$R < N$
			AQ:equivocal
			NG:$R < N$
Bouchard and Hare (1970)	5, 7, 9	$R < N$	–
Torrance (1970)			
Experiment 1	2	$R = N$	NO:$R < N$
Experiment 2	2	$R = N$	NO:$R < N$
Dillon, Graham, and Aidells (1972)	4	$R < N$	–
Bouchard (1972)			
Experiment 2	4	$R < N$	NG:equivocal
Bouchard, Drauden, and Barsaloux (1974)			
Conditions E and F	4	$R < N$	–
Street (1974)	3	$R < N$	–
Harari and Graham (1975)	4	$R < N$	–
Chatterjea and Mitra (1976)	3	$R < N$	–
Madsen and Finger (1978)	4	$R < N$	–
Maginn and Harris (1980)	4	$R < N$	–
Jablin (1981)	4	$R < N$	–
Barkowski, Lamm, and Schwinger (1982)	2	$R < N$	–
Pape and Bölle (1984)	2	$R = N$	NO:$R = N$

The following quality measures were used: total quality (TQ), average quality (AQ), number of original or unique ideas (NO), and number of good ideas (NG). Dashes indicate that quality was not assessed.
[a] Findings vary across different topics, subject groups, or experimental conditions.

received a score above a chosen cutoff point on a scale of quality ratings was classified as "good." Finally, some studies have assessed the number of unique or original ideas, having used the frequency with which the idea is suggested as a criterion.

The findings for quality appear to be heavily dependent on the type of measure used: In all six studies that assessed total quality, nominal groups performed better than real groups did.

No consistent pattern emerged for the other measures. Among those studies, findings were not only inconsistent between studies but even within the same study, if several topics, subject groups, or experimental conditions had been used.

Theories of Productivity Loss in Brainstorming Groups

In view of the accumulation of evidence for the superior productivity of nominal groups, at least in terms of the quantity of ideas produced, it is surprising that the reasons for their superiority have so far not been explained. The three major interpretations that have been offered to account for the lower productivity of real groups are *production blocking*, *evaluation apprehension*, and *free riding*. In the first part of this article, we discuss these interpretations in light of existing evidence. In the second part, we present four experiments conducted to evaluate these interpretations.

Production blocking

In their classic review, Lamm and Trommsdorff (1973) argued that the most important cause of the inferiority of real groups is the rule that only one group member speaks at a time. It is unclear, however, how production blocking operates. Although groups are typically given the same time limit as individuals, researchers have emphasized that there is ample time available and that even group members run out of ideas long before the end of a session. Thus, a lack of speaking time can hardly be the reason for the lower productivity of group members. It seems possible, however, that group members who are prohibited from verbalizing their ideas as they occur may forget or suppress them because they seem less relevant or less original at a later time. Finally, being forced to listen to the ideas of other group members may prove distractive and interfere with the subjects' own thinking.

Production blocking has never been tested directly and there is only limited indirect evidence. Thus, Bouchard and Hare (1970), who compared the productivity of 5-, 7-, and 9-person brainstorming groups with that of nominal groups, found that the productivity of the two types of groups diverged with increasing group size. This finding is consistent with a blocking interpretation, as the length of delay or the probability of delay is likely to increase with group size. Less relevant is a study by Barkowski, Lamm, and Schwinger (1982), in which the authors claimed to support a blocking interpretation by demonstrating that the advantage of the nominal groups disappeared when, instead of number of ideas, a ratio of numbers of ideas to numbers of words spoken was used as a measure of productivity. Because the number of ideas is likely to be correlated with number of words, it is not clear why this procedure should control for blocking.

Evaluation apprehension

An interpretation in terms of evaluation apprehension suggests that, despite brainstorming instructions, the fear of negative evaluations from other group members prevents subjects who are working in groups from presenting their more original ideas. Support for this hypothesis comes from a study by Collaros and Anderson (1969), who manipulated perceived expertise of group members in brainstorming groups. The authors reasoned that social inhibition would be greater the more group members perceived other members as experts. In their all-experts condition, each member of a brainstorming group was told that all other members had previously worked in such groups, whereas in a one-expert condition, members were told that only one unidentified member had had such an experience. In a third, a no-expert condition, no such instructions were given. Consistent with predictions, productivity was highest in the no-expert condition and lowest in the all-experts condition. Furthermore, subjects in the expert conditions indicated greater feelings of inhibition and reluctance to offer ideas in a postexperimental questionnaire than did subjects who brainstormed without receiving instructions as to the expertness of other group members.

In contrast, Maginn and Harris (1980), who manipulated evaluation apprehension in subjects working individually, could not demonstrate an effect of social inhibition on productivity. Maginn and Harris told subjects in half of their individual brainstorming conditions that there were three judges on the other side of a one-way mirror "who will be listening to your ideas and rating them for quality and originality" (p. 221). The authors reasoned that if evaluation apprehension accounted for the low productivity of real groups, introducing observers to the individual conditions should lower productivity in these conditions compared with that of the real groups. Contrary to the authors' expectations, individual productivity in the presence of observers was not significantly different from that of individual subjects working without observers. To account for their findings, Maginn and Harris (1980) suggested that their judges failed to induce evaluation apprehension because they were not in the same room as the subjects. This explanation does not seem very plausible, however, in light of findings from research on the impact of evaluation apprehension on social facilitation. These findings demonstrate "that threat of evaluation in the absence of an audience can produce energizing effects upon performance almost identical to those obtained when experts are observing the individual" (Henchy and Glass, 1968, p. 452).

Free riding

According to this interpretation, subjects are likely to work hard mainly because the experimenter has instructed them to produce as many ideas as possible. Thus, any factor that reduces the ability of the experimenter to monitor individual productivity is also likely to reduce subjects' motivation to work. Because group members expect their ideas to be pooled and analyzed at the group level only, they may feel tempted to free ride on the efforts of others. Subjects who participate in individual sessions, on the other hand, expect their productivity to be monitored individually and thus see no possibility to evade the control exerted by the experimenter. With physical tasks, the social loafing studies of Latané and co-workers (e.g., Latané, Williams and Harkins, 1979; Williams, Harkins and Latané, 1981) have produced results that are in line with this hypothesis.

A second reason for free riding in brainstorming groups can be derived from the economic theory of public goods (Olson, 1965; Stroebe and Frey, 1982). According to this theory, the temptation to free ride varies with group size not only because increases in size lower the *identifiability* of individual contributions, but also because they decrease the *perceived effectiveness* of individual contributions. Perceived effectiveness refers to members' perception of the difference it would make to the group or to themselves if they decided to contribute. In large groups, not all individual contributions are typically required for the group product; consequently, members may feel that their particular contribution is *dispensable*.

As Kerr and Bruun (1983) emphasized, "the dispensability of members' efforts (and hence, the likelihood of free-rider motivation losses) depends strongly on task features" (p. 80). By using the taxonomy of tasks Steiner (1972) developed, Kerr and Bruun argued that dispensability would be more important with disjunctive tasks (when only the best contribution counts as the group product) than with additive tasks (when the group product is the simple sum or average of individual contribution). Brainstorming is neither a purely additive nor a purely disjunctive task. Whereas the emphasis on quantity contained in the brainstorming rules would make it an additive task, the fact that the obvious purpose of the procedure is to come up with a number of good ideas would also make it a disjunctive task. Thus, the relative importance of dispensability as a source of free-rider motivation will depend to some extent on the subjects' conceptions of the brainstorming task.

The role of dispensability as a mediator of free riding has been examined for physical (e.g., Kerr and Bruun, 1983) as well as cognitive tasks (e.g., Harkins and Petty, 1982). Kerr and Bruun (1983) manipulated dispensability by varying task demands (disjunctive, conjunctive) and subjects' self-perceived ability. Consistent with predictions, low-ability subjects found their contributions dispensable and worked less than high-ability subjects under disjunctive task demands (i.e., when only the best score was counted). The reverse results were observed under conjunctive task demands (i.e, when only the worst score counted).

Similar findings were reported in a series of experiments conducted by Harkins and Petty (1982), who demonstrated with a modified brainstorming task (Experiment 4 of this article) that, even with identifiability held constant, an increase in dispensability lowers brainstorming productivity. Subjects in this study had to brainstorm in groups on the possible uses of an object. Subjects were asked to write their ideas on cards and to drop them into a common hopper, thus eliminating identifiability. Harkins and Petty manipulated dispensability by telling subjects either that all group members worked on the same object or that each worked on a different object. Consistent with predictions, subjects who believed every group member worked on a different object produced more ideas than did subjects who believed that all members had been given the same brainstorming task.

An interpretation in terms of free riding could resolve the apparent discrepancy between the results of Collaros and Anderson (1969) and Maginn and Harris (1980) and also account for the pattern of findings typically reported in the brainstorming literature. As applied to the Collaros and Anderson study, this analysis would suggest that the effect of perceived expertise on productivity was mediated by differences in perceived dispensability rather than in evaluation apprehension. Subjects should expect their own efforts to be more dispensable if they expect some members to be more qualified for the job than if they believe all group members to be equally qualified. The failure of the manipulation Maginn and Harris used to increase brainstorming productivity is consistent with a free-rider interpretation, because their manipulation should have affected neither dispensability nor identifiability, as both are already at a maximum with subjects who brainstorm individually.

The free-rider explanation can be used to interpret other findings in the brainstorming literature that previously could not be explained satisfactorily. For example, in some of his brainstorming groups, Bouchard (1972) required that participants contribute their ideas in a fixed sequence and that they announce a "pass" if they had nothing to say when their turn came. The free-rider interpretation would account for the observed increase in productivity by suggesting that taking turns essentially eliminates the temptation to free ride, by increasing the identifiability of individual contributions. The free-rider hypothesis would also account for the performance decrements Bouchard and Hare (1970) observed with increasing group size. This pattern, which has frequently been observed with physical tasks (e.g., Harkins, Latané, and Williams, 1980; Ingham, Levinger, Graves, and Peckham, 1974; Latané et al., 1979; Williams et al., 1981), could be due to both decreased identifiability and increased dispensability.

There is evidence that free riding does occur with brainstorming tasks (Harkins and Petty, 1982) and that the free-rider interpretation can account for certain inconsistent findings (e.g., Collaros and Anderson, 1969; Maginn and Harris, 1980). Nonetheless, only indirect support has been provided for the hypothesis that free riding is responsible for the difference in the productivity of real and nominal brainstorming groups, because Harkins and Petty (1982) did not compare the productivity of real and nominal groups within a given study. Therefore, we conducted Experiment 1 to test directly this free-rider interpretation.

Experiment I

If the difference in productivity between real and nominal groups is due to the fact that members of real groups are tempted to free ride because they know that the ideas of all group members will be pooled, then a direct manipulation of these expectations should eliminate the productivity difference between nominal and real brainstorming groups. To test this hypothesis, we asked subjects to brainstorm individually or in groups under instructions that either stressed personal or collective assessment of ideas. Thus, our major aim in this study was to demonstrate that the productivity difference normally observed between group and individual brainstorming is mediated by the implicit association of type of session and assessment expectations. It was not the purpose of this experiment to determine whether this effect is due to a variation in identifiability or dispensability (or both) as their impact on brainstorming productivity had already been demonstrated by Harkins and Petty (1982).

Method

Subjects
Subjects were 48 male students (aged 15–17) from a Tübingen, Germany, high school who were paid for their participation.

Task
As in all further experiments, brainstorming was conducted according to the usual four brainstorming rules. The issue of how to improve the relationship between the German population and the (foreign) guest workers was chosen, an important topic for these students.

Independent variables
Type of session (individual vs. group) Subjects brainstormed either individually or in 4-person groups.

Assessment instructions (personal vs. collective) Subjects were instructed that the purpose of the experiment was to compare the productivity of persons working individually with that of individuals working in groups. Subjects assigned to group sessions were then told that their performance would be compared with that of subjects working alone. Under personal-assessment instructions group members were informed that each member's individual perform-ance would be compared with that of a subject working alone. Those working under collective-assessment instructions were told that the group's performance would be compared with that of a nominal group, that is, the combined output of 4 subjects working alone. In individual sessions subjects working under personal-assessment instructions were told that their perform-ance would be compared with that of somebody working in a group, whereas subjects following collective-assessment instructions were informed that their ideas would be pooled with that of three other individuals to compare the productivity of this nominal group with that of real groups.

Procedure

Subjects were enrolled in 4-person groups. On arrival they were given their topic and informed of the brainstorming rules. Subjects were then either seated alone in small rooms (individual condition) or led into a somewhat larger room (group condition). Subjects were assigned to conditions on a predetermined random basis.

For group sessions, subjects were seated around a table and given clip-on microphones. They were instructed that they were in a group condition and should make suggestions on the guest worker topic. They were then given the assessment instructions and informed that they had 15 min for the brainstorming and that their responses would be tape-recorded. The experi-menter then left the room to switch on the tape recorder and stayed in the control room until the end of the session. On returning, the experimenter handed out the postexperimental questionnaire.

For individual sessions, subjects were seated individually in small rooms and given a clip-on microphone. They were told that they were in an individual condition and should make suggestions about their topic. These suggestions were tape-recorded. They were then given the assessment instructions and told that they had 15 min for the brain-storming. The experi-menter then left the room to switch on the tape recorder, stayed in the control room until the end of the session, and later returned to hand out the postexperimental questionnaire.

Dependent variables

The major dependent variables were the number of nonredundant ideas and the quality of ideas produced by real or nominal groups. The postexperimental questionnaire assessed subjects' understanding of the experimental instructions and also asked how at ease they felt in the brainstorming situation, how satisfied they were with their performance, whether they had suggested all the ideas that had occurred to them, and whether they had as much time as they wanted.

Scoring

Quantity   Ideas were transcribed from the tape recording by a research assistant, who was instructed to write each separate idea on a separate card. To test scorer reliability, a second research assistant repeated this task on the tapes of two nominal and two real groups. The correlation computed on the number of ideas per individual or group for the two scorers was $r = .94$. These cards were then compiled in sets that reflected either the performance of a real or a nominal group. An assistant who was blind as to whether a set constituted the work of a real or a nominal group was instructed to review these cards and eliminate any idea that had been suggested more than once within a given set. To assess the reliability of this decision, a second assistant repeated the procedure for a subsample of four sets. By relating the number of choices in which both raters agreed to the total number of possible pairs, we found that the raters agreed in 99.64% of the total number of possible pairs.[1]

Quality   Ideas were rated for originality and feasibility on two 5-point scales. The second assistant assessed reliability by performing these ratings on a subset of 190 items. Defining the two ratings as in agreement whenever both fell within one point of each other, the two raters agreed in 94.79% of the originality ratings and 94.27% of the feasibility ratings although the variance of the ratings was fairly high. The two measures of quality were not correlated.

Results

Table 15.2 presents the average number and quality of ideas suggested by nominal and real 4-person groups in the two assessment conditions. The quantity measure reflects the number of nonoverlapping ideas per group. Three measures of quality were used: the average for each of the two quality ratings (*originality, feasibility*), and the number of *good ideas*. A good idea was defined as one that received a rating of 1 on one rating scale and no worse than a rating of 2 on the other.

An analysis of variance (ANOVA) with a two-factor design (Type of session × Type of assessment) conducted on quantity scores resulted in two main effects. Nominal groups produced significantly more ideas than real groups, $F(1, 8) = 87.56, p < .01$ and subjects working under personal-assessment instructions produced more ideas than subjects working under collective-assessment instructions, $F(1, 8) = 8.13, p < .05$. There was no indication of an interaction.

Whereas the same two-factor ANOVA conducted on the measures of average originality and average feasibility did not yield any significant effects, results for number of good ideas tended to parallel those for number of ideas. Subjects produced more good ideas in individual sessions rather than in group sessions, $F(1, 8) = 10.38, p < .05$, and there was a tendency to produce more good ideas under personal-assessment instructions than under collective-assessment instructions, $F(1, 8) = 3.98, p < .10$. Even though the pattern of means (table 15.2) suggests that assessment instructions had their major impact in the individual session rather

Table 15.2   Average number and quality of ideas suggested by real and nominal 4-person brainstorming groups working under personal- versus collective-assessment instructions

Condition	Measure			
	Number of ideas	*Number of good ideas*	*Average originality*	*Average feasibility*
Real group				
Personal	32.33	3.00	2.52	2.90
Collective	23.66	2.00	2.49	3.07
Nominal group				
Personal	84.33	13.33	2.46	2.60
Collective	64.66	5.66	2.43	2.70

Lower numbers indicate higher originality and feasibility.

than in the group session, the Type of session × Type of assessment interaction did not reach an acceptable level of significance.

The items used to evaluate the understanding of the experimental manipulation indicated only a few misunderstandings. Thus, 5 subjects (two from the group session and three from the individual session) who had received personal-assessment instructions thought that they were following collective-assessment instructions, whereas 1 subject made the opposite mistake. The only two significant effects were main effects for type of session: Subjects reported that they had suppressed more ideas in group sessions than in individual sessions, $F(1, 44) = 4.64$. $p < .05$. Subjects also felt that there was slightly less time in group sessions than in individual sessions, $F(1, 44) = 6.53$, $p < .05$. However, the average difference between conditions was only half a unit on 5-point scale. Furthermore, the correlation computed between rated availability of time and individual productivity for the group condition was not significant ($r = -.21$). Finally, an analysis of the distribution of ideas over time indicated that more than 90% of the ideas had been expressed at the end of 10 to 12 min in group sessions and even earlier in individual sessions.

Discussion

The finding that subjects produced more ideas when working under personal-assessment as opposed to collective-assessment instructions is consistent with the assumption that subjects' expectations about the assessment of their contributions could account for some of the difference between real and nominal groups. However, the fact that the type of session affected productivity even though assessment expectations had been manipulated independently, and that descriptively, the impact of the type of session was much larger (accounting for 83.46% of the total variance) than that of assessment instructions (accounting for only 7.75%), suggests that assessment expectations are at best responsible for a small proportion of the total productivity loss observed in real groups.[2]

The quality ratings did not add a great deal to this evaluation. Our finding that despite their impact on quantity, the experimental manipulations did not affect average quality suggests that the increase in quantity was associated with an increase in poor as well as in good ideas. However, the number of good ideas was analyzed, the pattern of effects was similar to those observed with quantity ratings. Because the number of good ideas showed a correlation of $r = .82$ with the number of ideas, the additional information gained by looking at these quality ratings did not seem to justify the costly effort involved in conducting quality ratings. Therefore, we decided not to conduct quality ratings in further studies.

Although the results of this study give some support to the assumption that differences in free riding are partly responsible for the productivity difference typically observed between individual and group brainstorming, the results also suggest that there must be other processes contributing to the productivity loss. That free riding is not a major cause of productivity loss in brainstorming groups may be due to the fact that, unlike the physical tasks used in much of the social loafing research (e.g., Latané et al., 1979; Williams et al., 1981), brainstorming does not require a great deal of effort. According to the economic model (e.g., Olson, 1965; Stroebe and Frey, 1982), the temptation to free ride should vary as a function of the cost of contributing; consequently, there should be little temptation to free ride with a task that is practically effortless and that involves no time costs (i.e., subjects had to stay for a given period of time no matter what they did).

With free riding ruled out as a major explanation of productivity loss, we were left to consider evaluation apprehension and blocking as additional processes. Because social inhibition is such a pervasive feature of social life, Maginn and Harris's (1980) finding that brainstorming should somehow be exempted had always seemed puzzling. To clarify this issue, we tried to identify differences between our Experiment 1 and the Maginn and Harris study that might have minimized the impact of evaluation apprehension in their experiment.

One such feature could have been the nature of Maginn and Harris's problems. It seems plausible that individuals will be most likely to censor their responses if they fear that certain answers might reveal socially undesirable or even embarrassing aspects of themselves (e.g., lack of knowledge, ideological biases). It can be argued that none of these reasons for self-censure applied to the brainstorming topics Maginn and Harris (1980) used. Their "thumbs" problem ("What would happen if everyone after a certain date had an extra thumb on each hand?") was so obviously irrelevant that subjects even competed in producing silly ideas. The "energy problem" ("How can we reduce gasoline consumption?"), though more involving, was a problem that was uncontroversial and one that had been discussed extensively in the news media. Our topic, on the other hand, was highly controversial. Many potential solutions (e.g., that the guest workers should try harder to learn German and to adapt to German culture; that the government should offer financial inducements to motivate guest workers to return to their own countries) are considered "right wing" and cannot be mentioned in student circles.

If evaluation apprehension in our brainstorming groups was indeed partly caused by the fear of producing ideas that may reveal an unacceptable ideological position, it seems possible that a person's expectation of his or her performance being evaluated by peers would create more evaluation apprehension in this particular situation than would the anticipated evaluation of some unknown assessor. There are two reasons for this: First, the source of apprehension is not one's lack of knowledge but the risk of violating norms concerning political positions shared by one's peers (as opposed to some anonymous evaluator), and second, whereas one expects further interaction with peers, one might never again meet the evaluator.

Experiment 2

In Experiment 2, we examined these hypotheses by manipulating the nature of the brainstorming topics, the level of evaluation apprehension, and the source inducing this apprehension. Thus, subjects were to brainstorm individually on topics that were either rather uncontroversial or controversial and under low- or high-evaluation apprehension. We induced high-evaluation apprehension by telling subjects either that their ideas would be evaluated by some judges (who were not described further) or by their fellow students. If our hypotheses outlined previously were valid, the evaluation apprehension manipulation should affect brainstorming productivity for controversial topics but not for uncontroversial topics. Furthermore, on the controversial topics, we expected high-evaluation apprehension to lead to lower productivity if induced by a threat of peer rather than anonymous assessor evaluation.

Method

Subjects
Subjects were 36 male psychology students of the University of Tübingen who participated in the study as part of their course requirement.

Independent variables

Evaluation apprehension   Two different procedures were used to induce high-evaluation apprehension. In one condition (judges), modeled after Maginn and Harris (1980), a room with a one-way mirror was used and subjects were told that there were judges sitting on the other side of the mirror who would be listening to their ideas and rating them for quality and originality. In a second condition (peers), a videocamera was mounted in a corner and subjects were told that their performance would be videotaped and that these tapes would be used for demonstration purposes in social psychology classes.[3] To induce low-evaluation apprehension, there was no one-way mirror or videocamera and no instructions were given regarding experts or peers.

Type of topic (uncontroversial vs. controversial)   Two rather uncontroversial ("How can entertainment programs on television be improved?"; "How can life quality be improved in the suburbs?") and two controversial topics ("How can the number of guest workers be reduced?"; "How can economic growth be increased in West Germany?") had been selected for brainstorming on the basis of pretests.[4] A controversial topic was defined as one that subjects were forced to argue, not only against their own private opinion but also against a position widely shared by their fellow students. Subjects brainstormed on either the two controversial or the two uncontroversial topics, with the order counterbalanced within each condition.

Procedure

Subjects, who were randomly assigned to one of the six experimental conditions, were seated individually in small rooms. They were given taped instructions establishing one of three experimental conditions of evaluation apprehension (low-evaluation apprehension, high-evaluation apprehension/peers, high-evaluation apprehension/judges). They were then given the brainstorming rules and either an uncontroversial or a controversial topic and were told that they should speak their suggestions into the microphone. They were informed that they had 15 min for the brainstorming. At the end of the session the experimenter returned and gave the second topic to the subjects. After subjects worked for another 15 min the experimenter returned to hand out the postexperimental questionnaire.

Dependent variables

The major dependent variable was the number of nonredundant ideas produced by subjects working under the three experimental conditions. As in Experiment 1, the postexperimental questionnaire contained questions that checked the effectiveness of the experimental manipulations. To investigate the controversialness of topics, subjects were asked the extent to which they perceived a need for an improvement in entertainment programs and life quality or whether they believed that the number of guest workers should be reduced and economic growth be increased. They were also asked to indicate the opinions they would attribute to their fellow students on these issues. Finally, subjects had to rate how at ease they felt in the brainstorming situation and whether they had verbalized all the ideas that had occurred to them.

Scoring

The scoring of the number of ideas was performed according to the same procedure as in Experiment 1. Interrater agreement was $r = .87$ for number of ideas transcribed. Although not strictly necessary when only comparisons between individual conditions are planned, it was nevertheless decided to eliminate redundant ideas (within subjects) to increase the comparability between experiments. When this procedure was repeated on a subset of 299 ideas by a second scorer, the scorers agreed in their decision on 99.91% of the possible pairs.

Results

Table 15.3 presents the scores for the number of ideas individual subjects suggested under each of the three conditions of evaluation apprehension and for the two controversial and the two uncontroversial topics.

A two-factor ANOVA (Evaluation apprehension × Type of topic) was conducted collapsing across the two topics within each of the conditions. This analysis resulted in a marginal effect for type of topic, $F(1, 30) = 3.65$, $p < .10$. Thus, fewer ideas were produced when topics were controversial as opposed to uncontroversial. Two orthogonal contrasts were used to examine evaluation apprehension. Whereas an F value of less than 1 did not indicate a differential impact of the two conditions of high-evaluation apprehension (judges vs. peers), the contrast comparing the combined conditions of high-evaluation apprehension with low-evaluation apprehension was highly significant, $F(1, 30) = 14.25$, $p < .01$. Thus, regardless of the type of manipulation, the induction of high-evaluation apprehension resulted in a significant drop in productivity. There was no indication of the predicted interaction between evaluation apprehension and type of topic ($F < 1$). Because we modeled one of our evaluation apprehension conditions (judges) after the procedure Maginn and Harris (1980) used, our findings also confirmed that the evaluation apprehension main effect could be replicated when this condition only was used to represent high-evaluation apprehension.

The manipulation checks indicated that the controversialness manipulation was successful. Thus, subjects themselves agreed less, $F(1, 30) = 85.72$, $p < .01$, and also believed that their fellow subjects would agree less, $F(1, 30) = 56.30$, $p < .01$, with the controversial topic (i.e., need to reduce number of guest workers or need to increase economic growth) than with the uncontroversial topic (i.e., need to improve television programs; need to improve life quality). Subjects working under high-evaluation apprehension did not indicate less ease with the brainstorming situations than did those working under low-evaluation apprehension ($F < 1$).

Table 15.3 Average number of ideas suggested by individuals brainstorming under high- or low-evaluation apprehension discussing controversial or uncontroversial topics

Type of topic	Low-evaluation apprehension	High-evaluation apprehension	
		Peers	Judges
Controversial			
Economic growth	45.67	24.00	29.00
Guest workers	32.67	14.50	20.50
Uncontroversial			
Suburbs	62.67	36.50	31.33
Entertainment	45.17	28.33	21.83

Discussion

These findings are clearly inconsistent with those of Maginn and Harris (1980), even for the conditions that closely replicate those used in their study. Thus, in contrast to the findings of Maginn and Harris, our induction of evaluation apprehension reduced the quantity of ideas produced in this experiment, and this effect was independent of both the procedure by which evaluation apprehension had been induced and the controversialness of the topic.

These findings suggest that despite brainstorming instructions, the presence of outside observers motivates subjects to censor their own ideas (even when ratings in terms of originality are not made explicit). Because the identifiability of individual contributions is a necessary condition for inducing evaluation apprehension, the findings of this experiment could be considered inconsistent with those of Experiment 1, in which an increase in identifiability was associated with an increase in productivity. This apparent inconsistency becomes even more salient if one considers the findings of Harkins and Jackson (1985), who demonstrated that for identifiability to reduce the temptation to free ride, subjects must believe that their individual outputs could be evaluated by comparison with the outputs of other group members. When subjects believed that individual outputs were not comparable, and thus could not be evaluated, the identifiability induction did not reduce productivity.

The differential impact of the two manipulations was due to the different standards attributed to the evaluators. Our brainstorming instructions clearly indicated that the experimenter was mainly interested in quantity of ideas. Thus, subjects whose individual contributions were identifiable produced more than those whose contributions were not identifiable. The induction of evaluation apprehension, on the other hand, raised concerns about the quality of ideas and thus resulted in a decrease in the quantity of ideas produced due to self-censoring processes. The emphasis on quality was made explicit in the judges condition, and the fact that there was no difference in impact between judges and peers supports our contention that the anticipation of an evaluation through peers induces the same concerns.

Whereas our findings suggest the possibility that evaluation apprehension might be responsible for part of the productivity loss observed in brainstorming groups, they do not permit any definite conclusions, as the impact of evaluation apprehension was demonstrated only for individual brainstorming.

Experiment 3

To clarify whether the productivity loss in brainstorming groups is due to evaluation apprehension, an experiment was needed to manipulate both evaluation apprehension and type of session. We hypothesized that if the productivity loss in real brainstorming groups is partially or fully caused by the high level of evaluation apprehension induced by the group setting, then inducing evaluation apprehension should have a greater impact on individual brainstormers (who normally have low evaluation apprehension) than on subjects interacting in real groups (where apprehension is always at a high level).[5] We conducted Experiment 3 to test this hypothesis. However, to determine whether the two variables in combination could account for the productivity difference between nominal and real groups, we varied assessment instructions in addition to the type of session and evaluation apprehension.

Method

Subjects
Subjects were 64 psychology students (32 men, 32 women) from Tübingen University who participated in the study as part of their course requirements.

Task
Brainstorming on the guest worker topic used in Experiment 1 was performed in group sessions as well as in individual sessions.

Independent variables
Type of session (group vs. individual)   Subjects were assigned to brainstorm either individually or in 4-person groups. All groups were homogeneous with regard to sex composition, and an equal number of men and women were assigned to each of the experimental conditions.

Evaluation apprehension   High-evaluation apprehension was created by combining the two procedures used in Experiment 2. In the low-evaluation apprehension conditions, we told subjects that their suggestions would be recorded on audiotape. Evaluation by judges or for use in class demonstrations was not mentioned.

Assessment instructions (personal vs. collective)   The same instructions were used as in Experiment 1.

Procedure
The procedure for this experiment was almost identical to that of Experiment 1, with the following exceptions: Although 4 subjects were enrolled for sessions at any given time, sometimes fewer than 4 showed up for what had been planned as a group session. These subjects were then tested individually. The instructions used to induce evaluation apprehension were given after the information on type of session and assessment instructions.

Dependent variables
The major dependent variable was the number of nonredundant ideas produced by real or nominal groups. In addition, subjects had to complete a postexperimental questionnaire that evaluated their understanding of the experimental instructions and also asked how at ease they felt in the brainstorming situation and whether they had been given as much time as they wanted.

Scoring
The scoring of ideas was performed according to the same procedure as in Experiment 1. The interrater agreement was $r = .87$ for the ideas transcribed and 99.83% for the number of redundant ideas.

Results

Table 15.4 presents the group scores for each of the eight experimental conditions. A three-factor ANOVA (Type of session × Assessment instructions × Evaluation Apprehension)

Table 15.4   Average number of ideas suggested by real and nominal 4-person brainstorming groups working under high- versus low-evaluation apprehension and collective- versus personal-assessment instructions

	Type of assessment	
Condition	Collective assessment	Personal assessment
Real group		
Low-evaluation apprehension	34.50	52.50
High-evaluation apprehension	36.00	40.00
Nominal group		
Low-evaluation apprehension	82.00	102.00
High-evaluation apprehension	78.00	66.00

performed on these group scores yielded significant main effects for type of session and evaluation apprehension. Subjects who brainstormed individually produced significantly more ideas than did subjects who participated in group sessions, $F(1, 8) = 74.08, p < .01$. Similarly, subjects produced significantly more ideas when working under conditions of low- rather than high-evaluation apprehension, $F(1, 8) = 7.08, p < .05$. There was no main effect for assessment instructions but only an Assessment instructions $\times$ Evaluation apprehension interaction, $F(1, 8) = 5.76, p < .05$. Orthogonal contrasts that compared the impact of high- versus low-evaluation apprehension (across group and individual conditions) indicated a significant difference under personal assessment instructions, $F(1, 8) = 12.89, p < .01$, but not collective assessment instructions $(F < 1)$. Thus, inducing high-evaluation apprehension lowered productivity only when personal-assessment instructions had been given. When collective-assessment instructions were given, the evaluation apprehension manipulation had little effect.

Of the subjects, 93.75% correctly answered a multiple-choice item that checked recall of assessment instructions. The question asking how at ease subjects felt in the brainstorming session resulted in a weak main effect for type of session. Subjects felt somewhat less at ease under individual as opposed to group conditions, $F(1, 8) = 4.97, p < .10$. Similar to Experiment 2, evaluation apprehension did not affect these ratings. There was also a significant difference between individual and group brainstormers in their assessment of the time available for the task, $\chi^2(2, N = 64) = 14.35, p < .01$. Although the majority of responses for both conditions fell into the category "sufficient time," the distribution of the remaining responses differed between the two types of sessions. A sizable minority of individual subjects indicated that there was "too much time," yet subjects who had performed in groups felt that there was "too little time." There were again indications from the group discussion, however, that group members typically ran out of ideas some time before the end of a session.

Discussion

Although the three experimental manipulations had significant effects on brainstorming productivity, the pattern of findings is only partly consistent with our predictions. Type of session resulted in the usual main effect, with real groups producing less than nominal groups. When low-evaluation apprehension was used, the impact of the assessment instructions on productivity replicated the findings from Experiment 1. Again productivity was higher for subjects working under personal as opposed to collective instructions but, as in Experiment 1, assessment instructions did not eliminate the productivity difference between nominal and real groups.

The findings for evaluation apprehension are somewhat unexpected. The impact of evaluation apprehension seems to have been restricted to subjects who expected personal assessment. With personal-assessment instructions, subjects working under high-evaluation apprehension produced significantly fewer ideas than did those working under low-evaluation apprehension. However, the fact that evaluation apprehension did not affect performance of those following collective-assessment instructions suggests that the threat of evaluation does not seem to raise apprehension when the target of the evaluation is perceived as the group and not the individual. This pattern is similar to that Harkins and Jackson (1985) reported.

Furthermore, our results do not confirm the evaluation apprehension interpretation of the productivity loss in real groups. If evaluation apprehension were at least partially responsible for the low productivity of real groups, the evaluation apprehension manipulation would be expected to have less effect in groups than in individual sessions. Although there is a tendency for evaluation apprehension to be more effective in individual than in group conditions, this interaction did not even approach an acceptable level of significance. However, the failure of this interaction to reach statistical significance could be due to the small size of our sample. Also, as noted earlier (see note 5), the interaction prediction requires that evaluation apprehension already approaches its maximum possible value in brainstorming groups; the results of Experiment 4 tend to challenge this assumption.

Although assessment expectations and evaluation apprehension were manipulated in this experiment, type of session still accounted for more than 70% of the total variance in brainstorming productivity. Because our manipulation of evaluation apprehension used an external source of evaluation (judges and nonparticipating peers), it is possible that the evaluation apprehension could be stronger when aroused by members of one's own group hearing and evaluating arguments than by nonparticipating peers. Although we have no data on this issue, this assumption does not seem plausible because, unlike the group members, the external evaluators are not under instructions to be uncritical. Thus, although assessment expectations and evaluation apprehension have been shown to affect brainstorming productivity and can thus be assumed to contribute to the productivity loss in brainstorming groups, their impact has been minor when compared with that of type of session. This would suggest that there are still other powerful causes of the productivity loss that have not been identified in our experiments.

Experiment 4

We designed Experiment 4 to investigate production blocking as a factor contributing to the low productivity of brainstorming groups. Because production blocking cannot be eliminated in real groups, we examined its role by introducing blocking into individual sessions. If blocking were fully responsible for the low productivity of real brainstorming groups, the introduction of comparable blocking into individual sessions would be expected to lower the productivity of subjects brainstorming individually to that of subjects working in groups.

Design overview

The experiment contained five conditions: In addition to real group and individual brainstorming conditions included as baseline controls, there were three conditions in which blocking was manipulated for subjects working in separate rooms. This was done by signal displays connected to each subject's microphone through a voice-activated sensor. The display consisted of four lights (one green and three red), each light representing a subject. When a subject talked, the sensor switched on the green light for this subject and the red lights for the other subjects. The subject's light was switched off when he or she stopped talking. Because members of real groups usually speak only when others are silent, subjects in Conditions 1 and 2 were asked to talk only when all lights were off. Whereas in Condition 1 subjects could hear the ideas of the other "group members," this was not possible in Condition 2. The fact that subjects' ideas could not be heard in this latter condition eliminated evaluation apprehension within the group. In Condition 3 subjects were informed of the function of the lights (the same explanation as in Conditions 1 and 2) but were told to disregard them and to talk whenever they had anything to say. Thus, no blocking was expected in this condition. To keep expectations regarding assessment constant across conditions, all subjects were given personal-assessment instructions.

Method

Subjects
Subjects were 60 psychology students (20 men, 40 women) at the University of Tübingen who participated in the experiment as part of their course requirement.

Task
The brainstorming topic was: "How can unemployment be reduced in Germany?"

Procedure
Subjects were enrolled in same-sex, 4-person groups. On arrival at the laboratory, each group was assigned to an experimental condition according to a predetermined random order that assured that the proportion of male to female groups remained the same for all experimental conditions. All subjects were then given tape-recorded instructions explaining the brainstorming rules and telling them that the experiment was designed to compare the productivity of individuals who brainstormed individually or in groups. The instructions that follow varied according to conditions.

Group control   The instructions used in this condition were identical to those of the group sessions with personal assessment in Experiments 1 and 3.

Experimental Condition 1 (blocking, communication)   These subjects were also told that they were in a group condition, that their suggestions would be tape-recorded, and that their individual performance would be compared with that of another subject working individually. They were then informed that they would each work in a separate room and that they had to communicate with the other group members using intercoms that were connected to a signal system. The function of this system was explained as follows:

> There will be a display of four lights, three red and one green. Each of the lights represents one group member sitting in one of the rooms. Thus Room 1 is represented by Light 1, Room 2 by Light 2, etcetera. In each room, the member's own light is green; that of the other group members red. As soon as one person begins to talk, an acoustic sensor will switch on the light of this person. If a person stops talking for 1.5 seconds, his (her) light will be switched off automatically. Thus, everybody can see who is speaking at the moment. In addition you will hear through your earphones what is being said. Since in a group discussion only one person can talk at any moment, you should make your own contribution only when no other light is on.

Experimental Condition 2 (blocking, no communication)   The first part of the instructions for this condition was identical to that of Condition 1. Subjects were then told that they could not hear each other's ideas and that their terminals had lights and microphones but no earphones. After the function of the lights had been explained, subjects were told that "since this is a simulation of a group discussion, you are only allowed to speak when no other light is on."

Experimental Condition 3 (no blocking, no communication)   These subjects were told that they were in an individual condition, that their suggestions would be tape-recorded, and that their performance was to be compared with that of a person working in a group. Their terminals had lights and a microphone but no earphone. After the function of the lights had been explained, subjects were told that "everybody could talk whenever they wanted and that they need not pay any attention to the lights." However, the lights were left operating throughout the session.

Individual control   These subjects received the same instructions used in Experiments 1 and 3 for individual brainstorming sessions with personal assessment.

After instructions had been specified, all subjects were given a first brainstorming topic (discussed for 8 min only) to familiarize subjects in the experimental conditions with the signal system. These discussions were not recorded. At the end of this period, subjects were given the unemployment topic and told that they would now have 15 min to make suggestions.

Dependent measures

The dependent variable was the number of nonredundant ideas produced by real or nominal groups. The postexperimental questionnaire checked the subjects' understanding of the personal assessment instruction and also asked how at ease they were and whether they had verbalized all the ideas that had occurred to them. In addition, subjects had to rate the adequacy of the time available to them on a 5-point scale.

Scoring

Scoring of the ideas was performed according to the procedure described in Experiment 1. The interrater agreement was $r = .97$ for ideas transcribed and 99.72% for number of redundant ideas.

Results

Table 15.5 presents the group scores for each of the five experimental conditions. A one-way ANOVA indicated a significant difference between conditions, $F(4, 10) = 10.99$, $p < .01$. A

Table 15.5 Average number of ideas suggested by nominal versus real 4-person groups working under blocking and nonblocking conditions

Condition	Number of ideas
Group control	55.67
Condition 1 (blocking, communication)	37.67
Condition 2 (blocking, no communication)	45.67
Condition 3 (no blocking, no communication)	102.67
Individual control	106.00

planned contrast comparing the three conditions with blocking (group control, Conditions 1 and 2) against the two conditions without blocking (Condition 3, individual control) resulted in a highly significant effect, $F(1, 10) = 42.22, p < .01$. This analysis further revealed that 96% of the variance due to experimental conditions could be attributed to this comparison. A post hoc comparison of all means by Newman–Keuls confirmed that significant differences only occurred between (but not within) blocking and no-blocking conditions.

None of the postexperimental questions resulted in significant effects. Ratings of the availability of time in the various conditions were all above the midpoint on a scale ranging from *very short* to *very long*. Subjects seemed to feel that there was sufficient time available to discuss the problem; this was true under blocking as well as no-blocking conditions. A contrast that compared time ratings under blocking and no-blocking conditions resulted in an F of less than 1, indicating that there was no significant difference in the rated availability of time. That there was sufficient time for discussion even under blocking conditions was further supported by an analysis of the time spent on discussion in the group condition. It was found that talk (all comments) filled only 73% of the total time available.

Discussion

The findings of Experiment 4 provide strong support for the blocking interpretation. Working under conditions that allowed them to verbalize their ideas as they occurred, subjects produced approximately twice as many ideas as they did when working under conditions in which subjects had to wait their turn. However, the processes by which blocking reduces production are still somewhat unclear. In our earlier discussion of the blocking hypothesis we suggested that group members who are prevented from verbalizing their ideas as soon as they occur may reevaluate them in light of points made by other subjects or that they might simply forget some of these ideas as a result of the distraction provided by the group discussion. Both of these processes would require exposure to the group discussion. Thus, the finding that preventing subjects from overhearing each other's ideas did not significantly increase brainstorming productivity as long as blocking rules were imposed raises doubts about the validity of this interpretation. Because the knowledge that other group members will not be able to overhear one's ideas should eliminate perceptions of the other group members as a source of social inhibition, this last finding is also inconsistent with the evaluation apprehension interpretation of the productivity loss in brainstorming groups.

To control for a variation in assessment expectations, we tested all experimental conditions under personal-assessment instructions. This eliminated differences in assessment expectations as a confounding factor that could have contributed to the productivity difference observed between individual and group sessions. It should be remembered, however, that because assessment expectations were controlled, the findings of this study cannot rule out the possibility that free riding may contribute to the productivity loss in brainstorming groups.

General Discussion

The findings of these four experiments indicate that the type of session has a powerful effect on brainstorming productivity, accounting for more than two-thirds of the variance in the number of nonredundant ideas produced. Therefore, our evaluation of the three interpretations of the productivity loss not only addresses the question of whether evaluation apprehension, free riding, and blocking have a demonstrable effect on brainstorming productivity but also whether any of these processes is likely to be a major cause of the productivity loss. Obviously, our answers to the second concern have to be approximated for two reasons: First, we never manipulated all three variables within the same design, and second, we cannot be sure whether the potency of our experimental manipulations is representative of the strength of these variables in real group settings. However, in view of the facts that the potency issue does not arise for the manipulation of type of session, that the type of session was pitted against the other two factors, and that, in each of these comparisons, the type of session always accounted for an overwhelming share of the variance, we argue that our findings do permit statements about the relative importance of the three processes.

Evaluation apprehensions

In contrast to Maginn and Harris (1980), who failed to find an impact of evaluation apprehension on brainstorming productivity, the results of our Experiment 2 clearly demonstrated that the knowledge that peers or judges are evaluating one's performance significantly reduced the number of ideas produced in individual brainstorming sessions. However, the fact that our attempts to experimentally induce evaluation apprehension in both individual and group sessions in Experiment 3 did not significantly reduce the difference in productivity between the two types of sessions raises some doubt as to whether evaluation apprehension is a major cause of the productivity loss in brainstorming groups.[6] This doubt was strengthened by the finding of Experiment 4, that whether or not subjects could overhear each other's ideas made little difference to brainstorming productivity. Because brainstorming instructions are designed specifically to free group members from the inhibiting effects of criticism by other group members, it is plausible that members of brainstorming groups do not constitute powerful sources of social inhibition for each other.

Free riding

Although the free-rider interpretation fared somewhat better than the evaluation apprehension explanation, our findings raise considerable doubt as to whether free riding should be considered a major cause of the productivity loss in brainstorming groups. Thus, despite the explicit manipulation of assessment expectations in Experiments 1 and 3, the type of session was still shown to account for more than two-thirds of the total variance in brainstorming productivity. This finding, which suggests that there is little temptation to free ride in brainstorming groups, is quite consistent with the economic analysis (e.g., Olson, 1965; Stroebe and Frey, 1982). According to this model, the costs of the individual contribution (e.g., effort, money, time) are an important determinant of the motivation to free ride. Other things being equal, the temptation to free ride should be greater, the greater the cost of the contribution expected of the individual. Because suggesting solutions to the types of problems used in brainstorming research does not require great effort or concentration and because subjects are already committed to spending a set period of time in the laboratory, the costs of contributing are very low in brainstorming situations. The results of our experiments are, therefore, not inconsistent with the fact that studies using strenuous physical tasks like rope pulling (e.g., Ingham et al., 1974) and clapping and shouting (e.g., Harkins et al., 1980; Latané et al., 1979; Williams et al., 1981) typically reported sizable free-rider effects.

Blocking

The one interpretation our data supported most strongly was production blocking. The presence or absence of blocking accounted for most of the variance created by the experimental manipulations in Experiment 4. Because the impact of the blocking manipulation remained unaffected by a variation in group members' exposure to the content of the group discussion, the blocking effect does not seem to be due to a reevaluation of ideas in light of the points made by other group members or to a forgetting of ideas due to the distractive activity of listening to the discussion.

However, although subjects may not be forgetting ideas, the periods of delay due to blocking may prevent them from developing new thoughts. After all, storage space in short term memory is fairly limited, and individuals will only be able to store a small number of ideas at a given time. This would suggest that productivity in brainstorming groups could be improved if group members were allowed to write down their own ideas. Tentative support for this hypothesis comes from Street (1974), who found that 3-person groups increased their productivity if each subject wrote down his or her own ideas instead of dictating them to a group member who acted as a recorder.

A second factor contributing to the blocking effect could be the difference in the length of time available for suggesting ideas. Brainstorming research makes use of what has been called *equal man-hour comparisons* (i.e., participants under individual and group conditions are given the same amount of time), which allows more time for individual brainstorming.[7] However, if one defines productivity as the number of ideas developed per time unit (as the emphasis on quantity contained in the brainstorming instructions suggests), then time should be kept constant in a comparison of individual and group productivity. Furthermore, there seems to be little indication that group members lack sufficient time to express their ideas. Even in group sessions, subjects tend to run out of ideas toward the end of the allotted time period.

How, then, does the time limit influence brainstorming productivity? We would like to suggest an interpretation of blocking in terms of situational demands. This interpretation, which seems to be consistent with most of the evidence reported earlier, conceptualizes blocking as a source of motivation rather than as a coordination loss (Steiner, 1972). If individuals are given a time period in which to suggest ideas on some topic, they are likely to feel obliged to continue this activity for most of this time. Obviously, this task is less difficult for group members than for participants in individual sessions. Whereas group members can relax and let others do the talking, subjects in individual sessions have to fill all of the time by themselves. Even periods of silence might be more embarrassing in individual sessions, where subjects have nobody to blame but themselves, than in group sessions, where the responsibility is shared.

General implications

In view of the considerable effort that has been invested in developing and testing models that allow a comparison of individual and group productivity, it is surprising that solution time has received relatively little attention as a variable in group problem solving. Most individual and group comparisons relate group size only with the proportion of solvers, although it has been found that the analysis of solution times resulted in conclusions at variance with those that were based on the proportion of solutions. Thus Taylor and Faust (1952), who compared group and individual performance for the game of "Twenty Questions," concluded that although "group performances were superior to individual performance in terms of . . . elapsed time per problem . . . in terms of man-minutes required for solution, the performance of individuals was superior to that of groups" (p. 367).

Bray, Kerr, and Atkin (1978), who assessed performance of groups of different sizes in terms of both the proportion of solvers and the time of solution, found that although groups often worked up to their potential productivity with regard to the proportion index, those same groups fell below potential on the latency index. Bray et al. suggested the concept of *functional size* to explain this pattern. According to this notion, the number of nonparticipators in a group increases with group size, resulting in a functional group size smaller than the actual size. Bray et al. found that an analysis that was based on the assumption that groups function at the rate of the fastest member of the functional group resulted in a more accurate prediction of solution times than the assumption implied in the equalitarian model of Restle and Davis (1962). The latter model assumes that group functioning results in a slow-down of each solver's efficiency that is proportional to the number of nonsolvers in the group.

In addition to the theoretical importance of the study of solution times, this type of analysis also has practical implications (e.g., for the decision to have individuals work in groups rather than alone). As Taylor and Faust (1952) pointed out:

> It appears probable that there are many kinds of problems which a group will solve more quickly than an individual. If elapsed time in hours, weeks, or months is the primary consideration, then such problems should be undertaken by groups. However, it appears equally probable that few of those same problems will be solved more efficiently in terms of man-minutes or man-hours by groups than by individuals. (pp. 522–3)

Our findings suggest even more specific implications for the use of group discussion procedures. Because blocking slows down the generation of ideas in groups, it might be more effective to ask subjects first to develop their ideas in individual sessions and next have these ideas discussed and evaluated in a group session. The task of the group would then consist of evaluation rather than production of ideas. This procedure might combine the advantage of group and individual sessions without making unnecessary demands on individual time.

NOTES

The authors are indebted to Thomas Ostrom, Kenneth Gergen, and Margaret Stroebe for helpful comments on an earlier draft of this paper. We are also grateful to Rüdiger Arnscheid, Claudia Brandl, and Christl Fischer for their help in collecting some of the data.

[1] The following formula was used to assess the degree of agreement in decisions to eliminate redundant ideas:

$$100\left(1 - \frac{2d}{n(n-1)}\right)$$

where n = number of ideas and d = number of pairs of ideas for which raters arrive at discrepant decisions.

[2] The proportion of variance accounted for by each of the factors manipulated in an experiment depends on the relative strength of these manipulations. Therefore, statements about the amount of variance accounted for have little meaning in most studies that use social psychological variables, because there is typically no basis for determining on what points on the dimensional scale the manipulations are set. In the case of brainstorming, the situation is different, however, as standard instructions have been used in most of this research. Because our studies were designed to explore potential causes for the productivity difference between group and individual sessions, it is quite instructive to know that type of session accounted for 70% to 80% of the total variance in brainstorming productivity observed in our experiments, even when other variables assumed to mediate this difference were controlled.

[3] This variation in the immediacy of assessment had to be accepted to make the peer manipulation plausible. This was not considered crucial, however, because there is empirical evidence that delay of evaluation has no significant effect on impact (Henchy and Glass, 1968; Maginn and Harris, 1980). Furthermore, even if delay had somewhat reduced the impact of peer evaluation, this would not have interfered with the purpose of the study: that is, (a) to establish that the findings of Maginn and Harris could be replicated with the type of uncontroversial topics used in their study; (b) to establish that it would also hold for controversial topics; and (c) to test whether an even stronger manipulation of evaluation apprehension (i.e., the use of the film in classroom demonstrations) would reduce productivity.

[4] The opposition to economic growth is part of the "green" ideology that connects economic growth to the destruction of our natural environment. Thus, pretest subjects rejected the idea that economic growth should be increased in West Germany and they believed that their fellow students shared this position. Pretest subjects also rejected the notion that the number of guest workers should be reduced (and attributed the same position to their fellow students). With regard to the uncontroversial topics, subjects were in favor of improving entertainment programs and life quality and attributed the same position to their fellow students.

[5] This prediction assumes that there is a functional ceiling on felt evaluation apprehension. However, if no such ceiling exists, then the predicted interaction effect need not occur.

[6] But again, see note 5.

[7] As an alternative solution, it has been suggested that group members be given the same time as individuals who work on a problem by themselves (i.e., to give n-person groups $n \times$ the time period allotted to individuals). Thus with persons working for 15 min in our experiments, 4-person groups should be given 1 hr. However, even if members of groups were slightly more productive than persons working alone, they would have to be more than four times as productive to compensate for the greater need for time. Furthermore, because subjects might be able to think about the issue when others are talking, providing four times as much time to members of 4-person groups may give them an unfair advantage. Alternatively, one might think of making time discretionary (i.e., persons brainstorming in

groups or alone would be asked to continue until they had no more ideas). This would give subjects a chance to exhaust their repertory of responses regardless of context. However, this solution has the drawback of introducing time costs into the problem-solving situation. Whereas subjects working under set times had nothing to lose if they attended to the problem, subjects working under discretionary time limits would have no opportunity costs in terms of the activities they could have performed if they had left the laboratory earlier. Among other things, this should increase the temptation to free ride.

REFERENCES

Barkowski, D., Lamm, H., and Schwinger, T. (1982). Einfallsproduktion von Individuen und Dyaden unter "Brainstorming"-Bedingungen [Brainstorming productivity of individuals and dyads]. *Psychologische Beiträge*, 24, 39–46.

Bouchard, T.J. (1969). Personality, problem-solving procedure and performance in small groups. *Journal of Applied Psychology Monograph*, 53 (1, pt. 2).

Bouchard, T.J. (1972). A comparison of two group brainstorming procedures. *Journal of Applied Psychology*, 56, 418–21.

Bouchard, T.J., and Hare, M. (1970). Size, performance, and potential in brainstorming groups. *Journal of Applied Psychology*, 54, 51–5.

Bouchard, T.J., Drauden, G., and Barsaloux, J. (1974). A comparison of individual subgroup and total group methods of problem solving. *Journal of Applied Psychology*, 59, 226–27.

Bray, R.M., Kerr, N.L., and Atkin, R.S. (1978). Effects of group size, problem difficulty, and sex on group performance and member reactions. *Journal of Personality and Social Psychology*, 36, 1224–41.

Chatterjea, R.G., and Mitra, A. (1976). A study of brainstorming. *Manas*, 23, 23–8.

Cohen, D., Whitmyre, J.W., and Funk, D.W. (1960). Effect of group cohesiveness and training upon creative thinking. *Journal of Applied Psychology*, 44, 319–22.

Collaros, P.A., and Anderson, L.R. (1969). Effect of perceived expertness upon creativity of members of brainstorming groups. *Journal of Applied Psychology*, 53, 159–63.

Dillon, P.C., Graham, W.K., and Aidells, A.L. (1972). Brainstorming on a "hot" problem: Effects of training and practice on individual and group performance. *Journal of Applied Psychology*, 56, 487–90.

Dunette, M.D., Campbell, J., and Jaastad, K. (1963). The effect of group participation on brainstorming effectiveness for two industrial samples. *Journal of Applied Psychology*, 47, 30–7.

Gurman, E.B. (1968). Creativity as a function of orientation and group participation. *Psychological Reports*, 22, 471–8.

Harari, O., and Graham, W.K. (1975). Tasks and task consequences as factors in individual and group brainstorming. *Journal of Social Psychology*, 95, 61–5.

Harkins, S.G., and Jackson, J.M. (1985). The role of evaluation in eliminating social loafing. *Personality and Social Psychology Bulletin*, 11, 457–65.

Harkins, S.G., and Petty, R.E. (1982). Effects of task difficulty and task uniqueness on social loafing. *Journal of Personality and Social Psychology*, 43, 1214–29.

Harkins, S.G., Latané, B., and Williams, K. (1980). Social loafing: Allocating effort or taking it easy? *Journal of Experimental Social Psychology*, 16, 457–65.

Henchy, R. and Glass, D.C. (1968). Evaluation apprehension and the social facilitation of dominant and subordinate responses. *Journal of Personality and Social Psychology*, 10, 446–54.

Ingham, A.G., Levinger, G., Graves, J., and Peckham, V. (1974). The Ringelmann effect: Studies of group size and group performance. *Journal of Experimental Social Psychology*, 10, 371–84.

Jablin, F.M. (1981). Cultivating imagination: Factors that enhance and inhibit creativity in brainstorming groups. *Human Communication Research*, 7, 245–58.

Kerr, N.L., and Bruun, S.E. (1983). Dispensability of member effort and group motivation losses: Free-rider effects. *Journal of Personality and Social Psychology*, 44, 78–94.

Lamm, H., and Trommsdorff, G. (1973). Group versus individual performance on tasks requiring ideational proficiency (brainstorming). *European Journal of Social Psychology*, 3, 361–87.

Latané, B., Williams, K., and Harkins, S. (1979). Many hands make light the work: The causes and consequences of social loafing. *Journal of Personality and Social Psychology*, 37, 822–32.

Madsen, D.B., and Finger, J.R. (1978). Comparison of a written feedback procedure, group brainstorming, and individual brainstorming. *Journal of Applied Psychology*, 63, 120–3.

Maginn, B.K., and Harris, R.J. (1980). Effects of anticipated evaluation on individual brainstorming performance. *Journal of Applied Psychology*, 65, 219–25.

Milton, G.A. (1965). Enthusiasm vs. effectiveness in group and individual problem-solving. *Psychological Reports*, 16, 1197–202.

Olson, M. (1965). *The logic of collective action*. Cambridge, MA: Harvard University Press.

Osborn, A.F. (1957). *Applied imagination* (rev. edn). New York: Scribner.

Pape, T., and Bölle, I. (1984). Einfallsproduktion von Individuen und Dyaden unter "Brainstorming"-Bedingungen [Brainstorming productivity of individuals and dyads]. *Psychologische Beiträge*, 26, 459–68.

Restle, F., and Davis, J.H. (1962). Success and speed of problem solving by individuals and groups. *Psychological Review*, 69, 520–36.

Rotter, G.S., and Portugal, S.M. (1969). Group and individual effects in problem solving. *Journal of Applied Psychology*, 53, 338–41.

Steiner, I.D. (1972). *Group process and productivity*. New York: Academic Press.

Street, W.R. (1974). Brainstorming by individuals, coacting and interacting groups. *Journal of Applied Psychology*, 59, 433–6.

Stroebe, W., and Frey, B.S. (1982). Self-interest and collective action: The economics and psychology of public goods. *British Journal of Social Psychology*, 21, 121–37.

Taylor, D.W., and Faust, W.L. (1952). Twenty questions: Efficiency in problem solving as a function of size of group. *Journal of Experimental Psychology*, 44, 360–8.

Taylor, D.W., Berry, P.C., and Block, C.H. (1958). Does group participation when using brainstorming facilitate or inhibit creative thinking? *Adminstrative Science Quarterly*, 3, 23–47.

Torrance, E.P. (1970). Influence of dyadic interaction on creative functioning. *Psychological Reports*, 26, 391–4.

Vroom, V.H., Grant, L.D., and Cotton, T.W. (1969). The consequences of social interaction in group problem-solving. *Organizational Behavior and Human Performance*, 4, 77–95.

Williams, K., Harkins, S., and Latané, B. (1981). Identifiability as a deterrent to social loafing: Two cheering experiments. *Journal of Personality and Social Psychology*, 40, 303–11.

16   Social Influence in Groups

— —

Influence of a consistent minority on the responses of a majority in a color perception task

S. Moscovici, E. Lage and M. Naffrechoux

Theoretical Background

This study is noteworthy as the first widely available empirical demonstration that minorities, and not just majorities, can influence other members of a group (see Faucheux and Moscovici, 1967). To gain some sense of the excitement when it was first published, the reader must appreciate that until this time all that published studies in this area demonstrated, and all that they conceived of, was majority influence. Moscovici shows that the exclusive focus on majority influence ('conformity'), with the assumption that others are influenced solely because they are dependent on the majority in social and informational senses, is limited; it must be supplemented by an analysis of minority influence ('innovation'). This first experiment analyses the qualities which a minority (two members of a six-person group) must have in order to exert influence (changing the perceived colour of an objectively blue slide from 'blue' to 'green').

Since minorities within groups typically lack power over others, Moscovici and colleagues argue that their influence cannot be explained in terms of dependency. Something else must be responsible; that something else, the authors suggest, is the 'behavioural style' of the minority. In order to establish a new group norm or propose an innovative solution to the problem, the minority must adopt a behavioural style that connotes resolution, certainty, clarity of definition and coherence; Moscovici labels this style 'consistency'.

In this study the authors aim to demonstrate minority influence in a situation that might at first seem 'unfriendly' to such influence: they try to change the majority norm for an explicit or quasi-physical stimulus, namely the perceived colour of a stimulus. Moscovici and colleagues argue, however, that such a situation may facilitate minority influence: the majority will be most likely to seek to explain away differences in colour perception in personal terms (see the readings on causal attribution, chapter 7). But if the experiment is carefully designed to rule out explanations of defective colour vision in terms of the poor judgement of an individual (by

Sociometry (1969), 32:365–80.

getting at least two members – the 'active minority' – to perceive the alternative colour), then the minority is likely to influence the majority.

Hypotheses

The research tested the hypothesis that a minority would only exert influence over a majority when it answered consistently in terms of the new norm it sought to establish (i.e. always calling 'blue' slides 'green'). Additional hypotheses, implicit in variations introduced by Moscovici and colleagues, are that minority influence would be greater when (1) the two members of the minority sat further apart; (2) the sequence of colour responses was uninterrupted; and (3) minority influence might only appear on a more subtle measure of perceptual threshold, even when there was no influence on the explicit colour-naming response.

Design

No experimental design is stated explicitly. The reader's task is made somewhat more complex by the fact that three 'experiments' are distinguished, the results of which are sometimes collapsed, sometimes treated independently. The main comparisons are made clear in the summary of results, below.

Method

All three experiments used six-person all-female groups, of which four persons were naive subjects and two experimental confederates (or 'stooges'). The two confederates played the role of the minority, trying to introduce a new norm whereby the series of six clearly blue-coloured slides presented on a screen were designated 'green' on every trial. It is important to note that Moscovici and colleagues tested all subjects' colour vision, first to eliminate any subjects with defective vision, and second so that subjects could not attribute the confederates' deviant colour responses to their having abnormal vision.

All responses were given aloud, and subjects both named the colour they saw and gave a simple estimation of how bright the slides were. After practice trials, during which the confederates responded randomly, the series of six slides was shown six times (i.e. thirty-six slide-trials in all); and then subjects completed a post-experimental questionnaire.

Experiment I

Using thirty-two groups, this also varied the seating patterns of the two confederates and the stimulus presentation. In twelve experimental groups, the confederates were seated in positions 1 and 2 in a line of six group members facing the screen; in the other twenty groups, the confederates occupied positions 1 and 4. Moscovici and colleagues hypothesized that the second confederate would appear more independent (and the minority would, presumably, have greater influence) when seated further from the other minority member. In addition, in thirteen groups (with minority positions 1 and 4) the experimenters interrupted the sequence of responses somewhat by inserting a one-minute pause after each block of twelve trials. Presumably, minority influence would be weakened by this interruption.

Experiment 2

Using ten groups, this included a new dependent measure, taken after the main experiment and away from the confederates, which assessed the threshold for designating a colour 'blue' or 'green'. This was measured by getting subjects to judge ten times a series of sixteen colour disks (of which three were unambiguously green, three unambiguously blue, and ten might appear ambiguous). This measure was added to provide a more subtle indication of a shift in perception, and moreover one that occurred after the experiment.

Experiment 3

Using eleven groups, this was identical to experiment 1, except that the minority answered 'green' twenty-four times and 'blue' twelve times over the thirty-six trials, with the twelve blue responses being randomized.

Control group

Twenty-four subjects (or whom two were excluded) viewed an uninterrupted sequence of slides and were not exposed to any influence. Their responses were compared, in turn, with those of the experimental subjects from each experiment.

Results

The results are presented separately for the perceptual task ('green' responses), the discrimination test (threshold for blue and green colour judgements), and the post-experimental questionnaire.

Perceptual task

Moscovici and colleagues report data from 128 naive subjects in experiments 1 and 2. According to our calculations, there were thirty-two groups in experiment 1 and ten in experiment 2, making forty-two groups each composed of four naive subjects ($N = 168$). Moreover, since subjects participated *in groups* where their judgements and perceptions could, and most likely would, be affected by the responses of other group members, the group mean (based on all four naive subjects) should have been the unit of analysis. The importance of taking the group as the unit of analysis is made clear from the authors' own discussion of the results, where they indicate that in some groups subjects were influenced by the minority (43.75 per cent of the groups) and in others they were not. The reported analyses, however, appear to be based on the individual as the unit of analysis.

If a majority subject responded 'green' this might indicate the influence of the minority. In fact, only 8.42 per cent of all responses were 'green' in experiments 1 and 2. But this was higher than the 0.25 per cent 'green' responses from the control group (the significance of this difference was only evident with a one-tailed Mann–Whitney test). Within experiment 1, there were no differences on this measure as a function of seating position or stimulus presentation. Finally, in experiment 3, where the minority responded inconsistently, there were only 1.25 per cent 'green' responses. No statistical comparison between this 'inconsistent' minority and either the 'consistent' minority or the control group is reported.

The discrimination test

These data refer to experiment 2 (after three subjects were excluded from the analysis, because their responses were even more in the direction of blue than those of the control subjects). There was a slightly larger shift in the threshold for perceiving the colour green among experimental than among control subjects (with a one-tailed *t*-test). In other words, subjects exposed to a minority who claimed to see blue slides as green seemed to accept that a wider range of colours can be called 'green' (see table 16.1). Moscovici and colleagues also tested the idea that this shift might be greater for groups where the majority of subjects did *not* change their use of 'blue' responses to describe the colour names of the slides. They reported a non-significant tendency for the shift in 'perceptual code' to be greater for groups where the majority did not change, and a significantly higher number of 'green' judgements to be made by subjects in these groups on the discrimination test.

The post-experimental questionnaire

Moscovici and colleagues highlight two separate aspects of this questionnaire, although it is unfortunately again unclear which, or how many, subjects were included.

Cognitive activity
Subjects in the experimental groups were apparently more willing to accept the green responses than were control subjects, and they perceived more nuances of colour, especially those subjects influenced by the minority.

Perception of the consistent minority
Although all subjects knew that all participants had been tested for colour vision, they still judged the (minority) confederates' colour perception to be not as good as their own, or as that of other members of the group. There was also an unreliable tendency for subjects to acknowledge that the confederates were more sure of their responses.

Discussion

This study provided initial data supporting the idea that a minority was capable of influencing a majority, and not only vice versa. But it was less impressive in demonstrating the role of behavioural style – consistency – since no statistical comparison of influence ('green' responses) exerted by consistent (experiment 1) and inconsistent (experiment 3) minorities was reported. And since the perceptual-threshold measures were only taken in experiment 2, consistent and inconsistent minorities could not be compared.

Despite these and other shortcomings, this study changed a whole area of research, spawning many more studies on minority influence (see Wood et al., 1994). It also helped to generate Moscovici's (1980) influential 'conversion' theory of minority influence, which suggested that minority influence is more likely on private than on public responses, and on indirect than on direct measures (the prototypes of which are the threshold and colour-name judgements, respectively, in this study). This study also paved the way for Moscovici and Personnaz's (1980) celebrated study on the perception of colour after-images in response to majority versus minority influence. A feature of later work has been the explicit comparison of majority and minority influence (in this study we do not learn what influence would be achieved by a majority calling blue slides green), and, in some studies at least, improved experimental designs and statistical procedures, and more sophisticated analysis of the cognitive responses instigated by these two sources of social influence (see Maass and Clark, 1984).

FURTHER READING

Maass, A. and Clark, R.D. (1984). Hidden impact of minorities: Fifteen years of minority influence research. *Psychological Bulletin*, 95, 428–50. A detailed, narrative review of studies on social influence.

Moscovici, S. (1980). Toward a theory of conversion behavior. In L. Berkowitz (ed.), *Advances in Experimental Social Psychology* (vol. 13, pp. 209–39). New York: Academic Press. An elegant account of Moscovici's influential theory of how minority influence differs from majority influence.

Moscovici, S. and Personnaz, B. (1980). Studies in social influence: V. Minority influence and conversion behavior in a perceptual task. *Journal of Experimental Social Psychology*, 16, 270–82. The famous 'after-image' studies, which purport to show that a minority, but not a majority, can bring about subtle perceptual changes in the recipient of their influence.

REFERENCES

Faucheux, C. and Moscovici, S. (1967). Le style de comportement d'une minorité et son influence sur les réponses d'une majorité. *Bulletin de CERP*, 16, 337–60.

Wood, W., Lundgren, S., Ouellette, J.A., Busceme, S. and Blackstone, T. (1994). Minority influence: A meta-analytic review of social influence processes. *Psychological Bulletin*, 115, 323–45.

The Conformity Bias

Primary
Reading

Specialized literature commonly assimilates the process of influence to the process of conformity (Allen, 1965). On the one hand, the tendency is to assume that any type of influence leads to conformity, and moreover that conformity is the sole phenomenon achieved by means of influence. On the other hand, when examining the individual, it is always assumed that he asks himself the question "Should I follow the group or the minority?" or in other words he is faced with the alternative of conformity or deviance. On the contrary, an individual frequently poses the question in exactly the inverse manner: "What should I do so that the majority will adopt my point of view? How can I change the conception of others?" The multiplicity of such possible questions tends to contradict the aforementioned assimilation. Without going into the details stated elsewhere (Moscovici and Faucheux, 1969) we can consider the innovation as a form of social influence. In order to study theoretically and empirically this form, the analysis of the action of a minority upon the majority, the qualities which it must possess in order to make its point of view accepted, constitutes a sort of prolegomenon. This research proposes to show more clearly one of these qualities and to depart from the customary emphasis on attitudes which are linked to conformity.

Behavior Style as a Source of Influence

In almost all of the research done to date on social influence only one of its possible sources has been studied theoretically and experimentally: dependency.

Nonetheless, for certain reasons, we cannot make use of it in the study of innovation. First of all, it seems clear that dependency in relation to an individual or a subgroup which innovates is a consequence rather than a cause of an action aimed at exerting an influence. The necessity to heed the advice of electronics, computer or television experts follows the adoption of electronic equipment, computers, or television, or any kind of specific technical invention. A minority which truly innovates, which transforms social reality, only rarely has power at the outset. In addition, it is to be noted that the individuals or subgroups who change rules, values, or knowledge are not judged as being superior to others insofar as competence is concerned.

In short, dependency in relation to the phenomenon which interests us is neither a decisive independent variable, nor a differential factor which can account for influence which is exerted. Thus, we were prompted to seek another source of influence which is not subject to the limitations which we have just mentioned, and which comes closer to expressing the active, resolute character of a minority. We believe that we have found it in the behavioral style of the individual or those individuals who propose a solution to a problem, a new norm for a group. Good reasons exist to suppose that in the process of innovation, the way in which the behavior is organized and presented could suffice to provoke the acceptance or the rejection of a judgment or a proposed model during the course of social interaction. Moreover the consistency of the behavior of a minority, the fact that it resolutely maintains a well-defined point of view and develops it in a coherent manner, appears as if it ought to be a powerful source of influence, which under the circumstances would not be a result of an explicit dependency.

A series of experiments made by one of the authors in collaboration (Faucheux and Moscovici, 1967) has already shown the impact of a consistent minority upon a majority when preference judgments concerning equiprobable stimuli or the modification of an implicit norm are involved. In the present study, which is a continuation of the previous one, we should like to prove that this action is also possible when the majority norm to be changed is explicit or quasi-physical.

Why are we expecting such an effect? The presence of a norm can be distinguished in the spontaneous unanimity of those who share it, and in the expectancy that a high-probability response will occur in the face of a stimulus or a determinate object. The validity of judgments and opinions (Kelley, 1967) and the stability of relations with the environment are guaranteed owing to this norm only if these two criteria are expected.

Now, let us suppose that a subgroup diverges from this customary mode of response and that it provides an alternative mode of response to the same object, the same stimulus. The diversity which replaces uniformity in the group is a creator of uncertainty and of conflict; doubt is cast upon the hierarchy of responses of each person or of the group and the variability is increased. By insisting on its answer, a minority will not only engender a conflict, but will intensify the conflict, because it poses its own judgments and opinions as having the same value, as being equivalent to those of the majority (Worell, 1967). Moreover, this insistence proves that taking one's stand is not casual and that the subgroup has no intention of conceding or submitting to the group.

This exerts a tremendous pressure toward acceptance of the new and surprising response. We must also add that these conflict relations assume a particular character in the case where the stimulus is physical. The reality to be judged in these circumstances is not individual, arbitrary: it is common, in principle universal. No matter who, faced with such a reality, one is expected to react in the same way, and each one imagines that he is reacting as he is supposed to react.

In an experiment cited by Asch (1962), Sperling demonstrated that the influence exerted on an individual is much greater when he believes in the existence of an objective response than when he does not believe in it. Thus, the fact that a physical stimulus is involved does not necessarily work against the exertion of influence by a minority; on the contrary it may facilitate it. The majority has one single means to reduce the tension, to ignore the judgment of the minority: that is, to transform the conflict of response into a conflict of attribution. This means that it must be able to explain the difference not as being produced by the properties of the stimulus, but as being produced by those who perceive it: an anomaly of vision, a lesser judgment capacity. This is possible when the minority is an isolated individual (Moscovici, 1969).

In the event that nothing in the situation permits such an attribution and that members of the minority, constituting a dyad, cannot be distinguished from members of the majority by such traits, then the latter are even more obligated either to adopt the response of the minority or to reject it, i.e., to polarize. No other means is left to them to restore the invariability of response in their relation with the external world.

With these presuppositions in mind, in order to demonstrate the influence of a minority upon a majority within a group, we have conceived an experiment in which:

(a)   Response conflict is increased by the consistency of the minority and by the consensus among its members.

(b)   Objectivity is an implicit exigency of judgments.

(c)   The responses of the majority and minority are exclusive, constituting an alternative, without either one just negating the other, as, for example, if one were to say that two unequal amounts of dots were said to be equal.

(d)   The difference in judgment cannot be accounted for by individual qualities. (Thus it was necessary for the minority to be composed of more than one person.) Otherwise the conflict in response could be transformed into a conflict of attribution, permitting differences to be explained by personal eccentricities, for example.

(e)   The judgment of the majority in the laboratory is identical with that of any random sample outside the laboratory, so that the judgment of the minority can be expected to be directly counter to the normal expectations in society.

Experimental Procedure and Results

First experiment

The subjects were liberal arts, law and social science students. Given the nature of the experimental material female subjects were preferred because of their greater involvement in evaluating the color of an object. The stimuli used consisted of slides with two different types of filters mounted in them: (1) photo filters permitting the passage of a beam of light of the dominant wave length ($X = 483.5$) in the blue scale; (2) neutral filters which reduced light intensity in certain proportion.

In a set of six slides, three slides were more luminous than three others. These variations in light intensity were studied in order to make the task more realistic and less boring. Their effect in this experiment was controlled.

Each experimental group consisted of four naive subjects and two confederates. Once the subjects were seated in a row before the screen on which were to be projected the slides, they were told that this would be an experiment on color perception. At the same time they were informed that they would be asked to judge the color and variation in light intensity of a series of slides (a brief explanation of the meaning of light intensity was furnished). Before passing a judgment, the whole group was asked to take a Polack test collectively, in order to check the participants' "chromatic sense."

This test had a twofold objective: first, to eliminate those subjects who perchance might have visual abnormalities; second, to emphasize the fact that everyone in the group had normal vision, so that the confederates' response will not be attributed to a difference in vision, i.e., to a personal factor external to the experimental situation.

After the collective correction of the result to the test, and after having ascertained that everyone sees normally, the subjects were instructed what responses might be given and how the experiment would be conducted, to wit replying aloud and naming a simple color as well as estimating the light intensity in numerical terms (ranging from 0 for the dimmest to 5 for the brightest). Subjects were also told that the preliminary trial would be just for practice in which each subject would only make a light-intensity judgment.

The real purpose of these preliminary trials was to enable the subjects to get acquainted with the color of the stimulus and to immunize them in McGuire's (1964) sense of word against the future onslaught of the instructed minority which does not share the norm. During these preliminary trials the confederates answered at random. Following these trials, the series of six different slides was presented six times, the order of the slides varying systematically from one series to the next. Thus these were 36 trials, each one lasting 15 seconds, separated by approximately 5 seconds of darkness. In each trial the two confederates exerted influence by calling the color "green." In this manner, the confederates were both internally consistent from one trial to the next with each other, since they gave all the time the same response.

At the end of the experiment the subject filled out a questionnaire concerning the stimuli and the other members of the group. As usual, the real objectives of the experiment were explained before leaving the room.

Two variations were introduced regarding the seating of the two confederates and the presentation of the stimuli.

1 *Confederate variation:* in 12 groups the confederates were seated side by side and gave the first and second responses, while in the 20 other groups they were separated, and occupied the first and fourth places. The variation in the seating of the second confederate was aimed at modifying the interpretation of his behavior, that is to say, to make him appear more independent of the first confederate.

2 *The stimulus variation:* in order to test the impact of the commitment to the first response and to permit a possible change, we modified the mode of presentation of stimuli. In 13 groups which included those in which the confederates were seated in position 1 and 4, the continuity of the sequence of the stimuli was interrupted by introducing two one-minute pauses after a sequence of 12 slides.

The order of response of the subjects remained the same from one trial to the next for the duration of the experiment.

Second experiment

We wondered whether the subjects experienced an influence which, even if it did not result in a change in verbal response during the experiment, did have a lasting effect on their perception. We expected a shift in the blue–green designation threshold which would reveal a reaction that was repressed during the social interaction. Certain subjects did refuse to adopt openly the minority response, feeling compelled to remain loyal to the general norm, even when they themselves began to doubt its validity. Here one might expect a latent attraction manifesting itself by an extension of the designation "green" to stimuli in a zone which a control group would call blue. The opposite reaction (extension of the notion blue to stimuli in the green zone) would be the result of polarization.

The first stage of this experiment is identical to the preceding experiment, that is to say that the minority exerts its influence on the majority. At the end of this phase the experimenter thanked subjects telling them that another researcher, who was also interested in vision phenomena, would like to solicit their participation in another research project, independent of the one in which they had just participated. He left the room and the second experimenter entered immediately and repeated his request. The latter having obtained the agreement of the subjects seated them around a table and said to them that it was an experiment related to the effect of the exercise about the vision phenomena. He then described the material, isolated the subjects by means of cardboard screens and instructed them to write down the responses individually on a sheet of paper. The material consisted of 16 disks in the blue-green zone of Farnsworth 100-hue set perception test. Three disks from each end of the "blue" and "green" scale were absolutely unambiguous, but the other 10 stimuli might appear ambiguous. After having made sure that the subjects understood the instructions well, the experimenter announced the beginning of the test. Each disk was presented on a neutral background for a period lasting approximately 5 seconds; it was placed in the center of the table so that it would be visible to everyone. The series of 16 disks was presented 10 times in the continuous method. The order of presentation was randomized. After the discrimination test the first experimenter returned, the subjects filled in the postexperimental questionnaire and the experiment ended in the same manner as the previous one.

Ten groups participated in this experiment.

Third experiment

In this experiment, which was identical to the first one, only we diversified the consistency degree of the confederates. In this case they answered 24 times "green" and 12 times "blue," the dispersion of "blue" answers being randomized. Eleven groups participated to this experiment.

The control group was the same for the three experiments. For this group the presentation of the stimulus was continuous. The control subjects also took, of course, the discrimination test after the initial experimental phase. In all we had 22 control subjects, or four groups of 6 subjects, with the elimination of two subjects who failed to give the discrimination response according to the instructions.

Results

The perceptual task

"Green" responses (responses which express the influence of minority in the experimental groups) constituted 8.42 per cent of the answers of the 128 naive subjects in the two first experiments. There is no significant difference between the two series of groups on the perception tests nor on the postexperimental questionnaire. Among the 22 subjects of the control group, only one gave two green responses, representing 0.25 per cent of the responses of the uninfluenced subjects. That means that the latter perceived the stimulus as really blue and that this norm is firmly established socially.

The difference between control and experimental subjects on the basis of Mann–Whitney's U test ($Z = 2.10$) turns out to be significant ($p = .019$, one-tailed test). Other data show this influence as well. Subjects changed their response (giving 4 or more green responses) in 43.75 per cent of the groups. The percentage of individuals who yielded was 32 per cent. Thus we have two categories of groups, those in which no subjects were influenced and those in which subjects were influenced. In the latter, it can be seen that 57 per cent of the subjects or two subjects per group on the average gave the same response as the confederates; 18.70 per cent green responses were obtained in these groups.

Thus, the quantity of green responses which we obtained was not so much the result of isolated individuals who followed the confederate as the result of a modification of judgment within the group. The confederates' seating position, and the type of introduction – continuous or discontinuous – of the stimuli did not have any differentiation effect.

Moreover, we have noticed that even though no color contrast effect existed, the subjects were more similar to the confederates when light intensities were weak than when they were strong ($Z = 3.37$, $p < .003$, Mann–Whitney U test). This agrees with the Bezold–Brücke phenomenon concerning perception of color with different luminosities. Yet, irrespective of the luminosity the proportion of green response was significantly higher in the experimental groups than in the control groups.

In the third experiment, where one or several responses of the confederates were inconsistent, we obtained only 1.25 per cent green responses. A similar proposal was obtained in groups completely inconsistent (50 per cent blue–50 per cent green responses of the confederates). Although we have to explore more systematically the variation of inter- and intra-subject inconsistency, the results we have just mentioned are suggestive of a marked influence of the behavior style of a minority.

The discrimination test

The question here concerns whether the subjects who changed their social response under the influence of the consistent minority also changed their perceptive code. In addition, we also wanted to verify the hypothesis that the subjects who did not change their social response, *even in the group where the majority was not at all influenced at this level by the minority*, at least changed their perceptual code.

The measurement of the threshold makes it possible to verify this hypothesis. Our calculations bear on the threshold values, which were obtained by a graphic method on the smoothed-out curve of individual responses. We retained three values: (1) the 50 per cent threshold indicating the point in the ordered sequence of stimuli where the subject gives as many "blue" as "green" judgments; (2) the lower threshold value indicating the point where the subject gives 75 per cent green and 25 per cent blue judgments; and (3) the upper threshold value, where the subject gives 25 per cent green and 75 per cent blue judgments. To study the influence of the consistent minority, we subsequently eliminated the results of three subjects in the experimental groups who polarized. Their 50 per cent threshold was lower than that of all the control group thresholds. It was their lower threshold value which indicates a generalization of the notion of blue in the green zone. Then, by comparing the 50 per cent, 75 per cent, and 25 per cent thresholds of the experimental groups (37 subjects) and the control groups (22 subjects) we obtained (table 16.1) the expected shift.

All of the data reflect the effect of interaction between minority and majority in the modification of the perceptual code. This modification affects more subjects than the change of verbal responses. This proposition is supported by other data. On the one hand, if within the experimental groups a distinction is apparent between subjects who sometimes adopted the minority response and subjects who never adopted the minority responses, no such difference emerges in the discrimination test for the three thresholds under consideration. On the contrary, it must be observed that shift is even more pronounced for groups where the majority did *not* change than it is for those where it changed, and the Student's *t* of 1.50 is close to the 1.68 value, while it would be significant at .10.[1]

We had made the assumption that in the groups where there was no change in social response, or where the "green" response had been in some way "repressed" one would observe a greater *number* of "green" judgments in the discrimination test. One can see that this is indeed the case. The difference between the groups where the majority did not change and where the majority did change is significant ($\chi^2 = 14.94, p < .002$). We can conclude that the consistent minority has an even greater influence on the perceptive code of the subjects than on their

Table 16.1 Shift in the threshold for perception of the color green

Threshold	Control group Mean	SD	Experimental group Mean	SD	t	P (one-tailed level)
50	47.39	1.21	48.03	1.38	1.78	.038
75	46.16	1.42	46.85	1.54	1.68	.047
25	48.41	1.14	49.19	1.28	2.33	.01

verbal response to the slides. Of course the experimental technique employed was not without its faults.[2] But the results obtained should be mentioned only for the new research line it gives us.

The postexperimental questionnaires

The postexperimental questionnaires we had devised showed us that:

(a)   The divergence of opinion or response of the consistent minority constrains the subjects to a cognitive activity bearing upon the stimulus. The perceptive change is not produced by a pure attraction towards the minority.

(b)   The relative certainty of the majority is probably weakened as a result of the confrontation with the minority, and its problem was to explain not why it followed the minority, but why it *did not follow* it.

(a)   The cognitive activity of the experimental group

To begin with we can put forward that occasionally seeing green slides, or seeing green in blue slides, is not due to a simple acquiescence to the response of the minority.

Having raised the question: "To what extent is it possible for these slides to be perceived as green?" we ascertained that subjects in the experimental groups did not accept this possibility in a more significant degree than subjects in the control groups. On the other hand, however, subjects in the former groups did prove more inclined to *accept* the green response than subjects in the latter groups ($t = 2.64, p < .008$). Thus, we can infer that the desire to reach an agreement with the minority led to an inclination to see what the latter were seeing, to make an effort to look for green in the blue stimuli. With this in mind we asked the subjects: how many different nuances of color did you distinguish? Subjects in the experimental groups perceived more than two nuances, while subjects in the control groups saw at most one or two ($Z = 2.12, p < .0342$). A differentiation can also be made between subjects within the experimental groups. Subjects who yielded to the minority saw more nuances than those who did not yield to the minority. ($Z = 2.79, p < .005$). Moreover, whether they did or did not yield to the minority, subjects in groups in which a change in response occurred perceived more shades than those in groups where the majority maintained its position, and always responded blue ($Z = 1.78, p < .076$). Using an appropriate question, we then asked subjects to specify these shades by naming the colors which composed them. No matter what these shades were or how many were cited, for purposes of this analysis we retained only the highest percentage of green found on the response sheet, using it as an index of the extreme limit of a subject's attempt to find this color. All subjects in the experimental groups distinguished more green than those in the control groups ($Z = 2.99, p < .003$). Of course, in the experimental groups, subjects who yielded to the minority saw more than 30 per cent ($Z = 4.92, p < .001$). Everything tends to point to the fact that members of the majority made an effort to take into account the viewpoint of the minority, to verify the objective basis of its judgment. At no time did they remain passive, nor were they content blindly to accept or reject a norm opposed to their own. The effect of this was probably the modification, as we saw, of their own perception or their definition of green and of blue.

(b)   Perception of the consistent minority

Naive subjects, who constituted the majority in the experimental groups, were more inclined to see green in the blue slides than the control subjects (and actually did see more green). The psychological problem which they had to solve was the following: why, although having agreed that the minority's answer was not without foundation, did they not yield to it, since a physical stimulus was involved? The only possible explanation for such a contradiction was the assertion that they were less certain than the minority. Thus while they were interested by what was proposed to them, they considered themselves to be more competent than the minority, since they represented normal perception – therefore they had the right to yield or not to yield. Needless to say, these trends can be accounted for in other ways. In spite of the results of the Polack Test, subjects did not believe that a person who always perceived these slides as green could have a very good color perception. Even if he had good vision, his competency in the area of color must be inferior to that of the majority of people. On the other hand the consistent nature of the minority response in the face of the different judgments emitted by the majority supplied great self-assurance. Without coming to any definite conclusion, it can nonetheless be seen that the first interpretation applies to the two series of predictions considered together, while the second concerns each series separately.

Now let us examine the results obtained more in detail. In the first two questions subjects were asked to judge each of the persons who participated in the experiment, including themselves, on a 10-point scale (from good to bad), as to their capacity first to discriminate intensities and second to perceive colors. A comparison of the grades which subjects gave to themselves, confederates and other subjects for color perception is very instructive. On the whole, subjects considered that the confederates' color perception was not as good as theirs, both in the groups where the confederates were seated next to each other ($t = 9.98, p < .001$), and in the groups where they were separated ($t = 7.02, p < .001$). They also considered that confederates did not perceive colors as well the other members of the group ($t = 10.83, p < .001$). Nevertheless, it was felt that the second confederate had a better color perception than the first confederate ($Z = 2.04, p = .04$, Mann–Whitney U test). Thus the members of the majority judged themselves more competent than the minority, and they experienced little anxiety regarding their perceptive capacity.

What about certainty? In their postexperimental questionnaire subjects had to classify "the persons who participated in the experiment, according to whether they were more or less sure of their responses." Subjects judged confederates to be more sure of their responses than they were ($t = 5.02, p < .07$) and than other members of the group ($t = 4.42, p < .07$). A difference revealed itself also in the perception of the two confederates. The confederate seated in the first position was judged as being more sure of his response than the second confederate, both in the groups where they were seated next to each other ($t = 2.54, p < .07$) and in the groups where they were separated ($t = 3.22, p < .07$). These evaluations were shared by all subjects, whether they were among those who responded like the consistent minority, or whether they were in the groups where the majority resisted all influence. Three trends clearly emerge from these results: (a) subjects judged themselves more competent and less certain than confederates; (b) judgments of competence and of certitude of confederates had an inverse relation; (c) the confederate in the second position was perceived differently from the one in the first position and as being closer to other subjects. These trends corroborate observations made in other experiments. Thus, Brehm and Lipsher (1959) proved that perceived trustworthiness would be greater when the communicator took an extreme position on either side of the issue than when he took a moderate position. More recently, Eisinger and Mills (1968) studied the effect of the discrepancy of the communicator position upon his sincerity and competence. They proved that a communicator on the opposite side will be perceived as more incompetent and more sincere in comparison with a communicator who is opposed but more moderate. These experiments suggest that the response of an individual or an extreme subgroup has more weight. But what interests us here is the fact that obtaining the same results as ours, they offer indirect support in favor of the view that consistency, especially of a minority with a norm opposed to the norm of the majority, is at the same time an index of extremism. Now, this extremism, to the extent that it shows itself uncompromising, engenders an anxiety linked to the disagreement, and places the others in a situation where they must either concede or polarize in order to reduce this disagreement and diminish the anxiety. As nothing permits them to polarize, then, in certain groups, subjects yielded.

The trends discovered also enlightened us about the role of the second confederate. In a sense, he does not contribute any supplementary weight to the response of the "innovator," the first confederate. We make the hypothesis that his behavior serves as an example to the other subjects; he demonstrates that someone is capable of choosing the minority response, that there is a choice possible between the two alternatives, and to a certain extent justifies them. In short, if the effect of the first confederate is an influence effect, the effect of the second would be what economists call a demonstration effect. In any case the minority's influence cannot be attributed to a possible leadership recognized by the group. Questioned as to which persons in the group they would like to find themselves in a similar situation with, subjects did not choose confederates more frequently than any other member of the group. Likewise, when asked: "Who would you like to see lead the discussion (about the experiment) in the group?" a slight, nonsignificant trend can be observed to choose confederates less than other naive subjects.

Discussion and Conclusion

The experiment which we have just described shows, at least as far as female subjects are concerned, that by being consistent a minority is capable of influencing a majority at the level of verbal and perceptual responses. But this fact must be examined more closely.

Generality of the behavioral style as a source of influence

We have at the beginning of this article put forward the idea that the consistency of the behavior is a source of influence when a minority is concerned and when an innovation process is involved. And it clearly appears that conformity is an effect of consistency and not of dependence towards the majority of the group. To substantiate this conclusion, we will limit ourselves to Asch's experiments. We know that in these experiments a group-majority can induce a single individual to give answers going counter to perceptual evidence. The conditions required for this effect to occur are the usage of a nonambiguous stimulus, the need to respond publicly, and the presence of a unanimous majority. This majority, according to Asch (1962:497), gives rise to a propensity to adopt the erroneous "conformist" responses of the group. Our interpretation is, of course, different, but first let us look to the data and their meaning. We can consider that unanimity in a group corresponds to inter-individual consistency, to consistency which results from coincidence and identity of response of several subjects to a given stimulus. At the same time, the sequence of "erroneous responses," the identity of responses of each confederate through a series of stimuli, expresses internal, intra-individual consistency. What do we see when we examine Asch's results? We see that a *unanimous* majority from two to sixteen confederates provoked the acceptance of "erroneous" responses for one third

(32 per cent) of the responses of the naive subjects. The increase in the number of confederates to more than three has therefore no effect on the frequency of these responses. Thus, there is no direct relation between the magnitude of this social pressure and conformity. Now, only one single confederate in a group made up of seven or eight persons has to break the unanimity by giving correct answers for the number of conformist responses to drop to 10.4 per cent or 5.5 per cent. Thus, a group of three unanimous persons is more influential than a group of eight non-unanimous persons. This is tantamount to saying that it is the inter-personal consistency of, rather than the strength of, social pressure which is more important, and comes closest to accounting for the variation in the rate of influence.

Asch's (1955) and Allen and Levine's (1968) experiments give much weight to this innovation. They thought that if social support was important in order to reduce conformist constraint, the dissenter ought to give the response which the subjects privately considered to be correct. On the contrary, in the case of unanimity where group consistency was the critical variable, a dissenter's disagreement with the group, whether or not his responses were correct and in agreement with the subject's private judgment, was sufficient to decrease conformity. The results of the two experiments show that it is lack of unanimous consensus which is the decisive factor.

What is the effect of intra-individual consistency over time – of the identical repetition of subjects responses to a series of stimuli? As we know, Asch used two types of trials: "neutral" trials in which the confederates responded in a "correct" manner, and "critical" trials in which the confederates responded in an "erroneous" manner. Diachronistically, a group appeared all the more consistent with itself when there were more "critical" trials than "neutral" ones. Asch (1955) varied the proportion of the neutral trials in relation to the critical trials (1/6, 1/2, 1/1, 4/1) and although the differences were not significant, a decrease in the percentage of conformist responses was observed (50 per cent, 38.6 per cent, 36.8 per cent, 26.2 per cent) as the majority became less coherent in time. Iscoe and Williams (1963) obtained similar results. On the whole, considering the information we have at hand today, we can say that it is the behavioral style of a majority or a minority and not the pure amount of social pressure which is revealed to be at the origin of influence exerted.

Change of verbal and perceptual responses

We have seen that the alteration of the answer, while not negligible at the conscious social level, is more marked at the latent individual level. Our present state of knowledge does not enable us to ascertain whether it is of a perceptive or of a verbal nature (Goldiamond and Malpass, 1958). However, given that most of the experiments in this field (Tajfel, 1969), with the notable exception of Flament (1958), report influence at the verbal level and not at the level of perception, the results we have obtained are all the more remarkable. They oblige us to distinguish between a change in response and a change in code, between influence at the response level and influence at the code level. In this sense, we have the right to say that the consistent minority, in one experiment, provoked a real modification in the norm of the majority, and not only in its response.

If this phenomenon is rare in the laboratory, it is not in political life. Thus, a political party often adopts the ideas or the vocabulary of another party or social movement. Yet citizens continue to vote for this same party, to respond to this party's slogans. For example, in France the Gaullist government, in framing its own education program, adopted part of the rhetoric and the program proposed by students and workers in May 1968. Nevertheless, when a Frenchman votes for the Gaullist party he believes that he is "responding" to the same political body and in the same manner as he did in the past, although both it and its representatives have changed their opinions on very specific questions. Indeed, it is conceivable that minorities are more capable of changing the majority's code than its social response, while the majority would have more influence on the individual's verbal response than on his intellectual or perceptive code. This is an historical reality. Great innovators have succeeded in imposing their ideas, their discoveries, without necessarily receiving direct recognition for their influence. For example, many psychologists have assimilated notions elaborated by psychoanalysis, all the while refusing to recognize the value of psychoanalysis.

Thus, if we really want to understand the process of social influence, it is not enough to study more carefully the role of minorities and of innovation. We must begin to explore more subtle mechanisms of influence than those which are at work in direct and visible acceptance of norms and judgments proposed.

NOTES

S. Moscovici was Fellow (1968–9) at the Center for Advanced Study in the Behavioral Sciences. I also wish to acknowledge the assistance extended to me by the James Marshall Fund.
[1] Thomas and Bistey (1964) report a study using the same stimulus as our study and they found that subjects who called the stimulus "green" or "mostly green" showed significantly greater generalization toward the longer wave length than those who called it "blue" or "mostly blue." Our results are in the opposite direction.
[2] Using the same test, Brown and Lenneberg (1958) showed that there is a relationship between color naming and color recognition which is a function of stimulus exposure time. Thus we should have varied the exposure time. Nevertheless since we dealt with highly codable colors, we should be able to recover them from their name. But in general our study is in agreement with theirs which shows that inconsistency within the group corresponds to inconsistency and hesitation in the individual.

REFERENCES

Allen, V.L. (1965) "Situational factors in conformity." *Advances in Experimental Social Psychology* 2:133–75.
Allen, V.L. and J.M. Levine (1968) "Social support, dissent and conformity." *Sociometry* 31(June):138–49.
Asch, S.E. (1955) "Opinions and social pressure." *Scientific American* 193 (November):31–5.
Asch, S.E. (1962) *Social Psychology*. Englewood Cliffs: Prentice-Hall.
Brehm, J.W. and D. Lipsher (1959) "Communicator–communicatee discrepancy and perceived communicator 'trustworthiness'." *Journal of Personality* 27(June):352–61.
Brown, R.W. and E.H. Lenneberg (1958) "Studies in linguistic relativity." Pp. 9–18 in Maccoby, Newcomb, and Hartly (eds), *Readings in Social Psychology*. New York: Holt, Rinehart and Winston.
Eisinger, R. and J. Mills (1968) "Perception of the sincerity and competence of a communicator as a function of the extremity of his position." *Journal of Experimental Social Psychology* 4(April):224–32.
Faucheux, C. and S. Moscovici (1967) "Le style de comportement d'une minorité et son influence sur les réponses d'une majorité." *Bulletin du Centre d'Etudes et Recherches Psychologiques* 16(October–December):337–60.
Flament, C. (1958) Influence Sociale et Perception. *Année Psychologique* 58(Fascicule 2):378–400.

Goldiamond, I. and L.F. Malpass (1958) "Locus of hypnotically induced changes in color responses." *Journal of the Optical Society of America* 51(October):1117–21.

Iscoe, I. and M.S. Williams (1963) "Experimental variables affecting the conformity behavior of children." *Journal of Personality* 31(June):234–46.

Kelley, H.H. (1967) "Attribution theory in social psychology." Pp. 192–241 in D. Levine (ed.), *Nebraska Symposium on Motivation*. Lincoln: University of Nebraska Press.

McGuire, W. (1964) "Inducing resistance to persuasion." *Advances in Experimental Social Psychology* 1:191–229.

Moscovici, S. (1969) "Behavioral style as a source of social influence." Symposium on Social Influence, IXth International Congress of Psychology, London.

Moscovici, S. and C. Faucheux (1969) "Social influence, conformity bias and the study of active minorities." Center of Advanced Study in Behavioral Sciences, Strafford (Mimeo).

Tajfel, H. (1969) "Social and cultural factors in perception." Pp. 315–94 in Lindzey and Aronson (eds.), *The Handbook of Social Psychology*, vol. III (2nd edn), Reading: Addison-Wesley.

Thomas, D.R. and G. Bistey (1964) "Stimulus generalization as a function of the number and range of generalization test stimuli." *Journal of Experimental Psychology* 68(December):599–602.

Worell, J. (1967) "Some ramifications of exposure to conflict." *Progress in Experimental Personality Research* 4:91–125.

Behavioral study of obedience

S. Milgram

Editors' Introduction

Theoretical Background

Social influence emanates from many sources, including group members and the media. Milgram's research addresses a specific form of influence, namely obedience to an authority figure. The context for this research is provided, on the one hand, by Milgram's desire to understand just how the Nazi Holocaust (and all the individual acts of obedience involved in that systematic annihilation) could have taken place; and on the other hand, by his fascination with the trial in Jerusalem of the arch-architect of the 'Final Solution' Adolf Eichmann, as reported by the philosopher Hannah Arendt (1963) in her book *Eichmann in Jerusalem: A Report on the Banality of Evil*. If such evil was 'banal', then would most people show destructive obedience? Prior to his research Milgram doubted it, and indeed this study represents what was intended to be the 'baseline', a situation in which few people would obey. Later research was then to manipulate key variables and investigate their impact on rates of obedience (see Milgram, 1965, 1974). The study is without question the most celebrated experiment in social psychology, widely cited but often misreported, which in itself is a reason to read the original.

Hypothesis

The purpose of the study is to ascertain what degree of obedience, if any, would be observed in this paradigm.

Journal of Abnormal and Social Psychology (1963), 67:371–8.

Design

There is no experimental design as such; no factors are manipulated.

Method

Subjects were solicited via newspaper advertisements for a study on 'memory and learning' (it is important that no mention was made either in the advertisement or, later, in the experimental cover story of obedience). At the laboratory the teacher–learner scenario was explained and subjects were led to believe that roles had been determined by chance. The 'victim' was, in fact, an experimental confederate. The experimenter explained that, by means of a simulated shock generator, the subject (as 'teacher') was to deliver increasingly more intense electric shocks to the 'learner' each time the latter made a mistake on the learning task. In fact, no shocks were delivered, but the impact of the experimental scenario is so high that all subjects believe that they are shocking the learner.

The procedure is spelled out in some detail – including the descriptions of both experimenter and victim, and the apparatus. In a clever touch, Milgram ensured that each subject experienced the reality of a relatively low-intensity electric shock (45 v), so that it could not be claimed later that subjects did not *believe* they were really shocking the victim. The degree of scripting of both the victim's responses (a predetermined set of grunts, screams, etc.) and the experimenter's commands (the four levels of 'prods') are important. In this way Milgram ensures that his experimental scenario has a very high impact on subjects without sacrificing control over the situation. (Later theoretical discussion of why people obey placed great emphasis on the notion of 'entrapment' whereby the experimenter proceeds with a graduated set of instructions, rather than beginning with an outrageous demand which most subjects would probably have refused.)

As befits such an intrusive experiment, a detailed debriefing was given which included uniting the subject with the victim, and assuring him that he had not actually delivered any shocks.

Results

No statistics are reported on the data, nor are they needed, since no experimental variations were compared. The subjects clearly believed that they had administered painful shocks to the victim (their mean response was 13.42, on a fourteen-point scale where 14 denoted 'Extremely painful'). Milgram also reports on non-verbal and verbal signs of tension and distress shown by the subjects.

The primary dependent measure is the maximum shock a subject administers before refusing to go any further (on a scale of responses from '0', refusing to administer the first shock, to '30', a 450-v shock). Far from the minimal level of obedience predicted by Milgram's students, no subject stopped before administering a 300-v shock. Across the sample, maximal obedience was shown by twenty-six of forty respondents: 65 per cent (see table 16.3).

Discussion

This study should be understood in the context of a whole series of experiments later conducted by Milgram (see Milgram, 1965, 1974). The work has also been the focus of massive controversy, centred on ethical issues (see Miller, 1986). Ethics is an important, if too often neglected, topic in social psychology and this research provides a dramatic and fascinating arena for that debate. Milgram was severely criticized for inducing suffering in his subjects, in a procedure that would be impossible to replicate today given ethical guidelines for research. The study raises a host of questions which might serve to stimulate your further thinking on this topic. Could this extent of suffering be dealt with in normal debriefing? And what would be the effects on subjects of learning that they could be so easily deceived; and that they were – apparently – capable of committing great harm under instructions? Should the experiment ever have been carried out? Is the research sufficiently important to justify such deception of and stress experienced by participants?

Another valuable perspective on the research is whether the results are so surprising. Later critics suggested that the role of the experimenter was more obtrusive than is evident from this early report, and that the disobedience shown by 35 per cent of the subjects is itself remarkable. Whatever your view, this is a study every social psychologist should read and think about; as indeed is true for Milgram's innovative wider contributions to social psychology (see Blass, 1992).

FURTHER READING

Milgram, S. (1965). Some conditions of obedience and disobedience to authority. *Human Relations*, 18, 57–76. This later paper presents a fascinating series of variations on the theme of the first study, highlighting the situational determinants of (dis)obedience.
Miller, A.G. (1986). *The Obedience Experiments: A Case Study of Controversy in Social Science*. New York: Praeger. This volume steps back and looks at Milgram's research with distance and objectivity, including a detailed consideration of ethics.

REFERENCES

Arendt, H. (1963). *Eichmann in Jerusalem: A Report on the Banality of Evil*. New York: Viking Press.
Blass, T. (1992). The social psychology of Stanley Milgram. In M. Zanna (ed.), *Advances in Experimental Social Psychology* (vol. 25, pp. 277–330). San Diego, CA: Academic Press.
Milgram, S. (1974). *Obedience to Authority*. London: Tavistock.

Obedience is as basic an element in the structure of social life as one can point to. Some system of authority is a requirement of all communal living, and it is only the man dwelling in isolation who is not forced to respond, through defiance or submission, to the commands of others. Obedience, as a determinant of behavior, is of particular relevance to our time. It has been reliably established that from 1933–45 millions of innocent persons were systematically slaughtered on command. Gas chambers were built, death camps were guarded, daily quotas

Primary Reading

of corpses were produced with the same efficiency as the manufacture of appliances. These inhumane policies may have originated in the mind of a single person, but they could only be carried out on a massive scale if a very large number of persons obeyed orders.

Obedience is the psychological mechanism that links individual action to political purpose. It is the dispositional cement that binds men to systems of authority. Facts of recent history and observation in daily life suggest that for many persons obedience may be a deeply ingrained behavior tendency, indeed, a prepotent impulse overriding training in ethics, sympathy, and moral conduct. C.P. Snow (1961) points to its importance when he writes:

> When you think of the long and gloomy history of man, you will find more hideous crimes have been committed in the name of obedience than have ever been committed in the name of rebellion. If you doubt that, read William Shirer's "Rise and Fall of the Third Reich." The German Officer Corps were brought up in the most rigorous code of obedience . . . in the name of obedience they were party to, and assisted in, the most wicked large scale actions in the history of the world (p. 24).

While the particular form of obedience dealt with in the present study has its antecedents in these episodes, it must not be thought all obedience entails acts of aggression against others. Obedience serves numerous productive functions. Indeed, the very life of society is predicated on its existence. Obedience may be ennobling and educative and refer to acts of charity and kindness, as well as to destruction.

General procedure

A procedure was devised which seems useful as a tool for studying obedience (Milgram, 1961). It consists of ordering a naive subject to administer electric shock to a victim. A simulated shock generator is used, with 30 clearly marked voltage levels that range from 15 to 450 volts. The instrument bears verbal designations that range from Slight Shock to Danger: Severe Shock. The responses of the victim, who is a trained confederate of the experimenter, are standardized. The orders to administer shocks are given to the naive subject in the context of a "learning experiment" ostensibly set up to study the effects of punishment on memory. As the experiment proceeds the naive subject is commanded to administer increasingly more intense shocks to the victim, even to the point of reaching the level marked Danger: Severe Shock. Internal resistances become stronger, and at a certain point the subject refuses to go on with the experiment. Behavior prior to this rupture is considered "obedience," in that the subject complies with the commands of the experimenter. The point of rupture is the act of disobedience. A quantitative value is assigned to the subject's performance based on the maximum intensity shock he is willing to administer before he refuses to participate further. Thus for any particular subject and for any particular experimental condition the degree of obedience may be specified with a numerical value. The crux of the study is to systematically vary the factors believed to alter the degree of obedience to the experimental commands.

The technique allows important variables to be manipulated at several points in the experiment. One may vary aspects of the source of command, content and form of command, instrumentalities for its execution, target object, general social setting, etc. The problem, therefore, is not one of designing increasingly more numerous experimental conditions, but of selecting those that best illuminate the *process* of obedience from the sociopsychological standpoint.

Related studies

The inquiry bears an important relation to philosophic analyses of obedience and authority (Arendt, 1958; Friedrich, 1958; Weber, 1947), an early experimental study of obedience by Frank (1944), studies in "authoritarianism" (Adorno, Frenkel-Brunswik, Levinson, and Sanford, 1950; Rokeach, 1961), and a recent series of analytic and empirical studies in social power (Cartwright, 1959). It owes much to the long concern with *suggestion* in social psychology, both in its normal forms (e.g., Binet, 1900) and in its clinical manifestations (Charcot, 1881). But it derives, in the first instance, from direct observation of a social fact; the individual who is commanded by a legitimate authority ordinarily obeys. Obedience comes easily and often. It is a ubiquitous and indispensable feature of social life.

Method

Subjects

The subjects were 40 males between the ages of 20 and 50, drawn from New Haven and the surrounding communities. Subjects were obtained by a newspaper advertisement and direct mail solicitation. Those who responded to the appeal believed they were to participate in a study of memory and learning at Yale University. A wide range of occupations is represented in the sample. Typical subjects were postal clerks, high school teachers, salesmen, engineers, and laborers. Subjects ranged in educational level from one who had not finished elementary school, to those who had doctorate and other professional degrees. They were paid $4.50 for their participation in the experiment. However, subjects were told that payment was simply for coming to the laboratory, and that the money was theirs no matter what happened after they arrived. Table 16.2 shows the proportion of age and occupational types assigned to the experimental condition.

Personnel and locale

The experiment was conducted on the grounds of Yale University in the elegant interaction laboratory. (This detail is relevant to the perceived legitimacy of the experiment. In further variations, the experiment was dissociated from the university, with consequences for performance.) The role of experimenter was played by a 31-year-old high school teacher of biology.

Table 16.2 Distribution of age and occupational types in the experiment

Occupations	20–9 years n	30–9 years n	40–50 years n	Percentage of total (occupations)
Workers, skilled and unskilled	4	5	6	37.5
Sales, business, and white-collar	3	6	7	40.0
Professional	1	5	3	22.5
Percentage of total (Age)	20	40	40	

Total $N = 40$.

His manner was impassive, and his appearance somewhat stern throughout the experiment. He was dressed in a gray technician's coat. The victim was played by a 47-year-old accountant, trained for the role; he was of Irish-American stock, whom most observers found mild-mannered and likable.

Procedure

One naive subject and one victim (an accomplice) performed in each experiment. A pretext had to be devised that would justify the administration of electric shock by the naive subject. This was effectively accomplished by the cover story. After a general introduction on the presumed relation between punishment and learning, subjects were told:

> But actually, we know *very little* about the effect of punishment on learning, because almost no truly scientific studies have been made of it in human beings.
>
> For instance, we don't know how *much* punishment is best for learning – and we don't know how much difference it makes as to who is giving the punishment, whether an adult learns best from a younger or an older person than himself – or many things of that sort.
>
> So in this study we are bringing together a number of adults of different occupations and ages. And we're asking some of them to be teachers and some of them to be learners.
>
> We want to find out just what effect different people have on each other as teachers and learners, and also what effect *punishment* will have on learning in this situation.
>
> Therefore, I'm going to ask one of you to be the teacher here tonight and the other one to be the learner.
>
> Does either of you have a preference?

Subjects then drew slips of paper from a hat to determine who would be the teacher and who would be the learner in the experiment. The drawing was rigged so that the naive subject was always the teacher and the accomplice always the learner. (Both slips contained the word "Teacher.") Immediately after the drawing, the teacher and learner were taken to an adjacent room and the learner was strapped into an "electric chair" apparatus.

The experimenter explained that the straps were to prevent excessive movement while the learner was being shocked. The effect was to make it impossible for him to escape from the situation. An electrode was attached to the learner's wrist, and electrode paste was applied "to avoid blisters and burns." Subjects were told that the electrode was attached to the shock generator in the adjoining room.

In order to improve credibility the experimenter declared, in response to a question by the learner: "Although the shocks can be extremely painful, they cause no permanent tissue damage."

Learning task

The lesson administered by the subject was a paired-associate learning task. The subject read a series of word pairs to the learner, and then read the first word of the pair along with four terms. The learner was to indicate which of the four terms had originally been paired with the first word. He communicated his answer by pressing one of four switches in front of him, which in turn lit up one of four numbered quadrants in an answer-box located atop the shock generator.

Shock generator

The instrument panel consists of 30 lever switches set in a horizontal line. Each switch is clearly labeled with a voltage designation that ranges from 15 to 450 volts. There is a 15-volt increment from one switch to the next going from left to right. In addition, the following verbal designations are clearly indicated for groups of four switches going from left to right: Slight Shock, Moderate Shock, Strong Shock, Very Strong Shock, Intense Shock, Extreme Intensity Shock, Danger: Severe Shock. (Two switches after this last designation are simply marked XXX.)

Upon depressing a switch: a pilot light corresponding to each switch is illuminated in bright red; an electric buzzing is heard; an electric blue light, labeled "voltage energizer," flashes; the dial on the voltage meter swings to the right; various relay clicks are sounded.

The upper left-hand corner of the generator is labeled Shock Generator, Type ZLB, Dyson Instrument Company, Waltham, Mass. Output 15 Volts–450 Volts.

Details of the instrument were carefully handled to insure an appearance of authenticity. The panel was engraved by precision industrial engravers, and all components were of high quality. No subject in the experiment suspected that the instrument was merely a simulated shock generator.[1]

Sample shock

Each naive subject is given a sample shock on the shock generator, prior to beginning his run as teacher. This shock is always 45 volts, and is applied by pressing the third switch of the generator. The shock is applied to the wrist of the naive subject, and has its source in a 45-volt battery wired into the generator. This further convinces the subject of the authenticity of the generator.

Shock instructions

The subject is told to administer a shock to the learner each time he gives a wrong response. Moreover – and this is the key command – the subject is instructed to "move one level higher on the shock generator each time the learner flashes a wrong answer." He is also instructed to announce the voltage level before administering a shock. This serves to continually remind subjects of the increasing intensity of shocks administered to the learner.

Preliminary and regular run

Pretests revealed that the procedure of reading words and administering shocks requires some practice before it can be handled smoothly. Therefore, immediately preceding the regular run, the teacher is given a preliminary series of 10 words to read to the learner. There are 3 neutral words in the practice series (i.e., words that the learner answers correctly), so that shocks are administered for 7 of the words, with the maximum shock at 105 volts (moderate shock). Almost all subjects master the procedure by the time the preliminary run is over.

Subjects are then presented with a second list, and are told that the procedure is the same as for the first list; the experimenter adds, however:

> When you get to the bottom of the list, repeat it over again, and continue giving shocks, until the learner has learned all the pairs correctly.

The experimenter instructs the subject to,

> start from 15 volts and increase the shock level one step each time the learner gives a wrong answer.

Feedback from the victim

In all conditions the learner gives a predetermined set of responses to the word pair test, based on a schedule of approximately three wrong answers to one correct answer. In the present experimental condition no vocal response or other sign of protest is heard from the learner until Shock Level 300 is reached. When the 300-volt shock is administered, the learner pounds on the wall of the room in which he is bound to the electric chair. The pounding can be heard by the subject. From this point on, the learner's answers no longer appear on the four-way panel.

At this juncture, subjects ordinarily turn to the experimenter for guidance. The experimenter instructs the subject to treat the absence of a response as a wrong answer, and to shock the subject according to the usual schedule. He advises the subjects to allow 5–10 seconds before considering no response as a wrong answer, and to increase the shock level one step each time the learner fails to respond correctly. The learner's pounding is repeated after the 315-volt shock is administered; afterwards he is not heard from, nor do his answers reappear on the four-way signal box.

Experimenter feedback

At various points in the experiment the subject may turn to the experimenter for advice on whether he should continue to administer shocks. Or he may indicate that he does not wish to go on. It was important to standardize the experimenter's responses to these inquiries and reactions.

If the subject indicated his unwillingness to go on, the experimenter responded with a sequence "prods," using as many as necessary to bring subject into line.

Prod 1: Please continue. *or* Please go on.
Prod 2: The experiment requires that you continue.
Prod 3: It is absolutely essential that you continue.
Prod 4: You have no other choice, you *must* go on.

The prods were always made in sequence: Only if Prod 1 had been unsuccessful could Prod 2 be used. If the subject refused to obey the experimenter after Prod 4, the experiment was terminated. The experimenter's tone of voice was at all times firm, but not impolite. The sequence was begun anew on each occasion that the subject balked or showed reluctance to follow orders.

Special prods   If the subject asked if the learner was liable to suffer permanent physical injury, the experimenter said:

> Although the shocks may be painful, there is no permanent tissue damage, so please go on. [Followed by Prods 2, 3, and 4 if necessary.]

If the subject said that the learner did not want to go on, the experimenter replied:

> Whether the learner likes it or not, you must go on until he has learned all the word pairs correctly. So please go on. [Followed by Prods 2, 3, and 4 if necessary.]

Dependent measures

The primary dependent measure for any subject is the maximum shock he administers before he refuses to go any further. In principle this may vary from 0 (for a subject who refuses to administer even the first shock) to 30 (for a subject who administers the highest shock on the generator). A subject who breaks off the experiment at any point prior to administering the thirtieth shock level is termed a *defiant* subject. One who complies with experimental commands fully, and proceeds to administer all shock levels commanded, is termed an *obedient* subject.

Further records

With few exceptions, experimental sessions were recorded on magnetic tape. Occasional photographs were taken through one-way mirrors. Notes were kept on any unusual behavior occurring during the course of the experiments. On occasion, additional observers were directed to write objective descriptions of the subjects' behavior. The latency and duration of shocks were measured by accurate timing devices.

Interview and dehoax

Following the experiment, subjects were interviewed; open-ended questions, projective measures, and attitude scales were employed. After the interview, procedures were undertaken to assure that the subject would leave the laboratory in a state of well being. A friendly reconciliation was arranged between the subject and the victim, and an effort was made to reduce any tensions that arose as a result of the experiment.

Results

Preliminary notions

Before giving an account of the experimental results, it is instructive to consider how persons predict others will perform when commanded to administer powerful shocks to another person. Fourteen Yale seniors, all psychology majors, were provided with a detailed description of the experimental situation. They were asked to reflect carefully on it, and to predict the behavior of 100 hypothetical subjects. More specifically, they were instructed to plot the distribution of obedience of "100 Americans of diverse occupations, and ranging in age from 20 to 50 years," who were placed in the experimental situation.

There was considerable agreement among the respondents on the expected behavior of hypothetical subjects. All respondents predicted that only an insignificant minority would go through to the end of the shock series. (The estimates ranged from 0 to 3%; i.e., the most "pessimistic" member of the class predicted that of 100 persons, 3 would continue through to the most potent shock available on the shock generator – 450 volts.) The class mean was 1.2%. The question was also posed informally to colleagues of the author, and the most general feeling was that few if any subjects would go beyond the designation Very Strong Shock.

Result of Experiment I

Subjects accept situation

With few exceptions subjects were convinced of the reality of the experimental situation, that they were administering shocks to another person, and the most potent shocks were extremely painful. In the post-experimental interview subjects were asked: "How painful to the learner were the last few shocks that you administered to him?" Subjects were instructed to indicate their answers on a printed 14-point scale ranging from "Not at all painful" to "Extremely painful." The modal response was 14 (Extremely painful) with the mean at 13.42.

Signs of extreme tension

Many subjects showed signs of nervousness in the experimental situation, and especially upon administering the more powerful shocks. In a large number of cases the degree of tension reached extremes that are rarely seen in sociopsychological laboratory studies. Subjects were observed to sweat, tremble, stutter, bite their lips, groan, and dig their fingernails into their flesh. These were characteristic rather than exceptional responses to the experiment.

One sign of tension was the regular occurrence of nervous laughing fits. Fourteen of the 40 subjects showed definite signs of nervous laughter and smiling. The laughter seemed entirely out of place, even bizarre. Full-blown, uncontrollable seizures were observed for 3 subjects. On one occasion we observed a seizure so violently convulsive that it was necessary to call a halt to the experiment. The subject, a 46-year-old encyclopedia salesman, was seriously embarrassed by his untoward and uncontrollable behavior. In the post-experimental interviews subjects took pains to point out that they were not sadistic types, and that the laughter did not mean they enjoyed shocking the victim.

Distribution of scores

It had been conjectured that persons would not, in general, agree to administer shocks beyond the level designated as Very Strong Shock. The distribution of maximum shocks for this experiment is shown in table 16.3. The obtained distribution of scores deviates radically from the prediction.

Upon command of the experimenter, each of the 40 subjects went beyond the expected breakoff point. No subject stopped prior to administering Shock Level 20. (At this level – 300 volts – the victim kicks on the wall and no longer provides answers to the teacher's multiple-choice questions.)

Of the 40 subjects, 5 refused to obey the experimental commands beyond the 300-volt level. Four more subjects administered one further shock, and then refused to go on. Two broke off at the 330-volt level, and 1 each at 345, 360, and 375 volts. Thus a total of 14 subjects defied the experimenter. It is instructive to reprint their remarks at the point of defiance, as transcribed from the tape recordings:

[0124] I think he's trying to communicate, he's knocking. . . . Well it's not fair to shock the guy . . . these are terrific volts. I don't think this is very humane. . . . Oh, I can't go on with this; no, this isn't right. It's a hell of an experiment. The guy is suffering in there. No, I don't want to go on. This is crazy. [Subject refused to administer more shocks.]

Table 16.3   Distribution of breakoff points

Verbal designation and voltage indication	Number of subjects for whom this was maximum shock
Slight Shock	
15	0
30	0
45	0
60	0
Moderate Shock	
75	0
90	0
105	0
120	0
Strong Shock	
135	0
150	0
165	0
180	0
Very Strong Shock	
195	0
210	0
225	0
240	0
Intense Shock	
255	0
270	0
285	0
300	5
Extreme Intensity Shock	
315	4
330	2
345	1
360	1
Danger: Severe Shock	
375	1
390	0
405	0
420	0
XXX	
435	0
450	26

[0123] He's banging in there. I'm gonna chicken out. I'd like to continue, but I can't do that to a man. . . . I'm sorry I can't do that to a man. I'll hurt his heart. You take your check. . . . No really, I couldn't do it.

These subjects were frequently in a highly agitated and even angered state. Sometimes, verbal protest was at a minimum, and the subject simply got up from his chair in front of the shock generator, and indicated that he wished to leave the laboratory.

Of the 40 subjects, 26 obeyed the orders of the experimenter to the end, proceeding to punish the victim until they reached the most potent shock available on the shock generator. At that point, the experimenter called a halt to the session. (The maximum shock is labeled 450 volts, and is two steps beyond the designation: Danger: Severe Shock.) Although obedient subjects continued to administer shocks, they often did so under extreme stress. Some expressed reluctance to administer shocks beyond the 300-volt level, and displayed fears similar to those who defied the experimenter; yet they obeyed.

After the maximum shocks had been delivered, and the experimenter called a halt to the proceedings, many obedient subjects heaved sighs of relief, mopped their brows, rubbed their fingers over their eyes, or nervously fumbled cigarettes. Some shook their heads, apparently in regret. Some subjects had remained calm throughout the experiment, and displayed only minimal signs of tension from beginning to end.

Discussion

The experiment yielded two findings that were surprising. The first finding concerns the sheer strength of obedient tendencies manifested in this situation. Subjects have learned from childhood that it is a fundamental breach of moral conduct to hurt another person against his will. Yet, 26 subjects abandon this tenet in following the instructions of an authority who has no special powers to enforce his commands. To disobey would bring no material loss to the subject; no punishment would ensue. It is clear from the remarks and outward behavior of many participants that in punishing the victim they are often acting against their own values. Subjects often expressed deep disapproval of shocking a man in the face of his objections, and others denounced it as stupid and senseless. Yet the majority complied with the experimental commands. This outcome was surprising from two perspectives: first, from the standpoint of predictions made in the questionnaire described earlier. (Here, however, it is possible that the remoteness of the respondents from the actual situation, and the difficulty of conveying to them the concrete details of the experiment, could account for the serious underestimation of obedience.)

But the results were also unexpected to persons who observed the experiment in progress, through one-way mirrors. Observers often uttered expressions of disbelief upon seeing a subject administer more powerful shocks to the victim. These persons had a full acquaintance with the details of the situation, and yet systematically underestimated the amount of obedience that subjects would display.

The second unanticipated effect was the extraordinary tension generated by the procedures. One might suppose that a subject would simply break off or continue as his conscience dictated. Yet, this is very far from what happened. There were striking reactions of tension and emotional strain. One observer related:

> I observed a mature and initially poised businessman enter the laboratory smiling and confident. Within 20 minutes he was reduced to a twitching, stuttering wreck, who was rapidly approaching a point of nervous collapse. He constantly pulled on his earlobe, and twisted his hands. At one point he pushed his fist into his forehead and muttered: "Oh God, let's stop it." And yet he continued to respond to every word of the experimenter, and obeyed to the end.

Any understanding of the phenomenon of obedience must rest on an analysis of the particular conditions in which it occurs. The following features of the experiment go some distance in explaining the high amount of obedience observed in the situation.

1   The experiment is sponsored by and takes place on the grounds of an institution of unimpeachable reputation, Yale University. It may be reasonably presumed that the personnel are competent and reputable. The importance of this background authority is now being studied by conducting a series of experiments outside of New Haven, and without any visible ties to the university.
2   The experiment is, on the face of it, designed to attain a worthy purpose – advancement of knowledge about learning and memory. Obedience occurs not as an end in itself, but as an instrumental element in a situation that the subject construes as significant, and meaningful. He may not be able to see its full significance, but he may properly assume that the experimenter does.
3   The subject perceives that the victim has voluntarily submitted to the authority system of the experimenter. He is not (at first) an unwilling captive impressed for involuntary service. He has taken the trouble to come to the laboratory presumably to aid the experimental research. That he later becomes an involuntary subject does not alter the fact that, initially, he consented to participate without qualification. Thus he has in some degree incurred an obligation toward the experimenter.
4   The subject, too, has entered the experiment voluntarily, and perceives himself under obligation to aid the experimenter. He has made a commitment, and to disrupt the experiment is a repudiation of this initial promise of aid.
5   Certain features of the procedure strengthen the subject's sense of obligation to the experimenter. For one, he has been paid for coming to the laboratory. In part this is canceled out by the experimenter's statement that:

> Of course, as in all experiments, the money is yours simply for coming to the laboratory. From this point on, no matter what happens, the money is yours.[2]

6   From the subject's standpoint, the fact that he is the teacher and the other man the learner is purely a chance consequence (it is determined by drawing lots) and he, the subject, ran the same risk as the other man in being assigned the role of learner. Since the assignment of positions in the experiment was achieved by fair means, the learner is deprived of any basis of complaint on this count. (A similar situation obtains in Army units, in which – in the absence of volunteers – a particularly dangerous mission may be assigned by drawing lots, and the unlucky soldier is expected to bear his misfortune with sportsmanship.)
7   There is, at best, ambiguity with regard to the prerogatives of a psychologist and the corresponding rights of his subject. There is a vagueness of expectation concerning what a psychologist may require of his subject, and when he is overstepping acceptable limits. Moreover, the experiment occurs in a closed setting, and thus provides no opportunity for

the subject to remove these ambiguities by discussion with others. There are few standards that seem directly applicable to the situation, which is a novel one for most subjects.

8　The subjects are assured that the shocks administered to the subject are "painful but not dangerous." Thus they assume that the discomfort caused the victim is momentary, while the scientific gains resulting from the experiment are enduring.

9　Through Shock Level 20 the victim continues to provide answers on the signal box. The subject may construe this as a sign that the victim is still willing to "play the game." It is only after Shock Level 20 that the victim repudiates the rules completely, refusing to answer further.

These features help to explain the high amount of obedience obtained in this experiment. Many of the arguments raised need not remain matters of speculation, but can be reduced to testable propositions to be confirmed or disproved by further experiments.[3]

The following features of the experiment concern the nature of the conflict which the subject faces.

10　The subject is placed in a position in which he must respond to the competing demands of two persons: the experimenter and the victim. The conflict must be resolved by meeting the demands of one or the other; satisfaction of the victim and the experimenter are mutually exclusive. Moreover, the resolution must take the form of a highly visible action, that of continuing to shock the victim or breaking off the experiment. Thus the subject is forced into a public conflict that does not permit any completely satisfactory solution.

11　While the demands of the experimenter carry the weight of scientific authority, the demands of the victim spring from his personal experience of pain and suffering. The two claims need not be regarded as equally pressing and legitimate. The experimenter seeks an abstract scientific datum; the victim cries out for relief from physical suffering caused by the subject's actions.

12　The experiment gives the subject little time for reflection. The conflict comes on rapidly. It is only minutes after the subject has been seated before the shock generator that the victim begins his protests. Moreover, the subject perceives that he has gone through but two-thirds of the shock levels at the time the subject's first protests are heard. Thus he understands that the conflict will have a persistent aspect to it, and may well become more intense as increasingly more powerful shocks are required. The rapidity with which the conflict descends on the subject, and his realization that it is predictably recurrent, may well be sources of tension to him.

13　At a more general level, the conflict stems from the opposition of two deeply ingrained behavior dispositions: first, the disposition not to harm other people, and second, the tendency to obey those whom we perceive to be legitimate authorities.

NOTES

This research was supported by a grant (NSF G-17916) from the National Science Foundation. Exploratory studies conducted in 1960 were supported by a grant from the Higgins Fund at Yale University. The research assistance of Alan C. Elms and Jon Wayland is gratefully acknowledged.

[1] A related technique, making use of a shock generator, was reported by Buss (1961) for the study of aggression in the laboratory. Despite the considerable similarity of technical detail in the experimental procedures, both investigators proceeded in ignorance of the other's work. Milgram provided plans and photographs of his shock generator, experimental procedure, and first results in a report to the National Science Foundation in January 1961. This report received only limited circulation. Buss reported his procedure 6 months later, but to a wider audience. Subsequently, technical information and reports were exchanged. The present article was first received in the Editor's office on December 27, 1961; it was resubmitted with deletions on July 27, 1962.

[2] Forty-three subjects, undergraduates at Yale University, were run in the experiment without payment. The results are very similar to those obtained with paid subjects.

[3] A series of recently completed experiments employing the obedience paradigm is reported in Milgram (1964).

REFERENCES

Adorno, T., Frenkel-Brunswik, Else, Levinson, D.J., and Sanford, R.N. *The authoritarian personality*. New York: Harper, 1950.

Arendt, H. What was authority? In C.J. Friedrich (ed.), *Authority*. Cambridge: Harvard University Press, 1958. Pp. 81–112.

Binet, A. *La suggestibilité*. Paris: Schleicher, 1900.

Buss, A.H. *The psychology of aggression*. New York: Wiley, 1961.

Cartwright, S. (ed.) *Studies in social power*. Ann Arbor: University of Michigan Institute for Social Research, 1959.

Charcot, J.M. *Oeuvres complètes*. Paris: Bureaux du Progrès Médical, 1881.

Frank, J.D. Experimental studies of personal pressure and resistance. *J. gen. Psychol.*, 1944, *30*, 23–64.

Friedrich, C.J. (ed.) *Authority*. Cambridge: Harvard University Press, 1958.

Milgram, S. Dynamics of obedience. Washington: National Science Foundation, 25 January 1961. (Mimeo)

Milgram, S. Some conditions of obedience and disobedience to authority. *Hum. Relat.*, 1964, in press.

Rokeach, M. Authority, authoritarianism, and conformity. In I.A. Berg and B.M. Bass (Eds), *Conformity and deviation*. New York: Harper, 1961. Pp. 230–57.

Snow, C.P. Either-or. *Progressive*, 1961 (Feb.), 24.

Weber, M. *The theory of social and economic organization*. Oxford: Oxford University Press, 1947.

17 Intergroup Relations

Intergroup discrimination and self-esteem in the minimal group paradigm

L. Lemyre and P.M. Smith

L. Lemyre and P.M. Smith

Editors'
Introduction

Theoretical Background

This study deals with the important question of why people are apparently so inclined to discriminate in favour of their own group (the 'ingroup') and against another group (the 'outgroup') even on the basis of the most trivial criteria for group membership. That they are so inclined was first demonstrated by Tajfel and colleagues, using what they called the 'minimal group paradigm' (MGP; Tajfel et al., 1971). This paradigm, since replicated and varied in many ways, divides experimental subjects into two groups on the basis of 'minimal' criteria – preference for one of two abstract painters, tendency to overestimate or underestimate numbers of dots in a pattern, even the toss of a coin. Once categorized in this way, subjects tend to favour their ingroup at the expense of the outgroup, as shown by the way they allocated points between ingroup and outgroup members using specially constructed 'matrices' or tables of rewards (for a detailed exposition of the paradigm, see Bourhis et al., 1994). But why do people discriminate in favour of their own group?

Turner (1975) and Tajfel and Turner (1979) put forward an explanation in terms of 'social identity theory': they argued that in such situations social categorization triggers social comparisons between the ingroup and outgroup, with group members wanting to see their own group emerge as superior, thereby defending, maintaining or possibly enhancing their self-esteem. Lemyre and Smith were careful to keep an open mind about exactly how self-esteem might motivate intergroup discrimination: discrimination might be a response to a temporary threat to self-esteem (perhaps only 'restoring' self-esteem to its previous level, which had been lowered by the situation), or it might be a strategy for 'raising' self-esteem from its baseline value, by means of a social comparison in which the ingroup is made to do better than the outgroup.

Lemyre and Smith were not the first to test the relationship between discrimination and

Journal of Personality and Social Psychology (1985), 49:660–70.

self-esteem. But we have selected their paper because it is the most careful in its methodology and conclusive in its findings, providing also an insight into the minimal group paradigm and social identity theory. In particular, they point out that previous research by Oakes and Turner (1980) did not exactly equate experimental and control conditions (something that is always essential); and thus does not make clear whether the reported increase in self-esteem was caused by discrimination or by the mere act of being categorized within the MGP. Lemyre and Smith also point to the limitations of Turner and Spriggs's (1982) unpublished study, which could demonstrate only a correlational, and not an experimental, relationship between discrimination and self-esteem. Lemyre and Smith therefore sought to design a new experiment that could determine whether intergroup discrimination was a *necessary* condition for a change in self-esteem. A requirement of such an experiment is that it should have a 'no-categorization control condition', so that one can isolate the effect of mere categorization (independent of discrimination) on self-esteem.

Hypotheses

The main hypothesis tested was whether competitive comparison with, and/or discrimination against, an outgroup causes an increase in self-esteem. The main prediction is that subjects who were categorized *and* who discriminated would show the highest self-esteem.

Design

The eight conditions of the experimental design are set out clearly in table 17.1. The design is non-orthogonal, so appears rather complex, but the logic is simple and compelling. The eight conditions are created by varying three parameters. First, some of the conditions involve *categorization* into groups (C; conditions 3–8), others involve no categorization (NC; conditions 1–2). Second, several different types of *task* are used, whereby the subject allocates points to others. Some conditions allow the subject only to allocate points between members of their ingroup ('ingroup/ingroup matrices'; condition 5) or only between members of the outgroup ('outgroup/outgroup' matrices; condition 6); as compared with subjects who do have the opportunity to allocate points between ingroup and outgroup (conditions 3 and 4). Other conditions force the subject to be either fair (condition 7) or discriminatory (condition 8). Finally, for those subjects not categorized, one cannot allocate points between 'group' members, so they allocate points between others ('other–other' matrices; conditions 1 and 2). The third variable manipulated is the *order* of point-allocation and self-esteem tasks: in two conditions self-esteem is completed first (conditions 1 and 3); in all the other conditions self-esteem is completed second.

Despite this complexity, the core of the design is contained in a familiar 2 (categorization condition) × 2 (task condition) between-subjects factorial design, involving the four conditions: no categorization/categorization × no matrix task/matrix task before self-esteem measures (conditions 1, 2, 3, and 4). The logic of the experiment requires comparison of the typical MGP condition (4; where intergroup matrices precede self-esteem) with other conditions involving, for example: no opportunity to discriminate (5 and 6); forced to be fair (7) or to discriminate (8); self-esteem completed first, thus providing a baseline measure uninfluenced by discrimination (3); and no categorization (1 and 2).

Method

Students participated in the experiment during a normal class. They were randomly assigned to the eight conditions by drawing a slip of paper from a bag; those who were categorized were assigned to either a 'Blue' or a 'Red' group by the information on the slip of paper. (Given this minimal basis for group membership, the reported extent of discrimination and the link between discrimination and self-esteem reveal the power of social categorization.)

In varying orders, subjects completed both a booklet of matrices (illustrated in table 17.2) and the self-esteem measures. In conditions 7 and 8 the normal matrices were modified so that points allocated to ingroup and outgroup were always 'fair' (equal) or always discriminated in favour of the ingroup, respectively. The self-esteem measures consisted of a battery of items drawn from established scales.

Results

Manipulation checks

To ascertain whether subjects did in fact discriminate in favour of the ingroup in the categorization conditions, their allocated rewards on the matrices were analyzed for the use of various response strategies. The results show clearly that subjects in condition 4 did engage in intergroup discrimination (the one-sample 'Hotelling's T^2 statistic indicates that strategies were greater than zero for the Tajfel matrices, or differed from 1 for the Brewer matrices). Subjects in condition 4 also showed greater evidence of the favouritism strategy than those in condition 2, who were not given the opportunity to allocate points between ingroup and outgroup members.

Self-esteem

The five different measures of self-esteem were highly correlated, and a factor analysis yielded one main factor accounting for 63 per cent of the total variance. Despite this common factor, the authors preferred first to analyse the data using a 2 × 2 multivariate analysis of variance (MANOVA) on the five measures of self-esteem, followed by univariate analyses to examine which measures of self-esteem revealed the predicted interaction effect (which makes the results rather complex). Post hoc contrasts (with a controlled alpha level of .01, rather than the usual .05) did *not* reveal the predicted highest self-esteem for those subjects both categorized and given the opportunity to discriminate (table 17.3 shows that the mean index of self-esteem in condition 4 is not distinguishable from the mean in condition 1). However, self-esteem was lower in condition 2 (no categorization/matrix before self-esteem measure) than conditions 1 (no categorization/no matrix before self-esteem) and 4 (categorization/matrix first).

Subsequent analyses included focused (a priori) comparisons involving subsets of all eight conditions, using an index of self-esteem based on all five measures. The 'Bonferroni' procedure mentioned protects the researcher from making 'Type I' errors (concluding that the results are significant when, in fact, given the number of tests carried out, the 'significant' result is due to chance). The six contrasts tested are shown in table 17.4. The main findings were, for conditions in which subjects had been categorized, that: (1) subjects who could discriminate had higher self-esteem than those who could not: (2) subjects restricted to completing matrices about either two ingroup members or two outgroup members – i.e. intergroup discrimination was impossible – had equivalent levels of self-esteem, which were lower than the self-esteem of those subjects who could discriminate in favour of the ingroup; (3) subjects forced to discriminate had higher self-esteem than those forced to be fair, but not significantly different from those free to discriminate if/as they wished; (4) for subjects who could not engage in discrimination, completing the matrix task did not affect self-esteem.

Finally, within condition 4, the authors computed a multiple regression analysis in which they sought to predict self-esteem from the strategies subjects used in completing the matrices. The multiple regression coefficient was highly significant (.726) and the best two predictors were strategies reflecting 'maximum ingroup profit' and 'ingroup favouritism'.

Discussion

Although this experiment did not confirm the main hypothesis of highest self-esteem for those subjects who were categorized *and* who discriminated, it does support social identity theory, in showing that intergroup discrimination can raise self-esteem. Crucially, it rules out alternative accounts whereby raised self-esteem might be caused either by the mere fact of being categorized, or by the mere completion of a (matrix) task. But the authors honestly acknowledge that, although they obtained the predicted interaction between categorization and matrix task, the *form* of the interaction was unexpected. In fact, the level of self-esteem was equivalent for those subjects not categorized, but given no prior matrix task (condition 1), and those subjects categorized, and given a prior matrix task (condition 4). Self-esteem levels in both conditions were higher than in the other two conditions of the core design (2 and 3: no categorization/matrix and categorization/no matrix). This pattern of results does *not* indicate, as had been assumed, that discrimination 'enhances' self-esteem. Rather, the lowered self-esteem for subjects categorized, but given no prior matrix, compared with the no categorization/no matrix and categorization/matrix subjects, suggests that categorization lowers self-esteem and the opportunity to discriminate restores it. As Lemyre and Smith suggest, ingroup favouritism may reduce a threat to self-esteem, rather than raising self-esteem per se. This is an important qualification to social identity theory, and a correction to conclusions drawn from previous studies, although the motivational status of self-esteem in social identity theory remains an unresolved issue in intergroup relations (see Abrams and Hogg, 1988).

FURTHER READING

Abrams, D. and Hogg, M.A. (1988). Comments on the motivational status of self-esteem in social identity and intergroup discrimination. *European Journal of Social Psychology*, 18, 317–34. An important theoretical paper spelling out the determinants and consequences of self-esteem in research on intergroup discrimination.

Tajfel, H., Flament, C., Billig, M. and Bundy, R.F. (1971). Social categorization and intergroup behaviour. *European Journal of Social Psychology*, 1, 149–78. The first MGP study published, which explains the technique of minimal social categorization and the use of the matrices to measure intergroup discrimination.

REFERENCES

Bourhis, R.Y., Sachdev, I. and Gagnon, A. (1994). Intergroup research with the Tajfel matrices: Methodological notes. In M.P. Zanna and J.M. Olson (eds), *The Psychology of Prejudice: The Ontario Symposium* (vol. 7, pp. 209–32). Hillsdale, NJ: Erlbaum.

Oakes, P.J. and Turner, J.C. (1980). Social categorization and intergroup behaviour: Does minimal intergroup discrimination make social identity more positive? *European Journal of Social Psychology*, 10, 295–301.

Tajfel, H. and Turner, J.C. (1979). An integrative theory of intergroup conflict. In W.G. Austin and S. Worchel (eds), *The Social Psychology of Intergroup Relations* (pp. 33–47). Monterey, CA: Brooks/Cole.

Turner, J.C. (1975). Social comparison and social identity: Some prospects for intergroup behaviour. *European Journal of Social Psychology*, 5, 5–34.

Turner, J.C. and Spriggs, D. (1982). Social categorization, intergroup behaviour and self-esteem: A replication. Unpublished manuscript, University of Bristol.

- - - - -
Primary
Reading
- - - - - - - -

More than 20 experiments in which researchers used variants of the minimal group experimental procedure (MGP) support the hyothesis that under certain conditions, merely being categorized into an experimental group is sufficient to induce favoritism to the ingroup and discrimination against an out-group (e.g., Billig and Tajfel, 1973; Brewer, 1979; Brown, Tajfel, and Turner, 1980; Locksley, Ortiz, and Hepburn, 1980; Tajfel, 1970; Turner, 1978, 1980, 1983).

In these experiments, which have been extensively described elsewhere (Brewer, 1979; Tajfel, Flament, Billig, and Bundy, 1971; Turner, 1978; 1983), subjects are divided into groups on trivial or ad hoc bases, and then make decisions about rewards for anonymous in-group and out-group members. Reliably, they discriminate competitively in favor of their own group, striving not only for their own group's gain, but also for advantage relative to the other group even when this entails the sacrifice of absolute gain for one's own group.

The significance of competitive discrimination in the MGP is not only that it draws attention to the ease with which hitherto nonexistent criteria, which are in any case transient and usually trivial in the experiments, can become psychologically prominent as the focal point of social discrimination. Less striking, but in some ways more significant, is the fact that these criteria become the focal point of directed and reliable discrimination, taking the form of competitive in-group favoritism, in a context that is devoid of all the variables that are normally thought to determine group cohesion and intergroup antipathy.

The most satisfactory explanation of these findings to date is Tajfel and Turner's Social Identity Theory (SIT; Turner, 1982). This is based in part on an extension of Festinger's (1954) theory of social comparison, which postulates a human need to evaluate one's own opinions and abilities. Tajfel (1978) argued that not only individual opinions and abilities but group memberships as well are evaluatively important because they provide people with orientation and definition in society. He thus extended the social comparison idea to embrace intergroup as well as interpersonal evaluations. Just as Festinger hypothesized that there is a pressure towards obtaining favorable social comparisons for ability evaluations, Tajfel argued that this is true also in the case of intergroup comparisons.

To account for the fact that discrimination in the MGP systematically favors the in-group, Tajfel (1972, 1974) and Turner (1975; Tajfel and Turner, 1979) argued that social categorization more or less automatically stimulates comparisons between the in-group and outgroup and, furthermore, that there is a motivational tendency for people to resolve these comparisons in such a way as to defend, maintain, and possibly enhance their self-esteem. Social categorization in the MGP, they argued, triggers intergroup comparisons that have repercussions for group members' self-evaluations, thereby inducing them to engage in behavior that enhances the relative value of their own group when the opportunity arises. Turner (1975) called this *social competition*.

The need for positive self-esteem, in the sense of a relatively favorable self-evaluation, is afforded a prominent role in SIT as the motive underlying competitive discrimination. In only two experiments have researchers directly addressed the hypothesis that discrimination in the MGP contributes to personal self-evaluation. Oakes and Turner (1980) measured postexperimental self-esteem under two conditions. Subjects were first categorized on painting preferences and then were assigned either to an experimental condition, in which they completed the usual matrix booklet, or to a control condition, in which they read a newspaper article on which they would supposedly be questioned later. A the end of the session, all subjects completed a self-evaluation questionnaire. Experimental subjects, who indeed showed in-group favoritism on the matrices, expressed greater self-esteem than did control subjects. A factor analysis of the self-esteem measures yielded a single factor on which scores differed significantly across conditions. The experiment thus gave encouraging results. However, one can level the criticism that the experimental tasks in the two conditions were not of equal psychological significance: One was a decision-making task, whereas the other simply consisted of waiting. One could argue that the importance of the experimental task influenced self-esteem independently of the opportunity to discriminate. It would therefore be desirable to compare conditions in which the tasks are of comparable psychological significance. Moreover, the setting of the experimental condition made group membership much more salient, again independently of any actual discrimination response. Consequently, it is not clear which aspect of the experimental condition caused the difference in self-esteem: the significance of the task, the emphasis on comparison between in-group and out-group, or the discrimination itself.

Turner and Spriggs (1982) conducted another MGP experiment with self-esteem as one of the dependent variables. Two independent variables were manipulated. One was the instructions given to the subjects: They were instructed to be either cooperative or competitive. The second manipulation concerned the type of matrix. In the group condition, subjects were categorized on painting preferences, and they allocated points between in-group and out-group members, whereas in the individual condition, they were not explicitly categorized into groups, and they allocated points between themselves and another person, half of the time to someone who shared the same painting preference and the other half of the time to someone who did not. The self-esteem measures were the same as those used by Oakes and Turner (1980), namely, the Twenty Statements Test, semantic differential items, and Rosenberg's

(1965) Self-Esteem Inventory. Subjects in all conditions showed in-group favoritism, but they differed significantly according to the two expected main effects: More in-group favoritism was shown in the competition conditions than in the cooperation conditions, and more was shown in the group conditions than in the individual conditions. Two-way analyses of variance (ANOVAs) on each self-esteem scale revealed a main effect for competition versus cooperation, which was due to the tendency towards higher self-esteem on Rosenberg's scale, the semantic differential scales, and the common factor under competitive instructions. Surprisingly, self-esteem scores were higher under individual conditions (self vs. other matrices) than under group conditions (other vs. other matrices). No interactions were significant.

In that experiment the relation between competition and in-group favoritism seems to have mirrored that pattern between competition and self-esteem. Competitive instructions caused an increase in in-group favoritism and an increase in self-esteem, suggesting a relation between in-group favoritism and self-esteem. However, one cannot conclude that it is the amount of discrimination itself that caused the change in self-esteem; the relation between these two variables is correlational, and both could have been due to competitive instructions. Moreover, because subjects in all conditions were in situations of discrimination and showed in-group favoritism to some extent, one cannot judge whether intergroup discrimination was a necessary condition for a change in self-esteem; an appropriate control condition without discrimination was lacking.

Those two experiments partly addressed the hypothesis concerning the role of self-esteem in intergroup discrimination, but neither was conclusive. Our aim is to extend the contributions of Oakes and Turner (1980) and Turner and Spriggs (1982) in investigating the relation between social categorization, intergroup discrimination, and self-esteem, and to attempt to isolate the locus of the relation. Essentially, SIT is predictive of an increase in self-esteem after a successful competitive social comparison. Positive differentiation (i.e., discrimination) is a prerequisite of success in this respect. However, it is also conceivable that a change in self-esteem may be produced by other factors. For example, categorization in the MGP may itself elicit some positive self-evaluation in that it contributes in an admittedly minimal way to an individual's self-definition in a context in which the ambiguity of the experimental situation may elicit a search for meaning. Neither of the experiments just described included a no-categorization control condition against which one could compare the effects of categorization. Furthermore, it is possible that the opportunity for cognitive comparison and differentiation of the in-group and out-group, independently of any actual discrimination, may contribute to self-esteem because it makes group membership salient. Then, above and beyond the possible impact of categorization and cognitive differentiation, actual intergroup discrimination would of course bring into play the consequential process of social competition, which is the key factor according to SIT.

Method

Design and hypotheses

Our main objective was to determine whether competitive social comparison and discrimination against an out-group cause an increase in self-esteem. This presupposes a social categorization manipulation, as well as an opportunity to differentiate between groups. Eight experimental conditions were designed, as displayed in table 17.1.

Table 17.1 Summary of the experimental design

		Booklet	
Categorization		Part 1	Part 2
1	NC	Self-esteem	Other–other matrices
2	NC	Other–other matrices	Self-esteem
3	C	Self-esteem	In-group/out-group matrices
4	C	In-group/out-group matrices	Self-esteem
5	C	In-group/in-group matrices	Self-esteem
6	C	Out-group/out-group matrices	Self-esteem
7	C	Forced fairness matrices	Self-esteem
8	C	Forced discrimination matrices	Self-esteem

NC = no categorization; C = categorization.

The conditions varied on three parameters: (a) categorization into groups versus no categorization, (b) type of point-allocation task, and (c) the order of the point-allocation and self-esteem tasks. The core of the design consisted of the first four conditions, which formed, with respect to the dependent variable self-esteem, a 2 × 2 design: Categorization Versus Noncategorization × Matrix Task Versus No Matrix Task. To this block the four remaining conditions were affixed as supplementary controls.

The cornerstone of the design was Condition 4, which was to be compared on self-esteem with conditions in which subjects were categorized but could not express any in-group favoritism on the matrices because they were not confronted with both the ingroup and the outgroup simultaneously (Conditions 5 and 6) or because they were forced to be fair (Condition 7). In Condition 3 self-esteem was assessed before any possible discrimination, no explicit comparison or decision having yet been made. This permitted us to simulate a pre-postmeasure of self-esteem with respect to discrimination, without encountering repeated measure artifacts such as pretest sensitivity. Moreover, Condition 3 in conjunction with Condition 1, the baseline, permitted the evaluation of the impact of categorization alone on self-esteem. Condition 2 served as a control for the effect of the matrix task. Condition 8 provided an analogue to Condition 7 with respect to its forced character, and tested, when opposed to Condition 4, whether perceived freedom in discriminating against an out-group was a determinant of a change in self-esteem.

Concerning the 2 × 2 design, in our principal hypothesis we predicted a Categorization × Matrix interaction effect: Subjects who were categorized and who discriminated would show the highest self-esteem. As for the supplementary control conditions, the major prediction was that of all categorization conditions (3 through 8), self-esteem would be highest in those in which intergroup discrimination occurred (4 and 8). Further predictions were that Conditions 5 and 6 would not differ from each other on self-esteem and both would be lower than Condition 4; moreover, Condition 8 (forced discrimination) would be higher on self-esteem than Condition 7 (forced fairness). A comparison between Conditions 4 and 8 would help to reveal whether the constraints of a task in which in-group favoritism was imposed would interfere with the expected salutary effects of that strategy. Finally, we predicted that if completing a significant experimental task is in itself beneficial for self-esteem, then Conditions 5, 6, and 7 should be higher than Condition 3.

In summary, for the categorization conditions, our predictions for self-esteem were as follows: (a) It would be greater in Conditions 4 and 8 than in 3, 5, 6, and 7; (b) it would be the same in Conditions 5 and 6; (c) it would be greater in Condition 4 than in 5 than in 6; (d) it would be greater in Condition 8 than in 7; (e) it would be greater in Condition 5 than in 8; (f) it would be greater in Conditions 5, 6, and 7 than in 3.

Subjects

One hundred thirty-five undergraduates from an introductory psychology class at the University of British Columbia agreed to participate in this experiment during their class period. The 90 male and 45 female subjects were seated at individual desks separated from each other by about 0.5 m in a large auditorium.

Procedure

All the conditions in this experiment were run concurrently and subjects were randomly assigned to conditions. After a brief introduction, subjects were asked to sign a consent form. Then, following oral instructions about the overall procedure and the specific tasks to be performed, three teams each of two experimental assistants went around the classroom allowing each subject to draw a slip of paper from a bag and to take an experimental booklet. Subjects had been told that they would obtain an anonymous confidential personal code number by drawing a slip of paper. They would use this code number throughout the experimental session instead of their name, in order to protect their anonymity. In fact, all subjects drew "personal" code number 16. Moreover, three quarters of the slips of paper enabled us to perform a group categorization at the same time: According to these slips, the class was divided into two groups, Blue and Red, on a random basis, and the subjects who received these slips had been assigned by chance to Group Red. Secrecy of the slip of paper was stressed. Subjects had to read the slip, write down the information (code number and, if any, group membership) on the second page of their experimental booklet, fold up the slip of paper, and put it in an envelope already provided. The subjects then started work on their booklet, which contained two parts. One part was a point-allocation task involving matrices of rewards for two unknown persons identified by their code numbers and, in some conditions, by their group memberships. The other part of the booklet consisted of a self-esteem questionnaire. These two parts appeared in reversed order, depending on the condition. To prevent subjects from talking to one another, we also provided them from the beginning of the session with a filler task, a whole sheet of anagrams. They were instructed to solve these in their spare time, under the cover of establishing norms for somebody else's study. When everybody had finished answering their booklet, the experiment was declared over. Subjects were then asked to complete a postexperimental questionnaire with which we gathered their comments, hypotheses, perceptions, and suspicions. Finally, the subjects were debriefed about the whole procedure, the different conditions, and the hypotheses, and were given a brief summary of SIT.

Materials

As described earlier, we performed the categorization manipulation by using two types of slips of paper, which were drawn by the subjects; one type indicated only a code number and the other type also assigned a group membership, Red, to the subject. The core of the manipulations was accomplished through the booklets, whose composition changed according to the conditions. The booklets were made of 27 half-pages stapled together. The first page was left blank in order to cover the second page on which subjects had to write their code number and, in categorization conditions, their group membership. The matrix part consisted of a page of instructions followed by 16 pages of matrices. Eight matrices of Tajfel's (1970) 13-choice format alternated with eight of Brewer's (1979) two-choice type (for a full description of the matrices and their psychometric properties, see Brewer, 1979; Brown et al., 1980; Turner, 1978, 1983; examples are given in table 17.2). For each of these matrices two unknown persons were identified at the beginning of the rows by some randomly chosen code numbers and, for Conditions 3 through 8, by group memberships. This information was handwritten in ink corresponding to the color to the group labels, blue or red. For each matrix, subjects had to circle a column corresponding to the number of points they wished to allocate to the two persons identified on the page, and also to affirm this choice by copying the numbers in blank spaces provided on the page.

In Conditions 7 and 8 we used modified versions of the original matrices. For the forced fairness condition, the arrays of numbers were constructed in such a way that the points allocated to the in-group were necessarily equal to those given to the out-group. In the forced discrimination condition, the numbers were combined such that more points were always given to the in-group.

The self-esteem part consisted of a set of measures for which the instructions stressed the need for subjects to answer as they felt at that very moment ("State self-esteem"). The

Table 17.2 Examples of Tajfel's 13-choice and Brewer's 2-choice point-allocation matrices

						Tajfel's							
These numbers are rewards for												
Member 31 of Group Red:	19	18	17	16	15	14	13	12	11	10	9	8	7
Member 42 of Group Blue:	1	3	5	7	9	11	13	15	17	19	21	23	25
The chosen column gives												
to Member 31 of Group Red: ____												
to Member 42 of Group Blue: ____												

			Brewer's
These numbers are rewards for			
Member 31 of Group Red:	7	8	
Member 42 of Group Blue:	9	4	
The chosen column gives			
to Member 31 of Group Red: ____			
to Member 42 of Group Blue: ____			

Subjects are instructed to circle one column of numbers that represents their preferred allocation of points to the in-group and out-group members. They then copy these numbers in the appropriate spaces below the matrix. This enables the experimenter to check to see that subjects are explicitly aware of how the points will be distributed.

questionnaire included a half-length version of the Twenty Statement Test (Jones, Sensening, and Haley, 1974; Kuhn and McPartland, 1954; McGuire and Padawer-Singer, 1976), Rosenberg's (1965) 10-item Self-Esteem Scale extended to a 7-point Likert scale, 22 semantic differential scales consisting of Julian, Bishop, and Fiedler's (1966) nine items, and Sherwood's 13-item Self-Concept Inventory (Robinson and Shaver, 1973). Finally, there was a single 7-point rating scale with which we directly addressed the level of self-esteem (Hamilton, 1971).

The self-esteem questionnaire constituted Part 1 of the booklet for Conditions 1 and 3, and Part 2 for all other conditions. On the penultimate page of the booklet we asked for age and sex. On the final page, subjects were to write down what they thought the experiment was about.

Results

Manipulation checks

The matrix task served to operationalize the independent variable, intergroup discrimination. The encoding of the matrix choices allowed a manipulation check to see whether categorized subjects indeed discriminated.

In some conditions, constraints on the setting ensured that subjects did or did not discriminate. For others, though, subjects were left to their own will, and a verification was required to establish whether they did engage in in-group favoritism. This was particularly important for Condition 4, the pivot of the experiment. Five strategies, described by Turner (1978, 1983) and Brewer and Silver (1978), were analyzed: fairness (F), maximum joint profit (MJP), maximum in-group profit (MIP) maximum differentiation (MD), and a combination of the last two, in-group favoritism (FAV).

To test whether the categorized subjects of Condition 4 engaged in discrimination, we performed a one-sample Hotelling's T^2 on the strategy indexes. This procedure yielded experimentwise .95 confidence intervals that established whether Tajfel's (1970) pull scores were statistically equivalent to zero, and whether Brewer's (1979) strategy frequencies differed from 1, the chance level. The results show conclusively that subjects in Condition 4 engaged in intergroup discrimination. The pull of FAV on MJP was positive and statistically different from zero, C.I. = (1.4, 4.9); $t(17) = 3.82$, $p < .01$; the pull of MJP + MIP on MD was negative and significant, C.I. = (−3.6, −.5); $t(17) = −2.85$, $p < .02$. The frequency of FAV was different from 1, the chance expectation, C.I. = (1.29, 2.38). The results also supported the null hypotheses that the frequencies of F, MIP, and MJP were not different from 1, the chance level, and that the pull of F on FAV and of MJP on FAV were not different from zero.

Furthermore, because Condition 4 was to be compared with Condition 2 on self-esteem, it was particularly important to verify that these two conditions differed on discrimination indexes. Moreover, the replication of the role of categorization in discrimination was of interest here. A multivariate two-sample Hotelling's T^2 was run on the seven Tajfel indexes and three of Brewer's (Brewer's indexes entail linear dependency, as the frequency of three strategies determine the frequency of the fourth). Conditions 2 and 4 differed significantly (Wilks's lambda = .541), $F(10, 26) = 2.30$, $p < .05$; Heck value (1, 4, 12) = .459, $p < .05$. Namely, categorized subjects showed (a) more FAV, $t(35) = 4.18$, $p < .001$, (b) more FAV on MJP, $t(35) = 2.77$, $p < .01$, and (c) more FAV on F, $t(35) = 1.80$, $p < .08$. These results confirm that subjects in Condition 4 indeed engaged in intergroup discrimination, a prerequisite for an adequate test of our hypotheses.

Results on self-esteem

Five indices were obtained for self-esteem: the shortened Twenty Statement Test, the extended Rosenberg's (1965) Self-Esteem Scale, Julian et al.'s (1966) semantic differential scales, Sherwood's (Robinson and Shaver, 1973) Self-Concept Inventory items, and a single global rating scale.

For the Twenty Statement Test, two independent judges scored the responses as reflecting positive (1), negative (−1) or neutral (0) attributions. They agreed on 1,108 out of the 1,245 decisions, an agreement rate of 89%. For the other four measures, the subjects' responses were coded from 1 to 7, 7 being the positive anchor, and the average score on each measure was calculated for each subject.

Correlations among the five measures of self-esteem were all very highly significant ($p < .001$). They ranged from .55 to .75 except for those between the Twenty Statement Test and the other measures, which were lower, ranging from .34 to .46. In a common factor analysis we extracted one eigenvalue (3.14) greater than 1 that explained 62.8% of the total variance. The factor weights were .84 for the Sherwood inventory, .84 for the Julian et al. scales, .76 for the Rosenberg scale, .71 for the global scale, and .50 for the Twenty Statement Test.

The group means on each of the five self-esteem measures and on the first principal component are displayed in table 17.3. The first set of analyses concerns the 2×2 core design block, whereas later analyses include the supplementary control conditions. A two-way multivariate analysis of variance (MANOVA) was performed on the five measures of self-esteem. The first factor, categorization, had two levels: categorized (C) and noncategorized (NC). The second factor, order of the matrices in the booklet, also had two levels: matrix task before the self-esteem assessment (M) and no matrix before the measures (NM). The four cells of this 2×2 design were represented by Conditions 1 (NC–NM), 2 (NC–M), 3 (C–NM), and 4 (C–M).

Table 17.3 Group means on self-esteem measures and the first principal component

Condition	n	T	R	J	S	G	PC
1 (NC, SE, Mtx)	19	.140	5.895	5.444	5.583	5.316	.285
2 (NC, Mtx, SE)	19	−.353	5.356	4.912	5.419	5.444	−.225
3 (C, SE, I/O)	17	.007	5.418	5.039	5.602	5.353	−.028
4 (C, I/O, SE)	18	.122	5.822	5.475	5.457	5.611	.303
5 (C, I/I, SE)	13	−.162	5.346	4.915	5.201	5.333	−.275
6 (C, O/O, SE)	16	−.031	5.862	4.806	5.370	5.563	.002
7 (C–F, SE)	17	−.135	5.341	4.974	5.089	5.118	−.334
8 (C–D, SE)	16	−.040	5.850	5.278	5.446	5.563	.174

T = Twenty Statement Test, R = Rosenberg Self-Esteem Scale, J = Julian et al. semantic differential scales, S = Sherwood's Self-Concept Inventory items, G = global rating scale, PC = principal component score; NC = noncategorized SE = self-esteem, Mtx = matrix, C = categorized, I/O = in-group/out-group, I/I = in-group/in-group, O/O = out group/out-group, C–F = forced fairness condition, C–D = forced discrimination condition.

The two-way MANOVA showed neither a categorization effect ($p < .7$) nor a matrix task effect ($p > .3$). The interaction effect, however, was highly significant according to both the likelihood ratio criterion and the greatest characteristic root approach (Wilks's lambda = .700), $F(5, 63) = 5.39$, $p < .0001$; Heck value (1, 1.5, 30.5) = .300, $p < .01$. Because with the multivariate technique we demonstrated that the interaction was significant within the constraints of an experimentwise Type I error rate of .05 across the five measures, we performed two-day univariate tests (ANOVAs) to discover on which scales there were significant interactions. Two-way interactions were significant on the Twenty Statement Test, $F(1, 67) = 6.41$, $p < .02$; on the Rosenberg scale, $F(1, 67) = 4.97$, $p < .03$; and on the Julian et al. scales, $F(1, 67) = 5.40$, $p < .03$. For these three measures, post hoc comparisons were made via simple effect analysis. We carried out t tests at .01 Type I error rate, using mean square within as the best estimate of the error variance. These post hoc contrasts showed that Condition 2 (NC–M) was lower on self-esteem than Conditions 1 (NC–NM) and 4 (C–M), the latter two not being statistically different, and that Condition 3 (C–NM) was also lower than 1 and 4, except on the Twenty Statement Test, on which they were not different, Conditions 2 and 3 were equal on self-esteem, except on the Twenty Statement Test, on which 2 was significantly lower than 3. Conditions 1 (NC–NM) and 4 (C–M) were not statistically different on any scale. In summary, the two-way MANOVA showed that the interaction between categorization and the matrix task was significant, even with a highly controlled alpha rate, with Conditions 1 and 4 being highest (refer to the values in table 17.3).

In the next set of analyses we included the supplementary Conditions 5 to 8 and focused on some specific comparisons. A one-way MANOVA on the five self-esteem measures across all eight conditions was significant (Wilks's lambda = .661), $F(35, 507) = 1.50$, $p < .04$; Heck value (5, 0.5, 59) = .216, $p < .01$, yielding a clear, global, statistically conservative statement that the conditions differed significantly.

The problem posed by trying to describe these differences in more detail is not a trivial one. Multiple comparisons on each variable would offer no statistical power because there exist 140 possible pairwise contrasts alone. In this context it appeared more appropriate to apply univariate techniques on a global summary index of the five self-esteem indexes, taken here as the first principal component. To reduce the dimensionality of the self-esteem data, we applied a principal component analysis to the five dependent measures of self-esteem. Only one principal component with an eigenvalue greater than 1 was extracted, and it explained 62.8% of the variance. All the variables loaded about equally on this first principal component except for the Twenty Statement Test, which was somewhat lower. The weights were .61 for that, .82 for the Rosenberg scale, .86 for the Julian et al. scales, .86 for the Sherwood inventory, and .79 for the global scale. For each subject, we computed a principal component score, using these weights in linear combination. We then performed univariate analyses between experimental conditions on this new index.

Because only some specific comparisons were of interest in regard to the hypotheses, univariate a priori Bonferroni tests were executed on the first principal component. This powerful technique preserved a .05 experimentwise Type I error rate over the six contrasts that were relevant to the hypotheses. In table 17.4 we list the contrasts and their respective results. For conditions in which subjects had been categorized, subjects who could discriminate (Conditions 4 and 8) had higher principal component scores than those who could not (Conditions 3, 5, 6, 7). Categorized subjects filling in the matrices about two members of their own group (Condition 5) were equivalent on self-esteem to those who distributed points to two

Table 17.4   A priori Boneferroni *t* tests on the first principal component

Hypothesis about conditions	Actual value of contrast	Critical difference	Statistical decision
4, 8 > 3, 5, 6, 7	1.589	1.143	4, 8 > 3, 5, 6, 7
5 = 6	.277	.922[a]	5 = 6
4 > 5, 6	.879	.807	4 > 5, 6
8 > 7	.507	.460	8 > 7
4 > 8	.130	.461	4 = 8
5, 6, 7 > 3	−.521	.680	5, 6, 7 = 3

Experimentwise Type I error rate was .05; contrastwise error rate was smaller than .01. The inequalities and equivalences in the first and last columns refer respectively to expected and observed between-condition differences in scores on the first principal component. All tests were one-tailed, unless otherwise specified.
[a]Two-tailed test.

out-group members (Condition 6); subjects in both conditions were prevented from engaging in intergroup discrimination. Subjects in these two nondiscrimination conditions had significantly lower principal component scores than those who had in-group versus out-group matrices and could discriminate (Condition 4). Subjects in the forced discrimination condition (8) had higher scores than those in the forced fairness condition (7), but their scores were not different from those of subjects in the free discrimination condition (4). Finally, whether one performed the experimental matrix task did not influence self-esteem for those who could not engage in intergroup discrimination: Subjects in Conditions 5, 6, and 7 were equivalent to those in Condition 3.

In summary, we verified that, given categorization, subjects in the discriminative conditions had higher principal component scores than did nondiscriminative subjects (scores in Conditions 4 and 8 were higher than those in 3, 5, 6, and 7; were higher in 4 than in 5 and 6; were higher in 8 than in 7; were equal in 4 and 8, in 5 and 6, and in 5, 6, 7, and 3).

Moreover because the hypothesis was that discrimination led to higher self-esteem, we conducted an exploratory internal analysis of Condition 4. Our aim was to discover whether there was a relation between the extent of discrimination and the level of self-esteem. Correlations between principal component scores and the matrix indexes were computed within Condition 4, and a regression analysis was performed to predict principal component scores from the strategy indexes. We obtained a multiple regression coefficient of .726 ($p < .005$) from a stepwise regression analysis in which we used as the two best predictors two pulls reflecting in-group gain: MIP + MJP on MD ($\beta = .618$) and the pull of FAV on MJP ($\beta = .566$). A similar regression analysis was performed on the data from Condition 3, in which self-esteem was assessed before the matrix task, and it is of interest to note that no significant relations between principal component scores and the matrix indexes were obtained.

Postexperimental questionnaire

The postexperimental questionnaire was exploratory in nature, and was aimed at revealing signs of suspiciousness and demand characteristics. One hundred thirty subjects completed the questionnaire. None mentioned suspecting that different conditions were run simultaneously, nor that the drawing of the slip of paper was deceptive. A fair number of them even wrote their code on their answer sheet. No categorized subjects acknowledged any doubt about the existence of the two groups; many referred explicitly to Group Red and Group Blue. Most subjects focused on the self-esteem questionnaire in their comments. They perceived it as a personality trait or strength of character measure, and related it often to the anagram task. None actually stated a hypothesis in which he or she related self-esteem to intergroup discrimination.

Discussion and Conclusions

The results of this experiment support the main predictions of SIT concerning the effects of discrimination favorable to the in-group on self-esteem, and allow us to rule out alternative hypotheses that are based on the effects of either categorization or having completed a significant experimental task alone. Categorized subjects who discriminated showed higher postexperimental self-esteem than either categorized subjects who did not have the opportunity to discriminate or noncategorized subjects who engaged in a similar experimental task. Further support comes from the finding that the level of self-esteem in the forced discrimination condition was statistically indistinguishable from that in Condition 4 and higher than that in the forced fairness condition and in the other nondiscriminative conditions (5 and 6). Finally, there was suggestive evidence from the internal analysis of Condition 4 that indexes of in-group gain were significantly related to postexperimental self-esteem. This relation was not obtained in Condition 3, in which self-esteem was assessed before the point-allocation task.

In one respect, the form of the interaction between social categorization and the matrix task was quite different from what was expected. The level of self-esteem in Condition 1 (NC–NM) was equivalent to that in Condition 4 (C–M). Both were higher than those in Conditions 2 (NC–M) and 3 (C–NM). This configuration of results suggests that intergroup discrimination did not enhance self-esteem but rather restored and maintained it. Because in Condition 3 self-esteem was lower than in Condition 1, and in Condition 4 it was equal to that in Condition 1, a plausible interpretation is that in-group favoritism reduced a threat to self-esteem. Under this interpretation, categorization initiated a need for positive groupwise social comparison that was not experienced by the subjects in Condition 1. Because this comparison was as yet unresolved in Condition 3 when self-esteem was assessed, before the matrix task, it was perceived as threatening. Consequently, lower self-esteem was observed at that point. The noncategorized subjects in Condition 2 were involved in an individualwise comparison task in which the matrices did not allow them to contribute to their own position. Perhaps they suspected that other participants were making decisions about them, and they too consequently perceived a threatening, unresolved situation; as a result, their self-esteem was lower. As shown by the statistical results on the main effects, categorization in itself was not enough to raise self-esteem; neither was the matrix task if people could not act in favor of their relative position in the comparison. On the contrary, these two conditions (2 and 3) appeared to be threatening, compared with Condition 1. In-group favoritism, though, restored self-esteem for categorized subjects. Perhaps direct self-favoritism would have had the same beneficial impact, but in this experiment it was not an available solution.

An alternative interpretation attributes the decreased self-esteem to cognitive ambiguity. Subjects in Conditions 2 and 3 were confronted with, respectively, a puzzling task or an irrelevant categorization, whereas in Condition 4, subjects could use these two pieces of information together and engage in in-group favoritism. This "cognitive ambiguity" hypothesis, though, is weakened by the results from the supplementary conditions. The additional conditions demonstrated clearly that for categorized subjects, discrimination compared with nondiscrimination in favor of the in-group resulted in higher self-esteem. Subjects in Conditions 4 and 8 had higher self-esteem than those in 3, 5, 6, and 7. Forced and free discrimination resulted in equivalent self-esteem levels. In nondiscriminative conditions, it did not matter (a) whether self-esteem was assessed after the categorization (Condition 3), (b) whether a task had been making the group membership salient (conditions 4 and 5), or (c) whether the task had simultaneously opposed the in-group and the out-group (Condition 7). These four conditions did not differ statistically. These results are consistent with SIT: Given categorization, discrimination in favor of one's own group results in a relative increase in self-esteem. Categorization in itself was not sufficient, nor was cognitive differentiation of the in-group and the out-group if not paired with a comparative value differentiation as well. This experimental demonstration that intergroup discrimination can affect self-esteem is all the more significant because it was demonstrated in the minimal group paradigm and was based on a random categorization criterion. Group membership was determined simply on the basis of a slip of paper leading to the most trivial and temporary group membership. Yet subjects engaged in intergroup discrimination and, moreover, gained self-esteem as a consequence.

Apart from this, our main contribution is the discovery that social categorization in the absence of an opportunity for intergroup differentiation may attenuate self-esteem somewhat. This finding does not contradict SIT, which does not make predictions concerning the effects of social categorization alone on self-esteem. Unfortunately, this experiment does not permit one to make a clear decision as to whether the "perceived threat" or the "cognitive ambiguity" interpretation provides a better account of the observations, and future research will address this issue.

Eventual conclusions regarding the motivational role of the need for positive self-esteem in intergroup relations will clearly have to be based on observations made in a wide variety of contexts. In this sense, our research is very much a beginning, and the results must be interpreted cautiously, based as they are on students in an experimental setting. On the other hand, most of the features peculiar to this setting, such as minimal categorization, concurrent experimental conditions, and student subjects, seem intuitively to have militated against obtaining systematic effects on self-esteem. Nevertheless, such effects were observed. Furthermore, the tight operational control afforded here enabled us to disentangle the independent effects of previously confounded variables, and to make a discovery that would have been difficult, even impossible, to observe using groups with previous histories, in naturalistic situations in which the vehicles of differentiation are numerous and readily available.

The results of this experiment and others like it are troubling, because they imply that the conditions under which a sense of well-being is promoted within one's own groups entail a cost to others. Indeed, it is difficult to avoid the conclusion that people engage in in-group favoritism in order to promote this well-being (by whatever psychological process: reduction of threat or ambiguity, enhancement of group position, etc.), although the issue of intentionality has not been explicitly addressed here or elsewhere. In the final analysis, however, knowledge of the factors that underlie group conflict, though it may be the cause for some pessimism about human nature, is a necessary prerequisite to reducing this conflict. In this sense, SIT offers a very optimistic horizon.

NOTE

This research was completed in partial fulfillment of the masters degree by the first author, who acknowledges support received from the Social Science Research Council of Canada, from the FCAC research fund of Quebec, and from the University of British Columbia.

REFERENCES

Billig, M., and Tajfel, H. (1973). Social categorization and similarity in intergroup behavior. *European Journal of Social Psychology*, *3*, 7–52.

Brewer, M.B. (1979). In-group bias in the minimal intergroup situation: A cognitive–motivational analysis. *Psychological Bulletin*, *86*, 307–24.

Brewer, M.B., and Silver, M. (1978). Ingroup bias as a function of task characteristics. *European Journal of Social Psychology*, *8*, 393–400.

Brown, R., Tajfel, H., and Turner, J.C. (1980). Minimal group situations and intergroup discrimination: Comments on the paper by Aschenbrenner and Schaefer. *European Journal of Social Psychology*, *10*, 399–414.

Festinger, L. (1954). A theory of social comparison processes. *Human Relations*, *7*, 117–40.

Hamilton, D. (1971). A comparative study of five methods of assessing self-esteem, dominance and dogmatism, *Educational and Psychological Measurement*, *31*, 441–52.

Jones, K.A., Sensening, J., and Haley, J.V. (1974). Self-descriptions: Configurations of content and order effects, *Journal of Personality and Social Psychology*, *30*, 36–45.

Julian, J.W., Bishop, D.W., and Fiedler, F.E. (1966). Quasi-therapeutic effects of intergroup competition. *Journal of Personality and Social Psychology*, *3*, 321–7.

Kuhn, M.H., and McPartland, T.S. (1954). An empirical investigation of self-attitudes. *American Sociological Review*, *19*, 68–76.

Locksley, A., Ortiz, V., and Hepburn, C. (1980). Social categorization and discriminatory behavior: Extinguishing the minimal intergroup discrimination effect. *Journal of Personality and Social Psychology*, *39*, 773–83.

McGuire, W.J., and Padawer-Singer, A. (176). Trait salience in the spontaneous self-concept. *Journal of Personality and Social Psychology*, *33*, 743–54.

Oakes, P.J.T., and Turner, J.C. (1980). Social categorization and intergroup behavior: Does minimal intergroup discrimination make social identity more positive? *European Journal of Social Psychology*, *10*, 295–301.

Robinson, J.P., and Shaver, P.R. (1973). *Measures of social psychological attitudes*. Ann Arbor, MI: Institute of Social Research.

Rosenberg, M. (1965). *Society and the adolescent self-image*. Princeton, NJ: Princeton University Press.

Tajfel, H. (1970). Experiments in intergroup discrimination. *Scientific American*, *23*(5), 96–102.

Tajfel, H. (1972). La categorisation sociale [Social categorization]. In S. Moscovici (ed.), *Introduction a la psychologie sociale* (pp. 272–302). Paris: Larousse.

Tajfel, H. (1974). Social identity and intergroup behavior. *Social Science Information*, *9*, 113–144.

Tajfel, H. (1978). *Differentiations between social groups: Studies in intergroup relations*. London: Academic Press.

Tajfel, H., and Turner, J. (1979). An integrative theory of intergroup conflict. In W.G. Austin and S. Worchel (eds), *The social psychology of intergroup relations* (pp. 33–47). Montery: Brooks/Cole.

Tajfel, H., Flament, C., Billing, M., and Bundy, R.F. (1971). Social categorization and intergroup behavior. *European Journal of Social Psychology*, *1*, 149–78.

Turner, J.C. (1975). Social comparison and social identity: Some prospects for intergroup behavior. *European Journal of Social Psychology*, 5, 5–34.

Turner, J.C. (1978). Social categorization and social discrimination in the minimal group paradigm. In H. Tajfel (ed.), *Differentiation between social groups: Studies in the social psychology of intergroup relations* (pp. 101–40). London: Academic Press.

Turner, J.C. (1980). Fairness or discrimination in intergroup behavior? A reply to Branthwaite, Doyle and Lightbown. *European Journal of Social Psychology*, 10, 131–47.

Turner, J.C. (1982). Towards a cognitive redefinition of the social group. In H. Tajfel (ed.), *Social identity and intergroup relations* (pp. 15–40). Cambridge, England: Cambridge University Press.

Turner, J.C. (1983). Some comments on . . . "The measurement of social orientations in the minimal group paradigm." *European Journal of Social Psychology*, 13, 351–67.

Turner, J.C., and Spriggs, D. (1982). Social categorization, intergroup behaviour and self-esteem: A replication. Unpublished manuscript.

Intergroup contact: The typical member and the exception to the rule

D.A. Wilder

- - - - -
Editors'
Introduction
- - - - - - - -

Theoretical Background

Whereas the previous reading dealt with the instigation of intergroup conflict, or its causes, this reading considers how conflict between groups can be reduced, and negative stereotypes of the outgroup rendered more positive. The three studies (of which experiment 1 is the main one and is therefore covered in the article and here in more detail) address a number of key concepts in this area: intergroup contact, typicality, stereotype change and generalization.

Specifically, the three studies reported consider intergroup contact as a means of improving intergroup relations, and how it can be made more effective (see Miller and Brewer, 1984; Hewstone and Brown, 1986). As Wilder reports, people often react to positive, stereotype-disconfirming behaviour by an outgroup member not by changing their view of the outgroup as a whole, but by considering the positive outgroup member as 'the exception'. In order to overcome this tendency, Wilder suggests – somewhat paradoxically – that when we set up intergroup contact we should ensure that contact is with members of the outgroup who are clearly perceived to be 'typical' of the outgroup. Only then will positive contact with one or a few members of the outgroup 'generalize' to a new, more positive view of the outgroup as a whole. Negative contact, however, is likely to have a negative impact on outgroup perceptions whether the outgroup member one encounters is typical or atypical: negative behaviour is likely to be expected and thus reinforces negative expectations about the outgroup; it may also make the outgroup member appear more typical of the disliked outgroup than she or he actually is.

Journal of Experimental Social Psychology (1984), 20:177–94.

EXPERIMENT I

Hypotheses

Three hypotheses are tested:

1   A positive interaction with a *typical* member of the outgroup will have a favourable impact on evaluations of the outgroup.
2   A positive interaction with an *atypical* outgroup member will have little impact on outgroup evaluation.
3   A negative interaction with either a typical or an atypical outgroup member will have an unfavorable impact on outgroup evaluation.

Design

The experimental design was a three-factor, between-subjects design: 2 (college identity of confederate: Douglass/Rutgers) × 2 (behaviour of the confederate: positive/negative) × 2 (typicality of the confederate: typical/atypical). Thus there were eight experimental conditions in all, with two levels of each independent variable. Subjects were randomly assigned to one level of each of the latter two independent variables. Of course, they always experienced contact with a member of the outgroup (and data were later collapsed across college affiliation, since this factor was non-significant). There was also a control condition, which involved neither contact with nor the presence of a confederate.

Method

Because the study capitalized on natural groups (rival colleges) and took place outside the psychology-department laboratory, it might be described as a 'field experiment'. Also Wilder led participants to believe that they were taking part in a study on group performance (there was no mention of intergroup rivalry). Note that the experimental confederate used was 'blind' to the hypotheses; this is good practice. Also noteworthy is the extensive 'pre-testing' to identify what stereotypes students of the two colleges held about their own and the rival group, which formed the basis of the typicality manipulation. The manipulations of typicality and pleasantness of contact are clearly reported; note that Wilder was careful to make sure that pleasant and unpleasant contact was equated for success of the confederate's performance. The questionnaire including outgroup evaluations was also dissociated from the study itself by telling subjects that it was being handed out for a colleague from another college.

Results

Manipulation checks

Before analysing the main data, Wilder verified that he had successfully manipulated both typicality and pleasantness of contact. This was clear from ratings of the contact person.

Evaluation of the outgroup

The study predicts an interaction of typicality × pleasantness which should be reliable in the analysis of variance: evaluation of the outgroup should be most positive in the typical member/pleasant contact condition. This interaction was significant for the index assessing the quality of the other college, but not for the item indicating whether subjects would recommend the other college to an acquaintance (see table 17.5). However, in both cases ratings were most positive, as predicted, in the typical/pleasant condition, and only this rating was significantly different from the control.

Beliefs about the outgroup

There was almost no evidence that the contact manipulations, either typicality or pleasantness, affected participants' stereotypes (see table 17.6). Thus beliefs about the outgroup appear to be harder to change than evaluations of the outgroup.

EXPERIMENT 2

This study starts from the insight that the manipulation of typicality in the first study was based on beliefs about the outgroup that had no direct reference to the ingroup. Wilder wondered whether typicality would always function in this positive manner. He predicted, and found, that typicality based on stereotypes that had direct implications for the participant's own group would be less successful. Thus it would be unwise to try to increase the perceived typicality of an outgroup member if that involved getting him or her to display negative stereotypes directed at the ingroup (e.g. 'we are better than they are'). Once again, Wilder found changes in outgroup evaluation (see table 17.7) but not outgroup stereotypes.

EXPERIMENT 3

The final study tried to ascertain why, when contact is pleasant, typicality works as it does. The results indicate that, following pleasant contact with a typical outgroup member, participants find it easier to generalize *from* that outgroup member *to* other members of the outgroup (i.e. the outgroup member's behaviour is seen to be more highly predictive of outgroup behaviour in general).

Discussion

Wilder's results gave broad support to his main hypotheses and were crucial in highlighting the importance of typicality in intergroup contact (see also Hewstone, 1996; Rothbart and John, 1985). His thoughtful discussion of how and when stereotypes might change, even though he was unable to report change in his research, was also influential in guiding later research (see Johnston and Hewstone, 1992; Wilder, 1986). One limitation of the main study is that there was no actual contact between group members. They simply passed information on answer sheets between their separate booths. In this way interaction was carefully controlled, but perhaps participants never felt that they had really 'seen' enough to warrant changing their stereotypes.

FURTHER READING

Johnston, L. and Hewstone, M. (1992). Cognitive models of stereotype change: (3) Subtyping and the perceived typicality of disconfirming group members. *Journal of Experimental Social Psychology*, 28, 360–86. This study, using a quite different paradigm, shows that stereotype change is brought about by otherwise-typical members of the group behaving in stereotype-disconfirming ways.

Rothbart, M. and John, O.P. (1985). Social categorization and behavioral episodes: a cognitive analysis of the effects of intergroup contact. *Journal of Social Issues*, 41, 81–104. A more cognitive perspective than Wilder's, but one that comes to the same bold conclusions about the central role of typicality in promoting generalized change in outgroup attitudes.

REFERENCES

Hewstone, M. (1996). Contact and categorization: Social-psychological interventions to change intergroup relations. In C.N. Macrae, C. Stangor and M. Hewstone (eds), *Foundations of Stereotypes and Stereotyping* (pp. 323–68). New York: Guilford Press.

Hewstone, M. and Brown, R.J. (eds) (1986). *Contact and Conflict in Intergroup Encounters*. Oxford: Blackwell.

Miller, N. and Brewer, M.B. (eds) (1984). *Groups in Contact: The Psychology of Desegregation*. Orlando, FL: Academic Press.

Wilder, D.A. (1986). Social categorization: Implications for creation and reduction of intergroup bias. In L. Berkowitz (ed.), *Advances in Experimental Social Psychology* (vol. 19, pp. 293–355). New York: Academic Press.

Primary
Reading

Studies of intergroup relations have demonstrated that contact between members of hostile groups can be effective in reducing bias. Conditions conducive to successful contact include cooperation in the successful pursuit of common goals, contact between equal-status group members, and contact promoted by an authority (Allport, 1954; Amir, 1976; Riordin, 1978). As reviews of the contact literature indicate, even these favorable conditions do not guarantee a lessening of bias between the groups.

For one thing, conditions that are objectively favorable, from the vantage point of someone outside the relationship, may not be interpreted as such by the participants. Much of the social perception literature suggests that our responses to others are influenced by our attributions about the causes and motivations of their actions. Surely we would not expect a contact situation to be effective if the parties are coerced to be pleasant to one another. In that situation they would simply discount each other's behavior as externally mandated and not indicative of their true feelings.

Another way of discounting positive actions of out-group members is to dissociate them from their group. If they are judged to be atypical of the out-group, an "exception to the rule" so to speak, then their pleasant behavior need not disturb our existing cognitions about the out-group (Pettigrew, 1979). Many of us can recall instances in which persons who harbor prejudices against an out-group have nevertheless interacted amicably with specific out-group members. When called upon to explain their behavior, they reason that these out-group members are not like the rest. Indeed, to the extent the "pleasant exception" is different from typical out-group members, he/she may actually reinforce the perceiver's stereotypes of the out-group, thereby making a change in evaluation of the whole out-group unlikely. The pleasant exception is "proof" that typical members are unpleasant. Success of contact depends, therefore, on the perceived relationship between the contact person and the group he/she represents.

The "typical" out-group member should match many of the stereotypes held about the out-group while the "atypical" member confirms few of them. Research on stereotype change suggests that individuals resist information contrary to their stereotypes by subtyping the discrepant information (Weber and Crocker, 1983). In other words, they partition the "exceptions" as a subset of the out-group category and, by implication, not representative of the out-group as a whole.

Social categorization theorists (Brown and Turner, 1981; Tajfel and Turner, 1979) posit that social interactions vary along an interpersonal–intergroup continuum. To be successful in changing an evaluation of an out-group, favorable contact with an out-group member must be defined as an intergroup encounter. A weak association between the contact person and the out-group (atypical member) lessens the intergroup nature of the interaction. Furthermore, persons expect differences between groups and relative homogeneity within groups (Park and Rothbart, 1982; Quattrone and Jones,1980; Wilder, in press). Atypical out-group members violate that expectation and may more easily be dissociated from the out-group than be the source of a change in one's evaluation of the out-group. Three hypotheses follow from the above arguments:

1   A positive interaction with an out-group member will have a favorable impact on one's evaluation of the out-group when that member is perceived to be highly typical of the out-group; in other words, when he/she corresponds closely to one's expectations about members of that group.
2   A positive interaction with an out-group member will have little impact on one's evaluation of the out-group when that member is perceived to be atypical of the out-group.
3   A negative interaction with an out-group member will have an unfavorable impact on one's evaluation of the out-group regardless of how typical he/she is of that group. Clearly, an unpleasant interaction with a typical out-group member should be harmful to one's evaluation of the out-group. That the same should occur for unpleasant contact with an atypical member is less clear. To begin with, unpleasant behavior by any out-group member reinforces one's negative expectations of the out-group. Moreover, negative behavior by an atypical member may increase her/his perceived typicalness. Fulfillment of the negative expectations makes him/her appear to be more typical of the out-group than had events gone more favorably.

Experiment 1

To test hypotheses 1, 2, and 3, subjects were recruited from two ongoing groups that have some negative expectations about each other. Subjects were female students from two adjacent colleges. Although members of an ongoing social group, they participated in a short laboratory study. In this manner we were able to draw subjects from real social groups while retaining substantial control over their interactions. Subjects in the study interacted with a member of the out-group college over a 2-day period. The out-group member was a confederate who behaved in either a positive or a negative manner, and who appeared to be either very typical or atypical of the out-group. The experimental design was a 2 (college identity of confederate: Douglass College, Rutgers College) × 2 (behavior of confederate: positive, negative) × 2 (typicalness of confederate: high, low) between subjects factorial.

Method

Subjects

Subjects were 62 female undergraduates; 30 from Douglass College and 32 from Rutgers College. Eligibility was restricted to upperclasswomen who were not psychology majors. At the time of the research Douglass and Rutgers Colleges were two independent undergraduate Colleges comprising a part of Rutgers, the State University of New Jersey. Rutgers and Douglass women hold a fairly complementary set of stereotypes about each other (Wilder and Thompson, 1980). For instance, Rutgers women thought Douglass women were overly concerned with their appearance and good grades while Douglass women thought Rutgers women were interested in having a good time at the expense of scholarship. In addition, Douglass women were perceived to be rather conservative while Rutgers women were considered to be liberal. Pretesting indicated that students preferred their in-group college.

Procedure

The study was conducted in a classroom building a couple of miles away from the Rutgers psychology building. The confederate was blind to the hypotheses. The experimenter asked the subject and accomplice to wait in an adjacent room and introduce themselves while materials for the study were being assembled. The manipulation of typicalness occurred at this point.

Typical contact person   In half of the sessions the confederate dressed and presented herself in a manner designed to fit subjects' stereotypes of the out-group (either Douglass or Rutgers, depending, of course, on the college membership of the subject). When the confederate posed as a Douglass student, she wore a skirt and blouse and a moderate amount of makeup. She introduced herself as a junior from Douglass majoring in home economics (a major available only at Douglass). She mentioned that she hoped the experiment would be brief because she had a lot of studying to do. When the experimenter stated that subjects would have to return the next day to complete the study, she checked her appointment book to see if that conflicted with a meeting of her conservative political club. Thus, the typical Douglass student exhibited three characteristics (conservatism, neatness, studiousness) that were found in pretesting and earlier research to be attributed to Douglass women by Rutgers women (Wilder and Thompson, 1980).

When the confederate posed as a typical Rutgers student, she wore faded jeans, a plaid shirt that was too large, and no makeup. She introduced herself as a junior from Rutgers majoring in economics (one of the more popular majors at the college). She mentioned that she hoped the experiment would be brief because she had to get ready for a party that evening. When the experimenter stated that subjects would be required to return the next day, she checked her appointment book to see if that conflicted with a meeting of her liberal political club. Thus, compared to the typical Douglass student, the typical Rutgers woman was portrayed to be more liberal, less neat, and less studious.

Atypical contact person The confederate identified herself as a biological science major. When she hailed from Douglass College, the confederate dressed and behaved like the typical member from Rutgers College (as described above). When ostensibly a Rutgers student, she dressed and acted like the typical student from Douglass. Thus, the atypical contact person was the antithesis of what subjects expected a typical member of the out-group to be like.[1]

Once the introductions were completed, the experimenter led the participants to an adjacent room and asked them to sit in separate booths. He stated that he was interested in comparing the performance of groups of various sizes and member composition. The subjects were in the "two-persons-heterogeneous condition" because each was a student from a different college. He encouraged subjects to cooperate and do their best because their performance would be compared with that of other sized groups. This instruction was designed to promote cooperation between the participants because that has been shown to be an important condition for successful contact. Then the subject and confederate were given a set of problem-solving tasks that required 40 min to complete (short essays, anagrams, riddles). Each task was timed so that speed as well as accuracy affected the group's score. As they completed each task, they compared their responses by exchanging answer sheets between the booths. The pleasantness of the interaction was varied at this point.

Pleasant contact The confederate gave the correct or most popular responses to 60% of the exercises. (From pretesting, tasks had been selected so that subjects completed 70% of them within the time constraints.) In addition, the confederate wrote brief comments of approval about the subject's performance when she succeeded or agreed (e.g., "I agree," "good idea") and encouraging comments in response to failure or disagreement (e.g., "We'll do better next time," "I understand your opinion but feel differently").

Unpleasant contact The confederate succeeded on the same number of tasks. (Success was held constant so that any effect of the pleasant–unpleasant manipulation would be due solely to the affective relations between the two rather than to any differences in attributions about the confederate's competency.) But written reactions to the subject's performance were unhelpful and denigrating (e.g., "poor idea," "You blew it").

After completing the tasks, subjects were scheduled to return for a second session the following day. The tasks were similar but fewer, requiring a total of 20 min. The purpose of the second session was to reinforce the subject's initial impression of the out-group member. The accomplice's behavior was the same in both sessions, so it would be difficult for subjects to dismiss her behavior on the first day as due to some transitory mood or chance event. Again tasks were selected so that subjects and the confederate completed about 70% of them successfully.

At the conclusion of the second session, subjects completed a questionnaire designed to assess their impressions of the out-group member and their reactions to the study. Then the experimenter asked them if they would like to earn an extra dollar by completing a short questionnaire about college life ("Survey of College Life") for a colleague who taught at Livingston College (a third college in the Rutgers archipelago). In this manner the second questionnaire was dissociated from the subject's and confederate's colleges as well as the experimenter's study. Acting as a positive model, the confederate quickly agreed to do so, and all subjects followed suit. The second questionnaire contained items soliciting opinions about the five colleges in the Rutgers system (Cook, Douglass, Livingston, Rutgers, and University). At the top of the questionnaire there was a blank space in which the second experimenter indicated the college he was soliciting opinions about that day. He always wrote the out-group college (either Douglass or Rutgers) on each subject's questionnaire. After completing this questionnaire, subjects were debriefed and paid.

Finally, a fifth condition was included as a control or baseline. Subjects in this condition participated in the experiment individually. There was no confederate present at any time. They received the same instructions (with necessary modifications) and completed the same tasks, but there was no contact with a member of an out-group college.

Dependent measures

Three sets of measures were of particular interest: ratings of the contact person (confederate), evaluations of the out-group as a whole, and stereotypes of the out-group.

Three measures on the first questionnaire assessed subjects' reactions to the confederate. On 7-point bipolar scales they rated the helpfulness of the out-group person, their desire to have the out-group member as a partner again, and how typical the out-group member appeared to be of her college.

The second questionnaire, administered under the guise of a separate research project, contained three items evaluating the out-group as a whole. These were constructed as 11-point bipolar scales. (Eleven-point scales were used to make these items dissimilar in form from the seven-point items in the first questionnaire.) Two questions asked subjects to rate the quality of education and the quality of students at the out-group college. End points were labeled "poor" and "excellent." For the third item subjects indicated how strongly they would recommend that a high school acquaintance attend the out-group school. No item directly asked subjects whether they liked the out-group school. A direct query would be perceived as inappropriate in the context of the survey and would be highly reactive.

Three additional measures tapped stereotypes that members of the schools held about each other. Subjects were asked to rate women at "———College" (either Douglass or Rutgers) as a whole on the following 9-point scales: "conservative"–"liberal"; "neat"–"messy"; "studious"– "frivolous." These characteristics comprised part of the manipulation of typicalness described in the Procedure.

Results and discussion

Success of manipulations: ratings of the contact person

Helpfulness of partner   A $2 \times 2 \times 2$ analysis of this item revealed a main effect for the pleasantness factor, $F(1, 54) = 86.72$, $p < .001$. No other effects were significant. The confederate was rated as more helpful when she was pleasant ($M = 5.41$) than when she was critical ($M = 2.73$).

Desirability of partner   Again pleasantness was the only variable that had a significant impact, $F(1, 54) = 32.87$, $p < .001$. Subjects expressed greater willingness to work with the pleasant out-group member ($M = 5.14$) than the frustrating member ($M = 3.09$) on future tasks. Neither the college affiliation nor typicalness factors affected these ratings.

Typicalness of partner The 2 × 2 × 2 analysis yielded a marginal effect for college affiliation, $F(91, 54) = 3.55$, $p < .10$, and a strong effect for typicalness, $F(1, 54) = 21.11$, $p < .001$. Subjects rated the typical contact person as more typical of her college ($M = 4.90$) than the atypical out-group member ($M = 3.25$). Douglass subjects judged the contact person (allegedly from Rutgers) to be marginally more typical of her college ($M = 4.43$) than did Rutgers subjects ($M = 3.84$).

Evaluation of the out-group

It was hypothesized that pleasant behavior by a typical member of the out-group would generalize to a more positive evaluation of the out-group. Pleasant behavior by an atypical member or negative behavior by either a typical or atypical member would be ineffective in improving evaluations of the out-group as a whole. These hypotheses predict an interaction between the typicalness and pleasantness factors.

Quality of out-group college Two items assessed perceived quality of the out-group college: quality of education and quality of students. Data from these measures were significantly correlated, $r = .56$, $t(77) = 5.93$, $p < .01$. Responses were combined to form a single index of quality. The 2 × 2 × 2 analysis of these data revealed significant effects for the typicalness, $F(1, 54) = 4.02$, $p < .05$ and pleasantness factors, $F(1, 54) = 10.76$, $p < .001$. These effects were qualified by a significant typicalness × pleasantness interaction, $F(1, 54) = 6.80$, $p < .05$. As shown in the first line of table 17.5, subjects rated the out-group significantly more favorably when the contact person was typical and pleasant than in any of the other conditions.

Table 17.5 also includes data from the control condition in which subjects had no contact with an out-group member. (Data were collapsed across college affiliation because there were no differences between Rutgers subjects' ratings of Douglass and Douglass subjects' ratings of Rutgers.) Comparisons with the experimental conditions yielded a significant difference between the control group and the typical–pleasant condition, $t(29) = 2.53$, $p < .01$. Subjects in the latter condition were more favorable ($M = 5.93$) in their evaluation of the out-group than those in the control condition ($M = 4.71$).

Recommendation to a friend The main effect for pleasantness reached significance, $F(1, 54) = 9.73$, $p < .01$. Subjects recommended the out-group school more strongly when the contact person had been helpful ($M = 5.97$) than unhelpful ($M = 4.78$). The typicalness factor was marginally significant, $F(1, 54) = 3.36$, $p < .10$, but the typicalness × pleasantness interaction was not significant. Nevertheless, an examination of those means (second row of table 17.5) clearly indicate that the most favorable evaluation of the out-group (i.e., strongest recommendation) occurred when subjects had had pleasant contact with the typical out-group member. The typical–pleasant condition ($M = 6.57$) differed significantly from the typical–unpleasant ($M = 4.86$) and atypical–unpleasant conditions ($M = 4.63$) and marginally from the atypical–pleasant condition ($M = 5.37$).

Individual comparisons between the control and the four experimental conditions revealed that only the typical–pleasant condition differed significantly from the control, $t(29) = 2.69$, $p < .01$. Subjects who interacted with the helpful, typical member gave a more positive recommendation of the out-group ($M = 6.57$) than those who had had no contact with the out-group ($M = 5.06$).

Table 17.5   Evaluations of the out-group college (Experiment 1)

Measure	Pleasant contact		Unpleasant contact		
	Typical	Atypical	Typical	Atypical	Control
Quality of college	5.93ₐ	4.60_b	4.24_b	4.31_b	4.71_b
Recommend to friend	6.57ₐ*	5.37_ab*	4.86_b	4.63_b	5.06_b

Row means with completely different subscripts differed at the .05 level of significance or better (Fisher's LSD test). Means are based on 11-point scales.
*Mean values of 6.57 and 5.37 in the second row differed at the .15 level of significance (two-tailed).

Beliefs about the out-group

Conservatism   The Rutgers out-group was rated less conservative and more liberal ($M = 4.59$) than the Douglass out-group ($M = 5.63$), $F(1, 54) = 5.17$, $p < .05$. No other effects approached significance. These ratings did not differ significantly from the control means ($M = 4.75$ for ratings of Rutgers; $M = 6.11$ for ratings of Douglass). None of the contact manipulations affected subjects' beliefs about the conservatism of the out-group as a whole, even though the contact person expressed either a liberal or conservative orientation.

Neatness   Subjects attributed greater neatness to the Douglass out-group ($M = 6.47$) than the Rutgers out-group ($M = 5.25$), $F(1, 54) = 11.01$, $p < .001$. No other effects were significant. Control subjects also attributed greater neatness to Douglass ($M = 6.78$) than Rutgers ($M = 5.38$). Again, there was no evidence that the contact experience appreciably affected this belief about the respective out-groups.

Studiousness   The college × typicalness interaction reached significance, $F(1, 54) = 4.16$, $p < .05$ (table 17.6). Subjects thought the Douglass out-group more studious ($M = 6.20$) than the Rutgers out-group ($M = 4.81$) when they had interacted with the typical out-group member (who did, in fact, confirm this belief). But there was no difference between means when contact occurred with the atypical member. Differences in studiousness appears to be a weak assumption; although ordered as predicted, control means did not differ significantly for the Douglass and Rutgers out-groups.

Overall, there was no evidence that the contact manipulation affected subjects' stereotypes of the out-group on two measures (conservatism, neatness). For the studiousness item, however, contact with the typical out-group member appeared to reinforce the stereotype while contact with the atypical member diminished differences between groups. But this effect was small. Thus, unlike evaluations of the out-group, beliefs about the out-group seemed to be unchanged by the contact in this study.

The results of Experiment 1 have several implications. First, as hypothesized, the effectiveness of favorable contact with an out-group member on evaluations of the out-group depends on how typical the person is of her/his group. Second, changes in attitudes toward an out-group may occur without changes in stereotypes of the group (Brigham, 1971; Gurwitz and Dodge, 1997; Locksley, Hepburn, and Ortiz, 1982; Weber and Crocker, 1983). Contact with the pleasant, typical member of the out-group resulted in a more favorable evaluation of the out-

Table 17.6 Beliefs about the out-group; studiousness (Experiment 1)

Out-group	Experimental conditions		Control condition
	Typical contact	Atypical contact	
Douglass	6.20$_a$	5.40$_{a,b}$	5.89$_{a,b}$
Rutgers	4.81$_b$	5.50$_{a,b}$	5.25$_{a,b}$

Means with completely different subscripts differ at the .05 level of significance (Fisher's LSD test). Larger means indicate stronger attributions of studiousness.

group but no change in stereotypes of the out-group. Indeed, contact with a typical member may reinforce the prevailing stereotypes of the out-group because the contact person matches them so well.

But something about this argument does not seem quite right. If out-groups are disliked, in part, because they are thought to possess undesirable characteristics, then typical members will likely possess some of those undesirables. The more an out-group member confirms the negative expectations, the less effective he/she should be in producing a favorable evaluation of the out-group. Intuition suggests that the successful contact person be contrary to stereotypes of the out-group (e.g., Ashmore, 1970; Deutsch and Collins, 1951). The key to this apparent contradiction may lie in the specific stereotypes the contact person displays.

Stereotypes associated with the out-group vary in their relevance to the perceiver's in-group. Some stereotypes have direct implications, usually unfavorable, for the in-group (e.g., "they despise us"; "they think themselves superior to us") while others have no direct bearing on the in-group (e.g., "they are short"; "they are indolent"). The manipulation of typicalness in Experiment 1 employed beliefs about the out-group that had no direct references to the in-group (e.g., confederate's appearance, political orientation, studiousness, degree major). Furthermore, the contact person made no explicit comparisons between her group and the subject's in-group.

Experiment 2

A second experiment examined the effectiveness of contact with an out-group member who appeared to be very typical by confirming beliefs directly involving the subject's in-group. It was hypothesized that pleasant contact with this "typical" out-group member would be less successful than pleasant contact with the "typical" out-group member of Experiment 1. Employing the methodology of the first study, subjects had a pleasant interaction with an out-group member who confirmed stereotypes of the out-group that either involved no negative evaluation of the subject's in-group (irrelevant condition) or a negative evaluation of the in-group (relevant condition). Subjects in the irrelevant condition should generalize their positive experience with the contact person to a more positive evaluation of the out-group. But little generalization should occur in the relevant condition where the contact person, although pleasant, reinforced beliefs about the out-group that had negative implications for the in-group.

Method

Subjects

Subjects were 33 female undergraduates from Rutgers College. All were juniors and seniors; none were psychology majors. Three subjects expressed suspicion about the authenticity of the confederate's actions; their data were omitted. No subjects were recruited from Douglass College. Because there were no significant interactions involving college membership in Experiment 1, replication of this factor seemed an unnecessary expense.

Procedure

Typical-relevant condition   This condition was identical to the typical-pleasant condition of Experiment 1 with one qualification. In addition to displaying the "typical" characteristics described above, the contact person confirmed the belief that Douglass women thought themselves superior to Rutgers women. Pretesting had indicated that because Douglass College had maintained its original identity as a women's college. Douglass women were thought to be elitist. They were perceived to feel special and superior to those who chose to attend the coeducational colleges at Rutgers. The confederate capitalized on this belief by making some disparaging comparisons between Douglass and Rutgers. She mentioned during the introductions that she was offered a choice of attending Douglass or Rutgers. She was glad she chose Douglass because it provided women with a better opportunity to reach their potentials. She also felt that the Douglass campus was more beautiful than the Rutgers campus. Her experience taking courses at both colleges indicated that Douglass was more selective in attracting quality students and faculty. It is important to note that these comments were made at the beginning of the session, prior to participation in the tasks. The confederate was pleasant and helpful while working on the tasks.

Typical-irrelevant condition   The procedure was the same as in the preceding condition, with one modification. The target of the confederate's unfavorable comparisons was Livingstone College, not Rutgers College. Thus, the confederate's behavior was the same in both the relevant and irrelevant conditions. The only difference was whether the target of her elitist remarks was the in-group or another out-group.

Atypical-unpleasant-irrelevant condition (control)   This condition was identical to the atypical-unpleasant condition of Experiment 1. It was included to assess the effectiveness of the typicalness and pleasantness manipulations.

Dependent measures were the same as those employed in Experiment 1. Data from the items were analyzed in a single-factor design with three conditions.

Results and discussion

Success of manipulations: ratings of the contact person

Helpfulness   Conditions differed strongly, $F(2, 27) = 19.76$, $p < .001$. Subjects accurately reported that the partner was more helpful in the typical-relevant ($M = 5.10$) and typical-irrelevant conditions ($M = 5.50$) than in the control condition ($M = 2.60$).

Desirability   Subjects reported a greater desire to interact with the confederate when she was pleasant in the typical-irrelevant condition ($M = 5.30$) than when she was unpleasant in the control condition ($M = 3.00$), $F(2, 27) = 7.93$, $p < .01$. Although the confederate behaved pleasantly in the typical-relevant condition, she was viewed as significantly less desirable as a future partner ($M = 4.10$) than in the typical-irrelevant condition ($p < .05$). The typical-relevant and control conditions differed marginally ($p < .10$). Evidently the negative comments directed at the in-group poisoned the relationship between the subject and confederate somewhat, even though the latter's subsequent aid was recognized as such on the helpfulness item.

Typicalness   This manipulation was successful, $F(2, 27) = 5.24, p < .05$. Subjects rated the out-group member as more typical of the out-group in the typical-irrelevant ($M = 4.90$) and typical-relevant conditions ($M = 4.70$) than in the control condition ($M = 3.30$).

Overall, ratings of the confederate paralleled those found in the first study and indicated that the manipulations were successful.

Evaluation of the out-group
Quality of out-group college   Analysis of the combined scores for the quality of education and students measures yielded a significant effect, $F(2, 27) = 6.58, p < .05$ (Table 3). Ratings of the out-group were similar to those reported in Experiment 1 for the replicated typical-pleasant (typical-irrelevant in Experiment 2) and atypical-unpleasant (control in Experiment 2) conditions ($M = 6.30$ and $M = 4.90$, respectively). Subjects in the former condition evaluated the out-group more favorably. But evaluation of the out-group in the typical-relevant condition ($M = 5.08$) was no more favorable than in the control condition and significantly less positive than in the typical-irrelevant condition.

Recommendation to a friend   The same pattern of means emerged for this item, $F(2, 27) = 7.98$, $p < .01$ (table 17.7). Subjects in the typical-irrelevant condition were more willing to recommend the out-group college ($M = 6.90$) than were subjects in either the typical-relevant ($M = 5.50$) or control conditions ($M = 5.10$).

Stereotypes of the out-group   There were no differences among conditions on any of the three measures. Means for the two conditions replicated from Experiment 1 were nearly the same as those reported in Experiment 1. Condition means were as follows: conservatism, typical-relevant = 5.50, typical-irrelevant = 5.80, control = 5.10; neatness, typical-relevant = 5.90, typical-irrelevant = 6.00, control = 5.40; studiousness, typical-relevant = 5.70, typical-irrelevant = 6.00, control = 5.50.

In summary, Experiment 2 demonstrated that pleasant contact with a typical out-group

Table 17.7   Evaluations of the out-group college (Experiment 2)

	Condition		
	Typical-relevant	*Typical-irrelevant*	*Atypical-unpleasant (control)*
Quality of out-group college	5.08$_a$	6.30$_b$	4.90$_a$
Recommendation to a friend	5.50$_a$	6.90$_b$	5.10$_a$

Means with different subscripts differ at the .05 level of significance (Fisher's LSD test). Larger means indicate attributions of greater quality or a more favorable recommendation.

member can improve intergroup relations when the out-group member's typicalness is based on characteristics that do not involve negative actions directed at the in-group. Note that the typical out-group member confirmed a negative stereotype (elitism) in both the typical-relevant and irrelevant conditions. But it reduced the effectiveness of contact only when the target was the in-group. Thus, increasing the typicalness of contact persons will be counterproductive if that increase is purchased through the display of negative stereotypes involving the in-group.

Experiments 1 and 2 established the importance of the typicalness variable in contact settings. But neither study attempted to explain why the manipulation of typicalness led to the observed outcomes. A third study was designed to gather data relevant to the following explanations.

Consistency hypothesis If the typical out-group member closely fits the perceiver's image of the out-group, then the association between the typical member and the out-group category should be quite strong. Relative to the atypical member, the typical member is in a stronger unit relationship with the out-group, so pressures for a consistent evaluation of both should be greater (Heider, 1958). Consequently, the out-group as a whole benefits more from positive contact with the typical than the atypical member.

Representativeness hypothesis Because the typical out-group member possesses many of the characteristics thought to be common in the out-group, the typical member should be highly predictive of others in the out-group. Evidence that she is a pleasant, cooperative individual carries weight in judgments about the out-group as a whole. Although the pleasant, atypical member may be appreciated for her actions, her unrepresentativeness precludes generalizations from her behavior to the group as a whole.

Contrast hypothesis Given the existence of some intergroup animosity, pleasant contact should be less expected with the typical than the atypical out-group member. Favorable contact with the typical member may seem to be more positive than the same experience with the less typical member (analogous to contrast effects in interpersonal evaluations and judgments; e.g., Aronson and Linder, 1965; Sherif, 1967).

Status hypothesis Because the typical out-group member confirms more stereotypes of the out-group, she may be perceived as high in status and more influential than the less typical member. A pleasant interaction with the more powerful member may be more satisfying, resulting in a more favorable evaluation.

Two additional typotheses consider the possibility that the typicalness findings were unique to the population of Experiments 1 and 2. Perhaps the typical out-group member possessed more desirable characteristics than the less typical person (*desirability hypothesis*). Alternatively, the typical member may have been more similar than the atypical member to the perceiver (*similarity hypothesis*).

None of the six explanations is independent of the others. Nevertheless, to narrow the field somewhat, a third study was conducted partially replicating the first two experiments. Subjects interacted with a confederate who appeared to be a typical or atypical member of the out-group college. Then subjects were asked a set of questions that provided data relevant to the hypotheses outlined above.

Experiment 3

Method

Subjects
Twenty female undergraduates were recruited from Rutgers College. None were psychology majors and none were freshwomen.

Procedure
The purpose of Experiment 3 was to examine why the typical contact manipulation had a greater impact on evaluations of the out-group in the pleasant condition than the atypical manipulation. Subjects were randomly assigned to either of those two conditions from Experiment 1: typical-pleasant or atypical-pleasant conditions. The procedure of Experiment 1 was followed to the end of the first day's session. At that point subjects completed a questionnaire containing the dependent measures.

Dependent measures
The first item required subjects to list as much information about the other person (confederate) as they could remember "including what she told you, what she looked like, how she behaved, and anything else you can recall." Subjects were provided with 20 numbered blank lines to list information. No subject used more than 10 nor fewer than 5 lines. After completing this item, subjects turned to the second page and answered 9 questions constructed as 9-point scales. These questions were randomly ordered for each subject. At least one question was relevant to each of the interpretations of the typical/atypical finding. The number of questions was kept to a minimum to minimize potential artifacts due to demands and fatigue.

Consistency hypothesis The open-ended recall measure was examined for references to the contact person's affiliation with her in-group (Douglass College). To the extent the typical out-group member is perceived to be in a strong unit relationship with the out-group, that membership should be especially salient to the observer. Consequently, mention of the contact person's association with the Douglass group should occur more often and earlier in descriptions of the typical than the atypical member. This measure is a rough index of the perceived bond between the contact person and the out-group. Unfortunately, direct attempts to tap the "goodness of fit" between the typical manipulation and the out-group category proved fruitless with pretest subjects. (For instance, when asked how closely the typical member came to their image of the "ideal" out-group member, some subjects interpreted "ideal" as what they thought the out-group member ought to be like.) The recall item always appeared first in the questionnaire to avoid contamination by other measures that directed attention to specific aspects of the confederate.

Representativeness hypothesis Based on their interaction with the out-group member, subjects estimated the percentage of other out-group members (a) who had similar personalities and (b) who would behave like her. The 9-point scales were labeled from 10 to 90% in increments of 10.

Contrast hypothesis　On separate measures subjects rated (a) the helpfulness and (b) the extent to which they expected the contact person to behave as she did.

Status hypothesis　On 9-point scales subjects indicated (a) how influential and (b) how popular they thought the contact person was with her peers.

Desirability hypothesis　Subjects rated the extent to which the contact person possessed qualities that they would find desirable in a person.

Similarity hypothesis　Subjects rated the degree of similarity between the contact person and themselves.

　　Finally, subjects indicated how much they liked the out-group member based upon what they knew about her. A difference for the typical manipulation would be predicted by several of the hypotheses (Desirability, Similarity, Status, Contrast). Therefore, a significant difference would not be particularly supportive of any one interpretation, but no difference would help eliminate several hypotheses.

Results and discussion

Consistency hypothesis

All subjects mentioned the contact person's membership in the out-group (Douglass College) as part of their open-ended description of her. Interestingly, nearly twice as many subjects in the typical condition ($n = 7$) than in the atypical condition ($n = 4$) mentioned the out-group in the first half of their lists, suggesting a stronger connection between the typical member and her group. This difference, however, was not significant, $\chi^2(1) = .89$.

Representativeness hypothesis

Subjects who interacted with the typical out-group member thought that more others in the out-group shared her personality ($M = 5.60$, approximately 56%) than did subjects who interacted with the atypical out-group member ($M = 3.50$, approximately 35%), $t(18) = 3.04$, $p < .01$. Similarly, the behavior of the typical member was judged to be more predictive of the behavior of other out-group members in the typical condition ($M = 6.80$, approximately 68%) than in the atypical condition ($M = 4.90$, approximately 49%), $t(18) = 2.90$, $p < .01$. These findings suggest that the more positive evaluation of the out-group following contact with the typical member can be interpreted in terms of the ease with which subjects generalized from that person to others in the out-group. The personality and behavior of the typical member was considered to be more indicative of what others in the out-group would be like and how they would behave in that setting.

　　With one exception, analysis of the other measures failed to discern any differences between the typical and atypical conditions. Subjects like the contact person more when she was atypical ($M = 6.50$) than typical ($M = 5.50$) of her group, $t(18) = 2.07$, $p < .07$. Hence, there was no evidence to support the status, desirability, similarity, or contrast hypotheses. This does not necessarily mean that those interpretations have no impact on the success of intergroup contact; findings do suggest that they are inadequate explanations for the paradigm employed here.

General Discussion

There is consensus in the literature that face-to-face contact can be effective in improving intergroup relation if the contact occurs under cooperative conditions. The studies in this paper echoed that conclusion with pleasant, cooperative contact producing a more favorable evaluation of a rival out-group college. Moreover, the person with whom one has contact significantly affects the success of contact. Contact with a person who appeared to be highly typical of the out-group (i.e., matched several stereotypes of out-group members) led to a more favorable evaluation of the out-group than contact with a less typical member. Among the several possible interpretations of this finding, only one received support. Subjects judged the typical member's personality and behavior to be more indicative of how others in the out-group would act in the contact setting. Apparently, greater generalization of successful contact to evaluations of the out-group as a whole was due to the typical member being viewed as more predictive of the others in the out-group. Because she behaved favorably in the setting, there was a good chance that others would behave likewise.

Although contact with the out-group member affected evaluations of the out-group, contact had virtually no impact on stereotypes of the out-group. Subjects were no less likely to endorse prevailing stereotypes when the contact person was atypical than when she was typical. Perhaps a single contact experience is insufficient to change prevailing beliefs about the out-group as a whole; beliefs that may be based on multiple confirming examples (Rothbart, 1981). Characteristics of the contact person (e.g., neatness, studiousness, conservatism) may be "averaged" in some manner with the existing store of contact experiences, thereby diluting the effect of the present interaction. Multiple exceptions may also be subtyped without affecting beliefs about the out-group as a whole (Weber and Crocker, 1983). Rather than changing stereotypes, exceptions may simply reduce the likelihood of applying stereotypes in that setting (Gurwitz and Dodge, 1977; Locksley et al., 1982).

Alternatively, the construction of the measures may have facilitated a change in evaluation while hindering a change in beliefs about the out-group. The evaluation items (quality of education and students, recommendation to a friend) required that subjects make a global judgment of the out-group college. The stereotype measures (conservatism, neatness, studiousness) refer to more specific characteristics of out-group members; characteristics for which subjects can recall specific instances. Thus, the latter measures may have been more affected by frequency; that is, subjects were more likely to use other experiences with out-group members in responding to these items as well as the contact experience in the study.

Consideration of the typicalness factor in intergroup contact may help explain the mixed results that often follow contact. To cite one example, in an early study of intergroup contact Young (1932) had a class of graduate students interact over a semester with blacks who were quite favorable models and quite different from existing racial stereotypes (e.g., a doctor, a wealthy and cultured couple, a pianist). Despite the favorable contact over an extended period of time, attitude change was mixed. Some students showed little change; some became more prejudiced; and some became less prejudiced. With perfect hindsight one may wonder if the choices of "atypical" contact persons (relative to the students' expectations) contributed to the meager success of Young's project.

On the other hand, Hamill, Wilson, and Nisbett (1980) reported a strong effect for atypical information on judgments of an out-group. They provided subjects with a description of a humane prison guard who was atypical of guards in general. Subjects given that information judged prison guards to be more humane than a control group not provided with the exception to the rule. Their finding suggests that "contact" with an atypical member can have a powerful effect on evaluations of the out-group. On reflection, however, their work does not contradict our conclusions. In the Hamill et al. research, subjects were asked to make judgments about a group with which they had had little, if any, contact. Contrast that with situations in which subjects have had many contact experiences with both in-group and out-group members (e.g., racial groups, adjacent colleges). Even the "exception to the rule" should influence attitudes toward the out-group as a whole when both knowledge of the out-group and contact experiences are minimal.

The relationship found in Experiments 1 and 2 between typicalness of a contact person and attitude change toward the out-group presents a quandary for the individual out-group member who desires to elicit both a favorable reaction to his/her group and her/himself. Benefit from positive contact will accrue to the group to the extent the person is viewed as typical of his/her group. But maximum benefit for the individual may result from being dubbed an exception to the rule, particularly if that inference implies superior abilities and more favorable attributes relative to the "typical" out-group member. In our studies the atypical member was liked somewhat better than the typical member even though contact with the typical member was more beneficial to evaluations of the out-group as a whole.

In a relevant study Linville and Jones (1980) presented whites with a description of an applicant to law school who was either white or black and either well or poorly qualified. The black applicant was rated more favorably when well qualified and more unfavorably when poorly qualified than the comparable white applicant. Assuming whites have a narrower range of expected performance for blacks than whites (which would be consistent with the assumption of homogeneity in out-groups discussed in the introduction), one interpretation is that the qualified black was viewed as an exception, deserving of praise for rising above expectations. But a comparably qualified white was more "typical" of the broader expectations about the familiar in-group.

The fact that contact situations can become self-fulfilling prophecies further complicates an out-group member's dilemma. To the extent the person is perceived to be highly typical of the out-group, expectations about the out-group may influence the manner in which information is processed (e.g., Snyder, 1981). The degree of bias will be limited by the ease with which the contact person's behavior can be distorted. Clearly positive behavior, such as that found in Experiments 1 and 2, will be difficult to distort. But motives behind actions can always be questioned. For these reasons individual out-group members may attempt to maximize a positive evaluation of themselves by behaving so as to distance themselves from their group.

From this discussion of contact, it appears that members of a negatively evaluated out-group are in a bind. On the one hand, information that strengthens their association with their group should also strengthen the favorable impact of successful contact on evaluations of their group as a whole. But to the extent they appear to be typical of the out-group, they risk confirming unfavorable stereotypes about the out-group, thereby jeopardizing evaluations of themselves as individuals. On the other hand, information that weakens their association with the out-group may encourage more favorable evaluations of themselves as individuals. But to the extent they appear to be atypical of their group, successful contact should have less impact on evaluations of their group.

NOTE

[1] The atypical contact person matched stereotypes out-group members held about the subject's in-group. Perhaps subjects viewed the atypical person as similar to themselves. But remember that the stereotypes were those that each group had of the other; they were not beliefs subscribed to by subjects about their own groups. Pretesting had indicated that students at neither college shared the stereotypes each attributed to the other. Moreover, if the atypical member was more similar to the subject, that makes the hypotheses harder to confirm because they predicted the typical member would be the more effective representative of the out-proup.

REFERENCES

Allen, V.L., and Wilder, D.A. (1979). Group categorization and attribution of belief similarity. *Small Group Behavior*. 10, 73–80.

Allport, G.W. (1954). *The nature of prejudice*. Reading. MA: Addison-Wesley.

Amir, Y. (1976). The role of intergroup contact in change of prejudice and ethnic relations. In P.A. Katz (ed.), *Towards the elimination of racism*. New York: Pergamon.

Aronson, E., and Linder, D. (1965). Gain and loss of esteem as determinants of interpersonal attractiveness. *Journal of Experimental Social Psychology*, 1, 156–71.

Ashmore, R.D. (1970). Solving the problem of prejudice. In B.E. Collins (ed.), *Social psychology*. Reading, MA: Addison-Wesley.

Brigham. J.C. (1971). Ethnic stereotypes. *Psychological Bulletin*, 76, 15–38.

Brown, R.J., and Turner, J.C. (1981). Interpersonal and intergroup behavior. In J.C. Turner and H. Giles (eds), *Intergroup behavior*. Chicago: University of Chicago Press.

Deutsch, M., and Collins M. (1951). *Interracial housing: A psychological evaluation of a social experiment*. Minneapolis: University of Minnesota Press.

Gurwitz, S.B., and Dodge, K.A. (1977). Effects of confirmations and disconfirmations on stereotype-based attributions. *Journal of Personality and Social Psychology*, 35, 495–500.

Hamill, R., Wilson, T., and Nisbett, R. (1980). Insensitivity to sample bias: Generalizing from atypical cases. *Journal of Personality and Social Psychology*, 39, 578–89.

Heider, F. (1958). *The psychology of interpersonal relations*. New York: Wiley.

Linville, P.M., and Jones, E.E. (1980). Polarized appraisals of out-group members. *Journal of Personality and Social Psychology*, 38, 689–703.

Locksley, A., Hepburn, C., and Ortiz, V. (1982). Social stereotypes and judgments of individuals; An instance of the base-rate fallacy. *Journal of Experimental Social Psychology*, 18, 23–42.

Park, B., and Rothbart, M. (1982). Perception of out-group homogeneity and levels of social categorization: Memory for the subordinate attributes of in-group and out-group members. *Journal of Personality and Social Psychology*, 42, 1051–68.

Pettigrew, T.F. (1979). The ultimate attribution error: Extending Allport's cognitive analysis of prejudice. *Personality and Social Psychology Bulletin*, 5, 461–76.

Quattrone, G.A., and Jones, E.E. (1980). The perception of variability within ingroups and outgroups: Implications for the law of small numbers. *Journal of Personality and Social Psychology*, 38, 141–52.

Riordin, C. (1978). Equal-status interracial contact: A review and revision of a concept. *International Journal of Intercultural Relations*, 2, 161–85.

Rothbart, M. (1981). Memory processes and social beliefs. In D. Hamilton (ed.), *Cognitive processes in stereotyping and intergroup behavior*. Hillsdale, NJ: Erlbaum.

Sherif, M. (1967). *Group conflict and co-operation*. London: Routledge and Kegan Paul.

Snyder, M. (1981). On the self-perpetuating nature of social stereotypes. In D.L. Hamilton (ed.), *Cognitive processes in stereotyping and intergroup behavior*. Hillsdale, NJ: Erlbaum.

Tajfel, H., and Turner, J.C. (1979). An integrative theory of intergroup conflict. In W.G. Austin and S. Worchel (eds), *The social psychology of intergroup relations*. Monterey, CA: Brooks Cole.

Weber, R., and Crocker, J. (1983). Cognitive processes in the revision of stereotypic beliefs. *Journal of Personality and Social Psychology*, 45, 961–77.

Wilder, D.A. (1981). Perceiving persons as a group: Categorization and intergroup relations. In D.L. Hamilton (ed.), *Cognitive processes in stereotyping and intergroup behavior*. Hillsdale, NJ: Erlbaum.

Wilder, D.A. (in press). Predictions of belief homogeneity and similarity following social categorization. *British Journal of Social Psychology*.

Wilder, D.A., and Thompson, J.E. (1980). Intergroup contact with independent manipulation of in-group and out-group interaction. *Journal of Personality and Social Psychology*, 38, 589–603.

Young, D. (1932). *American minority peoples*. New York: Harper.

Part V
Epilogue

18   Applied Social Psychology

Social support and immune function among spouses of cancer patients

R.S. Baron, C.E. Cutrona, D. Hicklin, D.W. Russell and D.M. Lubaroff

Theoretical Background

Research on social support became fashionable during the 1970s, when health researchers developed an interest in the health consequences of being socially integrated. Although the relationship of social integration to health had been known a long time (e.g. Durkheim, 1897/1951; Farr, 1858/1994), the more recent interest was stimulated by a series of seminal lectures given in the mid-1970s (Cassel, 1976; Cobb, 1976) and fuelled by findings from prospective studies of large community samples which indicated that social support reduced mortality (e.g. Berkman and Syme, 1979; House et al., 1982). These studies found that individuals who lacked social integration (e.g. were unmarried, had few or no contacts with extended family or friends) at the time of the first measurement were more likely to die during the following nine-year period than individuals with more extensive contacts. This relationship was independent of physical health status at the time of the first measurement.

It is now well established that social support has beneficial effects on mental as well as physical health. It has further been shown that the positive health effect occurs not only when social support, as in the mortality studies, is measured in terms of the existence or quantity of social relationships (i.e. structural measures), but also when the individual's perception of the availability of others who provide certain support functions is assessed (i.e. perceived or functional social support). However, little is known about the processes which mediate this relationship. The issue of why having friends should make one live longer therefore remains something of a riddle. And to complicate matters even further, there is evidence that different mechanisms may be involved in mediating the impact of structural and of functional social support (Cohen and Wills, 1985).

With regard to functional social support, one of the most widely accepted hypotheses has been that it somehow protects (i.e.'buffers') individuals against the deleterious impact of

Journal of Personality and Social Psychology (1990), 59:344–52.

stressful life events (e.g. by making the event appear less stressful, or by directly influencing physiological processes). By linking social support to stress reduction, researchers were able to draw on knowledge about the physiological consequences of stress to account for the positive health effects of social support. One of the physiological consequences of stress, which had already been suggested by the pioneer of stress research Selye (1936), is that stress impairs the functioning of the immune system. It therefore seemed plausible that the protective effects of social support should be mediated by changes in immune functioning. And the study conducted by Baron and colleagues is one of the first to present evidence concerning the validity of this assumption.

Hypotheses

The extent to which individuals perceive social support will protect them against the impact of a stressful life event on their immune system. It is further assumed that social support has its positive effect on the immune system primarily by alleviating or preventing depression. Thus, depression (or better, lack of depression) is assumed to be a mediator of the protective effect of social support on immune function.

Design

The study is a field study with all measures taken at the same point in time (i.e. cross-sectional rather than prospective).

Method

Participants were spouses of urology cancer patients, thus undergoing a stressful life event (the incidence of additional life events was also measured with the Geriatric Social Readjustment Rating Scale; this was used a control variable).

Perceived social support was measured with the Social Provisions Scale, a scale assessing respondents' perception of the extent to which their relationships provide them with a number of different support functions (i.e. provisions). *Depressive symptoms* were measured with the Beck Depression Inventory (BDI), a widely used self-report instrument, which assesses the major symptoms of depression. *Immune function* was assessed using a number of different functional measures of immunocompetence (e.g. lympohocyte mitogen response, natural killer cell activity). These procedures measure how the immune system reacts to various agents. For example, the measure of the lymphocyte mitogen response examines how quickly each respondent's T-lymphocyte population proliferates (multiplies) in response to a 'mitogen' known to trigger such proliferation. The proliferation response to these mitogens is thought to model the body's response to challenge from infection. Thus, if an individual's immune system immediately dispatches a whole army of T-lymphocytes to attack the foreign intruder (i.e. the mitogen), we assume that it will do the same when attacked by some nasty bacteria. Each of the two mitogens was used in a number of different concentrations. The third functional measure of immunocompetence was an index assessing the ability of natural killer cells to destroy (or lyse) a target cell, an important index of a responsive immune system.

Results

Respondents were divided into high- and low-social-support groups on the basis of a median split. Data were analysed by means of mixed model analyses of variance (ANOVAs). Social support was used as a between-subject factor (i.e. high- and low-support groups contained different subjects). The measures of the immune system constituted a within-subject factor (i.e. repeated measures on the same subject, or in this case on the blood serum of these subjects). These analyses resulted in significant main effects of social support, for two of the three measures of immune function. Consistent with the hypotheses, subjects in the high-social-support group showed superior immune functioning.

To examine whether the positive association between social support and immunocompetence was mediated by depression, analyses of covariance (ANCOVAs) were used. These analyses allow one to determine whether social support affects immunocompetence only to the extent that it prevents depressive reactions to stressful events. If this is so, then statistically controlling for the level of depression by introducing the scores on the depression measure as covariate should eliminate the association between social support and measures of immune functioning. There was no evidence for mediation by depression.

Discussion

The findings of this study demonstrate that individuals who experience a severe and chronic life stress show evidence of better immunity if they experience high rather than low levels of social support. Thus, this study improves our understanding of the physiological processes which mediate the relationship between a psychological event (namely the perception of social support) and some physical health outcome. The assumption that we have to react with depression to stress in order for our immune system to be affected was not supported. This latter findings suggests that stress may impair our immune system even while we seem to be coping well and dealing with the stressful event without letting it get us down.

FURTHER READING

Cohen, S. and Wills, T.A. (1985). Stress, social support and buffering. *Psychological Bulletin*, 98, 310–57. Classic review article reconciling apparent inconsistencies in the social support literature by demonstrating that buffering vs. main effects of social support on health occur under different conditions.

House, J.S., Landis, K.R. and Umberson, D. (1988). Social relationships and health. *Science*, 241, 540–5. Reviews the major studies on the relationship between social integration and mortality.

REFERENCES

Berkman, L.F. and Syme, S.L. (1979). Social networks, host resistance, and mortality: A nine-year follow-up of Alameda County residents. *American Journal of Epidemiology*, 109, 186–204.

Cassel, J. (1976). The contribution of the social environment to host resistance. *American Journal of Epidemiology*, 104, 107–23.

Cobb, S. (1976). Social support as mediator of life stress. *Psychosomatic Medicine*, 38, 300–14.

Durkheim, E. (1897/1951). *Suicide: A Study in Sociology*. Glencoe, IL: Free Press.

Farr, W. (1858/1994). Influence of marriage on the mortality of the French People. In N. Humphreys (ed.), *Vital Statistics: A Memorial Volume of Selections from Reports and Writings of William Farr* (pp. 438–41). New York: Methuen (originally published in 1958).

House, J.S., Robbins, C. and Metzner, H.L. (1982). The association of social relationships and activities with mortality: prospective evidence from the Tecumseh Community Health Study. *American Journal of Epidemiology*, 116, 123–40.

Selye, H. (1936). A syndrome produced by diverse nocous agents. *Nature*, 138, 32.

- - - - -
Primary
Reading
- - - - - - - -

In recent years, social support has been found to have beneficial effects on a wide variety of health-related variables (e.g., Cobb, 1976; Cohen and Syme, 1985; Cutrona, Russell, and Rose, 1986; Jemmott and Locke, 1984; Pennebaker and O'Heeron, 1984; Seeman, Kaplan, Knudsen, Cohen, and Guralnik, 1987), and to buffer the physical and psychological effects of a wide range of stressors, including the death of a spouse (Pennebaker and O'Heeron, 1984), natural catastrophe (Murphy, 1984) and job loss (Linn, Sandifer, and Stein, 1985). In a recent review, House, Landis and Umberson (1988) point out that there are at least six prospective, large sample field studies in which mortality rates are substantially higher among those individuals in the sample who are lowest in social integration. They argue that the strength of the data linking social support variables to health outcomes is approximately as strong as that linking smoking to cancer in the 1964 Surgeon General's report. Given the generality and importance of these effects, several writers have emphasized the need to explore possible mechanisms linking social support and physical health (Cohen and Wills, 1985; Wortman, 1984). At least one possibility in this regard is that social support may in some way affect the immune system (Cohen, 1988; Jemmott and Locke, 1984), thereby influencing a wide variety of health-related outcomes.

This suggestion seems quite plausible given recent research in psychoneuroimmunology. There are now a number of studies indicating that psychological variables can affect the immune system. For example, research has established that various forms of stress can impair immunological functioning, including overcrowding (Boranic, Pericic, and Radicic, 1982), bereavement (Bartrop, Luckhurst, Lazarus, Kiloh, and Penny, 1977), marital strife (Kiecolt-Glaser, Fisher, et al., 1987), life-event stress (Dorian, Keystone, Garfinkel, and Brown, 1982), and academic examinations (Kiecolt-Glaser, Glaser, Strain, et al., 1986; Jemmott and Locke, 1984). In one study (Schleifer, Keller, Camerino, Thornton, and Stein, 1983), for example, spouses of women with advanced breast cancer were found to have deficiencies in T lymphocyte function. Other studies indicate that behavioral control and relaxation training improve immune functioning in times of stress (e.g., Jemmott and Magloire, 1988; Kiecolt-Glaser and Glaser, 1987; Kiecolt-Glaser, Glaser, Strain, et al., 1986; Kiecolt-Glaser, Glaser, et al., 1985; Maier and Laudenslager, 1985).

The current study was designed to examine the effects of social support on immunocompetence. Although there are very few studies addressing the association between interpersonal factors and the immune system, those data that exist are quite consistent with the view that social support may influence the ability of the immune system to respond to pathogens. Several studies indicate that lonely individuals have poorer immune function than nonlonely individuals (Kiecolt-Glaser, Garner, et al., 1984; Kiecolt-Glaser, Glaser, et al., 1987; Kiecolt-Glaser, Ricker, George, et al., 1984). Only two studies to date have examined the association between social support and immune function. In a community sample of the elderly, higher levels of social support were associated with total lymphocyte count and the ability of lymphocytes to subdivide when stimulated by a mitogen (Thomas, Goodwin, and Goodwin, 1985). Jemmott and Magloire (1988), focusing on a different measure, found that students with more adequate social support had superior immune functioning before, during, and after exam periods than did those with less adequate social support, as reflected by salivary measures of secretory immunoglobulin A.

This study extends these initial findings by testing the contribution of each of six different components of social support to blood-based measures of immune function among individuals exposed to substantial stress: the treatment of their spouse for urologic cancer. Furthermore, the role of depressive affect in the relation between social support and immunocompetence was examined. Specifically, we attempted to test whether the association between social support and immune function was due to the effects of social support on depressive affect, which may lead more directly to effects on immune function. In essence, a mediational model was tested in which social support effects immunocompetence only to the extent that it leads to lower levels of depressive symptoms. Finally, it has been argued that the apparent relation between social support and health outcomes may be due to the effect of social support on number of negative life events experienced, such that individuals with higher social support experience fewer negative life events (Thoits, 1982). Thus, a second mechanism by which low levels of social support may affect immunocompetence is through increasing the experience of stressful life events, which in turn may directly affect immune-system functioning. To provide some data on this issue, we administered a life-events' inventory so that we could ascertain whether the relation between social support and health was effected when life-events' scores were partialed out.

Components of Social Support

Most researchers argue that perceived social support can usefully be analyzed into several different components. Weiss (1974), for example, hypothesizes six different components or interpersonal provisions. These provisions include both instrumental and emotional forms of support. In Weiss's scheme, the instrumental provisions include reliable alliance (knowledge that one can count on tangible aid when it is needed) and guidance (advice and information from a trusted source). Emotional support provisions include reassurance of worth (recognition of one's abilities and competence), attachment (closeness and intimacy that foster a sense of security), social integration (belonging to a group with similar interests and concerns), and the opportunity to provide nurturance (feeling that one is needed by others). It is quite possible that some of these dimensions of support are more closely linked to immune function than others. In this study, we used a multidimensional measure of social support that assessed each of Weiss's six provisions, to permit an assessment of whether these factors relate to immune response in a differential fashion.

Mediation by Depression and Life Events

As previously mentioned, a question that remains unanswered is the role of depression in the tentatively established relation between social support and immunity. It has been proposed that depression may be a crucial mediating variable in this relation (Cohen and Wills, 1985; Jemmott and Magloire, 1988). Depression (especially during times of stress) may elevate the release of corticosteroids and catecholamines, substances known to produce immunosuppression (Borysenko and Borysenko, 1982). Consistent with this view, depression has been directly associated with impaired immunological functioning in several studies (e.g., Krueger, Levy, Cathcart, Fox, and Black, 1984; Linn, Linn, and Jenson, 1982). As a result, it seems possible that social support may have its effect on immunity primarily by alleviating or preventing depression, thereby damping the release of corticosteroids and catecholamines. A consistent finding in the social support literature is a negative correlation between social support and depression (see review by Kessler, Price, and Wortman, 1985). This association, however, does not rule out the possibility that social support and depression might have independent effects on immunity. This study addresses this issue by administering a well-known depression measure and using covariance analysis to examine the independent contribution of social support to immunity after variation in immunocompetence explainable by depression has been statistically controlled.

In an influential article, Thoits (1982) argued that the most frequently used method for evaluating the extent to which social support protects against the deleterious effects of negative life events actually confounds the effects of social support and life events. To the extent that individuals with high levels of social support are able to avoid negative events (e.g., as the result of guidance or assistance from others), typical analytic strategies do not distinguish between a direct effect of support upon health and an indirect effect, in which support is only beneficial to the extent that it lowers the number of negative life events encountered. All of the participants in the current study were experiencing the stress of a spouse afflicted by cancer, but it was anticipated that participants would vary in the number of additional negative life events encountered. The study sought to test directly the extent to which the effect of social support on immune function was mediated by the number of negative life events experienced.

Immune Function Assessment

The present research relied on three often used functional measures of immunocompetence. These measurement techniques go beyond assessing the basal level of key immunological components. Rather, these procedures assess how the immune system reacts to various agents. Accordingly, two of these measures examine how quickly each subject's T-lymphocyte population proliferates in response to mitogen known to trigger such proliferation. Two such mitogens are the plant lectins (i.e., seed extracts), phytohemagglutinin (PHA) and concanavalin A (Con-A), both of which stimulate T-lymphocyte proliferation. The proliferation response to these mitogens (referred to as *blastogenesis*) is thought to model the body's response to challenge from infection (Kiecolt-Glaser et al., 1985).[1]

Since different mitogens can affect lymphocytes uniquely, the present study used both Con-A and PHA as mitogenic agents. Similarly, since each batch of mitogen varies in its ability to stimulate cell division, we followed the usual procedure of conducting a variety of assays at differing mitogen concentrations. In these assays, the mitogen/lymphocyte mixtures are "bathed" in radioactive thymidine. A portion of this thymidine is incorporated into the DNA of the cell during cell division. As a result, after the excess thymidine is removed from solution, one can infer the degree of proliferation from the beta count in the assay. The amount of proliferation in response to Con-A and PHA represent our first two measures of immune response.

Our third functional measure of immunocompetence was an index assessing the ability of NK cells to destroy (or lyse) a target cell, an important index of a responsive immune system. In this assay, the target, a K 562 human myeloid (tumor) cell line (well known to be sensitive to lysis by NK cells), is fed a radioisotope that is incorporated into the cell. If lysis occurs then, the radioisotope will be released and detectable as an increase in the gamma count. Different effector (NK): target (K 562) ratios were used.

In addition to these dynamic measures of immunity, we used flow cytometry analyses to assess the overall percentage of lymphocytes and T-lymphocytes in the peripheral blood.

Method

Participants

Participants were spouses of urology cancer patients being seen at the University of Iowa hospitals and clinics. Thirty spouses of patients being treated for renal, bladder, prostate, or testicular cancer were asked to participate; 24 (80%) agreed, with one of these individuals being eliminated due to the use of medication. At the time of the study, the participants' spouses were undergoing extensive chemotherapy or radiation treatment or both, or they were at the end stages of their disease. After screening participants for medication and health problems, the final sample consisted of 2 men and 21 women.[2] The mean age for participants was 48.2 years, with approximately half of the sample over age 50 (range = 32 to 75 years).

Procedure

After a brief explanation of the study and obtaining informed consent, subjects were asked to complete three self-report questionnaires. Subjects completed measures of social support (Social Provisions Scale; Cutrona and Russell, 1987; Russell and Cutrona, 1984), depressive symptoms (Beck Depression Inventory, BDI; Beck, Ward, Mendelson, Mock, and Erbaugh, 1961), and life events (Geriatric Social Readjustment Rating Scale; Amster and Krauss, 1974). The approximate time to complete all three measures was 20 min. On completion of the self-report measures, blood samples were drawn by peripheral venipuncture into heparinized collection tubes. Within 1 hr after collection, samples were subjected to immunological analysis as described below. All samples were obtained between 8:30 a.m. and 11:00 a.m. when subjects accompanied their spouses to the hospital for cancer treatment. As a result, the data should be minimally affected by diurnal variation (Carandente, Angeli, De Vecchi, Dammacco, and Hallberg, 1988).

Self-report measures

Social support

Perceived social support was assessed using the Social Provisions Scale (Cutrona and Russell, 1987; Russell and Cutrona 1984). This scale was developed to assess the six relational provisions identified by Weiss (1974). The measure asks respondents to rate the degree to which their social relationships are currently supplying each of the provisions (guidance, reliable alliance, reassurance of worth, social integration, attachment, and opportunity to provide nurturance). Each provision is assessed by four items, two that describe the presence and two that describe the absence of the provision. For example, two of the items on the attachment subscale are "I have close relationships that provide me with a sense of emotional security and well-being," and "I lack a feeling of intimacy with another person." Reliability for the total support score in a previous study of elderly adults was .92, with reliabilities of the 4-item subscales ranging from .76 to .84 (Cutrona et al., 1986). Intercorrelations among subscales range from .27 to .74 ($M =$ .483 following an r to z transformation.) Confirmatory factor analysis supports the six-factor structure of the measure, and consistent differences in patterns of association with various outcome variables have been found for the six provisions (for a review, see Cutrona and Russell, 1987). Several studies provide evidence for the validity of the Social Provisions Scale among adolescent mothers (Cutrona, 1989), the elderly (Cutrona et al., 1986), public school teachers (Russell, Altmaier, and Van Velzen, 1987), and hospital nurses (Constable and Russell, 1986; Cutrona and Russell, 1987). The discriminant validity of the scale has been demonstrated against measures of mood (e.g., depression), personality (e.g., introversion–extraversion, neuroticism), and social desirability (Cutrona and Russell, 1987, 1990).

Negative life events

The incidence of major life events in addition to the spouse's illness was assessed using the Geriatric Social Readjustment Rating Scale (Amster and Krauss, 1974). This checklist consists of events that were judged by a group of gerontologists to be relevant to the life experiences of older adults. Previous studies of the elderly have found that scores on this measure are significantly related to measures of physical and mental health among the elderly (Amster and Krauss, 1974; Cutrona et al., 1986), supporting the validity of the measure. Only unambiguously negative events that cannot be explained as symptoms of psychiatric disorder were included in the version of the scale that we administered.

Depressive symptoms

The level of depressive symptoms was assessed with the BDI, a widely used 21-item self-report instrument. Validity of the scale for use with older adults has been documented (Gallagher, Breckenridge, Steinmetz, and Thompson, 1983).

Measures of immune function

Lymphocyte mitogen response

Measurement of the response of peripheral blood mononuclear cells to the mitogens PHA (Sigma) and Con-A (Sigma) were measured by [³H] thymidine incorporation microculture assay (Greiner, Reynolds, and Lubaroff, 1982). Briefly, mitogens were used at a final concentration of 1.0, 2.0, 4.0, 8.0 and 16.0 µg/ml for Con-A and .188, .38, .75, 1.5 and 3.0 µg/ml for

PHA. In this assay, the number of lymphocytes is held constant while the amount of mitogen varies. Fifty microliters of mitogen was added to 6×10^5 lymphocytes in 96 well flat-bottom microtitration plates (Costar) and incubated at 37° in a humidified chamber with an atmosphere of 5% CO_2 for 48 hr. Twenty microliters of tritiated thymidine (.5 μCi) was added to each well and the plates incubated at 37°C for 12 hr. Cells were harvested by aspiration onto glass fiber filters (Whatman GF/A) and radioactivity measured using a Beckman model beta scintillation counter.

NK assay

Natural killer cell activity was determined by a microtiter [51]Chromium release assay (Lubaroff, Reynolds, and Culp, 1979). Blood samples were diluted 1:2 in Rosewell Park Memorial Institute (BPMI) 1640 medium and a 20 ml diluted sample was layered onto 10 ml of Histopaque 1077 (Sigma). Samples were then centrifuged at 1,600 g for 25 min in a Sorvall RC3 centrifuge. Mononuclear cells were collected from the interface and washed by centrifugation three times to remove all Histopaque. The final cell pellet was resuspended in complete medium consisting of RPMI 1640 supplemented with 1% sodium pyruvate, 1% L-glutamine, 1% Eagles nonessential amino acids, and 10% heat inactivated fetal calf serum (Hyclone). Lymphocyte cell counts were determined by Coulter Counter and adjusted accordingly to 1×10^7 with complete media.

The myeloid cell line, K562, was used as the target cell in the assay. Target cells (5×10^6) were labeled with 100 μCi of the radioisotope $Na_2^{51}CrO_4$ (Amersham) for 30 min at 37°C. Cells were then washed twice and counted. Target cell concentration was adjusted to 1×10^5/ml in complete medium.

Serial 2-fold dilutions of the original lymphocyte suspension were added in triplicate 100 μl aliquots to wells of 96-well, conical bottom tissue culture plates (Costar) containing 100 μl of target cell suspensions. This produced NK to target cell ratios of .78, 1.56, 3.12, 6.25, 12.5, 25.0, 50.0, and 100.0. In addition, wells containing only target cell suspensions, and wells containing targets and detergent (1% NP40) were prepared to determine spontaneous released radioactivity and maximal lysis.[3] Plates were then centrifuged at 300 g for 5 min and incubated for 4 hr in a humidified incubator at 37°C with an atmosphere of 5% CO_2.

After incubation, plates were centrifuged at 800 g for 7 min and then 100 μl of supernatant was harvested from each well. Supernatants were counted on a Beckman 300-System gamma counter. Results are reported as percent lysis using the formula:

$$\% \text{ lysis} = \frac{\text{Experimental CPM} - \text{Spontaneous CPM}}{\text{Maximal CPM} - \text{Spontaneous CPM}} \times 100,$$

where CPM equals gamma counts per min.

This formula assesses what percentage of the maximal cell destruction (maximal being the proportion achieved with a detergent) occurs in a given NK/target cell sample after controlling for effects of spontaneous cell destruction occurring in the absence of NK activity.

Total lymphocyte and T-cell populations

The antihuman T-cell fluoresceine isothiocyanate (FITC) conjugated monoclonal antibody OKT11 (Ortho Diagnostics) was added (10 μl) to 100 μl of well-mixed whole blood. As a control, 10 μl of phosphate buffered saline (PBS; .01 M phosphate, .15 M NaCl) was added to a duplicate sample. Blood samples were mixed and incubated in an ice water bath for 30 min with occasional shaking. Following ice water incubation, samples were incubated at room temperature in lysing solution provided with the anti-T-cell antibody for 10 min and then collected by centrifugation at 4°C. Samples were then resuspended in 500 μl of cold PBS and analyzed immediately on a Beckton–Dickinson FACS IV cell sorter (flow cytometer).

Results

Descriptive statistics

Means and standard deviations for the full sample on the Social Provisions Scale, the BDI, and the Geriatric Social Readjustment Rating Scale are shown in table 18.1. When compared with published norms for the Social Provisions Scale ($N = 1,792$; Cutrona and Russell, 1987), means obtained in the current sample were about one standard deviation below those for community dwelling adults, suggesting a lower level of perceived social support. Social provision scores also appeared to be more variable in this sample compared to normative data. Specifically, the spouses of cancer patients showed greater variation than normative samples in terms of overall support ($SD = 16.4$ vs. 9.9), reliable alliance ($SD = 3.7$ vs. 1.9), and guidance ($SD = 3.4$ vs. 2.2). Mean number of negative life events (total score on the Geriatric Readjustment Rating Scale) reported by participants in the current study (2.2) was similar to the mean of 2.0 found in a community sample of elderly men and women using the identical measure (Cutrona et al., 1986). Mean scores on the BDI were higher than the mean ($M = 5.54$) reported by Gallagher, Nies, and Thompson (1982) for a community sample of elderly individuals. Although six

Table 18.1   Sample means and standard deviations for all measures

Measure	M	SD
Social Provisions Scale		
Reliable alliance	11.8	3.7
Guidance	11.6	3.4
Attachment	12.3	2.8
Social integration	12.3	2.7
Reassurance of worth	12.0	2.5
Opportunity to provide nurturance	12.1	2.3
Total support	72.1	16.4
Beck Depression Inventory	6.7	3.2
Negative life events	2.2	1.4
Immune function		
T-lymphocyte proliferation-PHA	4892.5	835.5
T-lymphocyte proliferation-Con-A	4060.8	374.1
Killer cell activity (percent lysis)	22.3	3.3
Percentage of lymphocytes	26.0	5.7
Percentage of T-lymphocytes	79.1	6.4

$N = 23$.

individuals (26%) scored in the range of *mild depression* (total scores of 10 to 14), no one scored in the *moderate* or *severe* depression range. Although scores on a self-report depression scale cannot be used to make accurate diagnoses, these results do not suggest a high prevalence of clinical depression in this sample.

Mean scores for the sample on the measures of immune function are also shown in table 18.1. In the table, values are averaged across concentration levels.

Effects of social support on immune function

After performing a median split on the total social provisions score (*Mdn* = 74.0), the PHA, Con-A, and NK data were each analyzed in repeated-measures ANOVA in which assay concentration was treated as the repeated factor. These ANOVAs used the multivariate approach for estimating the effects of the repeated measures factor (O'Brien and Kaiser, 1985).[4] High and low social support constituted a between-subjects factor.

PHA *assay*
The dependent variable in this assay and in the assay for Con-A was the difference between the amount of proliferation occurring at each concentration level (i.e., induced by some amount of mitogen) and that occurring spontaneously without mitogenic stimulation (Greiner et al., 1982). Since assays were conducted in triplicate, the measure used to represent these delta scores was the average (beta) CPM across the three samples at each concentration level.

Subjects reporting high social support had significantly higher delta scores (indicating greater T-cell proliferation in response to mitogenic stimulation) than subjects low in social support, $F(1, 21) = 5.86$, $p < .05$. In addition, delta scores were higher as the concentration of mitogen increased, $F(4, 18) = 240.62$, $p < .001$. The interaction between social support and concentration was not statistically significant. These results are presented in figure 18.1.

Con-A *assay*
Proliferation measures in response to Con-A were constructed in the same manner as scores for PHA. In an ANOVA testing the effects of social support and concentration on Con-A

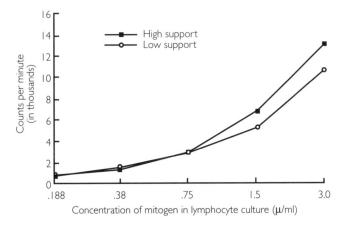

Figure 18.1 T-cell proliferation in response to phytohemagglutinin (PHA) as a function of concentration level and high versus low social support

stimulated proliferation, the only significant effect was the main effect for concentration, $F(4, 18) = 1539.70, p < .001$, with greater delta scores occurring at higher mitogen concentrations. Neither the main effect for social support nor the interaction between social support and concentration attained statistical significance.

NK cell assay

As noted previously, the dependent variable in this assay was the percent lysis occurring at each concentration (see Method section for formula). This measure represented the percentage of maximum possible cell destruction that was produced in a given NK/target cell sample. Once again, since assays at each concentration were conducted in triplicate, the score used to derive percent lysis was the average gamma count per minute averaged across the three samples. The results for NK mirrored the PHA results. Those high in social support had significantly higher percent lysis scores than those low in social support, $F(1, 21) = 7.91, p < .01$. In addition, there was a significant effect of concentration, $F(7, 15) = 272.35, p < .001$, with greater lysis occurring at stronger concentrations (i.e., where the effector:target cell ratio was greater). The interaction between social support and concentration was not statistically significant (see figure 18.2).

Thus, both the PHA and NK assays indicate that immune function is relatively more robust among individuals reporting high levels of social support. Although the interaction between social support and concentration was not significant in either of these assays, examination of figures 18.1 and 18.2 indicate that these effects are largely manifested at higher concentration levels.

Flow cytometry analyses

In addition to the dynamic measures of immune function, we also used flow cytometry analysis to assess the overall percentage of lymphocytes in the peripheral blood sample and to assess what percentage of the effectors were T cells. These assays were done in batches with no more than 3 subjects' data included in any one batch. In the analysis of the overall percentage of lymphocytes, the equivalent measure (% lymphocytes) was taken from a normal control subject

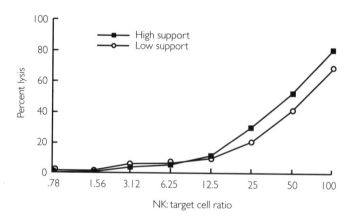

Figure 18.2   Natural killer (NK) cell activity (percent lysis) as a function of NK:target cell ratio and high versus low social support

for each batch. Blood samples from the experimenter (D.H.) were used to generate these control data for all batches. This control value was used as a covariate to adjust for variations in instrumentation. A one-way analysis of covariance (ANCOVA) on percentage of lymphocytes was conducted, with control percentage of lymphocytes used as a covariate and social support (high vs. low) as the independent variable. The main effect for social support was not significant, $F < 1$. Similarly, the main effect for social support on percentage of T-lymphocytes was not significant, $F < 1$.

The absence of statistically significant differences in total lymphocyte or T-lymphocytes between subjects high and low in social support despite significant differences in their ability to proliferate to PHA is not surprising. Results from the present study are consistent with a number of prior studies that find that functional measures of immunocompetence (e.g., mitogeninduced proliferation, cytotoxicity) are generally more consistently affected by psychological variables than are simple quantitative measures provided by the flow cytometry analyses (Calabrese et al., 1987; Kiecolt-Glaser and Glaser, 1988).[5] In addition, the differences between social support groups in the proliferative capacity of T-cells could be a function of changes in T-lymphocyte subset populations (e.g., CD4) not analyzed in these flow cytometry assays.

Depression as a mediating variable

To determine whether the relation between social support and immune function was mediated by level of depressive symptoms, a series of ANCOVAs was conducted. These analyses were designed to determine whether social support only affects immunocompetence to the extent that it prevents depressive reactions to stressful circumstances. If this is so, then statistically controlling for level of depression should eliminate the association between social support and measures of immune function.

Each subject's score on the BDI was used as a covariate in examining the impact of social support on PHA proliferation and NK activity to assess the extent to which the effects reported earlier were mediated by depression. The main effects for social support were largely unchanged for both PHA, $F(1, 20) = 4.91$, $p < .05$, and for NK, $F(1, 20) = 6.71$, $p < .05$. Furthermore, the effects of depression as a covariate were not statistically significant in either analysis. Thus, in the current study, no evidence was found for mediation by depression of the relation between social support and immune function.

Effects of additional negative life events

It has been argued that the effects of social support on health can be explained by the fact that individuals who have high levels of social support experience fewer negative life events (Thoits, 1982). That is, social support only enhances health outcomes to the extent that it prevents negative life events. To test the extent to which number of negative life events beyond the spouse's illness may mediate the relation between social support and immune function, a set of ANCOVAs was conducted parallel to the those reported above for depression, covarying scores on the life events measure (Geriatric Social Readjustment Rating Scale). Results showed that when statistically controlling for number of negative life events, the main effect of social support remained significant in both the analyses of PHA activity, $F(1, 20) = 6.60$, $p < .05$, and NK activity, $F(1, 20) = 4.89$, $p < .05$. Thus, no evidence was found that social support's effect on immune function was due to its effect on the number of negative life events reported by the spouse. Furthermore, negative life events did not emerge as a significant covariate in the analysis, so evidence was not found for an additional independent effect of life events on immunocompetence beyond the spouse's illness.

Individual components of social support

To determine whether the various components of social support relate differentially to immune function, the six subscales of the Social Provisions Scale (guidance, reliable alliance, attachment, social integration, reassurance of worth, and opportunity to provide nurturance) were correlated with overall immune function scores (averaged across concentration levels). These

Table 18.2 Simple correlations between social support and immune-function measures

Measure	Con-A proliferation	PHA proliferation	Killer cell activity
Reliable alliance	−.01	.70***	.53**
Guidance	−.03	.63**	.56**
Attachment	.05	.65**	.54**
Social integration	−.03	.62**	.56**
Reassurance of worth	−.07	.56**	.59**
Opportunity to provide nurturance	−.27	.53**	.41*
Total support	−.05	.66***	.57**

$N = 23$.
*$p < .05$.
**$p < .01$.
***$p < .001$.

Table 18.3 Partial correlations between social support and immune-function measures controlling for depression and life events

Measure	Control for depression			Control for life events		
	Con-A	PHA	Killer cell activity	Con-A	PHA	Killer cell activity
Reliable alliance	−.04	.69***	.51**	−.02	.69***	.47*
Guidance	−.06	.62**	.54**	−.04	.65**	.52**
Attachment	.02	.63**	.53**	−.04	.66***	.49**
Social integration	−.08	.59**	.53**	−.05	.63**	.49*
Reassurance of worth	−.11	.54**	.57**	−.08	.57**	.57**
Opportunity to provide nurturance	−.32	.51**	.38**	−.29	.55**	.35
Total support	−.10	.65**	.55**	−.07	.69***	.52**

$N = 23$.
*$p < .05$.
**$p < .01$.
***$p < .001$.

data are presented in table 18.2. The correlations indicate that all six subscales are strongly related to immune function as measured in the PHA and NK assays.[6] The percentage of variance in immune function accounted for by the various social support subscales ranged from 16% to 49%, with total social support scores accounting for 43% of the variance in PHA proliferation and 32% of the variance in NK activity. These results compare with those of Jemmott and Magloire (1988), in which social support was correlated .51 with a salivary measure of immunocompetence. To further illustrate the independence of the social support–immune function link, the partial correlations between social support and both NK and PHA function with depression and life event scores statistically controlled are reported in table 18.3.

Discussion

These data provide a clear replication of prior research reporting a positive relationship between social support and immune function under stress. Those participants who had greater social support had faster T-cell proliferation when stimulated by the mitogen PHA, and also were more effective at destroying target tumor cells in comparison to individuals who were below the median on reported social support. That these results were obtained in a participant sample exposed to intense and relatively prolonged stress extends the generality of prior reports of this nature (Thomas et al., 1985), and underscores the fact that social support can provide a powerful psychological benefit even under the most severe duress. In addition, the present data nicely complement Jemmott and Magloire's (1988) report that social support is associated with higher levels of salivary secretory immunoglobulin A, an alternative index of immunocompetence. The similarity of outcomes in these two investigations is provocative given that they involve different immunological systems.[7]

Two mediational models of the association between social support and immune function were tested. In the first model, possible mediation by level of depressive symptoms was examined. It has been hypothesized that social support affects health outcomes primarily through its effectiveness as a deterrent to depression (e.g., Jemmott and Magloire, 1988), which appears to have a suppressive effect on some aspects of immune function. However, no support for mediation by depression was found in the current study. Statistically controlling for depressive symptoms did not diminish the strength of the association between social support and either T-lymphocyte proliferation (in response to the PHA mitogen) or natural killer cell activity. It is noteworthy that an association was found between social support and immune function that did not depend on the mediation of depression. Clearly, some other mechanism operated to produce the obtained relation found in this sample.

Depression scores were not significantly associated with any of the measures of immunocompetence. The generally low level of depressive symptomatology in this sample may account for these results. Although a few participants scored above the cutoff for mild depression on the BDI, only one was in the moderate range and none scored in the severe range. Thus, it is unlikely that any of the participants suffered from a diagnosable major depression. Given the likelihood of greater physiological disruption in more severe depressions, the expected relation between depression level and immune function might have been found in a sample that included individuals suffering from diagnosable depression. In a sample of more severely depressed individuals, it is quite possible that depression might contribute to the relation between social support and immunity. Our data, however, indicate that such a contribution is not a necessary condition for finding a strong association between social support and immunocompetence. The second mediational model, in which the effects of social support are mediated by the incidence of negative life events, also was not supported. Statistically controlling for life events did not diminish the strength of the association between social support and immune function. Little insight into the precise mechanism through which social support affects immunocompetence was obtained through analyses of links to specific components of support. The two indices of immune function that were related to total social support scores had uniformly high associations with each of the six provisions.

Although these data are quite provocative, our interpretation of the findings must be restrained by several considerations. First, it is yet to be established that variations in immunological functioning produced by psychosocial variables such as social support have practical significance by altering health outcomes (Calabrese et al., 1987). Thus, while social support appears to be positively related to immunocompetence, we cannot yet be confident that it will also have an impact on morbidity. Related to this point, we do not know how the levels of immunocompetence evidenced by subjects in this study relate to immune system functioning among normal subjects. A natural assumption is that low levels of social support are associated with suppressed levels of immunocompetence, with higher levels of support serving to bring immunity up to normal levels. However, some studies have found that life stress can serve to enhance immunocompetence relative to normal levels (Jemmott and Locke, 1984; Dienstbier, 1989).[8] Similarly, it is possible that high levels of social support may serve to enhance immunocompetence above normal levels, even among populations experiencing high levels of stress. Future studies need to evaluate the effects of social support on immune system functioning among both stressed and matched nonstressed (normal) populations, to better understand the effects of both stress and social support on immunocompetence. A third limitation of the study concerns the correlational nature of the data. Results of any correlational study are open to alternative interpretations. For example, it may be that individuals with good physical health not only have highly competent immune systems, but also are more attractive as friends and therefore have more sources of social support. Future research designs should address the issue of causality, using experimental methods wherever possible. For example, the temporary effects of social rejection or isolation as well as those of positive social interactions on immune function should be investigated using tightly controlled experimental designs.

In the current study, individuals experiencing a severe and chronic life stress showed evidence of better immunity if they had high levels of perceived social support. These data suggest that the relation between social support and immunity is a strong one. Although the precise mechanism or mechanisms responsible for this relationship has yet to be specified, the association appears strong enough to encourage further research in this area.

NOTES

[1] The lymphocytes, or white blood cells, are composed of two general types of cells: T lymphocytes (T cells) and B lymphocytes (B cells). T cells and B cells provide two different but dependent types of immunity: cellular and humoral, respectively. Cellular immunity involves a complex cascade of events initiated by the invasion of an antigen. An antigen may be any molecule that is capable of stimulating an immune response. In general, cellular immunity is regulated by three classes of T lymphocytes: T-helper cells, T-suppressor cells, and cytotoxic or killer lymphocytes. The major role of T-helper cells is to signal B lymphocytes to produce antibody to specific antigens or to help other T-lymphocyte effector

cells in cell-mediated immunity. Proliferation is a major function of these T-helper cells. Obviously, the ability of T lymphocytes to proliferate (i.e., multiply) in times of stress is a crucial component in immune function. In contrast, T-suppressor cells turn off immune responses to an antigen. Cytotoxic T lymphocytes seek out antigen-bearing cells such as tumors and destroy them. An additional class of lymphocytes, natural killer (NK) cells, will also bind to tumor cells and cause their destruction.

The humoral response to antigens is mediated by the B cell. On activation by an antigen or T-helper cell, the B cell differentiates into an antibody-secreting plasma cell. Through complex processes, which are beyond the scope of this discussion, antibodies secreted by the plasma cell neutralize, kill, and eliminate the antigen from the body. As one can see, the proper functioning of T- and B-lymphocyte populations is essential for maintenance of immune system functioning and health. Thus, a reasonable strategy for evaluating the responsiveness of the immune system involves assessing the ability of lymphocytes to respond to well-known mitogens, the degree of natural killer cell activity in the lymphocyte population, and the overall percentage of T- and B-cell populations in the peripheral blood sample (cf. Calabrese, 1987, for a review).

[2] Subjects were screened for health problems (including weight change and sleep disturbance) as well as use of medication. We did not feel free to question this stressed population regarding substance abuse and diet, because of our desire to avoid questions that might annoy the subjects or produce complaints about the project to the clinic staff or both. Obtaining such background data would clearly be desirable in research on a less sensitive subject situation.

[3] By exposing target cells to a detergent, one determines the maximal amount of cell destruction that is reasonable to expect.

[4] A more powerful analysis of the effects of social support on immunocompetence would have involved using social support as a continuous score (Cohen and Cohen, 1983; see, for example, Jemmott and Magloire, 1988). Unfortunately, the multivariate analysis of variance (MANOVA) program did not permit the estimation of the support by concentration interaction term when support was specified as a continuous variable, since concentration level was a within-subjects factor. We also conducted repeated-measures analysis of variance (ANOVAs) using a multiple regression approach, as described by Pedhauzer (1982). In these analyses, the univariate approach to repeated measures was used, with social support treated as a continuous predictor variable. The results were virtually identical to the MANOVA results.

[5] One reason this may be true is that flow cytometry is relatively insensitive to small or transient changes in cell number (McElligott, 1985).

[6] Very high levels of covariation among the six social provisions scores, ranging from .72 to .93 ($M = .86$, following an r to z transformation), were found in this sample. This contrasts to average correlations ranging from .4 to .5 in investigations that have used the Social Provisions Scale with other stressed populations. Thus, it appears that little differentiation among different types of support was made by these subjects in completing the scale. Either the spouses were receiving high levels of all six forms of support, or they were receiving low levels of all six forms of support.

[7] Secretory immunoglobulin A (S-IgA) is an antibody class found in bodily secretions. It acts against bacteria and viruses by preventing them from becoming established in mucosal surfaces. As such, it limits infections in the upper respiratory, gastrointestinal, and urogenital systems. Thus, there are distinct differences between this form of immunological response and the blood-based processes assessed in the present study (Calabrese et al., 1987).

[8] We could like to thank an anonymous reviewer for raising this issue of normal immunocompetence.

REFERENCES

Amster, L.E., and Krauss, H.H. (1974). The relationship between life crises and mental deterioration in old age. *Journal of Gerontology*, 42, 107–13.

Bartrop, R.W., Luckhurst, L., Lazarus, L., Kiloh, L.G., and Penny, R. (1977). Depressed lymphocyte function after bereavement. *Lancet*, 1, 834–6.

Beck, A.T., Ward, C.H., Mendelson, M., Mock, J., and Erbaugh, J. (1961). An inventory for measuring depression. *Archives of General Psychiatry*, 4, 561–9.

Boranic, M., Pericic, D., and Radicic, M. (1982). Immunological and neuroendocrine responses of rats to prolonged or repeated stress. *Biomedicine*, 36, 23–8.

Borysenko, M., and Borysenko, J. (1982). Stress, behavior, and immunity: Animal model and mediating mechanisms. *General Hospital Psychiatry*, 4, 59–67.

Calabrese, J.R., Kling, M.A., and Gold, P.W. (1987). Alterations in immunocompetence during stress, bereavement, and depression: Focus on neuroendocrine regulation. *American Journal of Psychiatry*, 144, 1123–34.

Carandente, F., Angeli, A., De Vecchi, A., Dammacco, F., and Hallberg, F. (1988). Multifrequency rhythms of immunological functions. *Chronobiologia*, 15, 7–23.

Cobb, S. (1976). Social support as a moderator of life stress. *Psychosomatic Medicine*, 38, 300–14.

Cohen, J., and Cohen, C. (1983). *Applied multiple regression/correlation analysis for the behavioral sciences* (2nd edn). Hillsdale, NJ: Erlbaum.

Cohen, S. (1988). Psychosocial models of the role of social support in the etiology of physical disease. *Health Psychology*, 7, 269–97.

Cohen, S., and Syme, S.L. (eds) (1985). *Social support and health*. San Diego, CA: Academic Press.

Cohen, S., and Wills, T.A. (1985). Stress, social support, and the buffering hypothesis. *Psychological Bulletin*, 98, 310–57.

Constable, J.F., and Russell, D. (1986). The effect of social support and the work environment upon burnout among nurses. *Journal of Human Stress*, 12, 20–6.

Cutrona, C.E. (1989). Ratings of social support by adolescents and adult informants. *Journal of Personality and Social Psychology*, 57, 723–30.

Cutrona, C.E., and Russell, D.W. (1987). The provisions of social relationships and adaptation to stress. In W.H. Jones and D. Perlman (eds), *Advances in personal relationships* (vol. 1, pp. 37–67). Greenwich, CT: JAI Press.

Cutrona, C.E., and Russell, D.W. (1990). Type of social support and specific stress: Toward a theory of optimal matching. In I.G. Sarason, B.R. Sarason, and G.R. Pierce (eds), *Social support: An interactional view* (pp. 319–66). New York: Wiley.

Cutrona, C.E., Russell, D., and Rose, J. (1986). Social support and adaptation to stress by the elderly. *Psychology and Aging*, 1, 47–54.

Dienstbier, R. (1989). Arousal and physiological toughness: Implications for mental and physical health. *Psychological Review*, 96, 84–100.

Dorian, B.J., Keystone, E., Garfinkel, P.E., and Brown, G.M. (1982). Aberrations in lymphocyte subpopulations and functions during psychological stress. *Clinical and Experimental Immunology*, 50, 132–8.

Gallagher, D., Nies, G., and Thompson, L.W. (1982). Reliability of the Beck Depression Inventory with older adults. *Journal of Consulting and Clinical Psychology*, 50, 152–3.

Gallagher, D., Breckenridge, J., Steinmetz, J., and Thompson, L. (1983). The Beck Depression Inventory and Research Diagnostic Criteria: Congruence in an older population. *Journal of Consulting and Clinical Psychology*, 51, 945–6.

Greiner, D.L., Reynolds, C.W., and Lubaroff, D.M. (1982). Maturation of functional T-lymphocyte subpopulations in the rat. *Thymus*, 4, 77–90.

House, J.S., Landis, K.R., and Umberson, D. (1988). Social relationships and health. *Science*, 241, 540–5.

Jemmott, J.B., III, and Locke, S.E. (1984). Psychosocial factors, immunologic mediation, and human susceptibility to infectious diseases: How much do we know? *Psychological Bulletin*, 95, 78–108.

Jemmott, J.B., III, and Magloire, K. (1988). Academic stress, social support, and secretory immunoglobulin A. *Journal of Personality and Social Psychology*, 55, 803–10.

Kessler, R.C., Price, R.H., and Wortman, C.B. (1985). Social factors in psychopathology: Stress, social support, and coping processes. *Annual Review of Psychology*, 36, 531–72.

Kiecolt-Glaser, J.K., and Glaser, R. (1987). Psychosocial moderators of immune function. *Annals of Behavioral Medicine*, 9, 16–20.

Kiecolt-Glaser, J.K., and Glaser, R. (1988). Psychological influences on immunity: Implications for AIDS. *American Psychologist*, 43, 892–8.

Kiecolt-Glaser, J.K., Garner, W., Speicher, C.E., Penn, G., and Glaser, R. (1984). Psychosocial modifiers of immunocompetence in medical students. *Psychosomatic Medicine*, 46, 7–14.

Kiecolt-Glaser, J.K., Fisher, L.D., Ogrocki, P., Stout, J.C., Speicher, C.E., and Glaser, R. (1987). Marital quality, marital disruption, and immune function. *Psychosomatic Medicine*, 49, 13–34.

Kiecolt-Glaser, J.K., Glaser, R., Dyer, C., Shuttleworth, E., Ogrocki, P., and Speicher, C.E. (1987). Chronic stress and immunity in family caregivers of Alzheimer's disease victims. *Psychosomatic Medicine*, 49, 523–35.

Kiecolt-Glaser, J.K., Glaser, R., Strain, E.C., Stout, J.C., Tarr, K.L., Holliday, J.E., and Speicher, C.E. (1986). Modulation of cellular immunity among medical students. *Journal of Behavioral Medicine*, 9, 5–21.

Kiecolt-Glaser, J.K., Ricker, D., George, J., Messick, G., Speicher, C.E., Garner, W., and Glaser, R. (1984). Urinary cortisol levels, cellular immunocompetency, and loneliness in psychiatric inpatients. *Psychosomatic Medicine*, 46, 15–24.

Kiecolt-Glaser, J.K., Glaser, R., Williger, D., Stout, J., Messick, G., Sheppard, S., Ricker, D., Romisher, S.C., Briner, W., Bonnell, G., and Donnerberg, R. (1985). Psychosocial enhancement of immunocompetence in a geriatric population. *Heath Psychology*, 4, 25–41.

Krueger, R.B., Levy, E.M., Cathcart, E.S., Fox, B.H., and Black, P.H. (1984). Lymphocyte subsets in patients with major depression: Preliminary findings. *Advances*, 1, 5–9.

Linn, B.S., Linn, M.W., and Jenson, J. (1982). Degree of depression and immune responsiveness. *Psychosomatic Medicine*, 44, 128.

Linn, M.W., Sandifer, R., and Stein, S. (1985). Effects of unemployment on mental and physical health. *American Journal of Public Health*, 75, 502–6.

Lubaroff, D.M., Reynolds, C.W., and Culp, D.A. (1979). Immunologic studies of prostatic cancer using the R3327 rat model. *Transactions of the American Association of G.U. Surgeons*, 70, 60–3.

Maier, S.F., and Laudenslager, M. (1985). *Psychology Today*, 19, 44–9.

McElligott, D.L. (1985). Natural cell-mediated cytotoxicity in an animal model of prostatic cancer. Unpublished doctoral dissertation, University of Iowa, Iowa City.

Murphy, S.A. (1984). After Mount St. Helens: Disaster stress research. *Journal of Psychosocial Nursing and Mental Health Services*, 22, 9–18.

O'Brien, R.G., and Kaiser, M.K. (1985). MANOVA method for analyzing repeated-measure designs: An extensive primer. *Psychological Bulletin*, 97, 316–33.

Pedhauzer, E.J. (1982). *Multiple regression in behavioral research* (2nd edn). New York: Holt, Rinehart, and Winston.

Pennebaker, J., and O'Heeron, R. (1984). Confiding in others and illness rate among spouses of suicide and accidental death victims. *Journal of Abnormal Psychology*, 93, 473–6.

Russell, D., and Cutrona, C.E. (1984, August). The provisions of social relationships and adaptation to stress. Paper presented at the annual meeting of the American Psychological Association, Anaheim, CA.

Russell, D., Altmaier, E., and Van Velzen, D. (1987). Job-related stress, social support, and burnout among classroom teachers. *Journal of Applied Psychology*, 72, 269–74.

Schleifer, S.J., Keller, S.E., Camerino, M., Thornton, J.C., and Stein, M. (1983). Suppression of lymphocyte stimulation following bereavement. *Journal of the American Medical Association*, 250, 374–7.

Seeman, T.E., Kaplan, G.A., Knudsen, L., Cohen, R., and Guralnik, J. (1987). Social network ties and mortality among the elderly in the Alameda County study. *American Journal of Epidemiology*, 126, 714–23.

Thoits, P.A. (1982). Conceptual, methodological, and theoretical problems in studying social support as a buffer against life stress. *Journal of Health and Social Behavior*, 23, 145–59.

Thomas, P.D., Goodwin, J.M., and Goodwin, J.S. (1985). Effect of social support on stress-related changes in cholesterol level, uric acid level, and immune function in an elderly sample. *American Journal of Psychiatry*, 142, 735–7.

Weiss, R. (1974). The provisions of social relationships. In Z. Rubin (ed.), *Doing unto others* (pp. 17–26). Englewood Cliffs, NJ: Prentice-Hall.

Wortman, C.B. (1984). Social support and the cancer patient. *Cancer*, 53(May 15 suppl.), 2339–62.

The social psychology of eyewitness accuracy: Misleading questions and communicator expertise

V.L. Smith and P.C. Ellsworth

Editors'
Introduction

Theoretical Background

Eyewitness testimony often plays a decisive role in court proceedings. Members of the legal profession were therefore shaken by the empirical evidence on the malleability of the memory of eyewitnesses presented by Loftus and her colleagues in the 1970s (for a review, see Loftus, 1979). These studies demonstrated that eyewitnesses who were asked misleading questions about an event they had seen, typically suggesting the presence of details that in fact had not been there, tended during subsequent questioning to report as real the false information contained in the misleading questions. Loftus explained this phenomenon by suggesting that the false presuppositions contained in the misleading questions are incorporated into the witness's memory for the event.

Subsequent research demonstrated that the effect of misleading questions is less general than the results reported by Loftus and associates suggested. For example, findings of a study conducted by Yuille (1980) indicated that uncertainty was an important antecedent to the misleading question effect and that the effect did not occur for subjects whose memories already contained clear representations of the event. However, even these critics accepted the misleading question effect as a purely cognitive phenomenon.

The important contribution of this article by Smith and Ellsworth is to point out that the misleading question effect constitutes a social influence process and should therefore be affected by social-psychological factors such as communicator credibility. The authors argued that in practically all of these studies, the misleading information is presented to the subject by the experimenter, who, having designed or selected the witnessed event himself or herself, must be considered an expert. They therefore reasoned that the power of misleading questions to modify the memory of the witness might be dependent on the perceived credibility of the person asking the question.

Journal of Applied Psychology (1987), 72:294–300.

Hypotheses

1 Misleading questions will influence the memory of eyewitnesses only if asked by individuals perceived to be knowledgeable about the event. When asked by individuals not considered to be knowledgeable, no distortion will occur.
2 The perceived knowledge of the questioner should make no difference when questions are not misleading.

STUDY I

Design

The experiment used a factorial 2 (Questioner type: knowledge high/low) × 2 (Type of question: misleading/unbiased) between-subjects design.

Method

Student subjects first watched a videotaped clip of a crime and then were questioned about the crime by another subject, who was, in fact, a confederate of the experimenters. For the independent variables the questioner was presented either as unfamiliar with the crime or as very knowledgeable, and asked either unbiased or misleading questions (e.g. 'Did the other guy have a gun?' vs. 'What did the other guy's gun look like?'). For the dependent measure, subjects had to complete a questionnaire about the crime, which contained five items tapping the subject's memory for the critical details.

Results

The two hypotheses predict an interaction of questioner type and type of question on error rates (i.e. percentage of subjects making errors). Because the unit of measurement for proportions is almost never constant over the total scale, with differences at the extremes of the distribution being more important than at the midpoint, the authors conducted an arcsine transformation, which stretches the tails of the distribution (see Cohen and Cohen, 1983, pp. 265–7). But instead of following the elegant procedure suggested by Langer and Abelson (1972) for testing interactions among percentages in a 2 × 2 table with a single test, they then conducted a number of separate contrasts, checking the significance of differences between different conditions.

First, Smith and Ellsworth tested the prediction that the questioner's knowledge would not significantly affect error rates for unbiased questions. Although descriptively there appears to be a difference (43 per cent vs. 25 per cent), this failed to approach an acceptable level of significance, which could have been due to the small number of subjects in these conditions. As a next step, Smith and Ellsworth compared the error rates in the condition with the knowledgeable questioner asking misleading questions against the naive questioner asking misleading questions and the two unbiased conditions, and found a highly significant difference. Also in line with predictions, no differences in error rates were found between subjects who had been asked misleading questions by a naive questioner and those who had been asked unbiased questions by a naive questioner.

This study had a number of shortcomings recognized by the authors. Although the pattern of findings was generally consistent with predictions, there were a number of puzzling inconsistencies. There was a marked, albeit insignificant, difference in error rates for unbiased questions of subjects who had been interviewed by naive as compared to knowledgeable questioners. Furthermore, separate analyses conducted on the five biased questions showed that most of the effect was due to one item. More than half the subjects who were asked what the other robber's gun looked like by the knowledgeable questioner later 'remembered' seeing the non-existent gun, as compared to three of the thirty subjects in the other conditions. On the other items, misleading questions from the knowledgeable questioner had hardly any impact. The second study was conducted to resolve these inconsistencies.

STUDY 2

The second experiment was a replication of the first study but with three changes in procedure: (1) a different videotaped crime clip was used, (2) the number of subjects per cell was increased, and (3) the manipulation of the perceived knowledge of the questioner was strengthened. These changes in procedure did succeed in eliminating some of the weaknesses of the previous study and results were fully in line with predictions. However, individual analysis again indicated that most of the effect for misleading questions was due to two of the four misleading questions, suggesting that memory for some facts is relatively immune to misleading questions.

Discussion

The findings of this study suggest two important conclusions. First, the power of misleading questions to influence the memory of witnesses depends very much on the extent to which the witness perceives the interviewer as knowledgeable. The misleading-question effect occurs mainly when the witness assumes that the interviewer already knows the facts. When the interviewer is perceived as having little knowledge about the event, misleading questions have little impact. Second, memories of some facts are relatively immune to misleading questions, and these are facts about which the witness is apparently certain. The findings have practical implications for police questioning, namely that police officers should emphasize that they do not know what happened and that they should avoid asking misleading questions. Unless one can be assured that police follow this procedure, one has to be doubtful of the validity of eyewitness testimony.

FURTHER READING

Loftus, E.J., Miller, D.G. and Burns, H.J. (1978). Semantic integration of verbal information into a visual memory. *Journal of Experimental Psychology: Human Learning and Memory*, 4, 19–31, Empirical demonstration of the impact of misleading questions on eyewitness accounts.

Wells, G.L. and Loftus, E.F. (eds) (1984). *Eyewitness Testimony: Psychological Perspectives*. Cambridge: Cambridge University Press. Edited book which includes contributions from the major researchers on eyewitness testimony.

REFERENCES

Cohen, J. and Cohen, P. (1983). *Applied Multiple Regression/Correlation Analysis for the Behavioral Sciences* (2nd edn). Hillsdale, NJ: Erlbaum.
Langer, E.J. and Abelson, R.P. (1972). The semantics of asking a favor: How to succeed in getting help without really dying. *Journal of Personality and Social Psychology*, 24, 26–32.
Loftus, E.J. (1979). *Eyewitness Testimony*. Cambridge, MA: Harvard University Press.
Yuille, J.C. (1980). A critical examination of the psychological and practical implications of eyewitness research. *Law and Human Behavior*, 4, 335–45.

Legal scholars and experimental psychologists share a longstanding concern about the factors that make an eyewitness's testimony accurate and, perhaps more common in the experimental literature, the factors that impair accuracy. An important general issue raised in this work is the malleability of an eyewitness's memory. Is it possible to alter a person's memory for a crime, and if so, how does this process operate?

Primary Reading

The study of misleading questions and their effects on accuracy is the approach most commonly taken by recent researchers who have worked on the question of memory malleability. Misleading questions provide information that is inconsistent with the event witnessed, suggesting, for example, the existence of an object that was in fact not present. Elizabeth Loftus and her colleagues (Loftus, 1975, 1977; Loftus, Altman, and Geballe, 1975; Loftus, Miller, and Burns, 1978; Loftus and Palmer, 1974; Loftus and Zanni, 1975) have repeatedly demonstrated that subjects who are asked misleading questions tend, during subsequent questioning, to report the false information contained in the misleading questions they were asked. As a result, these subjects make significantly more errors in their reports of the event than do subjects who are asked unbiased questions. For example, in one experiment (Loftus, 1975), subjects watched a videotape of a traffic accident and then answered questions about the incident. One half of the subjects were asked, "How fast was the white sport car going when it passed the barn while traveling along the country road?" This question is misleading because it contains the presupposition that there was a barn in the clip, when in fact no barn was shown. The remaining subjects were simply asked, "How fast was the white sports car going while traveling along the country road?" When later asked if they had seen a barn, 17.3% of the subjects exposed to the misleading question reported having seen a barn, whereas only 2.7% of the control subjects made this error.

Loftus (1975, 1977) explained this phenomenon by proposing that the false presupposition contained in the misleading question is incorporated into the witness's memory for the event. When asked to recall the incident, the subject remembers a barn but fails to recall that the source of this memory was the question rather than the event itself. As a result, the information is recalled and reported as part of the event that the subject witnessed. Using this same general paradigm, Loftus and others (Clifford and Scott, 1978; Lesgold and Petrush (cited in Loftus, 1979); Loftus, 1977; Loftus et al., 1975; Loftus et al., 1978; Loftus and Palmer, 1974; Loftus and Zanni, 1975) have replicated these results with a variety of stimulus materials and have obtained error rates as high as 95% for subjects who are asked misleading questions (Clifford and Scott, 1978).

Critics have argued that this effect of misleading questions is actually less general than these high error rates imply. Dritsas and Hamilton (cited in Loftus, 1979) reported that memory for items that are salient and central to the witnessed event is significantly less likely to be altered by misleading information than is memory for peripheral details. These authors maintained that the high error rates reported by other investigators are attributable to the testing of peripheral details.

Yuille (1980) found that misleading information did not affect the accuracy of subjects whose memories already contained a correct representation of the implied object. Subjects viewed slides that depicted an accident involving an automobile and a pedestrian, and then described the event in writing. Following this free-recall stage, subjects completed a questionnaire about the accident that either did or did not contain misleading information about the type of traffic sign present at the intersection. Overall, the misleading question effect was replicated: subjects who were asked misleading questions were significantly more likely to be wrong about the traffic sign than were subjects who were asked unbiased questions. However, only subjects who failed to mention the sign in their original reports of the event were misled by the false information. Subjects who correctly described the type of traffic sign during the free-recall stage were relatively immune to the false information.

Together, the results of these two experiments indicate that uncertainty is an important antecedent to the misleading question effect. When the subjects's memory already contains a clear representation of the object, false information suggested afterward is not incorporated into memory. As proposed by Dritsas and Hamilton (cited in Loftus, 1979), the high error rates obtained by some investigators may be a function of their focus on tangential details that subjects did not carefully encode in memory.

So far, both the original researchers and their critics have considered the power of misleading questions to distort memory as a purely cognitive phenomenon. The vast social psychological literature on persuasion and attitude change (cf. McGuire, 1969) has not been brought to bear on the interactions between a questioner and a witness. In this article, we examine the effects on eyewitness accuracy of one of the classic social psychological variables – the expertise of the communicator (cf. Hovland and Weiss, 1951). Others have suggested that the credibility of the questioner may influence the accuracy of a witness's report (e.g., Yuille, 1980), but no systematic study of this issue has been undertaken.

Misleading information is typically presented to subjects on a questionnaire designed by the experimenter. Having designed the original event, the experimenter is necessarily well acquainted with it, and is therefore a highly credible source of information. The subject, having seen the event only once, assumes that he or she knows less about the details of the event than does the experimenter, and thus is likely to accept the information suggested by the experimenter without questioning its accuracy. The subject assumes that the new information is correct, and modifies his or her memory of the event to make it consistent with that information.

Suppose, however, that the source of the misleading information were less credible than the experimenter. When interrogated by someone known to be unfamiliar with the witnessed event, the subject would be less likely to accept the misleading information as accurate and therefore less likely to modify his or her memory of the event. Under these circumstances, asking misleading questions should not diminish the witness's accuracy. Thus, the influence of misleading questions may well depend on the witness's assumptions about how much the questioner already knows.

Investigation of the effects of the questioner's knowledge of the crime also has practical implications for the questioning of real-world witnesses. Experiments on eyewitness questioning have generally examined the effects of misleading information presented during the initial questioning of the subject. This situation is analogous to the questioning of real-world witnesses by police at the scene of the crime. Because the police are typically called to the scene after the crime has been committed, they do not know what actually happened, but must try to reconstruct the event from the witness's report. Although there are some situations in which a police questioner already knows (or thinks he or she knows) a great deal about the crime, the initial questioning of a witness is often conducted by naive police questioners. Thus, it is important to know whether communicator expertise is a significant moderating variable affecting the power of misleading questions.

We designed two experiments to compare the relative impact on accuracy of different levels of questioner expertise by manipulating the knowledge of the questioner. Consistent with previous research, one experimental condition portrayed the questioner as being well acquainted with the crime that the subjects witnessed. In the other experimental condition, the questioner was represented to subjects as being unaware of what had taken place. We predicted that when the questioner was seen as knowledgeable about the crime, the misleading question effect obtained in previous research would be replicated. However, when the questioner was represented as being naive to the witnessed event, we expected that the misleading question effect would disappear and that subjects in this condition would make no more errors than did control subjects.

Experiment I

Method

Overview

Subjects watched a videotaped clip of a bank robbery, after which a confederate of the experimenter asked the subject a series of questions about the crime. Two variables related to this questioning were factorially crossed. The first was the questioner's knowledge of the crime: Subjects were interrogated by a questioner who was either knowledgeable or naive about the crime the subject witnessed. The second factor manipulated was the type of question asked: One half of the subjects were asked misleading questions, and the other half were asked unbiased questions. After a 20-min filler activity, subjects completed a questionnaire about the crime that included critical questions designed to assess the effects of the misleading information.

Subjects

A total of 45 undergraduates enrolled in introductory psychology participated individually in the experiment, and were randomly assigned to one of the four experimental conditions. Fifteen subjects participated in each of the two misleading question conditions; the remaining 15 subjects were assigned to the unbiased question groups. Because no misleading information was given to subjects in the unbiased question conditions, it was expected that equivalent error rates would be obtained for these two groups, permitting their combination into a single control group with 15 subjects.

The data for 6 subjects were excluded from the experiment, with comparable subject loss in each condition. Three subjects were dropped because they did not give yes or no responses to the critical items on the crime questionnaire, but wrote ambiguous answers. Another was excluded because he recognized the film clip that was used and had some difficulty remembering what information he knew from the clip and what he remembered from the remainder of the film. Another was dropped because he was mistakenly asked the misleading questions while being assigned to the control condition. Finally, 1 subject was deaf, and thus unable to either process the auditory portion of the clip or understand the questions he was asked. Six additional subjects (randomly assigned) replaced those excluded so that the total number of subjects participating in the experiment remained at 45.

Two undergraduate men served as confederates. The confederate's task was to portray himself as another introductory psychology student taking part in the experiment for course credit. The confederates were trained to assume this role convincingly, with as much cross-confederate behavioral consistency as possible.

Procedure

On arriving at the laboratory, the subject was directed to one of two chairs positioned in front of a videotape monitor and was told that the experiment would begin as soon as the other subject arrived. The confederate always arrived a few minutes later than the subject did to avoid suspicion by subjects of experimenter–confederate collusion. The experimenter began the session by explaining that the study dealt with the questioning of eyewitnesses of criminal events and, particularly, with how complete and accurate a report of a crime someone could get by questioning an eyewitness.

The experimenter then went on to explain that one of the participants would assume the role of eyewitness and the other the role of questioner. The procedure for assigning the subject the role of eyewitness varied with the experimental condition. Subjects in the naive questioner conditions drew lots, arranged so that the subject was always the witness. In the knowledgeable questioner conditions, the experimenter explained that the role assignments had been randomly determined prior to the session, and identified the subjects as eyewitness and the confederate as questioner. The participants were then told that the questioner would move to another room while the witness watched a videotaped clip of a crime, and that the questioner should use this time to think of questions to ask the witness that would reveal as much detailed information about the crime as possible.

Questioner's knowledge Critical to the hypotheses being tested was the manipulation of the questioner's knowledge of the crime. To this point in the procedure the subject was led to believe that the confederate was merely another subject in the experiment and thus equally unfamiliar with the videotaped clip. For subjects in the naive questioner conditions, this assumption was preserved and the questioner was merely told, "To make your job (of questioning) a little easier, I'll tell you that the crime (<u>subject</u>) will witness is a bank robbery." For subjects in the knowledgeable questioner conditions, the confederate was portrayed as well acquainted with the crime. To make this salient to the subjects, the following interchange took place:

Experimenter (to subject:) To make (<u>confederate's</u>) job a little easier, I called and asked him to come in earlier today to familiarize himself with the videotaped clip you'll be seeing. He was given as much time as he needed to watch the clip over and over again and get a good idea of what happens, so that when the time came he could ask you good questions. He wasn't at that time asked to write down any questions: that's what he gets to do now.

Experimenter (to confederate): How many times did you end up seeing the clip?

Confederate: Oh, I don't know, 9 or 10 I guess.

Experimenter (laughing): Nine or 10? You probably know it better than I do.

Finally, the experimenter explained that later in the hour the subjects would be asked to fill out a questionnaire about the crime to see how effective the questioning process was. At this point, the confederate left the room and the subject watched the videotaped crime. The crime was a bank robbery that lasted just over 1 min.

Misleading and unbiased questions　After the subject had seen the crime, the confederate returned to the room with a list of 19 questions for the witness. These questions included the misleading information manipulation. For subjects in the misleading question condition, 5 of the questions contained misleading information; for subjects in the unbiased question conditions, the misleading information was removed. Table 18.4 lists the questions asked of subjects in the misleading question conditions, with the unbiased versions of the questions in parentheses. Because these questions were allegedly composed by the confederate during the time the subject watched the videotaped crime clip, they had to be carefully worded so as to arouse no suspicion by subjects of experimenter–questioner collusion.

Limitations on the content of the questions were imposed by the expertise manipulation. Because the same set of questions was asked by both knowledgeable and naive questioners, the topics covered had to be sufficiently general that the questions could logically be asked by both types of questioners. Thus, very specific questions about the robbery – such as, "Which police officer entered through the back of the bank?" – were avoided because they included details that could not possibly be known by a questioner who had never seen the crime clip. Note that in much of the previous research on this topic, the questions themselves imply expertise, perhaps further strengthening the subjects' impression that the experimenter must be knowledgeable. For example, it is highly unlikely that someone who knew nothing about an event would ever ask a question like, "How fast was the white sports car going when it passed the barn while traveling along the country road?"

The experimenter told the confederate that he would have 5 min to question the witness, stressed the importance of asking specific questions, and asked him to write down the witness's responses. The experimenter left the room during the interrogation, but returned at a predetermined point in the questioning process. Then, while the experimenter allegedly scored the questions and answers, the subject and the confederate completed a 20-min filler activity, which consisted of two questionnaires unrelated to the experiment.

Dependent measure　In the final stage of the experiment, subjects completed a 35-item questionnaire about the crime. This questionnaire was identical for subjects in all four conditions and contained 5 items tapping the subject's memory for the critical details: Were the robbers wearing gloves? Did you see a bank manager? Were any shots fired? Did both of the robbers have guns? Did you see a getaway car? Each of these questions required the subject to make a

Table 18.4   Interrogator's questions in Experiment 1

No.	Question
1	How many robbers were there?
2	What did they look like?
3	Were they wearing masks?
4	Were they wearing jackets? What kind? Color?
5	What kind of pants were they wearing?
*6	What kind of gloves were they wearing? (Were they wearing gloves?)
7	What kind of weapons did the robbers have?
8	Describe the gun the blue guy had.
	Was it small, large?
	Was it a pistol?
*9	What did the other guy's gun look like? (Did the other guy have a gun?)
	Was it small, large?
	Was it a pistol?
10	Did the robbers get away?
11	Were there any police there? How many?
12	How many tellers were there?
13	Not counting the tellers or the bank manager, how many witnesses were there? (Not counting the tellers, how many witnesses were there?)
*14	Where was the getaway car parked? (Was there a getaway car?)
15	What did the robbers say?
*16	How many shots were fired? (Were any shots fired?)
17	What time of day was the robbery?
18	Was anybody tied up?
19	Did everybody in the bank realize what was going on?

Asterisk denotes questions containing misleading information; the unbiased versions of the questions appear in parentheses.

yes or no response, and an error was recorded when the subject responded yes to one or more of the items.

Results

Percentages of subjects who made errors in each of the four conditions are shown in table 18.5. A z test on the arcsine transformed proportions (Langer and Abelson, 1972; Mosteller and Tukey, 1949) of subjects making errors in the two unbiased question groups revealed, as predicted, no significant difference in error rates for subjects questioned by a naive questioner and those questioned by a knowledgeable questioner, $z(\infty) = .74$, *ns*. Because the error rates obtained for the two unbiased question conditions did not differ significantly, these groups were combined for all subsequent analyses.

Two hypotheses examining the role of the questioner's level of expertise in producing the misleading question effect were tested. Specifically, it was hypothesized that (a) when the questioner was portrayed as more knowledgeable about the crime than were the subjects

Table 18.5   Experiment 1: percentage of subjects making errors

Questioner type	Type of question	
	Misleading	Unbiased
Knowledgeable	73 ($n = 15$)	43 ($n = 7$)
Naive	27 ($n = 15$)	25 ($n = 8$)

themselves, the misleading question effect obtained in previous research would be replicated, and (b) when the questioner was represented as naive to the crime, the misleading question effect would not be obtained and subjects in this condition would exhibit an error rate equivalent to that obtained in the unbiased question conditions.

Contrasts testing these two hypotheses were performed on the arcsine transformed proportions of subjects making errors in each condition (collapsed across the two unbiased question groups). As predicted, subjects who were asked misleading questions by a knowledgeable questioner made significantly more errors than did either subjects who were asked misleading questions by a naive questioner or subjects who were asked unbiased questions, $F(1, \infty) = 7.89$, $p < .01$. The second hypothesis was also confirmed: Misleading questions asked by a naive questioner produced no more errors than did unbiased questions, $F(1, \infty) = .13$, *ns*. Thus, the misleading question effect was obtained only in the condition in which the questioner was more knowledgeable about the crime than was the witness.

Examination of the data for each misleading question revealed that one of the questions accounted for the majority of the overall effect obtained in the knowledgeable questioner condition. The question, "What did the other guy's gun look like?" exhibited the highest error rate of the five misleading questions. A contrast performed on the data for this question alone revealed that, consistent with the overall effect, subjects who were asked misleading questions by a knowledgeable questioner made significantly more errors than did subjects in any other group, $F(1, \infty) = 9.85$, $p < .01$. The remaining four critical questions were associated with very low error rates in all conditions, precluding meaningful contrast analyses of these questions.

Separate chi-square tests were performed on the data for each critical question. Because our overall contrast analysis revealed no significant differences in the proportion of subjects who made errors when asked either misleading questions by a naive questioner or unbiased questions, these three conditions were combined for the chi-square analyses. As a result, our chi-square tests compared the frequency of error among subjects who were asked misleading questions by a knowledgeable questioner to the other three conditions combined. The question, "What did the other guy's gun look like?" yielded a highly significant chi-square value, $\chi^2(1, N = 45) = 10.15$, $p < .01$. Slightly more than one half of the subjects who were asked this question by a knowledgeable questioner later "remembered" seeing the nonexistent gun. Only 3 of the 30 subjects in the other experimental conditions made this mistake.

The other four critical questions failed to show significant effects for this chi-square analysis, $\chi^2(1, N = 45) < 2$, *ns*. What is important to note, however, is that these same four questions failed to show *any* effect of misleading information, even when the expertise manipulation was disregarded. Chi-square tests were performed on the data for these four questions collapsed across the expertise conditions. This analysis is consistent with the comparisons made in previous experiments of the misleading question effect; the frequency of error among subjects who were asked misleading questions was compared to the frequency of error among subjects who were asked unbiased questions. None of the four questions analyzed in this way showed significant differences in error for misleading versus unbiased questions, $\chi^2(1, N = 45) < 2$, *ns*. These results are consistent with the findings of Dritsas and Hamilton (cited in Loftus, 1979) and Yuille (1980) that were reported earlier: Not all questions are subject to the deleterious effects of misleading information on subsequent accuracy.

Discussion

On the critical question for which misleading information effectively impaired subsequent accuracy, effect was limited, as predicted, to subjects who were given the misleading information by a knowledgeable questioner. The same misleading information presented by a naive questioner did not decrease subjects' subsequent accuracy, with the error rate in this condition being equivalent to the error rate obtained in the two unbiased question conditions.

Experiment 2 was undertaken to address two issues raised by our Experiment 1 results. First, only one of the critical questions tested in Experiment 1 exhibited an error rate high enough to test our hypotheses regarding the role of questioner expertise in obtaining the misleading question effect. Although our results for this question were very strongly in the predicted direction ($p < .01$), we felt it was important to establish the generality of the findings by replicating the study with a new crime clip and a new set of questions.

Second, there is a seemingly large difference in the percentage of subjects who made errors in the two unbiased question conditions: 43% when asked by a knowledgeable questioner, and only 25% when asked by naive questioner. As we reported earlier, this difference did not approach significance, $z(\infty) = .74$, *ns*, but the number of subjects in each of these cells was small. In Experiment 2 we increased the number of subjects in each of these two conditions to allow a more adequate test of the possibility of a main effect of expertise.

Experiment 2

Method

Subjects
A total of 60 undergraduates enrolled in introductory psychology participated individually in Experiment 2; 15 subjects were randomly assigned to each of the four conditions of the experiment. Data from 2 subjects were excluded from the experiment because they suspected that the confederate was not really another subject. Two additional subjects, randomly assigned, replaced those who were excluded.

Procedure
The procedure for Experiment 2 was the same as that used in Experiment 1, with one exception. We discovered that some subjects in the naive questioner conditions failed to absorb the information that the questioner had no knowledge of the crime. Thus, to make the questioner's naivety in these conditions as salient as his knowledgeability in the other conditions, the following interchange took place:

Experimenter (to confederate): To make your job (of questioning) a little easier, I will tell you that the crime (<u>subject</u>) will witness is a bank robbery in which a hostage is taken.

Confederate (interrupting experimenter's next statement): Wait, you mean I don't get to see the clip?

Experimenter: No, you'll be in the other room writing your questions while (<u>subject</u>) watches the clip. All you get to know about it is that it's bank robbery in which a hostage is taken.

The addition of the confederate's question and the experimenter's response was quite effective in making the questioner's naivety salient to subjects.

Materials

The videotaped crime clip used in Experiment 2 was an excerpt from a police training film that lasted approximately 4 min. This clip also depicted a bank robbery in which a hostage was taken, but it was not the same clip as that used in Experiment 1.

The critical questions in the interrogation stage of Experiment 2 were as follows (with the unbiased versions of the questions in parentheses):

What did the fourth robber look like? (Was there a fourth robber?) Was the teller who was taken hostage a man or a woman? (Was the person who was taken hostage a man or a woman?) How many shots did he fire? (Did he fire any shots?) Which robber was carrying the bag with the money in it? (Were any of the robbers carrying a bag with money in it?)

As in Experiment 1, one half the subjects were asked the misleading form of the critical questions and the other half were asked the unbiased form: likewise, one half the subjects were questioned by a knowledgeable questioner and the other half by a naive questioner. Following a 20-min filler task unrelated to the experiment, all of the subjects completed a questionnaire measuring their accuracy for the critical details. Questions of interest on this questionnaire were

How many robbers were there? Answer the following about the robber in the red checked jacket who first noticed the police officer: [filler questions] Did he fire any shots? The hostage was a (check one) teller, other bank employee, customer, police officer. Were any of the robbers carrying a moneybag?

Results

As in Experiment 1, contrasts were performed on the arcsine transformed proportions of subjects making errors in each of the four conditions (see table 18.6). Consistent with the results of Experiment 1, (a) a significantly higher proportion (73%) of subjects made errors when asked misleading questions by a knowledgeable questioner than when questioned in any other condition (40%–53%), $F(1, \infty) = 3.93, p < .05$, and (b) the proportion of subjects making errors when asked misleading questions by a naive questioner did not differ significantly from the proportions obtained for the unbiased question groups, $F(1, \infty) = .68$, *ns*. Thus, subjects who were asked misleading questions by a knowledgeable questioner were significantly more likely to make errors in their subsequent reports of the crime than subjects who were asked unbiased questions. Subjects who were asked misleading questions by a naive questioner, on the other hand, did not exhibit such decreases in subsequent accuracy, relative to subjects asked unbiased questions.

Table 18.6   Patterns of error in Experiment 2

	Type of question	
Questioner type	Misleading	Unbiased
Percentage of subjects making errors		
Knowledgeable	73	40
Naive	53	40
Mean percentage error per subject		
Knowledgeable	41	13
Naive	18	13

The third orthogonal contrast tested for differences in the proportions of subjects making errors in the two unbiased question groups. These two groups yielded identical error rates, so the contrast was nonsignificant, $F(1, \infty) = .00$, *ns*. Thus, it appears that the discrepancy obtained in these two cells in Experiment 1 was not in fact due to a real effect of questioner expertise. As explained earlier, one of our objectives in conducting Experiment 2 was to test for a possible main effect of questioner expertise. Thus, an additional contrast for this main effect was tested, but was not significant, $F(1, \infty) = .66$, *ns*. These results indicate that an expert who asks unbiased questions does not affect witnesses' error rates.

Additional analyses on the Experiment 2 data examined differences in the average error rate per subject in each of the four conditions of the experiment. Table 18.6 shows the mean percentage of critical questions answered incorrectly in each cell. Consistent with the results reported earlier, the mean proportion of critical questions answered incorrectly for subjects who were asked misleading questions by a knowledgeable questioner is significantly higher than the means for the other three conditions, $F(1, \infty) = 11.35$, $p < .002$. Furthermore, the error rate obtained for subjects who were asked misleading questions by a naive questioner did not differ significantly from the error rates for the two unbiased question groups, $F(1, \infty) = .52$, *ns*, which in turn did not differ significantly from each other, $F(1, \infty) = .00$, *ns*.

Again, we performed separate chi-square analyses on the data for each critical question. Because our contrast analysis revealed no significant differences in error rates for subjects who were asked misleading questions by a naive questioner and subjects who were asked unbiased questions, these conditions were combined for the chi-square analyses. Thus, our chi-square tests compared the frequency of error for subjects who were asked misleading questions by a knowledgeable questioner to the frequency of error in the other three conditions combined.

Significant chi-square values were obtained for two of the critical questions: "Was the teller who was taken hostage a man or a woman?" yielded $\chi^2(1, N = 60) = 10.72$, $p < .01$, and "Which robber was carrying the bag with the money in it?" yielded $\chi^2(1, N = 60) = 17.31$, $p < .001$. Thus, for these two questions, the frequency of error for subjects who were asked misleading questions by a knowledgeable questioner significantly exceeded the frequency of error for the other three conditions.

The remaining two questions failed to produce significant chi-square values, χ^2s$(1, N = 60)$ < 1, *ns*. We then tested these questions to see if the misleading information significantly affected subjects' accuracy when questioner expertise was disregarded. Comparing the error rate of subjects who were asked misleading questions to the error rate of subjects who were asked unbiased questions (collapsed across expertise conditions), we found no significant effects of misleading information for these two questions, χ^2s(1, $N = 60$) < 1, *ns*.

As in Experiment 1 then, misleading information did not always interfere with accurate recall. However, for those questions which *do* show deficits in accuracy due to misleading information, we consistently find that the witness's assumption of questioner expertise is critical. The witness's perception that the questioner already knows about the crime determines whether the misleading information will impair subsequent accuracy.

Discussion

Two important findings emerged from the experiments reported here. The first is the critical moderating role played by questioner expertise in determining the effect of misleading information on accuracy. Our results indicate that the power of a misleading question to distort a listener's memory is not simply a matter of semantics or sentence construction, but involves the listener's perception of the social context.

As in previous research, misleading questions generated incorrect answers when the witness could assume that the interrogator already knew a great deal about the crime. In a situation like this, unless the witness has a very clear memory that contradicts the facts presupposed by the knowledgeable questioner, he or she is not likely to doubt the accuracy of those facts, and will later remember them as part of the event. But when the witness knows that the interrogator is ignorant of the facts, misleading questions have no effect. In a situation like this, the witness is the primary authority on the crime, and is unlikely to accept false presuppositions in the first place or to recall them later. Subjects who were asked misleading questions by an interrogator they knew to be naive were as accurate as subjects who were not asked misleading questions at all.

These findings do not raise questions about the validity of the misleading question effect so amply documented by Loftus and others, only about its generality. That facts presupposed in a question influence the respondent is not simply a cognitive phenomenon; it is also a social phenomenon. Social psychologists have known for decades that a direct communication, intended to persuade, will be more effective in changing attitudes if the source is seen as credible (Hovland and Weiss, 1951). A situation in which one person questions another is at least as much a social interaction as a situation in which one person attempts to persuade another, and it is not surprising that characteristics of the communicator should be influential in both. The same communicator qualities that affect the power of direct communications affect the power of indirect ones.

The second important finding highlighted by these experiments is one that has been suggested before but may be more general than is typically assumed: Memories for some facts are relatively immune to alteration by the presentation of misleading information. As we described earlier in this article, it appears that only memories that are somewhat indefinite are subject to distortion on the basis of subsequent information (Dritsas and Hamilton, cited in Loftus, 1979; Yuille, 1980). The differential effectiveness in distorting recall of the critical questions used in the two experiments reported in this article lends further support to this uncertainty hypothesis. Also consistent are the findings of a study reported by Marquis,

Marshall, and Oskamp (1972) that the accuracy of eyewitness testimony varies as a function of the difficulty of the questioned item, with higher error rates obtained for "difficult" items than for "easy" ones.

Although the potential exists to impair a witness's memory for a crime by asking misleading questions, this type of memory distortion is subject to certain preconditions. Two of these preconditions are the expertise of the person presenting the misleading information and some uncertainty about the facts. The mere presentation of misleading information is not sufficient to decrease a witness's accuracy.

Applications

The findings of the experiments reported here also have practical implications for police questioning. Given that accuracy is the goal in questioning eyewitnesses, our results suggest that police officers should avoid suggesting to witnesses that they already know something about the crime, because under these circumstances, if a misleading question is inadvertently asked, the accuracy of the witness's report is likely to suffer. If the police are successful in convincing witnesses that they are ignorant of what took place, misleading questions will generally not result in decreased witness accuracy.

But how do witnesses generally see the police officers who question them? One possibility is that the police are perceived as experts, using the witness to confirm and elaborate a scenario they already have in mind. This may occur because the police present themselves as more knowledgeable than they really are – for example, because they have a suspect in mind but no corroboration, because they have already obtained information about the crime from other witnesses, or because of their general knowledge of similar crimes. On the other hand, it may occur simply because the witness believes in the expertise of the police, regardless of the behavior of the particular officer who is asking the questions. In either case, the phenomenon described by Loftus would represent a real threat to the accuracy of the witness's report, and could increase the number of false arrests and convictions. Another possibility, however, is that witnesses generally believe that the police are asking questions because they really do not know what happened. When this is the case, it is much less likely that an officer's assumption about what "must have happened" could distort the witness's memory of what did happen.

In any case, when the police are seeking information they should go out of their way to convince the witness that they know little or nothing of what happened. But in order to know how serious a problem the misleading question effect currently is, it is important to move from the lab to the police station. We need to find out, first and most obviously, what kinds of questions police actually ask. How common are misleading questions, incorporating presuppositions based on specific information about the crime or general knowledge of similar crimes? Second, we need to know whether witnesses see the police as *knowing* or as *seeking* the truth. Finally, we need to know what it is the police do that may create a false impression of expertise in some or most witnesses, and what they can do to counteract it.

NOTES

This research was conducted while the first author was supported by a National Science Foundation Graduate Fellowship.

The authors are grateful to Robert Mauro for his help in various phases of this research, and to R. Edward Geiselman for providing the crime clip used in Experiment 2. We would also like to thank Pamela Burke, Craig Smith, and Anthony Ahrens for their helpful comments on an earlier version of this article, and Andrew Blaine, Gary Rothschild, Kazu Sano, and Michael Tuchin for serving as confederates in these experiments.

REFERENCES

Clifford, B.R., and Scott, J. (1978). Individual and situational factors in eyewitness testimony. *Journal of Applied Psychology*, 63, 352–9.

Hovland, C.I., and Weiss, W. (1951). The influence of source credibility on communication effectiveness. *Public Opinion Quarterly*, 15, 635–50.

Langer, E.J., and Abelson, R.P. (1972). The semantics of asking a favor: How to succeed in getting help without really dying. *Journal of Personality and Social Psychology*, 24, 26–32.

Loftus, E.F. (1975). Leading questions and the eyewitness report. *Cognitive Psychology*, 7, 560–72.

Loftus, E.F. (1977). Shifting human color memory. *Memory and Cognition*, 5, 696–9.

Loftus, E.F. (1979). *Eyewitness testimony*. Cambridge, MA: Harvard University Press.

Loftus, E.F., and Palmer, J.P. (1974). Reconstruction of automobile destruction: An example of the interaction between language and memory. *Journal of Verbal Learning and Verbal Behavior*, 13, 585–9.

Loftus, E.F., and Zanni, G. (1975). Eyewitness testimony: The influence of the wording of a question. *Bulletin of the Psychonomic Society*, 5, 86–8.

Loftus, E.F., Altman, D., and Geballe, R. (1975). Effects of questioning upon a witness's later recollections. *Journal of Police Science and Administration*, 3, 162–5.

Loftus, E.F., Miller, D.G., and Burns, H.J. (1978). Semantic integration of verbal information into a visual memory. *Journal of Experimental Psychology: Human Learning and Memory*, 4, 19–31.

Marquis, K.H., Marshall, J., and Oskamp. S. (1972). Testimony validity as a function of question form, atmosphere, and item difficulty. *Journal of Applied Social Psychology*, 2, 167–86.

McGuire, W.J. (1969). The nature of attitudes and attitude change. In G. Lindzey and E. Aronson (eds), *The handbook of social psychology* (pp. 136–314). Reading, MA: Addison-Wesley.

Mosteller, F., and Tukey, J.W. (1949). The uses and usefulness of binomial probability paper. *Journal of the American Statistical Association*, 44, 174–212.

Yuille, J.C. (1980). A critical examination of the psychological and practical implications of eyewitness research. *Law and Human Behavior*, 4, 335–45.

Author Index

Subject Index